Arms control after Iraq

This is a joint project of the United Nations University (UNU) and the International Peace Academy (IPA), in partnership with the Ritsumeikan Asia Pacific University, Beppu, and Ritsumeikan University, Kyoto

UNITED NATIONS
UNIVERSITY

International
Peace Academy

APU Ritsumeikan
Asia Pacific University

RITS Ritsumeikan
University

Arms control after Iraq: Normative and operational challenges

Edited by Waheguru Pal Singh Sidhu and Ramesh Thakur

**United Nations
University Press**

TOKYO · NEW YORK · PARIS

United Nations University Press
United Nations University, 53-70, Jingumae 5-chome,
Shibuya-ku, Tokyo 150-8925, Japan
Tel: +81-3-3499-2811   Fax: +81-3-3406-7345
E-mail: sales@hq.unu.edu   general enquiries: press@hq.unu.edu
http://www.unu.edu

United Nations University at the United Nations, New York
2 United Nations Plaza, Room DC2-2062, New York, NY 10017, USA
Tel: +1-212-963-6387   Fax: +1-212-371-9454
E-mail: unuona@ony.unu.edu

United Nations University Press is the publishing division of the United Nations University.

Cover design by Rebecca S. Neimark, Twenty-Six Letters
Cover photograph of Hiroshima Dome reproduced by kind permission of John Hobson ©.
www.johnhobsonphotography.co.uk

Printed in Hong Kong

UNUP-1131

92-808-1131-2

Library of Congress Cataloging-in-Publication Data

Arms control after Iraq : normative and operational challenges / edited by Waheguru Pal Singh Sidhu and Ramesh Thakur
    p.   cm.
 Includes bibliographical references and index.
 ISBN-13: 978-9280811315 (pbk.)
 ISBN-10: 9280811312 (pbk.)
 1. Nuclear nonproliferation. 2. Arms control. I. Sidhu, Waheguru Pal Singh. II. Thakur, Ramesh Chandra, 1948–
 JZ5675.A74   2006
 327.1′74—dc22   2006020917

Contents

Figures and tables

Contributors

Professor **Ramesh Thakur** is Senior Vice-Rector of the United Nations University, Tokyo, Japan, and Assistant Secretary-General of the United Nations

Dr **Waheguru Pal Singh Sidhu** is Faculty Member at the Geneva Centre for Security Policy, Switzerland, and was formerly Senior Associate at the International Peace Academy directing the *Iraq Crisis and World Order* project.

Brig. Gen. (ret.) **Shlomo Brom** is a Senior Research Associate at the Jaffee Center for Strategic Studies, Tel-Aviv University, Israel

Dr **Christophe Carle** is Deputy Director of the United Nations Institute for Disarmament Research, Geneva, Switzerland

Dr **Damon Coletta** is Deputy Department Head at the Department of Political Science, US Air Force Academy, Colorado, USA

Mr **Philippe Errera** is Deputy Director of the Centre for Analysis and Planning, Ministry of Foreign Affairs, Paris, France

Dr **Trevor Findlay** is Associate Professor at the Norman Paterson School of International Affairs, Carleton University, Ottawa, Canada

Dr **Kennedy Graham** is Fellow in the School of Law at the University of Canterbury, Christchurch, New Zealand

Professor **Kalevi J. Holsti** is Professor Emeritus of Political Science at the University of British Columbia, Vancouver, Canada

Dr **Wade L. Huntley** is Director of the Simons Centre for Disarmament & Non-Proliferation Research, Liu Institute for Global Issues, University of British Columbia, Vancouver, Canada

Dr **Rebecca Johnson** is Executive Director of the Acronym Institute for Disarmament Diplomacy, London, UK

Mr **Tsutomu Kono** is Political Affairs Officer of the United Nations Department for Disarmament Affairs, New York, USA

Dr **Patricia M. Lewis** is Director of the United Nations Institute for Disarmament Research, Geneva, Switzerland

Dr **Harald Müller** is Director of the Peace Research Institute Frankfurt, Germany

Ambassador **Gopalaswami Parthasarathy** is Honorary Visiting Professor at the Centre for Policy Research, New Delhi, India

Dr **William C. Potter** is Director of the Center for Nonproliferation Studies at the Monterey Institute of International Studies, California, USA

Professor **Jalil Roshandel** is Associate Professor and Director of the Security Studies programme in the Department of Political Science, East Carolina University, Greenville, NC, USA

Mr **Cyrus Samii** was formerly Senior Program Officer at the International Peace Academy, New York, USA, and is a PhD Candidate in Political Science at Columbia University, New York, USA

Dr **Heigo Sato** is Senior Research Fellow of the National Institute for Defense Studies, Tokyo, Japan

Professor **Mohammad El-Sayed Selim** is Director of the Centre for Asian Studies, Cairo University, Egypt

Ambassador **Mohamed I. Shaker** is the President of the Egyptian Council for Foreign Affairs, Cairo, Egypt

Professor **Dingli Shen** is Dean of Fudan University, Shanghai, China

Professor **John Simpson** is Director of the Mountbatten Centre for International Studies, University of Southampton, UK

Dr **Andrei Zagorski** is the Deputy Director of the Institute for Applied International Research, Moscow, Russia

Dr **Jiadong Zhang** is Lecturer at the Center for American Studies, Fudan University, Shanghai, China

1

Managing the nuclear threat after Iraq: Is it time to replace the NPT paradigm?

Ramesh Thakur

Nuclear arms control is back on the international agenda with a vengeance. It has three interlinked components: non-proliferation, arms control (for example, de-alerting and de-mating) and disarmament (the partial, limited or total abolition of nuclear weapons). According to the High-level Panel on Threats, Challenges and Change, there is a twofold threat of nuclear proliferation. First, some countries, from within the shelter of the Treaty on the Non-Proliferation of Nuclear Weapons (NPT), could either develop a full-fledged weapons capability covertly and illegally, or else acquire all the materials and expertise needed for a weapons programme and withdraw from the treaty when they are ready to proceed with weaponization. Second, there is genuine reason to fear an erosion and possible collapse of the whole NPT regime over the longer term.[1] The panel recalls US government fears in 1963 that over the following decades the number of nuclear-weapon states (NWS) would climb to 15–25, while others worried that the number could be as high as 50. Instead, as of 2004 only eight countries are known to have nuclear weapons.[2] A still greater surprise, historically speaking, is that they have not been used as an instrument of war since Hiroshima and Nagasaki in 1945.

There were two great pillars of the normative edifice for containing the nuclear horror: the doctrines of strategic deterrence, which prevented the use of nuclear weapons among those who had them, and the non-proliferation regime, centred on the NPT, which both outlawed the spread of nuclear weapons to others and imposed a legal obligation on the NWS to eliminate their own nuclear arsenals through negotiations – their only explicit multilateral disarmament commitment. At the start of the new millennium, both these pillars were at risk of crumbling. Some commentators fear that arms control is at an impasse and disarmament could be reversed. Treaties already negotiated and signed could unravel through non-ratification or breakouts. The testing of nuclear weapons could be resumed. Revelations of a previously unsuspected underground nuclear bazaar run by Abdul Qadeer Khan, the "father" of Pakistan's bomb, came as quite a shock. There is a lengthening list of proliferation-sensitive "countries of concern". Iran's confrontation with the International Atomic Energy Agency (IAEA) could lead it to pull out of the NPT altogether, following the example of North Korea. No one seriously advocates letting market forces triumph in order to level the killing fields for the whole world. A world in which anyone who wanted to and could get nuclear weapons was allowed to do so would be a far more dangerous place for all of us.

The NPT regime

The NPT came into force in 1970 as the centrepiece of the global non-proliferation regime, which codified the international political norm of non-nuclear-weapon status.[3] It tries to curb proliferation by a mix of incentives and disincentives. In return for intrusive end-use control over imported nuclear and nuclear-related technology and material, non-NWS were granted access to nuclear technology, components and material on a most-favoured-nation basis.

Proliferation refers to the dispersion of weapons, capabilities and technologies. Weapons can be sought for one or more of six reasons:[4] deterrence of enemy attack; defence against attack; compellence of the enemy to one's preferred course of action; leveraging adversary and great power behaviour;[5] status; and emulation.

There are eight categories of proliferation-sensitive actors:
- vertically proliferating NWS: those that increased their nuclear stockpiles and upgraded their nuclear lethality from inside the NPT regime, and by doing so undermined the non-proliferation regime and institutionalized international nuclear "apartheid";[6]
- NPT-irresponsible NWS: those that export nuclear-missile materials, technology and expertise in violation of international treaties, regimes and commitments;
- fragmenting NWS, or NPT splinters: when the old Soviet Union broke up, for instance, we faced the prospect of an additional three NWS

(Belarus, Kazakhstan and Ukraine) – fortunately, they were persuaded to forgo the nuclear option;

- NPT cheats: those that have signed the NPT but are engaged in activities in violation of their obligations;
- threshold NWS: those that do not claim possession of nuclear weapons, have not forsworn the nuclear weapons option, produce significant amounts of nuclear material or equipment, and refuse to accept international control over their material and equipment – with India and Pakistan coming out of the nuclear closet in 1998, and few left to deny Israel's nuclear weapons capability, the threshold status is in effect obsolete;
- nuclear terrorists: it defies credulity that nuclear weapons and materials can be kept secure in government inventories and never be obtained by any terrorist group – whereas a government's nuclear capability can be seized and destroyed, it is impossible to capture or kill every single terrorist and his/her last piece of dynamite, Semtex or timing mechanism;
- "virtual" NWS: the flow of enabling technologies, material and expertise in the nuclear power industry can be used, through strategic pre-positioning of materials and personnel, to build a "surge" capacity to upgrade to nuclear weapons within the timeframe of a crisis degenerating into conflict. Thus Ichiro Ozawa of the Japanese Liberal Party warned China not to forget that Japan could easily make 3,000–4,000 nuclear weapons;[7]
- missile proliferators: missiles are an acutely destabilizing form of weaponry because little defence is available against them; armed with biological, chemical or nuclear warheads, they can be lethal.

The specific causes of proliferation are many, diverse and usually rooted in a local security complex. Persuading key problem states to move to a non-nuclear-weapon status requires convincing them that the balance of advantage lies with forswearing the nuclear option. This necessarily includes not just the national security calculus, but also the internal political constellation, the regional security complex and considerations of international equity. The most crucial elements in preventing proliferation are "the creation and maintenance of political and security conditions which are conducive to nonproliferation".[8]

The barriers against the acquisition, spread and use of nuclear weapons include legal conventions, norms and the fact of their non-use for over 50 years. Norms, not deterrence, have anathematized the use of nuclear weapons as unacceptable, immoral and possibly illegal in any circumstance – even for states that have assimilated them into military arsenals and integrated them into military commands and doctrines. There have been several occasions since 1945 (the United States in Viet Nam; the former Soviet Union in Afghanistan) when nuclear weapons could have been used without fear of retaliation but were not, even at the price of defeat on the battlefield.[9]

The IAEA is part of the UN system and reports annually to the General Assembly on its work. One of its major functions is to apply safeguards to ensure that nuclear materials and equipment intended for peaceful uses are not diverted to military uses. The safeguards system constitutes the international community's first attempt to establish a control system over an industry of strategic importance. The IAEA is expected not to prevent the misuse of civilian nuclear facilities but to detect possible misuse soon enough to give early warning to the international community. The ex post facto revelations of South Africa's acquisition of nuclear weapons in the 1980s, the discovery of the extent of Iraq's pre-1990 clandestine nuclear programme while subject to IAEA safeguards and inspections, the continuing uncertainty over North Korea's nuclear programmes, the confessions by Libya of how advanced its programmes were, the revelations of the existence of an underground supermarket in Pakistan, and the continuing dispute with Iran have cumulatively eroded the IAEA's credibility as an early-warning system.

On the supply side, a major proliferation challenge is the globalization of the arms industry, the flooding of the global arms market and a resulting loosening of supplier constraints. Safeguards are the technical means to verifying compliance with non-proliferation obligations; export control regimes are the technical means to preventing dissemination of proliferation-sensitive materials. The industrial states gradually evolved a regime of technical denial for keeping nuclear weapons capabilities from potential proliferators through IAEA arrangements and export control guidelines. Safeguards provide early warning of possible proliferation. The risk of detection adds an element of deterrence. Export restraints add to the technical difficulty, raise the costs of the nuclear weapons option, compel proliferators to take a more circuitous path, introduce a longer lead-time and so buy time for offending governments to change their mind and the international community to organize a suitable riposte.

The NPT regime also includes a number of treaties restricting nuclear testing. The Partial Test Ban Treaty (1963) outlawed atmospheric, space and underwater nuclear testing. The Threshold Test Ban Treaty (1974) outlawed underground tests of more than 150 kt yield. The elusive goal of a total ban on nuclear testing was seemingly realized in 1996 with the endorsement by the UN General Assembly of the Comprehensive Nuclear-Test-Ban Treaty (CTBT). However, in part due to the rigid entry-into-force provisions of the CTBT,[10] and in part due to changed administrations in Washington and the changed climate of arms control after "9/11", the CTBT is unlikely to enter into force in the foreseeable future. Nor has the world been any more successful in the pursuit of a non-discriminatory, multilateral and verifiable convention banning the production of fissile material for weapons purposes that would greatly strengthen the non-proliferation regime.

Arms control efforts look too much to the past and are mostly reactive and curative. Nuclear-weapon-free zones are anticipatory and preventive integral components of the mosaic of international action on denuclearization and the de-legitimization of the entire edifice of nuclear weapons (possession, testing, deployment, doctrines, strategies and the associated infrastructure of warheads, delivery systems, bases). They help to embed and institutionalize the global non-proliferation norm at the regional level and thus offer a means of extending and reinforcing the NPT. Such zones cover virtually the entire southern hemisphere but are conspicuously scarce north of the equator.[11]

The nuclear landscape in 2005

The mushroom clouds on the horizon in 2005 appeared to be the darkest in years, although there were some silver linings. In December 2003, Libya entered into a "grand bargain": in return for a comprehensive dismantling of its WMD (weapons of mass destruction) capabilities, the United Kingdom and the United States agreed to lift sanctions and restore diplomatic relations. The implementation of the agreement was swift, international watchdog agencies started dismantling and destroying Libya's nuclear-related material and stocks, and Libya joined the CTBT and the Convention on the Prohibition of the Development, Production, Stockpiling and Use of Chemical Weapons and on Their Destruction (Chemical Weapons Convention). Moreover, Libya's disclosures exposed the global underground nuclear black market, led by the Pakistani metallurgist Abdul Qadeer Khan, which supplied sensitive nuclear technology to Iran, Libya and North Korea. Although many questions remained about the full extent of Khan's network and activities, President Pervez Musharraf pardoned him in exchange for his continued cooperation in rolling up the network. The improvement in the political atmosphere between Pakistan and India was sustained through the transition to a Congress-majority government in New Delhi. The nuclear rivals moved to more responsible nuclear stewardship of their programmes.

Non-state actors were the explicit focus of UN Security Council Resolution 1540. Adopted unanimously in April 2004, it called on all countries to refrain from supporting by any means such actors attempting to acquire, use or transfer nuclear, chemical or biological weapons and their delivery systems, and requires the establishment of domestic controls.

The bad news rather outweighed the good. The Conference on Disar-

mament, established in 1979 as the single multilateral disarmament negotiating forum of the international community, remained immobilized for
the ninth year in succession. Washington announced its commitment to
negotiate a legally binding fissile material cut-off treaty, but without verification provisions. Space talks remain blocked. Iran sent conflicting messages on compliance with NPT commitments and its pursuit of a nuclear
energy programme for peaceful purposes. The Six-Party Talks on the
North Korean nuclear programme made no visible progress in keeping
North Korea from establishing a fully functioning nuclear weapons programme. East Asia was further rattled with revelations of a series of supposedly "rogue" nuclear experiments by South Korean and Taiwanese
scientists. Concerns persist about the potential leakage of "loose nukes"
from Russia to terrorists. Worst-case scenarios see terrorists using nuclear
or radiological weapons to kill hundreds of thousands of people. As far
as we know, however, no terrorist group has the competence to build nuclear weapons. Nor is there any evidence so far to suggest that nuclear
weapons have been transferred to terrorist organizations.

The seventh NPT Review Conference in May 2005 ended in complete
collapse. It failed to address the vital challenges or to offer practical ideas
for preventing the use, acquisition and spread of nuclear weapons. The
first half of the conference was dogged by procedural wrangling and the
second was rancorous. The exercise ended in acrimony and recrimina-
tions over where the primary blame lay for the lost opportunity to bolster
the NPT. Most countries concluded that the nuclear powers had no intention of fulfilling their NPT-based disarmament obligations and agreed
commitments from the 1995 and 2000 conferences. This had a triple negative effect: it eroded support for US proposals for strengthening the
non-proliferation elements of the treaty, it weakened support for strong
action against possible Iranian and North Korean transgressions, and it
may soften adherence to NPT obligations over the long run.

China continues to modernize its arsenal. The United States has
retreated from several arms control and disarmament agreements, including the Anti-Ballistic Missile Treaty, the NPT and the CTBT. It is
asserting the right to develop new generations of earth-penetrating,
bunker-busting nuclear weapons and battlefield "mini-nukes" and refin-
ing the doctrines underpinning the deployment and possible use of nuclear weapons. The bilateral agreement between India and the United
States on civilian nuclear cooperation, signed during Prime Minister
Manmohan Singh's visit to Washington on 18 July 2005, proved extremely contentious. Supporters argued that it serves the strategic goals
of both countries while also advancing the global non-proliferation
agenda more realistically than any conceivable alternative. Opponents
countered that the gains were outweighed by the damage to the non-

proliferation cause. Still more disappointment came with the UN World Summit in September 2005. US insistence on dispensing with the NPT pillars of "disarmament, non-proliferation, and the peaceful use of nuclear energy" in favour of a focus solely on preventing the further spread of nuclear weapons gave ample cover for spoilers on the other side. Secretary-General Kofi Annan rightly called the failure to agree on any action on non-proliferation and disarmament "a real disgrace".

A paradigm shift?

In *The Structure of Scientific Revolutions*, Thomas S. Kuhn outlined the process by which a dominant paradigm in science is replaced by a new paradigm. Normal science is concerned with solving puzzles within a particular framework. In the course of ongoing research, however, anomalies are uncovered that suggest deficiencies in the theory or the existing paradigm and generate auxiliary hypotheses within the dominant paradigm to explain the anomalies. If the old paradigm proves unable to accommodate the anomalies, the pressure grows for a new paradigm to emerge. At this point "the anomalous has become the expected".[12] Might a similar process be under way (a) with regard to the NPT regime and, more generally still, (b) with regard to the dominant paradigm of the contemporary world order?

The central doctrine underpinning the contemporary Westphalian system holds that sovereign states are equal in effectiveness, status and legitimacy. In reality, states are not of equal worth and significance, either militarily, economically, politically or morally. An important lesson of peace operations is that impartial peacekeeping should not automatically translate into moral equivalence among the conflict parties on the ground. The Brahimi Panel on United Nations Peace Operations noted that, in some cases, local parties consist not of moral equals but of aggressors and victims, and consequently "peacekeepers may not only be operationally justified in using force but morally compelled to do so".[13] Can this insight be applied to the nuclear dilemma? It seems counterintuitive to postulate that, in the eyes of most people and countries, nuclear weapons in the hands of the United Kingdom and North Korea would pose equal risks to international peace and security. The United Nations, resting on the principle of the sovereign equality of member states, is compelled to assert the danger of nuclear weapons per se arising from their uniquely destructive properties. But, if the United Nations is not able or willing to distinguish between regimes with respect to the risks they pose and the threats they constitute, then either it must be reformed and reconfigured to enable such determination, or else we must accept the reality that concerned countries will make these tough decisions and act on them outside the UN framework. Such countries are not going to imperil their national security through an idealistic faith in the UN system of collective security resting on demonstrably false assumptions.

Since 1968, the symbol of the dominant arms control, disarmament and non-proliferation paradigm has been the NPT regime. Over the course of three decades, however, significant anomalies have accumulated and now weigh down the regime. The question is: are they so insubstantial that they can be accommodated within the NPT regime through reforms and auxiliary agreements, or are they of sufficient number and magnitude that the NPT needs total replacement? They can be grouped into five broad categories: a discrepancy between the legal definition and actual nuclear-weapon status; the dangerous gap in time between the threat of non-proliferation becoming evident and the capacity of the existing international modalities to respond effectively to it; the risks of lumping together biological, chemical and nuclear weapons under the one label of WMD; the tensions between norms and treaties, on the one hand, and compliance mechanisms and enforcement agents, on the other; and the difficulty of encouraging the acquisition of nuclear weapons as the deterrent of choice resulting from efforts at compulsory or pre-emptive disarmament.

Anomaly 1: Legal definition vs. strategic reality

The definition of a nuclear-weapon state is chronological, a function of countries having been nuclear powers before the NPT was signed, rather than analytical or existential. For example, the nuclear arsenals of India, Pakistan and Israel are NPT-illicit – these countries could test, deploy and even use nuclear weapons but they cannot be described as nuclear-weapon states.[14] In principle, the United Kingdom and France could dismantle their nuclear edifice and destroy their nuclear arsenals, but would still count as nuclear-weapon states. This is an Alice-in-Wonderland approach to affairs of deadly seriousness. When legal fiction comes into collision with strategic reality, either the legal fiction gives way or the world becomes a more dangerous place. Moreover, if the gap between strategic reality and the NPT world view is not bridged, in time it is the NPT that will become progressively less credible and relevant. Yet can the NPT definition be opened up for revision through a formal amendment of the treaty, with all the unpredictable consequences regarding the status of existing States Parties? The conceptual fudge is evident in the report of the High-level Panel asking Middle Eastern and South Asian countries to ratify the CTBT and negotiate regional nuclear-weapon-free zones.[15] Should India, Pakistan and Israel do so as nuclear-weapon states? If so, would this not formalize their nuclear status outside the NPT? Furthermore, why not make the same call to the other five nuclear powers? If not, w(h)ither realism?

Anomaly 2: Fast-paced threats, slow institutional response

The cases of Israel, India and Pakistan show that, decades after the problem arose, the international community is still unable to agree on an appropriate response within the existing NPT framework. In conducting 11 nuclear tests in May 1998, India and Pakistan confronted the world with a dilemma. A moderate response would have been self-negating. The nuclear hawks would have felt vindicated, saying that their country was being treated with respect because it had nuclear weapons. To accept India and Pakistan as nuclear-weapon states would reverse three decades of non-proliferation policy and victimize many countries that signed the NPT and CTBT on the understanding that the number of nuclear-weapon states would be limited to five. On the other hand, a harsh response would have been self-fulfilling. The hawks would have argued that a friendless India that is the target of hostile international attention needs an arsenal of nuclear weapons to defend its interests. Seven years later, trying to revert to the status quo ante in South Asia is as realistic as demanding an immediate timetabled framework for the elimination of all nuclear weapons. For India, Israel and Pakistan, the question is no longer if they are nuclear powers but what kind of nuclear powers they are going to be.

On Iraq, Washington did not help its case for war against Saddam Hussein by issuing a confused mix of motives and explanations. In the resulting "noise" of diplomatic traffic, answers were not forthcoming to two crucial questions: why Iraq, and why now? Any single answer to the first question – such as known/suspected links to terrorism or to weapons of mass destruction – would always complicate attempts to answer the second, since people could instantly counter with more compelling cases of the same pathology.

For instance, whereas evidence of nuclear weapons remained elusive in Iraq, North Korea did almost everything except actually conduct a nuclear test. The glib conclusion drawn by the anti-war lobby, therefore, was that Washington's inconsistent response to the simultaneous crises showed two things: Iraq did not possess usable nuclear weapons, and North Korea does not have oil. Yet, glibness aside, Washington could have constructed a powerful case for its action on Iraq precisely by linking the two crises. We know that Saddam had pursued the nuclear option in the past, had possessed and used biochemical weapons against his own people as well as against Iran, and had played a dangerous game of hide and seek with UN weapons inspectors for over a decade. Given that we cannot be certain that North Korea has not already crossed the nuclear threshold, what options are available to the international community for dealing with Pyongyang without causing grave damage to ourselves? The UN Security Council seems barely able to table the North Korean threat for discussion and resolution. Similarly, it would have been impossible to de-fang Saddam of nuclear weapons the day after he acquired and used them – the United Nations is incapable of doing so the day before – hence the American determination to do so instead. Thus the two questions (why Iraq and why now?) can be answered simultaneously and symbiotically.

The reality of contemporary threats – a virtual nuclear weapons capability that can exist inside non-proliferation regimes and be crossed at too short notice for international organizations to be able to react defensively in time, and non-state actors that are outside the jurisdiction and control of multilateral agreements whose signatories are states – means that significant gaps exist in the legal and institutional framework to combat them. If international institutions cannot cope with today's real threats, states will try to do so themselves, either unilaterally or in company with like-minded allies. If military action is strategically necessary and morally justified but not legally permitted, then the existing framework of laws and rules – not the anticipatory military action – is defective.

Recognizing this, a group of like-minded countries has launched a Proliferation Security Initiative (PSI) to interdict illicit air, sea and land cargo linked to WMD. Its premise is that the proliferation of such weapons deserves to be criminalized by the civilized community of nations. The PSI signals a new determination to overcome an unsatisfactory state of affairs through a broad partnership of countries that, using their own national laws and resources, will coordinate actions to halt shipments of dangerous technologies and materiel. Whereas the High-level Panel encouraged all states to join the PSI,[16] the Secretary-General simply welcomes the voluntary initiative.[17]

Anomaly 3: Weapons of mass destruction

Nuclear non-proliferation efforts must be viewed within the context of the broader proliferation environment, which in addition to nuclear weapons includes biological, chemical and conventional weapons and their delivery systems. The clandestine nature of all biological and chemical weapon programmes suggests that no prestige value attaches to them. They have been so successfully stigmatized and evoke such universal revulsion that they are not a source of national pride.

Language is not always neutral, and often contains powerful codes of permissible and impermissible behaviour. It is not clear that biological, chemical and nuclear weapons belong in one conceptual category. They differ in their technical features, in the ease with they can be acquired and developed, and in their capacity to cause mass destruction. Treating them as one category of weaponry can distort analysis and produce flawed institutional responses. In the long-lasting and particularly traumatic conflicts in Africa and Asia, the real weapons of mass destruction are small arms and landmines. There is also the danger of mission creep for nuclear weapons. The taboo against nuclear weapons use is so strong that it is difficult to imagine their use other than against enemy nuclear weapons.

The creeping tendency to redefine the mission to counter WMD has three consequences: it lumps together biological, chemical and nuclear weapons in one conceptually fuzzy category; it weakens the nuclear taboo; and it permits the nuclear powers to obfuscate the reality that they are the possessors of the most potent WMD.[18] If nuclear weapons are accepted as having a role in countering biological/chemical warfare, then by what right or logic can we deny a nuclear weapons capability to a country such as Iran that has actually suffered chemical weapons attacks? In other words, mission creep carries the attendant danger of cross-category horizontal proliferation. It also raises a further interesting question: why should there not be a universal nuclear weapons convention banning such weapons, comparable to the biological and chemical weapons conventions?

Anomaly 4: Enforcers as exemplars

The NPT-N5 (the five nuclear powers recognized as such by the NPT) preach nuclear abstinence but do not practise it. It defies history, common sense and logic to believe that a self-selecting group of countries can keep a permanent monopoly on any class of weaponry. Not a single country that had nuclear weapons when the NPT was signed in 1968 has given them up.[19] Moreover, their stockpiles are in defiance of the International Court of Justice's Advisory Opinion of July 1996 of a legal obligation to pursue in good faith and bring to a conclusion negotiations leading to nuclear disarmament. India and Pakistan breached no international treaty, convention or law by testing. For the five nuclear-weapon states to impose sanctions on the nuclear gatecrashers is akin on this issue to outlaws sitting in judgment, passing sentence and imposing punishment on the law abiding. Such behaviour fuels the politics of grievance and resentment.

There is profound scepticism about the country with the world's most powerful nuclear weapons using military force to prevent their acquisition by others. By attacking Iraq in defiance of world opinion without UN authorization, Washington exempted itself from the existing normative restraints on the use of military force. Many prudent national security planners around the world will be more attracted than they were before the Iraq war to nuclear weapons for deterring possible attack on their countries in the suddenly harsher jungle of international relations. They may begin to edge away from existing non-proliferation commitments and become interested in nuclear warheads and missiles as leveraging weapons in order to affect the calculus of US decision-making on wars.

The nuclear-weapon states are trapped in the fundamental paradox that, while they justify their own nuclear weapons in national security terms, they seek to deny such weapons to anyone else for reasons of global security. Ultimately, however, the logic of nuclear non-proliferation is inseparable from the logic of nuclear disarmament. Hence the axiom of non-proliferation: as long as any one country has them, others, including terrorist groups, will try their best (or worst) to get them.

For arms control regimes – the infrastructure of sustainable disarmament[20] – to be vested with legitimacy, they must incorporate a balance of obligations between the present nuclear haves and have-nots. The urgent requirement now is to put in place an increasing number of verifiable constraints on the policies, practices and arsenals of nuclear-weapon states. The lack of compliance and enforcement of NPT obligations on the nuclear-weapon states de-legitimizes the NPT's normative claims in the eyes of others. The historic and favourable changes in the world strategic situation must be embedded in structures that consolidate, deepen and reinforce the non-proliferation, arms control and disarmament regimes in their normative, technical-denial and compliance-cum-enforcement attributes. All the regimes must be invested with the requisite political will, fiscal means and intelligence support.

Anomaly 5: Utility vs. futility of nuclear weapons

During the Cold War, large numbers of US nuclear warheads were aimed at fixed enemy targets. Under the targeting system called "adaptive planning" based on "offensive deterrence", Washington would have the option of launching a pre-emptive strike with precision-guided conventional bombs or "special-purpose nuclear weapons" against hostile countries that posed a threat of WMD attack on the United States. Does contemplating and preparing for the use of nuclear weapons with lower yield and reduced fallout constitute a preparatory step too far?

The Nuclear Posture Review has the great merit of trying to reconcile the reality of nuclear weapons with operational military doctrines. The unique properties of nuclear weapons mean that they will continue to play critical roles. Their military-political utility ranges from assurance of allies and friends to dissuasion of competitors, deterrence of aggressors and defeat of enemies. In the process, however, nuclear weapons have advanced up the ladder of escalation from the weapon of last resort to a weapon of choice, and the underlying defence doctrine has changed from the Cold War's mutual assured destruction to the post–Cold War's unilateral assured destruction. Such doctrinal spread may have unhappy consequences, because the calculus of potential proliferators is bound to change in response to the new US doctrine. It is not possible to convince others of the futility of nuclear weapons when the facts of possession and the doctrines of use prove their utility for a self-selected few. Lowering the threshold of their use weakens the taboo against them, and thus inevitably lowers the normative barriers to nuclear proliferation.

A dramatic deterioration in the security environment hardens the determination of the "rogues" to acquire the most lethal weapons in order to check armed attacks they fear will be launched by the United States. Just as Iraq as a hotbed of terrorism became a consequence more than a cause of war, so proliferation of nuclear weapons may result from that war: some countries will have concluded that only nuclear weapons can deter Washington from unilateral wars of choice. Thus, as Washington throws off the fetters on the unilateral use of force and the universal taboo on nuclear weapons, it strengthens the attraction of nuclear weapons for others while simultaneously weakening the restraining force of global norms and treaties.

But this in itself is now less worrying to Washington. For yet another effect of 9/11 was to change dramatically the focus of concern from universal to differentiated nuclear proliferation. Previously, the NPT was the centrepiece and embodiment of the non-proliferation norm. Now the US concern may be not so much the NPT as the relations of the proliferators with Washington. US-friendly countries such as Israel have never evoked outrage over their nuclear weapons programmes. The failure to confront Israel's nuclear weapons increasingly complicates efforts to address nuclear concerns by others in the region. Since 9/11, even India and Pakistan have been lifted out of the ranks of countries of concern (with Pakistan being designated a major non-NATO ally) in favour of concentrated attacks on the axis of evil countries – that is, US-hostile proliferators. And of course the concern is no longer limited to state proliferators, but extends much more broadly to non-state groups and individuals as well, especially those who might some day contemplate acts of nuclear terrorism.

In turn this changes the basis of world order as we know it. And that might be the most profound and long-lasting significance of 9/11, which may indeed have changed the world and tipped us into a post-Westphalian world. US policy is full of contradictions within the Westphalian paradigm. How can the most prominent dissident in many global norms and regimes claim to be the world's most powerful enforcer of global norms and regimes, including non-proliferation? How can the most vocal critic of the very notion of an international community anoint itself the international community's sheriff?

The answer lies in a conception of world order rooted outside the framework of Westphalian sovereign equality. This also explains why some of today's most potent threats come not from the conquering states within the Westphalian paradigm but from failing states outside it. In effect, President Bush is saying that the gap between the fiction of legal equality and the reality of power preponderance has stretched beyond breaking point. Washington is no longer bound by such fiction. The Bush administration insists that the United States will remain as fundamentally trustworthy, balanced and responsible a custodian of world order as before – but of a post-Westphalian order centred on the United States. Other countries and leaders must pay their respects to Washington as the new imperial centre, or else Washington will make them pay for their disrespect.

Outline of the book

Can the International Atomic Energy Agency be transformed from an inspectorate into an international nuclear police force? Or even an international nuclear-ready reaction force, equipped, tasked and prepared to destroy unauthorized nuclear facilities by force? Alternatively, now that we know just how well the UN inspection machinery (UN Special Commission/UN Monitoring, Verification and Inspection Commission) worked in containing Saddam Hussein's nuclear ambitions, could they be transformed from ad hoc to standing institutions? The success of such ventures cannot be guaranteed, and they are high risk too in terms of precipitating conventional and nuclear wars and ecological disasters.

These and other questions are discussed and analysed from a variety of perspectives in this book. The key questions include: are the problems we now face old problems (such as those of non-compliance by states members of various regimes) or new problems (such as non-compliance by states not members of various regimes); are the gaps in the international institutions to deal with non-compliance the result of the lack of resources or of a lack of norms; are there lessons to be learned from other reforms, such as the Brahimi Panel on UN Peace Operations, which challenged the traditional notion of impartiality in peacekeeping? Is a similar norm applicable to non-proliferation? What weaknesses did the Iraq crisis expose in the non-proliferation regimes and in the UN system's role as a central arena for handling proliferation crises? What successful elements of the international community's policies vis-à-vis Iraq should not be forgotten? What are the lessons learned for devising international responses to proliferation challenges in the Middle East and in North-east Asia?

Part I (Chapters 2–4) looks at doctrinal issues regarding the use of force in general and at the implications of a shift in the utility of nuclear weapons from deterrence to compellence, and of an abandonment of the parallel pursuit of nuclear non-proliferation and disarmament in favour solely of non-proliferation. Part II (Chapters 5–8) examines the place and role of the United Nations in attempting to control the spread and use of nuclear weapons. In Parts III (Chapters 9–10) and IV (Chapters 11–13), we discuss the regional dynamics of proliferation concerns in North-east Asia and the Middle East, respectively. Parts V (Chapters 14–18) and VI (Chapters 19–20) look at the policy drivers of the NPT and extra-NPT nuclear powers. Finally, in Part VII (chapters 21–23), we conclude with a range of observations on the threats posed by the possible acquisition of nuclear weapons by non-state actors and by missiles, as well as the state of affairs after the Iraq war.

The three pillars of arms control

The goal of containing the genie of nuclear weapons was unexpectedly successful for three decades from 1968 to 1998, but it has suffered serious setbacks since then. The success rested on three pillars, each of which has been crumbling in the past few years: norms, treaties and coercion.

Norms are socially efficient mechanisms for regulating human behaviour from the family and village to the global setting. In conducting 11 nuclear tests in 1998, India and Pakistan did not violate any treaty they had signed. But they did breach the global anti-nuclear norm and were roundly criticized for doing so. By now they are increasingly being accepted back into the fold as de facto nuclear powers, which weakens the anti-nuclear norm still further.

Non-fulfilment of treaty obligations by the nuclear powers weakens the efficacy of the anti-nuclear norm in controlling the threat of proliferation. The five permanent but unelected members of the UN Security Council – the N5 – then have to resort to measures of coercion ranging from diplomatic and economic to military. But relying solely on coercion with little basis any longer in norms (morality) and treaties (legality) usually turns out to be counter-productive.

A norm cannot control the behaviour of those who reject its moral status. India had argued for decades that the most serious breaches of the anti-nuclear norm were being committed by the five nuclear powers, which simply disregarded their disarmament obligations under the NPT. Of late, Washington has engaged in a systematic belittling, denigrating and hollowing out of a series of arms control and disarmament agreements. Arguably, it has also been engaged in a similar frontal assault on the principle of global norms – from arms control, climate change and international criminal justice to conventions against torture and for the rights of children and planned parenthood. In doing so, Washington contributes to a worsening of the proliferation challenge by weakening the behaviour-regulating force of global norms.

Precisely because multilateral agreements are negotiated outcomes, they are typically imperfect bargains, reflecting the compromises that all sides had to make in the interests of getting an agreement that meets the minimum concerns of all parties while falling short of their maximum ambitions. Australia helped to broker the CTBT in the belief that technical improvements through continued nuclear testing were subordinate to the risks of nuclear proliferation if testing was not terminated. Canada was the catalyst for the ban on antipersonnel landmines because their marginal military utility is outweighed by their humanitarian carnage.

While the CTBT and the NPT, along with the chemical and biological weapons conventions, the Convention on the Prohibition of the Use, Stockpiling, Production and Transfer of Anti-Personnel Mines and on Their Destruction (the Ottawa Treaty) and other international instruments, raise the threshold of proliferation and use, they simultaneously lower the bar to collective international responses for ensuring regime compliance. They thus lower the threat, reduce the need for counter-proliferation preparation and strategies, and promote norms of acceptable international behaviour. In signing international arms control treaties, states accept binding obligations. If a state should seek to acquire nuclear weapons, NPT obligations give us significant leverage first to hold it to a legal contract, and second, if that is ignored, to fashion a collective response to non-compliance. It is far easier to form coalitions of the willing from those angered by non-compliance with international treaties and global norms – which is a good working definition of a rogue state.

Of course, no arms control regime can provide foolproof assurance against cheating. But the key issue, as in all aspects of life, is risk management. We do not stop driving or flying because of the risk of accidents. Rather, we take reasonable precautions, institute safety procedures, ensure minimum skills through approved testing procedures and set in place mechanisms and people for catching and punishing the violators of the collective norms of driving and flying. There is no country in which people do not violate traffic laws and seek to evade detection. Some even succeed. It would be as irresponsible as it would be irrational to conclude that driving licence requirements and traffic codes should therefore be thrown out in favour of a free-for-all on the nation's roads.

Some states and groups will surely try to cheat on their international obligations. But the verification and monitoring mechanisms built into arms control regimes give us a higher chance of catching them out in their efforts to cheat. The risk of detection acts as a deterrent against cheating, and the risk of being branded a cheat adds an element of compliance. The United States can leverage its hard and soft power assets to hold signatories to their international treaty obligations. If these are violated, the United States can leverage the same set of assets to forge coalitions of the willing, as in the Persian Gulf, Kosovo and Afghanistan wars over the past decade. The world needs American muscle and leadership on the side of the law-abiding.

In sum, there was great merit in relying on an integrated strategy of norms, treaties and coercion to keep the threat of nuclear proliferation in check. The NPT is tied to a frozen international power structure decades out of date, and it has become dangerously fragile. The road to the nuclear-free destination includes deep reductions in nuclear arsenals; further constraints on the extra-territorial deployment of nuclear weapons; the entry into force of the CTBT; a ban on missile test flights and the production of fissile materials; a pre-emptive ban on the nuclear militarization of outer space; and the de-alerting and de-mating of nuclear forces, warheads and missiles.

Confronted with a world that cannot be changed, reasonable people adapt and accommodate. Yet the turning points of history and progress in human civilization have come from those who set out to change the world instead. The only guarantee against the threat of nuclear war is the complete elimination of nuclear weapons. In most contexts, a step-by-step approach is the best policy, but such caution can be fatal if the need is to cross a chasm. In the case of nuclear weapons, the chasm over which we must leap is the belief that world security can rest on weapons of total insecurity. Such scenarios provoke dismissive comments from so-called "realists". *Realistically* speaking, what other option is there? A rollback to the pre-1998 status quo, in the name of realism? Unchecked proliferation? Rearmament? As with Winston Churchill's famous aphorism on democracy, the abolitionist option may well be unrealistic; all other conceivable options are even less realistic as strategies for our common security and survival.

Notes

1. High-level Panel on Threats, Challenges and Change, *A More Secure World: Our Shared Responsibility*, UN Doc. A/59/565 (New York: United Nations, December 2004), para. 108.
2. Ibid., para. 110.
3. I use the term "regime" loosely to refer to norms, rules and behaviour around which actor expectations converge in the issue-area of non-proliferation even in the absence of formal international organization. The non-proliferation regime includes the norms of international nuclear behaviour and the network of international treaties, institutions, export controls and nuclear trade agreements.
4. This is developed more fully in Ramesh Thakur, "Arms Control, Disarmament, and Non-Proliferation: A Political Perspective", in Jeffrey A. Larsen and Thomas D. Miller, eds, *Arms Control in the Asia–Pacific Region* (Colorado Springs: USAF Institute for National Security Studies, US Air Force Academy, 1999), pp. 39–61.
5. Many of the newer proliferating materials and processes are "leveraging" technologies that allow poorer countries to offset high-technology advantages. By demonstrating the acquisition of just a few key capabilities, developing countries can affect the perceptions and alter the decision calculus of diplomacy and war of the advanced military powers.
6. The use of the emotive word "apartheid" by critics of the NPT entails entirely negative connotations. Apartheid referred to a system in which a minority imposed its order on a majority by coercion. The NPT has been signed by a majority of the world's countries exercising their free choice.
7. *Japan Times*, 6 April 2002.
8. Hans Blix (then Director General of the IAEA), "Strengthening the NPT and the Nuclear Non-Proliferation Regime", *Disarmament: A Periodic Review by the United Nations*, Vol. 16, No. 2 (1993), p. 5.
9. See Nina Tannenwald, "The Nuclear Taboo: The United States and the Normative Basis of Nuclear Non-Use", *International Organization*, Vol. 53 (Summer 1999), pp. 433–468.
10. China joined the NPT regime in March 1992, followed by France in August, thereby bringing all five known nuclear-weapon states within the NPT fold. If analogous clauses had been written into the NPT, that treaty would never have entered into force.
11. See Ramesh Thakur, ed., *Nuclear Weapons-Free Zones* (London/New York: Macmillan and St. Martin's Press, 1998).
12. Thomas S. Kuhn, *The Structure of Scientific Revolutions* (Chicago: University of Chicago Press, 1962), p. 53.
13. *Report of the Panel on United Nations Peace Operations*, UN Doc. A/55/305–S/2000/809, 21 August 2000, para. 50.
14. The official UN formulation is that India and Pakistan are "non-NPT States that have conducted tests of nuclear devices". India describes itself as a declared possessor of nuclear weapons. See W. P. S. Sidhu, "India's Nuclear Use Doctrine", in Peter R. Lavoy, Scott Sagan and James J. Wirtz, eds, *Planning the Unthinkable: New Proliferators and the Use of Weapons of Mass Destruction* (Ithaca, NY: Cornell University Press, 2000), pp. 125–157; and Ramesh Thakur, "The South Asian Nuclear Challenge", in John Baylis and Robert O'Neill, eds, *Alternative Nuclear Futures: The Role of Nuclear Weapons in the Post-Cold War World* (Oxford: Oxford University Press, 2000), pp. 101–124.
15. High-level Panel, *A More Secure World*, para. 124.
16. Ibid., para. 132.
17. Kofi Annan, *In Larger Freedom: Towards Development, Security and Human Rights for All. Report of the Secretary-General*, UN Doc. A/59/2005 (New York: United Nations, 21 March 2005), para. 100.

18. The WMD issue was further clouded (no pun intended) with confirmation that US forces had used white phosphorus during their assault on Fallujah in November 2004. As the *New York Times* argued in an editorial, "U.S. demands for counter-proliferation efforts and international arms control ring a bit hollow when the United States refuses to give up white phosphorus, not to mention cluster bombs and land mines" – "Shake and bake" (the "unsettling military name" given to white phosphorus), *International Herald Tribune*, 30 November 2005.

19. The renunciations by Belarus, Kazakhstan and Ukraine after the breakup of the former Soviet Union do not alter the substantive claim, insofar as, for this purpose, the successor state is Russia.

20. See Ramesh Thakur, "Sustainable Disarmament", in Carl Ungerer and Marianne Hanson, eds, *The Politics of Nuclear Non-Proliferation* (St Leonards: Allen & Unwin Australia, 2001), pp. 11–30.

Part I

Strategic doctrine, norms of non-proliferation and disarmament, and world order

2

The use of force in international politics: Four revolutions

Kalevi J. Holsti

The proliferation of weapons of mass destruction (WMD) is a symptom of deep structural characteristics in the contemporary international system. Agents and actors obtain weapons systems for a variety of reasons, ranging from prestige, through compellence, to deterrence. The processes by which weapons systems migrate from community to community include sales and commerce, mimicry, indigenous research and development, spying and illegal purchases. There is nothing new about weapons proliferation. What distinguishes the current problem from its predecessors is (1) the extreme lethality of certain types of weapons, and (2) an assumed willingness on the part of the proliferators to use those weapons as instruments of terror, blackmail or irrational strikes against innocents. These are the nightmares of many contemporary defence analysts. In the contemporary mind, these threats are sufficiently great to generate and sustain not only specified weapons prohibition "regimes" but also coercive military action to disarm suspected violators of these regimes. The US attack on Iraq in 2003 was largely justified in terms of the threat that Iraq's asserted (but unproved) weapons of mass destruction posed to the United States and the international community.

Weapons proliferation is a sub-problem of the main issue in the relations between sovereign political communities in a system of anarchy. That issue is the use of force between those communities. The systematic study of the essential characteristics of international relations has traditionally focused on the problem of war, which, according to analysts such as Hobbes, Rousseau and contemporary Realists, is an inevitable outcome of anarchical systems. In gaining sovereignty from the old medieval order characterized by command and obedience relationships, the newly independent states gained their freedom to rule internally and to pursue their foreign ventures, but in the process created a system of perpetual insecurity. Hobbes and Rousseau did not specify when, where or over what issues the sovereigns were going to use force, so there is no known degree of threat at any time. In a system of anarchy, according to Hobbes, there is, like rain in England, a perpetual "disposition" to war. For Rousseau, in his famous parable of the stag hunt, war is inevitable because of the security dilemma and the lack of trust between states.

Throughout history, armed force has been a ubiquitous characteristic of the relations between independent polities, be they tribes, cities, nation-states or empires. For example, a striking feature of the relations between the Greek city-states in the period 700 to 300 BC was their propensity to engage in warfare; it was almost a constant activity for at least the greatest of the political communities, and undertaken for seemingly trivial reasons. Conquest was its most frequent outcome. Similarly, all the great historical empires – Roman, Mongol, Mogul, Spanish and Russian, for example – were created largely through military conquest. But, if we review the record of war in the past three centuries approximately, we can discern some critically important modifications in the long and dreary history of armed conflicts. There are at least four aspects of the use of force between polities that can be considered revolutionary. By revolutionary, I mean that common and historical practices have changed roles, tasks and functions (transformation); trends in practices have had a critical increase or decrease in incidence; or practices have become obsolete or disappeared. The revolutions are:
1. the significant decline in the incidence of war between states;
2. the de-legitimization of conquest;
3. a developing norm that requires *collective authorization* for the use of force to be legitimate;
4. the change in the purposes and tasks of armed force.

The incidence of inter-state war

Numerous statistical studies on the incidence of inter-state war exist but, because they use different definitions of war, different time periods and different databases, the details differ. However, the trends are roughly similar. Table 2.1 summarizes the frequency of inter-state war (war, not war involvement, is the unit of analysis) as noted in two recent studies.[1]

Several patterns emerge from these data. First, the raw amount of inter-state war has not declined in the past three centuries. Whereas a new war

Table 2.1 The incidence of inter-state war since 1495

Period	Number of states (average for period)	Number of inter-state wars[a]	Average interval between wars (years)	Inter-state war per state per year
Holsti data[b]				
1495–1600	18	40	2.6	0.15
1648–1714	20	22	3.0	0.15
1715–1814	19	36	2.8	0.15
1815–1914	21	29	3.4	0.16
1918–1941	30	25	0.9	0.36
1945–1990	145	38	1.2	0.06
1991–2005	181	8	1.9	0.01
Sarkees et al. data				
1816–1899	30	30	3.0	0.519[c]
1900–1997	98	49	2.0	0.283[c]

[a] Includes armed interventions with 1,000+ casualties as a result, but does not include wars of colonial conquest or pacification, or wars of "national liberation"–decolonization.
[b] Data for the 1495–1600 period come from Quincy Wright, *A Study of War* (2nd edn, Chicago: University of Chicago Press, 1965, pp. 641–642).
[c] Wars per system member.

began on average once every three years in the period between Westphalia and the Treaty of Utrecht (1715), in the period since 1991 there has been a new inter-state war or armed intervention almost every second year. As noted by many historians, the nineteenth century, compared with its successor, was an era of relative peace in Europe, with a new war or armed intervention taking place only once every 3.4 years on average. The worst record of warfare was the period between the two world wars of the twentieth century, when a new war or armed intervention became on average an annual event. Woodrow Wilson's characterization of World War I as the "war to end war" was tragically incorrect because it actually spawned an era of unprecedented armed violence and conquest between states. Similarly, George H. W. Bush's 1991 declaration of a "New World Order" has been succeeded by eight inter-state wars and major armed interventions rather than by peace.

However, these figures hide as much as they reveal. Because the number of states has increased from approximately 20 in the mid-nineteenth century to 191 current members of the United Nations, we would expect on a basis of probability that, as in increasing traffic densities, the incidence of accidents (war) would climb. Yet, the trend here is a dramatic reversal from the historical pattern. For the average state in an average year, the probability of using armed force against an external adversary has declined from one chance in seven during the era of the Enlightenment (1715–1814) to one chance in one hundred currently. Many areas of the world have known no war for more than a half-century (Western Europe, South America) and a few states have not been to war for almost three centuries (Sweden, Siam/Thailand). Hobbes' world of perpetual fear of attack and invasion has not come to pass. For millions, perhaps billions, of people, the main threats to their security and livelihood today come from domestic sources, not from outside attack.

States have used armed force, as Clausewitz suggested, for known political purposes. Over the centuries, these purposes have changed, and what we notice in drafting a map of conflict-generating issues over the period is that many of the purposes and values over which states so often went to war no longer generate lethal conflicts. In the eighteenth century, contests over trade, semi-official piracy, dynastic prestige ("glory" as it was called), colonial competition, succession issues and territory gave rise to the use of force. For example, Louis XIV's attack on Holland in 1672 was designed primarily to establish the king's "glory" and reputation as a warrior. In the same era, Holland and England went to war three times over issues of trade and the limits of territorial jurisdiction. Today, institutions such as the World Trade Organization or the International Court of Justice resolve such issues. Most of the uses of armed force of the recent past have involved issues of ideology, the composition of governments, national self-determination, state integrity, terrorist activity, the collapse of state authority and pre-empting the development of WMD (the Israeli bombing of Iraq's Osirak nuclear reactor in 1981; the US attack on Iraq in 2003). Territorial conquest, colonies, empire and glory no longer exist in the minds of most government leaders.

Historically, decisions to use armed force were made only after procedures to resolve issues through diplomatic and other non-violent means had failed. Many wars escalated from militarized crises; others expanded when alliance partners felt compelled to meet their treaty obligations; still others were forms of retaliation against earlier provocations. In most of these cases, the policy makers did not seek out opportunities to launch their armed forces. They went to war because other instrumentalities of persuasion failed; most were perceived as wars of necessity.

Aggression – a secretly planned, unprovoked war of choice, usually with a staged "incident" or some "intolerable" condition as a pretext – remains a relatively rare event in international life. Table 2.2 lists some of the more spectacular cases of aggression in the history of the contemporary states system.[2] Although this list is not comprehensive, its brevity – except for the 1930s – suggests that the unjustified use of force, not pre-

Table 2.2 Major military aggressions/conquests, 1648–present

Aggressor	Victim	Year	Incident
Louis IV	Holland	1672	
Frederick II	Austria	1740	
Napoleon	Multiple	Multiple	
Bismarck	France	1870	Ems telegram
USA	Spain	1898	Battleship "Maine"
Japan	Russia	1905	
Japan	Manchuria	1931	Mukden incident
Italy	Ethiopia, multiple	1935, 1939, 1940	
Japan	China	1937	Marco Polo Bridge
Germany	Poland, multiple	1939, 1940, 1941	Gleiwitz "canned goods" attack
USSR	Finland	1939	Mainila incident
Japan	USA	1941	
Israel, UK, France	Egypt	1956	
USA	North Viet Nam	1964	Gulf of Tonkin
Egypt, Syria	Israel	1973	
North Viet Nam	South Viet Nam	1975	
Indonesia	East Timor	1975	
Iraq	Kuwait	1990	
USA, UK	Iraq	2003	"weapons of mass destruction"

ceded by prior diplomatic means of conflict resolution and often legitimized by a phoney or staged "incident", is a rare form of statecraft. If
we exclude the serial aggressions of Napoleon, those of the dictators in
the inter-war period and imperial wars, there were only 16 cases of outright aggression/occupation in the more than 350 years since Westphalia.
As in the case of all inter-state war, the raw incidence of aggression has
not declined but, when adjusted for the number of states, its comparative
infrequency does constitute a major shift away from the historical pattern
of the use of armed force.

Armed force need not, however, involve war in the sense of a contest
of violence between the armed forces of two or more states. If we include
unilateral armed intervention as a form of armed force, then our first revolution needs to be qualified. Armed intervention, a relatively rare phenomenon in the eighteenth and nineteenth centuries, has become a hall-
mark of the use of force since the end of World War II. The purpose of
this type of armed force is not to achieve "victory" over an adversary's
military forces, but to sustain or change another polity's configuration of
public authority or political personnel. Since 1945, the United States, the

United Kingdom, the Soviet Union and France have employed force on numerous occasions for this purpose.

Overall, the figures in Table 2.2 show two remarkable shifts from historical trends: the significant decline in the incidence of conquest/ aggression and classic inter-state wars, offset by the increase in the great powers' propensity to use force unilaterally to prop up or depose regimes in the post-colonial world.

The obsolescence of conquest

Conquest was the common outcome of wars throughout history. The typical pattern was for the armies to fight in the field (or navies on the seas) and, once a victory had been gained, the victors physically occupied the city of the vanquished, put the military-age men "to the sword", and took women and children as slaves. If the victor did not wish to maintain hold of the vanquished city, it razed it.

The pattern of conquest in Europe going back to the seventeenth century is roughly similar, although the winning side in a war seldom killed off the peoples of the conquered territories (except in establishing colonies in the "New World"). Every war fought within Europe since the great Thirty Years War and until 1945 led to territorial revision of one type or another. Provinces, cities, duchies and whole countries were carved up, attached to the victors or divided among several parties. A sovereign, according to legal analysts, had a *right* of conquest, provided certain conditions were met.

Since the early nineteenth century, that right has been increasingly circumscribed and, today, eliminated. The Congress of Vienna began the process. Although not written into the final document, the main protagonists agreed in the Austrian capital and at subsequent Concert of Europe meetings that any great power that gained territory through the use of armed force had to seek the approval of the other great powers, and that in no case could a great power use military force against the interests of another great power. This norm was put to its severest test in the case of the Russo-Turkish war of 1877. The resulting peace treaty of San Stefano (1878) was subjected to revision at the Congress of Berlin in the same year, where Austria and England compelled Russia to give up some of its territorial gains made at the expense of Turkey. A conquest was partially undone.

The Great War and its aftermath spelled the death knell of the old sovereign right of conquest. In Article 10 of the League of Nations Covenant, member states agreed that the new League of Nations had as its main purpose the protection of the independence and territorial integrity of all states. The Kellogg–Briand Pact of 1928 outlawed aggressive war, and the Stimson Doctrine (1931), later adopted as a formal component of international law, stated that no new legal rights could emanate from territorial conquest. In the event, this meant that Japan's conquest of Manchuria and its establishment of the puppet state of Manchukuo had no legal standing and would not be recognized by the governments of the world. The final blow to the right of conquest came in the Charter of the United Nations, which, as in Article 10 of the Covenant, claimed that the main purpose of the Organization is to protect the independence and territorial integrity of its members. Force can be used legitimately only for self-defence or on the order of the Security Council. Moreover, any territorial revision brought about through armed force violates the principle of self-determination. This norm has been reiterated in the Helsinki Final Act (1976), the Pact of Paris (1990), and literally dozens of diplomatic notes sent by the United States and members of the European Union to the successor states of the Soviet Union and Yugoslavia. The message is now clear: there can be no territorial revision except through the consent of the parties involved in a dispute.

Conquest has been de-legitimized. But is this only the case at the rhetorical level? The answer is no. There have been few conquests since 1945 and, of those that have taken place, most were undone later. Indonesia was compelled to give up East Timor; the Arab territories occupied by Israel will not (with minor exceptions) become formally annexed to Israel (or will not be accepted as legal by other states); and all the attempts at conquest (Korea in 1950, Suez in 1956, Iraq in 1990) failed largely as a result of overwhelming international opposition. Although there have been a few minor territorial revisions (primarily disputes about the exact location of boundaries) achieved through military force since 1945, the only successful (i.e. permanent and internationally recognized) conquests of an established jurisdiction were India's annexation of Daman, Diu and Goa in 1961, and North Viet Nam's forced annexation of South Viet Nam in 1975–1976. The near-obsolescence of conquest stands in stark contrast to the previous patterns of war throughout recorded history.[3] This is a genuine revolution in the use of military force.

The collective legitimization of the use of force

Throughout that history, rulers seldom sought outside approval to unleash the sword. The doctrine of sovereignty is a negation of any authority above the state. No European dynast of the seventeenth or eighteenth century could have conceived that a decision to use armed force might require external authorization.

This exclusive domain of decision-making began to erode after the Napoleonic wars. The Concert of Europe was a loose consultative system among the great powers that developed important norms about when and in what circumstances a government could legitimately use force within Europe. The sovereigns of the era expected that (1) there would be consultations prior to the use of force, (2) no great power would use force that threatened the vital interests of another great power, and (3) any conquests (in Europe) required monitoring, review and possible revision.

The League of Nations did not go far beyond these ideas. The Covenant contained no specific requirement that any use of force must have prior *authorization* by the Council or Assembly. However, Articles 12–16 made it clear that all states had to exhaust numerous procedures (conciliation, mediation, court decisions, etc.) before they could legitimately use armed force.

The real revolution appears formally for the first time in the Charter of the United Nations. It dramatically circumscribes the use of force to two circumstances: for self-defence, and in applying sanctions under Chapter VII. The latter requires formal votes in the Security Council. That is, any use of force to be legitimate (except in self-defence) must obtain *authorization* from the Security Council. That authorization represents a mandate from the international community. Absent the mandate, the use of force (except in self-defence) is presumably illegal. This is a dramatically new norm in international relations. It has no historical precedent. As a metric of the international community's tolerance for the use of force, it raises the bar to unprecedented levels. Indeed, the bar may be so high that there will be a significant gap between the norm and actual behaviour. What do the figures show?

The United Nations Security Council has authorized collective military action 15 times since 1950. In addition, regional organizations have undertaken collective military activities on at least 36 occasions, all with the ultimate approval of the United Nations. Korea was the first authorization, although it must be recalled that South Korea and the United States launched military action prior to authorization by the Security Council. In 1991 and 2001, UN resolutions authorized member states to force the withdrawal of Iraqi troops from Kuwait and the United States to attack Afghanistan for harbouring al-Qaeda.

Although we know of these successes, *a majority of instances of the use of force between states since 1945 did not receive international authorization.* Inter-state wars and armed interventions have recurrently taken place in the absence of Security Council authorization. The Soviet Union, France, the United States, Israel, India, Pakistan, the United Kingdom, China, Viet Nam, Tanzania and many others have all launched military campaigns and armed interventions against their neighbours and more distant locales without any reference to an international organization, much less to a formal request for authorization. Some political leaders – most recently George W. Bush – have publicly claimed that they would never submit decisions relating to the security of their countries to external authorization. We can legitimately query, then, whether a norm that is systematically violated actually constitutes a norm that effectively constrains decision-making. Or, to put it another way, can we speak of a "revolution" in military affairs when in so many instances states behave unilaterally, as their predecessors did throughout history?

The existence of the norm is indicated by the strenuous debates surrounding the NATO armed intervention against Serbia in 1999 and the US aggression against Iraq in 2003. Most analysts have concluded that the NATO attack on Serbia was technically illegal because it failed to obtain Security Council authorization. However, there were compelling moral reasons in this case that vitiated the authorization requirement. Without military action, there would have been a humanitarian catastrophe, because the policy of the Serbian government was to force the Kosovars to leave their homeland. In this case, ethical requirements trumped legal obligations, just as in the case where a passer-by jumps in a lake clearly marked "no swimming" in order to save a drowning child. In the Iraq case, a large majority of UN members made it clear that no attack on Baghdad would be legitimate in the absence of an authorizing vote in the Security Council. The Secretary-General of the United Nations unequivocally characterized the US action as illegal. This position was also adopted by huge numbers of people throughout the world.[4] Governments that supported the United States against overwhelming domestic opposition (e.g. Spain) have had to pay an electoral price. All of this suggests that in the contemporary popular mind there is a strong supposition that, for any military action to be legitimate, it must have the imprimatur of an international organization, preferably the United Nations. This is at least circumstantial evidence about the existence of the norm. That it represents a revolutionary change in attitudes toward the use of force can be established if we compare the debates of 2003 with the complete freedom of action enjoyed by Louis XIV, Napoleon, Bismarck and the dictators of the twentieth century.

The fourth revolution: Re-inventing military tasks

Throughout history, military forces have been used for five essential purposes: (1) conquests and holding them; (2) defence against attack; (3) compellence; (4) dissuasion/deterrence; and (5) visual displays of prestige and power. In the Clausewitzian conception of war, the purpose of organized violence is to compel the adversary to surrender. In the past several decades, however, we have seen the rise of a new array of military tasks. These include peacekeeping (in the original sense of monitoring and separating combatants), peace enforcement and the plethora of roles and tasks involved in post-conflict "stabilization" and "nation-building". Most military organizations around the world now have training components that deal with the highly specialized tasks of peacekeeping, peace-making and peace enforcement, and many governments have created special units to undertake these tasks. I should add, as well, that many of the armed forces of post-colonial and post-Soviet states have as their main function the monitoring and policing of domestic society. Their main tasks are no longer to deter or defend against external threats, but to maintain domestic order and, as in so many current cases, to defeat secessionist and other types of domestic insurgencies.

This fourth revolution in the use of force is a symptom of the rise of private armed violence in an international system that contains numerous weak and collapsing states. The victory of the European state over other forms of organized armed strength was symbolized by the publication, in the 1820s, of Karl von Clausewitz's famous work *Von Krieg*. Clausewitz's work is notable for a number of reasons, but for our purpose its main points reflected the near-monopoly over the use of armed force that the states of Europe had achieved by the end of the Napoleonic period. Armed force, as Clausewitz famously noted, is a continuation of *state* policy by violent means. It is not organized plunder, medieval-type private violence or mayhem that feeds on itself – as was so typical in the Thirty Years War (1618–1648). War is a distinct form of violent confrontation, but one intimately linked to *public* purposes. Michael Howard provides a precise characterization of the Enlightenment conception of war:

> The prime characteristic of the military is not that they use violence, or even that they use violence legitimized by virtue of their function as instruments of the state. It is that they use that violence with great *deliberation*. Such violence, purposeful, deliberate, and legitimized is normally known as *force*, and the use of *force* between states is what we mean by war. War consists of such deliberate, controlled, and purposeful acts of force combined and harmonized to attain what are ultimately political objectives.[5]

State-organized, -controlled and -directed use of military capabilities does not encompass a significant amount of organized violence in the contemporary world. Today, the political landscape of many regions and states is populated by armed secessionist movements, millenarian religious groups and cults, organized terror cells, armed militias under little if any political control, armed, proto-criminal gangs parading as "liberation movements", private mercenary firms, armed dacoits, and the like. David Capie summarizes the characteristics and range of armed, non-state actors.

These groups [of armed non-state actors] vary enormously in terms of their size, behaviour, structure, motives, goals and resources. Some resemble traditional armies, with a formal, hierarchical command structure, while others operate with only loose controls between commanders and front line troops. Groups also have diverse motives. Some aspire to take over and control the state they are fighting, while others seek to create a new political community. Some fight to enrich themselves and their friends, while others pursue less tangible religious or spiritual objectives. Some groups exist in the open, associating with a political wing or party that advocates their cause, while others remain secretive and reclusive.[6]

The redefinition of military tasks is a response to this rise of private armed power and violence. As the line between criminality and classic military operations has become increasingly blurred in contemporary intra-state wars, so has the line between military and police tasks in the international responses to them.[7]

In terms of the proliferation problem addressed in this volume, weapons of mass destruction may not be the most compelling issue on the international security agenda. Although large numbers of innocent civilians may perish as the result of the use of nuclear or other mass-destruction weapons, to date the number of casualties resulting from WMD attacks and from terrorist incidents pales in comparison with the deaths attributed to conventional small arms used in civil wars and local insurgencies of various types. Conventional small arms rather than weapons of mass destruction or terrorist bombs killed 3 million in the Congo, almost 1 million in Rwanda and 100,000 in Darfur. If the number of actual or potential victims of violence is our measure of urgency, then the problem of licit and illicit trade and commerce in conventional weapons should take precedence over concerns about the proliferation of nuclear and other potential weapons of mass destruction. The probability that a "rogue" state would actually launch a nuclear attack on any other state is much smaller than the probability that privately armed groups will continue to kill hundreds of thousands of civilians within Burma, Kashmir, Chechnya, Sudan, Uganda, Nagorno-Karabakh, Congo and elsewhere. Nuclear weapons in the hands of non-state actors such as terrorist groups present a very serious threat but one that remains somewhat remote in comparison with intra-state violence commissioned with small weapons.

Responses to the problems of weak states, insurgency and private armed power

The purpose of the United Nations, as the Preamble to the UN Charter claims, is to "rid the world of the scourge of war". This signifies a global determination not to repeat the experiences of the 1930s, to place limits on the use of force between states and to provide procedures that must be used as alternatives to war. The founders of the United Nations can perhaps be excused for being backward looking – solving the problems of the past – and not foreseeing the explosion of civil wars, state collapse, wars of national liberation and the re-appearance of private armed power that are the legacies of colonialism. These, rather than wars between states, have formed most of the agenda of the United Nations during the past several decades.

The United Nations was created to protect states from their external enemies, meaning other states. It has now become primarily an organization to protect states from their internal enemies, be they secession movements, religiously or ideologically inspired insurgents, quasi-criminal organizations, terrorists, local militias or, sometimes, governments themselves. It is ironic that, in dealing with these new problems, the United Nations has transformed itself from an organization dedicated to the limitation and prohibition of public armed violence in the world to one that is seeking to decide how to use military force.[8] The primary question today is no longer how do we prevent war between states but in what circumstances and with what procedures can the international community legitimately use force to protect citizens from their own governments, massive abuses of human rights, humanitarian catastrophes, terrorist attacks, civil wars, proliferation of WMD and the resurgence of armed private groups? The United Nations is no longer an instrument of collective security against aggression so much as a collective life belt for endangered peoples and the states they inhabit.

The Enlightenment/Clausewitz conception of war contained an element of symmetry. The use of force involved a battle between the organized and centrally controlled armed forces of two sovereigns. The sole purpose of force was to induce the surrender of the opponent by defeating him on the battlefield, after which the diplomats would negotiate terms of peace. They would establish a new legal status quo. The tasks of contemporary collective force, in contrast, are highly variegated. In typical civil wars, the military forces may initially have only the task of separating the armed forces, roving militias and militarized gangs from the civilians upon whom they prey, but eventually they must provide overall security for citizens whose own governments are too weak, incompetent and/or corrupt to maintain law and order in their realms. Peacebuilding requires a host of civilian projects for which traditional armed forces were seldom trained. These include organizing elections, rebuilding infrastructure, training police, restoring civil society institutions such as courts, schools, hospitals and municipal services, relocating refugees, organizing amnesties or various forums for reconciliation, and the like. These multiple tasks have two aims: to establish conditions that will significantly lower the risk of new outbreaks of hostilities, after which the priority is to withdraw the intervening troops.

In terms of UN-sponsored peacemaking and peace-enforcing missions since the end of the Cold War (so-called "second generation" operations), the community military capabilities are impressive. At the height of these missions in the early 1990s, the United Nations had under its auspices more than 78,000 troops in the field – the equivalent of about five standard army divisions.[9] More than 800 peace keepers perished in this same period, a ratio of casualties to armed forces higher than US losses in Iraq since 2003. By 2001, there were 51 UN and UN-authorized ongoing peace operations, the majority including armed components. There were also 32 operations under the auspices of regional organizations.[10] The current debate over the conditions under which collective armed force can be used to prevent or put an end to humanitarian emergencies clearly accepts the basic procedural norm that any individual or collective intervention must receive collective authorization to be legitimate.[11] That issue has generated a near-universal consensus. The remaining issue is how to take effective action in the event that the Security Council is unable to authorize use of force owing to a veto.

A counter-revolution? The doctrine of pre-emptive attack

In 2003, Condoleezza Rice, the then National Security Advisor to President George W. Bush, wrote in a memorandum to her boss that "pre-emptive attack against terrorists or tyrants who control rogue states is a legitimate form of self-defense".[12] This is an even more extreme version of the pre-emptive war doctrines adopted as official policy by the United States in 2002. It asserts that the United States is justified in attacking any state or group that is even *suspected* of having or seeking weapons of mass destruction. There is no test of intent. Mere suspicion of potential possession is adequate justification for launching a military attack. This is the ultimate method of preventing proliferation, but it contradicts the essential norms governing the use of force in the UN Charter. The US attack on Iraq in 2003 established that the United States would act according to Ms Rice's advice. For there is mounting evidence that the president and his advisers knew before the attack, despite public rhetoric to the contrary, that Saddam Hussein did not possess weapons of mass destruction, or that at best he had only intentions to obtain them at some distant future date. The International Atomic Energy Agency in late February had certified that Iraq had no nuclear weapons programmes and, despite Saddam Hussein's attempts at deception and other cat-and-mouse games, by 19 March 2003 the Blix investigating commission had come up empty-handed in its search for evidence.

A major government that announces a fundamental change in military doctrine from deterrence to "attack-on-suspicion" risks creating a mimic problem. Even prior to the announcement of the Bush doctrine in 2002, Israel had long reserved for itself a right to act pre-emptively. But others could ignore that policy because it applied primarily to a limited geographical domain. Now, however, the United States has set a new (and significantly more risky) standard, which has been quickly followed by Australia and Russia. Others may claim the same "right", which means that the norms governing the use of force, evolved over almost two centuries, will become increasingly irrelevant.

However, the tension between the norms regulating the use of force and the problems associated with proliferation and the rise of private, subnational and transnational armed groups can be viewed in another light. We may be observing the development of a new profile of military violence that seems reminiscent of a "good guys, bad guys", "cops and robbers" metaphor. In this environment certain states, unilaterally or in ad hoc coalitions, take it upon themselves to deal with "rogue" states or non-state armed actors that pose the greatest threats to the international community at any given time. International relations then is no longer a game between sovereign equals, where war between them is the main problem to regulate (the fundamental assumption underlying the United Nations), but becomes a contest between anti-state and state forces. If this is the case, then the norms designed to deal with inter-state wars may not be relevant to the newer problems. We may be in the early stages of a new and prolonged contest between states and new kinds of actors that pay no attention to system-wide norms.[13]

What about the "nuclear revolution"?

After the two atomic bombs were dropped on Hiroshima and Nagasaki in 1945, military analysts were quick to proclaim a "nuclear revolution". These new weapons – enhanced many-fold by hydrogen bombs – caused such horrendous destruction that it was inconceivable they could actually be used as instruments of warfare. Their sole purpose, aside from serving as indicators of prestige, is deterrence – the prevention of war. Nuclear technology was making war obsolete. Should not this development constitute a fifth revolution in the use of armed force in international politics?

The contemporary concern with nuclear proliferation indicates that, in both popular and officials minds, nuclear weapons constitute a *continuity* of threats to international peace and security, not a break from the past. Whereas the leaders of both Cold War blocs and their allies insisted that *their* possession of nuclear weapons for purposes of deterrence was fully rational and a contribution to international peace and security, they perceived the expansion of nuclear capabilities to other states as a serious threat. The leaders of new states or "rogue" states could not be assumed to possess the rationality and moderation of leaders in Moscow, Paris, London or Washington. For some unexplained reason, the prudence learned by the nuclear great powers cannot be trusted to be learned by others. This view has prevailed despite evidence that, for example, the crisis between India and Pakistan in 2002 might well have resulted in war had their governments not feared that military necessity would demand the use of nuclear weapons. Nuclear proliferation is a serious problem, to be sure, but it must be differentiated. It makes a considerable difference whether additional aspirants to the nuclear club are well-established states such as India or Japan or non-state-based terrorist groups. Yet the conventional wisdom underlying the view of proliferation as a profound and continuing threat is that such weapons have not at all altered the calculus of war and that therefore the greater the number of states possessing these weapons, the greater the probability they will be used.

There are serious problems with this view, but there are more important reasons why nuclear weapons have not produced a revolution in the use of force. The record clearly indicates that for most crises, wars and armed interventions since 1945 nuclear weapons have been *irrelevant*. The possession of nuclear weapons undoubtedly moderated behaviour in a few crises, such as Berlin in 1961, Cuba in 1962 and Czechoslovakia in 1968, but, for the hundreds of other instances where force was used, they did not come into play in any meaningful sense. War has not become obsolete, states still possess armed forces primarily for "national security", and many states have launched those armed forces against their neighbours and more distant societies. Nuclear weapons may complicate defence decision-making, but by themselves they have not brought forth a revolution as defined earlier.

Conclusion

If we go back three millennia to explore the use of military force, we see a pattern of recurrence of violence, frequent conquest and uninhibited warfare. Westphalia did not terminate that long-run trend of war between independent polities. However, the Napoleonic wars resulted in such havoc, devastation and assault on Enlightenment sensibilities that the governments of the European states began thinking seriously about means to limit the frequency and consequences of war. World War I was a watershed event in the sense that it helped bring forth normative, public-opinion-based constraints on the use of force. It also gave effect to popular values dealing with the sovereignty and territorial integrity of states as well as national self-determination. Despite the systematic aggressions of Hitler, Stalin, Mussolini and the Japanese imperialists during the 1930s, millennia of conquests were about to come to an end. Although not endorsing a strict philosophy of historical progress, the revolutions in military affairs reviewed in this chapter give rise to the conclusion that the texture of international politics has changed dramatically in the past several centuries, and particularly since 1945. Kant predicted that humans would learn to overcome the urges to use military force only after suffering a series of ever-more catastrophic wars. His prediction has been borne out by subsequent events. The world wars of the nineteenth and twentieth centuries gave rise to immense normative changes that, in turn, affected the practices of states. Today – in stark contrast to the state of affairs at the time of Westphalia – there are important norms proscribing conquest and limiting the legitimate use of violence in the relations between states. The problem of war between states and unilateral armed intervention has not been solved by any means, but their frequency, given the greater number of states today, has declined significantly. Currently, it is primarily private armed insurgent groups and, often assumed though not proven, "rogue" states that pose the most urgent contemporary threats. Dealing effectively with them may require new techniques that are contrary to some of the norms regulating the use of force between sovereign states. If the declining incidence of classic inter-state wars approximates Kant's view of a peaceful world, the rise of new kinds of threats challenges this optimistic view of historical progress. To deal effectively with these threats, assuming that they are genuine and enduring, may require moving backward to prototypes of eras when war was unregulated, where conquest was normal and where unrestrained unilateralism was the predominant form of behaviour when it came to the use of force.

Notes

1. See K. J. Holsti, *The State, War, and the State of War* (Cambridge: Cambridge University Press, 1996), p. 22 and Appendix, updated in K. J. Holsti, *Taming the Sovereigns:*

Institutional Change in International Politics (Cambridge: Cambridge University Press, 2004), p. 310. Meredith Reid Sarkees, Frank Whelan Wayman and J. David Singer, "Inter-State, Intra-State, and Extra-State Wars: A Comprehensive Look at their Distribution over Time, 1816–1997", *International Studies Quarterly*, Vol. 47, No. 1 (2003), pp. 49–70. For more recent data using different categories and cut-off points for counting (25 battle casualties annually instead of the more conventional 1,000+), see Andrew Mack, ed., *Human Security Report 2005: War and Peace in the 21st Century*, Centre for Human Security, the Liu Institute for the Study of Global Issues, University of British Columbia (Oxford: Oxford University Press, 2005).

2. The list is not exhaustive. It does not include attacks to claim or re-claim small pieces of territory, reprisals, and the like. However, most cases involving formal occupation of conquered territory are included.

3. For systematic data on the declining use of force for effecting territorial change, see Mark W. Zacher, "The Territorial Integrity Norm: International Boundaries and the Use of Force", *International Organization*, Vol. 55, No. 2 (2001), pp. 215–250.

4. As David Cortright makes clear in his contribution to the companion volume to this one: "The World Says No: The Global Movement against War in Iraq", in Ramesh Thakur and Waheguru Pal Singh Sidhu, eds, *The Iraq Crisis and World Order: Structural, Institutional and Normative Challenges* (Tokyo: United Nations University Press, forthcoming).

5. Michael Howard, "*Temperamenta Belli*: Can War be Controlled?", in Michael Howard, ed., *Restraints on War: Studies in the Limitation of Armed Conflict* (Oxford: Oxford University Press, 1979), p. 3.

6. David Capie, "Armed Groups, Weapons Availability and Misuse: An Overview of the Issues and Options for Action", Armed Groups Project, Centre for International Relations, University of British Columbia, 2004, unpublished.

7. See Peter Andreas and Richard Price, "From War Fighting to Crime Fighting: Transforming the American National Security State", *International Studies Review*, Vol. 3 (Autumn 2001), pp. 31–52; Richard Price, "Hegemony and Multilateralism", *International Journal* (Winter 2004–2005), pp. 109–130.

8. See Adam Watson, "The United Nations and Humanitarian Intervention", in Jennifer Welsh, ed., *Humanitarian Intervention and International Relations* (Oxford and New York: Oxford University Press, 2004), p. 71.

9. Brian Job, "The United Nations, Regional Organizations, and Regional Conflict: Is There a Viable Role for the UN?", in Ramesh Thakur and Edward Newman, eds, *New Millennium, New Perspectives: The United Nations, Security, and Governance* (Tokyo: United Nations University Press, 2000), p. 230. At the end of 2004, the figure stood at 60,000.

10. Ibid., p. 233, based on data from the Stockholm International Peace Research Institute.

11. The position is clearly specified in the report (sponsored by the United Nations and organized by the Canadian government) by the International Commission on Intervention and State Sovereignty, *The Responsibility to Protect* (Ottawa: International Development Research Centre, 2001). The policy prescription of the "responsibility to protect" was accepted officially in modified form at the United Nations World Summit in 2005.

12. The National Security Adviser [*sic*], Memorandum to the President, "Impact of the 2002 National Security Strategy on Reshaping America's Military", 2002, available at ⟨http://www.ciaonet.org/wps/kol02/kol02_addendum.pdf⟩.

13. I am grateful to Damon Colette for suggesting some of these points.

3

From deterrence to compellence: Doctrinal implications of the Iraq crisis

Kennedy Graham

"The unleashed power of the atom has changed everything save our modes of thinking, and thus we drift toward unparalleled catastrophe."

(Albert Einstein, telegram, 24 May 1946)

The human capacity to devastate the planet is still, in evolutionary terms, a new phenomenon. Whereas non-use of a particular kind of weapon is, for the first time, a political and moral imperative, its non-possession has not become universal policy. The force of tradition in security thinking still prevails in the modern age, with the acquisition of nuclear weapons still valued as a symbol of power, and their deployment as a credible sign of readiness for use in extreme circumstances.

This chapter explains how the extended Iraq crisis (1990–2006) comprises a pivotal point in the continuing efforts at controlling nuclear weapons. Its importance derives from the confluence of "old" and "new" security threats – inter-state aggression and nuclear proliferation. Its significance lies in two facts of portent for the future. It is the first time a UN member state has been forcibly denied the potential ownership of nuclear weapons, and it is the first time in the post–Cold War era that regime change has been undertaken of a member state's government recognized at the United Nations. As such, the crisis signifies the beginning of an apparent move from one doctrinal age to another. Yet even the Iraq crisis must be placed in the larger context of the nuclear dilemma faced by the international community as a whole, involving other equally difficult crises elsewhere.

Collective security and self-defence: The Faustian relationship

Collective security, as enshrined in the UN Charter, and the strategic doctrine that emerged to govern the nuclear age are only distantly related. Collective security was fashioned as the mechanism by which states, employing their combined conventional might, could repel aggression once it had been committed. The security system it reflected was designed, not for the first time, to prevent the preceding war. Contemporaneously, the advent of new and more potent weaponry ensured, not for the first time, its immediate obsolescence. The development of nuclear weapons and their spread among the major powers within a decade generated a military game for which the retrospective institutional rules were not designed. Conventional collective security was emasculated with the bipolar nuclear stand-off that paralysed the Security Council. Strategic doctrines designed to ensure global stability took its place, operating independently of, if loosely compatible with, the Charter.

The rules governing the use of force in the UN era have correspondingly undergone a mutation from that originally envisaged. The plans of the 1940s for ensuring the avoidance of further global conflict posited one exception only for the use of military force – the collective response to aggression authorized by the Security Council. It was not until the San Francisco Conference itself, five weeks before the Charter was signed, that a second exception was entered as a compromise with those urging greater autonomy for regional security mechanisms. The right of individual and collective self-defence was included as a second exception for the use of force. Unlike collective security, self-defence is an "inherent right" that exists independently of Council authorization – the only requirement being to report to the Council on any armed action undertaken in its name. Self-defence is subordinated, however, to collective security insofar as the right lasts only until the Council takes the necessary measures to maintain peace.[1]

The compromise was to prove fateful for the international community. As collective security collapsed under the weight of the Cold War, self-defence moved centre-stage as the principal justification for the use of force, encompassing at the same time the novel phenomenon of nuclear weapons. Thus regional nuclear defence alliances sprang up as the central struts of the international security architecture for half a century. These tenets – self-defence and nuclear alliances – governed international security for 50 years. In the new era they continue to be pursued, but in scarcely recognizable form compared with only a few decades before.

The Cold War and deterrence: Son of Faust

During the Cold War, "deterrence" became the governing paradigm for strategic relations among the five nuclear powers (the United States, the United Kingdom, France, Russia and China) and "persuasion" became the governing paradigm for relations between the nuclear powers and the non-nuclear states. The five nuclear powers were "deterred" from mutual aggression and the hundred or so non-nuclear states were "persuaded" to agree to forgo such weapons.

Deterrence

Deterrence involves the threatened use of military power to induce an adversary not to undertake an action it might otherwise be disposed to do. It is achieved by making the adversary believe that the deterrer is able and ready to inflict unacceptable damage upon it if that action is undertaken. Although deterrence as a psychological concept has characterized political activity for millennia, it became the principal feature of global stability in the nuclear age. Before the nuclear age, the purpose of military strategy had been to win wars; since then, its chief purpose has been to avert them.[2]

During this period the doctrine evolved, at least in Western thinking, from "massive retaliation" to "mutual assured destruction" (MAD). MAD rested on two interdependent phenomena: the maintenance of a negotiated "rough parity" in strategic offensive nuclear forces and the foreswearing of strategic defence. Manifest in twin legal instrumentation – the Strategic Arms Limitation Talks (SALT) and Strategic Arms Reduction Treaty (START) on the one hand and the Anti-Ballistic Missile (ABM) Treaty on the other – strategic deterrence kept a cold, calculated and, ultimately, dangerous peace for two generations of policy makers.

Persuasion

While "deterrence" prevailed among themselves, "persuasion" was prosecuted by the leading nuclear powers towards all other states to construct an effective non-proliferation regime. The Treaty on the Non-proliferation of Nuclear Weapons (NPT) was a bargain between the desire for a nuclear-free world, or one close to it, and the concerns of the non-nuclear states over the discriminatory advantage of nuclear technology for the major powers. The *quid pro quo* for the non-nuclear states, in terms of national interest, was two-fold. Their energy needs could be met through national development of nuclear power for peaceful use, with assistance from the nuclear powers. Their security interests were met through inclusion in nuclear alliances or, for the non-aligned, the "positive security assurances" entered by the permanent members in the Security Council.[3] A third consideration was entered – a compromise over the broader issue of global security, namely a declaratory vision of the "total elimination of nuclear weapons from national arsenals" and a binding obligation on the nuclear-weapon states to negotiate nuclear disarmament "in good faith".[4]

This two-tier discrimination over nuclear weapons possession generates continuing political and legal controversy. The dichotomy enshrined by the NPT rests on a time-sequenced distinction between states that possessed nuclear weapons before 1967 and all others.[5] Politically this allowed the dual fiction that justified possession by the permanent five members of the Security Council (the P-5): their "superior" command and control systems and a special responsibility for peace and security under the Charter. Legally, however, the fact remains that membership of the NPT is a voluntary act by every state, each of which retains the right of withdrawal at three months' notice if "extraordinary events" jeopardize its "supreme national interests". Conversely, continued adherence to the Treaty requires, to this day, a judgement that nuclear non-possession is continuously in a country's national interests. If the "negative criterion" is not met, a withdrawing state is simply obliged to give notice to all other parties and to the Security Council, including a statement of the events that have jeopardized its supreme interests.

Such was the controversial nature of the NPT that it was originally struck for 25 years, with reviews undertaken every 5 years. Two nuclear powers remained outside the regime – China and France objecting to the discriminatory nature of the deal struck. Only half the UN member states immediately joined. Review conferences were tense and acrimonious. Several outside the Treaty moved purposefully towards nuclear-weapon status. "Persuasion" worked, but only partially and at an agonisingly slow pace in a fateful race against time.

The "war on terror" and compellence: Second son of Faust

The collapse of the socialist system and the move from bipolarity to unipolarity have transformed the strategic landscape. Deterrence retains a rhetorical element, with nuclear weapons deployed as "weapons of truly last resort" in statecraft, involving reduced force levels and lowered alert status on the part of some powers. But deterrence between the major powers is no longer politically centre-stage in global strategy, being consigned to the doctrinal closet for retrieval in the event of a revived strategic rivalry. Deterrence is now focused on pre-emptive tactical use against non-state actors.[6] Eclipsing deterrence politically is a new major power relationship – "nuclear collaboration", prosecuted through a newly assertive Security Council.

Collaboration

The strategic realignment of major power interests in the early 1990s created a heightened awareness of their common "superior" nuclear status, signalled by a policy change by China and France in support of the NPT. The hopes of the international community for a reinvigorated Security Council to govern the peace coincided with a more united nuclear pentarchy in the form of the P-5 claiming in common the two overarching symbols of global power: permanent Security Council membership and nuclear weapon possession. The post–Cold War development – a more effective Council with a generally pliant rump in the elected 10 members – is a novel scenario. Yet it shows sibling characteristics common to the nuclear family.

Since 1990 the Council has thus begun to evolve from the traditional, narrowly conceived instrument that responds to inter-state aggression envisaged by the framers of the Charter into a prototype body of global governance. Part of this has involved the manner in which the Council has started to act on the legal and enforcement aspects of the nuclear regime. The Council has begun to "legislate" in the matter of nuclear weapons. In the 1990s, the P-5, acting through the Security Council, moved away from the *quid pro quo* debate towards a new global strategy, one predicated on the presumption of the legality of their own nuclear weapons.

This trend has been strengthened by the deliberations of the International Court of Justice (ICJ). When the matter was submitted to it for an advisory opinion, the Court was unable to conclude that the use or threat of use would be illegal in an extreme circumstance of self-defence when the very survival of a state was at stake.[7] The Court added that a binding obligation existed on the nuclear powers to negotiate disarmament in good faith, which was widely regarded as simply a reiteration of the existing NPT provision. The implication, however, is that nuclear weapon use is not illegal when national survival is threatened and provided the requisite humanitarian principles are observed. In the view of most legal authorities, this is a contradiction in terms.

The departure from deterrence was marked by the US withdrawal from the ABM Treaty and the development of a rudimentary ballistic missile defence.[8] The move towards nuclear collaboration was marked by the 1992 Summit Statement of the Security Council that "the proliferation of all weapons of mass destruction constitutes a threat to international peace and security".[9] With that seminal "decree" the P-5 distinguished between their own possession of nuclear weapons as "guardians of the peace" and possession by others as "threats" to that peace.[10] Having delivered themselves of that distinction, the nuclear powers proceeded to signal their intention to retain nuclear weapons "for the foreseeable future".[11] The world is thus set for an indefinite two-tier system of oligarchic nuclear power.

Compellence

After securing the NPT's indefinite extension in 1995 and persuading nearly all the non-nuclear states to join,[12] the nuclear powers have moved, on a collaborative basis, to a more nuanced policy towards the non-nuclear world. A majority of states remain "persuaded" of their own accord that their national interests continue to reside in adherence to the NPT. But the past decade has witnessed a development that requires the calibration of "persuasion" with "compellence". Thus the P-5 have begun a historic move in global strategic policy: those that will not be "persuaded" to remain non-nuclear will be "compelled" to do so.

In fact the Council has developed a three-tiered policy in the past decade towards nuclear proliferators, namely:

- "persuasion" (bordering on coercion) of the majority of states that are "amenable";
- "exceptionalism" towards the three nuclear-weapon states (Israel, India and Pakistan) that were always outside the dragnet (the NP-3); and
- "compellence" towards those that seek to escape from within.

The successful "persuasion" effort had, by 1990, established a norm of universality in non-proliferation. Following the Soviet collapse, Kazakhstan, Ukraine and Belarus hosted nuclear weapons on their national territories. Yet the combined political pressure and financial incentives of the US Department of Defense's Cooperative Threat Reduction Program succeeded within the context of "persuasion". Apartheid South Africa's secret programme was terminated in 1990 by the democratic government, which joined the Treaty the following year. Ratification by Argentina and Brazil in 1995 and 1998, respectively, completed the policy of "persuasion" towards the major threshold countries. And in 2003 Libya terminated its weapons of mass destruction (WMD) programme, which included a nuclear component.

Three states, however, have escaped the tightening non-proliferation regime. Israel, suspected of having nuclear weapons since the 1960s, implacably maintains a policy of "nuclear ambiguity". Despite persistent efforts by the Arab League, the Security Council, facing a US veto, has never made a pronouncement on the matter, reducing the credibility and legitimacy of the pentarchic policy. India and Pakistan, never having joined the NPT, were denied, at the time of their nuclear tests in 1998, the "status of a nuclear weapon State ... in accordance with the NPT" – stretching the P-5 nuclear fiction to near breaking-point.[13] Notwithstanding its view that this constituted a threat to the peace, the Council merely condemned the development, failing even to apply economic sanctions.[14] South Asia is today the only region where nuclear deterrence directly underpins security in a political as well as a doctrinal stance.[15] With the NP-3, the Council's impotence with *faits accomplis* has been amply demonstrated.

Compellence or persuasion: Three critical tests

Three states – Iraq, North Korea and Iran – are the litmus test of the choice between "persuasion" and "compellence", which is expressed in doctrinal terms in the distinction between the US policy of pre-emption and the European policy of pre-emptive engagement.[16] These three countries are also listed by the United States as comprising the "axis of evil" – a characterization that, apart from inflaming political passions, obfuscates policy-making by conflating proliferation and terrorism to no constructive effect.

Iraq: Failing the first test

Iraq remains to this day the only complete case of "selective compellence". The multinational response to Iraq's aggression against Kuwait in 1990 showed the ability of the United Nations to make collective security work when the Council is united. Of equal significance, however, was the Council's readiness to apply a vice-like grip on Iraq's sovereignty over WMD. Its "decision" of April 1991 that Iraq would reaffirm its adherence to the NPT and the Biological Weapons Convention, and undertake all WMD disarmament under UN inspection, was a seminal move.[17] It was the first time the Council had, under binding authority, decided that a sovereign state would not be free to withdraw from a WMD treaty and manufacture WMD.[18]

Did the Council have the inherent authority to make such a decision, stripping a sovereign member state of its customary right to acquire any armaments it might deem necessary for its defence? Of the three judgements the Council can make to trigger enforcement powers, the first two – aggression and breach of the peace – pertain to acts of commission. They are territorially specific, amenable to empirical verification and involve the direct response of a military roll-back of an aggressor's forces. The third – a "threat to the peace" – is wide-ranging and inherently subjective. Yet the Council has had no compunction over the past decade in according itself considerable latitude in identifying what constitutes such threats.[19] In this case the Council's judgement did not derive directly from Iraq's aggression.[20] It came rather from its concern eight months later over the reports "in the hands of Member States" that Iraq had attempted to acquire material for a nuclear weapons programme "contrary to its obligations under the Treaty on the Non-Proliferation of Nuclear Weapons". It also deplored "threats made by Iraq during the recent conflict to make use of terrorism against targets outside Iraq and the taking of hostages by Iraq".[21] In April 1991 the Council was acting on new "facts on the ground" (nuclear proliferation) yet evoking enforcement powers derived indirectly from the earlier aggression.

By August 1991 the Council had already determined that Iraq's actions comprised "serious violations" of its obligations under, and thus a "material breach" of, the Council's disarmament resolution. It was not until October 1994 that the Council determined that subsequent post-invasion actions by Iraq, namely "any hostile or provocative action directed against its neighbours", constituted a "threat to peace and security in the region".[22] Economic sanctions – "mild compellence" – cost the world half a million Iraqi children, souls forever immortalized in the comment of one policy maker that their sacrifice had been worthwhile.[23]

The invasion of Iraq by the coalition in 2003 signified the potent force of the US policy of pre-emption in the name of self-defence – an action not authorized by the Council. But the debate in the Council was not, in early 2003, over whether it had the right to authorize intervention, but rather over when that authorization might be most appropriate and politically wise in light of the facts known at the time.[24]

North Korea and Iran: Searching for middle ground

Doctrinally, the Iraq crisis has run its course – the United States and the United Kingdom, if not the Council, will engage in compellence if necessary, and the United States will do it alone if necessary. Politically, however, the test for the future lies with the Democratic People's Republic of Korea (DPRK) and Iran.

These two axis cases are different from Iraq. Whatever lack of sympathy the North Korean regime may attract from beyond its borders, it advances a credible claim for WMD acquisition on grounds enshrined in the NPT and observed by the P-5 for themselves – national security in extreme situations. Legally, the ICJ's opinion that nuclear weapons cannot be judged illegal when "the very survival of the state is at stake" applies to the DPRK as much as to the P-5 and the NP-3. Is the DPRK free to exercise its right to withdraw from the NPT and acquire nuclear weapons? The Court, in 1996, implied it is. The Security Council, in 1992, indicated it is not. A legal loophole thus currently exists that is open to political exploitation.

The Korean crisis lies at the fulcrum of "persuasion" and "compellence". The DPRK's unprecedented withdrawal announcement of 1993, specifying joint military exercises by the United States and South Korea as a "nuclear war rehearsal" designed to disarm it and "strangle" its socialist system, elicited an unprecedented response.[25] The three NPT depositary governments issued a joint statement querying whether the events cited by North Korea did, in fact, constitute "extraordinary events" that jeopardized North Korea's "supreme interests".[26] Legally that judgement remains within the sovereign discretion of the state concerned – the NPT explicitly accords neither the depositary governments nor the Security Council the authority to query the national view. Despite this, the Security Council noted the scepticism of the depositary powers, condemned the DPRK move and called for negotiations to resolve the crisis.[27] The 1994 US–DPRK Agreed Framework offered sufficient incentives (guaranteed heavy oil supplies, upgraded nuclear technology) to "persuade" the DPRK not to proceed with withdrawal. But the security situation again deteriorated in Pyongyang's view, and in January 2003 it simply announced its withdrawal (rather than an intention) on the grounds of the security situation on the Peninsula arising from the "aggressive actions of the US", this taking effect in April. The DPRK alternately acknowledges and denies nuclear weapons possession.[28] The six-power dialogue with North Korea suggests that "persuasion" is preferred to "compellence", reflecting a natural Asian instinct for dialogue and also American preoccupations with the difficulties of compellence elsewhere. Yet a pre-emptive strike, considered by the United States in the mid-1990s, is still not ruled out.

Iran, like Iraq, denies it has a nuclear weapons programme and, given the inadequacies of national intelligence advice over the Iraq crisis, prudence may be in order. Yet the International Atomic Energy Agency (IAEA) remains concerned over Iranian insistence on its "inalienable right" to peaceful nuclear technology and its refusal to suspend its enrichment programme. The Agency's Statute requires it to refer any violations of the NPT to the Security Council.[29] To date it has chosen not to do so, but Tehran's acrimonious rhetoric towards Israel of October 2005 may change that. Meanwhile there exists continuing apprehension over the possibility of a pre-emptive strike by Israel, with tacit US encouragement and support. Israel's 1981 strike on Iraq's nuclear reactor, unanimously condemned by the Council but without any punitive action, remains a de facto precedent.[30]

Dealing with the sibling – Iraq and problems of "compellence"

The halting move from "deterrence–persuasion" to "collaboration–compellence" reflects the international community's attempts at a nuanced calibration of policy in an increasingly complex world.

There is an acute distinction in human behaviour and state policy between coercion (compellence) and cocrccd volition (deterrence). As Schelling put it in the 1960s, the difference was "between taking what you want and making someone give it to you, between fending off assault and making someone afraid to assault you".[31] Deterrence and compellence differ in both objectives and means. Deterrence aims to influence an adversary to refrain from undertaking an action. Compellence aims to force an adversary to stop doing something it has started to do. Deterrence involves only the threat of force. Compellence involves the actual use of force before the action is performed. Given that no nuclear power can "compel" another to surrender its nuclear weapons, the only option is to influence them not to use them and to collaborate in keeping the numbers down. With respect to non-nuclear states, however, the option of compellence exists in the event that persuasion fails.

Thus the fundamental distinction has to be drawn between the nuclear/nuclear relationship and the nuclear/non-nuclear relationship. In the former case, stability among the nuclear powers, locked in Cold War adversarial rivalry, was held to rely only upon deterrence. As the relationship thawed, deterrence could cede to collaboration, albeit of modest proportion as befits major global players. In the latter case, persuasion towards non-nuclear states was required when the concept of national sovereignty retained the commanding heights of the Westphalian terrain, but could cede, in extreme cases of the post–Cold War era, to compellence when the major powers judged it necessary and feasible to breach the conceptual norm. It is a passing irony that Schelling advanced the concept of compellence, linking it with deterrence and persuasion, during Cold War days, but that a clearer matrix of these concepts is emerging in the post–Cold War era.

Compellence strategy rests, in the first instance, on regulatory controls (through the IAEA, the Nuclear Suppliers Group and the Missile Control Technology Verification Regime), tightened recently in the Proliferation Security Initiative. If these fail, the Council must decide on the legal merits of intervention and regime change. The latter, however, cannot be legally sanctioned purely on grounds of violations of NPT obligations. Nor can it be sanctioned by any judgement of the Security Council (or "willing coalition") over the nature of their political systems, whether communist or Islamic.

The weaknesses of compellence strategy in the twenty-first century – essentially a magnification of those of deterrence in the twentieth century – have to do with credibility borne of mutual understanding. In deterrence strategy it was recognized that conveying the appearance of irrationality introduces uncertainty in the adversary's decision-making calculus.[32] The same applies to compellence. Any assumption that military force will ultimately induce compliant behaviour in recalcitrant states carries the risk of miscalculation. Such a state may be motivated by rational considerations more than is presumed, and the pressure applied by the major powers may simply induce the opposite behaviour to that intended because of an adversary's different value system.

These shortcomings were portrayed in the Iraq crisis in three ways. Because compellence involves force, Iraq's prevarication required the Council to decide how to react. The question of when to use armed force against Iraq for alleged material breaches of its disarmament "obligations" had vexed the Security Council since the mid-1990s.[33] In 2003, the Council's divisions stemmed from disagreement not over shared suspicions of Iraqi WMD possession but over how to enforce its disarmament. The majority view that the "logic of peace" (UN inspections backed by an over-the-horizon military presence) should prevail over the "logic of war" (immediate invasion and regime change) signified a preference for "persuasion" over "compellence". The coalition's rationale for compellence – securing compliance by Iraq with the Council's disarmament conditions[34] – was deemed by the UN Secretary-General, a majority of states and global opinion to be lacking in legitimacy[35] and, indeed, to be "illegal".[36]

Secondly, compellence relies on credibility on the part of those applying the compulsion. The coalition's rationale was subsequently shown to be false, as the US congressional inquiry established. Iraq in fact had consistently denied possessing any WMD,[37] an assertion incorrectly branded by the United States as a "lie".[38] The "replacement rationale" advanced in the occupation phase – "removing tyranny" and "fostering freedom and democracy" – involves goals for which armed force is not sanctioned in the Charter. This constraint is undergoing change – "principles of intervention" reflecting the emerging norm of "responsibility to protect" were advanced by the 2004 report of the High-level Panel on Threats, Challenges and Change and endorsed by the Secretary-

General.[39] But, at its 2005 World Summit, the General Assembly kept the norm confined to a "case-by-case" basis.[40]

Thirdly, compellence also invites resistance, which, if it is based on reasonable legal grounds, can be politically potent. In response to the invasion of Iraq, the Arab League sought an urgent session of the Security Council with regard to "halting the American-British aggression and the immediate withdrawal of the invading forces".[41] The refusal of the Council to consider this request revealed, not for the first time, the body's structural shortcomings, further undermining its credibility in the General Assembly.[42] The popular Arab response to the Secretary-General's judgement over the illegality of the invasion was to claim legitimacy for the Iraqi resistance, repudiating at the same time the atrocities committed in its name.[43] Support for such resistance extends beyond the Arab world, influencing the debate elsewhere.

Misjudging the psychological calculus may have more lethal significance in relation to dissident non-state actors, involving their possible acquisition of nuclear or radiological weapons. That twenty-first-century spectre introduces qualitatively different reasoning for global strategy. In the twentieth century, the adversary was perceived by each side to be a rational actor, pursuing national interests through traditional statecraft. Each side felt the need to deploy nuclear weapons, yet neither wished to use them. The mutual strategy was thus designed to heighten that disinclination. In the war on terror the potential adversary is taken to be less rational, less predictable and more inclined to use nuclear weapons. Yet non-state actors are seen by many as also more rational than establishment rhetoric suggests. Extreme behaviour, including sacrificial and brutal actions (suicide bombings, civilian massacres), is not *ipso facto* irrational. It simply reflects visions and values that may be alien to the modern establishment power structure. For non-state actors, the utility of nuclear weapons lies in their potential not as military instruments of war but as "political instruments of terror".[44] In the past, nuclear weapons were seen as symbols of stability for the preservation of the status quo. Now they are sought by non-state actors as potential agents of radical global change. That heightened readiness for potential use drives the logic of the pre-emption doctrine, heightening concern over the erosion of international law.[45]

Pre-emptive intervention in support of a WMD prevention policy thus remains problematic. The United States cites "UN enforcement" in the Security Council but "self-defence" in the domestic debate ("no 'permission slip' is required"....). That degree of pre-emption for self-defence is not what the framers of the Charter had in mind, yet that document, framed principally by the thirty-second US president, appears to matter less to the forty-third. Current US policies – effecting withdrawal from the ABM Treaty but denying that right for the NPT, and threatening the use of nuclear weapons to deny them from others[46] – take the "discrimination double standard problem" to new heights.

Some prescriptive thoughts from the Iraq crisis

If compellence is to become acceptable to a majority of states, there will be a need for improvements in the procedures by which it is prosecuted. Two areas in particular are worthy of consideration.

First, the conceptual confusion deriving from the Iraq crisis has been largely clarified by the November 2004 report of the Secretary-General's High-level Panel.[47] The Panel's prudent judgement that the UN Charter was sufficient to accommodate the "new realities" of the twenty-first century, and did not require amendment, is useful guidance to a divided world, and it was reiterated by the 2005 World Summit.[48] The Panel's view that this applied to both the self-defence provision (Article 51) and the broader collective security provisions of Chapter VII has clarified the division between the "pre-emptive strikers" (the United States) and the "pre-emptive engagers" (the European Union). Pre-emptive self-defence under Article 51, the Panel thought, can legally be used against a terrorist threat provided that this is imminent and cannot be deflected otherwise, and that proportional means are employed. Preventive action against a WMD proliferator, however, is a longer-term threat and the use of force in such cases is a matter of collective security requiring Council approval (and not self-defence, which requires only notification).

In this received wisdom, compellence clearly falls into the latter category, requiring Council approval. Pre-emptive military action against proliferators cannot be unilaterally undertaken in the name of national self-defence. In making this clear, the Panel has usefully drawn the distinction between terrorism and proliferation, in effect implying that the Iraq invasion was illegal.

The second area concerns the way the Council makes decisions. The High-level Panel's recommendation was for an expanded Council of 24, which is unlikely to be acted upon any time soon. Certainly an expanded Council would increase its legitimacy and enhance its authority. Yet even an expanded Council will make mistakes of judgement and policy if procedural reform is not introduced as well. As the Iraq crisis showed, many procedural shortcomings remain that make the Council ineffective in times of crisis. As a remedial measure in this respect, five procedural improvements could be contemplated, namely:

- a mechanism for factual verification that serves the Council when enforcement powers are at stake, with a "firewall" established between the multilateral verification and national intelligence functions, and stricter procedures governing the admissibility of evidence for decision-making;
- more clarity on the legal merits of the use of force – in advance of a decision;
- greater precision in the language used in any resolution authorizing force;
- a time limitation on resolutions authorizing force (three months) – whose objective is explicitly identified;
- a procedural threshold for the use of force through an announcement by the Council president, it being understood that any use of force without that announcement is deemed illegal.

The first two improvements would require the Council to establish subsidiary organs – a Verification Committee and a Legal Committee. Both could be composed of diplomatic and expert representatives of Council member states. They would have advisory functions only and would be subordinate to the plenary powers of the Council as a whole. But, together, they would help "stabilize" and, to some extent, "de-politicize" Council deliberations. The other three suggestions would simply require innovation in customary behaviour.

Persuasion and compellence are at either end of a political spectrum but there is a logical contradiction between them. Although persuasion is the preferred route, the moment it fails it is too late for compellence. Yet if compellence is introduced prematurely, it undermines persuasion. So the two are antithetical. As long as nuclear weapons remain subject to national control, that catch-22 will haunt policy makers as they continue to deal with the Faustian dilemma of our times. Meanwhile, civilizational tensions are on the boil. We are in for a tough century.

Notes

1. UN Charter, Article 51.
2. B. Brodie, ed., *The Absolute Weapon: Atomic Power and World Order* (New York: Harcourt, Brace, 1946), p. 76.
3. UN Security Council Resolution 255 on Security Assurances to Non-Nuclear-Weapon States, UN Doc. S/RES/255, 19 June 1968.
4. NPT, Preamble, para. 11, and Article VI, respectively.
5. The permanent five members of the Security Council (the P-5) met that threshold, notwithstanding that two of them (China and France) remained outside the regime until the early 1990s.
6. A new US contingency plan for nuclear weapon use (CONPLAN 8022, 2003), implementing National Security Presidential Directives 14 and 17 of 2002, makes operational

the contingent first-use of US nuclear weapons against suspected weapons of mass destruction (nuclear, chemical or biological) in hardened deep bunkers, whether possessed by states or by non-state actors. This is a change from longstanding Western nuclear policy of first-use only in response to aggression with overwhelming conventional force.

7. "[T]he threat or use of nuclear weapons would generally be contrary to the rules of international law applicable in armed conflict, and in particular the principles and rules of humanitarian law; However, in view of the current state of international law, and of the elements of fact at its disposal, the Court cannot conclude definitively whether the threat or use of nuclear weapons would be lawful or unlawful in an extreme circumstance of self-defence, in which the very survival of a State would be at stake" (ICJ Advisory Opinion, *Legality of the Threat or Use of Nuclear Weapons*, 8 July 1996, para. 2E, ⟨http://www.icj-cij.org⟩). The Court was split seven to seven on this paragraph, and the president cast the deciding vote. This part of the Opinion in particular has given rise to considerable dispute over interpretation.

8. The US withdrawal from the Treaty was legally valid under Article XV, which requires identical criteria to those in the NPT but six months' notice rather than three. The United States asserted that withdrawal did not imply total strategic defence against major powers but a shield against the "stray" missiles of a hostile "mini-nuclear power" (such as North Korea). Yet China claims it undermines the deterrent effect of its 18 intercontinental ballistic missiles, and Russia is implacably opposed to US withdrawal.

9. UN Security Council statement, Project on Chemical and Biological Warfare, UN Doc. S/23500, 31 January 1992.

10. "NATO's nuclear forces continue to contribute, in an essential way, to war prevention. They are maintained at the minimum level sufficient to preserve peace and stability" (*NATO Handbook*, Brussels: NATO Information Office, 2001, p. 53). Non-NATO nuclear powers evince the same intentions.

11. *The Alliance's Strategic Concept*, 24 April 1999, para. 46, ⟨http://www.nato.int/docu/pr/1999/p99-065e.htm⟩.

12. NPT states comprise 189 countries (the P-5 plus 184 non-nuclear-weapon countries).

13. UN Security Council Resolution 1172, on Peace and Security – Nuclear Tests by India and Pakistan, UN Doc. S/RES/1172, 6 June 1998.

14. The United States and some other countries applied bilateral sanctions, which were lifted over time as Pakistan supported the war on terror. Pakistan is now listed as a "non-allied friend" of the United States.

15. Neither the Middle East nor the Korean Peninsula currently exhibits the same balance of mutually assured destruction, the quintessential feature of deterrence.

16. *The National Security Strategy of the United States of America* (New York: The White House, September 2002), ⟨http://www.whitehouse.gov/nsc/nss.pdf⟩; "An International Order Based on Effective Multilateralism", in *A Secure Europe in a Better World: European Security Strategy* (Brussels, December 2003), ⟨http://ue.eu.int/uedocs/cmsUpload/78367.pdf⟩.

17. UN Security Council Resolution on Iraq–Kuwait, UN Doc. S/RES/687, 3 April 1991.

18. The Versailles Treaty had imposed draconian disarmament measures on a defeated Germany in 1920, but this was the first occasion in the modern era and the first such decision on weapons of mass destruction.

19. See K. Graham and T. Felicio, *Regional Security and Global Governance* (Brussels: VUB Brussels University Press, 2006), pp. 40–51.

20. The Council resolution at that time determined only a "breach of international peace and security" (Resolution 660 on the situation between Iraq and Kuwait, UN Doc. S/RES/660, 2 August 1990) and called for the restoration of Iraq's forces to the position *ex ante bellum*.

21. S/RES 687, 3 April 1991.
22. UN Security Council Resolution 949, demanding that Iraq immediately complete the withdrawal of all military units recently deployed to southern Iraq to their original positions and that Iraq not again utilize its military or any other forces in a hostile or provocative manner to threaten its neighbours, UN Doc. S/RES/949, 15 October 1994.
23. US Secretary of State Madeleine Albright in CBS "60 Minutes" interview, 12 May 1996. Subsequently, Ms Albright in effect retracted the statement (*Madam Secretary: A Memoir*, New York: Miramax Books, 2003, p. 275).
24. See, for example: "The UN's rules governing the use of force, laid out in the charter and managed by the Security Council, had fallen victim to geopolitical forces too strong for a legalist institution to withstand. By 2003, the main question facing countries considering whether to use force was not whether it was lawful. Instead, as in the nineteenth century, they simply questioned whether it was wise" (Michael Glennon, "Why the Security Council Failed", *Foreign Affairs*, Vol. 82, No. 3, May–June 2003, p. 16).
25. "Letter of 12 March 1993 from the Permanent Representative of the DPR Korea transmitting the letter from the Minister for Foreign Affairs to the President of the Security Council concerning its decision to withdraw from the NPT", UN Doc. S/25405, 12 March 1993.
26. "Letter of 1 April 1993 from the Russian Federation, the UK and the USA transmitting the statement by the depository Governments of the NPT concerning the decision by the DPR Korea to withdraw from the NPT", UN Doc. S/25515, 2 April 1993.
27. UN Security Council Resolution 825 on the Democratic People's Republic of Korea, UN Doc. S/RES/825, 11 May 1993.
28. "The nuclear deterrent of the DPRK constitutes a legitimate self-defensive means to counter the ever-growing US nuclear threat and aggression against the DPRK and reliably defend sovereignty, peace and security of the country" (DPRK Statement to UN General Assembly, 27 September 2004, ⟨http://www.un.org/webcast/ga/59/statements/dprkeng040927.pdf⟩.
29. IAEA Statute, Article XII.C.
30. UN Security Council Resolution 487 on Iraq–Israel, UN Doc. S/RES/487, 19 June 1981. The Council also noted Iraq's membership and Israel's non-membership of the NPT, and called upon Israel to place its nuclear facilities under IAEA safeguards. This was ignored, yet the Council dropped the matter.
31. Thomas Schelling, *Arms and Influence* (New Haven, CT: Yale University Press, 1966), p. 2.
32. See Glen H. Snyder, *Deterrence and Defense* (Princeton, NJ: Princeton University Press, 1961), pp. 25–27.
33. In 1997 the Council determined that Iraq's "unacceptable decision" to impose conditions on the UN Special Commission created a situation that continued to constitute a "threat to international peace and security" (Security Council Resolution 1137 on the situation between Iraq and Kuwait, UN Doc. S/RES/1137, 12 November 1997).
34. "Letter dated 20 March 2003 from the Permanent Representative of the United States of America to the United Nations addressed to the President of the Security Council", UN Doc. S/2003/351, 21 March 2003.
35. Statement by UN Secretary-General, *UN News*, 3 April 2003.
36. Statement by UN Secretary-General, *BBC News*, 16 September 2004.
37. "The influence of any international organization is based on the conviction and trust of the community in which it exists, once the Organization declares that it has been established to serve goals important to that community.... We know that those who pressed the case in the Security Council ... have objectives other than to ascertain that Iraq has developed no weapons of mass destruction.... [S]end the inspectors to Iraq to ascertain

as much, and if their conduct is thoroughly supervised to ensure it is lawful and professional, everyone will be assured that Iraq has produced no nuclear, chemical or biological weapons of mass destruction" (Letter from Iraq Foreign Minister to UN Secretary-General, UN Doc. S/2002/1242, 13 November 2002).

38. "Why We Know Iraq Is Lying", US National Security Adviser, Condoleezza Rice, *New York Times*, 23 January 2003, available at ⟨http://www.whitehouse.gov/news/releases/2003/01/20030123-1.html⟩.

39. *A More Secure World: Our Shared Responsibility*, Report of the Secretary-General's High-level Panel on Threats, Challenges and Change, UN Doc. A/59/565, 20 November 2004, paras 199–203; and *In Larger Freedom: Towards Security, Development and Human Rights for All*, Report of the Secretary-General, UN Doc. A/59/2005, 21 March 2005, para. 132.

40. *2005 World Summit Outcome*, UN Doc. A/60/L.1, 15 September 2005, para. 139.

41. "Letter dated 24 March 2003 from the Permanent Representative of Iraq to the United Nations addressed to the President of the Security Council", UN Doc. S/2003/362, 24 March 2003.

42. See, for example, the statement by the Secretary-General of the League of Arab States before the Council: "In fact the Council was right when it refused to give a license or authorization to a single State to declare war on Iraq. The Council was also right when it refused to qualify the war as legitimate. Once the war started, the Council's role was discarded completely. Fighting raged for more than three weeks yet the Council remained silent, and this silence has seriously affected its credibility and role" (UN Doc. S/PV.4739, 11 April 2003). Within months, the Council retroactively legitimized the coalition's occupation, the Iraqi Interim Governing Council, and renamed the occupying force a "multinational force" – with the acquiescence of the Arab League.

43. "This testimony by the UN secretary general means that the US and Britain were in breach of international law, when they waged an unlawful war against a weak and besieged country that led to its total destruction and the death of more than 25,000 of its children" (*Al-Quds al-Arabi*, London); and "Annan's confirmation that war in Iraq was unlawful and [US Secretary of State Colin] Powell's confession that pretexts to wage war were concocted are a clear signal for the international community to do its best to support the courageous Iraqi resistance" (*Al-Jumhuriyah*, Cairo). *BBC News*, 16 September 2004.

44. Carl Builder, *The Future of Nuclear Deterrence*, Rand Report P-7702 (Santa Monica: RAND, 1991), p. 12.

45. Secretary-General Kofi Annan: "we must start from the principle that no one is above the law, and no one should be denied its protection. Every nation that proclaims the rule of law at home must respect it abroad" (Address to the General Assembly, 21 September 2004, ⟨http://www.un.org/apps/sg/sgstats.asp?nid=1088#⟩).

46. The United States has plans for a new generation of smaller "bunker-busting" nuclear weapons to penetrate suspected secret WMD programmes underground.

47. *A More Secure World*, paras 183–198.

48. *2005 World Summit Outcome*, para. 79.

4

"Do as I say, not as I do": From nuclear non-proliferation to counter-proliferation

Rebecca Johnson

Introduction

From its beginnings in the 1960s, the Treaty on the Non-Proliferation of Nuclear Weapons (Nuclear Non-Proliferation Treaty, or NPT) was primarily designed to prevent the horizontal spread of nuclear weapons *after* their acquisition had already been accomplished by a small number of states. That is unsurprising, since the concept of non-proliferation was largely promulgated by three of those nuclear powers – the United States, the Soviet Union and the United Kingdom – with a view to stabilizing the world in conformity with their perceived strategic interests. The objective of nuclear disarmament was insisted on by a number of non-nuclear-weapon states, but the best they were able to obtain was a very vague commitment in Article VI, which came after other incentives, such as the right to share in the benefits of nuclear energy and "peaceful" nuclear explosions. Though the arsenals continued to grow in size during the Cold War, the next three decades witnessed the progressive recognition of disarmament as an essential component of the concept of non-proliferation. However, this appearance of a stronger normative relationship was largely due to UN politics, including diplomatic strategies promoted by the non-aligned states, together with pressure from civil society; it would be a mistake to assume that the increased levels of political gesture and lip-service ever signified any genuine acceptance of the necessity of disarmament by the major nuclear powers.

As the Cold War ended, governments cemented their approach to chemical weapons threats by establishing a non-discriminatory prohibition regime that required all the existing chemical weapons arsenals to be verifiably dismantled and destroyed. By comparison with the NPT, which had differentiated the obligations of those already possessing nuclear arsenals from those that were to undertake never to acquire such weapons, the universal approach taken by the Chemical Weapons Convention (CWC)[1] was revolutionary. By the end of the 1990s, no one seriously challenged the relationship between disarmament and non-proliferation where biological and chemical weapons were concerned. By contrast, the strategic and political roles assigned to nuclear weapons made it much harder for the nuclear-weapon states to accept that the progressive elimination of their own nuclear arsenals might likewise be a prerequisite for effective non-proliferation.

The original brief for this chapter was to examine changes in the normative relationship between disarmament and non-proliferation, which led to the conclusion that progress on nuclear disarmament – as opposed to arms limitation – has largely been illusory, taking place in the realm of diplomatic gesture rather than being incorporated into policy and practice. As this chapter will explore, the salient shift that has actually occurred in conjunction with the war on terrorism is from norm-based non-proliferation to counter-proliferation, involving self-selected coalitions of the willing backed up by the threat or use of force. Driven by US policy changes, illustrated also in the war on Iraq, the counter-proliferation approach has been pursued on several fronts, though it is far from being internationally accepted. This approach carries inherent limitations for efforts to prevent the spread of nuclear weapons. The problem goes beyond debates about whether there has been adequate progress to reduce nuclear arsenals. For disarmament to have a structural and normative impact on non-proliferation, the existing nuclear weapons possessors would need to incorporate it as a genuine policy imperative, which would mean confronting the fundamental problem of the use and threat of use of nuclear weapons embedded in their own doctrines. The counter-proliferation approach avoids this challenge by focusing on "the bad guys". Although counter-proliferation can contribute useful tools, especially for dealing with non-state actors, there is a risk that, by de-linking disarmament from non-proliferation and failing to address the complex motives and causes underlying proliferation, its advocates will undermine the non-proliferation regime, rendering it less effective and authoritative.

1968–2000: Establishing a universal regime, from the NPT to the Thirteen Steps

Nuclear non-proliferation was an idea that came to the fore in the 1960s. The NPT developed out of a joint US–Soviet draft designed to reflect their own strategic interests, even though the idea had originated with non-nuclear countries, spearheaded by Ireland. Chastened by the Cuban missile crisis and trying to cope with the uncertainties of the bilateral nuclear relationship, President John F. Kennedy had looked at the possibility of 20–25 nuclear-weapon states by the 1970s and shuddered. The United States and the Soviet Union recognized that the spread of nuclear weapons would undermine both the perceived military and political utility of their own nuclear forces and their efforts to impose their version of bilaterally controlled stability on the rest of the world.

Arms control itself was a relatively new concept for the nuclear powers, and was developed to manage the US–Soviet nuclear relationship. Though disarmament proposals and zero options were periodically advanced by one side or the other during the Cold War, they were chiefly for propaganda purposes. The Partial Test Ban Treaty (PTBT),[2] which entered into force in 1963 (though without France, which started nuclear testing in 1960), was more significantly a measure of environmental protection than arms control, though one purpose of forbidding above-ground nuclear testing was to slow would-be proliferators down. Having crossed the nuclear threshold themselves, the first three nuclear-weapon states had no intention of renouncing nuclear weapons, but they were concerned about significant nuclear programmes in countries ranging from Sweden and India to China and Japan. The urgency of pursuing non-proliferation was underscored when China conducted its nuclear-testing rite of passage in 1964 and became the fifth nuclear power.

Developed as an additional instrument for managing Cold War international relations, non-proliferation differed from arms control in that it was designed to constrain the rest of the world. By seeking to ban the production and possession of a particular weapon, the nuclear non-proliferation regime departed from earlier multilateral instruments, which regulated use. For example, in response to the gassing of soldiers in World War I, which had come to be viewed in retrospect as more abhorrent and unsoldierly than conventional weaponry, the 1925 Geneva Gas Protocol prohibited the use of asphyxiating and poisonous gases and bacteriological methods of warfare, but did not ban the production, possession or stockpiling of the weapons.[3] Two years after the NPT entered into force, and following a US decision unilaterally to renounce the production and use of bioweapons and toxins, the Biological and Toxin Weapons Convention (BTWC)[4] was concluded in 1972. This banned both the weapons and their production, but lacked any verification and implementing authority. Though the BTWC did not explicitly prohibit the use of biological or poisonous weapons, it made clear that the 1925 prohibitions remained valid. It differed fundamentally from the NPT in imposing the same legal conditions and restraints on all States Parties, regardless of whether they had bioweapons programmes or not.[5]

Though there were continuing efforts towards prohibiting chemical weapons, it took the end of the Cold War and Saddam Hussein's use and stockpiling of chemical weapons to create the conditions and urgency for the CWC to be concluded in 1992. It emulated the BTWC by treating all States Parties alike, but reflected an important post–Cold War shift by including an elaborate multilateral verification regime.

By contrast, eschewing a universal approach to banning nuclear weapons, the nuclear powers in the 1960s sought the trickier objective of maintaining their own capabilities but preventing others. This was not acceptable to some of the leading non-nuclear-weapon states, which insisted on introducing disarmament by the nuclear-weapon states into the non-proliferation equation. They queried the dominant powers' logic that the problem was not the weapons but their spread, with its concomitant assumption that nuclear weapons were essential for deterrence and their own security but too dangerous or unsuitable for other countries to develop. Although they were prepared to accept that unbridled proliferation would be bad for international security and could increase the risks of nuclear accident or war, the non-nuclear-weapon states pointed out that for them to renounce weapons of such awesome power for the foreseeable future made security sense only if the overall objective was the complete elimination of those weapons from the face of the Earth. Since the United States, the Soviet Union and the United Kingdom were eager to sign up as many non-nuclear countries as possible, the outcome of these negotiations was Article VI, a watered-down pledge to pursue in good faith the cessation of the nuclear arms race, nuclear disarmament and general and complete disarmament. The relationship between these three objectives, and whether they should be treated as linear steps or dependent conditions, has been a source of endless politicking ever since. The non-nuclear countries were also given some conditional security assurances, not in the treaty itself but via the UN Security Council (Resolution 255 (1968)). As part of a different bargain, Article IV pledged that the treaty would not affect an "inalienable right" to nuclear energy for peaceful purposes, which has come to haunt modern efforts to combat nuclear threats. In addition, the initial period of the treaty's operation was set at 25 years, requiring a further decision in 1995 if it were to remain in force for longer.

Though the NPT did not address the use of nuclear weapons, a growing public awareness of the effects of nuclear weapons had contributed to the effective establishment of a taboo on the use of nuclear weapons. Though never formally acknowledged, this taboo was an important factor in deterrence and self-deterrence. It arose from the perception that the mounting nuclear arsenals made surviving a nuclear war less and less plausible. Theories of deterrence were borne from policy makers' realization that nuclear war was unplannable and would result in the incineration of their homelands. By the 1970s, the nuclear governments bought voters' acceptance for their nuclear arsenals chiefly by arguing that they were there not to be used but to prevent use. Although the doctrines of the NATO weapon states kept open the option of using nuclear weapons if required to avoid defeat in a conventional war, it was clear that most of their citizens would prefer occupation (which might be survived and overcome in the future) to nuclear obliteration, seen as more terrible and final.

In real terms, the United States accepted defeat rather than use nuclear weapons in Viet Nam, as did Russia in Afghanistan. In effect, nuclear weapons were legitimate only if never used; the justification for their possession was to deter anyone from using them. Deterrence came to be elevated into an article of faith, although some practitioners later claimed that its success rested chiefly on luck.[6] The non-nuclear-weapon states, meanwhile, continued to assert that the only sure way to prevent the use of nuclear weapons was to prohibit and eliminate them altogether.

As more states acceded to the NPT, the nuclear non-proliferation bargain was progressively reinterpreted, with the nuclear states' failure to halt testing and make progress on nuclear disarmament becoming the focus of non-nuclear – and especially the non-aligned – states' complaints. Proliferation was portrayed as having two equally important axes: horizontal proliferation – the spread of weapons and their technology to new states – and vertical proliferation, referring to qualitative developments, modernization and quantitative increases in existing arsenals. Disarmament and non-proliferation came to be seen as two sides of the same problem, which was nuclear insecurity.

The momentous upheavals of the 1980s changed the nuclear calculations forever. First came the 1987 Intermediate-Range Nuclear Forces (INF) Treaty, which removed land-based Cruise, Pershing and SS20 missiles from Europe. Dictated by political developments and civil society pressure, the INF Treaty pre-dated the fall of the Berlin Wall. In conjunction with the extraordinary debates between Presidents Reagan and Gorbachev at the Reykjavik Summit a year earlier, it was both a reflection of and factor in the upheavals that ended the Cold War. The START (Strategic Arms Reduction Treaty) process followed, but where the INF Treaty may be characterized as a genuine disarmament measure, eliminating state-of-the-art nuclear weapons, the bilateral START agreements and unilateral reductions of the early 1990s had the primary effect of rationalizing military and budgetary burdens.

Even as they claimed credit for cutting the numbers and types of nuclear weapons, France, Russia, the United Kingdom and the United

States emphasized the importance of their nuclear "deterrents" for security, which suggests that disarmament per se was not in their sights. China quietly carried on with its programme of nuclear modernization, while periodically calling for the "complete and thorough prohibition and destruction of nuclear weapons" and a multilateral agreement on no first use. The non-nuclear-weapon states, however, took the opportunity to push the cause of irreversible nuclear disarmament, starting with the Comprehensive Nuclear-Test-Ban Treaty (CTBT), which had been languishing on the non-proliferation agenda since the 1950s. They were also successful in linking disarmament principles and objectives with the 1995 decision on extending the NPT. Again the product of difficult negotiations with nuclear-weapon states which did not want to make measurable or accountable commitments to nuclear disarmament, the paragraphs on disarmament specified the CTBT and a ban on fissile material production (fissban) already in the pipeline, and then tailed off into fudged references to "the determined pursuit ... of systematic and progressive efforts to reduce nuclear weapons globally, with the ultimate goal of eliminating those weapons".[7] This was as generalized as they could get away with, but nevertheless an improvement on the vagueness of Article VI.

These developments were followed in 1996 by an Advisory Opinion from the International Court of Justice (ICJ) on the legality of the use or threat of use of nuclear weapons. Reflecting established geo-strategic and political interests, it was inevitable that the Opinion was ambiguous in several places. Most importantly, however, there was consensus among the judges that "[t]here exists an obligation to pursue in good faith and bring to a conclusion negotiations leading to nuclear disarmament in all its aspects under strict and effective international control".[8] The point here was that the goal of disarmament must be realized, not just evoked with political gesture. In a further split decision, carried by the president's casting vote, the Court determined that "the threat or use of nuclear weapons would generally be contrary to the rules of international law applicable in armed conflict, and in particular the principles and rules of humanitarian law".[9] Soon after, the Canberra Commission on the Elimination of Nuclear Weapons published its report, which dissected and debunked nuclear deterrence and recommended several practical steps for reducing nuclear dangers, including: taking nuclear forces off alert; removing warheads from delivery vehicles; ending the deployment of non-strategic nuclear weapons; ending nuclear testing; initiating negotiations to further reduce US and Russian nuclear arsenals; and reaching agreement among the nuclear-weapon states regarding reciprocal no-first-use undertakings (i.e. that they would not be the first to use or threaten to use nuclear weapons against each other) and also undertakings that they would not use or threaten to use nuclear weapons in any conflict with a non-nuclear-weapon state – a position going beyond the conditional security assurances currently in place.[10]

During the 1990s, nuclear weapons became viewed increasingly as a security problem, even by the weapons states. Though it is debatable whether policy makers in the nuclear-weapon states (NWS) were ever convinced that eliminating their own nuclear weapons would contribute to their security, the concepts of disarmament and the non-use of nuclear weapons had become integral normative components of non-proliferation. However slow their progress in eliminating the existing arsenals, disarmament was at least an objective that the NWS had to pretend to accept.

Though eagerly taken up by civil society and the non-aligned states, the ICJ and Canberra Commission reports received little policy attention from the major powers. After the NPT was indefinitely extended in 1995 and the CTBT concluded in 1996, the world was rocked by a series of nuclear tests by India and Pakistan in May 1998. A month later, a group of foreign ministers from Africa, Latin America, Europe and the Pacific issued a declaration entitled "A Nuclear Weapons Free World: The Need for a New Agenda".[11] Coming at a time of crisis for non-proliferation, the New Agenda Coalition attracted great interest, with significant support and high-level opposition. Building on the ICJ Opinion and the Canberra Commission's practical steps, the New Agenda played a crucial leadership role for the non-nuclear-weapon states, developing the ideas, the teamwork and the strategies that enabled the NPT Review Conference in May 2000 to adopt a substantive set of agreements. Known now as the "Thirteen Steps" – though the 13 numbered paragraphs actually comprise more than 13 principles, objectives and specific measures – the NPT 2000 plan of action on nuclear disarmament included a groundbreaking "unequivocal undertaking by the nuclear weapon states to accomplish the total elimination of their nuclear arsenals leading to nuclear disarmament to which all States parties are committed under Article VI". A number of unilateral, bilateral, plurilateral and multilateral steps were specified in a multi-stranded approach that recognized the need for different measures to be promoted singly or together, depending on political or international conditions or the particular circumstances of the different weapons states. These include: support for the CTBT, and a moratorium on nuclear testing pending its entry into force; negotiations on banning fissile materials for weapons; implementation of deeper reductions in deployed strategic nuclear forces (the START process); further unilateral reductions in nuclear arsenals; further reductions in non-strategic nuclear weapons; increased transparency and confidence-building measures; reduction in the operational status of nuclear weapons systems; a diminished role for nuclear weapons in security policies, thereby minimizing the risk of their ever being used (which could encompass no first use or strengthened security assurances); negotiations involving all the nuclear-weapon states; and verification to build confidence in the implementation of agreements.

Though the apparent breakthrough was heralded as an important stage forward in the tortuous route to disarmament, the years since the adoption of the "Thirteen Steps" have seen disarmament become more marginalized and the regime put under increasing pressure from new proliferators and arrogant weapons states. The "war on terror" has conveniently provided a context for reinterpreting the meaning of non-proliferation.[12] Going beyond the Clinton administration's attempts to square nuclear possession with non-proliferation in the early 1990s, neoconservative doctrine seeks to direct attention away from the special destructiveness of nuclear weapons and the disarmament objectives implicit in the wider concept of non-proliferation and focus selectively on keeping such weapons out of the hands of "bad guys".

2001–2004: The shift to counter-proliferation

Well before the Twin Towers were brought down on 11 September 2001, Bush administration strategists had been working on a new nuclear and security strategy for the United States and, by extension, its allies. Published in February and September 2002 respectively, the Nuclear Posture Review (NPR) and National Security Strategy (NSS) echoed the late 1940s and early 1950s, when military and political superiority was the overriding objective and nuclear weapons were not subject to deterring taboos but regarded as a powerful but specialized tool in the military arsenal. Instead of communism, terrorism is being packaged for the twenty-first century as the military and ideological enemy of "the Free World". Though non-state armed groups that perpetrate bombings, hijackings and other atrocities against civilians are the putative target, some states are also demonized within the category. In January 2002, Iraq, Iran and North Korea were dramatically castigated by President Bush as an "axis of evil", though they were clearly not in concert with one another.[13] In the war on terror, the reasons for targeting particular countries appear elastic: some (but not all) proliferators of technology or materials for weapons of mass destruction (WMD); some (but not all) totalitarian regimes with appalling human rights records against their own citizens or aggressive postures towards their neighbours; some (but not all) governments believed to sponsor or harbour armed groups bent on the destruction of other religious, ethnic or national ways of life. As with nuclear-armed communism, the United States has reason to view terrorism as a threat; but, like the paranoia over communism in the 1950s, it appears that the terrorist accusation is all too easily stretched to silence or undermine those who are merely guilty of being critical of US actions or having conflicting or competitive interests. One consequence of the ideology underpinning the war on terror may be a new era of witch-hunts to root out "un-American" behaviour, internationally as well as domestically, backed up by draconian (if frequently irrational) immigration restrictions and arbitrary arrest, interrogation and deportation powers.

It can be argued that several elements of the National Security Strategy were laid down under the Clinton administration, in part owing to the influence of the Republican majority in Congress, but the Bush administration has gone considerably further. On nuclear policy, President Clinton accomplished some useful agreements, but signally failed to get to grips with the challenges of the end of the Cold War. Although many agreed with Les Aspin (Clinton's first Secretary of Defense, whose term was cut short by serious illness) that it was in US security interests to take the lead in nuclear disarmament, Clinton fudged his historic opportunity to restructure US defence and foreign policy and contribute more profoundly to international security. Aspin had understood that the world was changing profoundly, and that nuclear weapons, once symbols of military sophistication, power and status, would become more accessible to weak leaders who would seek them as leverage or levellers against strong powers such as the United States.

Faced with what the 1999 Tokyo Forum for Nuclear Non-Proliferation and Disarmament characterized as "a choice between the assured dangers of proliferation or the challenges of disarmament",[14] Clinton dodged the challenge and went for arms control business-as-usual, augmented by the Nunn–Lugar cooperative threat reduction programme to reduce threats arising from the crumbling Soviet infrastructure and loose nukes. Rather than thinking through the future security environment and its requirements, he took the easier path of continuing to engage the Russians in the plodding bilateral measuring game of START II, while he also became embroiled in expanding the North Atlantic Treaty Organization (NATO), to appease some European governments and US defence contractors (for whom the expansion opened up lucrative new markets under the rubric of interoperability). Though the influence of the Republicans in constraining and hounding his administration must not be underestimated, Clinton's eight-year presidency in the first decade of post–Cold War reconstruction represented a real lost opportunity for foreign and security policy.

It is to the Bush administration's credit that it did not shirk the post–Cold War challenges. Less creditably, its analysis was largely driven by ideology, which seriously distorted the policy options. By fundamentally reframing the strategic triad in 2002, the Pentagon recognized that the large nuclear arsenals of the past were unusable and a drain on resources. The administration was more than happy to see deep cuts from Cold War levels of deployment. It appeared to demote reliance on nuclear weapons by elevating the strategic role of conventional forces, but leaked excerpts from the NPR showed that downgrading the strategic role of nuclear weapons went hand in hand with more tactical and "adaptive" nuclear capabilities to deal with contingencies. Taken together, these proposals would undermine deterrence and the normative taboo on the use of nuclear weapons, while also lowering the threshold for nuclear use. That this is intentional is borne out in public statements and the ways in which US security assurances have been reinterpreted. Depending in part on how other states respond, the Bush administration policy risks destabilizing international norms and non-proliferation in several other ways. The Pentagon persistently sought funding to develop robust nuclear earth penetrators (aka bunker busters) and smaller, more flexible tactical nuclear weapons, though Congress remained unconvinced, particularly as the defence budget and the occupation of Iraq were both spiralling out of control. The latest buzz from the US laboratories is now the "reliable replacement warhead" (RRW), which Britain also seems keen to embrace for its successor to the Trident nuclear submarine system.

The 2002 NPR envisages employing nuclear weapons in three broad circumstances: against targets able to withstand non-nuclear attack; in retaliation for the use of nuclear, biological or chemical weapons; or "in the event of surprising military developments", which is understood to extend to preventive or pre-emptive strikes. The first leg, as noted above, envisages a strategic role for conventional as well as nuclear weapons. The second leg encompasses defence, notably missile defence. In a remarkable innovation, capability-based planning was introduced as the third leg of the triad: "A revitalized defence infrastructure that will provide new capabilities in a timely fashion to meet emerging threats". Replacing strategic planning based on threat assessments, capability-based planning effectively rules out disarmament, though it allows for the rationalization of arsenals and withdrawal of redundant or obsolete weapons. Most importantly for the Republicans, capability-based planning would enable the Pentagon to support its defence industry indefinitely, making necessity-justified financial claims on taxpayers for research, development and testing. Hence, it would drive its own solitary, expensive, escalatory arms race to keep all options open to beat all possible future threats, whether feasible or fanciful.

The shock of 9/11 was real, but the timing was extraordinarily convenient for the Bush administration, which moved swiftly to consolidate the political construction of an unlimited, Orwellian war on terror. The NPR named North Korea, Iraq, Iran, Syria and Libya as countries that could threaten the United States and pose the kind of "immediate, potential or unexpected" contingencies to warrant nuclear-strike plans. Whereas threat-based planning required intelligence to be carefully sifted and rationally assessed as part of a process of identifying targets and priorities, the new approach has intelligence marshalled to legitimate a previously chosen target, as was seen in the build-up to the Iraq war.

Presaging the new policies, the Bush administration scuppered the BTWC verification protocol, which had taken six years to negotiate, in part to avoid reciprocal intrusive monitoring of US biotech industries or defence establishments. Bush also withdrew from the Anti-Ballistic Missile (ABM) Treaty and inaugurated a missile defence programme intended to provide interception (and attack) capabilities on land, sea and air platforms, with plans also to extend to weapons in outer space, the "fourth medium of warfare". In the wake of the NPR and the NSS, the agencies hurried to change US diplomatic positions in other areas too. Although the United States had been "out front pulling" for the CTBT during the Clinton years, and had played a constructive role in negotiating the Thirteen Steps in 2000, during 2002–2005 the United States spoke and voted against the CTBT and nuclear disarmament in concept and practice at numerous meetings of the United Nations and the NPT.[15] At the 2005 NPT Review Conference, the United States tried to steer NPT meetings away from disarmament, seeking condemnation of Iran and North Korea for violating their non-proliferation obligations, and taking credit for the Proliferation Security Initiative (PSI) and Libya's deproliferation.[16]

The PSI exemplifies the shift from non-proliferation approaches based on the multilateral NPT regime to counter-proliferation as a policing operation. It was launched in September 2003 as "an initiative to develop political commitments and practical cooperation to help impede and stop the flow of WMD, their systems and related materials to and from states and non-State actors of concern".[17] Billed as "a response to the growing challenge posed by the proliferation of weapons of mass destruction, their delivery systems, and related materials worldwide",[18] it followed on from the "Container Security Initiative" undertaken in the wake of the 2001 terrorist attacks. Six specific actions are authorized: not to allow anyone to transport or assist in transporting cargoes deemed to be proliferation sensitive; boarding and searching proliferation-suspected flagged ships, whether in internal or international waters; permitting another PSI member to board and search flagged vessels and seize any proliferation-related cargoes; enforcing conditions on vessels entering or leaving ports;

grounding and searching proliferation-suspected aircraft or denying them air space; and carrying out inspections at ports, airports and other shipping facilities, with seizure of any proliferation-relevant cargoes.

Referring to "the increasingly aggressive efforts by proliferators to stand outside or to circumvent existing nonproliferation norms",[19] the PSI was described by the White House as "a broad international partnership of countries which, using their own laws and resources, will coordinate their actions to halt shipments of dangerous technologies to and from states and non-state actors of proliferation concern – at sea, in the air, and on land".[20] France put a slightly different emphasis on PSI, underlining that its role in reducing "the risk of WMD falling into the hands of terrorists" must be seen as "part of the overall effort in support of nonproliferation" that can contribute to the "full implementation of and compliance with commitments under this regime, in particular multilateral non-proliferation agreements".[21] The PSI, which has to date coordinated 10 interdiction exercises, quickly grew to 15 members,[22] with more expected. Others, including India, have agreed to abide by the rules, and Panama and Liberia have made bilateral agreements with the United States to permit vessels carrying their flags to be boarded and searched in accordance with the principles of the PSI.

Most Western states quickly welcomed the PSI, particularly after its successful interdiction in October 2003 of the *BBC China* (belonging to BBC Chartering and Logistic, Germany), en route to Tripoli from Dubai carrying thousands of centrifuge components that might be used to enrich uranium. Reports differ on whether this seizure precipitated Libya's decision, announced on 19 December 2003, to come clean and renounce its WMD programmes, or whether the interdiction was made possible as a result of Libyan information as part of its decade-long normalization negotiations with the United Kingdom and the United States. In any case, the interdiction of the *BBC China* is generally presented as a spectacular first success for the PSI. Similarly, Libya's renunciation of WMD has been hailed by the United Kingdom and the United States as resulting from the "decisive actions" and "no tolerance" approach epitomized by the war on Iraq.[23] Libya clearly had an active chemical weapons programme, but its nuclear programme was aspirational rather than real, which made it doubly shocking for investigators to find that Gaddafi had acquired a warhead blueprint. Though Libya's return to full compliance with the NPT and its accession to the CWC and CTBT are undoubtedly welcome, the real importance of the Libyan revelations was in bringing into the open the long-suspected black market network centred on the "father" of Pakistan's bomb, Abdul Qadeer Khan. Khan's public confession on 4 February 2004 has removed him from the active hub and infor-. mation has been gained about the illicit trade in WMD-related technology and materials with North Korea, Iran and others, and industrial connections have been exposed from the United Kingdom to Malaysia, and Germany to South Africa. But US reliance on Pakistan in the war on terror's theatre in Afghanistan meant that the world was forced to acquiesce in General Musharraf's decision to pardon Khan, thereby ensuring that no information embarrassing to Pakistan's government or nuclear industry would emerge in a trial. Hence, although it has clearly been crippled, no one can say with assurance that Khan's nuclear supermarket has ceased trading.

The PSI's members have been at pains to underline that it is consistent with international law and the implementation of the UN Security Council presidential statement of 31 January 1992, and also in line with the Kananaskis and Evian G-8 Summit declarations as well as recent EU statements, but many others are concerned that the PSI lacks international legal authority and enables a cartel of states to act outside the institutions established to oversee and implement the WMD regimes, operating coercively to suit the interests of the powerful and impede legitimate trading or technology transfers among developing states.

In consequence, and to gain further international support while heavily bogged down in Iraq, the United Kingdom and the United States circulated a draft UN Security Council resolution. The initial draft was essentially the PSI principles written into a resolution; it heavily emphasized terrorism and made scant reference to the treaties governing chemical and biological weapons, with no mention at all of disarmament or the NPT. In order to get consensus, the resolution underwent several changes, with input from both PSI supporters and sceptics on the Security Council. It was eventually adopted on 28 April 2004, as UNSC Resolution 1540 on WMD.[24]

Resolution 1540 extends the reference to the January 1992 UN Security Council presidential statement by calling on UN members "to fulfil their obligations in relation to arms control and disarmament and to prevent proliferation in all its aspects of all weapons of mass destruction".[25] It affirms "support for the multilateral treaties whose aim is to eliminate or prevent the proliferation of nuclear, chemical or biological weapons", removing the reference in an earlier draft to "illicit acquisition", which could have been construed as legitimizing the nuclear weapons acquired by the NWS and non-NPT nuclear weapons possessors. The multilateral regimes are brought in several times in the final resolution, including a new paragraph that encourages member states "to implement fully the disarmament treaties and agreements to which they are party", which could be open to exclusive or inclusive interpretation. Nevertheless, it is politically important to recognize that such endorsements of the treaty regimes and disarmament appear in the preamble. The operative part of

the resolution is almost exclusively concerned with setting out the obligations and powers of states in nationally implementing non-proliferation
agreements and in underlining their responsibilities for dealing with
non-state and industrial activities in order to prevent terrorist acquisition
of WMD. In particular, Resolution 1540 requires that states refrain from
providing any support to non-state actors seeking to develop WMD and
that they adopt and enforce domestic controls and national procedures
and laws to prevent and prohibit non-state actors from acquiring WMD.
It also established for up to two years a Committee of the Security Council to report back on the resolution's implementation.

Though Resolution 1540 treats nuclear, biological and chemical weapons similarly, they are not the same in law and strategic thinking. Disarmament and prohibition are now embedded in the biological and chemical weapons regimes, and no one is suggesting that this be revoked.
By contrast, US strategies at the 2005 NPT Review Conference appeared
designed to reinforce the NPT's division between haves and have-nots,
despite the obvious fact that the non-nuclear-weapon states (at least)
would feel more secure in a world without nuclear weapons. In particular, a major factor in the NPT conference failure was the attempt by the
Bush administration to repudiate its disarmament commitments by side-
lining the outcome of the 2000 Review Conference. Hence, what had appeared to be the progressive acceptance of disarmament as an inextric-
able component of non-proliferation in the 1990s has been exposed during
the early twenty-first century as little more than gesture politics. A growing number of military officers and officials in the weapons states may be
willing to acknowledge (usually off the record) that nuclear weapons no
longer have a rational military utility, but they still occupy the strategic
high ground, as the policies of the P-5 and the nuclear declarations of India and Pakistan after their 1998 nuclear tests demonstrated. Underlining
this fact, despite widespread opposition among Members of Parliament
and the British public, the government of the United Kingdom is now
planning to spend over £25 billion on a successor nuclear weapon system
for when Trident reaches the end of its service life around 2024. The end
of the Cold War could have changed this salient fact, but did not.

Countervailing trends and implications

Whereas 2003 was dominated by US policies based on selective uses of
intelligence, unilateral action and "coalitions of the willing", as illustrated by the Iraq war and PSI, the lessons from 2004–2005 suggest that
Washington is becoming conscious again of the need for multilateral cooperation, assistance and legitimacy. Resolution 1540 is regarded positively (although sceptics question what it has achieved in real terms),

but the failure of NPT States Parties to make progress on strengthening compliance, accountability and the implementation of disarmament commitments at the 2005 Review Conference is regarded as a setback.

Even before this failure, international experts were sounding the alarms. In 2004, the international High-level Panel (HLP) on Threats, Challenges and Change made a thoughtful contribution to the debate on terrorism, but stressed the necessity for a more comprehensive concept of collective security, which included wider concerns about non-compliance and the health of the regimes, particularly the "precarious state of the nuclear non-proliferation regime".[26] The HLP report is based around four basic themes and offers 101 recommendations, nearly half of which address ways of making the United Nations more effective for the twenty-first century. The themes are the need for a new security consensus, taking account of non-state actors as well as states; comprehensive, collective security, recognizing the challenges of prevention and the limits of self-protection (ranging from WMD to infectious diseases and environmental degradation), covering conflict within and between states; security and the use of force; and security architecture, with particular emphasis on improving the effectiveness and accountability of the United Nations.[27] In his response, *In Larger Freedom: Towards Development, Security and Human Rights for All*, the Secretary-General expanded on the Panel's approach and linked non-proliferation and security closely with development and human rights objectives. The first recommendation argues that the nuclear-weapon states should honour their commitments under Article VI of the NPT, "take several steps to restart disarmament" and "reaffirm their previous commitments not to use nuclear weapons against non-nuclear weapon states". The bulk of the recommendations, however, concern better enforcement of existing instruments, relying on four layers of defence and prevention: reducing demand; reducing supply; better enforcement capabilities; and better public health and emergency planning defences.[28] Although the non-discriminatory prohibitions against the production, possession and use of biological and chemical weapons have helped to create powerful norms against such weapons, even for terrorists, and disarmament would undoubtedly reduce demand for nuclear weapons, it is revealing that neither the HLP nor *In Larger Freedom* gave much attention to nuclear disarmament. This is indicative of the penetration into international thinking of the US-led shift from non-proliferation to counter-proliferation.

The counter-proliferation approach: A world of sheep and goats

UK defence and foreign policy officials, who followed the Americans in renaming their non-proliferation departments "counter-proliferation" departments, are fond of characterizing their new approach in terms of sheep and goats. Though they have not yet applied the metaphor to disarmament, to which they still pay lip-service as an "ultimate" goal, they do use it to justify PSI-type coalitions of the willing or to explain why the United Kingdom opposes multilaterally imposed fuel-cycle restrictions on the enrichment of uranium or reprocessing of spent fuel: equal and universally applied constraints are portrayed as putting an unnecessary and onerous burden on the law-abiding sheep, when it is only really the troublesome goats that ought to be stopped.[29]

Though evident in developments pre-dating the terrorist attacks of 9/11, the attractiveness of sheep-and-goats counter-proliferation reflects dissatisfaction with the operation of the treaty-based regimes when confronted with states that shelter within treaties while pursuing clandestine weapons programmes, such as Iraq, North Korea and potentially now Iran. Concerns about the inadequacy of the regimes for dealing with state non-compliance were exacerbated after 9/11 by the heightened fear of non-state acquisition and use of WMD, which the treaties had not been designed to address. Such concerns are widely shared, but there have been profound disagreements about the means used to address these shortcomings.

Few would dispute the value of adopting national implementation measures to reinforce treaty obligations on states and hold national governments accountable for WMD-related transactions emanating from their territory. Most would applaud the strengthening of international powers and collective action to prevent terrorists from acquiring WMD capabilities, providing these actions are consistent with international law. Much of the world's population, however, would consider *any* use of WMD, particularly nuclear weapons, to be unlawful and inherently terrorist. Their security concerns could be met only through a disarmament-based approach. Instead, counter-proliferation initiatives are intended to exempt certain states and governments from interdiction or punitive action. Here lies a core problem for the legitimacy and effectiveness of counter-proliferation.

Why, for example, are ballistic missiles or warhead components transported between the United Kingdom and the United States or plutonium products regularly shipped to Japan from the British and French reprocessing plants at Sellafield and La Hague not considered proliferation sensitive, whereas dual-use aluminium tubes would be deemed a reason to board a Chinese or Malaysian ship under the PSI? The neoconservative response is to dismiss such legal or definitional problems with impatience, as if the identity and malign purpose of the designated targets are self-evident. This cavalier attitude to international legal checks and balances has most clearly been demonstrated in the war on Iraq, but its legacy has seeped into other areas of international relations and underpins the shift from non-proliferation to counter-proliferation.

To compound the problem, much of the debate on the PSI has been couched in adversarial terms, as if its supporters are bent on undermining the multilateral and normative regimes. Although it is undeniable that certain neoconservatives within the Bush administration have done their utmost to marginalize a range of arms control and disarmament agreements that constrained US freedom of action, and that they viewed the PSI as another weapon in that armoury, this simplistic attitude is not shared by most PSI members or by many US officials responsible for implementing security policy. It is desirable that the operation of the PSI be open for critiquing and evaluation, but treating it as a regime-breaker merely plays into the hands of those who prefer their treaties to be weak or non-existent.

Without glossing over its limitations, the final text of Resolution 1540 can be welcomed for contextualizing PSI-type operations, policing controls and national responsibilities in conformity with arms control and disarmament treaties and agreements. Indeed, as used in Resolution 1540, the word "agreements" is diplomatic code intending to encompass the consensus final document of the 2000 NPT Review Conference, which contains the nuclear disarmament plan of action. Multilateral treaties provide legal parameters, norms, rules and authority; far from being in competition with unilateral or plurilateral enforcement initiatives, their implementation has invariably evolved to include a mix of incentives and controls that might not have been envisaged or that it might not have been possible to put in the original treaty. For example, security assurances and export controls provided incentives and supply-side restrictions not contained in the NPT text but widely accepted as integral to the NPT-based regime. Whereas some treaties were written with national implementation measures explicitly stated, these were missing from the NPT and BTWC, so spelling out the responsibilities and requirements through the PSI and Resolution 1540 is a sensible way to plug that gap. Regional measures may also be selective but necessary instruments for reinforcing international regimes. The European Union (EU), for example, which has long applied a human rights condition to its trade and aid contracts, recently expanded this to include the proliferation of weapons of mass destruction.[30] The imposition of the EU non-proliferation condition has been credited with creating the right kind of pressure and incentives to get certain reluctant countries finally to accede to the CWC.

On the negative side, counter-proliferation portrays nuclear weapons as security problems only if sought or acquired by terrorists or the "wrong" states. The United States has recently treated NPT meetings as occasions to accuse others of violating their obligations, while downgrading disarmament commitments already undertaken, but it also opposes reforms that would give NPT States Parties greater institutional powers to address non-compliance. At the same time, US allies in the "war on terror", which include the three states that have pursued nuclear weapons outside the NPT, have been given a relatively easy ride, notwithstanding Israel's violation of Security Council resolutions, India's provocative nuclear tests and role in driving a regional arms race, and Pakistan's record on terrorism and Dr Khan's nuclear black market. The United States is not alone in its bid to co-locate India, Israel and Pakistan with the NPT regime "as if" they were nuclear-weapon states. The HLP also eschewed the ritual call for these states to join the NPT, instead calling on them to "pledge a commitment to non-proliferation and disarmament, demonstrating their commitment by ratifying the CTBT and supporting negotiations for a fissile material cut-off treaty".[31]

Disarmament: An ideological distraction or integral to non-proliferation?

An important factor in the development and stability of deterrence had been that nuclear weapons were understood to cause such massive annihilation and suffering that they were regarded as essentially suicidal and, to all intents and purposes, their use became subject to quite a powerful, if unacknowledged, taboo. The 9/11 attacks provoked fears that terrorists would neither be swayed by norms or taboos nor be deterred by nuclear forces. Although fear of terrorist use has rightly driven efforts to prevent nuclear materials and technology from falling into unauthorized hands, we look in vain for policy changes reflecting that nuclear weapons are useless for deterring, defending against or retaliating against terrorists or irrational leaders.

Having failed to take the opportunity to remove the Damoclean sword of nuclear war by getting rid of their nuclear weapons, the weapons states for a while considered it expedient to espouse the goal of disarmament, in part because they were faced in the 1990s with newly energized multilateral institutions, bolstered by resurgent civil society participation. Yet even though disarmament aspirations were at the heart of the successful NPT Review Conference in 2000 and nuclear-weapon-free zones were established to cover the Southern hemisphere and beyond, disarmament commitments were never significantly embedded in the policies of the weapons states or their allies.

These developments beg the question: is nuclear disarmament a necessary and integral aspect of non-proliferation, as many NPT States Parties assume, or an ideological distraction when faced with threats from terrorists or undemocratic states, as the nuclear-weapon states would have us believe? A point emphasized by the nuclear powers, with which few analysts would disagree, is that proliferators act principally on the basis of national and regional calculations rather than international norms, and so there is no direct or causal link between arms control or disarmament and the decisions of other nuclear weapons possessors or aspirants. It is true that, if the weapons states were to go forward with nuclear disarmament, this alone would not be enough to ensure non-proliferation, but that misses the point, for a disarmament decision would never be taken in isolation. It is axiomatic that, if any of the nuclear powers were to cease to rely on nuclear weapons, they would become very active in creating favourable security conditions for their disarmament by putting pressure on others and promoting a host of measures to prevent proliferation and ensure that no one else could threaten them with nuclear weapons or capabilities. Proponents of nuclearized defence invariably ignore the costs and opportunity costs of retaining nuclear weapons. If the weapons states do not go forward towards disarmament they make the long-term prevention of proliferation impossible. In other words, though proliferation may be slowed by supply-side denial of access to nuclear technologies and materials imposed by the dominant supplier states, backed up by coercive military force, as sanctioned by the PSI, Resolution 1540, export controls and the G-8 initiatives, such approaches do not halt nuclear weapon ambitions. Such coercive approaches may actually act as drivers, though they may also drive clandestine programmes further underground.

To halt proliferation it is necessary to pay equal attention to the demand side. If non-proliferation is narrowed down to "rogue" states and terrorists, this fails to address the political problems of a discriminatory approach to security in which certain haves are privileged above the majority of have-nots. As long as selective non-proliferation allows the major powers to assert the security value and military utility of *their* nuclear weapons, they are undermining the security incentive that is essential for stable, sustainable non-proliferation. Moreover, they make it harder for governments to justify not pursuing nuclear weapons for national security, as demonstrated by the public clamour in India, Pakistan and, most recently, Iran. Finally, safety and physical protection problems are made worse when nuclear facilities and bases are kept operating and nuclear weapons and materials continue to be transported around half the world.

Conclusion

The war on Iraq, the adoption of the PSI and the decisions at recent meetings of G-8 heads of state and NATO reflect and promote the reframing of non-proliferation as a policing operation rather than a regime-building process. The United States appears to have been successful in carrying most if not all its fellow nuclear weapons possessors in this narrow interpretation of non-proliferation because it feeds directly into their own desires to retain and, in some cases, develop their nuclear arsenals. Even New Delhi, erstwhile champion of non-aligned pressure for nuclear disarmament, will happily go along with narrow non-proliferation provided that India is accepted as a member of the nuclear club, as is increasingly the case (though not in terms of the NPT). This approach carries dangerous risks for world security. Confidence is already eroding in regimes that are so obviously unsupported by the world's major power. US policy, exemplified by the Bush administration's strategic triad, doctrine of prevention and military action in Iraq, is having the perverse effect of once again elevating the importance of nuclear weapons and eroding the taboo on nuclear weapons use. The contradictions in US policy towards Iraq and North Korea may also lead other isolated or beleaguered states to consider that a credible and demonstrable (if not necessarily proven) nuclear weapon capability is a necessary deterrent to prevent US military action.[32]

This chapter has argued that the apparent trend towards centralizing and embedding disarmament as an essential component of non-proliferation, exemplified by the successes of civil society and the non-nuclear-weapon states during the 1990s, was illusory: disarmament remained largely on the level of diplomatic gesture politics. That lip-service is now being discarded as the United States uses the "war on terror" to shift international support from regime-based non-proliferation to counter-proliferation under the auspices of willing cartels or coalitions of the self-proclaimed "good guys". Nothing illustrates the Bush administration approach more vividly than the way in which Ambassador John Bolton eliminated all references to disarmament and development from the 2005 World Summit outcome document.

The theoretical question underpinning this chapter is "do regimes matter?" If they do, then disarmament must be taken seriously, because it will progressively reduce incentives and access to dangerous materials. If not, then we are likely to see a further erosion of international norms against proliferation, to be replaced by regional and coercive counter-proliferation approaches. These may provide useful tools in the short term, but they will not achieve non-proliferation. It is also important to recognize that, if leading countries seek to control others while keeping all options open for their own military and commercial interest groups, they will undermine the credibility of the regimes, whether or not that is an intended objective.

Without regime norms, principles and rules, it may be much harder to sustain the coalitions of the willing required for the PSI, Resolution 1540 and other disparate non-proliferation efforts, especially in the long run. Disarmament, if integrated with better policing and progressively pursued with effective monitoring and verification of the dismantling of facilities and the elimination and disposal of weapons and materials, can do much to reduce nuclear threats and keep dangerous materials out of the hands of those who might be tempted to use them. This is now un-equivocally accepted in the parallel WMD cases of biological and chemical weapons. Delinking disarmament from non-proliferation narrows the zone of political, technical, legal and physical options within which effective non-proliferation policies can be developed. A comprehensive approach needs to be consensual, which implies reciprocity and the diminishing of the current levels of institutional privilege accorded to certain haves above the majority of have-nots. It needs to offer greater security and other incentives, with regional as well as international measures put in place. Finally, the task of keeping weapons and materials safe and out of terrorist hands would be greatly strengthened if nuclear facilities and bases were closed down and nuclear weapons were dismantled and their materials properly safeguarded and disposed of, instead of being paraded before eager-eyed wannabe nuclear terrorists. "Do as I say and not as I do" is the worst possible example to set in the post-colonial, post–Cold War era.

Notes

1. Convention on the Prohibition of the Development, Production, Stockpiling and Use of Chemical Weapons and on Their Destruction.
2. Treaty Banning Nuclear Weapon Tests in the Atmosphere, Outer Space and Under Water.
3. Though chemical weapons were not employed directly during World War II, they were not wholly absent: the Nazis used gas in the extermination camps and Japan conducted chemical weapons experiments on Korean and Chinese prisoners.
4. Convention on the Prohibition of the Development, Production and Stockpiling of Bacteriological (Biological) and Toxin Weapons and on Their Destruction.
5. The BTWC was the first treaty to prohibit the production, possession and use of a mass destruction weapon. This established an important norm, but the treaty lacked verification, and so the norm was hardly enforceable; indeed, most of the major powers continued to conduct research and develop bioweapons long after signing the BTWC, though some of this was in the guise of biodefence programmes.
6. For example, General Lee Butler US Air Force (Ret.), Commander-in-Chief, United States Strategic Command (1991–94), speaking in Wellington, New Zealand, 2 October 1997, called deterrence "a dialogue between the blind and the deaf, born of an irreconcilable contradiction".
7. Decision 2 on Principles and Objectives for Nuclear Non-Proliferation and Disarmament, 1995 Review and Extension Conference of the Parties to the Treaty on the Non-Proliferation of Nuclear Weapons, Final Document, Part I (New York, 1995), NPT/CONF.1995/32 (Part I). For a fuller account of the process and politics of the 1995 Conference, see Rebecca Johnson, *Indefinite Extension of the Non-Proliferation Treaty:*

Risks and Reckonings, ACRONYM 7 (London: The Acronym Consortium, September 1995).

8. Decision F, *International Court of Justice Reports 1996*, p. 225 (reported for 8 July 1996, General List No. 95). The full decision, documentation and dissenting decisions also formed the Annex to "Advisory Opinion of the International Court of Justice on the legality of the threat or use of nuclear weapons", Note by the Secretary-General, United Nations General Assembly, UN Doc. A/51/218, 15 October 1996, pp. 36–37.

9. Decision E, *International Court of Justice Reports 1996*, ibid. Though the split appeared to be 7 to 7, it is important to note that there were two conflicting reasons for opposing the decision: three of the seven judges opposed because they disagreed with the caveat in the second paragraph, which stated: "However, in view of the current state of international law and of the elements of fact at its disposal, the Court cannot conclude definitely whether the threat or use of nuclear weapons would be lawful or unlawful in an extreme circumstance of self defence, in which the very survival of a State would be at stake." As their statements made clear, those three judges supported the first paragraph but disagreed with the second because in their opinion there were no lawful circumstances for the use of nuclear weapons. More accurately, therefore, the ICJ split in favour of the view that the use of nuclear weapons would be contrary to international law was 10 to 4.

10. *Report of the Canberra Commission on the Elimination of Nuclear Weapons* (Canberra: Commonwealth of Australia, 1996), pp. 11–12.

11. At the time of the 2000 NPT Review Conference, the New Agenda Coalition (NAC) comprised Brazil, Egypt, Ireland, Mexico, New Zealand, South Africa and Sweden. The NAC originated in a declaration by eight foreign ministers on 9 June 1998, entitled "A Nuclear Weapons Free World: The Need for a New Agenda". Their declaration was in part a response to a perceived crisis in non-proliferation, a marked deterioration in international and security relations, and the South Asian nuclear tests of May 1998. Slovenia, one of the original group (but also an EU and NATO applicant), was pressured into withdrawing from the coalition by strongly expressed US, UK and French opposition. See "8-State Call for New Nuclear Disarmament Agenda", *Disarmament Diplomacy*, No. 27 (June 1998), pp. 27–31.

12. See, for example, President George W. Bush, Address to the UN General Assembly, 23 September 2003, ⟨http://www.whitehouse.gov/news/releases/2003/09/20030923-4.html⟩.

13. See George W. Bush, State of the Union Address, 29 January 2002, http://www.whitehouse.gov/news/releases/2002/01/20020129-11.html⟩.

14. *Facing Nuclear Dangers: The Report of the Tokyo Forum for Nuclear Non-Proliferation and Disarmament* (Japan Institute for International Affairs and Hiroshima Peace Institute, July 1999), Recommendation 2, p. 57.

15. For example, US Under-Secretary of State John Bolton told the NPT parties at the 2004 Preparatory Committee (PrepCom) meeting, "we cannot divert attention from the violations we face by focusing on Article VI issues that do not exist". Significantly, at the 2003 UN General Assembly, the United States took the unusual step of not merely abstaining but voting against Japan's very moderate NPT-supporting resolution "A Path to the Total Elimination of Nuclear Weapons" (UNGA 58/59). This negative vote was repeated at the 2004 and 2005 General Assemblies.

16. In accordance with the policy shifts, US and UK non-proliferation departments became "counter-proliferation" departments in title and, more importantly, focus. See, particularly, Rebecca Johnson, "Troubled and Troubling Times: The 2003 UN First Committee Considers Disarmament and Reform", *Disarmament Diplomacy*, No. 74 (December 2003), and "Politics and Protection: Why the 2005 NPT Review Conference Failed", *Disarmament Diplomacy*, No. 80 (Autumn 2005).

17. French Ministry of Foreign Affairs, "Meeting of the Proliferation Security Initiative, Press statement released under the responsibility of the Chair, Paris, September 4", 2003, ⟨http://www.france.diplomatie.fr/actu/article.gb.asp?ART=36865⟩.
18. "Statement of Interdiction Principles", declaration issued by the Proliferation Security Initiative (PSI), Paris, 4 September 2003, ⟨http://www.whitehouse.gov/⟩.
19. Ibid.
20. "Principles for the Proliferation Security Initiative", Statement by the Press Secretary, The White House, 4 September 2003, ⟨http://www.whitehouse.gov/⟩.
21. French Ministry of Foreign Affairs, "Meeting of the Proliferation Security Initiative".
22. Australia, Canada, Denmark, France, Germany, Italy, Japan, the Netherlands, Norway, Poland, Portugal, Singapore, Spain, the United Kingdom and the United States.
23. This characterization of Libya's renunciation as an early domino falling as a consequence of the war on Iraq has been assiduously stressed by US and UK spokespeople. However, set against this analysis is the fact that, for economic and domestic reasons, Colonel Gaddafi has been seeking normalization and the lifting of sanctions and embargoes in talks with the Americans and British for several years, during which he gave the accused Lockerbie bombers up for trial and promised compensation.
24. Security Council Resolution 1540 on non-proliferation of weapons of mass destruction, UN Doc. S/RES/1540, 28 April 2004, ⟨www.un.org/Docs/sc/unsc_resolutions04.html⟩.
25. Ibid.
26. *A More Secure World: Our Shared Responsibility, Report of the Secretary-General's High-level Panel on Threats, Challenges and Change*, UN Doc. A/59/565, 2 December 2004.
27. With regard to the use of force, the HLP considers pre-emption and prevention and develops five criteria of legitimacy for the use of force: seriousness of threat, proper purpose, last resort, proportional means and balance of consequences (ibid.).
28. *In Larger Freedom: Towards Development, Security and Human Rights for All*, Report of the Secretary-General, UN Doc. A/59/2005, 21 March 2005.
29. Quite why this metaphor presents sheep as more virtuous than goats is somewhat puzzling. Looked at another way, goats are considered far more intelligent – if also more aggressive and unpredictable – than sheep, who are generally portrayed as rather silly and passive. There is also a danger that frustrated non-nuclear-weapon states might employ this metaphor, with some reason, casting the nuclear weapons possessors as goats. However, UK officials do not seem to want to pursue the further logic of their metaphor.
30. See Council of the European Union, *EU Strategy against the Proliferation of Weapons of Mass Destruction*, adopted 12 December 2003; *Action Plan for the Implementation of the Basic Principles for an EU Strategy against WMD Proliferation*, 13 June 2003; Council of the European Union, *A Secure Europe in a Better World. European Security Strategy*, 12 December 2003; Council of the European Union, *EU Strategy against Proliferation of Weapons of Mass Destruction – Draft Progress Report on the Implementation of Chapter III of the Strategy*, 10 June 2004; and Council of the European Union, *Progress Report on the Implementation of Chapter III of EU Strategy against the Proliferation of Weapons of Mass Destruction*, 3 December 2004.
31. *A More Secure World.*
32. A similar point was emphasized in the 2004 introduction to the Stockholm International Peace Research Institute (SIPRI) Yearbook. See Alyson J. K. Bailes, "Iraq: The Legacy", *SIPRI Yearbook 2004* (SIPRI and Oxford University Press, 2004), p. 8.

Part II

The centrality of the United Nations in non-proliferation and disarmament?

5

The Security Council's role in addressing WMD issues: Assessment and outlook

Tsutomu Kono

The Security Council's engagement in WMD issues: An overview

With the exception of its pre-eminent role in the disarmament of Iraq's weapons of mass destruction (WMD), the United Nations Security Council has rarely addressed WMD issues. In fact, the question of Iraq's disarmament represents a unique case in the work of the Security Council over the past six decades. Whereas the Council adopted dozens of resolutions on Iraq, it passed only eight resolutions on other WMD issues.[1] These numbers underline that the Council's involvement in WMD issues constitutes a small fragment of its work, given that it has adopted over 1,600 resolutions since its inception.

In early years, the Security Council considered reports of the Atomic Energy Commission, which was created by the first resolution of the General Assembly in 1946, but took only procedural measures by adopting three resolutions that transmitted the Commission's reports and resolutions to the General Assembly.[2] Although the General Assembly recommended in December 1946 that the Security Council facilitate the work of the Atomic Energy Commission and expedite consideration of its reports,[3] the Council soon ceased to address WMD issues. Thus, for most of the post-war period, with the notable exception of Iraq, WMD issues were generally discussed outside the Security Council, mainly in the General Assembly and the Conference on Disarmament (and its predecessors). More significantly, the most crucial negotiations regarding

WMD disarmament and arms control were held outside the United Nations, especially in the context of bilateral talks between the United States and the Soviet Union (and its successor, the Russian Federation).

However, the Security Council did address a number of major WMD issues, making important policy statements and establishing valuable precedents. Aside from the question of Iraq's disarmament, the Security Council addressed the questions of (1) security assurances to non-nuclear-weapon states; (2) nuclear non-proliferation in the Middle East; (3) investigations into the use of chemical weapons in the Iran–Iraq war; (4) North Korea's withdrawal from the Treaty on the Non-Proliferation of Nuclear Weapons (NPT); and (5) nuclear tests by India and Pakistan. The Council's engagement in these five WMD issues is summarized in Table 5.1.

The Security Council has also made a number of significant policy pronouncements on WMD. In particular, on 31 January 1992, when the Council held its first ever summit-level meeting, it declared that "the proliferation of weapons of mass destruction constitutes a threat to international peace and security". The Council further stated that its members "committed themselves to working to prevent the spread of technology related to the research for or production of such weapons and to take appropriate action to that end".[4] But this was also a product of an exceptional circumstance in which the international community was gravely concerned about the spread of WMD following the discovery of Iraq's vast clandestine unconventional weapons programmes. When the heads of state and government of the members of the Security Council again gathered in September 2000 and in September 2005, they did not address WMD issues, instead adopting resolutions on the maintenance of peace and security, particularly in Africa; international terrorism; and conflict prevention, particularly in Africa.[5] This reflected the reluctance of the Council's permanent members (the P-5) – all nuclear-weapon states – to address the question of WMD in the Council.

The terrorist attacks of 11 September 2001, however, brought about a significant change in the Security Council's dealing with issues related to WMD. A sense of urgency aroused by the nexus between terrorism and WMD prompted the United States and other P-5 countries to negotiate a new resolution that would require all states to adopt and enforce the necessary legislative measures to prevent a transfer of any WMD and related materials to non-state actors and establish domestic control over them. The resolution, adopted under Chapter VII of the UN Charter as Security Council Resolution 1540 (2004) on 28 April 2004, established a subsidiary committee of the Council and called on states to submit a first report on the above measures to the Committee by 28 October 2004. The Council's action not only represented a departure from its previous

Table 5.1 The Security Council's involvement in WMD issues other than Iraq and WMD terrorism

Security Council actions	Background
North Korea's withdrawal from the NPT	

Presidential Statement of 8 April 1993 (S/25562)

Encouraged the IAEA to continue its consultations with North Korea for proper settlement of the nuclear verification issue in the country.	Pyongyang declared its intention to withdraw from the NPT in March 1993. The IAEA Board of Governors declared on 1 April 1993 that North Korea was in violation of its Safeguards Agreement with the Agency and its commitments under the NPT, and referred the matter to the Security Council.

Resolution 825 (1993) of 11 May 1993

Called on Pyongyang to reconsider its decision to withdraw from the NPT, honour non-proliferation obligations under the NPT and comply with its Safeguards Agreement with the IAEA; and requested the Director General of the IAEA to continue to consult with the North.

Presidential Statement of 31 March 1994 (S/PRST/1994/13)

Called on Pyongyang to allow the IAEA inspectors to complete their inspection activities, and stated its decision to remain actively seized of the matter and undertake further consideration if necessary.	In March 1994, North Korean officials refused to allow inspectors to enter and examine the reprocessing facilities and conduct broad sweeps for radiation throughout the Yongbyon facility. The Director General of the IAEA reported to the Security Council on 22 March 1994 that the IAEA was unable to draw conclusions as to whether there had been either diversion of nuclear material, reprocessing or other operations.

Presidential Statement of 30 May 1994 (S/PRST/1994/28)

Strongly urged North Korea to proceed with the discharge operations at the 5 MW reactor only in a manner preserving the technical possibility of fuel measurements in accordance with the IAEA's requirements and called for immediate consultations between the IAEA and North Korea on the necessary technical measures.	In April and May 1994, a dispute arose between North Korea and the IAEA over the refuelling of the Yongbyon reactor.

Table 5.1 (cont.)

Security Council actions	Background
Presidential Statement of 6 November 1994 (S/PRST/1994/64)	
Expressing satisfaction with the "Agreed Framework" and took note of Pyongyang's decision to remain a party to the NPT and to come into full compliance with the safeguards agreement with the IAEA; and requested the IAEA to take all necessary steps to verify the accuracy and completeness of North Korea's initial report on all nuclear materials in the country and its full compliance with its Safeguards Agreement.	On 2 June 1994, IAEA Director General Hans Blix informed the UN Secretary-General that the Agency could no longer perform its basic function in North Korea: to determine with good confidence the non-diversion of plutonium for weapons purposes. Following high-level diplomacy between the United States and North Korea, most notably former President Jimmy Carter's visit to Pyongyang, on 21 October 1994 they signed an overall resolution of the nuclear issue on the Korean Peninsula, better known as the "Agreed Framework", in which North Korea agreed to freeze activity at its existing reactor and the reprocessing site and permit IAEA inspections in exchange for an assurance by the United States not to use nuclear weapons against North Korea and for economic assistance including provision of two light-water reactor systems and oil shipments.
In 2003, no action	
After postponing discussion on North Korea's withdrawal from the NPT for two months, the Security Council discussed the issue in informal consultations on 9 April, but took no action because China and Russia opposed any formal action by the Council, favouring quiet diplomacy.	Pyongyang discontinued its cooperation with the IAEA, expelled its inspectors in December 2002, and announced its withdrawal from the NPT on 10 January 2003. On 12 February, the IAEA Board of Governors declared that North Korea was "in further non-compliance" with its Safeguards Agreement and agreed to report the matter to the Security Council.
Nuclear tests conducted by India and Pakistan	
Presidential Statement of 14 May 1998 (S/1998/PRST/1998/12)	
Strongly deplored nuclear tests by India and urged it to refrain from further tests; affirmed the crucial importance of the NPT and the Comprehensive Nuclear-Test-Ban	India conducted three underground nuclear tests on 11 May 1998 and two further tests two days later.

Table 5.1 (cont.)

Security Council actions	Background
Treaty (CTBT); appealed to India and all other states that had not yet done so to become parties to the NPT and to the CTBT; and encouraged India to participate in the proposed negotiations for a fissile material cut-off treaty.	

Presidential Statement of 29 May 1998 (S/1998/PRST/1998/17)

Strongly deplored a nuclear test by Pakistan on 28 May 1998, and urged India and Pakistan to refrain from further tests. This statement generally replicated the earlier Presidential statement of 14 May on India's nuclear tests.	Pakistan conducted an underground nuclear test on 28 May 1998.

Resolution 1172 (1998) of 6 June 1998

Condemned the nuclear tests conducted by India and Pakistan and demanded that they refrain from further nuclear testing; called upon India and Pakistan to stop their nuclear weapon development programmes immediately, to refrain from weaponization or from the deployment of nuclear weapons, and to cease development of ballistic missiles capable of delivering nuclear weapons and any further production of fissile material for nuclear weapons; requested India and Pakistan to confirm their policies not to export equipment, materials or technologies that could contribute to WMD or missiles capable of delivering them, and encouraged all states to prevent the export of equipment, materials or technology that could in any way assist programmes in India or Pakistan for nuclear weapons or ballistic missiles capable of delivering such weapons; recalled that, in accordance with the NPT, India or Pakistan cannot have the status of a nuclear state, and urged them to become parties to the NPT	Pakistan conducted a second underground nuclear test on 30 May 1998

Table 5.1 (cont.)

Security Council actions	Background
and the CTBT; requested the Secretary-General to report urgently to the Council on the steps taken by India and Pakistan to implement this resolution, and expressed its readiness to consider further how best to ensure the implementation of the resolution.	

Nuclear non-proliferation in the Middle East

Resolution 487 (1981) of 19 June 1981

Strongly condemned Israel's military attack against the Iraqi reactor in clear violation of the UN Charter and the norms of international conduct; considered that the attack constitutes a serious threat to the entire safeguards regime of the IAEA; noted that Israel has not adhered to the NPT and called upon Israel urgently to place its nuclear facilities under the safeguards of the IAEA; and requested the Secretary-General to keep the Council regularly informed of the implementation of the resolution.	Israel undertook air strikes on the Osirak reactor in Iraq on 7 June 1981.

Resolution 687 (1991) of 3 April 1991

Noted in paragraph 14 that the actions to be taken by Iraq in the fulfilment of its disarmament obligations represented steps toward the goal of establishing in the Middle East a zone free of weapons of mass destruction and all missiles for their delivery and the objective of a global ban on chemical weapons.	Following military action to force Iraq to withdraw from Kuwait and Iraq's surrender to the coalition forces, the Security Council passed a resolution formalizing a ceasefire between Iraq and the coalition.

In 2003, no action

The Syrian draft on a WMD-free zone was never put to a vote because it failed to gain the necessary support from Council members. Syria put forward the same draft resolution at the end of 2003, but the Council again failed to take action on it.	Shortly after the beginning of military action against Iraq in the spring of 2003, Syria tabled a draft resolution calling for the establishment of a WMD-free zone in the Middle East.

Table 5.1 (cont.)

Security Council actions	Background

Security assurances to non-nuclear-weapon states

Resolution 255 (1968) of 19 June 1968

Recognized that aggression with nuclear weapons or the threat of such aggression against non-nuclear-weapon states would create a situation in which the Security Council, and especially its nuclear-weapon-state permanent members, will act immediately in accordance with the relevant provisions of the UN Charter.	In efforts to canvass broad support for the NPT, the United Kingdom, the United States and the Soviet Union tried to address the legitimate interest of non-nuclear-weapon States Parties to the NPT to receive security assurances.

Resolution 984 (1995) of 11 April 1995

Took note of the statements made by each of the nuclear-weapon states, in which they give security assurances against the use of nuclear weapons to non-nuclear-weapon states that are parties to the NPT; and reiterated that the Security Council, and above all its nuclear-weapon-state permanent members, will act immediately in accordance with the relevant provisions of the UN Charter in the event that such states are the victim of an act of, or object of a threat of, aggression in which nuclear weapons are used.	In 1995, as part of their harmonized efforts to secure the indefinite extension of the NPT at its Review and Extension Conference in April and May 1995, the United Kingdom, France, Russia and the United States negotiated and agreed on the text of a statement providing security assurances to non-nuclear-weapon States Parties to the NPT. Each of the four countries, along with China – which has an unqualified non-first-use pledge – provided this text as their respective statements to the Security Council.

Investigation into the use of chemical weapons in the Iran–Iraq conflict

Presidential Statements of 30 March 1984, 25 April 1985, 21 March 1986 and 14 May 1987

Expressed profound concern or deep dismay about the unanimous conclusions of the specialists that chemical weapons had been used on many occasions; condemned the continued use of chemical weapons in clear violation of the 1925 Geneva Protocol; and demanded that the provisions of the Geneva Protocol be strictly observed.	Between 1984 and 1987, the Security Council considered annually the reports of the missions of specialists dispatched by the Secretary-General to investigate allegations of the use of chemical weapons.

Table 5.1 (cont.)

Security Council actions	Background

Resolution 582 (1986) of 24 February 1986

Deplored the escalation of the conflict, especially, *inter alia*, the violation of international humanitarian laws and other laws of armed conflict and, in particular, the use of chemical weapons contrary to obligations under the 1925 Geneva Protocol.

In February 1986, the hostilities intensified in the Fao peninsula, and renewed allegations of the use of chemical weapons were made in the conflict.

Resolution 612 (1988) of 9 May 1988

Condemned vigorously the continued use of chemical weapons in the conflict; expected both sides to refrain from the future use of chemical weapons; and called upon all states to continue to apply or to establish strict control of the export to the parties to the conflict of chemical products serving for the production of chemical weapons.

Following Iraq's chemical weapons attacks in Halabja in March 1988, the Secretary-General dispatched a mission of specialists to investigate allegations of the use of chemical weapons in the Iran–Iraq conflict.

Resolution 620 (1988) of 26 August 1988

Called on all states to continue to apply, to establish or to strengthen strict control of the export of chemical products for the production of chemical weapons, in particular to the parties to a conflict; encouraged the Secretary-General to carry out promptly investigations in response to allegations brought to his attention by any member state concerning the possible use of chemical and biological weapons that might constitute a violation of the 1925 Geneva Protocol; and decided to consider immediately, taking into account the investigations of the Secretary-General, appropriate and effective measures in accordance with the UN Charter, should there be any future use of chemical weapons in violation of international laws, wherever and by whoever committed.

Despite Iran's acceptance in July 1988 of Resolution 598 (1987), which demanded a ceasefire under Chapter VII of the UN Charter, Iraq continued its offensives and allegations of the use of chemical weapons persisted. To investigate these allegations, the Secretary-General dispatched missions of specialists, whose reports concluded that there had been continued use of chemical weapons in the conflict and such use against Iranians had become more intense and frequent.

aversion to WMD issues but also sparked a controversy on the role of the Council in addressing them. In particular, the new resolution's global legislative nature and relationship with the existing disarmament treaty regime raised serious questions regarding how the international community would address a wide range of WMD issues.

This chapter will examine the roles of the Security Council in two prominent cases (Iraq and WMD terrorism), assess its roles and functions on WMD issues, and finally shed light on challenges and problems it is likely to encounter in the future.

Iraq: Coercive disarmament

The disarmament regime established for Iraq pursuant to Resolution 687 (1991) was exceptional in many respects. It was imposed on Iraq as a condition for a ceasefire. It was linked to a sweeping economic embargo and was backed by military threats. For these reasons, it is called a "coercive" disarmament regime, as opposed to normal disarmament regimes, which are constructed on voluntary agreements into which states enter out of their free will. However, various measures taken by the Security Council since 1991 to disarm Iraq delineate the parameters for the Council's future action in addressing serious non-proliferation and disarmament issues. Despite its unfortunate ending, the disarmament regime established and operated first by the United Nations Special Commission (UNSCOM) in Iraq and then by the United Nations Monitoring, Verification and Inspection Commission (UNMOVIC), as well as by the International Atomic Energy Agency (IAEA), serves as a useful model for coercive WMD disarmament, setting important examples for a range of fairly effective mechanisms for addressing WMD issues in their various aspects.

Inspections, verification, investigation and dismantlement

By Resolutions 687 (1991) and 1284 (1999), the Security Council established independent inspection agencies – UNSCOM and UNMOVIC – to verify the disarmament of proscribed programmes. The Council gave them a sweeping inspection mandate and an unprecedented invasive authority regarding access to sites, personnel and information. Their powers were further reinforced by Resolution 1441 (2002). The Special Commission established pursuant to Resolution 687 (1991) started as an ad hoc commission comprising a group of commissioners and a small number of staff seconded by member states and the UN Secretariat, but over time it grew into a permanent bureaucracy known as UNSCOM. Following

Iraq's rejection of UNSCOM in the wake of Operation Desert Fox in December 1998 and a controversy over spy charges against it, the Security Council held lengthy discussions on disarmament issues. In early 1999, the Council created an expert panel chaired by the permanent representative of Brazil to the United Nations, Ambassador Celso Amorim. The panel, also known as the Amorim Panel, put forward a series of recommendations, including those on the structure of the inspection agency.[6] When the Security Council adopted Resolution 1284 (1999) on 17 December 1999, these recommendations were incorporated in its provisions regarding the establishment of UNMOVIC. As a result, the new inspection agency was made more impervious to external political influence and, while remaining accountable solely to the Security Council, acquired a number of attributes associated with the UN Secretariat.[7]

When the Security Council adopted Resolution 687 (1991), it envisaged a simple verification scheme in which UN inspectors were to verify Iraq's disclosure of its proscribed programmes and the dismantling of WMD and associated facilities. In the Council's vision, the burden of proof rested with Iraq. However, since the Iraqi government chose to conceal the bulk of its WMD and ballistic missile programmes, particularly its nuclear and biological weapons programmes, the Special Commission and the IAEA were forced to engage in lengthy search and investigative operations. Moreover, their investigations were confounded by Iraq's unilateral destruction of its proscribed weapons in the summer of 1991, a flagrant violation of Resolution 687 (1991), which provided for the dismantling of Iraq's illegal weapons under international supervision. Thus, Iraq succeeded in shifting the burden of proof to the United Nations, and a decade-long cat-and-mouse game ensued. Consequently, UNSCOM and the IAEA developed a highly sophisticated information-gathering capacity, establishing working relationships with national intelligence services. Although UNSCOM's close relationships with US and Israeli intelligence agencies tainted its independence, such collaboration enabled it to uncover evidence of Iraq's biological weapons programmes.[8] Likewise, information provided by national intelligence services was also crucial to the IAEA's discovery of Iraq's nuclear weapons programme in the early 1990s.[9] Following the damaging espionage charges against UNSCOM, the executive chairman of UNMOVIC, Hans Blix, taking into consideration the Amorim Panel's recommendations, instituted a more independent system of intelligence-sharing, in which intelligence flowed in only one direction, from national intelligence bodies to UNMOVIC.

Finally, the IAEA, UNSCOM and UNMOVIC all demonstrated their capabilities in dismantling proscribed weapons programmes. In particular, UNSCOM destroyed large volumes of weapon stockpiles, production facilities and equipment, and precursors and growth agents in the chemical, biological and ballistic missile areas. During a short period of time, UNMOVIC also supervised the destruction of dozens of Al-Samoud 2 missiles and a small amount of mustard and 155 mm artillery shells used for mustard gas.

The monitoring mechanism

Resolution 687 (1991) envisaged a monitoring plan for Iraq to ensure that Iraq would never reconstitute banned WMD programmes. In accordance with the Ongoing Monitoring and Verification (OMV) plan approved by Resolution 715 (1991), UNSCOM and the IAEA established and operated a meticulous monitoring system throughout Iraq. In addition, these agencies jointly established an export/import monitoring mechanism for Iraq pursuant to Resolution 1051 (1996), which was designed to ensure that dual-use goods imported by Iraq for civilian uses would not be diverted for military purposes. Resolution 1051 (1996) required both Iraq and exporting countries to submit semi-annual declarations to UNSCOM, which could serve as a useful transparency measure. Moreover, in an effort to streamline the economic sanctions, the Security Council approved the Goods Review List (GRL) by adopting Resolution 1409 (2002). This list is a comprehensive compilation of dual-use items that could be used for military purposes. Although the GRL was adopted to rationalize the sanctions regime, it can be utilized to establish international controls over the trade in these items, thus significantly contributing to global efforts to combat WMD proliferation.

The sanctions regime/oil-for-food programme

Although highly controversial, the economic sanctions imposed on Iraq by Resolution 661 (1990) provide valuable lessons for the future use of sanctions. Despite its deficiencies, the embargo against Iraq was still a relatively effective, evolutionary regime. To alleviate its negative humanitarian impact, the Security Council repeatedly modified the sanctions regime, particularly establishing and expanding the Oil-for-Food programme, which allowed the Iraqi government to sell billions of dollars worth of oil and to purchase foodstuffs, medicine and other essential civilian goods.[10] Furthermore, when the Security Council adopted Resolution 1284 (1999), it also removed the ceiling on the amount of oil that Iraq was allowed to export, thus virtually ending the oil embargo. As a result, the Oil-for-Food programme became the largest humanitarian programme in UN history, with the Iraqi government earning over US$60 billion from the end of 1996 to the spring of 2003. Furthermore, as the sanctions regime began to erode, the Security Council instituted so-called "smart sanctions" by adopting an extensive dual-use Goods Review List, while liberalizing the import of civilian goods.[11] Although it became clear that the Oil-for-Food programme was seriously compromised by Baghdad's abuses, collusion by member states and a degree of misman-agement by the UN Secretariat, the fact remains that the programme served as the only lifeline for Iraqi people. Following the coalition's inva-sion in the spring of 2003, it also became clear that economic sanctions played a crucial role in preventing Baghdad from reconstituting its pro-scribed weapons programmes. When the Security Council contemplates the possibility of imposing sanctions on non-compliant parties in the fu-ture, the experience with the Iraqi economic sanctions and humanitarian programme could serve as a useful guide in designing a more effective and humane sanctions regime.

The disarmament of Iraq: Assessment

The failure to find a significant WMD stockpile in Iraq has already prompted reassessments of the effectiveness of the disarmament regime and economic sanctions.[12] Although the results of these post mortems are encouraging, significant caveats and counterfactual assumptions un-derline that a number of questions remain unanswered. In particular, the difficult situation UNMOVIC was facing before the United States be-gan to threaten military action against Iraq prompts us to look again at why the multilateral disarmament and sanctions regimes in Iraq were widely regarded as unworkable. There were no inspections in Iraq be-tween December 1998 and November 2002 because UNMOVIC and the IAEA were not allowed to return to the country. It was only after the United States threatened military invasion in September 2002 that Iraq accepted UN inspections in the hopes of averting US military action. As early as the autumn of 1998, the Clinton administration concluded that the UN inspection regime was not working because Iraq had learned how to manipulate Security Council members. Operation Desert Fox was not designed to bring Iraq back into compliance with Security Coun-cil resolutions. It was aimed at degrading Iraq's WMD capabilities.[13] The lengthy list of unresolved disarmament issues, submitted to the Security Council pursuant to Resolution 1284 (1999) in March 2003, also under-scores the difficulties encountered by UNMOVIC inspectors in verifying Iraq's WMD programmes.

In addition, during the absence of inspectors, economic sanctions grad-ually eroded as Iraq launched an aggressive campaign to weaken the sanctions regime with the assistance of various countries friendly to Iraq, including key members of the Security Council. Baghdad subverted the Oil-for-Food programme and siphoned billions of dollars into its coffers, which allowed it illegally to import various materials for its military programmes. The Bush administration tightened the UN sanctions regime by adopting the Goods Review List but, despite the new mechanism, sanctions violations continued and contraband goods continued to flow into Iraq. When UN inspectors returned to Iraq and coalition officials started their search for WMD, they found clandestine procurement networks and various military and dual-use items imported in violation of UN sanctions.

In retrospect, the performance of the disarmament regime for Iraq hinged upon three crucial requirements: international legitimacy; sustained military threats; the unity of the Security Council. In the early 1990s, these three factors ensured the efficacy of the disarmament regime. Starting in the mid-1990s, however, these requirements, particularly the unity of the Security Council, became increasingly absent, which led to the significant deterioration of the disarmament regime.

International legitimacy

A series of actions by Iraq, starting with its invasion of Kuwait and continuing with its resistance to UN inspections, helped the Security Council maintain international legitimacy regarding the UN disarmament and sanctions regimes. In the 1990s, the international community accepted a wide array of invasive measures and punitive actions against Iraq taken by the Security Council. These included the continuation of comprehensive economic sanctions, the creation of the UN Compensation Commission for the victims of Iraq's invasion of Kuwait, and even the military humanitarian intervention in northern Iraq known as Operation Provide Comfort. The disarmament regime for Iraq enjoyed a fairly high degree of international legitimacy but, as time elapsed, international support for the regime began to erode. Despite Baghdad's continued non-compliance with its disarmament obligations, prolonged inspections gradually weakened international support for the disarmament regime. Even key Security Council members, such as Russia, France and China, grew tired of the lengthy disarmament process and began to challenge UNSCOM and question its work and credibility. The situation was exacerbated when Iraq and its allies began to condemn what it saw as UNSCOM's complicity with the United States. In the wake of Operation Desert Fox, and with the revelation of UNSCOM's close relationships with Israeli and US intelligence services, three permanent members of the Council, particularly

China and Russia, focused their efforts on discrediting UNSCOM. In the absence of support from key Council members and facing Iraq's rejection of further inspections, UNSCOM was unable to complete its mandate.

Under the leadership of Hans Blix, the executive chairman of the new inspection agency, UNMOVIC, the international legitimacy of the disarmament regime for Iraq was restored. With Blix's conscious effort to create an independent and competent inspection agency, UNMOVIC gradually gained international credibility and enjoyed broad support from the international community. However, as the international community continued to witness the Iraqi people's sufferings under the economic embargo, it began to question the legitimacy of the sanctions regime. In the late 1990s, three permanent members of the Security Council – Russia, France and China – vigorously called for a lifting of sanctions on humanitarian grounds. Russia and France joined Iraq in its effort to tear down the sanctions regime by challenging the air embargo. The Oil-for-Food programme created economic stakes, which conferred powerful leverage on Baghdad. As many countries pursued their economic interests in Iraq, international support for the economic embargo on Iraq began to wane. The Security Council took various measures to alleviate the adverse effect on the humanitarian situation in Iraq by expanding the Oil-for-Food programme and adopting the Goods Review List, but questions still remained about how much longer the international community would support such a comprehensive economic embargo.

Military threats

When the Security Council established the disarmament regime for Iraq in 1991, there were expectations that Iraq's non-compliance would trigger a resumption of military action by the coalition. Although the Iraqi government still sought to subvert the disarmament mechanism by concealment and deception, it largely accepted inspections by the Special Commission and the IAEA. Even in those early days, however, in the absence of a clear threat of immediate military action, Iraq defied the orders of UN inspectors and refused to surrender equipment and documents relevant to its proscribed weapons programmes. As the inspection process became more prolonged, immediate military threats began to recede. The coalition also became less willing to take military action in response to Baghdad's non-compliance.

In the meantime, Iraq gradually learned how to cope with military threats and absorb military action, and started to abuse the inspection mechanism. Between the autumn of 1996 and the end of 1998, it became a pattern that Saddam Hussein's brinkmanship prompted Washington to send its armada to the Persian Gulf to force him to accept inspections, only to bring it back after his last-minute about-face rendered military action unnecessary. But such massive long-distance military deployments cost Washington billions of dollars, and aroused resentment and fatigue among Clinton administration officials. It was little surprise that, in the course of the impasse in the Security Council over Iraq after Operation Desert Fox, the Clinton administration quietly disengaged from Iraq and left its Iraq policy, by and large, on automatic pilot. Accordingly, with the exception of the continued enforcement of the no-fly zones, US military threats over Iraq were diminished significantly, which in turn encouraged Iraq's resistance to UN inspections. It was also during this period that the economic sanctions began to unravel.

As Washington's immediate military threats subsided, Baghdad hardened its position on weapons inspections. In the absence of immediate military threats, Iraq adamantly rejected anything associated with Resolution 1284 (1999), especially UNMOVIC, its executive chairman, Hans Blix, and a high-level coordinator on the issues of missing persons and Kuwaiti property, Yuli Vorontsov. In his dialogue with Iraqi Foreign Minister Mohammad Sahaf in the spring of 2001, the UN Secretary-General sought to focus on the return of weapons inspectors. But Sahaf tried to belittle weapons inspections by claiming that no major disarmament issues remained, while attempting to shift the focus of discussions to the mechanism of lifting sanctions, no-fly zones, US threats against Saddam Hussein's government, and the creation of a WMD-free zone in the Middle East (as mentioned in paragraph 14 of Resolution 687 (1991)). The Iraqi leadership was well aware of Washington's unwillingness to use force, and it did not have to use its trump card – weapons inspections – to stave off US strikes.

As the Bush administration stepped up its threat to change the Iraqi regime by force, Baghdad's attitude toward weapons inspections changed significantly. In early 2002, the Iraqi leadership sought to resume dialogue with the UN Secretary-General, hinting at the possibility of accepting weapons inspections. The Iraqi delegation began to engage in substantial discussions with Hans Blix and his UNMOVIC staff, as well as with Mohamed ElBaradei, the Director General of the IAEA, and his staff. No sooner had President Bush challenged the United Nations to enforce resolutions on Iraq in his address to the General Assembly in September 2002 than Saddam Hussein accepted UN weapons inspections in his attempt to thwart US military action. This raises an important question about UNMOVIC: had the United States not decided to use force, would Iraq have allowed UN weapons inspectors back in? No less significant, in the absence of US military threats, the Council continued to face a serious credibility problem in the face of Iraq's continued defiance and non-compliance.

The unity of the Security Council

The Charter concept of maintaining peace and security is based on the power of the permanent members of the Security Council. In the absence of agreement among these five veto-holding countries, the United Nations does not work properly. The P-5 must come to a broad agreement on Council actions while respecting their various interests, and cooperate in implementing Council decisions. Unfortunately, in the case of Iraq, such agreement among the P-5 proved largely elusive. Their differences ranged from the Council's response to Iraq's resistance to inspections, judgements on the results and methods of inspections, the organization and management of inspection agencies, economic sanctions, the Oil-for-Food programme, the legality of the no-fly zones, and the role of the Secretary-General to their position on the use of force, which all but paralysed the Security Council.

In the face of a recalcitrant party, the UN inspection regimes need broad and strong international political support. The history of UNSCOM demonstrates that strong political support from the Security Council for the inspection agency is not only a prerequisite for UNSCOM's success but also its lifeline. Between 1996 and 2003, however, the Security Council was deeply divided over Iraq and unable to take effective measures. Serious divisions in the Council, particularly among its permanent members, highly politicized the disarmament process, undermined UNSCOM's work in Iraq and eventually prevented it from implementing its mandate. As Iraq's influence grew in the Council, UNSCOM's integrity was questioned, and attempts were made to shift the burden of proof to UNSCOM. Operation Desert Fox deepened the Council's schism, because Anglo-American military action angered the other permanent members.

Divisions within the Security Council also overshadowed the work of UNMOVIC. Throughout 1998, a paralysed Security Council was not able to agree on a new omnibus resolution establishing a new inspections system. Even when the Council finally adopted Resolution 1284 (1999) on 17 December 1999, its division was manifested by abstentions by three permanent members, which seriously weakened UNMOVIC's mandate at its inception. It was little surprise that Iraq quickly rejected the new mandatory resolution adopted under Chapter VII.

The Council's continued divisions also had negative effects on the sanctions regime. As the humanitarian situation gravely deteriorated – mainly as a result of Iraq's refusal to implement the Council-mandated humanitarian programme over five years – Russia, China and France also became staunch advocates of Iraq's humanitarian cause. Iraq finally accepted the Oil-for-Food programme in April 1996, but the programme accorded Iraq powerful economic leverage in the Council. Since the programme allowed Iraq to choose its trade partners, Baghdad actively exploited the programme to cultivate its influence in the Council and mobilize its allies to change the Council's policy by granting them lucrative trade deals. The Clinton administration's relatively hands-off policy toward Iraq in the wake of Desert Fox lent a hand to Iraq.

Iraq's influence in the Security Council grew significantly as a result of a dramatic increase in its oil revenues. Baghdad was thus able to extract numerous concessions from the Council in humanitarian areas, such as removal of the ceiling on oil exports, rehabilitation of its oil industry and expansion of the scope of civilian imports. These concessions greatly helped ease the sanctions against Iraq and permitted it to restore trade relations with the rest of the world. But growing economic interests in Iraq also impeded the Council from taking effective measures against Iraq's efforts to circumvent the sanctions regime through smuggling and illegal surcharges on its oil exports. In the autumn of 2000, a paralysed sanctions committee was unable to act on Baghdad's bid to erode the sanctions, which allowed Baghdad to restore international air links.

As the Bush administration began to threaten to change the Iraqi regime openly, however, the Security Council gradually restored its unity on disarmament. As Iraq continued to reject weapons inspections, China and France became more critical of the Iraqi government and began to press it to accept UNMOVIC inspections. Russia also began to pressure Iraq to accept UN inspections. By 2002, UNMOVIC came to enjoy full support from the Security Council, which unanimously demanded that Iraq accept its inspections. Meanwhile, the Council also began to restore its unity on the sanctions regime. Washington's active diplomacy resulted in French and Chinese agreement to restructure the sanctions regime by adopting the Goods Review List (GRL) in May 2001. In the face of active lobbying by Iraq, Russia initially opposed the new initiative.[14] In the wake of the 9/11 terrorist attacks, however, Russia joined the US effort to fight terrorism, and the relationship between the two countries warmed considerably. In November 2001, Moscow joined the consensus on Resolution 1382 (2001) in which the Council expressed its intention to adopt the GRL within six months. This led to the adoption of Resolution 1409 (2002) in May 2002 – the most sweeping restructuring of the sanctions regime – and the Council was able to restore unity on the most important humanitarian issue.

Despite the Council's unity regarding the new sanctions regime and the resumption of weapons inspections, there remained a number of differences over issues related to Iraq. For example, although agreeing to the "smart sanctions" in the sanctions committee, Russia continued to oppose the Anglo-American effort to suppress Iraq's unauthorized revenues earned through illegal surcharges. More significantly, the Council was sharply divided over the way forward on the issue of disarmament in Iraq, particularly the prospects of the use of force. Russia, China and France were not ready to support US military action even if Iraq continued to reject weapons inspections. They also disagreed with Washington's declared objective of overthrowing the regime of Saddam Hussein. It is little surprise that the different stands on the use of force among the P-5 eventually came to the fore when the Council discussed Iraq's compliance with Resolution 1441 (2002) and finally became deadlocked over the matter in March 2003.

Dealing with WMD terrorism: Resolution 1540

Following the 9/11 terrorist attacks, greater international concern about the possible acquisition of nuclear weapons by terrorists has added a new dimension to the effort to combat nuclear proliferation. The IAEA has stepped up its efforts to help member states improve the physical security of their nuclear materials against risks of theft and terrorism, and the Secretary-General's Policy Working Group on terrorism has focused on the linkage between terrorism and weapons of mass destruction. Following President George W. Bush's call in September 2003 for the adoption by the Security Council of an anti-terrorism resolution, the Council's permanent members began their consideration of a draft resolution.[15] After five months of intensive consultations, the P-5 agreed on a draft resolution, and one month later the Security Council unanimously adopted Resolution 1540 (2004) on 28 April 2004, which represented the Council's first attempt to address an important WMD non-proliferation issue in a systematic manner.

In this resolution, the Security Council, acting under Chapter VII of the UN Charter, decided that all states should refrain from providing "any form of support" to non-state actors that seek to acquire certain weapons of mass destruction or their means of delivery. The Council also required all states to adopt and enforce "appropriate effective laws" to this effect and, more generally, required all states to establish various types of domestic controls "to prevent the proliferation" of such weapons.[16] To ensure global implementation of the resolution, the Council decided to establish a Committee of the Security Council to review the implementation of the resolution and, to this end, called upon states to present a first report to the Committee on steps they had taken or intended to take to implement this resolution within six months of the adoption of the resolution. The Council also called on all states to take cooperative action to prevent illicit trafficking in such items and related materials, which was meant to encourage arrangements that allow interdiction of cargo ships suspected of carrying WMD or related materials.[17] Finally, the resolution envisaged the possibility of international assistance to states that might require help in implementing the provisions of the resolution.

Although Resolution 1540 (2004) was a fresh attempt by the Security Council to address WMD proliferation issues on a global scale, it was a logical extension of the Council's effort to combat terrorism. In Resolution 1373 (2001), the Council noted with concern the close connection between international terrorism and transnational organized crime, illicit drugs, money-laundering, illegal arms trafficking, and illegal movement of nuclear, chemical, biological and other potentially deadly materials, and emphasized the need to enhance coordination of efforts on various levels in order to strengthen a global response to this serious challenge. The reporting mechanism established by Resolution 1540 (2004) is fashioned after that of the Counter-Terrorism Committee, as well as that of the al-Qaeda/Taliban Committee established by Resolution 1267 (1999).

From the disarmament/proliferation perspective, the adoption of Resolution 1540 (2004) was rather controversial. Critics of the resolution contend that the Security Council went beyond its mandate by acting as a global legislature imposing law on all states, usurping the sovereign right of states to enter into treaties out of their free will.[18] As a matter of fact, WMD issues have usually been discussed outside the Security Council, and such a long-established practice seems to have contributed to the understanding that addressing these issues, particularly those of a general nature, is beyond the competence of the Security Council. From a legal standpoint, the Security Council does have the mandate to address the issue of WMD terrorism. According to the UN Charter, UN members confer on the Security Council primary responsibility for the maintenance of international peace and security and agree that, in carrying out its duties under this responsibility, the Council acts on their behalf (Article 24). Moreover, UN members agree to accept and carry out the decisions of the Security Council in accordance with the Charter (Article 25). Furthermore, acting under Chapter VII, the Council determines the existence of any threat to the peace and decides to take appropriate measures (Article 39). In the preamble of Resolution 1540 (2004), the Council affirmed that proliferation of WMD and their means of delivery constitutes a threat to international peace and security, and therefore acted within the powers granted to the Council by the Charter. Also, this is not the first time the Council has imposed a wide range of obligations on states. Resolution 1373 (2001) had already established such a precedent.

From a political standpoint, however, the Security Council's sweeping action in the area of disarmament and non-proliferation caused jarring repercussions in the diplomatic community. Prior to the adoption of Resolution 1540 (2004), a number of member states had expressed concern about the resolution's potential impact on the existing disarmament regime. A number of non-aligned countries criticized the draft resolution for focusing only on non-state actors while ignoring states, expressed concern that the new obligations imposed by the resolution went beyond what is required from States Parties to the NPT, the Chemical Weapons Convention (CWC) and the Biological Weapons Convention (BWC), and faulted its exclusive focus on non-proliferation.[19] A mere passing reference to disarmament in the preamble only aroused concern among non-nuclear-weapon states that the resolution would further tip the balance between disarmament and non-proliferation – which had been carefully maintained through tireless negotiations – in favour of non-proliferation.

To allay these concerns, Council members sponsoring Resolution 1540 (2004)[20] stressed the imminence and gravity of the threat posed by terrorists' acquisition of WMD and the need for closing a gap in the existing international instruments. However, although the co-sponsors accommodated these concerns by revising its preamble, the Council adopted Resolution 1540 (2004) without incorporating major amendments sought by many UN members. It is still unclear whether these concerns may affect the implementation of the resolution, but broader acceptance of the resolution by a wide UN membership is crucial in order to ensure full implementation. Although Resolution 1540 (2004) was adopted under Chapter VII of the UN Charter, there were some doubts about the extent to which this resolution would be implemented by the UN membership. Several Council members have already made clear the intention to narrow the scope of their implementation by interpreting only the first three paragraphs as legally binding on them.[21]

Several Council members' ambivalence was also reflected in the work of a new Committee established pursuant to the resolution. The 1540 Committee, which came to be known as such owing to disagreement about the title of the Committee and which consists of the same members of the Security Council, could not meet for about one month because of disagreement over its chairmanship.[22] In mid-June, the Committee finally started its work, but it took the Committee about two months to agree on guidelines on the conduct of its work and another month to agree on guidelines for hiring experts to be recruited. Since the Committee makes its decisions by consensus, there is always the danger that its work could be blocked or delayed by a single Committee member.

As of November 2005, the 1540 Committee had received and considered the first reports from 124 member states and one regional organization (the European Union). In response to the Committee's replies to these reports, 29 states submitted second national reports. But, given that its current mandate will expire on 28 April 2006, the Committee has not yet decided how to proceed with the examination of these reports. Although about two-thirds of UN member states have submitted their first reports, much remains to be done to ensure full implementation of Resolution 1540. Committee experts reported that significant gaps exist between measures in place and measures required under the resolution. The Committee also has yet to address the problem of non-reporting and inadequate reporting, as well as the issue of technical assistance. The Security Council therefore needs to revisit the Committee's mandate soon, define the scope of its work and establish an appropriate timeframe for fulfilling such work.

The Security Council: Roles and functions in WMD issues

An examination of the Security Council's past involvement, particularly the cases of Iraq and WMD terrorism, indicates that it has already assumed a wide range of roles and functions in addressing WMD issues. The following are an indicative but not exhaustive list of these functions:
1. guaranteeing compliance with multilateral disarmament/proliferation regimes;
2. promoting multilateral disarmament/proliferation regimes;
3. investigating alleged uses of WMD or suspected WMD facilities;
4. verifying and monitoring compliance;
5. dismantling WMD and related facilities and disposing of related materials;
6. promoting preventive measures against WMD proliferation and WMD terrorism;
7. enforcing disarmament.

The Security Council has already performed these functions in various cases. As the ultimate guardian of international peace and security, the Council dealt with non-compliance cases such as Iraq and North Korea. It also took steps in the event that serious threats emerged to the existing multilateral regime. Israel's military attacks on the Iraqi nuclear reactor, the use of chemical weapons in the Iran–Iraq conflict and India and Pakistan's nuclear tests are cases in point. Whenever the Security Council dealt with these specific issues related to WMD, the Council affirmed the importance of existing disarmament and non-proliferation regimes and promoted their universalization by calling on non-adherent states to accede to these treaties. The Council repeatedly utilized the Secretary-General's investigative role during the Iran–Iraq conflict. In the area of monitoring compliance, the Council asked UNSCOM and the IAEA to establish the OMV system with a view to ensuring that Iraq would not reconstitute its WMD programmes. Although disarmament inspections proved particularly difficult, both agencies found that the monitoring operations were implemented smoothly and with full cooperation from the Iraqi government. The 1540 Committee has been monitoring states' implementation of the resolution by examining their reports. UN-SCOM, UNMOVIC and the IAEA discharged their mandate in dismantling WMD assets and programmes in Iraq. These dismantling operations were not as contentious as intrusive inspections carried out by UN-SCOM, and the Iraqi government exhibited a relatively high degree of cooperation with UN agencies. The Security Council also embarked on a preventive function by adopting Resolution 1540 (2004), which requires all states to take and enforce a broad array of legislative and enforcement measures. In the area of enforcement, the Security Council has a particularly large dossier regarding Iraq's disarmament. Although the case of Iraq is exceptional in many respects, the Council accumulated numerous lessons drawn from its enforcement measures, ranging from economic sanctions and the humanitarian programme to use of force.

Yet how effective were the functions of the Security Council in addressing WMD issues? Did Iraq stop using chemical weapons? Did Israel join the NPT? Did India and Pakistan cease their nuclear weapons development programmes? Did Iraq completely abandon its WMD ambitions? Did the Council stop North Korea from developing nuclear weapons? Unfortunately, the answers to these questions are mostly in the negative. As in other areas, the Security Council has a poor record of following up its decisions on the issues related to WMD. But this does not mean that the Council's roles in addressing WMD issues are likely to be ineffectual. On the contrary, the past record suggests that the Security Council has underutilized certain functions and could well be more effective in the future.

For example, the Security Council could again utilize its investigative function in the event of alleged uses of WMD in the future. The Council's experience over the use of chemical weapons in the Iran–Iraq conflict indicates its tendency to moderate or equivocate its position on concrete cases of chemical warfare. Most of the resolutions and presidential statements adopted by the Security Council between 1984 and 1988 avoided specifying the party guilty of violations.[23] This reflects the Council's desire not to antagonize the belligerent in seeking a political settlement to the conflict. The reports of the Secretary-General's missions revealed similar political sensitivity. Nonetheless, the Secretary-General and the Security Council established a useful template for investigating the use of chemical weapons in the future. In particular, the Council needs to match its actions with its strong pronouncements contained in Resolution 620 (1988), in which the Council encouraged the Secretary-General promptly to carry out investigations into allegations of possible use of chemical and biological weapons and, taking into account the investigations of the Secretary-General, decided to consider appropriate and effective measures immediately should there be any future use of chemical weapons.

Since the Iran–Iraq conflict, there has been no conspicuous use of chemical weapons that has affected international security.[24] There has not been a chance to test the Council's resolve to deal resolutely with possible use of chemical weapons in the future. In 1997, the Chemical Weapons Convention took effect, banning an entire category of chemical weapons and establishing the Organisation for the Prohibition of Chemical Weapons (OPCW) to carry out the functions of inspections and verification. However, the precedent established during the Iran–Iraq war still provides a useful model for the Council's use of the Secretary-General's investigative function concerning alleged uses of chemical weapons. The Security Council or the Secretary-General can turn to the OPCW for such investigations. More significantly, the Council can create a stronger mandate than that given to the OPCW by the CWC.

In this regard, UNMOVIC's expertise and experience could also be utilized, particularly in biological and ballistic missiles areas. Critics argue that there are no criteria for compliance in these areas owing to a lack of a verification mechanism or a global norm. However, the Security Council itself can set such criteria and establish standards for compliance.[25] Although UNSCOM and UNMOVIC were created for a specific purpose in extraordinary circumstances, their expertise could be utilized once the Council provides a new mandate. Since military action against Iraq in the spring of 2003 and the US-led Iraq Survey Group took over the search and dismantling mission for Iraq's WMD programmes, the multilateral disarmament mechanism created by the Security Council has been sidelined. UNMOVIC did not receive either any information or a request for assistance from the Iraq Survey Group until 8 October 2004, when Charles Duelfer, Special Advisor to the US Director of Central Intelligence for Iraq's Weapons of Mass Destruction, visited UNMOVIC following the release of his comprehensive report to the public.[26] In May 2003, the Security Council expressed its intention to revisit the mandate of UNMOVIC and the IAEA and reaffirmed this intention in June 2004.[27] The Iraq Survey Group concluded its work in 2005 with the revision of the comprehensive report and the publication of its addendums. Yet the Security Council has not initiated serious discussion on their mandates.

At the moment, discussion of the Council's role in addressing WMD remains clouded by its unfortunate experience with Iraq. But, as mentioned above, the Council's long engagement in Iraq's disarmament also could provide useful ideas and templates for dealing with a variety of issues. What is required is to sort out political baggage and extract the purely technical merits of the Iraqi file.

Obstacles and challenges

An overview of the Council's engagement in past WMD issues also suggests that it may encounter major obstacles in the future. Among these obstacles, the following three seem particularly important: political gridlock; legitimacy; and marginalization.

Political gridlock

In fulfilling its role as ultimate guarantor of international peace and security, the Security Council is faced with the dilemma that, although the unity of the Council (particularly among the P-5) is indispensable to instituting effective measures to deal with cases of non-compliance, there is no guarantee of such unity. In particular, the P-5 have different priorities regarding disarmament and non-proliferation issues and pursue different interests in dealing with non-compliant parties. These differences among the P-5 also cast a shadow over the Council's future action on North Korea and Iran. The cases of Iraq and North Korea highlight the problem of a "veto umbrella". When a veto-holding permanent member seeks to protect non-compliant parties, the Council is unable to take effective action. In theory, the Security Council can take strong measures, including economic sanctions and even military action. This power constitutes the basis for its role as guarantor of compliance with multilateral disarmament treaties and provides teeth to the Council's decisions. However, if one of the permanent members does not wish to take a coercive step, the Council cannot play the role of such a guarantor.

The unity of the Security Council is critical to shoring up the authority of inspection agencies. Iraq, North Korea and Iran all argued that inspection agencies became an instrument of the foreign policy of major powers, particularly the United States. Iraq repeatedly made this point regarding UNSCOM. It went further to argue that the Security Council also became a policy instrument of the United States, and adamantly refused UNMOVIC inspections. North Korea also suggested that the IAEA had become a tool of US diplomacy. Iran too has repeatedly warned the IAEA against yielding to pressure from the United States. Discrediting inspecting agencies and international organizations is a common strategy pursued by recalcitrant states that are subjected to special inspections. The Council's experience with Iraq indicated that a divided Council strengthened Iraq's hand in pursuing this strategy.

The question of the use of force is particularly problematic. Generally speaking, Russia and China and, to a lesser extent, France are more cautious about coercive action, particularly military action. And the issue of military action is related not only to a permanent member's "veto umbrella" but also to their own power relationship. As the Iraq crisis clearly demonstrated, China, France and Russia are wary of the Bush administration's unilateral tendencies, especially regarding its perceived haste in resorting to military force. In order to counter Washington's power and constrain its freedom of action, these countries resort to the Security Council, where they can raise the issue of legitimacy and appeal to international opinion.[28] They share the view that only the Security Council can authorize the use of force – a view to which the United Kingdom is also sympathetic. Increasingly unsettled by US power and its growing unilateral tendencies, these states might seek to check US military action through the United Nations. US primacy may be indisputable outside the United Nations, but the United States remains equal to these other nations as a veto-wielding permanent member in the Security Council. Unfortunately, the lopsided distribution of power, resources, commitments and responsibilities only encourages the P-5 to pursue divergent policies. Furthermore, Russia and China are particularly averse to the use of force, as was demonstrated during NATO's military campaign in Kosovo. They also have serious concerns about the implications of the use of force for issues of their own concern.

Legitimacy

A second obstacle concerns the legitimacy of actions taken by the Security Council on behalf of the UN membership. Because disarmament and proliferation issues often relate to the vital question of national security, states are more reluctant to accept the Council's unilateral edict. UN members are more or less accustomed to the long-established practice in post-war intergovernmental disarmament parlance in which they maintain their sovereign right to negotiate and enter into treaties, so they would resist a greater role played by the Security Council in this specific area (although the fact is that it is only the Security Council that can force reluctant states to accept certain disarmament/non-proliferation measures.). Moreover, since the Security Council is a 15-member club dominated by 5 veto-wielding nuclear-weapon states, there are strong sentiments among UN members that disarmament and proliferation should be achieved in more universal and non-discriminatory forums, especially the Conference on Disarmament. Therefore, it can be reasonably assumed that the wider UN membership would not welcome the Council's attempt to assume greater responsibility for global disarmament and non-proliferation. If fully implemented, Resolution 1540 (2004) would contribute hugely to global efforts to prevent the spread of WMD, particularly to non-state actors. However, its implementation hinges upon the degree to which states will accept the provisions in the resolution. Hence, when the Security Council plays a more active role in the area of disarmament and non-proliferation in the future, it should take into account concerns and views expressed by the UN membership. In particular, the permanent members need to address non-nuclear-weapon states' concerns, especially the slow progress in nuclear disarmament, an increasing emphasis on non-proliferation and security assurances against the use of nuclear weapons.

Marginalization

Another problem the Security Council may encounter in addressing WMD issues is that the United States may sideline the Security Council and create a coalition of like-minded countries. Washington's current promotion of the Proliferation Security Initiative and its exclusion of UNMOVIC and the IAEA from search and dismantling operations in Iraq underline this problem. Since the P-5's differences are directly linked to lopsided geopolitical imbalances, there are always temptations for Washington to resort to unilateral measures or ad hoc arrangements outside the United Nations that can be established much more easily. US officials who advocated marginalizing the Security Council may have found a good case for their argument in the Security Council's experience with Iraq. Although Russia, France and China agreed with the United States and the United Kingdom that Iraq was in non-compliance with Security Council resolutions, they did not participate in enforcing compliance by joining the US military operations. They also agreed that Iraq's military and WMD programme constituted a threat to regional security, but they did not contribute to the Anglo-American effort to maintain peace and security in the Gulf. In supporting the containment policy of Iraq, the United States and the United Kingdom (and France initially) maintained the no-fly zones, but Russia and China played virtually no role in this regard. In fact, as Iraq began to challenge the no-fly zones as illegal and tried to shoot down US and UK airplanes, Russia and China joined Iraq's effort by condemning US and the UK military actions, which they insisted were reactions of self-defence. Rather than criticizing Iraq's provocation, they sought to dismantle the no-fly zones. In particular, China's assistance to Iraq in upgrading its anti-aircraft facilities highlighted competing interests between the permanent members of the Security Council.

Although such experience may have strengthened the impulse to bypass the Security Council, it became clear to other Council members that, despite their strong opposition, the United States was undeterred from using force. The sad ending of the Iraq crisis in March 2003 attests to this point. The irony is that adamant opposition from other Council members will only drive the United States away from the Security Council, with the ominous consequence of further marginalizing the Council and the United Nations. That is, recourse to military force by the United States and other countries without explicit authorization from the Security Council certainly undermines the Council's authority and credibility, but this also means the power and prestige accorded to the other permanent members are similarly diminished. Russia, France, China and the United Kingdom are well aware of this dilemma, which suggests that they may realize that it would be in their interests to work out a formula for the use of force that is acceptable to the United States and can be authorized by the Council as a whole. The question of the use of force does not come to the Security Council so often. But it is in the interests of all permanent members of the Security Council to accommodate one another's interests, find a common position on WMD issues and thus avoid the marginalization of this august body.

Conclusions

The Security Council has played an important role in addressing the issues of WMD proliferation and disarmament. The Council's past engagement in these issues provides useful models and templates for its future role, but also underscores the complex political constraints on effective Council action, particularly in cases that touch upon the deep differences between permanent members in addressing issues of WMD proliferation and non-compliance. The case of Iraq highlights a stark divergence of permanent members' goals and approaches, which clearly reflect their conflicting interests. The United States and the United Kingdom focused on Iraq's complete disarmament of WMD and compliance with Security Council resolutions, and primarily dealt with Iraq by pursuing a policy of containment through economic sanctions and no-fly zones. Russia, France and China focused on humanitarian and economic issues, and pursued a policy of engagement with Iraq by seeking to lift the economic embargo and expand their commercial gains from the Oil-for-Food programme. Regarding WMD disarmament, the United States and the United Kingdom sought "complete" disarmament, whereas Russia, France and China aimed at its "early" conclusion and transition to monitoring. These stark differences often prevented the Council from taking effective action on Iraq's non-compliance.

Iraq's economic power also undermined the Council's efforts to take effective action. The economic stakes in Iraq became particularly important for Russia and France – to which Iraq owed billions of dollars – and, to a lesser extent, China, as Iraq manipulated the Oil-for-Food programme to dispense oil and humanitarian contracts on the basis of political preference and awarded these nations billions of dollars worth of contracts. As the economic and commercial interests of Iraq and these permanent members converged, the latter began to represent and defend Iraq's interests in the Security Council. In the meantime, the United States and the United Kingdom were spending billions of dollars to deal with Iraq by maintaining aerial patrols in the no-fly zones, enforcing the sanctions through a multilateral interdiction force deployed in the Gulf, and, in responding to Iraq's non-compliance, deploying a large military presence in the region. Iraq penalized US and UK companies for their governments' political stance, discriminating against them in implementing the Oil-for-Food programme.

The Iraq case also revealed other potential constraints on effective Council action: protection of a non-compliant party by a permanent member's "veto umbrella"; and political rivalry between permanent members and their use of the Council as a counterweight to a predominant power. In hindsight, Iraq's continued defiance was encouraged by the protection offered by its veto-holding allies in the Security Council. By threatening to exercise their veto, these permanent members shielded Iraq from more stringent measures against it. In addition, there were indications that these pro-Iraq P-5 members utilized the Security Council as an arena in which they could counterbalance US power. Such indications were particularly evident when the United States and the United Kingdom sought to use military force against Iraq. In reality, as long as the Council's permanent members enjoy equal status and veto power, they can use these powers to equalize their real-world power relationships and thwart any action sought by another permanent member. This political constraint may persist as long as the power distribution among the permanent members is lopsided and their status and privileges fail to reflect their actual power relationships. Also, if the United States pursues its policies, particularly when resorting to military action, other permanent members, with the possible exception of the United Kingdom, are enticed to undercut US power and prevent such unilateral action.

To address critical issues of nuclear breakout and non-compliance, the Security Council must overcome these political constraints. In the wake of the Council's failure to address Iraq's non-compliance, there seems to be a growing reluctance to refer non-compliance issues to the Security Council. Many fear that referral to the Council could lead to enforcement measures, particularly military action. The current debate on Iran's nuclear programme is a case in point. But it has highly politicized the IAEA Board of Governors, which used to be a technical body. This raises a serious question regarding the role of the Security Council in the collective security system. If the Council avoids dealing with WMD issues, particularly those involving non-compliance, this sends the erroneous message that non-compliance will have no serious consequences, thus weakening the existing non-proliferation regimes.

The permanent members of the Security Council have a special responsibility and must cooperate to overcome the political constraints associated with WMD issues. After all, the Security Council remains the most important source of international legitimacy in dealing with questions of international peace and security. At the last session of the General Assembly of the League of Nations in 1946, the veteran French statesman Joseph Paul Boncour stated prophetically: "The strength and weakness – I repeat the strength and weakness – of the new institution is that it depends on agreement between the five permanent Great Powers."[29]

Notes

The views expressed in this chapter are my personal views and do not represent those of the United Nations.

1. Among those Security Council resolutions are Resolution 255 (1968) on security assurances to non-nuclear-weapon states, Resolution 487 (1981) on Israel's military attack on Iraq, Resolutions 612 (1988) and 620 (1988) on the use of chemical weapons in Iran and Iraq, Resolution 825 (1993) on North Korea's withdrawal from the Treaty on the Non-Proliferation of Nuclear Weapons, Resolution 984 (1995) on security assurances to non-nuclear-weapon states, Resolution 1172 (1998) on nuclear tests by India and Pakistan, and Resolution 1540 (2004) on WMD non-proliferation.
2. Security Council Resolutions 20 (1947), 52 (1948) and 74 (1949) on atomic energy and international control.
3. The General Assembly adopted Resolution 41(1) on 14 December 1946. In this resolution, the General Assembly also recommended that the Council expedite consideration of a draft convention or conventions for the creation of an international system of control and inspection, these conventions to include the prohibition of atomic and all other major weapons adaptable now and in the future to mass destruction and the control of atomic energy to the extent necessary to ensure its use only for peaceful purposes.
4. "Note by the President of the Security Council", 31 January 1992, UN Doc. S/23500.
5. Security Council Resolutions 1318 (2000), 1624 (2005) and 1625 (2005). In the process of negotiating the declaration contained in Resolution 1318, a couple of non-permanent members of the Security Council made earnest efforts to include references to WMD, but the permanent members did not agree.

6. "Report of the First Panel Established Pursuant to the Note by the President of the Security Council on 30 January 1999 (S/1999/100), concerning disarmament and current and future ongoing monitoring and verification issues", UN Doc. S/1999/356, 27 March 1999.

7. In Resolution 1284 (1999) of 17 December 1999, the Security Council recognized "the need for an effective, cooperative management structure for the new organization, for staffing with suitably qualified and experienced personnel, who would be regarded as international civil servants subject to Article 100 of the Charter of the United Nations, drawn from the broadest possible geographical base, including as he [the Executive Chairman] deems necessary from international arms control organizations, and for the provision of high quality technical and cultural training" (UN Doc. S/RES/1284 (1999), p. 3).

8. Tim Trevan, *Saddam's Secrets: The Hunt for Iraq's Hidden Weapons* (London: Harper-Collins, 1999).

9. Scott Ritter, *Iraq Confidential: Untold Story of Intelligence Conspiracy to Undermine the UN and Overthrow Saddam Hussein* (New York: Nation Books, 2005).

10. Security Council Resolutions 986 (1995) and 1153 (1998).

11. Security Council Resolution 1409 (2002), 14 May 2002.

12. Hans Blix, *Disarming Iraq: The Search for Weapons of Mass Destruction* (New York: Pantheon Books, 2004; London: Bloomsbury, 2005 – an updated edition with a new chapter); Michael Friend, *After Non-Detection, What? What Iraq's Unfound WMD Mean for the Future of Non-Proliferation*, UNIDIR/2003/38 (United Nations Institute for Disarmament Research, 2003); Joseph Cirincione, Jessica Tuchman Mathew and George Perkovich, *WMD in Iraq: Evidence and Implications* (Washington, DC: Carnegie Endowment Report, January 2004); George A. Lopez and David Cortright, "Containing Iraq: Sanctions Worked", *Foreign Affairs*, Vol. 83, No. 4 (July/August 2004).

13. William Jefferson Clinton, "Battling the Rogue State: The Weapons Inspection Crisis", Address to the Nation, White House, Washington, DC, 16 December 1998, in Alvin Z. Rubinstein, ed., *The Clinton Foreign Policy Reader: Presidential Speeches with Commentaries* (Armonk, NY: M. E. Sharpe, 2000), p. 231.

14. Russia initially agreed to the new initiative "in principle" by adopting Resolution 1352 (2001) in June 2001, which extended the Oil-for-Food programme for one month to give Russia more time to consider the new measure. The adoption of this resolution marked the restoration of the Council's unity for the first time in many years. However, Iraq's aggressive lobbying led Russia to threaten to veto the draft resolution on the GRL one month later.

15. In his Address to the General Assembly on 23 September 2003, President Bush said that the new anti-proliferation resolution should call on all members of the United Nations to criminalize the proliferation of weapons of mass destruction, to enact strict export controls consistent with international standards, and to secure any and all sensitive materials within their own borders.

16. These control measures include: (a) measures to account for and secure such items in production, use, storage and transport; (b) effective physical protection measures; (c) effective border controls and law enforcement efforts to detect, deter, prevent and combat the illicit trafficking and brokering in such items; and (d) export and transhipment controls over such items, including controls on providing funds and services related to such export and transhipment, end-user controls and criminal or civil penalties for violations of such export control laws and regulations. The resolution also called upon all member states to pursue the development of such lists.

17. Earlier drafts of this resolution contained a direct reference to interdiction, reflecting Washington's desire to promote the Proliferation Security Initiative (PSI). However,

this reference was deleted at the request of China (see Security Council meeting of 22 April 2004, UN Doc. S/PV.4950, p. 6).

18. Although Pakistan voted in favour of Resolution 1540 (2004) on 28 April 2004, its Permanent Representative to the United Nations stated after the vote that Pakistan shared the general view of the UN membership that the Security Council cannot assume the stewardship of global non-proliferation and disarmament issues, since it is not a representative body and it cannot enforce the obligations assumed by the P-5, which retain nuclear weapons, since they possess the right of veto in the Council (see Security Council meeting of 28 April 2004, UN Doc. S/PV.4956, p. 3).

19. During the open debate held on 22 April 2004, the Permanent Representative of South Africa to the United Nations made these points, which were echoed by a number of other non-Council members (UN Doc. S/PV.4950, p. 12).

20. France, the Philippines, Romania, the Russian Federation, Spain, the United Kingdom and the United States.

21. Pakistan stated upon the adoption of Resolution 1540 (2004) that, "under this resolution, legally binding obligations under Chapter VII arise only in respect of paragraphs 1, 2, 3, 4 and 5, which start with the word 'decides' and which, at our request, have been grouped together for presentational purposes". Pakistan further noted that "this offers reassurance that the provisions of the resolution will not serve to impose non-proliferation obligations on States or to transfer the general responsibility for global non-proliferation and disarmament to the Security Council" (UN Doc. S/PV.4956, p. 3).

22. Failing to break the stalemate over the selection of the chairman of the 1540 Committee through bilateral consultations by its president, the Security Council had to meet again at the ambassadorial level to resolve this problem in June.

23. As exceptions, in its Presidential Statement issued on 14 May 1987 after considering the report of the mission of specialists sent by the Secretary-General, the Security Council expressed deep dismay at the unanimous conclusions of the specialists that there had been repeated use of chemical weapons against Iranian forces by Iraqi forces, that civilians in Iran had also been injured by chemical weapons, and that Iraqi military personnel had sustained injuries from chemical warfare agents. In its preamble, Resolution 620 (1998) also expressed deep dismay at the missions' conclusions that the use of chemical weapons against Iranians had become more intense and frequent.

24. Aum Shinrikyo, a Japanese religious cult, used a sarin gas in the Tokyo subway and elsewhere, but, as an internal matter, it was not taken up by the Council.

25. Resolution 687 (1991) prohibited ballistic missiles with a range greater than 150 km. Resolution 1540 (2004) defined "means of delivery" as missiles, rockets and other unmanned systems capable of delivering nuclear, chemical or biological weapons that are especially designed for such use.

26. UNMOVIC's 14th, 15th, 16th, 17th, 18th and 19th quarterly reports: S/2003/844 of 28 August 2003, S/2003/1135 of 26 November 2003, S/2004/160 of 27 February 2004, S/2004/435 of 28 May 2004, S/2004/693 of 27 August 2004 and S/2004/924 of 26 November 2004.

27. Security Council Resolutions 1483 (2003) and 1546 (2004).

28. Michael J. Glennon, "Why the Security Council Failed", *Foreign Affairs*, Vol. 82, No. 3 (May–June 2003), pp. 16–35.

29. Brian Urquhart, *Life in Peace and War* (New York: W. W. Norton, 1987), pp. 105–106.

6

Dealing with WMD crises: The role of the United Nations in compliance politics

Harald Müller

The problem

Weapons of mass destruction, by their very nature, pose security problems. Because of their destructive and lethal character, their mere existence endangers the survival of states. Even if this statement is entirely true only for nuclear weapons, it applies in certain, very specific circumstances for biological weapons; chemical weapons would have less significant consequences, and only if used in large quantities against undefended civilian populations.

The menace is most acute in the immediate environment of the state possessing such weapons. But it can be equally virulent for states living in a hostile relationship with a far-away power that possesses long-distance power projection and WMD delivery capabilities. WMD's inherent threat of complete destruction presents the world with its single most menacing risk. The interaction of rival or hostile states in the context of the security dilemma,[1] fostered by misperception, misunderstanding and the fear of becoming the victim of a devastating and disarming first strike, could precipitate a WMD disaster even against the better interests and conscious will of the participating parties. This risk haunted strategists throughout the Cold War[2] and remains a nightmare wherever states armed with WMD face each other in an ongoing conflict.

On the other hand, weapons of mass destruction are seen by quite a few people as the solution to security problems and the guarantor of (eternal) peace. Through their capacity to inflict immense damage, they are be-

114

lieved to implant a grain of caution in the minds of otherwise hot-headed national leaders. Such leaders might contemplate the use of force to bolster the supposed national interest if they were not dissuaded by the threat of total annihilation or at least the unbearable cost invested in the WMD of the potential enemy.[3] As guarantors of peace, WMD may sometimes look attractive even to countries with quite a pacifist attitude.[4] For small powers, WMD appear to offer the guarantee of survival in a world in which lurk great powers with predatory motivations (ranging from ordinary territorial expansion to morally preferred regime change).

The trouble with this positive view of WMD is that, the more widely it is shared, the more WMD proliferation is likely to occur. It is improbable that a country in conflict with another state that is procuring WMD would watch these activities with sanguinity. Rather, reciprocal action is to be expected. The more WMD-endowed state dyads there are, the greater the probability that the unintentional escalation scenario will actually happen. As an unwelcome side-effect, with more and more countries possessing WMD, the opportunities for unauthorized, non-state actors to access such weapons and/or their materials and technologies rise.[5]

The international community was and is therefore well advised to uphold and strengthen those regimes that have been devised to provide for the disarmament and/or non-proliferation of WMD and have been the first and most important line of defence against the risks of spreading WMD.[6] These regimes rest largely on the voluntary renunciation of WMD by their members (a commitment the nuclear-weapon states have still to emulate) and the firm determination of the overwhelming majority of the regimes' members to abide by their undertakings.[7] However, this strength would be fatally undercut if the regimes did not include reliable and robust mechanisms to be applied when the compliance of a party with its basic obligations was in serious doubt.[8]

The suspicion or the proof of non-compliance with undertakings regarding WMD perforce have an impact in one way or another on international peace and security. This was the finding of the UN Security Council summit meeting in January 1992, when the Council declared the proliferation of WMD in all their forms to be a threat to peace and international security, and was reconfirmed in Security Council Resolution 1540 in April 2004. It is thus inevitable that the United Nations, and the Security Council in particular, should be involved in all cases where the spectre of WMD non-compliance is rising. Non-involvement, in turn, raises the immediate question "why?".

The compliance procedure ideally rests on a triad: verification, compliance activities, and enforcement if and when compliance cannot be ensured by other means. In this chapter, I focus on compliance and enforcement – and the role of the United Nations therein – and neglect verification, which has been the subject of much previous work. It must be emphasized, however, that verification – or, if not available, other means to collect evidence on the behaviour of a state suspected to be in non-compliance with its undertakings – is the basis for all compliance and enforcement procedures: without solid information, all such procedures are no more than a frantic dance in the fog.

Beware of circumstances: Reasons for non-compliance

There is too great an inclination nowadays to start discussing military action as soon as concerns about non-compliance arise. Although military pre-emption might be justified in certain circumstances to prevent worse consequences, all military enforcement engenders undesirable and morally deplorable consequences that are described very inadequately by the euphemism "collateral damage". In military action, however surgical it might be intended to be, innocents will die or be maimed. The boy who lost his arms and legs in the US/UK operation to "liberate" Iraq should never be forgotten. These personal disasters, which are, I repeat, an inevitable part of all warfare even if it is conducted with the most humane of intentions, are a serious counter-argument to engaging in military enforcement. This moral aspect is too easily forgotten in the current rediscovery of the notion of a "just war", which looks at the general justification for military action and the observation of the rule of proportionality and overlooks the individual calamities that occur even if the decision to go to war is well covered by the "just war" argument.[9] It is always morally suspect to weigh a human life against another human life, or against other values. In any case, to be justified in deciding to attack in order to forestall the development, or use, of hostile WMD one needs very good knowledge about the circumstances on the ground, a well-founded conviction that avoiding military action would lead to even worse results (with more innocent lives at stake), proof of a complete lack of promising alternatives, and a reliable assessment that the prospects are very good that military action will be successful in an enforcement procedure.

An in-depth look at the circumstances surrounding the acquisition of WMD by a state that has undertaken not to do so is thus required (of course, one has to deal with WMD procurement by states not bound by such an obligation as well – but this is not the subject of this chapter). To start with, there are very trivial cases of non-compliance, such as the failure of several states with no nuclear activities on their territory to negotiate and sign the required Safeguards Agreements with the International Atomic Energy Agency. I shall ignore all such cases of non-compliance related to secondary obligations under the relevant treaties, and instead focus on those that concern serious attempts to acquire prohibited WMD.

The degree of the threat to international peace and security emanating from states newly acquiring WMD does not rest on the technical capabilities of the weapons – their destructive potential – alone. It is also determined by the motivations of the particular government.[10] If a government has no intention whatsoever of using these weapons except in the most dire of circumstances when national survival is at stake (the case that is exempted in the International Court of Justice Advisory Opinion on the legality of nuclear weapons[11]), this represents less of a threat than if the WMD are meant to be instruments of aggressive and expansive designs. It is thus necessary to consider the motivations that might drive a state and its government to seek to acquire these weapons.[12]

The most likely motivation is national security. States embroiled in ongoing rivalry and conflicts that have already resulted in a serious war and inflicted destruction and loss of life might seek recourse to WMD as a general deterrent for preventing new outbreaks of war. The hope of forestalling further violence between this state and its neighbours might prove illusory, but that is not the point here. What is decisive is the purely defensive motivations behind the proliferation. Likewise, a state facing an overwhelming threat might seek WMD as an asymmetric deterrent against this threat. This could be the case if a major power declared this state an enemy, if the state was confronted with conventionally superior forces of a state or an alliance, or if the threatening state itself possessed WMD.

State security is generally viewed as a legitimate concern. This is why the international instruments relating to WMD contain withdrawal clauses. A state that feels compelled to take the proliferation route for security motivations is thus under an obligation to do so in a legal and orderly way. However, it is in precisely the situations where a real or perceived threat drives states to acquire WMD that they can be expected to be most reluctant to reveal their activities until they are completed. If their intentions are betrayed, the security threat they face might become an attempt at prevention, provoking exactly the violence that the acquisition of WMD was meant to forestall. It is thus not surprising – though strictly it is illegal – when security-motivated states try to conceal their activities as long as they can.

Proliferation for security motivations does not immediately increase the risk of intentional, premeditated use of WMD. We are left in this case with the risk of further chains of escalation, with an inevitable rise in the probability that WMD use will emerge from counter-intentional escalation processes, and of unauthorized use or easier access by non-state actors to WMD owing to the greater numbers of these weapons and of sites where they can be acquired.

A second motivation is to enhance a nation's status. Today, the continued possession of nuclear weapons by the United Kingdom or France can hardly be justified by any serious security considerations.[13] These two countries do not want to give up their nuclear weapons lest their international standing be diminished. And status considerations have played a major role in India's acquisition of nuclear weapons too.[14] Status motivations do not propel intentional use, and the remaining risks are the same as for the security motivation: proliferation chains through mimicry (which is particularly strong if status is in effect accorded to the new WMD possessor), escalation out of the security dilemma, and terrorist access.

It is the integration of WMD in aggressive political designs that poses the gravest threat to peace and international security. WMD can be employed to intimidate and blackmail a non-possessing state into concessions that it would not otherwise have made, to prevent external powers from coming to the aid of a threatened or attacked state under Article 51 of the UN Charter, or to force another state into surrender by threatening to use or actually using WMD in war. In these circumstances, possession of WMD by this kind of actor significantly enhances the probability of their use.

These three types of motivation call for quite different treatment in terms of compliance policy. A state facing a real or perceived threat that it tries to avert is acting in the legitimate tradition of sovereign statehood. Preventive military action would certainly not be justified, and it would mean adding insult to injury if the threat emanated from a WMD-armed power that then carried out the act of disarmament, ostensibly in the name of international law. What is called for is thoroughly addressing the states' grievances with a view to changing the security environment in a way that would persuade the state to stop its WMD activities because national security can be achieved in a different and less risky way.

If, however, proliferation cannot be stopped in this way, rather than enhance the level of international violence by going to war against the proliferator, the international community would probably be better advised to acquiesce in the undesirable increase in the number of WMD-armed states and to try to contain and mitigate the concomitant danger. The risks and costs of military action would probably outweigh the risks arising from the proliferation case itself, especially if the attacked state already possessed some WMD capability. However important the objective of non-proliferation, it would not be worth the cost in lives in a war for disarmament if containment of the proliferator would be likely to forestall the use of its WMD and prevent attacks on neighbours that this state might consider if the international community did not erect a credible deterrent posture against this possibility.

A state acquiring WMD for status may be harder to stop because of the irrational and intangible nature of that motivation. If a substitute for according status is available it should be offered, though with great care lest other states be induced to follow the same route to glory. Alternatively, a state that stubbornly pushes for WMD in order to enhance its international standing might be isolated and have sanctions imposed in order to deter others from emulating this example. In this case, thorough containment of this state is needed to protect its neighbours from possible security threats; positive security assurances loom large in this scenario.[15] But, again, fighting a war of disarmament appears to be a disproportionate response given the limited character of the emerging threat.

Of course, WMD in the context of an aggressive state actor are a quite different matter. Here, the risks for the international community and the immediate neighbourhood of the perpetrator are considerable. They might be big enough to justify preventive action if the prospects of success are reasonable high and diplomatic efforts to dissuade the government in question from its illegal activities have borne no fruit. Diplomacy would still be the first line of defence, but the "big stick" must already be visible in the background while diplomatic efforts arc going on.

The forensic and the political: What compliance politics involves

The preceding discussion has already revealed some requirements of an orderly compliance process. Compliance policy consists to a large degree of the necessity to determine what the situation on the ground really is and what means are appropriate to deal with the realities of this situation. In a nutshell, compliance politics is very much about *proliferation forensics* and, inasmuch as this process is politically charged, it shows similarities to a criminal trial.

The first question that must be answered is whether there is indeed a case of non-compliance, that is, a serious attempt to acquire weapons of mass destruction. Evidence must be collected and assessed to give the best informed answer possible. Experience shows that this is not always easy. Verification is helpful in supporting that determination, as is intelligence. But neither verification nor intelligence is foolproof, and either may be confronted with attempts at concealment and deception. In many cases, thus, evidence will be less self-explanatory and unambiguous than one would wish.

It is this ambiguity that opens the door wide for politicking. In jurisprudence, procedures are shaped to grant as impartial a treatment of evidence as possible. In politics, national interests, traditional amity and enmity, national prejudices and idiosyncrasies or blatant ignorance enter the picture. It would be necessary to devise procedures that at least curb these distorting influences on compliance policy. To start with, it must be understood by everybody, including the governments of the United States and the United Kingdom, that their justification of the invasion of Iraq through the allegation of large WMD programmes in Iraq, and the subsequent complete failure to find such weapons, parts or related production facilities in Iraq, mean that national intelligence assessments will not be accepted as a reliable basis for decision-making on WMD noncompliance for at least a generation.

On the basis of the experience in Iraq, information gathered through international verification should generally be rated as of higher quality and reliability than intelligence.[16] Intelligence information should be included in an overall threat assessment only if confirmed either by two sources independent of each other or by international verification following the intelligence lead. In the case of two intelligence sources confirming each other, care should be taken that there is true independence and that the confirmation is not the result of a "quotation chain", where one intelligence agency quotes information obtained from the other without admitting this.

If factual evidence has been dealt with and the case has been established that a serious proliferation concern exists, it would still be necessary to gain insights into the motivation behind the WMD activities. That they are illegal for a State Party to one of the regimes is beyond doubt. But, as the discussion in the previous section has shown, the illegal character of the act does not yet determine the kind of response without an in-depth attempt to understand the forces behind that state's breach of the rules.

Assessing motivations is naturally even harder than assessing concrete facts. One has to look at the past behaviour of the accused state, the personal attributes of its leaders, the threats it is facing, its policies towards its neighbours, and also its overall military capabilities as related to explicit political objectives. All this implies very politically charged judgements. To discuss these issues openly about a sovereign state is, even in the best of circumstances, a fairly delicate matter. Yet it cannot be avoided in a complete and orderly compliance procedure.

Again, the influence of national idiosyncrasies on these deliberations should be curbed as much as possible. It would be necessary to look at the supposed intentions from every possible perspective. For example, it was stated before the 2003 Iraq war that Saddam Hussein did not respond to deterrence. That stands in stark contrast to several accounts that he was deterred from using chemical and biological weapons in 1991. Although it is certainly true that his risk calculus was different from that of Western and Eastern bloc states during the Cold War, it was clear that he was not willing to go to extremes with no regard for the consequences.[17] It is thus necessary that, in determining the threat by estimating the intentions of a proliferator, states do not just utter their prejudices but approach the debate with an open mind, willing to listen until all relevant facts have been put on the table. It would be useful to have some independent institution involved in this process, although it is clear that this goes beyond the brief and the competence of the various verification agencies.

A final comment on intentions concerns the actual possibility of saying anything reasonable about them at all. Sometimes it is argued that, since intentions are within the brain and the brain of political leaders is a black box that cannot be opened, speculation about intentions is in vain and capabilities are the only indicator on which a judgement can be based. This might be true in terms of developing social science theory, but it fails to recognize that we work on the basis of estimated intentions in quite a few fields. Again, it is useful to employ the analogy with the criminal trial. Here, assessing intentions is part of the regular procedure; intent and neglect are powerful legal categories that lead judges to distinguish between different degrees of gravity of a crime or misdemeanour; the assessment of the presence and the type of intent, for example, is instrumental in the distinction between murder and other, lesser forms of homicide. Without exaggerating the analogy, it is obvious that an assessment of political intent should not in principle be beyond the reach of compliance procedures.

Lastly, one has to decide how to respond. Both the technical parameters of the situation and the findings on motivations must inform this decision. As discussed above, the response must depend primarily on the gravity of the threat – measured by the maturity of the WMD programme in question and the type of motivation behind the programme. If, and only if, intention of future use is rated very high does pre-emption become a viable option. The choice of response should also depend on the prospects of success. An essential criterion in this consideration is proportionality. A second criterion is the expected effectiveness of the chosen instrument: a country whose attitude to security is close to paranoia is unlikely to be swayed by the threat of sanctions; a country looking for status is probably immune to the lure of security guarantees; a state in poor economic shape might be more open to economic incentives than to status promises, and so on. Lastly, the probable effects of the response on third parties must be taken into account. If concessions are likely to arouse envy and lead to emulation of the proliferator's illegal action, if containment is not adequate to mitigate security concerns in the neighbourhood, or if threats of pre-emption send a whole region into panic, the choice of response was probably poor and must be reconsidered.

Justice, fairness and truth: Substantial and procedural requirements

The previous section discussed some substantive and procedural criteria that compliance procedures must satisfy; these were very much of a practical, functional nature, meant to ensure the adequacy and effectiveness of the assessment and the concomitant response. Another set of criteria could be described as "moral". They concern moral values that are common across world cultures, notably justice, fairness and truth. It is suggested that disregard for these criteria undermines international support for compliance measures, especially those containing an enforcement component. Without such support, the non-proliferation/disarmament regimes would very rapidly lose legitimacy and might no longer be robust enough to resist challenges internally as well as externally.[18]

The basic principle of justice that applies to our cases is that what is valid for one is valid for all. The rule of equal standards is one of the most fundamental notions of justice in world cultures and is very pertinent to WMD non-compliance responses. First of all, it is relevant to the way we treat individual cases of non-compliance. Vast differences in approach towards the same type of non-compliance raise serious questions. As stated above, differential treatment might make sense if the response would engender different risks or, because of the proliferators' different motivations, deliver results with very varying levels of reliability and efficiency. However, these different strategies are then explainable in terms of the regimes themselves, their superior goals, or other aspects of peace and international security. It is quite another matter if different strategies can be explained only by patterns of sympathies, antipathies, biases and prejudices, or by vested interests in particular relationships (e.g. with an oil producer). Variation of this kind tends to undermine the legitimacy of the response to non-compliance.

The other dimension of substantive justice concerns the overarching balance of undertakings within the regimes as they relate to non-compliance. This problem is most obvious in the Treaty on the Non-Proliferation of Nuclear Weapons (Nuclear Non-Proliferation Treaty, or NPT). This Treaty consists of a careful balancing of rights and duties between unequal sets of parties: nuclear-weapon states and non-nuclear-weapon states. The balance is inherently asymmetrical because the duties of non-nuclear-weapon states are stated in fairly clear terms and are subject to verification and assessment, whereas those of the nuclear-weapon states remain vague and lack a verification and assessment procedure. This asymmetry would be tolerable if there was a credible attempt by the nuclear-weapon states to implement their obligations. In the eyes of many, though, this credibility is lacking. It is thus a very sensitive situation that it is the permanent five members of the Security Council (the P-5), which also happen to be the five nuclear-weapon states and the erstwhile sinners, as it were, that decide upon enforcement measures and are the ones on which enforcement, if it is imposed, has to rely. The asymmetry of obligations and the imbalance in implementation create feelings of injustice that, in turn, detract from the legitimacy of compliance and enforcement measures.[19]

The term "fairness" as used here relates to procedural justice, the principle that decision-making should involve all those affected by the decision and ensure that all relevant aspects, opinions and interests can be expressed during the proceedings.[20] I have already exposed the complexity of procedural fairness in alluding to the participatory privileges of the P-5. The P-5 would be well advised to exert some self-restraint in these proceedings and to rein in their politicking. Doubts about their impartiality and their willingness to solve the issue at stake in a manner compatible with the interests and values of the international community are likely to undermine the credibility of the UN Security Council as the ultimate arbiter on war and peace and detract from the legitimacy of, and international support for, the WMD regime. In this regard, the Iraqi case was a full-scale disaster.

We need to recognize other aspects too. First, the accused country must be given an opportunity to defend itself. Equally importantly, if the spectre of war is looming the neighbouring countries have such a stake in the matter that their views should be taken fully into consideration when counter-measures against the proliferator are debated. Finally, a decision on preventive or pre-emptive military intervention is a grave and fateful occasion that affects the whole international community. Even if formal participation in the eventual decision cannot be granted, an input by the international community as a whole can be enabled through open sessions of the Security Council and a full debate in the General Assembly on the matter under consideration.

Compliance procedures in existing regimes: Tools, levels, strengths, weaknesses

All three regimes covering weapons of mass destruction contain ways and means to address non-compliance. The NPT lacks a treaty organization,

which creates some problems in terms of reliable compliance procedures.[21] The International Atomic Energy Agency (IAEA) is charged
with verifying compliance by non-nuclear-weapon states. Its verification
tools have been greatly strengthened by the adoption of an Additional
Protocol that grants it extended access rights. The empowerment to
draw on all kinds of sources and to apply up-to-date technology has improved the Agency's capability to detect clandestine, undeclared activities. It falls on the IAEA Secretariat to report on non-compliance cases
to the Board of Governors, which then determines if a case of non-
compliance exists; non-compliance, that is, with the Safeguards Agreement the state had concluded with the IAEA, not with the NPT as a
whole. The board can take such a decision by a majority, though there is
always an effort to achieve consensus. If the board considers the case to
be sufficiently grave, it reports it to the United Nations General Assembly and Security Council. The procedure is not written directly into the
NPT, but follows stipulations in the Safeguards Agreement and the
IAEA Statute (Article XII).

The Convention on the Prohibition of the Development, Production,
Stockpiling and Use of Chemical Weapons and on Their Destruction
(Chemical Weapons Convention, or CWC) puts the review of compliance
squarely into the hands of the Organisation for the Prohibition of Chemical Weapons (OPCW). As in the nuclear case, the Secretariat reports on
the findings of its inspections and the Board of Governors makes the decision. In addition to the tools available in the nuclear sector, the CWC
has a clarification procedure involving the Executive Council and can
deploy the instrument of challenge inspection: a member state suspecting
another member state of cheating can call for such an inspection at any
particular site. The procedural prescriptions are such that the inspection
proceeds within a timeframe that makes it very difficult for the inspected
state to conceal evidence before the inspectors actually arrive on the
spot. The inspection will occur unless it is blocked by three-quarters of
the executive board of the IAEA, which is a very high hurdle. If the clarification process does not progress satisfactorily, or if a challenge inspection gives an indication of non-compliance, the matter is forwarded to
the Conference of States Parties. Following a determination of non-
compliance, the Conference of States Parties will consider suspending
the rights and privileges of the perpetrator under the Convention, recom-
mending collective measures to States Parties of the CWC, and, in grave
cases, referring the case to the UN General Assembly and Security
Council (Article XII).

A similar procedure was foreseen in the Draft Protocol to the Convention on the Prohibition of the Development, Production and Stockpiling
of Bacteriological (Biological) and Toxin Weapons and on Their De-

struction (Biological Weapons Convention, or BWC). However, since the Draft Protocol was rejected by the United States, States Parties are left with the devices written into the regime itself. Article V calls for states that have doubts about the compliance of a fellow member state to seek clarification of the matter bilaterally or through the appropriate international procedures. Article VI entitles states to go directly to the Security Council with their complaint if they are not satisfied with the results of the clarification process or feel otherwise that the matter is grave enough to concern the Council (BWC, Articles V and VI). In addition, the UN Secretary-General has been given the task by UN Security Council resolutions of acting as the investigator of alleged uses of biological (and chemical) weapons relating to the Geneva Protocol.[22] For this purpose, a "mechanism" has been set up, which simply consists of a list of experts on whom the Secretary-General can draw if an investigation is to be conducted and a list of laboratories that would be available for analysing samples taken by the experts in the course of an investigation. Investigations have taken place with regard to the alleged use of chemical and biological weapons in South-east Asia (1981/82), during the Iran–Iraq war in 1984–1988, and in Mozambique and Azerbaijan in 1992.[23]

Looking at the strengths and weaknesses of these procedures, it must be emphasized that, in the nuclear and chemical sectors, the link between the relevant regimes and the Security Council is sensible and well designed. The technical expert community works on the collection of technical data and evaluates them. The Security Council enters the stage only when there has already been an assessment of the evidence. That should normally serve to constrain the involvement of vested interests and politicking that would otherwise be possible. Yet, the lack of established procedures and of the involvement of neutral, international institutions in the decision-making process leaves much to be desired. Security Council decision-making involves just the usual negotiation over a Council resolution and is not adapted to the specific forensic requirements of WMD non-compliance cases. Given the relevance to international security of the spread of weapons of mass destruction, the very difficult assessments the Security Council has to make, and the specifics of the decision-making process, notably its forensic character, this situation is not satisfactory.

In addition, non-compliance with the BWC lacks any intermediate step between bilateralism (the consultation process) and the Security Council, where the spectre of Chapter VII casts a shadow over all proceedings from the very beginning. Moreover, owing to the lack of an international expert organization, no routine technical procedures have been established and there is no experienced crew of specialists, accustomed to working together in an investigative capacity, available to collect, analyse and assess evidence before the diplomats become concerned with the matter. This is undoubtedly a very serious weakness. The Geneva Protocol mechanism is only a weak substitute for a robust and authoritative expert organization. There is no established procedure for dealing with a case of non-compliance. Moreover, the lists that make up the mechanism are disastrously outdated.

The role of the United Nations in legal and political terms

As elaborated in the discussion about the compliance mechanisms written into the WMD regimes, the Security Council and, to some extent, also the Secretary-General play important roles in ensuring the completion of a compliance process. In particular, the Security Council is where the major enforcement decisions take place. This is entirely appropriate because these decisions have to be taken when international peace and security are at stake – as with all WMD proliferation – and when the use of force might be considered as a remedy. Since this does not involve a situation of immediate self-defence, only the Security Council has the authority, if need be, to impose military sanctions on a perpetrator.

The General Assembly shares with the Council the responsibility for international security and peace, but in a deliberative rather than a decision-making capacity. It can thus choose to concern itself with matters related to WMD compliance without, however, pre-empting the Council's prerogative. In the nuclear non-proliferation regime, the GA membership is to be informed by the IAEA Board of Governors about all cases of non-compliance with the Safeguards Agreement referred to the Security Council, and by a state withdrawing from the NPT about its reasons for doing so. The General Assembly is then free to take up the issue and deliberate on it. If the Executive Council of the Chemical Weapons Convention reports a case to the Security Council, the General Assembly is also to be informed.

The Secretary-General could play a more active and prominent role than in the past. This role could be based upon Article 99 of the UN Charter, which gives the Secretary-General the right to bring any issue before the Security Council that, in his view, concerns international peace and security. This might well be the case if a non-compliance incident is ignored by the Council for whatever reason, or if information not available to Council members – or to the organizations dealing with WMD – is brought to the attention of the Security Council, for example by a member state without a Council seat. In this case, the Secretary-General would have to weigh the pros and cons of approaching the Council. The Secretary-General currently lacks the necessary technical expertise to evaluate information conveyed to him, so this task can hardly be fulfilled in an appropriate manner.

The way the Security Council has tackled WMD non-compliance issues cannot be rated effective or satisfactory. In the case of the Democratic People's Republic of Korea (DPRK), the Security Council looked at the issue in 1993 and then left it to bilateral negotiations between the United States and the DPRK to find a solution. This might still be regarded as a wise and appropriate decision, because – for the time being – the case was solved politically without the use of force. However, it was solved by suspending the rules of the NPT, thereby clearly transgressing the boundaries of existing legal obligations.[24] When North Korea breached its undertakings under the Agreed Framework of 1994, the Security Council did not act because of Chinese opposition.

Even worse, it also did not act when North Korea declared its withdrawal from the NPT, which it had violated before. This is deplorable, because the procedure prescribed by Article X(2) of the NPT requires the withdrawing state to inform all other parties as well as the Security Council about the reasons for withdrawal, which must relate to the "extraordinary events related to the subject-matter of the Treaty" which have "jeopardized the supreme interest" of the withdrawing state and thereby motivated the decision to withdraw, and have a substantial relation to the subject matter of the Treaty. The Security Council could have scrutinized the reasons given by the DPRK to check whether they really met the criteria. It should also have determined whether North Korea had abused its membership of the NPT to acquire technology that helped in its illegal endeavour to produce nuclear weapons. Finally, the Security Council should have passed judgement on whether a state not in good standing with the treaty is entitled to make use of Article X(2) in the first place. In light of all these deliberations, the Security Council could still have decided to give the six-nation talks the power to find a diplomatic solution to the crisis, but it would clearly have played its legitimate role in the compliance process.

Instead, China refused to take the issue up lest its client, North Korea, be confronted with sanctions, a move China deemed counter-productive and also not in its own interests (even though China is not enthused by the idea of nuclear weapons on the Peninsula). The United States, for its part, did not want to challenge the reasons of another country, not even North Korea, for using a withdrawal clause to escape from a treaty because the United States itself wishes to reserve its right to withdraw from treaties it no longer likes (as it did in the case of the Anti-Ballistic Missile Treaty) and does not want its reasons to be challenged. Politics, in other words, prevented the Security Council from fulfilling at least its formal role in the NPT compliance procedure.[25]

The Iraqi case of 2002–2003 is unique because the breach of its obligations related to the armistice Resolution 687 and its corollaries, not to the WMD regimes as such. Here, the Security Council lost its active role in the second half of the 1990s. For political and economic reasons, France and Russia were opposed to active pressure to improve Iraqi cooperation with the UN Special Commission, or to force the return of the inspectors or the entry of the successor UN Monitoring, Verification and Inspection Commission (UNMOVIC). The United States and the United Kingdom, in contrast, insisted on keeping wholesale sanctions that impinged more on the population than on the regime in the vague hope that this would force a regime change, and they were willing to enforce Resolution 687, if necessary, by the unilateral use of military force, as in Operation Desert Fox.

In 2002, things appeared to take a turn for the better. Under the umbrella of a US/UK military threat, the Security Council forced Iraq to open up to new inspections and established an elaborate system of reports by the inspectors, deliberation, and new and specific demands on the Iraqi government. The system worked: inspections were carried out whose findings (no weapons programmes), as we know today, were correct, and Iraqi cooperation improved incrementally. In early March 2003, UNMOVIC and the IAEA had a clear plan to complete their work within the set time-limits and to produce a final assessment of Iraq's weapons of mass destruction then.[26] On this basis, the majority of the Security Council was not willing to vote for military action – in this sense, the procedure functioned perfectly. What did not function was the political decision-making in Washington and London, where leaders decided on the basis of distorted evidence, and against the rules of international law, to go to war on their own.

What was wrong with the Security Council procedure on WMD noncompliance in general came to the fore on 5 February 2003, when US Secretary of State Colin Powell presented the evidence on Iraq available to the war-inclined parties. After his speech to the Council, there was no scrutiny in the Council of the validity and reliability of this evidence. Rather, Powell's one-hour multimedia presentation was followed by the reading of prepared statements by the other foreign ministers. There was never really a careful probing of the reasoning of those opting for war, just retaliatory propaganda.

In recent attempts to defuse the crisis over Iran's nuclear programme, the Security Council has played the background role of the "bad cop" while diplomatic efforts are focused on the IAEA and the EU-3 negotiation process, whereby France, Germany and the United Kingdom have offered Iran a package of incentives in exchange for Iran's readiness to halt its fuel-cycle activities, which, in due course, could lead to the production of nuclear weapons. Although it might be wise to postpone, for the time being, deliberation of the Iranian issue under Chapter VII, it appears strange that the Security Council should not even take note of, and stand seized on, an issue when the IAEA Board of Governors has already determined a breach by Iran of its Safeguards Agreement pursuant to the NPT. Having an issue like that before the Council does not necessarily and automatically imply sanctions (the North Korean case amply proves that). But it serves as a signal that the international community takes the issue seriously and that the state concerned must make an effort to remedy the situation lest the Security Council take a more proactive role.

It should also be noted that the Security Council has never been occupied with alleged breaches of the Chemical Weapons Convention or the Biological Weapons Convention. Despite many allegations – some of them made public – about some states, or even particular states, having breached their obligations, there has never been a request for either a challenge inspection under the CWC or a Security Council investigation under the BWC. Likewise, these rumours and allegations have never motivated the Security Council to act on its own – as it clearly could under the UN Charter – even though many of these allegations emanate from one of the P-5.

The balance is thus not positive. The Security Council has acted too rarely and then in a very selective and not very efficient manner. In the Iraqi case, it had finally found a good way to handle the issue, but it was undermined by the unilateral action of some of its members. Politics and national idiosyncrasies repeatedly got in the way of fair and appropriate decision-making on WMD non-compliance. States overlook too easily that weakening the Security Council ultimately runs counter to their own interests. Although the lack of wisdom in the capitals of major powers can, in the end, not be helped, better decision-making procedures might at least improve the prospects of the Security Council coming closer to doing its duty in WMD crises than it has done in the past.

Institutional and procedural options

In principle, cases of (suspected) non-compliance should progress through a three-layer system: first, the routine procedures contained in the treaties and their protocols; second, extraordinary actions by the relevant treaty community; third, the United Nations, with a non-exclusive focus on the Security Council.

Layer one: The treaty organizations

The role of the routine procedures attached to the treaty regimes is to collect relevant evidence through the respective organizations and to use their decision-making bodies to determine whether there is a case of non-compliance, whether the organization has the tools available to remedy it, and, if the case turns out to be intractable and serious enough, whether to move it to the Security Council. Both the IAEA and the OPCW possess a considerable collection of verification instruments for putting evidence on the table. This evidence may be complemented by information made available to member states in the course of the deliberations, though it has to be emphasized that member states having such information would usually be expected to have inserted it already in the collection exercise by the organization. It goes without saying that commercial satellite images and open sources are also available to them.

One sensitive issue that arises in this context and that the international community might tackle in the future is the potential synergy that could exist among the various verification agencies (including, in this case, the Comprehensive Nuclear Test-Ban-Treaty Organization or CTBTO) in cases of suspected non-compliance. Complementing the "lead agency" with insights gained by the other agencies might help to clarify the situation (given, for example, that a reprocessing plant is basically a chemical industrial facility, or that radionuclides of interest to the IAEA might be picked up by the CTBTO's monitoring system). Presently, however, the legal authority does not exist to exchange such information, because the organizations are responsible to different treaty communities, and the treaties do not contain the authority to give away information gained during treaty-related inspections to other treaty-unrelated entities. However, it is conceivable that a state that is under suspicion, but innocent, would have an interest in providing as much information on its activities as possible to avert suspicion of non-compliance. To prepare for this contingency, the executive (governing) boards of the organizations could empower their secretariats to transfer case-specific information to the agencies investigating the non-compliance case unless the state under investigation objects. It is clear that the state would have to be consulted in advance before the information transfer took place.

Although this might work well with nuclear and chemical weapons, there are no such devices in the biological weapons sector. The Draft Protocol had proposed quite sophisticated processes to address the issue of potential non-compliance and had envisaged establishing an organization responsible for implementation. Lacking this organization, there are only the meagre prescriptions in Articles V and VI of the Convention to fall back on. It is therefore important to explore whether it would be possible to establish a level of non-compliance procedure short of the highly politicized Security Council.

Such an option might be available if the technical capability for dealing with biological weapons issues were established at UN Headquarters, as proposed by the Secretary-General's Advisory Board on Disarmament Matters.[27] Such a unit, if well trained and endowed with access to further, external expertise and laboratory services, could fill the gap opened by the failure to adopt the protocol. Countries suspecting other countries of illegal biological weapons activities could approach the Secretary-General in his capacity under Article 99, which gives him a general responsibility for oversight of matters concerning peace and international security.

Such countries could ask for advice on whether or not the evidence available to them is serious enough to alert the Security Council, and leave it to the Secretary-General to take action to concern the Security Council with the matter. Depending on the results of the ensuing analysis, the complainant state might go back to the consultative stage with the suspected state, be satisfied that its suspicions are defused and thus drop the case, call for an extraordinary meeting of the States Parties, or put the case to the Security Council. Whatever direction is chosen, there would be a first layer of investigation before the Security Council takes up the matter.

Layer two: The community of States Party to the treaties

The second layer comprises the States Parties themselves. Although the Security Council is the trustee of the treaty regimes, it does not own them. The "shareholders" are the parties. It is sort of perverse that, in the most pressing circumstances, when one of the States Parties is under suspicion of violating its sacred duties towards the rest of them, the parties should trot sheepishly to the Security Council and let the big guys deal with the matter. It is equally perverse that Review Conferences, which are meant to look at compliance with the treaty and at ways and means to improve it, have been unable so far to take up non-compliance cases, not least because the accused state was present at the conference and could block the adoption of a final declaration naming it because of the consensus rule.

It is high time to devise a way for the treaty communities to address this issue. In the course of the NPT Preparatory Commission (PrepCom) process, Germany proposed, in a working paper, an extraordinary conference of States Parties if a party declared withdrawal.[28] It would make sense to extend the scope of such a conference in order to deal with cases of non-compliance as well (for example if a certain proportion of its membership so requests). It would even be conceivable for Review Conferences to establish themselves as extraordinary conferences to deal with cases of non-compliance.

The rules of these conferences should be significantly different from Review Conferences, with a view to avoiding a one-country veto by the perpetrator. There are two possible ways to handle this. First, in extraordinary conferences, the credentials of the accused party would be automatically suspended, and its participation would be possible only without voting rights. Second, there could be a rule that decisions in extraordinary conferences are taken principally by resolution, not by consensus declaration, with a large majority (say, 75 per cent of the membership) needed for approval. This would eliminate the possibility not only of a one-country veto but equally of clientele relations preventing an appropriate decision.

What, after all, should be the substance of such decisions? The conference would act on the basis of evidence and assessments presented by the relevant organization (for the BWC, see above). If it comes to the conclusion that there is a real case of non-compliance, all parties will be aggrieved because the violator has breached its commitment to each of them. Being aggrieved justifies measures in response. Breaking out of the treaty – reciprocal action in kind – is obviously not a reasonable answer if the parties believe that the treaty should be upheld and strengthened. Parties could thus agree among themselves to punish the perpetrator by, for example, withholding economic and scientific cooperation in the relevant technology. It is also conceivable that a far-reaching economic embargo could be agreed if it is deemed proportional and likely to succeed. It has to be emphasized that, in contrast to the Security Council acting under Chapter VII of the UN Charter, such agreements would be non-mandatory and would certainly not affect the rights and duties of non-parties. But they would send a powerful signal and, if largely observed, could have a serious impact on the economic interests of the perpetrator.

Beyond that, they would serve as a persuasive signal to the Security Council. A decision by a very large number of UN members that charges, or exonerates, a state that has come before the Security Council for consideration would certainly influence Security Council membership. To take a stand against a large majority of the members of the particular treaty, which have made up their mind on the basis of expert advice and assessment, would not be an easy political decision and would certainly require extra justification. It is likely that this would act as a definite, if not the ultimate, constraint on the usual politicking that has reigned over non-compliance deliberations in the Council.

Layer three: The United Nations

However, this by no means implies that the Security Council should not make a serious effort to arrive at its own conclusion. Given that it has to decide on what to do – possibly in mandatory form, and involving the use of force – it must draw on, but cannot entirely rely on, the assessments prepared at the previous stages. In this regard, the Council is acting as a kind of "court of appeal" for the case in question.

It has been argued throughout this chapter that there are some analogies between a non-compliance procedure before the Security Council and a criminal court case. Taking this aspect seriously, one must explore whether elements from criminal court procedures could be imported into the proceedings of the Security Council.

First, there should be rules about the evidence that is admissible in the deliberations of the Council. Whatever the treaty organizations present to the Council must be admitted. National intelligence, however, should be used as an element of evidence only when independently confirmed by two sources. States might be free to present single-source evidence but, as in court cases where the jury is requested by the judges to ignore certain pieces of irregular evidence in their deliberations, single-source intelligence should be ignored if not confirmed independently (although no one can prevent the presenting state, if it is a member of the Council, from taking its own intelligence into account). All pieces of national intelligence presented should be subject to independent review and the Council should be given a review report.

Second, consideration might be given to the introduction of a procedure of advocacy. One state might act as prosecutor and one as defender of the accused state (in addition, the accused state must be given the opportunity to defend itself as well). None of these states must necessarily be a member of the Council. If one is, it should be obliged to abstain from voting on the case.

Third, the Council must make a major effort to assess the motivations and intentions of the perpetrator, since, as argued above, this is essential in deciding on an appropriate response. This would be the most sensitive part of its deliberations. It might be most appropriate to entrust an independent expert group, appointed by the Security Council pursuant to a proposal by the Secretary-General, with this difficult task. The expert group would look at the available evidence, request information from the state concerned, and listen to neighbouring states' assessment of the situation. It would also draw on intelligence provided by member states, although with the same caveat as applies to the deliberations of the Council itself.

In determining the extent of the danger and deciding upon an appropriate response, the Security Council would rely on the report and the expertise of the group of experts, who should be available for a hearing, on statements from neighbouring countries and, of course, on information and assessments from the member states themselves. Opinions offered by the General Assembly would also be considered. On this basis, the Security Council would be in a position to assess the threat and the risks facing the international community should the perpetrator succeed in achieving its objectives. These risks must include not only the immediate consequences for the neighbourhood, but also the potential impact on the cost–benefit assessments of other states that might feel compelled to emulate the perpetrator's example, in other words, the possibility of a "proliferation chain".

After the assessment of threats and risks, the Council would proceed to considering counter-measures tailored to the motivations and the degree of threat and risk. As mentioned above, a broad range of options is available, from accommodation and incentives to military action with a view to eliminating the dangerous capabilities and, if the political will to acquire WMD and use them is seen to be connected to the specific features of a particular leadership, to effecting a regime change as well.

The choice of options cannot be made by assessing the cost. The Security Council must be sure that the medicine will not be worse than the illness to be cured. Economic sanctions could be imposed that target the specific industrial sector, or the whole realm of dual-use and high technologies and/or the personal assets of the leadership responsible for non-compliance. Given the experiences with the sanctions on Iraq in the 1990s, a thorough assessment of the impact of such measures on the welfare of ordinary people is required. It would be helpful to obtain an informed impact assessment from the regional/country experts of the International Monetary Fund, the World Bank and the United Nations Development Programme.

As for military options, an assessment of the expected "collateral damage" and regional repercussions is indispensable. In terms of regional consequences, the opinion of neighbouring states is of great importance. As for "collateral damage", a calculation by military experts of the effects of possible military operations is imperative. Although the High-level Panel on Threats, Challenges and Change has proposed the dissolution of the defunct Military Committee, it might gain a new function in this context.[29] The Military Committee could be given the task of bringing together a group of experienced military officers to simulate various military options and calculate the resulting casualties. This estimate could be handed over for comments to the military staffs of countries willing to conduct operations under a Security Council mandate. It is obvious that these states cannot be expected to detail their planned operations or they would lose the tactical surprise and increase the risks to their own troops. But an informed comment on the calculations of the Military Committee's expert group would enhance the information available to the Security Council.

As result of this analysis, the stages of "determination of non-compliance", "assessment of motivations, threat and risks", and "the costs and risks of response options" should be obligatory items on the Security Council agenda whenever a non-compliance case is tackled.

The need for independent assessment capacity

Throughout these considerations, the availability of "second opinions" or independent analytical and technical capacity has been emphasized. This is inevitable given the Iraq experience where purely national-based assessments have been all too thoroughly discredited. This does not eliminate the need for national inputs in the deliberations at all three levels. However, there is the need for double-checking, and in this section I try to develop viable and not too costly options for such double-checking in order decisively to enhance international confidence in the competence and impartiality of the Security Council and the integrity and appropriateness of its decisions.

Of course, for nuclear and chemical weapons contingencies, the main bodies will always be the IAEA and the CWC. It would be helpful, however, to have some additional expertise. This could be quite modest, with just the capacity to screen the reports of these two organizations and, if necessary, collect and coordinate questions on their reporting at UN headquarters, not as supervisors but as facilitators of the contacts. Full responsibility for the relevant assessments would continue to rest with these organizations. For biological weapons, pending the adoption of a verification protocol to the BWC, the biological weapons expert staff members of UNMOVIC should be transferred to the Department of Disarmament in the Secretariat as a permanent body for investigation and verification missions in the BW field. This would be better than locating them directly at the Security Council because the Secretary-General needs to be able to make use of them in his capacities related to the Geneva Protocol and Article 99 of the UN Charter.

Expert groups to assess motivations should be brought together as required, because it would be impossible to keep a large group covering the whole world idle for relatively low-probability contingencies. As for the military expertise to assess the consequences of military action, it is conceivable that it could be marshalled ad hoc, but it might also be worthwhile to have a small permanent military staff, (relatively) independent from member states, as UN employees who would have the necessary skills (notably gaming and computer simulation) and could, as required, draw on additional experts seconded by the member states.

The Secretary-General and the UN General Assembly

As a consequence of the above considerations, the role of the Secretary-General in dealing with cases of non-compliance will inevitably be enhanced. First and foremost, invoking his rights and duties under Article 99 gives him a more proactive role, all the more so if this is taken, as proposed, as a stopgap measure for the missing or fledgling compliance procedures under the BWC. Secondly, the location of technical expertise, especially in the BWC sector, clearly enhances the importance of the Secretariat and therefore of the Secretary-General as head of the Secretariat. Third, bringing together the various expert groups and providing for the necessary logistical support and secretarial services further enlarges the Security Council's responsibility for an orderly and smooth working of the procedures.

As I have already stated, the General Assembly must be involved in order to ensure the legitimacy of the Security Council's decision. It should be informed and, where appropriate, invited to deliberate the case in its own right. The General Assembly might even decide to pass resolutions in order to convey the opinion of the whole international community to the Security Council when the Council is tackling the difficult task of defining an appropriate response.

The General Assembly might even go further if the Security Council is incapable of reaching a decision (for example because of the veto) and a large majority in the General Assembly is of the opinion that inaction is causing grave dangers to peace and international security. In that case, the General Assembly might consider using the "Uniting for Peace Resolution" procedure, under which the Assembly can, in a situation where peace and international security are severely jeopardized and the Security Council is not capable of acting, invite member states to take appropriate measures.[30] Such a resolution, although not mandatory like Security Council resolutions, would command much more legitimacy than the unilateral decision of a single nation-state or of self-appointed "coalitions of the willing". As a procedure of last resort, it should not be ruled out completely as an option in non-compliance cases.

Conclusions

Current procedures to deal with alleged or proven non-compliance with undertakings under the WMD regimes are not satisfactory. They lack reliability, completeness, impartiality and effectiveness. The analysis in this chapter was intended to uncover these weaknesses and to come up with helpful proposals on how to remedy them.

I am aware that quite a few of the options considered sound utopian, especially given the current attitudes of some of the major powers towards the United Nations. Nevertheless, we need a major rethink about the ways and means to be employed by the international community if the proliferation of weapons of mass destruction is on the agenda. National decision-making has not proven capable of producing fruits of wisdom regularly, to put it mildly. Broad participation is much more likely to bring to the table all the information and all the perspectives that have to be taken into account.

Some features stand out:

1. The emphasis on a second layer between treaty organizations and the United Nations, consisting of related activities of the treaty communities.
2. The urgent need for an independent assessment capacity at UN level, to deal with all the difficult issues that must be taken into account in decision-making.
3. The need to be fully aware of the forensic character of a considerable part of this decision-making, and to shape procedures accordingly.
4. The importance of paying due attention to justice, fairness and truth, terms that are disdained by so-called realists, who believe that international relations is just about power, but that are nevertheless a shaping force in world politics whose neglect comes at a heavy price.
5. The advisability of admitting the synergies between the insights of the separate verification agencies.
6. The inevitable enhancement of the Secretary-General and its Secretariat, not at the cost of but rather to the benefit of the Security Council member states charged with the very difficult task of coming up with viable decisions in a crisis that is seriously affecting peace and international security.

Some of the proposed measures cost money – installing additional positions in the Department for Disarmament Affairs, bringing together expert groups, seeing through a complex decision-making process in the shortest possible time. However, compared with the costs of the "war on terror" of US$80 billion per year, the necessary investments of maybe tens of millions of dollars to enable the international community to cope better with one of the main security challenges of our time are paltry.

Notes

1. Robert Jervis, "Cooperation under the Security Dilemma", *World Politics*, Vol. 20, No. 2 (1978), pp. 167–214; Barry Buzan, *People, States and Fear: An Agenda for Interna-*

tional Security Studies in the Post Cold War Era (2nd edn, New York: Harvester Wheat-sheaf; Boulder, CO: Lynne Rienner, 1991).

2. Bruce G. Blair, *Command and Control of Nuclear Forces: Redefining the Nuclear Threat* (Washington, DC: Brookings Institution, 1985).

3. Kenneth N. Waltz, *Nuclear Proliferation: More May Be Better* (London: International Institute for Strategic Studies, 1981).

4. Simone Wisotzki, *Die Nuklearwaffenpolitik Großbritanniens und Frankreichs. Eine konstruktivistische Analyse* (Frankfurt/M: Campus, 2002), pp. 333–359.

5. *A More Secure World: Our Shared Responsibility. Report of the Secretary-General's High-Level Panel on Threats, Challenges and Change* (New York: United Nations, 2004).

6. UN Advisory Board on Disarmament Matters, *Multilateral Disarmament and Non-proliferation Regimes and the Role of the United Nations: An Evaluation*, Contribution of the Advisory Board on Disarmament Matters to the High-Level Panel on Threats, Challenges and Change, Department for Disarmament Affairs Occasional Paper 8 (New York: United Nations, 2004).

7. Abram Chayes and Antonia Handler Chayes, *The New Sovereignty. Compliance with International Regulatory Agreements* (Cambridge, MA: Harvard University Press, 1995).

8. Harald Müller, "Compliance Politics: A Critical Analysis of Multilateral Arms Control Treaty Enforcement", *Nonproliferation Review*, Vol. 7, No. 2 (2000), pp. 77–90.

9. Michael Walzer, *Just and Unjust Wars. A Model Argument with Historical Illustrations* (3rd edn, New York: Basic Books, 2000); John Rawls, *The Law of Peoples* (Cambridge, MA: Harvard University Press, 1999).

10. Peter R. Lavoy, ed., *Planning the Unthinkable: How New Powers Will Use Nuclear, Biological and Chemical Weapons* (Ithaca, NY: Cornell University Press, 2000).

11. International Court of Justice, *Year 1996, Legality of the Threat or Use of Nuclear Weapons*, General List No. 958 (The Hague: IGC, July 1996).

12. For example, Richard K. Betts, "Paranoids, Pygmies, Pariahs and Non-Proliferation", *Foreign Policy*, Vol. 26 (Spring 1977), pp. 157–183; Stephen M. Meyer, *The Dynamics of Nuclear Proliferation* (Chicago: University of Chicago Press, 1984); Jozef Goldblat, *Non-proliferation: The Why and the Wherefore* (London: Taylor & Francis, 1985); Harald Müller, ed., *European Non-Proliferation Policy. Prospects and Problems* (Oxford: Clarendon Press, 1987).

13. Wisotzki, *Die Nuklearwaffenpolitik Großbritanniens und Frankreichs*.

14. George Perkovich, *India's Nuclear Bomb. The Impact on Global Proliferation* (Berkeley: University of California Press, 1999).

15. Virginia Foran, ed., *Security Assurances, Implications for the NPT and Beyond* (Washington, DC: Carnegie Endowment for International Peace, 1995).

16. Hans Blix, *Disarming Iraq* (New York: Pantheon Books, 2004).

17. Anthony H. Cordesman, *The Deterrence Series. Case Study 3: Iraq* (Washington, DC: Chemical and Biological Arms Control Institute, 1998).

18. On this concept, see Thomas M. Franckk, *The Power of Legitimacy among Nations* (New York/Oxford: Oxford University Press, 1990).

19. Rebecca Johnson, "Incentives, Obligations and Enforcement: Does the NPT Meet Its States Parties' Needs", *Disarmament Diplomacy*, No. 70 (April/May 2003), pp. 3–10.

20. John Rawls, *Justice as Fairness. A Restatement* (Cambridge, MA: Belknap Press, 2001).

21. Rebecca Johnson, "Incentives, Obligations and Enforcement".

22. General Assembly Resolution 42/37C (1987), "Measures to uphold the authority of the 1925 Geneva Protocol and to support the conclusion of a chemical weapons convention", UN Doc. A/RES/42/37, 30 November 1987; General Assembly Resolution 43/74A (1988), "Measures to uphold the authority of the 1925 Geneva Protocol and to sup-

port the conclusion of a chemical weapons convention", UN Doc. A/RES/43/74, 7 December 1988.

23. Jonathan Tucker, "Strengthening the BWC: A Way Forward", *Disarmament Diplomacy*, No. 78 (July/August 2004), pp. 24–30.

24. William E. Berry, *North Korea's Nuclear Program: The Clinton Administration's Response* (Colorado Springs: Institute for National Security Studies, 1995).

25. *The North Korean Nuclear Calculus: Beyond the Six Power Talks*, Hearings, 108th Congress, Second Session, Senate Committee on Foreign Relations, 2004.

26. Blix, *Disarming Iraq*.

27. UN Advisory Board on Disarmament Matters, *Multilateral Disarmament and Nonproliferation Regimes and the Role of the United Nations*.

28. Chair's Summary, in *Disarmament Diplomacy*, No. 77 (May/June 2004), p. 25.

29. *A More Secure World*.

30. Norman Paech and Gerhard Stuby, *Völkerrecht und Machtpolitik in den internationalen Beziehungen* (Hamburg: VSA-Verlag, 2001), pp. 578–582.

7

Lessons of UNSCOM and UNMOVIC for WMD non-proliferation, arms control and disarmament

Trevor Findlay

Introduction

The long crisis over Iraq's actual and presumed weapons of mass destruction (WMD) capabilities has produced not only agonizing dilemmas for the international community but also novel ways of attempting to deal with the problem. In particular it has led to the establishment by the UN Security Council of two bodies designed to monitor, verify and assist in Iraq's disarmament. Both were given powers of inspection and information-gathering in relation to a sovereign member state that are unprecedented in the history of the United Nations. Both were withdrawn from Iraq in the face of Iraqi non-cooperation, which was judged by two permanent members of the Security Council – the United Kingdom and the United States – to warrant the use of military force.

This chapter considers the lessons for non-proliferation, arms control and disarmament that might be learned from the experience of the UN Special Commission (UNSCOM) and the UN Monitoring, Verification and Inspection Commission (UNMOVIC). Since both UNSCOM and UNMOVIC cooperated closely with the International Atomic Energy Agency (IAEA), which was given responsibility for the Iraqi nuclear "file", the experiences of that agency will also be considered where relevant.

140

Background

The UN Special Commission

The UN Special Commission was established in 1991 as an integral part of the arrangements for ending the fighting between Iraq and the coalition of states that, with Security Council authorization, had driven Iraqi forces from Kuwait. Part C of Security Council Resolution 687 of 3 April 1991 required Iraq unconditionally to accept the destruction, removal or rendering harmless, under international supervision, of all of its weapons of mass destruction and of all materials and facilities that could be used for WMD, including means of delivery.[1] Iraq was required to submit detailed reports of its inventories in the nuclear, chemical and biological fields as well as of missiles with a range exceeding 150 km. It was also obliged to accept "urgent on-site inspections" in order to verify the capabilities mentioned in Iraq's declarations as well as of any additional locations chosen by the Special Commission. Whereas UNSCOM was given the chemical, biological and missile files, the IAEA was charged, in cooperation with UNSCOM, with handling the nuclear portfolio.

UNSCOM was the first subsidiary body ever established by the Security Council for such a purpose. It was given uniquely intrusive powers of inspection in relation to a sovereign UN member state. It was also extraordinary in having to be built from scratch, having been mandated to conduct urgent inspections even before it had any capacity to do so.

In just a few months the Commission's hastily assembled staff developed the plans and procedures and garnered the resources needed to fulfil UNSCOM's mandate. In May 1991, just one month after the creation of the disarmament regime, UNSCOM conducted its first inspection. It also began assessing Iraq's declarations in detail, as well as planning and in some cases executing the destruction of declared weapons and capabilities. When it became apparent that Iraq's declarations were incomplete and that Iraq's cooperation would not be unconditional, UNSCOM turned its attention to identifying the gaps and seeking hidden or undeclared facilities and items.

Organizationally, UNSCOM comprised a College of Commissioners, who provided policy and other advice to an executive chairman, Swedish diplomat Rolf Ekeus. He had a small headquarters staff. The majority of inspection team members were seconded, on request, by supportive governments, mostly Western. UNSCOM also rapidly acquired techniques and technology not normally available to UN bodies. In August 1991, the United States provided the services of a U-2 high-altitude reconnaissance aircraft to support on-site inspection (OSI) planning and industrial infrastructure monitoring and to search for undeclared facilities. In 1991 and 1992, UNSCOM acquired low-altitude aerial capabilities in the form of helicopters and ultimately an Aerial Inspection Team, which provided overhead security at inspection sites and conducted aerial photography. Finally, and controversially as it turned out, UNSCOM began to seek and receive information, including intelligence information, from governments. This began with supplier information to permit UNSCOM to track Iraqi imports, but later expanded to include sensitive information obtained from so-called National Technical Means, such as satellites, and human intelligence.

It became clear as early as the end of 1991 that what many thought would be a quick accounting and verification exercise would turn into a tug of war with the "host" government. In October 1991, UNSCOM reported to the Security Council that "[t]he elements of misinformation, concealment, lack of cooperation and violation of the privileges and immunities of the Special Commission and IAEA have not created any trust in Iraq's intentions".[2] In June 1991, acting on information provided by the United States, a nuclear inspection team tried to examine two facilities suspected of containing undeclared components of the Iraqi nuclear programme. Iraq barred the inspectors from both facilities and fired at inspectors at one of them. In response, the Security Council passed Resolution 707 condemning Iraq's actions as a "material breach" of the ceasefire, language that would resonate more than a decade later in the Security Council debate over whether or not to invade Iraq. Three months later, another fabled incident occurred in which inspectors, again acting on external information, raided several facilities in Baghdad in search of documents relating to Iraq's nuclear programme. When inspectors seized documents, the Iraqis took some of the papers back and then besieged inspectors in a car park to force them to surrender the remainder. The incident ended only after the inspectors managed to transmit the incriminating data electronically to Washington.[3]

Whereas UNSCOM was able to piece together the details of and eventually almost completely destroy Iraq's nuclear and chemical weapon capabilities, Iraq was particularly unforthcoming about its biological weapons (BW) activities. UNSCOM had continuing suspicions about the extent of the programme, especially because of the large amount of biological growth media that Iraq had imported. Iraq admitted that it had a BW programme only after this was revealed by the defection in 1995 of President Saddam Hussein's son-in-law, General Hussein Kamal Hassan.

Between 1995 and 1998 UNSCOM embarked on an intensified series of investigations and developed more intrusive techniques in an effort to clear up the remaining mysteries about Iraq's capabilities.[4] These included digging up sites where Iraq claimed to have unilaterally destroyed and buried weapons and other materials; interviews with Iraqi personnel; and attempts to penetrate Iraq's concealment, deception and denial activities.

Inevitably, Iraq reacted badly and attempted to end UNSCOM's activities once and for all. In October, it ejected all US nationals participating in UNSCOM. In November, it refused all cooperation with the Commission on the grounds that the organization had been used as a cover for Western espionage – a charge that unfortunately had some truth to it. The United Kingdom and the United States carried out a series of bombing raids in December 1998 in an attempt to force Iraq to comply. When Baghdad refused, the Council disagreed about how to proceed and ultimately even the United Kingdom and the United States allowed their focus to shift away from the Iraq issue. UNSCOM remained in a hiatus for a year, able to observe Iraq only from afar, while the Council decided what to do.

Among the achievements of UNSCOM and the IAEA's Iraq Action Team – which was responsible for nuclear inspections in Iraq – were the discovery of an offensive biological weapons programme, a VX nerve agent capability, long-range missiles capable of delivering weapons of mass destruction and a clandestine nuclear programme. The inspectors successfully destroyed significant quantities of ballistic missiles, chemical munitions and agents, and closed down a BW facility and an entire nuclear weapons research and production capability.

But Iraq never did produce a credible complete and final accounting of its capabilities and what had become of them, particularly in respect of biological weapons. UNSCOM and IAEA inspectors were faced with persistent Iraqi non-cooperation, harassment and dissembling. They had therefore not been able to verify Iraqi disarmament completely or to finish putting in place the planned long-term Ongoing Monitoring and Verification (OMV) system, which was designed to prevent Iraq from reacquiring WMD capabilities. Unfortunately, UNSCOM ended its life in controversy. The organization was accused by Iraq of having become a Trojan horse for Western intelligence operations, and its second executive chairman, Richard Butler, was seen as too heavy-handed and as having become too close to the United States.[5]

The UN Monitoring, Verification and Inspection Commission

UNSCOM was abandoned in December 1999, after a year of debate in the Council, to be replaced by UNMOVIC. Created by UN Security Council Resolution 1284 on 17 December 1999, the new body inherited its predecessor's responsibilities, as well as being mandated to strengthen the OMV, now to be known as the Reinforced Ongoing Monitoring and

Verification (R-OMV) system. The IAEA retained its separate role with regard to nuclear matters. Swedish diplomat Dr Hans Blix, former Director General of the IAEA, was appointed UNMOVIC's executive chairman.[6] A 16-member College of Commissioners was also appointed that would meet at least every three months to provide the chairman with advice and guidance. The proposed role and membership of the commissioners elicited allegations that UNMOVIC would have less political independence than UNSCOM, but such fears never materialized.[7]

Organization and capabilities

UNMOVIC drew heavily on the experience of its predecessor, as well as acquiring its assets and archives and some of its personnel. However, it became a much more capable organization than UNSCOM had been, partly because UNSCOM had done much of the groundwork but also because UNMOVIC used the three years between its establishment and the deployment of its inspectors to Iraq to great advantage. It also implemented many of the recommendations of the Amorim Panel, named after Brazilian Ambassador Celso Amorim, which had been appointed by the Security Council to suggest ways forward after Iraq refused all cooperation with UNSCOM.[8]

The reforms included engaging all UNMOVIC staff, including inspectors, as UN civil servants, rather than accepting them on secondment and in the pay of governments. All staff would therefore be obliged to act on behalf of and in the interests of the world organization. This was in part an attempt to avoid the possibility of national intelligence agents, still beholden to their national authorities, being planted in the inspection teams. This intention was reinforced by Blix's determination that the flow of intelligence information would be strictly "one-way traffic", that is from national intelligence services to UNMOVIC.[9] In addition, the post of deputy executive chairman was abolished, since, as Blix puts it, "it had always been a direct channel to the authorities in Washington".[10] Internally, intelligence information would be restricted to the executive chairman and a "special officer", an intelligence conduit trusted by supplier governments. In the event that intelligence information was needed for directing the location or conduct of an on-site inspection, the head of operations and the team leader would also be included in the "loop", as agreed with the intelligence provider.

Another UNMOVIC innovation was to establish multidisciplinary analytical and inspection teams to avoid the "stove-piping" of information into the three types of WMD, which could result in missed leads and lost opportunities. Training courses were established to reflect the need for cross-disciplinary thinking.

A key difference between UNMOVIC and its predecessor was that

UNSCOM was launched straight into inspections, whereas UNMOVIC had the benefit of three years of preparation. UNMOVIC was able to use the waiting period to determine priority sites for inspection, carefully analyse the huge amounts of information on Iraq's WMD programmes and capabilities that UNSCOM had collected, consolidate and learn from the experiences of its predecessor, create a well-trained force of inspectors and refine its monitoring and inspection methods.

As instructed in Resolution 1284, UNMOVIC focused on identifying "unresolved disarmament issues" and "key remaining disarmament tasks". To this end, it assembled the unresolved issues into interrelated clusters to obtain a better overall picture of Iraq's WMD programmes and to assess the significance of gaps in its knowledge and hence what still needed to be verified.[11]

Staff training – under UNSCOM largely the responsibility of member states – was now organized and conducted solely by UNMOVIC (but with some support from governments).[12] Because UNSCOM had been accused of cultural insensitivity, the training included an Iraqi cultural training package that covered the history, economy, politics and society of Iraq, with regional, social and religious themes. With the completion of the first training courses and the recruitment of 42 professional core staff in New York, UNMOVIC was in a good position by the end of 2002 to commence inspections at short notice. Courses were still running in February 2003 when UNMOVIC was withdrawn from Iraq, bringing the total of experts on the UNMOVIC roster to 380 from 55 nations.

UNMOVIC also had better technological capabilities than UNSCOM. Surveys and inspections were greatly assisted by significant improvements in technology after 1998. Detection devices were smaller, lighter, faster and more accurate. They included miniature radiation sensors, portable chemical and biological weapon detectors and ground-penetrating radar.[13] The IAEA used environmental sampling techniques developed for improved nuclear safeguards verification to monitor water, air and vegetation. The equipment used to survey Iraq's watercourses was so sensitive that it could detect the permitted use by Iraq of radio-isotopes for medical applications. Information technology developments also helped UNMOVIC. For instance, the IAEA and UNMOVIC databases were linked and cross-disciplinary analysis not previously available was used to look for patterns and linkages.

UNMOVIC's capabilities were also to be enhanced by the establishment of two regional offices (in Basra and Mosul), the freedom to fly into Baghdad rather than an airport several hours' drive away, a fleet of British, Canadian and Russian helicopters, access to colour satellite images – including from commercial providers – and use of Mirage and U-2 aircraft for reconnaissance (although the latter took some time to arrange).

It was also planned to obtain data from unmanned aerial vehicles, but these could not be deployed before UNMOVIC's premature withdrawal.

The build-up to UNMOVIC's entry into Iraq

The first signs of movement in the Iraqi position on allowing inspectors to return began in the early part of 2002, prompted by US and UK intimations that the use of force could not be ruled out if Iraq continued to defy the Security Council.[14] Pressure was increased by the US release in September of intelligence information on Iraq's alleged import of aluminium tubes for use in uranium enrichment centrifuges. The now infamous UK dossier on Iraq's alleged weapons of mass destruction was published on 24 September 2002.[15]

On 8 November 2002, the Council unanimously adopted Resolution 1441, declaring that Iraq had been and continued to be in "material breach" of its obligations and calling on it to cooperate "immediately, unconditionally and actively" with UNMOVIC. It ordered Baghdad to provide UNMOVIC and the IAEA with "immediate, unimpeded, unconditional, and unrestricted access to any and all, including underground, areas, facilities, buildings, equipment, records, and means of transport which they wish to inspect".[16] The two bodies could impose no-drive and no-fly zones around suspect sites and could destroy, impound or remove any armaments, materials or records. They were also entitled to receive comprehensive lists of and "immediate, unimpeded, unrestricted, and private access to all officials and other persons" whom they wished to interview in a mode or location of their choosing, without the presence of Iraqi observers. Gone were the special procedures for the inspection of the eight so-called presidential sites negotiated by UN Secretary-General Kofi Annan in February 1998,[17] as were the confidential "understandings" previously reached with Iraq by Ekeus. Inspectors' premises were to be protected by UN guards, and UNMOVIC and IAEA personnel were to have unimpeded entry to, and exit from, Iraq and the right to import and export any equipment and material they required.

Not only was UNMOVIC's mandate now tougher and more intrusive than that of UNSCOM, but it was also politically more compelling. Unlike the resolution establishing UNSCOM, UNMOVIC was now specifically authorized under Chapter VII of the UN Charter, leaving no doubt that compliance with the resolution was mandatory. Furthermore, the resolution was, unlike the initial UNSCOM resolution, adopted unanimously (even Syria voted in favour). Resolution 1441 also explicitly stated that failure to comply at any point "shall constitute a further material breach of Iraq's obligations", which would be reported to the Security Council for immediate assessment, with the possibility of "serious consequences". This was the first time that such a direct threat of force had been made in a resolution concerning the UN inspection regime. Previously, it had been linked indirectly as part of Iraq's ceasefire obligations.[18]

Several deadlines were imposed by Resolution 1441 – 7 days for Iraq to notify the Council that it would comply and 30 days for it to provide a "currently accurate, full and complete declaration of all aspects of its programmes to develop chemical, biological and nuclear weapons, ballistic missiles, and other delivery systems". UNMOVIC was to begin inspections within 45 days and report to the Council 60 days thereafter, but earlier if Iraq was failing to comply.

On 13 November 2002, Iraq informed the Council of its decision to comply with the resolution "without conditions". An advance team of 30 lost no time in travelling to Baghdad. Led by Dr Blix and IAEA Director General Dr Mohamed ElBaradei, they held talks on 18 November with Iraqi officials on practical arrangements for the return of inspectors and began to prepare premises and organize logistics to permit the resumption of operations. On 7 December a crucial deadline was met when Iraq provided, more than 24 hours before it was required to do so, what purported to be the required "accurate, full and complete declaration". Comprising over 11,807 pages, with 352 pages of annexes and 529 megabytes of data, the declaration was detailed, technical and partly in Arabic.

UNMOVIC in Iraq

The first inspectors arrived in Iraq on 25 November 2002. There were just 11 experts but they covered all areas of UNMOVIC's work. This paved the way for inspections to begin early, just two days later, on 27 November, when three sites previously inspected by UNSCOM were visited. Several more inspections were conducted, unimpeded by the Iraqis, on successive days. These early inspections were low-key affairs designed to test Iraqi cooperation. On 3 December, the first presidential site was inspected, again without serious incident, although access was delayed.

The pattern of inspections by UNMOVIC and the IAEA's Iraq Action Team – renamed the Iraq Nuclear Verification Office (INVO) – had two distinct phases. From November 2002 until the beginning of 2003, the focus was on re-establishing a baseline for the declared sites by assessing any changes made in activity, personnel or equipment after inspectors had left in 1998. Newly declared sites were also visited and all sites assessed against Iraq's 7 December declaration. From 14 December inspections began in earnest, averaging eight per day, with discipline-specific teams focusing on their own particular area of interest. Inspection teams ranged from 2 to 40 inspectors, 8 being the average. From mid-January 2003 onwards, UNMOVIC and the INVO began a second, investigative phase, designed to identify and pursue leads obtained from inspections, Iraqi documents or information from other sources, including intelligence. This phase included the re-inspection of key sites.

In its 111 days in Iraq UNMOVIC conducted 731 inspections at 411 sites – of which 88 had not been inspected previously[19] – and the INVO conducted 237 nuclear inspections at 148 sites, including 27 new sites, covering over 1,600 buildings.[20] Most of the sites were located around Baghdad or the northern city of Mosul, the latter facilitated by the opening of a regional field office there.[21] Despite the intensity of UNMOVIC's activity, the United States, convinced that there were WMD to be found, was becoming increasingly impatient. Vice President Dick Cheney, fearful that a drawn-out inspection process would permit Iraq indefinitely to delay the US invasion that was being secretly planned, publicly expressed disdain for UNMOVIC.[22]

By mid-March 2003, differences in the Security Council over continuing Iraqi non-compliance reached a head. China, France, Germany and Russia on the one hand and the United States and the United Kingdom on the other clashed heatedly over the US/UK proposed resolution declaring Iraq in material breach of Resolution 1441 and authorizing the use of force. When France indicated that it would not support any such resolution, the United States, with UK support, contended that it needed no second resolution after all and interpreted Resolution 1441 as permitting it to act unilaterally. On 18 March 2003, two days after Washington advised the United Nations that the inspectors should leave for their own safety, UNMOVIC and the IAEA withdrew from Iraq. So ended the second round of international inspections. Bombing by US and UK aircraft began on 20 March and the coalition invasion began soon after.

UNMOVIC's achievements

Many observers and significant numbers of Security Council member states, including China, Russia, France and all of the non-permanent members except Bulgaria and Spain, felt that UNMOVIC had not been given enough time to fulfil its mandate. Although Iraq had not been proactive in assisting the inspectors and continued to prevaricate about its past programmes, it had nonetheless cooperated sufficiently to permit UNMOVIC and the IAEA to carry out their tasks unhindered and had consistently backed down on specific issues when pressure was applied by the Council.

UNMOVIC had barely been in the country three months. It had not yet completed its second phase, had only just begun receiving overhead imagery and had not installed monitoring equipment. It had yet to open an office in Basra, which would have opened up southern Iraq to more thorough inspection and increased the element of surprise. In the end only seven sites were inspected in the southern third of the country. UNMOVIC had also interviewed only a tiny number of the scientists and officials that it wished to.

UNMOVIC appeared at all times to act professionally and efficiently, despite the adverse conditions. Among these were at the time a perceived failure by the Western states to provide adequate, reliable intelligence information early enough and fully enough to permit inspections to move more quickly. It turns out, in retrospect, that no reliable intelligence information was available, which is why the United States and the United Kingdom were so coy in providing it. Also difficult for UNMOVIC were the insinuation and carping from critics within or associated with the US administration about its alleged shortcomings. Blix, as the head of an international organization that was supposed to balance the interests of all UN member states, including Iraq, could clearly not engage in an open, all-out debate with his critics without further harming UNMOVIC's reputation. On the contrary, his official reports to the Security Council and public comments were a model of tact, balance and diplomacy.

If there was one failure by UNMOVIC in fulfilling its mandate, which was much criticized by US officials, it was Blix's understandable reluctance to attempt to remove Iraqi scientists (accompanied presumably by their families) from Iraq for interview. However, plans were being developed, before UNMOVIC's withdrawal, for this to occur in another Arab state or possibly Cyprus. This probably would not have helped much. Scientists might still have felt too intimidated by the Iraqi regime to have divulged much information of use. Even after the invasion, the United States had little success in inducing Iraqis to talk and, when it did succeed, its interlocutors revealed little or actually denied the existence of WMD programmes or plans.

The failure of US and coalition forces and the Iraq Survey Group (ISG) subsequently to uncover anything more of substance than had UNMOVIC has retrospectively gilded the UN inspector's reputation.[23] Calls for the ISG to be given more time and vastly greater resources reinforced the notion that UNMOVIC itself should have been afforded these. The difficulty for UNMOVIC, even if had been given more time and resources, was the perennial challenge that all verifiers, including the ISG, face – that of verifying a negative, in this case the absence of Iraqi WMD capabilities. The professional duty of verifiers to give honest assessments of the probabilities involved in seeking verifiable certainty provides openings for those with political motives to invoke worst-case scenarios that are ultimately unverifiable. The fact that no WMD were found does not, as some observers claim, indicate that UNMOVIC was not tested; in fact the opposite is true – it is much easier to verify the existence of weapons than to verify their non-existence.

The strategic lessons of UNSCOM and UNMOVIC

The first strategic lesson to be drawn from the cases of UNSCOM and UNMOVIC and the experiences of their partner in the nuclear field, the IAEA, is that international verification can work effectively even in the most disadvantageous of conditions. Despite Iraq's non-cooperation and deliberate attempts at sabotage, both bodies broadly succeeded in their verification mission. Both demonstrated that an international inspection body can perform creditably: both were able to prepare themselves well, deploy quickly, use technology skilfully, organize efficiently, maintain their impartiality and produce sober, balanced reports of a high technical standard. They were also able successfully to follow intelligence leads and reach quick and decisive, albeit suitably caveated, conclusions.

The findings of UNSCOM and UNMOVIC respectively have subsequently been vindicated as largely true: Iraq did destroy the bulk of its WMD capabilities, either unilaterally before inspections commenced or under international supervision. In the nuclear area the IAEA's closure of the nuclear file on the grounds that Iraq no longer possessed significant nuclear capabilities or the possibility of swiftly rejuvenating them has proved correct. Similarly, UNMOVIC determined that the chemical weapons programme had, with a few innocuous exceptions, largely gone by 1991, a fact that the Central Intelligence Agency (CIA) now admits was correct.[24] In the biological weapons area, although substantive questions remained after UNSCOM's withdrawal, some of which even now have never been satisfactorily explained, the more outlandish claims by US intelligence, such as the existence of mobile BW laboratories and pilotless drones for BW dissemination, were credibly rebuffed by UN inspections. In the missile area, where question marks remained after UNSCOM's departure, UNMOVIC did detect Iraqi violations and was in the process of removing them when it was withdrawn.

A second strategic lesson, though, follows from the first. The experience of both UNSCOM and UNMOVIC demonstrated once more that the full support of the Security Council, or at least its permanent membership, is essential for a multilateral verification endeavour to succeed in the face of opposition from the country being verified. In the UN-

SCOM case, a significant cause of its ultimate failure was French and Russian reluctance to press Iraq to comply and to give UNSCOM full political support for its intrusive inspections. Without a united Security Council, the executive chairman was simply unable to force the Iraqis to back down.

In the case of UNMOVIC, the re-admission of inspectors to Iraq and the substantive success of the process, even up to the very end of their presence in the country, were undoubtedly the result of the steeling of the Council's nerve by the United States and the United Kingdom. The threat of the use of force in the event of continuing Iraqi non-compliance and a growing UK–US military presence on Iraq's doorstep undoubtedly were key factors in forcing Iraq to back down. In turn, the premature withdrawal of UNMOVIC was caused by the flouting of the majority view of the Council, not by Iraq but by the United States and the United Kingdom. The Bush administration's pretence of growing impatience with the inspection process, seeking to mask a predetermined preference for military means irrespective of UNMOVIC's performance,[25] split the Council irredeemably.

A third strategic lesson is that an international monitoring and verification system backed by military pressure, and in combination with economic sanctions and control of militarily significant imports and exports, can provide effective containment of a renegade regime. Having, as it turned out, successfully disarmed Iraq of its WMD capabilities, it can now be seen that the planned Ongoing Monitoring and Verification regime, which was never fully implemented, would likely have proved effective in detecting any future moves by Iraq to reacquire its lost capabilities.

In addition to these strategic lessons there are numerous institutional, operational and technical lessons that have been learned as a result of the UNSCOM/UNMOVIC/IAEA experience in Iraq.

Institutional lessons

Institutionally, there was a direct lineage between UNSCOM and UN-MOVIC, but also some evolution. Both were established by the Security Council and remained under its control and direction, rather than becoming part of the UN Secretariat. This had advantages for the political credibility of the organization, in that there was a direct line of authority to the Council. Both UNSCOM and UNMOVIC were headed by executive chairmen with strong executive powers and answerable to the Security Council (although appointed by the UN Secretary-General) and a College of Commissioners.

Iraq could have been under no illusion that it was dealing with another toothless part of the sprawling UN bureaucracy under a Secretary-General obliged to act in accordance with diplomatic niceties. Indeed, Richard Butler resisted attempts by UN Secretary-General Kofi Annan to manage him, criticizing Annan for his alleged over-solicitousness towards the Iraqis.[26] The United States too was critical when it appeared that Annan had weakened UNSCOM's inspection powers in respect of the so-called presidential sites in his February 1998 agreement with Iraq (it turned out that the agreement made very little difference either way). All this reinforces the necessity for the head of future such verification operations to be independent of the UN Secretary-General and Secretariat to the extent possible.

Finance is also critical to organizational independence. UNSCOM had been funded for the first six months from the UN Working Capital Fund and subsequently by individual, mostly Western or pro-Western, UN member states (notably Australia, France, Japan, Kuwait, Norway, Saudi Arabia, the United Kingdom and the United States). By funding UNMOVIC through the Iraq Oil-for-Food programme escrow account (0.8 per cent), the independence of the organization, as well as the ready availability of funding, was assured. Had UNSCOM or UNMOVIC been set up under the UN Secretariat or by the UN General Assembly, their budget would have been scrutinized by the Advisory Committee on Administrative and Budgetary Questions and undoubtedly been whittled down by those states that had political objections to their existence. UNSCOM's reliance on seconded staff provided and paid by UN member states (in addition to seconded personnel from various UN agencies) had called into question its independence, as well as being managerially unsatisfactory. Independent funding enabled UNMOVIC to hire the necessary staff quickly, an essential requirement when inspections have been urgently mandated by the Security Council.

Although the vast majority of UNSCOM personnel undoubtedly behaved professionally and in the best interests of the international community, UNSCOM was to some extent subject to undue influence by some UN member states. This occurred in two ways. First, the nature and pace of inspections may have been influenced without the agreement of UNSCOM's executive chairman. Former US National Security Advisor Richard Clarke claims that he "set up" the confrontational nuclear inspections under UNSCOM, with British connivance, although it is not clear whether this was approved by the executive chairman in advance.[27] A second misuse of UNSCOM was the reported planting of listening devices by the United States on UNMOVIC's monitoring equipment and the use of inspections for national intelligence-gathering purposes as a result of inspectors reporting back to capitals.

Compared with UNSCOM, UNMOVIC more successfully avoided being taken advantage of by any UN member state, managed not to offend Iraqi sensibilities unnecessarily and was able to parlay strong Security Council support into achieving Iraqi cooperation, if not proactive engagement and full compliance.

Operational lessons

Intelligence information and verification

There are continuing lessons to be learned from both UNSCOM and UNMOVIC with regard to the relationship between intelligence information and multilateral verification. Clearly intelligence information can be of great assistance to multilateral verifiers. It may, for instance, derive from highly sophisticated National Technical Means that are beyond the reach of international bodies. High-resolution satellite photography is one example, although one that is declining in importance with the advent of cheap commercial satellite photography with resolutions below 1 metre.

But, as in the Iraq case, national intelligence information can also largely consist of analysis of human intelligence sources obtained by national intelligence agencies or through electronic eavesdropping. As the various inquiries by legislatures in Australia, the United Kingdom and the United States have revealed, such intelligence information may be based on unreliable, self-interested and/or malicious sources. National intelligence agencies, adopting worst-case scenarios or under political pressure, can dangerously inflate their analyses. By the time such analyses and "information" are provided to multilateral verifiers they may have lost their qualifiers, their context and often, in an effort to protect the source, their provenance. International verification bodies therefore need to be extremely wary of taking intelligence information provided by states at face value, even when it is provided in good faith.

It appears that UNMOVIC did learn from the difficulties that UNSCOM experienced in what was later regarded as too cosy a relationship with national intelligence agencies. There was, however, a price to pay. In seeking to formalize the relationship between UNMOVIC and national agencies by restricting it to the highest levels and a single designated "conduit", UNMOVIC may have cut itself off from valuable contacts and information at the working level. This may, however, be necessary to keep the intelligence/verification nexus as pristine as possible.[28] The relationship between any future inspection agency and national intelligence needs thorough review and careful thought.[29] It is encouraging, however, that UNSCOM, the IAEA and UNMOVIC were never accused of leaking classified information and, indeed, were successful in establishing systems to safeguard it. This should help rebuff critics who claim that UN bodies inevitably "leak like sieves".

Verification and public relations

A key lesson for the future that has been identified by the IAEA, but which applies equally to UNMOVIC as well, is that multilateral verification bodies need to make better use of the media to convey their achievements to the public and to decision makers.[30] In part because of the multilateral nature of such bodies but also because traditionally UN bodies have not been adept in defending their case, it was relatively easy for ill-informed and hostile observers to impugn the intentions and capabilities of the inspectors. Naturally there are constraints on how virulently UN bodies can engage in self-defence in these circumstances, especially when critics can be as senior as a US Vice President. Nonetheless, they should have public information and media capacities to enable their case to be injected clearly into the public arena.

Deception and denial

Initially, UN inspections in Iraq may have begun in the naive hope that they would be concluded within weeks if not months, but UNSCOM quickly entered a steep learning curve in terms of the degree of deception and denial that Iraq was willing and able to undertake. UNSCOM, the IAEA and UNMOVIC all ended up participating in a "deception and denial" race, in which the Iraqis attempted increasingly sophisticated means that the international bodies sought to counter with innovative schemes of their own. Just one example relates to prior notification of inspections: after realizing that pre-notification allowed the Iraqis to clear intended sites of any traces of WMD, the inspectors developed techniques of setting off vaguely in one direction, while leaving their actual destination a mystery until the last possible moment. Learning such counter-deception techniques is unusual for a UN body but clearly necessary in the circumstances. The lessons of such campaigns need to be collated and analysed for use when future challenges to verification arise.

Technical lessons

The technical lessons that may be gleaned from the UNSCOM/UNMOVIC/IAEA experience are too numerous to be detailed in this

chapter. Nonetheless several broad categories of lessons are readily identifiable. One is the need for rapid deployment. All three verification
bodies fared well in this respect, but future such endeavours would be facilitated by pre-contracted airlift, pre-positioned equipment and standing
contracts with inspection personnel, rosters of experts and pre-authorized
analytical laboratories. A second lesson is that UN verification bodies are
clearly capable of rapidly absorbing and even advancing the latest verification techniques. Examples from the Iraq experience include U-2
overflights, ground-penetrating radar and environmental sampling. This
should give pause to those who claim that UN bodies will always be behind the technology curve.

An innovation of UNSCOM and UNMOVIC, one acted on most stri-
dently by David Kay as an IAEA inspection team leader, was the search
for and use of a paper trail – documents that would reveal WMD capabilities and intentions – rather than searching endlessly for the capabilities
themselves.[31] A further innovation of UNMOVIC was what might be
termed "verification archaeology", the digging up of sites to detect
buried weapons or weapons components or to determine destruction
techniques and timelines. UNMOVIC did this fruitfully in relation to
both missiles and chemical weapons. Finally, the role of UNSCOM and
UNMOVIC in seeking information from UN member states about Iraqi
imports of weapons-related technology and materials and those of a dual-
use character, and about the companies and organizations involved, was
also unprecedented for a UN body. The IAEA has followed such success
in attempting to trace the reach of the Abdul Qadeer Khan network in
facilitating nuclear proliferation in the cases of Libya and Iran. Such
precedents are valuable for future counter-proliferation efforts.

Perhaps the greatest legacy of the Iraq verification experience is the
size of the verification cadre that it has produced. Literally hundreds of
inspectors have been trained and have gained field experience in all areas
of WMD verification. Not only has this benefited the standing verification
bodies such as the IAEA and the Organisation for the Prohibition of
Chemical Weapons (OPCW), but it will be useful for any future biological weapons investigations under the UN Secretary-General's mandate or in a future BW organization. Such experience and capacity
should be retained and nurtured, including by considering a permanent,
standing verification body to succeed UNMOVIC that would be available
for future Iraq-style non-compliance challenges.

Further lessons relate to health and safety and environmental issues,
which may seem minor and parochial but which can assume great significance. UNSCOM initially underestimated the time it would take to ensure the safety and security of its personnel in a hostile political and
physical environment. If such considerations are not taken into account,

verification can stop dead in its tracks, with enormous political ramifications. Several UNSCOM inspectors suffered damaging exposure to toxic chemicals; UNMOVIC was much more careful in this respect, having learned the correct lessons. Similarly, the United Nations cannot be seen to be flouting environmentally sound practices and international conventions in its rush to destroy WMD. In the early days of UNSCOM, for instance, chemical weapons were simply dynamited in open pits. Criticism of verification activities on environmental grounds can provide yet one more political excuse for opposing such multilateral action and should be avoided by proper planning and organization.

Conclusion

The experiences of the three international bodies involved in verification in Iraq have been both salutary and path breaking. They have added greatly to the store of verification know-how and capacity that can be utilized in future such endeavours.[32] Lessons learned have already been fed into the standing multilateral verification bodies and were notable in the UNSCOM–UNMOVIC transition. The task for the international community is to ensure that such capacities as have been developed are preserved and strengthened for future use. Giving the United Nations the capacity for launching intrusive, highly capable verification operations when required may give pause to the small number of states that are tempted to violate international treaties and norms relating to WMD.

Acknowledgements

This chapter was written when I was executive director of the Verification Research, Training and Information Centre (VERTIC) in London. I am now Associate Professor, Norman Paterson School of International Affairs, Carleton University, Ottawa, Canada. I am grateful for the research assistance of Benjamin Armbruster, VERTIC intern.

Notes

1. UN Security Council Resolution 687, UN Doc. S/RES/687 (1991), 3 April 1991.
2. "Note by the Secretary-General", UN Doc. S/23122, 8 October 1991 (Report of the sixth IAEA inspection team).
3. A team of inspectors apparently read out the documents to a secretary in the US State Department, who typed them up for the UN Secretary-General and the President. See

Richard A. Clarke, *Against All Enemies: Inside America's War on Terror* (New York: Free Press, 2004), pp. 67–69.

4. For details, see Stephen Black, "Verification under Duress: The Case of UNSCOM", in Trevor Findlay, ed., *Verification Yearbook 2000* (London: Verification Research, Training and Information Centre, 2000), pp. 122–125.

5. There are varying assessments of Butler's performance. Clearly a tough executive chairman was needed to deal with the Iraqis, who were engaged in an increasingly sophisticated denial and deception campaign against UNSCOM. Butler himself had throughout his career been notably critical of US policy and could hardly be considered a US lackey. Nonetheless, it obviously suited the Iraqis and their supporters to portray him that way.

6. The Security Council had been unable to agree on the Secretary-General's first choice, Rolf Ekeus, Swedish head of UNSCOM from 1991 until 1997.

7. Richard Butler, *Saddam Defiant: The Threat of Weapons of Mass Destruction, and the Crisis of Global Security* (London: Phoenix, 2000), p. 239.

8. "Report of the First Panel established pursuant to the Note by the President of the Security Council on 30 January 1999 (S/1999/100), concerning disarmament and current and future ongoing monitoring and verification issues", UN Doc. S/1999/356, 27 March 1999.

9. Hans Blix, *Disarming Iraq: the Search for Weapons of Mass Destruction* (London: Bloomsbury, 2004), p. 50.

10. Ibid., p. 49.

11. "Unresolved Disarmament Issues – Iraq's Proscribed Weapons Programmes", UNMOVIC working document, 6 March 2003, which was presented informally to the Security Council. Paradoxically, a draft work programme was submitted to the Council for its approval on the very day that UNMOVIC completed its last inspection before leaving Iraq ("Draft Work Programme", UNMOVIC document, 17 March 2003).

12. The Commission instigated a rolling programme of training on a wide range of topics: the past work of UNSCOM; the origins, mandate and legal framework of UNMOVIC; the scope and nature of Iraq's weapons programmes; monitoring and inspection techniques; and health and safety.

13. Multi-channel analysers were used to detect and analyse gamma radiation from radioisotopes and neutron radiation from plutonium, and a gamma spectrometer was used to identify highly enriched uranium. Importantly, because nuclear activities often require exotic metals, X-ray fluorescence spectrometers were used to distinguish between various metal alloys.

14. Foreign Minister Tariq Aziz held talks with the UN Secretary-General on 7 March 2002 and again on 1 and 3 May. Technical talks were also held with an Iraqi delegation, headed by General Amir al-Saadi, the main point of contact for UNSCOM on chemical and biological weapons.

15. *Iraq's Weapons of Mass Destruction: The Assessment of the British Government* (London: The Stationery Office, 24 September 2002).

16. Security Council Resolution 1441, UN Doc. S/RES/1441 (2002), 8 November 2002.

17. "Memorandum of Understanding between the United Nations and the Republic of Iraq", UN Doc. S/1998/166, 23 February 1998.

18. Although Resolution 1154 of 2 March 1998 had come close in asserting that "any violation would have severest consequences for Iraq".

19. "Thirteenth Quarterly Report of the Executive Chairman of UNMOVIC to the Security Council", UN Doc. S/2003/580, 30 May 2003. For a detailed log of the inspections, see the Verification Research, Training and Information Centre's (VERTIC) online database of UNMOVIC and IAEA weapons inspections: ⟨http://www.vertic.org/onlinedatabase/unmovic⟩.

20. "Fifteenth Consolidated Report of the Director General of the International Atomic Energy Agency under Paragraph 16 of the UNSC Resolution 1051 (1996)", Vienna, 11 April 2003.

21. Of the UNMOVIC inspections, 219 (30 per cent) were conducted by missile teams, 205 (28 per cent) by biological teams, 161 (22 per cent) by chemical teams and 146 (20 per cent) by multidisciplinary teams. In addition to inspections, the INVO conducted 125 surveys, including 42 at locations not previously visited by the IAEA. The surveys included land- and vehicle-based sampling, travelling over 8,000 km to visit state-run industrial and military locations as well as urban areas. They also conducted a radiometric survey of Iraq's main watercourses from 9 to 19 December.

22. Some in the US administration believed Blix was deliberately withholding findings about Iraqi WMD for fear that this would be a *casus belli* for war, a somewhat absurd allegation considering that US intelligence agencies were by this stage watching both UNMOVIC and Iraq like hawks. See Bob Woodward, *Plan of Attack* (New York: Simon & Schuster, 2004), pp. 239–240.

23. Frank Ronald Cleminson, "What Happened to Saddam's Weapons of Mass Destruction?", *Arms Control Today*, Vol. 33, No. 7 (September 2003), ⟨http://www.armscontrol.org⟩.

24. Greg Miller, "CIA Corrects Itself on Arms", *Los Angeles Times*, 1 February 2005, ⟨http://www.latimes.com/news/nationworld/world/la-fg-cia1feb01,1,4146281.story⟩.

25. Richard Clarke records that in the days after the 11 September 2001 attacks on the United States, when he expected to be talking about strategy to deal with al-Qaeda, he instead "realized with almost a sharp physical pain" that Defense Secretary Donald Rumsfeld and Under Secretary of Defense Paul Wolfowitz were "going to take advantage of this national tragedy to promote their agenda about Iraq" (Clarke, *Against All Enemies*, p. 30). Quizzed in an ABC television interview about the "hard fact that there were weapons of mass destruction, as opposed to the possibility that [Saddam] might move to acquire those weapons", President George W. Bush replied revealingly, "What's the difference?" (ibid., p. 266). Clarke also notes that Charles Duelfer, former deputy executive chairman of UNSCOM and head of the Iraq Survey Group, was the leading US expert on Iraqi WMD and he had thought in 2002 that there were no remaining large and threatening stockpiles left in Iraq. He was ignored by the US administration until appointed to the ISG (ibid., p. 267).

26. "Deeply alarming", says Butler, "was the behaviour of ... Kofi Annan, who repeatedly tried to deal with the problems raised by an outlaw regime by papering them over with diplomacy". See Richard Butler, "Why Saddam Is Winning the War", *talk*, Vol. 1, No. 1 (September 1999), pp. 196–201.

27. Clarke, *Against All Enemies*, pp. 67–69.

28. For further analysis of the verification/intelligence relationship, see Brian Jones, "Intelligence, Verification and Iraq's WMD", in Trevor Findlay, ed., *Verification Yearbook 2004* (London: VERTIC, 2004).

29. Jessica Tuchman Mathews, "What Happened in Iraq? The Success Story of the United Nations Inspections", Keynote Address Delivered at the International Peace Academy Conference, Weapons of Mass Destruction and the United Nations: Diverse Threats and Collective Responses, 5 March 2004, Carnegie Endowment for International Peace, ⟨http://www.ceip.org⟩.

30. Jacques Baute, "Timeline in Iraq: Challenges and Lessons Learned in Iraq", *IAEA Bulletin*, June 2004, p. 67.

31. Blix notes that "I came to recognize in 1991 that both David Kay and UNSCOM had a better instinct than I: namely, on the importance of searching for relevant documents ... the rich caches of documents which Kay seized that year showed that such a search

could be highly rewarding – providing you had good intelligence on where to look"
(Blix, *Disarming Iraq*, p. 26).

32. For analysis of issues relating to the future role of UNMOVIC post-Iraq, see Trevor
Findlay, "A Standing United Nations Verification Body: Necessary and Feasible",
Compliance Chronicles No. 1, Canadian Centre for Treaty Compliance, Carleton University, Ottawa, December 2005.

8

Why we got it wrong: Attempting to unravel the truth of bioweapons in Iraq

Patricia Lewis

What we firmly believe, if it is true, is called *knowledge* ... What we firmly believe, if it is not true, is called *error*.
           (Bertrand Russell, "Knowledge, Error, and Probable Opinion")[1]

What the intelligence professionals told you about Saddam Hussein's programs was what they believed. They were simply wrong.
           (Letter to President George W. Bush from the WMD Commission, 31 March 2005)[2]

Intelligence estimates that Iraq possessed weapons of mass destruction (WMD), including biological weapons, were the major rationale for the US-led invasion of Iraq in early 2003. Yet to date – and following the formal closure of the Iraq Survey Group's field operations – no biological weapons have been found and indeed they are judged to have been destroyed over 10 years previously.[3] Given the significance of the concerns over the Saddam Hussein regime's continuing possession of bioweapons in the decision to go to war, it is incumbent on the international community to understand how we got it so wrong and how we can help prevent similar grave misjudgements happening again.

It is time to take stock of what we have learned about what we previously thought we knew about the existence of bioweapons in Iraq.[4] It is important to understand that it was not just the intelligence agencies of the United Kingdom and the United States that had misjudged the extent of the WMD programmes in Iraq in 2002–2003. Independent analysts all over the world had similar assumptions, including those in the United Nations. It is fair to say that many academic analysts were more cautious in their conclusions and were certainly more open to the implications of the lack of evidence produced by UN inspectors in early 2003 than were certain key politicians in the lead-up to the war. Nonetheless, that there was no significant bioweapons programme in Iraq and that it is almost certain now that the Iraqi government was telling the truth when it declared that it had destroyed most, if not all, of its bio-agents in 1991, came as a surprise to most experts. In addition, some analysts still find this impossible to accept and continue to postulate theories about the transfer of bioweapons to a neighbouring country or the burial of the capability in the desert.

Attempting to prove the non-existence of something is far harder than the reverse. But enough is now revealed that we can have strong assurance that, in 2003, the prevailing view that Iraq still possessed a considerable WMD capacity was an error. It was an error that cost tens of thousands of lives. The central question of this chapter is: how could such a mistake over the continuing possession of bioweapons in Iraq have been made and what can we learn from this mistake so that structures are put in place to prevent the like of such errors being made again?

To frame this issue, it is necessary to go back to the period between 1991 and 1995, when inspectors from the UN Special Commission (UN-SCOM) began searching for evidence of Iraq's bioweapons programme. Features of the search for Iraqi bioweapons in that period have important consequences for the later drumbeat of war and invasion.[5]

That Iraq had an extensive and ambitious bioweapons programme since the 1980s is now well documented. However, it is worth noting that, in 1991, many Western intelligence analysts were of the opinion that Iraq did not have a significant bioweapons capability.[6] This initial lack of high-level concern over Iraq's bioweapons potential led to some serious mistakes being made in the early days of UNSCOM.[7] These mistakes were soon rectified and UNSCOM did a superb job of uncovering the extent of the bioweapons programme in Iraq long before the defection of Hussein Kamal Hassan, Saddam Hussein's son-in-law, who was in charge of and spilled the beans on the whole Iraqi WMD effort in 1995.[8] However, it may be true that this initial misjudgement led to an over-reaction later and a worst-case analysis of the possible continuation of the Iraqi WMD programmes.[9] This was exacerbated by the continual lies and deliberate obfuscation by the Iraqi government during the 1990s. How does one believe a liar, even when he is telling the truth?

Production, destruction and UNSCOM

Dr David Kelly led the first UNSCOM bioweapons inspection in August 1991. Before the first inspection, Iraq declared – incompletely – 11 major bio-facilities with dual-use equipment. Following discussions with Iraqi officials in the first bioweapons inspection, where UNSCOM inspectors found key pieces of equipment,[10] the UNSCOM team reported that "Iraqi officials admitted that Iraq had carried out a programme of biological research for military purposes which, it was made clear, could be used for both defensive and offensive purposes".[11] Iraq also disclosed that it had a military biological programme and Dr Kelly stated in his report that, "during the inspection, it was apparent that the emphasis was offensive research".[12] At that point, however, there was no real expectation of a fully weaponized capability.

Iraqi officials handed over a collection of over 70 unused, original vials of microbial materials including bacillus anthracis, clostridium botulinum, clostridium perfringens and brucella in August 1991.[13] They claimed that all microbial cultures had been ordered to be destroyed in late 1990 through a process of autoclaving with superheated steam.[14] Iraq admitted to other biological facilities and activities as early as 1991, but not to their full purpose.[15] Through to the end of 1994, Iraq attempted to conceal the full extent of its programme. However, from their findings, UNSCOM inspectors were able to report that "conclusive evidence that Iraq was engaged in an advanced military biological research programme has been collected".[16] Even though the Iraqi bioweapons programme, including the role of Al Hakam, was well understood by Western intelligence agencies, it should be noted that UNSCOM inspectors did not visit there until late 1995.[17]

Iraq finally admitted to the production of bulk bio-warfare agents in July 1995,[18] although by then UNSCOM inspectors had gathered so much incriminating evidence that the admission contained few surprises. In August 1995, following the defection of Hussein Kamal Hassan, Iraq admitted weaponizing bio-agents prior to the 1991 Gulf war, including the filling of 166 bombs and 25 Al Hussein warheads. Altogether, Iraq admitted to the production of 19,000 litres of botulinum toxin, 8,500 litres of anthrax and 2,200 litres of aflatoxin; of these, some 10,000 litres of botulinum toxin, 6,500 litres of anthrax[19] and 1,580 litres of aflatoxin were reported to have been filled into weapons. These admissions were detailed in a report from Iraq in October 1995. In 1996, the Iraqi government claimed that, in May–June 1991, an oral order was given to destroy the bio-munitions and the bulk agent. Some 8,000 litres of botox, 2,000 litres of anthrax and 340 litres of gas gangrene were said to have been emptied into the septic tank at Al Hakam.[20] UNSCOM took samples at the sites in 1994 and 1996 and, at the time, found elevated levels of anthrax spores.[21] Recent genotypic analysis of the samples showed that the anthrax strain from the Al Hakam site is the same as the strain declared by Iraq to have been used in its agent production and the strain analysed in the R-400 bombs excavated by Iraq under the supervision of the UN Monitoring, Verification and Inspection Commission (UN-MOVIC) in early 2003 from the Al-Aziziyah firing range.[22] The R-400 bombs were found to contain liquid and not dry anthrax, thus verifying Iraq's declaration of 1995. In addition, analysis of potassium permanganate, nucleic acids, bacilli and spore-forming bacteria from the sites supports Iraqi claims that large amounts of B. anthracis were deactivated and destroyed prior to 1997. It is now clear that the most likely fate of the B. anthracis was destruction in 1991–1992.[23]

The lack of documentation on the destruction contradicts all the normal practice of the Iraqi military and scientific efforts in WMD development, and so UNSCOM inspectors, for the most part, assumed that Iraq was lying, as it had lied so often – a natural assumption to make, but one that now appears to have been in error. Indeed, in August 1995, Rolf Ekeus, the head of the UNSCOM inspection team, was taken to a chicken farm that had belonged to Hussein Kamal and was handed numerous boxes filled with over half a million pages of documents, photographs, disks, etc. pertaining to the Iraqi WMD programme. Buried in the boxes were documents that had previously been described as destroyed or non-existent. It seemed, at the time, naive to believe that Iraq had undertaken a large-scale destruction of its bio-agents without being able to produce written evidence of an order to that effect and so an in-depth investigation of such claims was judged to be a waste of time. In fact, Iraq admitted officially that, since the outset of the Commission, it had been withholding important information and that its disclosures over a number of years had been deliberately misleading.[24]

There is now evidence that in 1991 the Iraqi government decided to destroy the bioweapons and bulk agents in order to hide its capacity whilst retaining expertise and equipment for the future. In addition it would seem that Hussein Kamal preferred not to use written orders in sensitive situations but to deliver them in person.[25] It is now understood that, as a result of the UN sanctions and far more thorough UN inspections than he had expected, Saddam Hussein decided to abandon the WMD programmes and ordered the unilateral destruction of the bioweapons stockpile.[26] According to the report by the WMD Commission, only six or seven senior officials are likely to have known about this order.[27] In addition, the Iraq Survey Group concluded that, owing to Saddam's tight control on decision-making, instructions to subordinates were rarely documented and often shrouded in uncertainty.[28] So the lack of documentation in this respect is perhaps not so inexplicable.

From mid-February 1996, the new open approach from Iraq appeared to close again[29] until late 1997, when Iraq provided another "Full, Final and Complete Disclosure", which, according to the executive chairman of UNSCOM, also failed to give "a remotely credible account of Iraq's biological warfare programme".[30] This opinion was endorsed by an international panel of experts.[31]

UNMOVIC, the hiatus and the march to war

In March 1999, the Amorim Panel Report stated that UNSCOM had a detailed but incomplete picture of Iraq's procurement activities for its bio-weapons (BW) programme.[32] The Panel recognized that Iraq continued to possess the capability and knowledge base through which BW agents could be produced quickly and in volume. Following this report, the UN Monitoring, Verification and Inspection Commission (UNMOVIC) was established in December 1999.[33] There were no inspections in Iraq between late 1998 and late 2002. In the interim period UNMOVIC was formed as a successor to UNSCOM and, at the beginning of the inspection period, UNMOVIC inspectors had to carry out three tasks in parallel: to re-establish baseline information; to check out the information supplied in the Iraqi declaration; and to investigate the claims made by the United Kingdom, the United States and others over specific sites and weapon systems.

There was also no immediate prospect for the return of inspectors and, despite a sanctions regime against Iraq, there was concern that key equipment and pathogens for WMD R&D programmes were slipping through the net. In addition, there were several indications that Iraq was generating funds through bartering goods or illicit sales of oil. Because of suspicions that Iraq still had the motivation, the money, the capability and the intention to continue its WMD programme, such developments were viewed as potent signs that Iraq had managed to thwart the sanctions and the Oil-for-Food programme.[34]

For example, the most high-profile import was said to be a convoy of large trucks that had been adapted as mobile BW agent production facilities. They were revealed in the UK government's September 2002 dossier as evidence from defectors, with a confirmation from "recent intelligence" that the Iraqi military had developed mobile facilities.[35] US Secretary of State Colin Powell brought them to the attention of the United Nations during his presentation to the Security Council in February 2003.[36] One defector's testimony was made public in May 2002.[37] However, the Iraqi government repeated the claim that Iraq had been bio-weapon and bio-agent free since 1991 and expressed astonishment at the allegations of mobile laboratories.[38] Of course, by then few people believed any statement that came from the Iraqi government. It turned out, however, that Iraq was speaking the truth (see below).

In the December 1998–December 2002 period there were sporadic press articles referring to intelligence on Iraq's BW capabilities. Defector reports, on the ground human intelligence information (humint), satellite images and signals intelligence information (sigint) formed the most part of the basis for the reports. However, the UK dossier cautioned that intelligence rarely offers a complete account of activities that are designed to remain concealed and that Iraq was a difficult target for the intelligence services. Despite this, Prime Minister Blair stated that he believed that the assessed intelligence had established beyond doubt that Saddam had continued to produce chemical and biological weapons and that the policy of containment had not worked sufficiently well to prevent Saddam from developing these weapons.

Back to Iraq

Thanks to skilful diplomacy (not altogether appreciated by some key countries) by the UN Secretary-General, Dr Hans Blix and others, UNMOVIC finally got the chance to clear up the issue of WMD in Iraq and possibly prevent the seemingly inevitable war. Most experts expected UNMOVIC to discover a continuing bioweapons programme and thus call Iraq's bluff on the issue and give everyone a chance to sort things out through the Security Council.

In the first three weeks of inspections in late 2002, UNMOVIC inspected 44 sites that had been declared by Iraq or had been previously inspected by UNSCOM/IAEA. By January 2003, UNMOVIC was using helicopters to conduct surprise inspections and aerial surveillance planes to monitor activities. Early in the process, UNMOVIC's chairman expressed great frustration at the lack of information that he was being given by those who said they had it.[39] From February, Iraq provided more substantive cooperation. The Iraqi government released more documentation on the bioweapons programme and provided more information on its claims that the bio-agents were destroyed in 1991, including a re-excavation of a disposal site. It also produced remnants of over 92 bombs and 8 intact liquid-filled R-400 bombs and the results of investigations to quantify the amount of unilaterally destroyed anthrax dumped at a site.[40] Yet the work of UNMOVIC in Iraq came to a halt and the United States and the United Kingdom led the attack on Iraq.

It is now widely accepted that halting the inspections was a mistake. It was becoming clearer and clearer that the inspections were revealing evidence that conflicted with the prevailing view of the US and UK intelligence agencies. Had more information come to light through UNMOVIC inspections, it might have been possible to call a halt to military offensive action and finally bring Iraq to book in the Security Council vis-à-vis its compliance with UN Security Council resolutions. Certainly it can be argued that parliaments in democracies around the world would have taken a different view of the justness of the cause for war had it become clear that Iraq's WMD possession was not as definite as had been thought and, indeed, in the case of nuclear and biological weapons, did not even exist, let alone pose a threat.

Post-war inspections

Following the war in Iraq, the US military was charged with the immediate search for WMD. That responsibility was passed to the Iraq Survey Group (ISG) in June 2003, commanded by General Keith Dayton. The inspections were originally led by Dr David Kay (from July 2003 to January 2004) and then, until their close in January 2005, by Charles A. Duelfer. According to Duelfer in September 2004, the ISG had found no direct evidence that Iraq was conducting BW-specific work after 1996 and since the mid-1990s there appeared to have been a complete absence of interest in BW at the presidential level.[41] The ISG has judged that in 1991 and 1992 Iraq appeared to have destroyed its undeclared stocks of BW weapons and remaining holdings of bulk BW agent, although there was not enough evidence to document the complete destruction.[42] In addition, research carried out in Iraq prior to 2003 was judged to be unconnected to any BW programme[43] and, in spite of exhaustive investigation, there was no evidence that Iraq possessed or was developing mobile bio-agent production facilities.[44] Indeed, information has now been revealed that shows a complete misjudgement on this issue from at least three intelligence agencies. The primary source for the information on the mobile bio-labs was in fact fabricating the evidence, probably in exchange for a visa to live abroad, and was thus an unsound source. The other two corroborating sources for this information were already considered unsound.[45]

So what does all this mean for arms control?

First, we have a strong case that a combination of inspections, export controls and sanctions worked better than anybody believed it would. In 1998, it was generally believed that bioweapons inspections in Iraq had failed to uncover the bio programme fully and that the regime had managed to hide away its bioweapons capability. This had major implications for the negotiation of the protocol to strengthen the Biological and Toxin Weapons Convention. The negotiation collapsed in 2001 largely due to the belief from the United States that effective verification of the Convention was not feasible. Much of this belief was based – erroneously as we now know – on the understanding that, despite highly intrusive inspections in a go anywhere, anytime manner, UN inspectors had failed to unravel the bioweapons programme in Iraq. In truth, well before the defection of Hussein Kamal, UNSCOM had unravelled the full extent of the bioweapons programme. They had not found the vast quantities of weapons produced due to one simple fact – the weapons had been destroyed. In addition, it is now clear that the efficacy of the UNSCOM inspections coupled with the sanctions regime was the deciding factor in Saddam Hussein's decision to destroy stocks of WMD. So the major pillar on which the belief that an effective verification regime for bioweapons is impossible turns out to be a false premise. If only the clock could be turned back.

The absence of bioweapons in Iraq has remarkable implications for arms control more generally. Indeed, the former head of inspections of the ISG stated that "the U.N. inspection process achieved quite a bit.... Inspections accomplished a great deal in holding a program down, and that's where the surprise is. In holding the program down, in keeping it from break out, I think the record is better than we would have anticipated."[46] Dr Hans Blix has also come to the conclusion that "inspections and monitoring by the IAEA, UNMOVIC and its predecessor UNSCOM, backed by military, political and economic pressure, had indeed worked for years, achieving Iraqi disarmament and deterring Saddam from rearming. Containment had worked."[47]

This should give us optimism for the future. Arms control, including intrusive verification measures, is a useful tool for international peace and security and should be restored to its rightful place. Arms control is not a panacea and verification cannot tell us everything – neither, for that matter, can intelligence-gathering. However, arms control treaties are legal instruments that hold countries to account for their behaviour. The verification regimes for such treaties are the mechanisms through which we build trust in compliance or else gather information to challenge a miscreant. Intelligence-gathering and verification regimes can work side by side as complementary and mutually reinforcing tools for international peace and security. The key issue in both cases is to be aware of the limits of each technique and the uncertainties and ambiguities inherent in each and to factor these limits and uncertainties into the decision-making equations.

How should we have treated the information we had?

In 2002, it was accepted as "fact" that Iraq had not destroyed its BW capability. Iraq had lied and lied again, and so it was natural not to believe it when it said that it had destroyed all the weapons and bulk agents, particularly when it could produce no documents to support such statements.[48]

However, not believing is very different from believing the opposite. It was completely justifiable to be sceptical of Iraq's statements, but inspectors, intelligence analysts, academics, journalists and politicians should also have kept in mind that there was no hard proof that Iraq still had such weapons. Yes, there was evidence of production and weaponization that had originally been hidden but there was no evidence of the continued existence of bioweapons. That should have been borne in mind and decision makers should have been a little less certain about their assumptions. Indeed, given the hiatus in inspections between the end of 1998 and the end of 2002, the uncertainties inherent in the human sources of the intelligence agencies (such as single-source concerns, motivations, ambiguities, fabrication, exaggeration) should have been given greater weight than they were.

Indeed, by spring 2003, the continuing lack of evidence from the UNMOVIC inspections was giving the United Nations plenty of pause for thought. At first it was hard to understand why the UNMOVIC inspections had found nothing at sites that had been classed as sure bets by the intelligence agencies. Unsure of the implications, Drs Hans Blix and Mohamed ElBaradei increased the note of caution in their reports to the UN Security Council, urging the continuation of the inspection effort until things became clearer one way or another. In addition, from what we now know, it would seem that, even before 1998, the yardsticks by which Iraqi compliance was being judged might well have produced a false impression. For example, the issue of "missing growth media" turns out to have been a red herring. It was all down to measurement error in the end: out of 42 tonnes of growth media, only 142 kg was unaccounted for – an amount well within normal measurement errors over a period of seven years. Moreover, concerns over the purchase of a spray drier were unfounded: it had not been bought in 1989 as had been thought.[49]

What would have been the impact of continuing the inspections for another year?

We must recognize that the inspections resumed at the end of 2002 only because of the threat of war. It would be disingenuous to forget the salient fact that UNMOVIC inspectors were allowed to return to Iraq only because the Iraqi regime was given the distinct impression that continued denial of access would mean war. So it would have been vital for that threat to have remained real and worrying to the Iraqi Ba'athist regime in order to retain its cooperation. Could such a threat have been maintained for another six months, or even a year? It would have been difficult but, with the benefit of hindsight, it clearly would have been better to have tried that approach. The inspections in Iraq were yielding such unexpected results that this alone should have warranted some pause for reflection and more information-gathering. The UK and US intelligence agencies had already stressed caution about the information they had presented,[50] and so presidents and prime ministers would have done well to have been less sure of what they "knew".

If the inspections could have been continued for, say, another six months, what might have been the outcome? Would there have been war nonetheless? Although we would have known more, we still would have had large uncertainties. Given how long it took the Iraq Survey Group in a post-conflict, US-occupied Iraq to feel certain enough to publish its findings, imagine how long it would have taken UN inspectors in a pre-war environment to be sure that Iraq had no bioweapons and then to have their findings accepted by the UN Security Council.

Or would Iraq have come clean about everything and convinced the United Nations, the United States, the United Kingdom and others of the absence of WMD? This last scenario is unlikely and not supported by the available evidence.[51]

However, there clearly was a strong and growing case for continuing the inspections and delaying an invasion. The legal basis for war, as it was understood and put by the proponents of that war, was the non-compliance of the Iraqi government with the UN Security Council resolutions on disarmament. As full an investigation of Iraqi compliance as was possible was therefore morally, ethically and legally warranted. This was particularly so in light of the fact that inspections had not taken place for four years and there could be no certainty over the issue of Iraqi compliance with the resolutions. Even though the inspections would have continued to be inconclusive in this regard, the continuing lack of evidence could eventually have led states to a new understanding of Iraqi behaviour and the WMD programmes. War could have been prevented. On the other hand, even if the lack of evidence was dismissed on the grounds that lack of evidence does not necessarily mean non-existence, at least due attention would have been paid to the process of gathering evidence.

Intelligence and information

We need to reassess the interaction between intelligence assessments and arms control. The information gleaned from intelligence methods is different from the information gathered through inspections in arms control measures. For one thing, information gleaned from intelligence methods is secret. It is scrutinized by a small, closed set of analytical minds. Those conducting the analysis mostly come from one particular culture and thus tend to interpret information in similar way. When there are differences of opinion, it is usually owing to relative emphases on the weight of different pieces of information relevant to the issue. Information gleaned from human sources is often the most suspect. People providing such information have a variety of motives (spite, greed and betrayal, as well as higher motives of whistle-blowing and prevention of conflict). Furthermore, such sources are often not fully aware of the facts. They may have heard rumours that are untrue, they may be unwittingly being used to pass deliberately false information or they may have interpreted a piece of information in the wrong way and passed it on as "fact".[52] Intelligence gleaned from technical sources, such as signals, radio communications and remote imaging by aircraft or satellite, may be more likely to be value free, but such sources are still subject to deliberate deception and inadvertent misinterpretation – or simply being missed and thus not factored into the debate.[53]

Information from arms control inspections tends to go to a wider analytical set. It is given to all states involved, including the inspected state. It is not covert – quite the reverse in the case of on-site inspections. Indeed, the concern is often the amount of notice given, which can give a miscreant time to hide evidence of clandestine activities (this happened on more than one occasion in 1991–1998 in Iraq). Information from national or multinational technical means is written into an agreement and thus can be used by the parties to that agreement. Obviously, the capabilities of national technical means still have to be protected – as in the case of intelligence-gathering – so as not to give away details that would allow a treaty violator to subvert them.

In addition, the role of open source information and how that is factored into the equation must be addressed. How the different strands of information from intelligence-gathering, verification activities and open sources interact is important and very few analysts pay adequate attention to this. In particular, the problem of the "world view"[54] or "group think" or the development of a "prevailing wisdom" has to be addressed.[55] Major Richards J. Heuer, Jr, wrote that "intelligence failures are usually caused by failures of analysis, not failures of collection. Relevant information is discounted, misinterpreted, ignored, rejected, or overlooked because it fails to fit a prevailing mental model or mind-set ... A mind-set is neither good nor bad. It is unavoidable. It is, in essence, a distillation of all that analysts think they know about a subject. It forms a lens through which they perceive the world, and once formed, it resists change."[56] Dealing with "group think" and "mind-sets" is paramount. Doubt has to be encouraged, competing hypotheses have to be regularly tested against the available evidence and we – including politicians – have to be able to live with uncertainty. On the other hand, decisions – life and death decisions – have to be made and leaders have to come down on one side of the evidence or the other. Not to act is often more risky than to take action, and it is easy to criticize such decisions from an armchair in the university library; it is far harder to be the person making that decision while holding the security of your citizens in your hands. This is all the more reason that politicians should be fully apprised of the uncertainties and dissent involved in reaching intelligence estimates. It is vital for the future of humanity that presidents, ministers, parliamentarians, journalists and citizens are treated not as children to be protected from complexity but as fully functioning adults, educated to be able to cope with subtleties and uncertainty and still make difficult decisions. It is time we stopped pretending that through intelligence-gathering we can know everything – we can't – or that a verification regime has to provide us with 100 per cent certainty for it to be valuable or even admissible. We live with uncertainties every day of our lives and we cope. We can try to find out everything politicians want to know, but we'll always understand far less than we need to.

Getting things right from now on

One of the lessons we can take from the tragedy of the hunt for bioweapons in Iraq is that we need a way of obtaining information on compliance with the Biological and Toxin Weapons Convention (BTWC) as well as compliance with a range of other WMD measures. For nuclear non-proliferation we have the IAEA safeguards; for chemical weapons prohibition we have the Organisation for the Prohibition of Chemical Weapons (OPCW); for bioweapons we have no international way to check compliance with the treaty or other laws. There have been a number of proposals to address this deficit.

First, there is the possibility of resurrecting the attempt to strengthen the BTWC with a protocol that includes a verification regime. Currently such an attempt is generally judged to be politically impossible.[57] Moreover, many experts agree that the protocol as it was constructed by 2001 was not adequate to the task of verifying compliance in the long term, given the rapid changes in biotechnology. Thus, a resurrection of the protocol, although a long-term goal, would need such a high degree of political consensus that it would have to be constructed again from its foundations.

A second approach would be to extend the life and mandate of UN-MOVIC. UNMOVIC's mandate was to verify Iraq's compliance with its obligation to be rid of its weapons of mass destruction (chemical and biological weapons and missiles with a range of more than 150 km), and to operate a system of ongoing monitoring and verification to ascertain that Iraq did not reacquire the same weapons prohibited to it by the Security Council. UNMOVIC's mandate could be extended to all states. In terms of nuclear weapons, UNMOVIC's role would be to carry on working in partnership with the IAEA, as it has done from its inception, and a similar arrangement could be forged with the OPCW. In effect, UNMOVIC would not have any direct responsibility for monitoring compliance over nuclear or chemical weapons. In the case of bioweapons and missiles, however, UNMOVIC has an unparalleled degree of expertise in terms of knowledge of materials, experience in inspections and background knowledge of illegal markets, transfers and procurement. Such expertise and all the archived materials and in-depth analysis from UN-SCOM and UNMOVIC should be retained and used for international peace and security.[58]

Third, since 1987 and the use of chemical weapons in the Iraq–Iran war and on Kurdish towns and villages in Iraq, the UN Secretary-General has a General Assembly mandate to carry out fact-finding missions to investigate the alleged use of biological and chemical weapons.[59] An updated roster of trained experts should be maintained so that, at the very least, the Secretary-General can implement this mandate in the event of such an allegation.

Fourth, a form of self-regulation of scientists and technologists in the sphere of biotechnology is being pursued by a number of august bodies. Notably the Biotechnology, Weapons and Humanity initiative of the International Committee of the Red Cross[60] is working with professional bodies such as the Royal Society, the British Medical Association and the US Academy of Sciences to develop a Code of Conduct for people working in the life sciences. In 2005, States Party to the BTWC discussed – at both expert and political levels – the content, promulgation and adoption of codes of conduct for scientists. Other work on codes of conduct and codes of practice is being formulated,[61] along with training for industrial and academic scientists in the issues of biotechnology security and prevention of proliferation. Codes of conduct and practice are necessary for the life sciences and will need to be incorporated into any national or multilateral efforts to control biotechnology and ensure that it develops for the benefit of humanity.

Knowledge

Knowledge is a resource that, like life, builds on what came before. Each generation is faced with the questions: What is it we know? What is it we understand? Each generation has to build on the knowledge acquired by their ancestors and thus will find flaws in past understandings and gaps in our knowledge. We already know that. What we handle so badly is the extent of our ignorance. For some reason, leaders – be they politicians, teachers or parents – feel the need to pretend to know things when they don't. Thus we can embark on a programme of self-delusion and deception, not through any malicious intent, rather through feelings of inadequacy when faced with our own ignorance. Bertrand Russell, like many philosophers before and after him, grappled with the concept of knowledge. Russell also dedicated much of his life to the pursuit of peace and the abolition of weapons of mass destruction and was a thorn in the side of successive British governments. He has something to say to us today as we struggle to make sense of our collective ignorance and our inability to admit what has been done.

Philosophy may claim justly that it diminishes the risk of error ... To do more than this is not possible in a world where mistakes must occur; and more than this no prudent advocate of philosophy would claimed to have performed.[62]

Notes

1. Bertrand Russell, "Knowledge, Error, and Probable Opinion", in *The Problems of Philosophy* (London: Oxford University Press, first published 1912, taken from sixteenth impression, 1989), p. 81. Russell goes on to explain that what we firmly believe, if it is neither knowledge nor error, is probable opinion. Probable opinion is also what we hesitatingly believe – owing to it being, or derived from, something that has not the highest degree of self-evidence. "Thus the greater part of what would commonly pass as knowledge is more or less probable opinion."
2. Letter to President George W. Bush from the Commission on the Intelligence Capabilities of the United States Regarding Weapons of Mass Destruction, 31 March 2005, ⟨http://www.wmd.gov/report/transmittal_letter.pdf⟩ (accessed 23 February 2006).
3. *Comprehensive Report of the Special Advisor to the DCI on Iraq's WMD. Volume 3: Biological Warfare*, 30 September 2004, ⟨http://www.foia.cia.gov/duelfer/Iraqs_WMD_Vol3.pdf⟩ (accessed 23 February 2006), p. 2 and pp. 50–53.
4. This chapter is a sequel to Patricia M. Lewis, "Armes biologiques irakiennes: ce que nous savons, ce que nous ignorons et ce que nous pourrions apprendre [Bioweapons in Iraq: What We Knew, What We Still Don't Know and What We May Be Able to Learn]", *Politique étrangère*, Vol. 2 (2004).
5. This chapter will consider only the issue of biological and toxin weapons and agents. For chemical weapons and agents, nuclear materials and technology and missiles, the reader

should go to reports by the United Nations Monitoring, Verification and Inspection Commission (UNMOVIC) and the International Atomic Energy Agency (IAEA) and well as the *Comprehensive Report of the Special Advisor to the DCI on Iraq's WMD*, ⟨http://www.cia.gov/cia/reports/iraq_wmd_2004/⟩ (accessed 23 February 2006), and *The Bomb in My Garden* by Mahdi Obeidi and Kurt Pulitzer (New Jersey: John Wiley, 2004).

6. Tim Trevan, *Saddam's Secrets: The Hunt for Iraq's Hidden Weapons* (London: Harper-Collins, 1999).

7. Mistakes such as not being aware of the significance of information on Al Hakam (Iraq's most sophisticated and largest biological weapons factory) and not taking samples from the disposal site at Al Hakam at a time when the veracity of Iraq's claims of destruction of the bio-agents would have been clearer. For a fuller discussion see Lewis, "Armes biologiques irakiennes".

8. A persistent error in analyses of the Iraqi bioweapons programme is the erroneous belief that, until Hussein Kamal's defection, there was no evidence of Iraqi bioweapons.

9. For a comprehensive explanation of this see *Review of Intelligence on Weapons of Mass Destruction. Report of a Committee of Privy Counsellors*, Chairman: The Rt Hon The Lord Butler of Brockwell (London: The Stationery Office, July 2004), pp. 48–53. Also see Commission on the Intelligence Capabilities of the United States Regarding Weapons of Mass Destruction (WMD Commission), *Report to the President of the United States*, 31 March 2005, ⟨http://www.wmd.gov/report/wmd_report.pdf⟩ (accessed 23 February 2006), "Overview", p. 9.

10. Jonathan B. Tucker, "Lessons of Iraq's Biological Warfare Programme", *Arms Control: Contemporary Security Policy*, Vol. 14, No. 3 (December 1993), p. 252.

11. Graham S. Pearson, *The UNSCOM Saga: Chemical and Biological Weapons Nonproliferation* (London: Palgrave Macmillan, 1999), p. 129.

12. Unpublished report of the UNSCOM7/BW1 inspection team (New York: United Nations, 1991), cited in Graham S. Pearson, *The Search for Iraq's Weapons of Mass Destruction* (London: Palgrave Macmillan, 2005), p. 83; Pearson provides a full list of all the UNSCOM BW inspections and a detailed analysis of the UNSCOM and UNMOVIC experience.

13. UNMOVIC, *Fifteenth Quarterly report on the activities of the United Nations Monitoring, Verification and Inspection Commission in accordance with paragraph 12 of Security Council resolution 1284 (1999)*, UN Doc. S/2003/1135, 26 November 2003, Appendix 1, para. 6.

14. *Chemical Weapons Convention Bulletin*, No. 14 (December 1991), p. 5, cited in Tucker, "Lessons of Iraq's Biological Warfare Programme", p. 253.

15. UNMOVIC, *Fifteenth Quarterly report*, Appendix 1, para. 7.

16. Pearson, *The UNSCOM Saga*, p. 129.

17. "Status of Biological Weapons: Detail on the Location of Iraq's Biological Weapons", August 1991 (cia_62856_62856_01.txt), available at ⟨http://fas.org/irp/gulf/cia/960531/62856_01.htm⟩ (accessed 23 February 2006).

18. UNMOVIC, *Fifteenth Quarterly report*, Appendix 1, para. 10. Note that this report, in which the chairman of UNSCOM reported to the UN Security Council on Iraq's fully fledged offensive bioweapons programme, was made prior to the defection of Hussein Kamal Hassan.

19. According to the Iraq Survey Group and UNMOVIC, Iraq had produced greater quantities of anthrax than was declared, probably thousands of litres more (UNMOVIC, *Nineteenth Quarterly report*, UN Doc. S/2004/924, 26 November 2004, para. 18).

20. Pearson, *The UNSCOM Saga*, tables 5.5 and 5.6, pp. 145–150.

21. UNMOVIC, *Fifteenth Quarterly report*, Appendix 1, para. 14.

22. Ibid., para. 5.

23. UNMOVIC, *Nineteenth Quarterly report*, para. 19, and *Comprehensive Report of the Special Advisor to the DCI on Iraq's WMD. Volume 3: Biological Warfare*, p. 2. and pp. 50–53.

24. *Report submitted by the Executive Chairman of UNSCOM to the United Nations Secretary General pursuant to paragraph 9 (b) (i) of Security Council resolution 687 (1991)*, UN Doc. S/1996/258, 11 April 1996, para. 7.

25. Obeidi and Pulitzer, *The Bomb in My Garden*, pp. 57, 137, 158.

26. *Comprehensive Report of the Special Advisor to the DCI on Iraqi WMD. Volume 1: Regime Strategic Intent*, 30 September 2004, ⟨http://www.foia.cia.gov/duelfer/Iraqs_WMD _Vol1.pdf⟩ (accessed 23 February 2006), p. 46.

27. WMD Commission, *Report to the President of the United States*, "Regime Decisionmaking", p. 155.

28. *Comprehensive Report of the Special Advisor to the DCI on Iraqi WMD, Volume 1*, pp. 8–9.

29. *Report submitted by the Executive Chairman of UNSCOM to the United Nations Secretary General*, S/1996/258, para. 9.

30. *Report submitted by the Executive Chairman of UNSCOM to the United Nations Secretary General pursuant to paragraph 9 (b) (i) of Security Council resolution 687 (1991)*, UN Doc. S/1997/774, 6 October 1997, para. 83.

31. Ibid., Annex II, paras 2–5.

32. *Report of the First Panel Established Pursuant to the Note by the President of the Security Council on 30 January 1999 (S/1999/100), Concerning Disarmament and Current and Future Ongoing Monitoring and Verification Issues*, UN Doc. S/1999/356, 27 March 1999, ⟨http://www.un.org/Depts/unmovic/documents/Amorim%20Report.htm⟩ (accessed 23 February 2006).

33. Patricia Lewis, "From UNSCOM to UNMOVIC: The United Nations and Iraq", *Disarmament Forum: The Middle East*, No. 2 (2001), pp. 63–68.

34. Now that the outside world is more apprised of the situation through the reports from the Independent Inquiry Committee into the United Nations Oil-for-Food Programme (⟨http://www.iic-offp.org⟩), it is obvious why intelligence agencies made the assumption that Iraq had the means to continue its WMD programmes – at least as regards R&D and procurement attempts.

35. *Iraq's Weapons of Mass Destruction: The Assessment of the British Government* (London: The Stationery Office, 2002).

36. Transcript of US Secretary of State Colin Powell's presentation to the UN Security Council on the US case against Iraq, "U.S. Secretary of State Colin Powell Addresses the U.N. Security Council", 5 February 2003, ⟨http://www.whitehouse.gov/news/ releases/2003/02/20030205-1.html⟩ (accessed 23 February 2006).

37. Interview with David Rose, *Vanity Fair*, May 2002, p. 120.

38. "Iraq's Reply on Blair's Report", INA News Agency website, Baghdad, in English, 2 October 2002, available at ⟨http://news.bbc.co.uk/1/hi/world/middle_east/2296223.stm⟩ (accessed 23 February 2006).

39. Edith M. Lederer, "Blix Defends Inspectors' Credibility", Associated Press, 10 June 2003. According to the Intelligence Services Committee, *Iraqi Weapons of Mass Destruction – Intelligence Assessments*, Cm 5972 (London: The Stationery Office, 2003), UN inspectors were content with the support they had received from the United Kingdom and that the United Kingdom had provided UN inspectors with all the intelligence support it could within third-party rules.

40. Hans Blix, "Briefing of the Security Council, 7 March 2003: Oral introduction of the 12th quarterly report of UNMOVIC", ⟨http://www.un.org/Depts/unmovic/new/pages/ security_council_briefings.asp#7⟩ (accessed 23 February 2006).

41. *Comprehensive Report of the Special Advisor to the DCI on Iraq's WMD. Volume 3: Biological Warfare*, "Findings", p. 1.
42. According to the ISG, Saddam Hussein authorized Hussein Kamal to destroy, unilaterally, Iraq's stocks of BW agents. According to accounts this began in mid-1991 and was over by the autumn.
43. *Comprehensive Report of the Special Advisor to the DCI on Iraq's WMD. Volume 3: Biological Warfare*, "Findings", p. 2.
44. Ibid., p. 3.
45. WMD Commission, *Report to the President of the United States*, "Biological Warfare", pp. 80–111.
46. Dr David Kay, Testimony to the Senate Armed Services Committee, 28 January 2004, response to questions from Senator Clinton, ⟨http://www.ceip.org/files/projects/npp/pdf/Iraq/kaytestimony.pdf⟩ (accessed 23 February 2006).
47. Hans Blix, *Disarming Iraq* (New York: Pantheon Books, 2004), p. 272.
48. In January 1999, UNSCOM reported to the Security Council that, with regard to its BW programme, Iraq had made fraudulent statements, given false and forged documents and misrepresented the roles of people and facilities and other specific acts of deception (UNSCOM, *Report: Disarmament*, 25 January 1999, Annex C, available at ⟨http://www.fas.org/news/un/iraq/s/990125/dis-bio.htm⟩, accessed 23 February 2006).
49. This was another victory for arms control. The exporting country had not been satisfied with Iraq's requirements for the spray drier and had refused an end-user certificate and thus refused an export licence. So, although Iraq had all the papers for the spray drier, it had in fact never been allowed into the country.
50. Select Committee on Intelligence, United States Senate, *Report on the U.S. Intelligence Community's Prewar Intelligence Assessments on Iraq*, 7 July 2004, p. 184, available at ⟨http://www.gpoaccess.gov/serialset/creports/iraq.html⟩ (accessed 23 February 2006).
51. WMD Commission, *Report to the President of the United States*, 31 March 2005, Chapter 1, pp. 152–153.
52. For a comprehensive comparison of intelligence-gathering and arms control verification, see Michael J. Herman, "Intelligence and Arms Control Verification", in VERTIC, *Verification Report 1991* (New York: Apex Press, 1991), pp. 187–196.
53. For an excellent, highly detailed analysis of intelligence, how it connects with assessments on WMD and how, in the United States at least, it could be improved, see the complete report of the WMD Commission, *Report to the President of the United States*, 31 March 2005.
54. For an excellent appraisal of world views and intelligence analysis, see Richards J. Heuer, Jr, *Psychology of Intelligence Analysis* (Washington DC: Center for the Study of Intelligence, Central Intelligence Agency, 1999).
55. On "Group-think" see *Review of Intelligence on Weapons of Mass Destruction*.
56. Heuer, "Keeping an Open Mind", in *Psychology of Intelligence Analysis*, Chapter 6.
57. Jez Littlewood, "Managing the Biological Weapons Problem: From the Individual to the International", The Weapons of Mass Destruction Commission, Paper No. 14, ⟨http://www.wmdcommission.org/files/no14.pdf⟩ (accessed 23 February 2006).
58. Barbara Hatch Rosenberg, "Enforcing WMD Treaties: Consolidating a UN Role", *Disarmament Diplomacy*, No. 75 (January/February 2004); Terrence Taylor, "Building on the Experience: Lessons from UNSCOM and UNMOVIC", *Disarmament Diplomacy*, No. 75 (January/February 2004); Trevor Findlay, "Preserving UNMOVIC: The Institutional Possibilities", *Disarmament Diplomacy*, No. 76 (March/April 2004); Trevor Findlay and Angela Woodward, "Enhancing BWC Implementation: A Modular Approach", The Weapons of Mass Destruction Commission, Paper No. 23, ⟨http://www.wmdcommission.org/files/No23.pdf⟩ (accessed 23 February 2006).

59. UN General Assembly Resolution 42/37C (1987), "Measures to uphold the authority of the 1925 Geneva Protocol and to support the conclusion of a chemical weapons convention", UN Doc. A/RES/42/37, 30 November 1987.

60. See ⟨http://www.icrc.org/web/eng/siteeng0.nsf/htmlall/bwh⟩ (accessed 23 February 2006).

61. See Center for International and Security Studies at Maryland, Controlling Dangerous Pathogens Project, ⟨http://www.cissm.umd.edu/pathogensproject/⟩ (accessed 23 February 2006).

62. Bertrand Russell, "The Limits of Philosophical Knowledge", in *The Problems of Philosophy*, p. 88.

Part III

Proliferation challenges and international responses in North-east Asia

9

Nuclear threat reliance in East Asia

Wade L. Huntley

Introduction

This chapter offers a regional perspective on proliferation challenges in East Asia, to complement the country-based analyses of other contributors to this volume. The analysis consists of two sections.

The first section presents an analytical framework for the dynamics in the region and the challenges that these dynamics pose to the non-proliferation regime. This section outlines two key new features of an emerging new structure of regional relations: the relatively more autonomous role of nuclear policy as distinct from nuclear armament levels, and the relatively greater importance of regional over global security environments in security perceptions.

The second section adopts these analytical precepts to review the current nuclear weapons policies of six governments whose behaviour shapes the security environment of East Asia: the United States, China, Japan, North Korea, South Korea and Taiwan.[1] This section focuses on how reliance on nuclear threat-making by both nuclear-armed and non-nuclear governments responds primarily to regional threat perceptions.

The chapter concludes by underscoring the importance of regional collective security mechanisms to easing nuclear threat reliance and to promoting arms control and non-proliferation, and by noting the links between these regional dynamics and contemporary trends in the global non-proliferation regime.

The new nuclear age

Nuclear weapons were born into a world defined by the pitched ideological confrontation of the United States and the Soviet Union. Consequently, the dilemmas of the nuclear age were defined by this "bipolar" structure and rarely conceived of outside it. Nuclear weapons also deepened the shadow the superpower competition cast over more localized inter-state disputes, from concern that even the smallest spark could ignite a nuclear conflagration.

Accordingly, the focus of efforts toward nuclear arms control, nonproliferation and eventual disarmament was on the United States and the Soviet Union. Bilateral arms reductions were an immediate priority, and stemming "horizontal" proliferation of nuclear technology to more states was intrinsically linked to rolling back "vertical" proliferation by the two superpowers – a linkage enshrined in the "grand bargain" of the Treaty on the Non-Proliferation of Nuclear Weapons (Nuclear Non-Proliferation Treaty, NPT), which committed the five "permanent" nuclear-weapon states to the ultimate goal of disarmament. Control of nuclear weapons hinged upon the willing participation of the two superpowers.

The end of the Cold War's pitched ideological confrontation allowed immediate progress in non-proliferation and arms control efforts. Achievements included unilateral actions, bilateral accords and multilateral agreements, reaching a symbolic zenith with the indefinite extension of the NPT in 1995. However, this progress then languished. The 1998 nuclear tests by non-NPT members India and Pakistan and the US Senate's refusal to ratify the Comprehensive Nuclear-Test-Ban Treaty (CTBT) augured the closing of the post–Cold War "window of opportunity" for significant progress towards nuclear disarmament.

The failure to realize the hope for reducing nuclear dangers that the end of the Cold War initially offered has many sources, including failures of political will, the pernicious effects of parochial military and economic interests, and the continuing appeal of nuclear weapons as strategic tools and symbols of prestige in an anarchic world. Few of these explanations, however, question the understandings of the basic workings of the nuclear age bestowed by Cold War era analyses blinkered by the bipolar, ideologically driven competition defining that era.

The end of the Cold War initiated a new, second era of the nuclear age. In this new era, dissipated ideological confrontation has liberated ethnic, national and religious aspirations. Global relations are not structured bipolarly but shaped by crosscutting forces of US primacy, multipolar interaction and transnational globalization. On this new global terrain, nuclear weapons have fundamentally altered roles. The slowness of arms control and non-proliferation advocates in adjusting their thinking accordingly is an important and under-appreciated reason for the waning of progress towards disarmament at the start of the twenty-first century.

Two elements of the changed circumstances of this new era are particularly relevant to understanding proliferation pressures in East Asia. The first is the relatively more autonomous role of nuclear policy as distinct from nuclear armament levels. The second is the relatively greater importance of regional security environments, as opposed to the global environment, in nuclear strategizing and decision-making. The remainder of this section outlines these two elements.

Nuclear arms and nuclear policy

The distinction between nuclear capabilities (deployed nuclear weapons and associated material assets) and policies pertaining to those capabilities (including both military planning and nuclear threat-making by national leaderships) is in practice sometimes opaque but conceptually vital. Nuclear policies function as the conduit through which nuclear weapons capabilities and practices, on the one hand, and prevailing political-security conditions, on the other, interact synergistically (see Figure 9.1)

In the Cold War era, concern for the *autonomous* role of nuclear policies was relatively muted because, in its ideologically polarized climate, both nuclear strategists and nuclear abolitionists tended to regard nuclear weapons issues as largely independent of politics. For the strategists, the existence of nuclear weapons imposed a logic of its own: theories of deterrence and war-fighting held for any "rational actor". For the abolitionists, a parallel logic obtained: the cataclysmic potential of widespread nuclear warfare rendered their use as a weapon of war "unthinkable" and established the primacy of the imperative of nuclear disarmament. Both communities implicitly held that the driving feature of the nuclear age was the existence of the weapons themselves; policies were derivative.

The manner by which the Cold War ended belies this contextual autonomy of nuclear weapons. Elimination of the Cold War's ideologically driven animosity dramatically reduced the perceived threat of deliberate nuclear war between the United States and Russia, despite force levels and launching capabilities as lethal as ever, and so enabled (rather

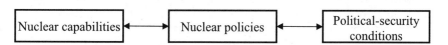

Figure 9.1 The intermediate role of nuclear policies.

than followed) the subsequent dramatic nuclear arms reductions, which quickly dwarfed Cold War achievements. The historical lesson is that evolving political conditions are more determinative than abstract strategic logic or operational doctrines of the ultimate role and disposition of nuclear weapons.

Because the emerging autonomous role of nuclear policies was underappreciated, efforts to reduce state reliance on nuclear threats in security policies did not match efforts to reduce nuclear weapons levels. The inevitable stalling of progress in the control of nuclear (and other nonconventional) weapons capabilities both reinforced reliance on the nuclear threats and obstructed resolution of security tensions wherever such threats were tangible. Regional relations in East Asia and the Middle East exemplify these patterns most prominently.

Regional and global dynamics

Cold War superpower competition, with its nuclear dimension, imposed itself on many generically regional conflicts, leading to the presumption that control of nuclear weapons needed to be pursued at the global level. Pursuing disarmament through regional initiatives was often viewed as supplemental to globally focused efforts, rather than as principally useful in its own right.

The end of the Cold War has "loosened" world politics by lessening the influence of overarching global security circumstances on many regional security environments. More geographically proximate and immediate security concerns have taken on higher priority in state security policy-making, driving the emergence of regionally identifiable security environments that have, in turn, taken on a greater role in shaping the overarching global security motif. Thus, although the global and regional security "levels" continue to interact bi-directionally, the end of the Cold War has shifted the weight of influence from the global to the regional level, as Figure 9.2 depicts.

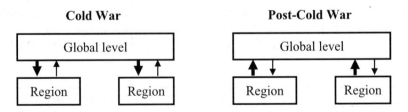

Figure 9.2 Regional influences on nuclear policies.

Developments in East Asia exemplify how nuclear policy decision-making has followed this trend. As reviewed in the following section, the nuclear policies of each of the principal governments of the region are now primarily responsive to regional conditions. In some cases (for example, China and Japan) this marks a notable shift from the primary considerations of the Cold War era. Similar thinking also underlies the nuclear policies of governments in South Asia, the Middle East and even Russia.

Although the United States emerged from the Cold War as the world's only truly global power, its nuclear weapons policies are also evolving towards greater regional specification. During the Cold War, the United States established a network of alliance relationships, girded by extended nuclear deterrence guarantees, as a bulwark against Soviet expansion. With the end of the Cold War removing this overarching strategic motivation, the United States' extended nuclear deterrence alliance relationships are now increasingly justified as protecting US interests and allies from threats of nearer origin.

Thus, the regional determinants of all states' reliance on nuclear threats and nuclear capabilities (latent or extant) are now of vital concern to the pursuit of nuclear arms control and non-proliferation. In place of the implicit Cold War assumption that regional progress would follow progress at the global level, and could not be realized in its absence, the question now becomes what states in a specific region can do to move towards nuclear disarmament more locally, and thereby facilitate global non-proliferation in the process.

Nuclear threat reliance in East Asia

Developments in East Asia since the end of the Cold War exemplify how proliferation of nuclear capabilities and propagation of nuclear threats now proceed primarily along regional lines and for regionally defined purposes. All the principal states and governments in East Asia – including those lacking nuclear weapons capabilities – now rely upon some form of nuclear deterrence or coercion in their security postures.

This section reviews the nuclear weapons policies of six governments whose behaviour shapes the nuclear environment of East Asia: the United States, China, Japan, North Korea, South Korea and Taiwan. Operating from the analytical viewpoint of the preceding section, this review focuses on how these states' reliance on nuclear threat-making pursues security goals derived mainly from regional-origin security concerns.

US nuclear policy

During the Cold War, the United States employed extended nuclear deterrence to protect overseas interests and allies against perceived Soviet global ambitions. In East Asia, extended nuclear deterrence applied primarily to Japan, South Korea and Taiwan. To bolster the credibility of the retaliatory threat at the heart of extended deterrence, the United States deployed an array of tactical and battlefield nuclear weapons in the region offering "limited" nuclear options to implement "warfighting" and "flexible response" nuclear strategies.[2]

The end of the Cold War threat that Soviet conventional forces had posed in Europe and Asia fundamentally changed prevailing political and military conditions. Responsively, the United States made unilateral cuts in the absolute size of its nuclear arsenal and drew back most of its forward-deployed nuclear forces, including those on the Korean peninsula and on surface naval vessels. But US policy continued to rely on Cold War era extended nuclear deterrence as a core pillar of the US posture in East Asia. Thus, the end of the Cold War saw dramatic changes in both East Asian political-security conditions and the operational US nuclear posture in the region, but not in the extended nuclear deterrence policies mediating them.

The curtailed ability of US nuclear policy to perform its linking function between East Asia's transformed political-security conditions and reduced nuclear forces introduced new, pernicious sources of regional instability. Russia, China and North Korea perceived continued US adherence to flexible response strategies as evincing US determination to compel and coerce them, rather than merely to deter them. These perceptions encouraged destabilizing responses, including North Korean nuclear ambitions and more assertive Chinese nuclear policies (as discussed below). Meanwhile, for Japan and South Korea, continued US reliance on extended deterrence raised questions about the credibility of security guarantees in some circles while in other circles spawning perceptions that US policy was unsympathetic to these allies' newer security concerns, fuelling restiveness in the relationships across the board.

Instead of revisiting nuclear policies, however, US strategic planners began working to bring US military capabilities and threat perceptions in East Asia back in line with reliance on extended nuclear deterrence. This effort has neared culmination under the George W. Bush administration: the 2002 Nuclear Posture Review (NPR)[3] calls for developing a new generation of smaller, versatile nuclear weapons to restore the type of tactical capabilities that girded extended deterrence throughout the Cold War, but now aiming to deter attacks – or even compel disarmament – by "rogue" states armed with weapons of mass destruction, among which North Korea ranks most prominently.[4]

Given the United States' pre-eminent position at the global level, its expanded reliance on nuclear weapons threats in regional contexts may motivate other, conventionally weaker states to seek "equalizing" nuclear capabilities.[5] Certainly, emphasis on nuclear threat-making by the world's conventionally strongest state works to undermine nuclear non-use and non-proliferation norms in East Asia and other key regions, as well as at the global level.

Chinese nuclear policy

In the wake of the collapse of the Soviet Union, China appeared to some to be poised to emerge as the new Asian hegemon, exercising the greatest influence over (if not posing the greatest threat to) security in the region.[6] In terms of nuclear weapons policies, the impact of the end of the Cold War on China has been somewhat the opposite of this. Consistent with the increasing salience of regional over global considerations, China no longer views its nuclear weapons as a means of independence from the Cold War superpower competition, but sees them as an instrument of foreign and security policies focused on the country's immediate region.[7]

At the top of the list of China's security concerns is protection of its claims to sovereignty over Taiwan. Many in Beijing believe that only Chinese threats to respond with force deter an overt declaration of independence by Taiwan. Although the 1972 US–China Shanghai Communiqué formally recognized China's sovereignty over Taiwan, the 1979 Taiwan Relations Act pledges US "defensive" support of the island to ensure that "the future of Taiwan will be determined by peaceful means".[8] This US commitment, although deliberately ambiguous, raises the prospect of direct US–China conflict over Taiwan. That prospect has a clear strategic dimension: China possesses a small arsenal of intercontinental ballistic missiles (ICBMs) capable of carrying nuclear weapons to targets in the continental United States, and it has undertaken a strategic modernization programme to improve the size, accuracy and survivability of these forces.[9]

Because China's ICBM forces will remain smaller and less capable than US forces for the foreseeable future, US analysts see little prospect that China would initiate a nuclear conflict.[10] However, China's capacity to *threaten* such an attack poses a politically meaningful coercive instrument: in the event of a conflict over Taiwan, US war planners would have to factor a possible Chinese nuclear attack into their decision-making. Deterring (or at least moderating) any US intervention in a

Taiwan conflict is now the principal function of China's strategic forces – evincing the primacy of local over global considerations in China's strategic policies. This same regional primacy also drives China's concerns over other US strategic plans, particularly missile defence and the potential weaponization of space, because these are the elements most imperilling China's nuclear threats relative to Taiwan.[11]

In the aftermath of the 11 September 2001 attacks, tensions between the United States and China over Taiwan, missile defence and nuclear threats became muted as China moved from "strategic competitor" to anti-terrorism "partner" in the Bush administration's eyes. But, as the impact of 9/11 slowly recedes, concern over the threat of a "rising China" has begun to re-emerge in Washington. Over the long run, ongoing interactions over Taiwan and the Korean peninsula are most likely to orient US–China strategic relations.[12] Success in moderating nuclear weapons proliferation on the Korean peninsula and in building a US–China relationship sturdy enough to manage the volatile issues surrounding Taiwan could help reduce reliance on nuclear threats in the region by both countries.

North Korean nuclear policy

Throughout the Cold War, North Korea's ruling regime saw itself directly threatened by US nuclear forces, particularly those deployed in and near South Korea. Pyongyang met that threat through its own economic and military power and the support of both China and the Soviet Union. By the end of the Cold War, however, both these pillars had collapsed: support from the dissolved Soviet Union evaporated, China was liberalizing its economy and had opened burgeoning trade relations with South Korea, and North Korea's own economy had disintegrated into energy and famine crises.

This is the context in which North Korea began pursuing an independent nuclear capability. Although nuclear research may have begun in the 1950s, a dedicated nuclear weapons programme appears to have begun in the mid-1980s with construction of the research reactor and plutonium reprocessing facilities at Yongbyon. North Korea joined the NPT in 1985 but did not reach a Safeguards Agreement with the International Atomic Energy Agency (IAEA) until 1992, at which time the country was already suspected of having extracted enough nuclear material from the reactor to fabricate at least one explosive device.[13] From this point on, North Korea's regional relationships have evolved against the backdrop of its potential possession of nuclear weapons.

Ensuing IAEA inspections soon produced evidence of North Korean reprocessing activities, escalating to a full confrontation resolved only by direct US intervention. The 1994 US–North Korea Agreed Framework froze North Korea's plutonium-based nuclear programme, but left the spent plutonium stockpile in the country pending construction of two new nuclear reactors – allowing North Korea to retain the threat to resume its nuclear programme on relatively short notice. This circumstance provided the Pyongyang government with a latent nuclear threat that it utilized to considerable effect for the next decade. Uncertainties over whether North Korea had already weaponized the material extracted earlier did not impinge on its ability to use its latent nuclear capability coercively.

The 1994 agreement unravelled following US charges in October 2002 that North Korea was developing a second nuclear weapons programme based on uranium enrichment. By the end of 2002 North Korea had expelled IAEA inspectors from Yongbyon, removed seals and monitoring equipment from its safeguarded nuclear facilities, and prepared to resume reprocessing of the spent nuclear fuel. Early the following year the IAEA referred North Korean "chronic noncompliance" with its Safeguards Agreements to the UN Security Council.[14]

In 2003 the United States reportedly detected evidence that reprocessing of the spent fuel stockpile was under way in multiple hidden locations, and by 2004 it estimated that North Korea had "at least eight" functional nuclear devices.[15] Pyongyang's own claims to its capabilities escalated steadily, culminating in early 2005 with the first explicit declaration that the regime possessed nuclear weapons.[16] With both its plutonium and uranium programmes unfettered, North Korea may eventually be able to produce between 29 and 56 weapons per year, yielding between 120 and 250 nuclear weapons by the end of the decade.[17]

North Korea with a growing nuclear arsenal heightens regional insecurities and uncertainties, threatens the integrity and sustainability of the NPT regime, and creates new potential for fissile material proliferation. US policies under the Bush administration's first term – trading prior US engagement for contempt and lack of interest, and planning vigorous expansion of US nuclear capabilities and policies clearly aimed at North Korea – have only fuelled Pyongyang's nuclear ambition while offering little alternative to confrontation.[18] In its second term, the Bush administration has moderated its posture toward North Korea, and the Six-Party Talks agreement on 19 September 2005 offered grounds for limited optimism; however, a full resolution of the confrontation will still be long and hard in coming.[19]

North Korea's behaviour well illustrates how nuclear threat-making links nuclear capabilities to prevailing political conditions. In the short run, the number of functioning nuclear warheads Pyongyang actually has at hand is secondary – the prospect of its nuclear armament alone is enough to garner the regime useful coercive leverage. Indeed, from this point of view, threatening to test a device is more valuable to the regime's purposes than actually doing so.

To be sure, Pyongyang's motivations for relying on nuclear threats probably include preserving the regime's domestic authority as well as protecting territorial sovereignty. Nevertheless, spending decades subject to US nuclear threats has clearly instructed the regime on the potency of that instrument. If in Pyongyang's eyes its nuclear motivations are domestic as well as regional, so they are also for North Korea's neighbours: amelioration of conditions within North Korea (with or without the cooperation of the current leadership) is an essential component of the improvement of the regional security environment upon which reducing reliance on nuclear threats in East Asia relies. A comprehensive negotiated settlement, addressing North Korea's nuclear capabilities but aimed at a general resolution of energy, economic and political conditions on the Korean peninsula, is thus also a precondition for moving from the immediate challenges posed by North Korea's proliferation activities to a more encompassing agenda of eliminating the role of nuclear weapons threats in East Asia comprehensively.

Japanese nuclear policy

Although Japan does not possess nuclear weapons, the country's security policies rely fundamentally on nuclear weapons threats. This reliance takes two forms: acceptance of the role of US nuclear threats in deterring attacks on Japan, and the coercive resource flowing from Japan's latent capacity to develop nuclear weapons of its own.

US policy threatening potential nuclear responses to attacks on Japan – the "nuclear umbrella" – has constituted the central pillar of the relationship between the United States and Japan since the end of World War II. During the Cold War this nuclear guarantee was mainly aimed at deterring both attacks on and coercion of Japan by the Soviet Union. Over this period, Japanese governments' embrace of the nuclear umbrella was often far more fulsome than commonly realized.[20]

The end of the Cold War and the subsequent US decision to remove all nuclear weapons from surface naval vessels and overseas deployments reduced US nuclear force presence around Japan and eliminated tensions over the US naval presence in Japanese ports. However, reliance on nuclear deterrence in the US–Japan security relationship remained as deep as ever, focused now more proximately on North Korea. Deepening US–Japan military collaboration, including expanding the range of Japanese activities under joint auspices and Japanese participation in US-sponsored missile defence research and planning, has been viewed by defence planners in both countries as underscoring mutual alliance commitment, including bolstering the credibility of extended US nuclear deterrence guarantees.[21]

The second form of Japan's reliance on nuclear weapons threats is the coercive resource flowing from Japan's latent capacity to develop nuclear weapons of its own. Japan sustains a peaceful nuclear power programme that generates enriched plutonium, a space launch capability and the technical expertise to reorient these activities into a sophisticated nuclear weapons development effort if it chose to do so.[22] Over time, a small submarine-based intercontinental nuclear missile force, providing Japan with a secure second-strike capability and making it a nuclear peer of China and Russia, is likely within Japan's technical and financial capabilities.

The prospect of North Korea gaining overt nuclear weapons capability fuels speculation that Japan would develop nuclear weapons in response.[23] Few Japanese leaders openly favour development of nuclear weapons, which lacks a compelling strategic logic[24] and directly contradicts widespread Japanese public commitment to the country's non-nuclear status.[25] Nevertheless, Japan could do more demonstrably to limit its capacity to develop nuclear weapons one day, by both limiting its material potential and more aggressively pushing to de-nuclearize the region.[26] Japan refrains from taking these steps, in part, because they would entail surrendering the coercive capacity provided by Japan's latent threat to gain nuclear arms.

The spectre of a nuclear-armed Japan fuels longstanding concern among Japan's neighbours over reawakened Japanese militarism and regional ambitions. US and Japanese policy makers justify maintaining the US "nuclear umbrella" and deepening joint defence ties as serving regional interests by supplanting the need for Japan to develop nuclear capabilities of its own. Japan's latent nuclear threat helps Japan mollify its neighbours over the expanding of both Japanese and US forward presence in the region, such as envisioned in the 1997 revisions of the US–Japan guidelines for security cooperation.[27] This leverage also helps Japan keep US policy makers attentive to Japan's regional security concerns, such as developments in Korea.

Japan is unlikely to pursue nuclear weapons anytime soon. Although Japan would perceive North Korea's development of an overt nuclear weapons capability (or the emergence of a nuclear-armed unified Korea) as specifically threatening, confidence in US security guarantees is probably the crucial tipping point among many Japanese defence planners. So long as that confidence endures, many Japanese strategists will quietly appreciate that Japan's threat to go nuclear is far more useful in current regional relations than would be actually going nuclear. Unfortunately,

Japan's reliance on both this latent threat and the US nuclear umbrella obstructs the reduction of the role of nuclear weapons threats in the region and the development of viable non-nuclear cooperative security mechanisms.

South Korean nuclear policy

For South Korea, as for Japan, extended US nuclear deterrence has been a vital component of national security policy, and in the Cold War represented an allied response to overarching threats. Unlike with Japan, extended deterrence in South Korea also applied to the specific local threat of North Korean aggression. But, in the aftermath of South Korean President Kim Dae-jung's "Sunshine Policy", North–South relations have warmed considerably. Only a minority now view the North as a principal threat, whereas views of the United States are increasingly ambivalent.[28]

The South Korean public also do not share the popular aversion to national nuclear capability found in Japan: a poll in 2004 showed 51 per cent of the South Korean public supporting the acquisition of nuclear weapons.[29] Some South Koreans envision eventually "inheriting" North Korean nuclear capabilities, enabling a newly unified Korea to "balance" China and Japan and provide for its security without reliance on the United States.[30] Public opposition, a key factor restraining Japan from developing nuclear weapons, seems absent in South Korea.

Reflecting these sentiments, South Korean leaders have previously contemplated acquiring nuclear weapons. In the 1960s and 1970s, perceptions of waning US commitment to South Korea's defence helped motivate several attempts to develop a nuclear weapons programme, which were ultimately thwarted largely by intensive US pressure.[31] Some officials in South Korea's nuclear establishment continued to aspire to plutonium reprocessing capability, ostensibly in order to "close the fuel cycle", but resenting discriminatory US treatment allowing Japan but not South Korea to possess reprocessed plutonium.[32]

These lingering issues were rekindled with South Korea's twin revelations in September 2004 that technicians affiliated with the Korea Atomic Energy Research Institute (KAERI) undertook uranium enrichment activities on two separate occasions, in 1979–1981 and 2000, and also separated a small amount of plutonium in 1982. KAERI's suppression of this information prevented the Ministry of Science and Technology (MOST) from reporting these activities to the IAEA, putting South Korea in violation of its IAEA Safeguards Agreements.

In the 2000 incident, KAERI researchers enriched 0.2 grams of uranium to an average of 10.2 per cent concentration of U-235. The 1979–

1981 experiments enriched 700 grams of uranium to an average of 0.72 per cent concentration of U-235. KAERI hid these activities until it realized that South Korea's ratification of the IAEA Additional Protocol in February 2004 would expose the experiments.[33]

The plutonium separation activity is more disturbing insofar as current information reveals more deliberate KAERI subterfuge and a measure of US culpability. In 1981, KAERI technicians irradiated a fuel assembly containing 2.5 kg of depleted uranium, and then in 1982 separated approximately 40 mg of plutonium from the fission products. However, South Korea reported to the IAEA that this fuel assembly remained in the reactor and subsequently became part of a "measured discard", explicitly misleading the IAEA about its nuclear activities (rather than simply failing to disclose them). The United States, tracking these activities closely and therefore aware of the reprocessing, also did not disclose this information to the IAEA. Ironically, South Korea's NPT obligations did not restrict this activity; only its failure to report it constitutes a violation.[34]

These reported activities fell far short of providing South Korea with a latent nuclear weapons capability and do not seem to indicate a South Korean government desire to develop nuclear weapons, but they are troubling for several reasons. One is the absence of South Korean public concern: more than two-thirds appear not to have been alarmed by KAERI's surreptitious nuclear activities, some apparently viewing them as justifiable "balancing" of North Korea's nuclear ambitions.[35] Second is the apparent deficiency of civil regulation of South Korea's nuclear facilities; MOST officials may have known informally about at least some of the KAERI activities, suggesting a wider tolerance for bending the rules that would also reflect public attitudes. Thirdly, revelation of the concealed experiments opened South Korea (and to an extent the United States) to charges of hypocrisy in challenging North Korea's violations of its IAEA Safeguards obligations – although far less egregious than North Korea's behaviour, South Korea's deceptions were similar enough in principle to carry symbolic weight.

The South Korean revelations do offer hope that the improved IAEA inspection system will be effective. But this optimism must be tempered. No inspection regimen can be 100 per cent effective against wilful deception. Moreover, the very success of the new system may increase the reluctance of other states to embrace it too fulsomely.

The South Korea experience indicates again that materials control treats only the "supply" side of nuclear proliferation. Quelling "demand" – that is, instilling a desire to abide by commitments – requires easing regional political tensions to undermine the utility of the nuclear threat-making capacities that nuclear capabilities enable.

Taiwan's nuclear policy

Taiwan's interest in nuclear explosives dates at least to the 1950s, and it has undertaken several covert nuclear weapons programmes. Soon after Taiwan began operating a plutonium-producing research reactor in 1973, the US Central Intelligence Agency concluded that Taiwan might develop a nuclear weapon within five years. IAEA inspectors in early 1976 discovered that fuel rods containing about 500 grams of plutonium could not be located, sparking concern that Taiwan might have secretly reprocessed them. Further suspicious discoveries elicited strong US pressure, leading eventually to Taiwan's shutting down the research reactor; however, the status of the diverted materials was never resolved. Concerns re-emerged in the late 1980s when Taiwan began building a new reprocessing facility; again, US pressure led eventually to its dismantling and no plutonium separation is thought to have taken place.[36]

US intervention has been instrumental in restraining Taiwan's nuclear ambitions owing both to Taiwan's dependence on US security guarantees and to Taiwan's unique status under the Nuclear Non-Proliferation Treaty. Taiwan signed the NPT in 1968; however, United Nations recognition of the People's Republic as the sole representative of China in 1971 led to Taiwan's expulsion from the IAEA. The United States and the IAEA subsequently agreed informally to continue an existing trilateral arrangement for maintaining NPT-type safeguards on Taiwan's nuclear materials and facilities.

Taiwan today seems to have no active plans to develop nuclear weapons and has implemented the IAEA's newer safeguards. However, how quickly Taiwan could build nuclear weapons if it chose to is unknown. Most estimates of the amount of plutonium Taiwan reprocessed fall far short of the quantity needed for a nuclear weapon, but this work is likely to have yielded important knowledge; Taiwan probably possesses the technological expertise to develop nuclear weapons if it were able to obtain the requisite fissile materials. As in Japan, some Taiwanese strategists believe Taiwan's security vis-à-vis China benefits from the perception that Taiwan could quickly develop effective nuclear strike capabilities should the need arise. Unlike with Japan, however, US interests vis-à-vis China are less served by Taiwan wielding this latent threat, helping to explain lesser US tolerance for Taiwanese nuclear ambitions.

As with Japan, US security support reduces Taiwan's incentives for nuclear acquisition. Since the 1979 adoption of the Taiwan Relations Act, US policy has entailed a crafted ambiguity concerning US intentions actively to aid Taiwan in the event of an outbreak of hostilities with China, which is aimed at discouraging both sides from precipitous action.[37] Taiwan's resumption of nuclear weapons ambitions would likely

lead at least to curtailed US assistance to Taiwan's nuclear power programme and perhaps to retraction of US security support, while simultaneously disrupting Taiwan's regional economic relations, undermining its
efforts to enhance its political legitimacy and inviting a Chinese pre-
emptive strike to prevent nuclear acquisition.

For this reason (and unlike with Japan and South Korea), too much
US support, as well as too little, might induce Taiwan to revive a nuclear
weapons programme by reducing the disincentives for Taiwan to establish more independence from China generally. For example, President
Bush's indications of more overt US commitment to defend Taiwan –
criticized for increasing the dangers of conflict[38] – have dovetailed with
renewed interest in Taiwan in developing an "offensive capability" aiming to "deter" a Chinese attack on the island by posing "credible threats
to China's urban population or high-value targets".[39] If such a strategy,
albeit conventionally based, increased the prospects of Chinese pre-
emptive attack, reliance on it could then induce Taiwan to develop a retaliatory nuclear threat rather than retreat from the policy.

Skilful US–China management of their relationship could pull back the
nuclear shadow over the Taiwan Strait, as was noted earlier. Taiwan's security posture, with its latent nuclear ambitions, adds a volatile complica-
tion to this imperative.

Conclusion: Proliferation and non-proliferation in East Asia

In East Asia today, the United States, China and now North Korea rely
in key ways on explicit nuclear threats. Japan, South Korea and Taiwan
may now all be "virtual" nuclear-weapon states able to cross the line and
make nuclear arms more quickly than the international community could
effectively respond.[40] Such nuclear threat usage offers an "equalizer"
with unique application in the more autonomous multipolarity of the
post–Cold War region, offering redress of conventional weaknesses with
fewer complications than the alternative of costly alliances.

Nuclear threat reliance in this setting also creates the potential for an
explosive nuclear arms race. Any erosion of the several relatively improved regional relationships (such as between China and South Korea)
could incite rapid escalations in nuclear acquisitions. Thus, the creation
of durable cooperative security structures in the region, desirable in its
own right, is also vital to reducing nuclear threat reliance and dampening
proliferation incentives.

Developments in East Asia also interact with circumstances elsewhere.
The US-led attack on Iraq appears to have fuelled Pyongyang's nuclear
ambitions by challenging its confidence that its conventional threat

against South Korea alone would deter a US attack.[41] North Korea's own proliferation activities have exacerbated proliferation threats elsewhere in the world and challenge the durability of the NPT regime overall.

Reflecting such global impacts, the UN Secretary-General's office has identified nuclear proliferation as a paramount global security danger and called for both renewed commitment to disarmament by the world's nuclear-armed states and new efforts to prevent nuclear proliferation to new states or terrorist groups.[42] But this trade-off, the foundation of the NPT, has become increasingly strained, as evinced by the deadlock of the 2005 NPT Review Conference and the failure of the 2005 United Nations World Summit even to address the issue of nuclear proliferation.[43]

Pressing *all* states, nuclear-armed or not, to reduce reliance on nuclear threats in their security postures offers opportunities to circumvent this paralysis by highlighting a non-discriminatory nuclear disarmament obligation. Moreover, the post–Cold War disaggregation of world security relations creates the potential for progress towards reducing nuclear threat reliance in separate regions independently. Thus, fostering durable non-nuclear collective security mechanisms in East Asia would also be a vital contribution to non-proliferation efforts throughout the world.

Notes

1. Note that terming Taiwan a "government" capable of pursuing independent nuclear policies conveys no judgement of its sovereignty status.
2. Policy makers often defended these nuclear policies strictly in terms of bolstering deterrence; see, e.g., Casper W. Weinberger, "A Rational Approach to Nuclear Disarmament", *Defense* (August 1982).
3. The NPR was first publicly summarized at a Department of Defense briefing on 9 January 2002. The classified review was subsequently obtained by the *Los Angeles Times* and the *New York Times*. Substantial excerpts of the review are available at ⟨http://www.globalsecurity.org/wmd/library/policy/dod/npr.htm⟩.
4. For an expansion of this assessment, see Wade L. Huntley, "Threats All the Way Down: U.S. Strategic Initiatives in a Unipolar World", *Review of International Studies*, Vol. 32, No. 1 (January 2006), pp. 49–67.
5. See, e.g., Jeffrey Record, "Bounding the Global War on Terrorism", US Army War College, December 2003, pp. 29–32, ⟨http://www.carlisle.army.mil/ssi/pubs/2003/bounding/bounding.htm⟩.
6. For an early representative example, see Denny Roy, "Hegemon on the Horizon? China's Threat to East Asian Security", *International Security*, Vol. 19, No. 1 (Summer 1994).
7. For a good discussion of Chinese strategic policy, see Alistair Iain Johnston, "China's New 'Old Thinking': The Concept of Limited Deterrence", *International Security*, Vol. 20, No. 3 (Winter 1995–1996).
8. *Taiwan Relations Act*, US Public Law 96-8, 96th Congress, 1st session (10 April 1979).

9. The United States considers China to have "about 20" deployed single-warhead silo-based ICBMs; estimates for 2015 range "from about 75 to 100 warheads deployed primarily against the United States". The current modernization includes development of mobile, solid-fuelled ICBMs and possibly multiple independently targetable warheads. See National Intelligence Council, "Foreign Missile Developments and the Ballistic Missile Threat Through 2015", December 2001, ⟨http://www.cia.gov/nic/pubs/other _products/Unclassifiedballisticmissilefinal.htm⟩ or ⟨http://www.fas.org/irp/nic/bmthreat-2015.htm⟩.

10. Department of Defense, *Annual Report on the Military Power of the People's Republic of China*, Pursuant to the FY2000 National Defense Authorization Act, June 2000, available at ⟨http://www.defenselink.mil/news/Jun2000/china06222000.htm⟩.

11. For an expansion of this analysis, see Wade L. Huntley, "Missile Defense: More May Be Better – for China", *Nonproliferation Review*, Vol. 9, No. 2 (Summer 2002).

12. On China's evolving regional and global roles, see Evan S. Medeiros and M. Taylor Fravel, "China's New Diplomacy", *Foreign Affairs*, Vol. 82, No. 6 (November–December 2003).

13. Joseph Cirincione, Jon Wolfsthal and Miriam Rajkumar, *Deadly Arsenals* (Washington, DC: Carnegie Endowment for International Peace, 2002), pp. 243–244.

14. IAEA Director General Mohamed ElBaradei, "Introductory Statement to the Board of Governors", Highlights of IAEA Press Briefing, Vienna, 12 February 2003, ⟨http:// www.iaea.org/worldatom/Press/Statements/2003/ebsp2003n004.shtml⟩. In the context of the impending US-led attack on Iraq, the IAEA simultaneously reported that in Iraq it had been able to maintain its accounting of safeguarded nuclear materials even during the 1998–2002 suspension of inspections and had found no evidence of a revived nuclear programme during resumed inspections in the preceding months.

15. David E. Sanger and Thom Shanker, "North Korea Hides New Nuclear Site, Evidence Suggests", *New York Times*, 20 July 2003; "N. Korea Nuclear Estimate to Rise", *Washington Post*, 28 April 2004, p. A01.

16. James Brooke and David E. Sanger, "North Koreans Say They Hold Nuclear Arms", *New York Times*, 11 February 2005.

17. Jon B. Wolfsthal, "Estimates of North Korea's Unchecked Nuclear Weapons Production Potential", Carnegie Non-Proliferation Project, *Proliferation News*, 29 July 2003, ⟨http://www.ceip.org/files/projects/npp⟩.

18. For an elaboration of these points, see Wade L. Huntley, "Ostrich Engagement: The Bush Administration and the North Korea Nuclear Crisis", *Nonproliferation Review*, Vol. 11, No. 2 (Summer 2004).

19. See Wade L. Huntley, "Waiting to Exhale: The Six-Party Talks Agreement", *Foreign Policy in Focus*, 25 October 2005, ⟨http://www.fpif.org/fpiftxt/2903⟩.

20. See Hans M. Kristensen, "Japan under the Nuclear Umbrella: U.S. Nuclear Weapons and Nuclear War Planning in Japan during the Cold War", Nautilus Institute, July 1999, ⟨http://www.nautilus.org/library/security/papers/Japan.pdf⟩.

21. For a discussion, see U. Tetsuya, "Missile Defense and Extended Deterrence in the Japan-US Alliance", *Korean Journal of Defense Analysis*, Vol. 12, No. 2 (Winter 2000), pp. 135–152; Patrick M. Cronin et al., "The Alliance Implications of Theater Missile Defense", in Michael J. Green and Patrick M. Cronin, eds, *The US–Japan Alliance: Past, Present, and Future* (New York: Council on Foreign Relations, 1999).

22. For contrasting views on this potential, see Selig S. Harrison, ed., *Japan's Nuclear Future: The Plutonium Debate and East Asian Security* (Washington, DC: Carnegie Endowment for International Peace, 1996); see also Shaun Burnie and Aileen Mioko Smith, "Japan's Nuclear Twilight Zone", *Bulletin of the Atomic Scientists*, Vol. 57, No. 3 (May–June 2001), pp. 58–62, and Eiichi Katahara, "Japan's Plutonium Policy:

Consequences for Nonproliferation", *Nonproliferation Review*, Vol. 5, No. 1 (Fall 1997).

23. Marc Erikson, "Japan Could 'Go Nuclear' in Months", *Asia Times Online*, 13 January 2003. Some representative examples in Japanese language media include: Kazuyasu Akashi, "Japan Is Okay to Arm with Nuclear Weapons", *World Affairs Weekly*, 4 February 2003; Shintaro Ishihara and Kazuya Fukuda, "Conversation", *Shokun*, 1 February 2003; Yoshiko Sakurai, Tadae Takubo and Nagao Hyodo, "We Have an Option for Nuclear Weapons", *Shokun*, 1 January 2003.

24. For a good concise discussion of why Japan is unlikely to go nuclear, see Matake Kamiya, "Nuclear Japan: Oxymoron or Coming Soon?", *Washington Quarterly*, Vol. 26, No. 1 (Winter 2003), pp. 63–75.

25. Analyses of Japanese domestic conditions include P. Katzenstein and N. Okawara, "Japan's National Security: Structures, Norms, and Policies", *International Security*, Vol. 17, No. 4 (Spring 1993), and T. Berger, "From Sword to Chrysanthemum: Japan's Culture of Anti-Militarism", *International Security*, Vol. 17, No. 4 (Spring 1993).

26. For one such conception, see A. DiFilippo, "Can Japan Craft an International Nuclear Disarmament Policy?", *Asian Survey*, Vol. 40, No. 4 (July–August 2000), pp. 571–598.

27. T. Akaha, "Beyond Self-Defense: Japan's Elusive Security Role under the New Guidelines for US–Japan Defense Cooperation", *Pacific Review*, Vol. 11, No. 4 (1998), pp. 461–483.

28. See "Korea Backgrounder: How the South Views Its Brother from Another Planet", International Crisis Group Asia Report No. 89, Seoul/Brussels, 14 December 2004.

29. Chicago Council on Foreign Relations, "US–Korean Comparative Report", *Global Views 2004*, 30 September 2004, ⟨http://www.ccfr.org/globalviews2004/sub/news _korrelease.htm⟩.

30. See "New Nuclear Powers in Asia", CEIP Non-Proliferation Conference, 14 November 2002, ⟨http://www.ceip.org/files/projects/npp/resources/conference2002/ newnuclearpowersinasia.htm⟩.

31. Peter Hayes, *Pacific Powderkeg: American Nuclear Dilemmas in Korea* (Lanham, MD: Lexington Books, 1991).

32. Jungmin Kang et al., "South Korea's Nuclear Surprise", *Bulletin of the Atomic Scientists*, Vol. 61, No. 1 (January–February 2005), pp. 40–41.

33. Ibid., pp. 43–46; Jungmin Kang, Tatsujiro Suzuki and Peter Hayes, "South Korea's Nuclear Mis-Adventures", Nautilus Special Report, 10 September 2004, ⟨http://www. nautilus.org/archives/pub/ftp/napsnet/special_reports/0435-ROK.html⟩.

34. Kang et al., "South Korea's Nuclear Surprise", pp. 46–47; this report speculates that MOST probably also knew about the plutonium reprocessing activities from the outset. See also Jungmin Kang, "South Korea's Past Nuclear-Material Experiments", paper presented at the Conference on Moving beyond Missile Defense, Hiroshima, Japan, 8–11 October 2004.

35. Kang et al., "South Korea's Nuclear Mis-Adventures".

36. For a good description of the history of Taiwan's nuclear weapons acquisition efforts, see David Albright and Corey Gay, "Taiwan: Nuclear Nightmare Averted", *Bulletin of the Atomic Scientists*, Vol. 54, No. 1 (January–February 1998).

37. For a more extensive treatment of US–China strategic relations with respect to Taiwan, see Huntley, "Missile Defense: More May be Better – for China".

38. See Michael D. Swaine, "Trouble in Taiwan", *Foreign Affairs*, Vol. 83, No. 2 (March–April 2004).

39. David M. Lampton, "Is Taiwan Acquiring an Offensive Capability?", *The National Interest*, Vol. 3, No. 30 (28 July 2004).

40. William J. Broad, "Plowshare or Sword?", *New York Times*, 25 May 2004.

41. Howard W. French, "North Korea Says Its Arms Will Deter U.S. Attack", *New York Times*, 7 April 2003, p. 13.
42. *A More Secure World: Our Shared Responsibility. Report of the High-level Panel on Threats, Challenges and Change* (New York: United Nations, 2004), pp. 39–47; *In Larger Freedom: Towards Development, Security and Human Rights for All. Report of the Secretary-General*, UN Doc. A/59/2005, 21 March 2005, pp. 28–29.
43. See Kofi A. Annan, "A Glass at Least Half Full", *Wall Street Journal*, 19 September 2005.

10

Non-proliferation after 9/11 and beyond: A Japanese perspective

Heigo Sato

Introduction

The terrorist attack of 11 September 2001 refocused a global concern about the risks of a connection between international terrorist networks and the proliferation of weapons of mass destruction (WMD). The threat was recognized long before the dreadful attack, but it was re-confirmed when the international community was faced with covert nuclear development by Iraq and North Korea. Coupled with concern that international terrorist groups might use WMD for terrorist attacks, non-proliferation was put centre-stage in global security.[1]

However, the current non-proliferation policy is faced with three problems. First, as is apparent in the case of Iraq and North Korea, the peaceful use of nuclear energy, as assumed in Article IV of the Treaty on the Non-Proliferation of Nuclear Weapons (NPT), is not a menu for giving up the military development of nuclear energy but a menu of choice for those who aspire to nuclear development. Second, a regime-based non-proliferation strategy is insufficient to deal with non-state actors, including terrorist groups and the nuclear black market. Third, the political complexity surrounding NPT violators may limit the option to use coercive measures by the countries concerned. The Iraq war revealed the divisions within the existing non-proliferation scheme.

Despite these problems, a global focus on non-proliferation provided both an opportunity and a challenge to Japan's security policy. On the positive side, it allowed Japan to exercise political leadership, especially in the Asia-Pacific, to persuade countries in the region to comply with the global effort on non-proliferation. Japan justified its growing activism on the international scene by arguing that it had "international responsibility" for the peace and stability of the existing global order. Domestically, Japan emphasized its status as a major beneficiary of the current international system. The Japanese government has repeatedly emphasized the importance of the international non-proliferation regimes and of global cooperation and collaboration on non-proliferation.

The key challenges to the global effort on non-proliferation came from the basic framework on which Japan depends for its political legitimacy. Particularly when faced with the putative North Korean nuclear development and North Korea's declaration of withdrawal from the NPT, Japan as well as the rest of the world faced the reality that the existing non-proliferation regime alone cannot prevent a determined country from acquiring weapons of mass destruction. Furthermore, as the focus of proliferation issues moves from latent and first-tier proliferation to second-tier proliferation and beyond, as explained by Braun and Chyba,[2] the networks of proliferation must be addressed with new sets of measures that would prevent and detect, or even destroy, such networks.

These complex features of proliferation required multiple measures, including strengthening the non-proliferation regime, enforcing strict export control mechanisms domestically, promoting coercive measures to prevent proliferation, and exercising the military option to remove "rogue" regimes.[3] Some of these measures were traditional and already enforced, but some measures were completely new and required existing international law and rules to be redefined. The Iraq war, in particular, provoked a debate within the international community about the role of the United Nations and the desirability of the United States' unilateralist security policy.

As a faithful adherent of international norms and rules and an ally of the United States, Japan faced the question of how to reconcile both positions in cooperating with the global effort to prevent a proliferation of WMD and related materials. Indeed, the North Korean threat made the Japanese position unambiguous, but Japan still went on with a debate domestically to answer this question. By following the development of Japan's non-proliferation policy after 9/11, this chapter explains an impact of the Iraq war and its aftermath on its nuclear non-proliferation policy.

Continuity and discontinuity in Japan's non-proliferation policy

Policy framework

Japan is a signatory of the major non-proliferation regimes. It has been an NPT signatory since 1970 (the NPT was ratified in 1976), is subject to a Safeguards Agreement with the International Atomic Energy Agency (IAEA) and became a signatory to the IAEA Additional Protocol in December 1998 (and ratified it in December 1999).[4] Japan is also a signatory of the Comprehensive Nuclear-Test-Ban Treaty (CTBT), which was ratified in 1997. A brief outline of Japan's active participation in and contribution to the various non-proliferation regimes serves to affirm its commitment to global non-proliferation efforts.[5] Compliance with the non-proliferation regimes and their norms and terms is a core objective of Japan's arms control and disarmament diplomacy.[6] Japan's commitment supports its position as a strong advocate of those global norms. Japan believes that its position is further reinforced by its domestic arrangements, such as the Three Non-Nuclear Principles, and its policy of denial towards the arms trade.

Japan reconfirmed the significance of non-proliferation after 9/11, and the succeeding war on terror and the North Korean nuclear showdown reinforced its conviction that the world would be better off if universal compliance with the existing non-proliferation regimes were accomplished. The Japanese prime ministers and other political leaders have repeatedly emphasized the value of non-proliferation regimes on various occasions, both before and after 9/11. For example, at the UN General Assembly in 21 September 1998, Prime Minister Keizo Obuchi stated, "the existing format certainly is not perfect, but there is no feasible, realistic alternative if we are to ensure stability in our international community". He proposed five points for further promoting non-proliferation: the nuclear non-proliferation regime should become more universal; strict export controls should be placed on equipment, materials and technologies that relate to nuclear weapons and missiles in order to complement the NPT and ensure nuclear non-proliferation; any further nuclear testing should be prevented (by encouraging universal support for the CTBT); nuclear disarmament should be further promoted by nuclear-weapon states sincerely implementing their obligations under the NPT; each nation should reach an early conclusion on a fissile material cut-off treaty.[7]

Four years later, in September 2002, Prime Minister Koizumi stated at the UN General Assembly that four challenges were facing the international community: the fight against terrorism; the consolidation of peace and nation-building; the simultaneous achievement of environmental protection and development; and nuclear disarmament. As regards the fourth challenge, Prime Minister Koizumi stated:

I believe that Japan, as the only country in human history to have suffered nuclear devastation, has a significant role to play in nuclear disarmament and non-proliferation. Japan will continue its efforts to realize a peaceful and safe world, free of nuclear weapons, as early as possible. To that end, we will propose a draft resolution titled "A path to the total elimination of nuclear weapons" at this session of the General Assembly, and will redouble our efforts to achieve the early entry into force of the Comprehensive Nuclear-Test-Ban Treaty.[8]

In fact, although Japan's policy on non-proliferation was not affected by 9/11, it was closely linked with the introduction of a missile defence system. Japan valued a regime-based approach to non-proliferation, but was realistic about its limits and therefore sought defensive measures. In a joint statement issued on 30 June 2001, US President Bush and Prime Minister Koizumi of Japan announced that "recognizing the growing threat from the proliferation of weapons of mass destruction and ballistic missiles, the two leaders emphasized the need for a comprehensive strategy to address this threat, including a variety of defense systems and diplomatic initiatives, such as arms reductions", and "the President and the Prime Minister agreed that the two governments should continue to consult closely on missile defense, together with strengthened non-proliferation and counter-proliferation measures".[9] Japan was involved with joint technology development with the United States at that time, but did not make a decision to join the full ballistic missile defence system until 19 December 2003.[10]

The limits of the traditional regime-based approach to non-proliferation[11] were keenly felt when faced with the Iraq and North Korea cases. At a press conference on the issue of Iraq on 20 March 2003, Prime Minister Koizumi asked: "What would be the consequences were dangerous weapons of mass destruction to fall into the hands of a dangerous dictator?" He answered: "I believe that all people are now aware that we would all be facing grave danger", adding that "how to prevent this is a matter of concern to the entire world". Koizumi justified his support for the US and UK military operation in Iraq by criticizing Iraq, which "has unfortunately ignored, or has not taken seriously, or even ridiculed the United Nations resolutions. I do not believe that Iraq has acted with sufficient sincerity."[12] An interesting point in this speech is Koizumi's reasoning for supporting the US action. Although he emphasized the danger posed by the possession of WMD by "a dangerous dictator", he put most weight on Iraq's repeated ignoring of UN resolutions. This revealed Japan's concern about the deficiencies in the existing regime, and that the regime-based approach depends on the sincerity of political leaders, which is not always dependable.

Looking at the limitations of regime-based non-proliferation, there appear to be political and institutional elements. The first political limitation that Japan experienced was a conflict between political necessity and the application of the policy's principles. The norms and rules of non-proliferation and disarmament regimes are valid when universal application is sustained or the wider international community is working toward that end. This includes unilateral or coordinated sanctions against violators. Under this principle, Japan enforced sanctions against India and Pakistan after their nuclear tests in 1998. In October 2001, however, the Koizumi administration announced that Japan would terminate these sanctions. The Cabinet Secretary Yasuo Fukuda issued an announcement stating that "Japan highly values India and Pakistan's efforts to contribute to strengthening the international coalition against terrorism. It is vitally important that Pakistan remains stable and cooperative with the international society in this combat against terrorism." As for India, Japan's concerns were India's role in combating terrorism in South Asia. Regarding non-proliferation, the announcement said, "both India and Pakistan have been maintaining their moratoria on further nuclear tests for the past three years and declaring their intention to maintain it. Furthermore, both countries have stated that they will ensure strict controls of nuclear and missile related goods and technologies. To that extent, Japan's measures have obtained due achievement."[13]

The 1998 statement of economic sanctions against these two countries had demanded the termination of further nuclear tests and of nuclear development, as well as the unconditional signing and ratification of the NPT and the CTBT. Judging from the announcement made by Cabinet Secretary Fukuda in 2001, Japan clearly had not obtained what it demanded. Rather, Japan made a policy shift out of political necessity and justified it on the basis of future promises by these two countries. Japan introduced a new agenda into the bilateral relationship, which was to support India and Pakistan in the war on terror. The irony is that the policy principle had to compromise with political needs for the sake of keeping up with the United States on the war on terror.

The second political limitation of the "regime-based" approach for Japan is US policy towards non-proliferation. If we simplify the assumption behind Japan's non-proliferation policy, it is that there is no contradiction between support for the United States and for the international community. Thus, the United States represented the global public will and provided the de facto global standards on non-proliferation. This is the logic behind Prime Minister Koizumi's emphasis on the coexistence of the Japan–US alliance and cooperation with the international community.[14] On this basis, Japan was able to accept counter-proliferation and anti-proliferation measures conducted through military means, although they were not welcomed. However, another important element of Japan's foreign policy is to support an increasing and crucial role for the United Nations in global issues involving non-proliferation.[15] The emphasis on support for both the United States and the United Nations could be conflictual if one side implements a policy without due consideration of the interests of the other.

As the United States elaborated its comprehensive non-proliferation strategy, Japan was faced with a dilemma. In a speech at the National Defense University in February 2004, President Bush outlined a forward strategy on non-proliferation. Following this speech, John Bolton, US Under Secretary for Arms Control and International Security, explained the strategy in June at the American Enterprise Institute and said "the frontlines in our nonproliferation strategy must extend beyond the well-known rogue states to the trade routes and entities that are engaged in supplying the countries of greatest proliferation concern". He outlined a number of measures, including sanctions, interdiction and credible export controls, through which to disrupt procurement efforts. In his speech, Bolton valued the lessons of the Iraq war: the United States had "gained enormous, immensely valuable and even decisive credibility from our actions there" because "our intervention in Iraq has made this seminal message both possible and credible for the first time".[16]

The question of whether Japan should accept Bolton's reasoning on the value and lessons of the Iraq war is a tricky problem in terms of both global norms and Japanese domestic politics. According to the forward strategy on non-proliferation, a "regime-based" approach or utilization of the international legal architecture comprises a part of the US non-proliferation policy and is designed specifically to dissuade WMD aspirants and their diversion networks from pursuing WMD development. Therefore, if the doctrine of regime change through preventive attack provides some clue to the emerging non-proliferation challenge, should Japan welcome this approach and compromise its pacifist security policy with "effective" non-proliferation measures? In fact, faced with a warning from the North Korean regime that any move to impose economic sanctions on Pyongyang would be seen as a "declaration of war", it was clear to the Japanese government that it is a delicate decision even to make a formal condemnation of nuclear development and/or kidnapping cases.

Although acknowledging that the Iraq and Afghanistan campaigns have compromised Libya's nuclear ambitions, Japan strongly opposes the "war of choice" approach in dealing with North Korea. Therefore, Japan was in desperate need of international coordination and authorization to encircle North Korea politically to deal with the threat. Particularly after 9/11, Japan was an active promoter of an international consensus on non-proliferation in North-east Asia, which included sub-regional (the Six-Party Talks, the Trilateral Coordination and Oversight Group), regional (the ASEAN Regional Forum, Asia-Pacific Economic Cooperation, the Association of Southeast Asian Nations, ASEAN+3, etc.), and global (the G-8, the United Nations, etc.) mechanisms.

The irony of this approach is that its success depends on the degree to which the United States refrains from the unilateral solution after the Iraqi experience. The solution may involve military as well as diplomatic measures. For example, China, Japan and South Korea – three of the members of the Six-Party Talks – have been urging the United States to take a more "realistic" approach instead of its current insistence on complete disarmament before rewarding North Korea, but the United States has refused to do so because it would send the wrong message to Pyongyang.[17] The Japanese government will publicly support the United States' position, but is aware that the lack of flexibility may lead to a political impasse, which will give North Korea time to further develop its nuclear weapons programme.

Institutional architecture

On the institutional side, the limitations of the existing approach are felt on many fronts. On the high-enriched uranium (HEU) issue, President Bush made a statement on February 2004 that, under the NPT, "regimes are allowed to produce nuclear material that can be used to build bombs under the cover of civilian nuclear programs" and he proposed to close this treaty's "loophole".[18] In March 2004, the IAEA's Director General, Mohamed ElBaradei, told the agency's Board of Governors that "the wide dissemination of the most proliferation-sensitive parts of the nuclear fuel cycle – the production of new fuel, the processing of weapons-usable material, and the disposal of spent fuel and radioactive waste – could be the 'Achilles' heel' of the nuclear nonproliferation regime".[19]

The HEU issue represents one of the major problems facing the NPT regime. Under current mechanisms, the NPT cannot prevent ambitious states from making use of civil facilities for weapons development purposes because it allows peaceful nuclear development as a right for the non-nuclear states under the regime. Furthermore, it cannot punish states or non-state actors that illegally try to acquire nuclear weapons either. If an individual state or group of states is the only actor willing to punish or coerce nuclear aspirants to make them subject to international rules and norms, trust in the non-proliferation regime would soon evaporate. The doctrine of compliance makes its way to the heart of non-proliferation because, as John Bolton, Under Secretary of State, says: "we are determined to use every resource at our disposal – using diplomacy regularly, economic pressure when it makes a difference, active law enforcement when appropriate and military force when we must."[20]

A similar problem exists in export control. The uncovering of a nuclear smuggling ring headed by Pakistani scientist A. Q. Khan revealed the fragility of the measure itself. The fact that even tough domestic control does not guarantee the prevention of technology diversion to the smuggling network or terrorists was one of the contributing factors to Japan's introduction of the "catch-all" provision in the Foreign Exchange and Foreign Trade Law. Japan introduced the provision in April 2002. Following a recommendation by the project group organized by the Ministry of Economy, Trade and Industry (METI) in December 2001, METI amended the Foreign Exchange and Foreign Trade Law and introduced a licence requirement for the items listed in the Export Control Regulations Item 16 and the Foreign Exchange Regulations Item 16.[21]

The amendment featured a major change to Japan's export control mechanism after 9/11. The need for a "catch-all" provision was first proposed in the early 1990s and Ichita Yamamoto of the Liberal Democratic Party and Keiichiro Asao of the Democratic Party claimed in 1999 that it would be useful to punish North Korea.[22] However, Japan's introduction of the "catch-all" provision was late compared with the United States and the European Union, partly because the Ministry of International Trade and Industry (which became METI in 2001) was reluctant to impose an administrative burden on the export industry, and also because it had doubts about the utility of the "catch-all" mechanism. MITI had introduced the so-called "Know Regulations" under a supplementary export control initiative in the early 1990s.[23] However, owing to increased concern over the proliferation of WMD and related materials, the effectiveness of existing non-proliferation regimes and treaties became a major issue, and the enforcement of national export controls became a focus of domestic debate.[24] In an interim conclusion paper issued in December 2001 by the Security Trade Control Subcommittee of the Industrial Structure Advisory Committee, the nuclear development of Iraq and North Korea, missile proliferation, and possible chemical attack by international terrorist groups were listed as major concerns in terms of the proliferation of WMD and related materials.[25] This clearly shows that 9/11 contributed to the policy shift.

It is true that the success of export control is less visible and, if illegal transfers occur behind the scenes, there is no way to judge if the system is defective. The Myoshin case, in which the export of a condenser to North Korea was successfully prevented, showed the utility of the catch-all regulation.[26] However, the success and failure of export control are mostly determined behind the scenes. Furthermore, export control will never be effective if there is no universal enforcement. The four export control regimes have no legally binding measures and many developing countries are outside the regimes. It is often pointed out that the catch-all provision is only one of the solutions to the complicated export procedures.

To summarize the institutional limitations of the non-proliferation effort, the inability to distinguish legitimate and peaceful transfers of critical technologies from potentially destabilizing transfers, the lack of enforcement and compliance measures, and a less-than-universal non-proliferation regime have the potential to derail non-proliferation efforts.

These factors point to the necessary measures to meet future challenges. First, the reinforcement of non-proliferation norms is particularly significant. In this realm, the role of the United Nations is still the mainstay of global efforts, since the United Nations can provide an overarching agenda with a sense of legitimacy. UN Security Council Resolution 1540 (2004) affirmed that "proliferation of nuclear, chemical and biological weapons, as well as their means of delivery, constitutes a threat to international peace and security".[27] Together with repeated references to this resolution during the Iraqi debate from late 2002 to early 2004, it is undeniable that the authority of the United Nations is still large and significant. In this regard, Japan has consistently supported UN initiatives on non-proliferation.

However, the reinforcement of non-proliferation norms does not necessarily involve the accumulation of declarations or pledges and persuasion of non-compliant parties by member states. There need to be active and passive measures to reinforce non-proliferation. One of the active measures is the use of force. Supposedly backed by UN Resolution 1540, it may be true that the use of force against WMD aspirers is justifiable if those parties do not comply with requests from the international community. Although the UN member states must recognize their responsibility to deal with threats to international peace and security, the ways in which active measures are applied may vary depending on the issue area and the region.

In the case of Iraq, the US goal was non-proliferation as well as regime change in Iraq, whereas the United Nations was seeking Iraqi compliance with UN resolutions. Indeed, there were shared goals, but the United States put as much emphasis on the wider implications for the security order of the Middle East and the peace and security of the wider international community by demonstrating its will and power in this case. In the case of North Korea, on the other hand, given the complexities of the issues involved, the United States and the members of the Six-Party Talks are reluctant even to submit this case to the United Nations. It is interesting to compare the US reaction to these two cases, since North Korea had declared its possession of nuclear weapons on several occasions. Besides the trustworthiness of North Korea's declaration, it might be true that lessons in one particular case cannot be transferred to other cases where the nature of the threat and the regional dynamics may differ.

The passive measures on non-proliferation are equally significant. The most basic passive measure is reinforcement of the existing regime and treaty. In a working paper submitted to the Third Session of the Preparatory Committee for the 2005 Review Conference of the Parties to the NPT, Japan listed as important areas: nuclear disarmament; non-proliferation; peaceful uses of nuclear energy; universality and compliance; nuclear-weapon-free zones and negative security assurance; and strengthening dialogue with civil society and future generations. Particularly in the nuclear disarmament field, Japan stated that "nuclear-weapon States are urged to respond to such resolute determination on the part of non-nuclear-weapon States by demonstrating tangible progress towards nuclear disarmament". For Japan, the crucial issues in nuclear disarmament are: the early entry into force of the Comprehensive Nuclear-Test-Ban Treaty; negotiations on a fissile material cut-off treaty; a reduction in nuclear weapons by nuclear-weapon states; a reduction in non-strategic nuclear weapons; assistance for denuclearization in the former Soviet states; and regular report by States Parties on their efforts towards nuclear disarmament.[28] It is fair to argue that Japan's interests are concurrent with global efforts on the issue of non-proliferation.

An equally important passive measure would be an outreach programme aimed at raising awareness among non-regime members about non-proliferation and strengthening their domestic control mechanisms. The awareness-raising can take the form of either government-to-government lectures or public education. Through a government-level lecture programme, officials in developed countries talk about the value and lessons of their export control system and encourage, or in some cases help, developing countries to establish such a system. This would benefit the developed countries because they can export technologies to the developing country without worrying about third-party transfer or technology diversion if full compliance is implemented. As regards public education on non-proliferation, papers were submitted to the Third Session of the Preparatory Committee for the 2005 Review Conference of the Parties to the NPT by individual states. Japan's paper shows that it is actively involved in the promotion of public education about non-proliferation.[29]

Other measures deal with enforcing compliance on defectors and neglectors. The introduction of the Proliferation Security Initiative (PSI) was intended to fill the gap between the domestic measures and military operations. Many analysts welcomed the initiative because of its implications for Japan's North Korean policy, particularly its curtailment effect on North Korea's external revenue sources. Through PSI, Japan was able to impose de facto "economic sanctions" on North Korea in the name of international consensus and cooperation, thus avoiding being criticized for unilateral self-interested sanctions. This might be called a side-effect of non-proliferation.

Japan's initiative on global and regional non-proliferation

Japan's initiative on non-proliferation is built on three layers: regime compliance, global and regional commitment, and norm-building. Within these layers, Japan incorporates a new development of the issues and measures to overcome the political and institutional limits noted earlier.

Regime compliance

Japan is proud of having been an active supporter of the non-proliferation regime throughout the recent history of Japanese foreign policy. Its stance is further enhanced by its initiatives on conventional weapons such as landmines and small arms. For example, Ambassadors Mitsuro Donowaki and Kuniko Inoguchi showed strong leadership in the matter of small arms, with Professor Inoguchi being appointed Chairperson-Designate of the United Nations First Biennial Meeting of States on Small Arms and Light Weapons, held in New York in July 2003. This represented one of Japan's commitments toward promoting non-proliferation.

Indeed, Japan's approach to regime compliance can be broken down into two aspects: regime participation/adherence and self-restraint. The former aspect is demonstrated in Japan's active participation in the non-proliferation regime, while the latter aspect explains Japan's determination not to be a source of proliferation through technology diversion.

In addition to strictly controlling military and dual-use technology exports to prevent technology diversion, Japan is determined not to become equipped with nuclear weapons. Japan's Three Non-Nuclear Principles, which state that Japan will not possess, produce or allow the transhipment of nuclear weapons, have been enforced since the 1960s and are still in place despite the Chinese nuclear programme in the late 1960s and North Korean nuclear developments in the early 1990s and beyond. It is true that a legal interpretation by the Director of the Cabinet Legislative Bureau, Hideo Sanada, in 1978 would allow Japan's possession of nuclear weapons as not unconstitutional, but Japan maintains the principles for political purposes.[30] The issue of Japan's nuclear possession resurfaced in May–June 2002 because a private and off-the-record speech at Waseda University by Deputy Cabinet Secretary Shinzo

Abe was intentionally misinterpreted and leaked, but Chief Cabinet Secretary Fukuda reiterated the government's traditional position in the Diet.[31]

Japan nonetheless periodically faces doubt and suspicion from neighbouring countries and especially from academics about possible nuclear development and possession. According to realist theory, it would be rational for Japan to develop and possess nuclear weapons because it is surrounded by hostile states with nuclear weapons. In fact, it is widely believed that Japan has the technological foundation to develop nuclear weapons and delivery systems in a short period of time. Japan's nuclear option was highlighted when Dr Masashi Nishihara, president of Japan's National Defense Academy, wrote to the *Washington Post* about the non-aggression pact between the United States and North Korea in August 2003. Dr Nishihara argued that "such a pact would in fact lead only to a withdrawal of U.S. troops from South Korea and perhaps even to justifying the development of its own nuclear weapons".[32]

The Japanese government strongly counters these doubts and suspicions. First, as Defense Minister Shigeru Ishiba explained in November 2002, Japan is a faithful supporter of the NPT and "must respect and extend the spirit of the NPT regime".[33] Second, the Japan-US alliance provides security guarantees and the US presence in the Asia-Pacific works as a stabilizing factor in this region. Japan also benefits from the US nuclear umbrella. The Japanese government further explains that joining the ballistic missile defence (BMD) system would supplement the US security guarantee and reinforce Japan's protection from missile attacks. Chief Cabinet Secretary Fukuda announced that "Japan will take all possible measures to ensure national defense and prevention of proliferation of weapons of mass destruction, by ensuring transparency and encouraging international understanding on BMD, and by promoting further cooperation with the United States on technology and operation".[34]

The negative side of this approach is that an over-reliance on the US deterrence capability might remove Japan's freedom of action in many areas of its security policy. Critics argue that Japan has become a poodle (often termed *pochi* in Japanese, which means "faithful dog to his master") of the United States and could not stop US unilateralist policy even if it wished to do so. This argument has surfaced from time to time since 9/11 and is used to criticize Prime Minister Koizumi's policy towards the United States. However, at a press conference on the issue of Iraq on 20 March 2003, Prime Minister Koizumi opposed this view by arguing that "the people of Japan should not forget that the fact that the United States deems the attack to Japan as an attack to itself is serving as a great deterrence against any country attempting to attack on Japan".[35]

Global and regional commitment

Global commitments

Japan continues to support a global commitment on non-proliferation and has been an active promoter of the various initiatives. In a statement of global partnership against the proliferation of WMD issued at the G-8 Summit in Canada in 2002, the G-8 leaders declared that "we commit ourselves to prevent terrorists, or those that harbour them, from acquiring or developing nuclear, chemical, radiological and biological weapons; missiles; and related materials, equipment and technology". The G-8 called on all countries to join them in a commitment to six principles on non-proliferation: promote the adoption, universalization, full implementation and strengthening of multilateral treaties and other international instruments; account for and secure such items in production, use, storage and domestic and international transport; develop effective physical protection measures applied to facilities; develop effective border controls, law enforcement efforts and international cooperation to detect, deter and interdict in cases of illicit trafficking; develop effective national export and transhipment controls over items on multilateral export control lists; manage and dispose of stocks of fissile materials designated as no longer required for defence purposes, eliminate all chemical weapons, and minimize holdings of dangerous biological pathogens and toxins.[36] These principles became the guidelines of Japan's non-proliferation efforts.

The diversion of weapons, technology and personnel engaged in WMD development is one of the most serious issues facing the international community, and the former communist countries were deemed to be major sources of supply because of a lack of resources to prevent diversion. Cooperation projects in Russia had started years before the G-8 statement. In fact, the Russian disposal of nuclear waste in the Sea of Japan had been pointed out in the early 1990s, and both governments engaged in cooperation to deal with this problem. Since 1993 Japan has provided US$70 million to the Committee for Cooperation to Assist the Destruction of Nuclear Weapons Reduced in the Russian Federation and has undertaken a programme to assist in the denuclearization of Russia. A bilateral initiative agreed in May 1999 – the Japan-Russian Federation Joint Efforts for Disarmament and Environmental Protection – identified three areas in which to promote cooperation: the dismantling of decommissioned nuclear submarines in the Far East region; promoting the conversion of military resources to the private sector; and the management and disposal of surplus Russian weapons-grade plutonium by using Russia's BN600 fast reactor.[37]

In fact, the issue was first put on the global agenda at the G-7 Tokyo

Summit in 1993. The Political Declaration stated that "enhanced cooperation is necessary in combatting the danger of proliferation of weapons of mass destruction and missiles". One of the goals was to "encourage the countries concerned of the former Soviet Union to ensure rapid, safe and secure elimination of nuclear weapons in accordance with current agreements, providing effective assistance to this end".[38] Japan supported participation by the former communist countries in the non-proliferation regimes after the Cold War. Furthermore, it provided financial support to Russia, Ukraine, Kazakhstan and Belarus to dismantle their nuclear weapons, a project established in line with the United States' Cooperative Threat Reduction programme. Unfortunately, the project was terminated because the funds provided by the Japanese government were not disbursed. However, Japan announced at the G-8 Summit in Canada that it would provide US$200 million to the non-proliferation programme in Russia.[39] Japan reached an agreement on 28 June 2003 to the pilot project of dismantling one Victor III-class submarine at Zvezda Shipyard, Primorye.

Regional commitments

Japan is actively engaged in an outreach programme in the Asia-Pacific, which has two tracks. The first track is the Asian Export Control Seminar hosted by the Center for Information on Security Trade Control (CISTEC). CISTEC, established in 1989, is a private organization with strong ties to the Japanese government, especially with METI. CISTEC started the Asian Export Control Seminar in 1993. The idea behind the seminar was to invite export control administrators and practitioners in the Asia-Pacific to Japan and to help them learn the significance and practical benefits of establishing their own export control system. It was part of Japan's regional responsibility to monitor the progress of the legal development of export controls in the Asia-Pacific region, which was shared under the framework of the Coordinating Committee for Multilateral Export Controls. In October 2004, the 12th Asian Export Control Seminar was held in Tokyo. Reflecting the increasing awareness of the significance of international cooperation on export controls, Hong Kong and Singapore changed their status from "participating country" to "cooperating country", the category to which Australia, Germany, South Korea and the United States belong.

The second track is the Asian Senior-level Talks on Non-Proliferation (ASTOP) hosted by the Japanese Ministry of Foreign Affairs (MOFA). ASTOP started in November 2003 by inviting 12 Asian nations, namely, Brunei Darussalam, Cambodia, Indonesia, Japan, the Republic of Korea, Laos, Malaysia, Myanmar, the Philippines, Singapore, Thailand and Viet Nam, together with Australia and the United States as participants.

ASTOP is a senior-level dialogue among the Asian countries dedicated specifically to the discussion of the non-proliferation of WMD. In conducting the ASTOP, the Japanese government refers to various documents, including the G8 Declaration on Non Proliferation of Weapons of Mass Destruction adopted in June 2003, the Political Declaration on Prevention of Proliferation of Weapons of Mass Destruction and Their Means of Delivery adopted by the ASEM (Asia Europe Meeting) foreign ministers in July 2003, the Joint Declaration on the Promotion of Tripartite Cooperation among Japan, the People's Republic of China and the Republic of Korea, and the APEC (Asia Pacific Economic Cooperation) Leaders' Declaration adopted in October 2003. It is clear that the idea for ASTOP arose from the growing emphasis on non-proliferation within the international community after 9/11.

In his opening statement at the first ASTOP meeting in November 2003, Ambassador Yukiya Amano argued that the "proliferation process consists of several phases – the export phase, traveling phase and import phase". For the export phase, he argued that "export control as well as customs security must be duly reinforced in the respective countries in order to stop the flow of the sensitive items". Explaining the transportation and import phases, he argued that "sensitive materials travel across borders because there may be those who wish to acquire them in our countries", so that "we must also seriously consider ways to illegalize the acquisition of sensitive materials for criminal use and seek for ways to duly penalize the end-users of concern"; he also stressed "the importance of taking a more proactive approach to stop shipments of proliferation concern in their traveling phase".[40] In this regard, Ambassador Amano emphasized the importance of the PSI. To encourage security cooperation on the high seas, MOFA hosted the Asia Non-proliferation Seminar in May 2004, and invited officials from Cambodia, Indonesia, Malaysia, the Philippines and Thailand to provide lectures on law enforcement on the high seas.

Comparing these two tracks of Japan's outreach effort in the Asia-Pacific, the first initiative is conducted and managed by a METI-influenced institution, and the second is undertaken by MOFA itself. Although ASTOP's status in Japan is high in bureaucratic terms, and its policy implications are considered significant, export control is actually managed by trade, police and military officials, so that the Asian Export Control Seminar deals with the more pragmatic elements of non-proliferation. This shows that the Japanese government has taken the significance of non-proliferation very seriously since the early 1990s. Thus, developments since 9/11 have merely helped to accelerate the various initiatives that were already under way, although they have added a new dimension that emphasizes the importance of enforcement measures such as the PSI and the Container Security Initiative (CSI). However, interestingly, Japan understood the importance of the military measures but did not elaborate on when and how military operations might be justified as a part of the non-proliferation strategy.

Norm-building

The Japanese government is active in promoting a variety of measures in relation to norm-building, including norm formation, the promotion of awareness and enlightenment, and the education of young people.

Norm formation

Japan encourages both academics and practitioners jointly to develop new norms and to hold symposiums and seminars to elaborate problem-solving methods. For example, after the nuclear tests by India and Pakistan, the Japan Institute of International Affairs and the Hiroshima Peace Institute, supported by the Ministry of Foreign Affairs, hosted the Tokyo Forum for Nuclear Non-Proliferation and Disarmament in May 1998. The Tokyo Forum made 17 key recommendations in July 1999, which were submitted to UN Secretary-General Kofi Annan. Another example was an international seminar titled "Nuclear Non-Proliferation Regime: In the Face of a Possible Renewed Nuclear Arms Race", which was held just before the NPT Review Conference in April–May 2000 to discuss how to lead the conference to success. In August 2000, the Japan Institute of International Affairs hosted the "International Workshop on Nuclear Disarmament and Non-Proliferation", which considered how to implement the practical steps towards nuclear disarmament and non-proliferation agreed on at the Review Conference. Thus, most of these initiatives started before 9/11.

The promotion of awareness and enlightenment

MOFA anticipates a role for non-governmental organizations (NGOs) in promoting awareness and enlightenment about nuclear issues. For example, the Hiroshima and Nagasaki peace movements perform a crucial role in supporting Japan's insistence on the complete elimination of nuclear weapons, since they are able to convey the true picture of the effect of nuclear weapons. MOFA and the Japanese government also anticipate that NGOs will be involved in the disarmament domain. It is deemed appropriate for NGOs to act as implementation bodies in landmine clearance, and the Japanese government is keen to support their activities through the Japan Platform, which provides emergency relief in natural disasters and refugee situations.

The education of young people

In educating young people, Japan supports the United Nations Disarmament Fellowship Programme and its seminars. Japan also invites teachers in the Asia-Pacific to help develop teaching techniques on nonproliferation. Most of the programme was developed after 9/11, but its importance was recognized before 9/11.

Conclusion

It is not clear that the 9/11 attacks and the Iraq war had an impact on Japan's non-proliferation policy. In fact, most of the initiatives highlighted under the banner of the war on terror and the non-proliferation strategy were already under way before 9/11. Unfortunately, despite Japan's conviction about the inseparable relationship between arms control, disarmament and non-proliferation under the NPT regime, Japanese efforts and initiatives are fragmented by political realities and strategic demands. For example, there is an implied contradiction in the fact that Japan relies on the extended deterrence of the United States while proclaiming the elimination of nuclear weapons at the United Nations. Furthermore, the future direction of the PSI indicates that there might be a demand for more joint operations with other militaries to promote nonproliferation, whereas Japan maintains a strict restriction on the use of force other than for territorial defence purposes.

The Iraq crisis revealed the weakness of the non-proliferation regime and its role in the UN system. This weakness has two dimensions. First, there were no concrete measures to deal with deliberate violations of the existing norms and procedures. Second, in spite of many promises by the international community on various occasions, it was extremely difficult to achieve international consensus when positive action was required and necessary. Therefore, if we wish to transfer the lessons of the Iraq war to other regions, measures need to be situation driven rather than derived from the universal application of principles. In this regard, a "war of choice" will be just one option in dealing with the proliferation problem. Within this logic, unfortunately, a pre-emptive strike against potential and/or actual proliferators could be irregular policy means in the future, since sensitive management of any ad hoc coalition is necessary, which is a key to effective military operations. It is true that the United States has a special role and responsibility in international society. However, US-led initiatives are not a substitute for global nonproliferation. The irony is that international society cannot live without US initiatives in dealing with non-proliferation, but nor does it wish to give the United States dominance over the issue. This ambivalence creates a split in non-proliferation, and the Iraq war can be seen as a means of filling the gap before the divergence grew any bigger.

In these circumstances, countries are obliged to cooperate with the United States, while complaining about its unilateral attitude towards the issue. Japan and other countries should therefore utilize the US policy to benefit their interest but also undertake their own initiatives based on their limitations and interests. In this course of action, however, an international society must face the question of the legal foundations of US policy and the role of the United Nations, and how it accommodates this dissension will be one of its greatest challenges in the future.

Notes

1. "Fact Sheet: Strengthening International Efforts against WMD Proliferation" (New York: The White House, 11 February 2004).
2. Braun and Chyba define latent proliferation as an activity by NPT member countries that develops nuclear capabilities despite their formal obligations under the Treaty. First-tier proliferation is defined as technology diversion from a private company or from a nuclear development assistance programme of the nuclear state to non-nuclear states. Second-tier proliferation is defined as mutual technology assistance among the developing countries. Chaim Braun and Christopher F. Chyba, "Proliferation Rings: New Challenges to the Nuclear Nonproliferation Regime", *International Security*, Vol. 29, No. 2 (Fall 2004), pp. 5–6.
3. Perkovich et al. assign proliferation threats to three categories – nuclear terrorism and transfers; regional proliferation and conflict; and the breakdown of the non-proliferation regime – and outline the necessary measures as strengthening enforcement, blocking supplies and reducing demand (George Perkovich et al., *Universal Compliance: A Strategy for Nuclear Security*, Washington, DC: Carnegie Endowment for International Peace, June 2004).
4. Japan's ratification was sixth overall.
5. Ministry of Foreign Affairs (MOFA), *Japan's Disarmament and Nonproliferation Diplomacy* (Tokyo: MOFA, April 2004).
6. For the contents of Japan's disarmament and non-proliferation policy, see MOFA, *Japan's Disarmament and Non-Proliferation Policy*; MOFA, *Japan's Disarmament Policy*, March 2003.
7. Address by Mr Keizo Obuchi, Prime Minister of Japan, to the Fifty-third Session of the General Assembly of the United Nations, UN Doc. A/53/PV.8, 21 September 1998, pp. 16–17.
8. Address by H.E. Mr Junichiro Koizumi, Prime Minister of Japan, to the Fifty-seventh Session of the General Assembly of the United Nations, UN Doc. A/57/PV.4, 13 September 2002, p. 18. Japan has submitted a resolution on "A path to the total elimination of nuclear weapons" annually since the late 1950s.
9. "Partnership for Security and Prosperity", Joint Statement by President Bush and Prime Minister Koizumi, 30 June 2001, ⟨http://www.whitehouse.gov/news/releases/2001/06/20010630.html⟩ (accessed 24 February 2006).
10. Statement by the Chief Cabinet Secretary on "Introduction of Ballistic Missile Defense

System and Other Measures" (Tentative Translation), 19 December 2003, ⟨http://www.kantei.go.jp/foreign/tyokan/2003/1219danwa_e.html⟩ (accessed 24 February 2006).

11. Jon B. Wolfsthal, "The Nuclear Third Rail: Can Fuel Cycle Capabilities Be Limited?" *Arms Control Today* (December 2004).

12. Press Conference by Prime Minister Junichiro Koizumi on the Issue of Iraq (Provisional Translation), 20 March 2003, ⟨http://www.kantei.go.jp/foreign/koizumispeech/2003/03/20kaiken_e.html⟩ (accessed 24 February 2006).

13. MOFA, "Announcement by the Chief Cabinet Secretary on Discontinuation of Measures in Response to Nuclear Testing Conducted by India and Pakistan", 26 October 2001, ⟨http://www.mofa.go.jp/region/asia-paci/india/announce0110.html⟩ (accessed 24 February 2006).

14. Prime Minister Koizumi's answer to a question from Hon. Kentaro Kiba at the Budget Committee, House of Councillors, 156th session. *The Minutes of the Diet (Kokkai Kaigiroku)*, Vol. 7, 6 March 2003, p. 14.

15. In the Basic Principles of Defense Policy, which was approved by the cabinet in 1957, the first item on the list was to "Support activities by the United Nations".

16. John R. Bolton, Under Secretary for Arms Control and International Security, speech to the American Enterprise Institute, Washington DC, 24 June 2004.

17. *Financial Times*, 2 December 2004.

18. "Remarks by the President on Weapons of Mass Destruction Proliferation", Fort Lesley J. McNair – National Defense University, 11 February 2004, ⟨http://www.whitehouse.gov/news/releases/2004/02/20040211-4.html⟩ (accessed 24 February 2006).

19. Quoted in Wolfsthal, "The Nuclear Third Rail".

20. *Financial Times*, 6 September 2004.

21. Under the catch-all provision, all exports except food and timber-related items are subject to licensing requirements, apart from exports destined for 26 "white countries". For the details of Japan's export control system, see METI's website, ⟨http://www.meti.go.jp/policy/anpo/⟩ (accessed 25 February 2006).

22. Ichita Yamamoto and Keiichiro Asao, "The List of North Korean Companies", Bungei-Shunju, 1999.

23. The "Know Regulation" is the equivalent of the catch-all provision, but its scope was more modest. Jun-ichi Ozawa and Takeshi Ito, "Export Control Policy in Japan: The Current System and Stream of Change", in Gary K. Bertsch, Richard T. Cupitt and Takeshi Yamamoto, eds, *U.S. and Japanese Nonproliferation Export Controls: Theory, Description and Analysis* (Lanham, MD: University Press of America, 1996), pp. 103–126.

24. Enforcement of national export control law and the introduction of the catch-all provision were a major subject of debate in the Industrial Structure Advisory Committee, which met five times between October 2001 and January 2004. The committee was established under METI to make policy recommendations.

25. Security Trade Control Subcommittee, Industrial Structure Advisory Committee, *Direction of Export Control for the Nonproliferation of WMD: Introduction of Japanese Version of Catch All* (translated by the author), December 2001.

26. *Asahi Shinbun*, 9 May 2003.

27. UN Security Council Resolution 1540 (2004), UN Doc. S/Res/1540, 28 April 2004, preamble.

28. "Working Paper by Japan" submitted to the Third Session of the Preparatory Committee for the 2005 Review Conference of the Parties to the NPT, NPT/CONF.2005/PC.III/WP.11, 28 April 2004.

29. "Working Paper on Disarmament and Non-Proliferation Education submitted by Egypt, Hungary, Japan, Mexico, New Zealand, Peru, Poland and Sweden", NPT/

CONF.2005/PC.III/WP.17, 29 April 2004, and "Japan's Efforts in Disarmament and Non-proliferation Education: Working Paper submitted by Japan", NPT/CONF.2005/PC.III/WP.18, 29 April 2004.

30. The government's interpretation of the possession of nuclear weapons presented at the Budget Committee, House of Councillors, 84th session. *The Minutes of the Diet (Kokkai Kaigiroku)*, No. 23, 3 April 1978, pp. 2–3.

31. Cabinet Secretary Fukuda was interviewed on 31 May 2002 about the constitutional interpretation of Japan's nuclear weapons. Secretary Fukuda was severely criticized by the opposition parties for touching upon the issue. He appeared before the Appropriations Committee of the House of Councillors on 6 May and explained that the Koizumi government would not change its policy.

32. *Washington Post*, 14 August 2003.

33. Statement by Defense Minister Ishiba, 155th Session, House of Councillors, Security Committee, No. 2, 5 November 2002.

34. Statement by the Chief Cabinet Secretary, "On Introduction of Ballistic Missile Defense System and Other Measures", 19 December 2003, ⟨http://www.kantei.go.jp/foreign/tyokan/2003/1219danwa_e.html⟩ (accessed 25 February 2006).

35. Press Conference by Prime Minister Junichiro Koizumi on the Issue of Iraq, 20 March 2003, ⟨http://www.kantei.go.jp/foreign/koizumispeech/2003/03/20kaiken_e.html⟩ (accessed 25 February 2006).

36. "The G8 Global Partnership: Principles to prevent terrorists, or those that harbour them, from gaining access to weapons or materials of mass destruction", The G8 Global Partnership Against the Spread of Weapons and Materials of Mass Destruction, Statement by the Group of Eight Leaders, Kananaskis, Canada, 27 June 2002, ⟨http://www.state.gov/e/eb/rls/othr/11514.htm⟩ (accessed 25 February 2006).

37. Japan-Russian Federation Joint Efforts for Disarmament and Environmental Protection, 29 May 1999, ⟨http://www.mofa.go.jp/region/europe/russia/fmv9905/joint.html⟩.

38. *Tokyo Summit Political Declaration: Striving for a More Secure and Humane World*, 8 July 1993, ⟨http://www.g8.utoronto.ca/summit/1993tokyo/political.html⟩ (accessed 25 February 2006).

39. G8 Senior Group, *G8 Global Partnership Annual Report*, June 2004, ⟨http://www.kantei.go.jp/foreign/koizumispeech/2004/06/G8GLOBALPARTNERSHIP_e.pdf⟩ (accessed 25 February 2006).

40. "Opening Statement by Ambassador Yukiya Amano, Director-General for Arms Control and Scientific Affairs, Ministry of Foreign Affairs of Japan, On the occasion of Asian Senior-level Talks on Non-Proliferation (ASTOP)", 13 November 2003, ⟨http://www.mofa.go.jp/policy/un/disarmament/arms/astop/state0311.html⟩ (accessed 25 February 2006).

Part IV

Proliferation challenges and international responses in the Middle East

11

From bomb to fuel! Iran and the question of weapons of mass destruction

Jalil Roshandel

Since the mid-1980s, Iran's nuclear programme has been subjected to intense international attention. For much of the first half of this period, concerned countries in the region and the West, although accusing Iran of having a secret nuclear weapons project, could make no progress in unravelling the mysteries of Iran's nuclear objectives. Iran itself did not succeed in taking great leaps forward in developing its nuclear capability and the more it approached countries with nuclear capabilities the less it secured their cooperation and technical assistance. This absurd international search for assistance in fact turned global attention to Iran. In addition, Israeli sensitivity concerning Iranian nuclear plans made it harder for Iran to find reliable partners. The hardship experienced did not, however, lessen the Iranian desire to develop a nuclear capability.

Revolutionary Iran had initially refuted the necessity to have advanced weapons systems such as the American AWACS aircraft and had interrupted development of its nuclear reactors ordered under the Shah. By the mid-1980s, however, it was clear that the mind-set within the religious leadership of the country had shifted from rejection of advanced technology to appreciation of it and was hankering after some sort of weapons of mass destruction. The most convincing and concrete reason must have been that, had Iran been in possession of any of such devices, the Iran–Iraq war might have been avoided all together or at least would have lasted for far fewer than eight years and been brought to an end with much more positive results for Iran. Other than this, there was a secondary incentive: the Bushehr nuclear plant, which was started by the Shah in the 1970s, reminded people of the Shah's plan to make Iran a regional superpower. Until the mid-1980s, the Islamic Republic was unable to take significant steps towards the physical completion of the construction of the plant, but suddenly the decision to continue the project was taken. Whether there was a particular interest group behind the decision remains a mystery, but there are other factors that must have induced Iran to follow up its plans. This chapter will explain the process and argue that, based on a specific interpretation of the text of the Treaty on the Non-Proliferation of Nuclear Weapons (NPT), Iran sees no reason to abandon what it calls a peaceful nuclear programme; it seems that the decision has also been designed to extend the programme as far as possible while giving the International Atomic Energy Agency (IAEA) full access to its sites.

Although the IAEA expects Iran to stop its processing of nuclear fuel because of its potential as a dual-use technology, Iran shows no interest in doing so. As we shall see, the continuation of the Iranian project for more than two decades has transformed it into the main issue that is directly related to Iranian national honour and dignity. Therefore, any attempt to stop the project or militarily to destroy the facilities would definitely jeopardize regional security even more than the Iranian nuclear capability per se. Within Iranian society, a nuclear capability is to some extent viewed not only as a military necessity in light of Iran's nuclear-armed neighbours but as a symbol of the greatness of Iran and the nation's independence in the face of pressure from the hostile West. Should Iran succeed in acquiring a nuclear capability of some sort, civilian or military, the chances of that force being brought to bear against Israel seem slim. Despite the longstanding animosity between Iran and Israel and the Islamic regime's continuous support of Hezbollah and Hamas, it seems unlikely that Iran would risk the consequences of a nuclear attack upon Israel. Having seen the immediate and overwhelming force applied by the West against Saddam Hussein during the Persian Gulf war, or since March 2003 to oust him from power, Iran is certainly aware that the successful launch of a nuclear weapon against Israel could only result in a severe backlash from both Israel and the West. Given the probability that a nuclear-armed Iran would not use that technology unless threatened, it is important to examine the potential consequences of Western military action to intervene in the creation of that technology. Should the West decide to end the Iranian nuclear programmes militarily, the project's stature in the minds of the Islamic regime and the minds of Iranians would surely provoke a significant response, perhaps including conventional weapon attacks on Western interests within the Middle East. Given the instability stemming from so many pressure points within the region, Iran's introduction as a hostile player on the regional stage could easily and significantly exacerbate existing tensions and conflicts and, in such circumstances, Israel would most certainly be Iran's target of choice. It may not be desirable to stand idly by while Iran develops its nuclear capability, but the potential consequences of military intervention might easily dwarf the threat posed by a nuclear-capable Iran, given the Islamic regime's inability actually to use a military nuclear capability.

Background

Since the ceasefire with Iraq in 1989, Iran's security calculations have shifted from the old concerns about the Arab world and the Persian Gulf states' rivalries to greater threats that supposedly target both the territorial integrity and the cleric structure of the Iranian regime. The Iran–Iraq war proved how Saddam Hussein was rewarded for his aggression against Iran, leaving Iranians defenceless and with practically no allies. Seen from Tehran, Saddam was rewarded for his aggression because his success would put an end to Iran's Islamic regime, which was making many Europeans and Americans unhappy. In fact, more than disagreements over borders, what was really at risk was Iran's Islamic identity. Maintaining the system meant something far beyond "distrust" of a hostile neighbourhood and would take much more than the human shield and conventional defences that were used (and perhaps overused) during the war with Iraq. The acquisition of some sort of nuclear capability for deterrent purposes would naturally be the most appropriate answer.

New threats

This period coincided with the collapse of the Soviet Union and the emergence of the newly independent Central Asian and Caucasian republics, which transformed Iran's perception of post–Cold War regional threats. It also brought some hope of obtaining nuclear materials or perhaps scientists from the expanded market that opened up during this period.

In this new environment, the major threats to Iran's security stemmed not only from the hostile Arab states of the Persian Gulf, "whom Iran feared would actually form a US-aided and abetted anti-Iranian Arab front",[1] but also from geo-strategic changes under way on Iran's northern borders with the former Soviet Union and the Caspian Sea. The new threats arose from the distinctive geopolitical environment that directly resulted from the so-called New World Order.

The creation of an Arab front united against Iran, however hypothetical, was one of the scenarios Iran feared most. Despite the fact that the Arab world has never reached such a consensus, an Iran surrounded by unfriendly nations was and still is facing a threat to its survival. One might argue that most of Iran's neighbours are unlikely to be real sources of threat or to have the military strength necessary for that purpose. This is true, yet one cannot ignore Kautilya's notion of "enmity", which defines the "natural relation between neighbors".[2] Added to the magnitude of this perception was the US military presence in the Persian Gulf after the Iran–Iraq war, a presence that increased in size after the Iraqi invasion of Kuwait.

One of the imperatives in the post–Cold War era for Iran has been to equalize its relationship with Iraq because UN Security Council Resolution 598 only declared a ceasefire between the two belligerents and did not create a treaty for peace. Indeed, immediately after the end of the war with Iran, Iraq, helped by the international community, was able to reorganize its army and deploy it in another act of aggression – the occupation of Kuwait. Following and as a result of the war with Iraq, Iran was not in a position to defend itself by conventional means. The Islamic regime was facing severe international isolation and embargoes and was well aware that the theocratic nature of the regime was attracting the ire of much of the world. This was enough to convince the decision makers within Iran that any strategic weapons (such as ballistic missiles and nuclear, chemical or biological warheads) would make the regime safer and reduce its vulnerability to a completely hostile international system. In addition, they believed that advanced weapons systems would put Iran into a different category in the world order and bring international recognition of its capabilities.

From studying the Iranian land forces, air force, ground-based air defence forces, naval forces, mine and amphibious-warfare capabilities, and anti-ship missile forces, Anthony Cordesman argues that, in almost all areas, the Iranian military capability falls far short of "sustained capability". By "Gulf standards", the Iranian forces may have significant superiority in some fields, but Cordesman confirms Iran's inability to pose an operational threat against neighbours such as Iraq or Saudi Arabia. He also believes that Iran's "Southern Gulf neighbors are modernizing and expanding their forces at a much faster rate than Iran. In spite of [the] currently programmed force cut, the United States retains the capability to decisively intervene in the Gulf. It can rapidly achieve naval and air supremacy, and while it cannot rapidly deploy land forces against Iran, it can carry out the kind of strategic-bombing campaign it carried out against Iraq. In spite of Iraq's defeat in the Gulf War, it is still a superior military power and still poses a potential threat to Iran."[3] It is very likely that the revolutionary regime had reached similar conclusions and had decided that a nuclear capability would go far in addressing the gap and balancing military power in the Persian Gulf.

A less significant argument put forward by Iran was to consider nuclear technology as an appropriate field for creating new jobs and as a source of non-market-oriented production. One should remember that, with low oil prices in those years and an increasingly young population, Iran's concern was quite legitimate and any small steps could have had a positive impact on the Iranian job market. These arguments were of course never made in public, which is why there was little or no evidence and there was very little visible evidence of Iranian nuclear plans and intention. The only visible military activity was the development of a parallel and related capability of medium- to long-range ballistic missile – the Shihab series.

In the face of such weaknesses and vulnerabilities, Iran did have other options available to it and in fact several of them were explored. Regional cooperation seems to have been the first option examined during President Rafsanjani's administration from 1989 to 1996. In his first term, Rafsanjani was finally able to accept a ceasefire with Iraq. However, he was unable to meet people's post-war economic demands. It was only his family, "who rose from modest origins as pistachio farmers", who became more involved in economic activities, and his "clan" gradually "took key positions" in rich ministries such as the Ministry of Oil.[4] Unfortunately, he followed a patriarchal policy and, as a consequence of his autocratic weight, gradually pushed Ayatollah Khamenei towards more conservative policies. Rafsanjani's role behind all decisions during this period cannot be contested, yet he has to be credited with limited attempts at regional cooperation.

Another option was to reduce international tension. Iran tried, however inadequately, to approach some countries and sent calculated signals to the United States – not good enough to melt the ice, but they did create hope for the people who were beginning to demand better relations with the West, particularly with the United States, while constantly pressuring for more freedoms at the domestic level. Rafsanjani's second term is a clear example of this policy: Rafsanjani's hidden political flirtations led to a minor opening with the Arab states of the Persian Gulf, somewhat less tense relations with Europe and a lucrative contract for the Russians to finish the construction of the nuclear plant in Bushehr. This same period, however, produced no significant achievements in relations with the United States.

The unexpected and undesirable (for the conservatives) ascendance of Mohammad Khatami to power in 1997, followed by the insulting behaviour of reformists in the process of the sixth parliamentary election (which eliminated Rafsanjani from parliament), had some direct and perhaps indirect results that affected Rafsanjani and the decisions made under his patriarchy:

- Rafsanjani received a new mandate of authority at the head of the newly empowered Expediency Council, which had its own Centre for Strategic Studies. The centre was soon inviting university professors, distinguished scholars and former policy makers to work for the centre and for the council.
- All strategic decisions made under Rafsanjani's patriarchal rule, including the decision to go nuclear, became increasingly invisible, although Iran did not abandon its nuclear ambitions.
- Although a reformist government was formed and later had the support of an ultra-reformist parliament, society was under the kind of control that is reminiscent of the military Junta in Greece. The reformists were apparently free to say, ask and demand anything they wanted, but they could not expect their adversaries to be restrained. On the contrary, vigilante groups were free and even encouraged to act against the reformists. This had a significant impact on the strategic decisions made by the reformists and gradually led to the eventual stalemate.

In this chaotic situation (which was often wrongly interpreted as freedom), the implementation of the government's promises – internally and externally – and of the government's international commitments became more and more difficult. Once in power, Khatami signed more international agreements than had all previous presidents under the Islamic system since 1979, yet, especially since his second term, it has been completely impossible to consider his words and signature as legally binding on Iran's policies if they have not been confirmed by the clerics or the patriarchal institutions that often act as a second government.[5] Under Khatami's presidency, Iran's slow walk towards democracy engaged the whole world. New hopes and expectations were aroused and everything pointed to a new political and social life for Iran.

While the world's attention was diverted by the fate of democracy and the reform movement in Iran, nuclear issues became less important. Though the transparent part of Iran's nuclear programme was under IAEA control, the invisible part in fact managed to buy more time and was continued in secrecy. On the diplomatic side there was a very valuable understanding between the IAEA and Iran's formal government, but the shadow government was making secret deals with Pakistani nuclear scientists (perhaps because of the low cost). With the transfer of technology and equipment, Iran took several steps forward. Although there was not enough time to take the final step to bulk production of weapons-grade materials, a considerable level of expertise in highly important dual-use industry was assembled. In August 2002, when an Iranian opposition group first revealed publicly that Iran was building a uranium enrichment facility near Natanz (north of Isfahan), the IAEA quickly characterized the site as "sophisticated and the culmination of a large, expensive effort".[6] The world was puzzled when commercial satellite images, taken in 2002, made it clear that the facility was using gas centrifuges. Small, negligible and perhaps unimportant parts had been patched together to produce an industrial system and potential that was unthinkable for the West. Part of this enrichment chain was imported from other countries, but the major infrastructure and the primary engineering of the large underground structures were carried out solely by Iranians. Iran's operating centrifuge, assembly facilities and a centrifuge pilot plant suddenly became an international focal point, although not operating with uranium as of late March 2006 when this chapter was edited.

After almost 20 years of observation, control, sanctions, continued alarms (mainly issuing from Israel) and continuous monitoring of Iran's interaction with countries with nuclear know-how, it is now clear that Iran has progressed so far in the industry that the assessment by the Institute for Science and International Security (ISIS) – even though "preliminary" – claims that "Iran has demonstrated a capability possessed by only about ten countries".[7] However, during the past few years Iran has always insisted that its capability is for peaceful purposes only.[8] Even the Director General of the IAEA, Mohamed ElBaradei, has stated that:

Iran has no nuclear weapons program, but I personally don't rush to conclusions before all the realities are clarified. So far I see nothing which could be called an imminent danger. I have seen no nuclear weapons program in Iran. What I have seen is that Iran is trying to gain access to nuclear enrichment technology, and so far there is no danger from Iran.[9]

Between the two extremes

The past 20 years of Islamic rule in Iran have been filled with clashes between the Iranian political system – despite domestic factional rivalries – and the West. In a word, the West does not want Iran to be one of the world's nuclear-capable states, because the United States and Europe think this would violate the NPT. Iran had itself signed the NPT and accepted its extension in 1995 (incidentally under President Rafsanjani). At the diplomatic level, Iran has always called attention to its signing of the extension of the NPT as signalling its acceptance of and respect for the efforts by the United Nations for disarmament. However, during his last months in power, President Khatami found himself increasingly powerless in the face of a parliament dominated by hard-liners and he was under pressure to follow North Korea's example and quit the NPT. For instance, in September 2004, the conservative parliamentary representative Hassan Kamran prepared a bill for submission to parliament that would have forced the government to set a November deadline for the UN nuclear watchdog to take Iran off the agency's agenda,[10] otherwise Iran might consider withdrawal from the treaty; the bill was not passed.

The IAEA threatened to take tough action against Iran at its November 2004 meeting if Iran defied the agency's call to stop uranium enrichment. In the face of this threat two different reactions were demonstrated:

- The hard-liners almost unanimously pressured for withdrawal from the NPT.
- The reformists advocated staying under the non-proliferation regime. They have so far insisted that Iran is not seeking a nuclear bomb and that the network of nuclear facilities is geared to producing nuclear fuel for the atomic reactors and not a nuclear weapon.

At times even the clerics have refuted the accusation by saying that it is against Islamic ethics to produce weapons of mass destruction. Whereas, in 2003, demonstrators were shouting "no compromise, no surrender" and asking to "get out of the NPT";[11] in August 2004, President Khatami reassured that "We are ready to do everything necessary to give guarantees that we won't seek nuclear weapons".[12]

Confusing messages from the two extremes of the Iranian political spectrum make it impossible for scholars or professionals to support Iran's claim that it does not have a hidden agenda. The Iranian decision makers need to speak with one voice and build confidence through practical measures. So far Iran has always insisted that its nuclear programme is peaceful and that the ultimate goal is only to be self-sufficient and to produce nuclear fuel for its own nuclear plants.

The question is whether access to a nuclear capability for peaceful purposes is permitted by the NPT. The answer is definitely negative. That brings us to a second question: Why can Iran not have access to a capability that it has achieved with limited or no assistance from the industrial West? The answer is not as straightforward as it might seem. Everyone knows the answer, but no one wants to spell it out. The world does not want an Islamic Iran to become a nuclear-capable state.

The clerics in Iran are well aware of this trend in the West. They know that, if democracy prevails, their role and usefulness in Iranian society will be limited and therefore they will do whatever is necessary to strengthen their position. They sometimes bribe the Europeans against the Americans and try to get support from the Arabs against Israel, but this is not sufficient to get a green light on nuclear issues. What is wrong? What needs to be changed? The fact is that Iran and the West represent two extremes. The problem of Iran's nuclear capability cannot be solved in current circumstances. It may seem extremely improbable, but it really does not matter if sometime in 2006 Iran's case is submitted to the Security Council. The Security Council will have a hard time reaching unanimity on Iran's case. There is also a strong probability that Iran will decide to withdraw from the NPT.

Recent developments in Iran have only complicated Iran's nuclear case. First, there was a change in the configuration of parliament and then the presidential elections in June 2005 brought the hard-line candidate Mahmoud Ahmadinejad to power from 3 August 2005. In fact the positions taken by the hard-liners do not reassure the international community about Iran's intentions. Ahmadinejad's statement to the UN Summit in New York on 14 September 2005 and his "Israel must be wiped off the map" rhetoric in October,[13] which irritated the international community, did little to advance Iran's "peaceful" purposes.

Other factors

Although it is not possible to discuss all the aspects of the Iranian nuclear file in this short chapter, there are a few related issues at the international level that merit further elaboration.

The inadequacies of the existing disarmament regime under the NPT

It is a fact today that the NPT is not able to regulate relations between the haves and the have-nots. As long as the language used in the treaty leaves loopholes for legal arguments and new interpretations of the treaty, it cannot be used against countries that wish to be a nuclear state, let alone against Iran with its constant declarations about respecting the treaty and justifying what has been achieved so far, which is the direct result of full implementation of the treaty. As a member of the NPT, Iran has bound itself to a commitment to cooperate with the components of the treaty, including extensive IAEA monitoring. Iran's decision not to withdraw from the NPT yet can be interpreted in one of two ways: either Iran is legitimately seeking to make itself self-sufficient in nuclear fuel and the NPT is allowing it to create some degree of transparency in its nuclear programmes; or the IAEA's relatively ineffectual means of assuring compliance with the NPT offer Iran the chance to appear cooperative while easily concealing dual-use plans. Whatever the reason, Iran is to some extent held in check by the mere fact that it is a signatory of the NPT and some provisions of the treaty have been enforced within Iran.

Countries such as Israel, Pakistan and India have built up their nuclear capability by refusing to sign the treaty; these nations, though not perceived as threats to the West, are in reality loose cannons in the global nuclear non-proliferation movement. However, this problem is not exclusive to the NPT – all treaties and formal agreements are effective in regulating the activities only of their signatories. Although Israel has never admitted to possessing a nuclear arsenal of any kind, the assertion that Israel does possess such a capability is rarely disputed. Close ties with the West have permitted Israel in large measure to avoid the magnifying glass of the international community, reinforcing Iranian concerns about the asymmetrical application of the treaty. Israel, like a few other nuclear-capable non-NPT nations, has avoided becoming an NPT signatory in large part owing to the freedom of action it possesses outside the treaty. Even with a promise to support India's entry into the world's industrial nations, it appears that Germany could not convince Manmohan Singh, the Indian prime minister, to sign the NPT. He rejected it by saying that the circumstances were not "ripe".[14]

Challenges to the authority of the United Nations and the IAEA

The United Nations and the IAEA, as the sole authorities that can – among other responsibilities – authoritatively implement the binding clauses of the treaty, are facing tremendous challenges from within and without. Any organizational difficulties within the IAEA may affect Iran. Before the reappointment of ElBaradei as the IAEA's Director General, there were rumours that he was at odds with US preferences. Iran calculated that, until this was resolved, the IAEA might experience some internal difficulties that in the short run would work in favour of Iran. After ElBaradei was reappointed on 13 June 2005, the Iranian position changed, in the belief that the reappointment has political implications and will negatively affect Iran's case.

After his nomination for the Nobel Peace prize, ElBaradei's statement that the prize was "a shot in the arm" for his agency and would reinforce its resolve in dealing with Iran and North Korea was taken as some sort of conspiracy to encourage ElBaradei to facilitate the transfer of Iran's case to the UN Security Council. This time again, the hard-liners' interpretation prompted the political will (even a conspiracy) internationally to put extra pressure on Iran.

Externally, the IAEA is facing obstruction by non-member states. For instance, according to the Iranian news agency (Islamic Republic News

Agency) in October 2004 Pakistan said that the IAEA could not be allowed to meet or interview its nuclear scientists.[15] If this is correct, then it reveals a different form of resistance to the IAEA investigation. Any access could shed light on how Pakistani equipment has been exported to the black market and to Iran.[16] No doubt Israelis have similar excuses for categorically ignoring international calls for transparency in their nuclear programme.

Iran has been relatively more cooperative with the IAEA, but the reformist government has frequently been criticized by the hard-liners for giving access to "spies". In a resolution adopted on 13 March 2004 by the IAEA Board of Governors, the agency reported that Iran "[has] been actively cooperating with the Agency in providing access to locations requested by the Agency", but that "Iran's cooperation so far had fallen short of what was required".[17]

This can be interpreted in several ways. First, the IAEA has not found any significant proof of Iran's nuclear activities other than what is considered to be normal and peaceful. Second, in the case of Iraq, the IAEA is unhappy about the way its findings were used to justify the war and therefore does not want to play the same role again in Iran. This (if combined with Kofi Annan's statement about the illegality of the war in Iraq[18]) reveals concerns about the role of the IAEA and ultimately of the United Nations in the international security arena and about how their findings could have been used to condone and justify the war on Iraq. The United Nations' function as the only international organization dealing with issues related to global peace and war is constantly being jeopardized by US unilateralism under the current Bush administration. According to *Al-Sharq al-Awsat*, ElBaradei considered that referring Iran's case to the UN Security Council "for violating the provisions of the Nuclear Non-Proliferation Treaty (NPT) would be the worst-case scenario".[19] Yet, many interest groups and even some Iranian expatriates in the United States were extremely pleased that the IAEA Board of Governors, despite a more positive report in 2005, took a major step by the phased referral of Iran's case to the UN Security Council.[20]

Conflict between US global policies and other nations' interests

US unilateralism is widely contested by the international community and, unless other states change their considerations and expectations, there are going to be major disagreements between US global policies and other nations' interests. In the short run, small states such as Iran, pursuing their national interest, can benefit from this global discontent and lack of consensus. Iran has forged separate relations with Russia and Europe to the extent that both have direct and considerable economic interests in Iran. The existence of mutual interests makes it difficult if not impossible to support any Security Council resolution against Iran and therefore Iran can expect such resolutions to be vetoed.

Debates since the 2004 US presidential election indicate that neither the United States nor Israel is eager to take military action against Iran. For obvious reasons, economic sanctions have so far had more negative impacts on US corporations than on Iranians. However, an indirect threat to take military action against Iran has always been one of the options and at times there have been reports about preparations for targeting Iran's nuclear facilities.[21] For instance, in an interview in January 2005 with NBC regarding the US administration's willingness to use military force against Iran, President Bush specified that he would "never take any option off the table" as long as the international community continued to suspect Iran of a nuclear weapons programme.[22] More recently, the US options have always included the military option, but in most cases it looked like a warning to Iran rather than a real decision to use military action.

US involvement in Iraq and US–European involvement in Afghanistan put Iran in a key position. The situation is very similar to the late 1990s when Pakistan used such an opportunity to test its bomb. If Iran had the same type of relationship and had been supportive of the US war in Iraq and Afghanistan, then it could definitely expect a blind eye to be turned to its nuclear activities.

The complexity of regional security issues

Israel has never stopped sounding the alarm – sometimes false, sometimes true – about Iran's alleged nuclear bomb. At the same time, it has increased its own nuclear and conventional capabilities, which threaten the entire Middle East. The Israelis' major concern is based on the fact that Iran supports Hezbollah in Lebanon and Hamas in Palestine and that, if Iran achieved nuclear capability, it would use that capability against Israel.[23] This assumption contains some elements of both myth and truth, given that Iran has never recognized the legitimacy of the State of Israel. However, this rejection of recognition has been purely a matter of rhetoric. At times this rhetoric has even unwisely been used by Iranian leaders. Shortly after Ahmadinejad's comment that "Israel must be wiped off the map" was condemned by the United Nations, the Iranian foreign ministry declared: "The Islamic Republic of Iran is committed to its obligations under the United Nations Charter and has never used or threatened to use force against any other state."[24]

As I shall discuss further, Iran needs to reassure the international community with more transparency and by taking practical steps towards reducing the tensions it has created in the world. Torn between Islamic idealism and reformist optimism, Iran cannot decide which way to go and, because it cannot reassure the international community, its commitment to its international undertakings may be judged ambiguous and uncertain. Iran's multiple decision-making centres and shadow government, which usually overrule the formal government's decisions, threaten its international credibility.

Comprehending the past

I have so far explained in this chapter how the Iranian desire to have the legal right to a nuclear capability evolved from a basic intention to produce a nuclear bomb, scaled down to a desire to produce nuclear fuel. Iran's quest for nuclear capability was always beset by difficulties, and, eventually, the state concluded that if producing a nuclear weapon was currently unlikely its focus should shift toward the production of fuel to be used within the nation's nuclear reactors. Producing a nuclear weapon during the first few years of the war with Iraq was felt to be necessary because of concerns about the regime's sustainability, but this is no longer the case. Several years of trial and error proved that this might not be so easy to achieve as Tehran initially thought.

The completion of the two nuclear plants in Bushehr became a question of the regime's efficiency and later on a matter of the military efficiency of the revolutionary army. Although the lack of technological support and international pressure had made it almost impossible for Iran to produce its bomb, it seemed that producing nuclear energy would be a workable plan. As a result, Iran turned toward international suppliers and, to cut a long story short, finally turned to Russia. This approach had two goals: first, to complete the reactors, which had become a matter of national dignity and pride; and, second, to build up technologies that would eventually help Iran to produce the capability needed to assemble an atomic weapon within one month in the event of an imminent threat. At the same time, Iran has made considerable progress in developing its ballistic missile technology. However, the missiles have no proven targeting efficiency with conventional warheads. It is also unclear how many of these missiles have been produced.

Iran's inability to secure sufficient technological and material components for a bomb, on the one hand, and extreme international pressure and lack of cooperation, on the other, presumably compelled the system to shift its focus from weapons to the more viable and feasible product – nuclear energy. If this assumption is true, then in theory Iran will stay as close to nuclear capability as possible so that a shift from one usage to the other would be possible in the shortest possible time. Parallel to technological progress a broader interpretation of the Non-Proliferation Treaty was adopted. This interpretation is consistent with the approach by India and Pakistan and is based on both the discriminatory nature of the treaty and the fact that Iran's commitments under the NPT do not require it to stop its progress in fuel production. The discriminatory nature of the NPT is nothing new – many nations including Pakistan, Israel and India have never joined the NPT, and even today the prime minister of India would agree with this decision.[25]

Based on the above approach and also on Iran's need for fuel for its nuclear plants, Iran decided to convert its own natural uranium into processed uranium that could be used in future nuclear reactors. This seemed rational and legitimate, and in addition it had incontestable national support. Small pieces of knowledge and expertise here and there, together with considerable help from Pakistan combined with Iranian experts, have made it possible for young technicians trained by Russians to take the lead. In 2003, about 400 Iranian technicians trained in Russia were intended to replace the 1,000 Russian technicians who were installing "peripheral" equipment in Bushehr. Another 300 finished their training later and were supposed to start working at Iranian nuclear plants. Some Iranian experts originally graduated from European universities and were then sent to Russia to get more specialized training.[26] For the most part, however, such activities have been kept hidden and in undisclosed locations.

Iran also finds itself within range of Israeli missile and air attacks and is convinced that Israel would not miss a moment in attacking Iran's nuclear sites the same way it attacked Iraq in 1981. The most recent US planned delivery of "smart bombs" to Israel increases the existing concerns about an air raid over Iran's nuclear facility.[27] Despite the very good relationship established with the IAEA on the continuation of work on the Bushehr nuclear reactors and some other sites where everything was transparent and the IAEA had full access, it is widely believed that Iran might still have some facilities kept secret like the one in Natanz.

Occasionally, the Russians have stalled Iran's rush toward nuclear power by delaying their agreement for various reasons, including delivering or not delivering centrifuge units or disputing the way nuclear wastes should be returned. The possibility of returning nuclear fuel wastes is in fact technically in doubt.[28] Yet, as Russian Foreign Minister Sergei Lavrov arrived in Tehran in October 2004 for an official visit to discuss future nuclear relations, the official Itar-Tass news agency declared that "Moscow's principled stance is that Iran must develop the nuclear program within the framework of the IAEA regime and nuclear Non-Proliferation

Treaty".[29] Earlier, Iranian newspapers had mentioned that the two countries would also discuss the modality of returning fuel waste to Russia, and the Russian news agency MosNews had said that Sergei Lavrov "may discuss missiles with Iran".[30] Usually, the Russian position is to support Iran as long as the United States has no objections, but, when the Americans apply more pressure, the Russians too try to slow down the process. In the absence of more secure economic relations with the rest of the world and facing tremendous economic hardship, the Russians do not want to jeopardize their long-term hard currency income from Tehran.

The rest of the Iranian file is clear. An opposition group that still has some influence inside the country reveals the sites. International pressure increases and Iran sticks to its legal interpretation of the NPT. In response, the conservative right insists on withdrawal from the NPT. At the time, President Khatami and the (then) reformist parliament, which supported his policies, did not want to create a hostile environment and tried to solve the problem by approaching the Europeans. This seemed to be working for a while, but later even the Europeans decide to follow the US and Israeli policy of asking Iran to halt all nuclear activities, including the production of nuclear fuel.

Policy recommendations in the guise of a conclusion

With the latest developments in Iranian domestic politics and the return of the hard-liners to power, Iran's case becomes more and more complicated. What are the options available to both sides of the Iranian nuclear stalemate? Would Iran be willing to give up its existing potential for nuclear fuel processing and probably other capabilities? I shall now try to make some policy recommendations.

Iran's missile and nuclear programmes irritate the Americans and alarm the Europeans, although not as much as they frighten the Israelis (see note 23). Iran has tremendous security problems involving a vast array of implications, which range from territorial disintegration to civil war and from direct external military threats to more immediate threats to its survival as an Islamic entity. The fact that the Soviet Union collapsed while it was a nuclear superpower proves that the nuclear bomb cannot save ideology. At the domestic level there is little doubt that no military would be able to compel people to give up their claims and that a nuclear bomb would not be used in a domestic situation. In other words, the Iranian nuclear capability is not intended to be used against its own people. In the international arena, any step towards transparency and confidence-building will pay off, reducing tension, whereas aggression will only deepen the existing crisis. It is therefore more appropriate to see what could be done by both Iran and the international community to reduce tension and maintain peace and tranquillity in a region where the flames of war have not yet died down since 1980.

Iran

It is absolutely vital to demonstrate that there is only one voice and that it comes through the legal and formal channels of the government. No ultra-governmental channels or shadow government should be permitted to put any pressure on the decision-making process or reverse agreements already made. As a society and a state in which the clerics and the regime's core leaders possess so much power in ultimately setting the Iranian agenda, much progress is needed towards consolidating power within formal structures and limiting the influence of the extremists in setting the main policy agenda. Iran should put an end to inappropriate statements by hard-liners and limit their room for manoeuvre and action on highly sensitive policy issues. Their intervention in Iran's foreign and security policies and provocation of fanatical groups for ideological purposes have only been destructive. Their illegal financial activities are increasingly destabilizing and could gradually connect them to non-state players that are jeopardizing international security, including Iran's own security.

In an era of unilateral action by the United States in the pursuit of its national interest, Iran needs to strengthen its ties with international organizations such as the IAEA and the United Nations, yet it also needs to mend its ties with the United States. If Iran decides to continue its animosity toward the United States and its allies, and reduce its level of cooperation with the United Nations and its organizations, it will automatically isolate itself further and, instead of saving one of the most historic cultures and civilizations of the world, it will work only to fragment it and jeopardize its very existence.

The IAEA and the United Nations

The ambiguity of the NPT is a major obstacle that has to be addressed in the twenty-first century. If today the number of countries considered nuclear capable (formal or informal makes no difference) is less than a dozen, it is not because of the NPT. The Non-Proliferation Treaty is a completely inefficient means of policing international supply and demand and the situation will undoubtedly only worsen in the future. The consumption of oil is rapidly increasing. New markets are opening for the oil-producing countries and populations and local consumption are also on the rise. Nuclear energy may not be enough to satisfy ever-increasing demands because it, too, depends on another shrinking natural resource.

The international community needs a well-defined code of conduct and set of rules to face future problems in all areas. This may include the role of the United Nations and its related organizations such as the IAEA. The IAEA cannot continue to supervise the NPT as long as there is no clear and internationally accepted interpretation of its content. It is time to ink a new treaty or at least to draw new lines on interpretation and implementation of the existing treaty and to re-engage member states or invite non-members to accept the IAEA's supervisory role.

The existence of an international black market in nuclear materials and equipment reveals to what extent the NPT is incapable of regulating international atomic energy issues. As long as other nations in the Middle East and the Indian sub-continent are stockpiling nuclear materials and helping to spread know-how for economic reasons, the IAEA will have a hard time accomplishing its goals. ElBaradei righteously warned in June 2004 that universal non-proliferation would not succeed as long as India, Pakistan and Israel remained uncommitted.[31] It is time thoroughly to revise the treaty and strengthen it for the security of future generations.

The Islamic regime is not an attractive one. Its human rights record, its tolerance for opposing ideas and opposing thoughts, its respect for religious and intellectual minorities, and its support for fanatical groups are all among the factors that distinguish it negatively among other members of the international community. But the NPT is not about the suitability of a political system; it does not define nuclear capability in terms of political ideology or desirability of the political system. The hard-liners in Iran feel surrounded by hostile neighbours, some of them nuclear, and they see the IAEA putting significant pressure on an activity they presume to be fully legal and within the norms of the NPT. They also have the impression that IAEA requirements are infringing the state's sovereignty.

The NPT has no interdiction or prohibition on fuel-cycle works. The clerics – contested as their political regime might be – are even ready to guarantee that their activity has no military objectives. It is precisely on this point that the international community and its supervisory body, the IAEA, could sit and talk to Iran, engage it in a network of obligations and commitments, rather than blackmailing and threatening a nation that is fighting internally for a common cause: democratic rights. Before pushing Iran out of the treaty, and pushing the Islamic regime towards further radicalism, one should try alternatives and give the nation the opportunity to put the nuclear power plant into operation. Full supervision could be imposed and the deal could apparently be fully reversible. At a time when non-members of the NPT profit from freedom of action in their nuclear activities, the IAEA's stubborn and exacting relationship with its member states goes against the peaceful mission of the agency.

Notes

1. Patrick Clawson, ed., *Iran's Strategic Intentions and Capability*, McNair Paper No. 29 (Washington, DC: National Defense University, April 1994), p. 163.
2. Hakan Wiberg, "Small Nation's Strategies", in Yoshikazu Sakamoto, ed., *Strategic Doctrines and Their Alternatives* (New York: Gordon & Breach Science Publishers, 1987), p. 217.
3. Anthony H. Cordesman, "Iranian Military Capability and 'Dual Containment'", in Gary Sick and Lawrence Potter, *The Persian Gulf at the Millenium* (New York: St. Martin's Press, August 1997), p. 192. Also see *Iran: A Country Study* (4th edn, Washington, DC: United States Government, 1989), p. 242.
4. See Paul Klebnikov, "Millionaire Mullahs", *Forbes*, 21 July 2003, ⟨http://www.forbes.com/global/2003/0721/024_print.html⟩.
5. In May 2004 Iran Air had contracted the operation of Iran's new airport to a Turkish–Austrian consortium. The armed forces objected to the contract on the ground that the country's "security" and "dignity" would be jeopardized by such an agreement. They closed down the airport a few hours after its formal operations had started. It was only after the new airport had been closed down that the Supreme National Security Council annulled the contract.
6. See, for instance, David Albright and Corey Hinderstein, "The Iranian Gas Centrifuge Uranium Enrichment Plant at Natanz: Drawing from Commercial Satellite Images", Institute for Science and International Security, 14 March 2003, ⟨http://www.isis-online.org/publications/iran/natanz03_02.html⟩.
7. More details of the facility can be found at ⟨http://www.isis-online.org/publications/iran/natanz03_02.html⟩.
8. On 12 September 2005, a 131-page "Note Verbale" submitted by the Permanent Mission of the Islamic Republic of Iran in Vienna, containing a document entitled "Iranian Nuclear Policy and Activities", explains the Iranian position on its nuclear activities. The full document is available at ⟨http://www.iaea.org/Publications/Documents/Infcircs/2005/infcirc657.pdf⟩.
9. See, for instance, ElBaradei, "Iran Has No Nuclear Weapons Program", 2 October 2004, cited at ⟨http://www.aljazeera.com/cgi-bin/news_service/middle_east_full_story.asp?service_id=5051⟩.
10. "Iran's Hardline Lawmakers Want Withdrawal from NPT", Reuters, 28 September 2004; available at ⟨http://www.iranian.ws/cgi-bin/iran_news/exec/view.cgi/2/3927⟩.
11. As reported by AFP, 24 October 2003.
12. "Iran Ready to Provide Nuclear Guarantees", 28 August 2004, cited at ⟨http://www.aljazeera.com/cgi-bin/news_service/middle_east_full_story.asp?service_id=3277⟩.
13. Cited by Al Jazeera, "Ahmadinejad: Wipe Israel off map", 26 October 2005, ⟨http://english.aljazeera.net/NR/exeres/15E6BF77-6F91-46EE-A4B5-A3CE0E9957EA.htm⟩.
14. See, among other source of news, Amit Baruah, "Circumstances Not Ripe for Signing NPT: Manmohan", *The Hindu*, 8 October 2004, ⟨http://www.hindu.com/2004/10/08/stories/2004100809990100.htm⟩.
15. See ⟨http://www.globalsecurity.org/wmd/library/news/pakistan/2004/pakistan-041002-irna01.htm⟩.
16. The authorities in Islamabad rejected the IAEA's request to visit the Pakistani scientist

Dr Qadeer Khan on the grounds that they trust their own system of investigation and the IAEA cannot hold Pakistan responsible because Pakistan is not a signatory of NPT. "On the same grounds, Israel refused to discuss its nuclear programme with the IAEA, as Tel Aviv is reportedly involved in illicit nuclear black market while carrying out an ambitious clandestine nuclear programme." See Naveed Ahmad, "IAEA Can't Meet Pak Scientists: FO", *The News International*, 2 October 2004, ⟨http://www.jang.com.pk/thenews/oct2004-daily/02-10-2004/main/main5.htm⟩.

17. IAEA Resolution GOV/2004/21, 13 March 2004, cited in "Implementation of the NPT Safeguards Agreement in the Islamic Republic of Iran: Report by the Director General", Doc. GOV/2004/34, 1 June 2004, ⟨http://fas.org/nuke/guide/iran/iaea0604.pdf⟩.

18. See, among others, Evan Augustine Peterson III, "Was the Iraq War Legal, or Illegal, under International Law?", *Information Clearing House*, 17 September 2004, ⟨http://www.informationclearinghouse.info/article6917.htm⟩.

19. As quoted by Al Jazeera, 3 October 2004, ⟨http://www.aljazeera.com/cgi-bin/news_service/middle_east_full_story.asp?service_id=5051⟩.

20. In fact the resolution adopted on 24 September 2005 by the IAEA Board of Governors refers Iran to the UN Security Council without specifying an exact date. The articles of the resolution leave no doubt that the next step could be a referral to the UN Security Council:

"1. Finds that Iran's many failures and breaches of its obligations to comply with its NPT Safeguards Agreement, as detailed in GOV/2003/75, constitute non compliance in the context of Article XII.C of the Agency's Statute;

"2. Finds also that the history of concealment of Iran's nuclear activities referred to in the Director General's report, the nature of these activities, issues brought to light in the course of the Agency's verification of declarations made by Iran since September 2002 and the resulting absence of confidence that Iran's nuclear programme is exclusively for peaceful purposes have given rise to questions that are within the competence of the Security Council, as the organ bearing the main responsibility for the maintenance of international peace and security." For the full text of the resolution, see "Implementation of the NPT Safeguards Agreement in the Islamic Republic of Iran. Resolution adopted on 24 September 2005", Doc. GOV/2005/77, 24 September 2005, ⟨www.iaea.org/Publications/Documents/Board/2005/gov2005-77.pdf⟩.

21. Seymour Hersh writing in the *New Yorker* magazine, 17 January 2005, quoted by CBS News, "Hersh: Iran in U.S. Crosshairs", 18 January 2005, ⟨http://www.cbsnews.com/stories/2005/01/18/world/main667670.shtml⟩.

22. Cited in "Talk of Military Action against Iran 'Unhelpful': ElBaradei", *Sydney Morning Herald*, 31 January 2005, available at ⟨http://www.smh.com.au/news/World/Talk-of-military-action-against-Iran-unhelpful-ElBaradei/2005/01/30/1107020260943.html?oneclick=true⟩.

23. There is a huge uncertainty as to how Iran could use a nuclear bomb against a country that is less than 22,000 km^2 including the West Bank and the Gaza Strip. With current standards, could Iran target any part of Israel without destroying the third-holiest city of Islam, Jerusalem, and without killing many thousands of Palestinians living in the country? I have always doubted that Iran's nuclear capability would deter Israel from an offensive war against Iran.

24. Iranian foreign minister's statement on 29 October 2005, as quoted at ⟨http://www.globalsecurity.org/wmd/library/news/iran/2005/iran-051029-irna01.htm⟩.

25. This has been India's position from the early days of the NPT. Most recently it reiterated its view on the discriminatory nature of the NPT. See Prime Minister Manmohan Singh's interview with Charlie Rose from the Public Broadcasting Service, 21 September

2004. The text is available on the Indian Embassy website, ⟨http://www.indianembassy. org/pm/pm_charlie_rose_sep_21_04.htm⟩.

26. See *Iran Report*, Vol. 6, No. 11 (17 March 2003), ⟨http://www.globalsecurity.org/wmd/ library/news/iran/2003/11-170303.htm⟩.

27. On 27 September 2004 it was revealed that Israel's military arsenal was about to receive US$319 million worth of air-launched ordnance, including some 500 satellite-guided "bunker buster" warheads capable of penetrating 2 metre thick cement walls, plus 2,500 one-ton bombs, 1,000 half-ton bombs and 500 quarter-ton bombs. See ⟨http://la. indymedia.org/news/2004/09/117130.php⟩.

28. The distance from Bushehr to Russia is close to 2,000 miles and the cargo would have to transit through Azerbaijan and reach Russia either through Chechnya or through Turkmenistan and Kazakhstan.

29. Cited by the Islamic Republic News Agency (IRNA), 24 October 2004, ⟨http://www.irna. ir/en/news/view/line-17/0410240773173419.htm⟩.

30. See "Russian Foreign Minister May Discuss Missiles with Iran", MosNews, 7 October 2004, ⟨http://www.mosnews.com/news/2004/10/07/iranmissiles.shtml⟩.

31. See ⟨http://www.iranwatch.org/international/IAEA/iaea-elbaradaei-ceipconference-062104.htm⟩.

12

Arab perspectives on the question of WMD proliferation in the Middle East

Mohammad El-Sayed Selim

Since the end of the Iraqi invasion of Kuwait in 1991, the question of weapons of mass destruction (WMD) has been dominating Middle Eastern politics. The catalyst of this domination was the issue of Iraq's compliance with Security Council resolutions that obliged Iraq to remove its WMD arsenal as a prelude to the elimination of all WMD from the Middle East. Whereas the first task of eliminating the Iraqi WMD has been achieved, the second regional one has stagnated. The regional task was considered within the framework of the Arab–Israeli multilateral talks initiated after the Madrid peace conference of October 1991, especially in the Working Group on Arms Control and Regional Security (ACRS). This Group witnessed major duels between the Egyptians and the Israelis over the modalities of removing WMD from the Middle East, and its meetings were halted without reaching an agreement. The issue surfaced once more in 2002 as the US and UK governments began to argue that Iraq had WMD in violation of the Security Council resolutions and then invaded Iraq in 2003 in order to remove them. However, it was found that Iraq had no such weapons and that the question of WMD was used to camouflage other strategic goals. The issue continued to dominate the region as the Western powers shifted gear towards Iran. It is in this context that Arab countries began to advocate new strategies to deal with the question of WMD in the Middle East.

The objective of this chapter is to review and assess the perceptions of Arab countries (except Egypt) of the question of WMD in the Middle East and their likely impact on the global and regional debate on this issue. This chapter will deal with the following main questions:

1. How have Arab states used and relied upon the current WMD non-proliferation regimes, and how do WMD figure in the strategies of these countries? And what are the key pressures within the region?
2. What are the responses of Arab states to the current non-proliferation agenda of the United States as embodied in the invasion of Iraq, the Proliferation Security Initiative, the resumption of nuclear weapons development (e.g. "mini-nukes"), and the diplomatic approaches vis-à-vis Iran and North Korea?
3. What are the perceptions of Arab states of the factors which account for the failures of WMD non-proliferation regimes?
4. What are the main shifts in Arab approaches towards the issue of WMD in the wake of the invasion of Iraq?
5. How do Arab countries perceive the question of the potential possession and use of WMD by terrorist groups?

I shall conclude with a presentation of a policy framework that reflects the emerging consensus among Arab countries on the question of WMD.

In dealing with these questions, I shall focus on the cases of Syria, Saudi Arabia, Libya and Algeria. This is because the Egyptian case is dealt with in a separate chapter in this book (Chapter 13) and because these countries are the main Arab countries directly involved in the question of WMD in the Middle East, now that Iraq has been removed from the Middle Eastern debate on WMD.

WMD in the strategies of Arab states

No Arab country has nuclear capabilities. Algeria has a 10–15 MW reactor built in Ain Oussera with Chinese assistance. It also has a 1 MW reactor (Nur) at Draria, on the coast, which produces radioactive isotopes. Algeria has signed and ratified the Treaty on the Non-Proliferation of Nuclear Weapons (Nuclear Non-Proliferation Treaty, NPT) and in 1996 signed a comprehensive Safeguards Agreement with the International Atomic Energy Agency (IAEA), providing for IAEA inspections of all Algeria's nuclear facilities. The agreement came into effect on 7 January 1997. In the meantime, Algeria is expanding the use of nuclear power for the production of medical isotopes. There is no evidence of Algeria's deployment or possession of chemical or biological weapons. It has Scud-B missiles with a range of 300 km. In addition to the NPT, Algeria is a full member of the Chemical Weapons Convention (CWC) and the Biological Weapons Convention (BWC).

Libya used to have chemical weapons involving blister and nerve agents and a modest biological research programme, as well as Scud-B, Scud-C and No-dong missiles and some nuclear programmes, which were never turned into weapons. In March 2004, Libya handed over all technical data, material and weapons production equipment for its nuclear programmes to the United States and allowed full IAEA inspection. It also abandoned its chemical weapons programme and missiles with a range over 150 km. Libya has ratified the NPT and acceded to the CWC and the BWC, although it has not developed or produced biological weapons.

Syria has a 30 kW neutron research reactor built in cooperation with China. It is widely believed it has stockpiled 500–1,000 metric tonnes of chemical agents, which include persistent (VX) and non-persistent nerve agents (Sarin), as well as blister agents. It is believed that Syria has some biological capabilities and has Scud-B, Scud-C and SS-21 missiles. Syria is a full member of the NPT but has not signed the CWC or the BWC and did not sign the Additional Protocol of the NPT.

As for Saudi Arabia, it has no known nuclear, chemical or biological capabilities, but does have CSS-2 missiles with a range of 2,650 km and a payload of 2,150 kg. These were purchased in 1988 from China. It has been reported that Saudi Arabia has attempted to benefit from Pakistani nuclear expertise, but this has not been confirmed with any degree of certainty. Saudi Arabia is also a full member in the three global WMD regimes.[1]

Among the four Arab states, Syria is the country that has made the most serious attempts to develop WMD capabilities. This was essentially to compensate for its strategic weakness vis-à-vis Israel, especially after the break-up of the Soviet Union, its main arms supplier during the Cold War. After the end of the Cold War, Syria was surrounded by hostile powers (Israel and Turkey). In addition to its strategic inferiority, the Syrian decision to seek WMD capability was influenced by Israel's possession of nuclear weapons and delivery systems, including three submarines capable of deploying nuclear warheads, purchased from Germany by the mid-1990s. Another factor is Israel's occupation of Syrian territories (the Golan Heights) since 1967, and its decision to annex them to Israel in the early 1980s. The Syrian quest for WMD capability was an attempt to create a rough strategic balance with Israel so as to be able to enter into meaningful negotiations to retrieve the Golan Heights. The Syrians were strongly influenced by a book by Amin Howeidi, a former Egyptian chief of intelligence, published in 1983 in which he encouraged Arab countries to develop non-conventional capabilities (chemical and biological) to counterbalance Israel's nuclear capabilities. He argued that, because it is difficult for Arab countries to gain nuclear capabilities, it is more feasible to develop chemical and biological weapons and use the protection they provide to develop nuclear capabilities.[2]

The Syrian decision was also influenced by Israel's strategic doctrine, which does not limit WMD to a purely deterrent role. In 1962, Shimon Peres, the architect of the Israeli nuclear programme, referred to the idea of "non-conventional compellence", that is, the use of nuclear weapons to force the Arabs to accept Israel's view of the future of the region. In fact, it was revealed that Israel had actually deployed its nuclear warheads against the Egyptians during the early days of the October 1973 war. Later on, Yitzhak Mordekhai, the former defence minister of Israel, suggested that Israel "had tactical nuclear weapons and would be prepared to use them".[3]

A third factor that influenced the Syrian quest for WMD capability was the Iran–Iraq war, which witnessed the massive use of chemical weapons and the success of such weapons to achieve their objective of halting the advance of Iranian forces on Iraqi territory. The Syrians thought that a chemical capability could serve to stop a possible Israeli advance on Damascus. In summary, the main Syrian motive for developing WMD capability was to achieve strategic parity with Israel and to serve as a deterrent and a bargaining chip.

The Libyan decision to seek WMD capabilities was influenced by the mismatch between Libya's strategic vulnerability and its ambitions to gain strategic regional weight. Libya's population is around 2 million, but the country's vast area and long coasts made it almost impossible to provide a credible deterrent. This problem was aggravated by Libya's ambitions for change not only in the Middle East but also in the world. Because these ambitions brought military responses from the West (the US attack against Libya in 1986 and Europe's establishment of rapid intervention forces in the Mediterranean), the Libyans decided to embark on and accelerate their WMD programmes, especially when it became apparent from the Soviet response to the 1986 attack that it was no longer in a position to provide any protection to Libya.

The Saudi motives to obtain long-range missiles were mainly a result of the changes in the Gulf region after the outbreak and prolongation of the Iran–Iraq war in 1981. The main goal was to provide a deterrent against a possible Iranian assault as the war extended to other Gulf countries, namely Kuwait. Iran was thought to have considered a possible attack against Saudi Arabia in response to the latter's support of Iraq, which had resulted in a serious deterioration in Saudi–Iranian relations. Gulf security considerations, rather than the Arab–Israeli conflict, were the main motive for Saudi Arabia to seek long-range missiles.

Likewise, Algeria sought WMD capabilities in order to gain strategic advantage in its north African region. The major motives in its decision were its protracted conflicts with Morocco over the demarcation of the border and the Western Sahara, and its concern about the erratic behaviour of the Libyan regime, which it suspected was developing WMD capabilities.

The decisions of the four Arab countries to acquire WMD capabilities were mainly an outcome of changes in their immediate regional environment. None of them has ventured operational use of these capabilities, and only in the case of Syria was the main target Israel.

Arab responses to the American WMD agenda in the context of the invasion of Iraq

The Anglo-American invasion of Iraq in 2003 was rationalized on the basis of Iraq's possession of WMD in violation of Security Council resolutions. However, it was found that Iraq had no WMD because they had been destroyed either during the 1991 war or by the UN inspectors. The United States continues to pursue a WMD agenda that focuses on countering proliferation in hostile countries such as Iran and North Korea. After the re-election of President George W. Bush, Syria was added to the agenda. Further, in September 2003 the United States announced a Proliferation Security Initiative (PSI), which provided for the interdiction of the transfer or transport of WMD, their delivery systems, and related materials to and from states and non-state actors "of proliferation concern" to Western countries. The countries "of proliferation concern" were not specified in the PSI – the decision to identify them was left to the judgement of the signing powers. Four issues emerged from the new US policy and agenda. These were the US quest to remove WMD from Iraq, the US decision to resume the production of "mini-nukes", the PSI, and the US engagement with Iran and North Korea. A brief review of Arab responses to these issues may be in order.

In responding to the United States' new WMD agenda, Arab countries were reluctant to articulate anti-American views on these issues lest the United States should turn against them. The survival instinct led most of them to express their views cautiously so as not to offend the United States and as a result become a target of US wrath. Indeed, some Arab countries, especially Egypt, subscribed to the American agenda of removing Iraq's presumed WMD; President Hosni Mubarak had argued before the invasion that Iraq had WMD and it should abide by the UN resolutions. Saudi Arabia also provided some logistical support to the American invading troops. However, from the public debate, governmental and non-governmental, around these issues, one can identify some major trends.

Most Arab countries were silent on the issue of the linkage between the invasion and Iraqi WMD. Only Syria argued that the invasion was not related to the question of WMD but reflected strategic objectives to dominate the region. It continued to argue that the United States should admit the illegality of the invasion and withdraw from Iraq as soon as possible. Syria, in conjunction with other Arab countries, argues that the question of Iraqi WMD should lead the big powers to embark on the task of removing WMD from the Middle East as a whole, as stipulated in Security Council Resolution 687 of 3 April 1991, which set out the conditions of the ceasefire with Iraq (Article C/14). The main argument of these countries was that a pan-regional approach should be adopted and that no single country should be exempted from Article C/14.

The second issue was the US decision of May 2003 to resume the production of "mini-nukes". Arab countries expressed concern about this decision, which was initially triggered by the US Senate Armed Forces Committee's repeal of a longstanding ban on the development of small nuclear bombs. The decision was viewed as a setback to US obligations under the NPT. Among these obligations is the eventual global removal of nuclear weapons, including those possessed by the legitimate nuclear powers.

Arab countries also expressed some concern about the PSI. The PSI was launched outside the UN system and as such failed to take into consideration all members of the international community. Further, the PSI focuses on countries that attempt to acquire WMD and pays no attention to those that already possess them through indigenous capabilities, such as Israel. These countries are outside the PSI regime. It was also argued that the PSI would legitimize international piracy because it delegates the interdiction decision to certain countries that are under no legal global obligation to observe any rules.

Finally, the Syrians came out in support of the Iranian decision to pursue a programme for the enrichment of uranium, arguing that this programme was consistent with the NPT; they also called for Israel to be treated similarly. Only the Libyans called on Iran to pursue the Libyan model and give up its WMD; they did not call upon Israel to do likewise. Arab countries have not expressed a specific policy stance on the North Korean nuclear issue. They feel that they already have enough problems without engaging in a remote issue such as the North Korean case, especially if this would create trouble with the United States. Relations between Arab countries and Japan and South Korea could also account for the reluctance of Arab countries to address the North Korean issue. Arab silence reflects sympathy with North Korea, which had been a traditional supplier of missiles to Egypt and Syria. This sympathy never came to the forefront of the debate on WMD. However, Arab countries have noted the difference between the United States' militaristic approach to Iraq and its political approach to North Korea.

These views were mostly advocated by intellectual élites in Arab countries. Their governments were reluctant to make strong statements about American policies because of the new American strategy of military interventionism. Moreover, the Libyan appeal to Iran was widely criticized in the Arab world for its failure to address Israel's nuclear capabilities as well.

Arab perceptions of the failures of the WMD regimes

Despite its adherence to the NPT and the BWC, Iraq had developed an elaborate WMD arsenal. It was on the verge of developing a nuclear bomb, and had already developed chemical and biological capabilities. This situation is considered by some actors as indicating the failure of the global regimes for the control of WMD, and they call for another strategy to prevent the proliferation these weapons. The dominant view in the Arab world holds Western powers accountable for this failure. The failure lies not in the regimes themselves, as is widely argued in the West, but in the West's selective approach to these regimes.

Arab countries argue that the failure preceded the Iraqi case, and should be attributed to the West's unbalanced strategies in the Middle East. They contend that the West facilitated Israel's development of nuclear weapons and protected it from any international control. France had supplied Israel with nuclear reactors, and the United States did its best to make sure that Israel would develop nuclear capabilities. Iraq considered WMD capabilities only when Israel possessed them. Even after the 1991 war, which resulted in the destruction of most of Iraq's arsenal of WMD and was followed by Iraq's acceptance of Security Council Resolution 687, the West continued to refuse any meaningful debate on the question of Israel's nuclear weapons in the deliberations of the Working Group on Arms Control and Regional Security (ACRS), which was part of the multilateral track resulting from the Madrid Peace Conference of 1991, and did not take any steps towards implementing Article C/14 of Resolution 687. It was also Western powers, especially the United States, that supplied Iraq with chemical weapons during the Iran–Iraq war and condoned their use against the Iranians.

Further, Western powers dealt a major blow to the NPT when they violated two major articles in that treaty. The first is the one that stipulates that "legitimate" nuclear powers will eventually remove their nuclear weapons. These powers have not taken serious steps towards those goals. On the contrary, in the 1990 London Declaration, NATO countries asserted that they would keep nuclear weapons indefinitely because new threats had emerged that required them to be retained. The 1993 Strategic Arms Reduction Treaty between the United States and the Soviet Union (START II), which obliged both parties to make drastic reductions in their nuclear weapons, was not implemented and was replaced by the Moscow Treaty of 2002. Although this mandated both countries to reduce their nuclear warheads from 6,000 to 2,200, the removed warheads would not be destroyed but "stored" and as a result could be made operational if needed.

Arab countries also argue that, according to Article IV of the NPT, they are entitled to be given access to nuclear technology for peaceful means. In fact, the NPT rewards countries that ratify it by giving them preferential treatment in gaining access to nuclear energy. However, no such technology was provided. The main case was Egypt, which had a programme to build six nuclear reactors to generate electricity. The West made Egypt's ratification of the NPT a condition for selling it these reactors. Once Egypt had ratified the NPT in 1981, the West, and especially the United States, made every effort to deny Egypt access to nuclear technology.

The policy implication of these assessments is that, if the global regimes for the control of WMD are to have any real credibility, the great powers should pursue a balanced approach to the elimination of these weapons. The solution is not a further tightening of the system of controls, as envisaged by the PSI, but the pursuit of a new approach. This approach will be reviewed in the following section.

Arab approaches to the question of WMD

One may differentiate two main approaches to WMD among the four Arab countries studied in this chapter. According to the first approach, the Arabs should, immediately and unilaterally, rescind any ambitions to possess WMD. Arabs should abide by all global regimes without waiting for Israel to do likewise. This approach makes no linkages between various regional actors' possession of WMD. This is the approach advocated by Libya since it handed over all its WMD programmes and weapons to the United States.

The second approach is mainly advocated by Syria, although Syria's approach went through two main stages: the first stage lasted from 1992 until the Anglo-American invasion of Iraq; the second stage emerged as a result of that invasion. Before the invasion, Syria advocated the comprehensive elimination of WMD from the Middle East, but this should be preceded by an Arab–Israeli political settlement. An Israeli commitment to a "no-first use" of its nuclear weapons would be the first step in the process of their inclusion in the projected arms control regime. Ballistic missiles would not be included in that regime because they are a stabilizing factor given Israel's air superiority. Certain measures could be introduced to minimize the risk of their use, such as pre-notification of the testing of missiles.[5] The main emphasis was thus on the political process, which would lead eventually to the question of WMD being dealt with. This explains why the Syrians boycotted the deliberations of the ACRS, arguing that these deliberations should come after a political settlement had been reached. Ironically, the Syrian approach was congruent with the Israeli one. Israel too focused on reaching a political settlement before dealing with the issue of WMD in the Middle East.

The Syrian approach drastically changed after the Anglo-American invasion of Iraq, to give priority to the elimination of all categories of WMD from the Middle East. In April 2003, Syria presented a draft resolution to the Security Council that called upon the Security Council to adopt the following measures: (i) to emphasize the role of the Security Council in adopting a global approach to countering the spread of all WMD in the countries of the Middle East without exception, (ii) to urge the implementation of the Security Council resolutions, in particular Resolution 487 (1981) and Resolution 687 (1991), which are aimed at freeing the Middle East region from all WMD, in particular nuclear weapons, (iii) to call upon states of the Middle East, as non-nuclear-weapon states, to accede to the NPT, the BWC, the CWC and the Comprehensive Nuclear-Test-Ban Treaty, (iv) to determine to prevent the threat posed by the possession of WMD by terrorist groups, and (v) to request the UN Secretary-General to submit a report within one month from the date of this resolution on the implementation of its provisions. This draft resolution did not link the elimination of WMD with the political resolution of the Arab–Israeli conflict. The Syrians hoped to capitalize on the momentum created by the United States concerning the question of Iraqi WMD to extend the Anglo-American agenda to the Middle East. The Syrian draft resolution did not define the Middle Eastern countries that would be affected by the mechanisms of the resolution if it were adopted. For example, it was not clear if Turkey would be included in the scope of the resolution. Turkey considers itself outside the deliberations on arms control in the Middle East. The draft resolution was also vague on the question of the nuclear weapons already developed by Israel. In any event, under US pressure, the Syrians were forced to withdraw their draft resolution.[6] However, Syria is still advocating the comprehensive and immediate elimination of WMD from the Middle East. This has brought Syria in line with the approach that Egypt has been advocating in the multilateral Middle Eastern talks.

Arab perceptions of WMD terrorism in the Middle East

The attacks on 11 September 2001 in the United States brought to the forefront the question of the potential possession and use of WMD by terrorist groups. In fact, this issue was being discussed after the fall of the Soviet Union because of the resulting vulnerability of the WMD arsenal possessed by its heir states to potential theft from insiders. Advances in technology have also made terrorism using WMD easier to carry out.[7]

The dominant view in the West, China and Russia is that WMD terrorism is a real possibility and as such it represents a threat. The US Central Intelligence Agency warned in October 2004 that Iraqi resistance groups were attempting to acquire nerve gas materials in addition to biological weapons to be used against US forces.[8] Some American academics have also outlined scenarios for the possible use of WMD by terrorist groups.[9] A Chinese scholar has expressed concerns about the threat of WMD possession by terrorist groups.[10] Mohamed ElBaradei, the Director General of the IAEA, encouraged world leaders to make more effort to prevent terrorists from obtaining nuclear materials that could be used for operational purposes, arguing that there had been 650 cases of the smuggling of nuclear radioactive materials during the last few years.[11]

The issue has been discussed in the Middle Eastern context in many ways. In its draft resolution to the Security Council, Syria referred to the potential use of WMD by terrorist groups and used that scenario to advocate a pan-regional approach to WMD elimination. One may also refer to the initiative developed by some Arab non-governmental organizations (NGOs) to eliminate WMD from the Middle East. The initiative is entitled "A Message to the NGOs and Governments participating in the Treaty on the Non-Proliferation of Nuclear Weapons Concerning their Elimination from the Middle East". The initiative was widely discussed at a conference held under the auspices of the Egyptian Council for Foreign Relations and the Afro-Asian Peoples Solidarity Organization in Cairo on 15 March 2005. The initiative pointed to the threat that terrorist groups could possess WMD, and used that argument to plead for a global non-discriminatory approach to WMD elimination. The 2003–2004 volume of the *Arab Strategic Report* published in Cairo also referred to "scenarios of nuclear terrorism after September 11".[12]

The dominant view in the Arab world is that the issue of WMD terrorism has been blown out of all proportion and is being used to legitimize Western aggression and a discriminatory WMD agenda. Prince Turki bin Abdel-Aziz, the former Saudi chief of intelligence, has said that he had received no information concerning WMD possession by terrorist groups.[13] The *Arab Strategic Report* also concluded that nuclear terrorism was unlikely owing to the complexities involved in manufacturing a nuclear weapon. It added that the acquisition of a ready-made nuclear bomb would not help because such a bomb will be a "dead device" in the hands of the terrorists.[14]

Conclusion

One of the major features of Arab approaches to the question of WMD is the convergence between the Syrian and Egyptian approaches. Both approaches advocate the immediate and pan-regional elimination of all categories of WMD without waiting for the completion of the Middle East peace process. Implicit in these approaches is a concern about the United States' new selective counter-proliferation strategy and the advocacy of a linkage approach. These linkages include (i) linking the elimination of all categories of WMD – nuclear, chemical and biological – and their means of delivery, (ii) linking the elimination of WMD and the establishment of a pan-regional arms control regime because conventional weapons could be as devastating; and (iii) the simultaneous linking of the elimination of destructive weapons from all Middle Eastern countries, including Israel.

In the judgement of Arab countries, the worst scenario would be to deepen the present strategic imbalance in the Middle East by keeping Israel outside the global WMD regimes. This scenario is unlikely to lead to a genuine peace process. What is new in the Arab discourse on WMD is the involvement of Arab NGOs in the debate, as reflected in the March 2005 conference held in Cairo where they expressed concern about the new American agenda. In my judgement, Arab approaches and concerns are not likely to be reflected in the debate over the question of WMD in the Middle East, as these views are being expressed from a position of strategic inferiority and global unipolarity.

Notes

1. In reviewing the WMD capabilities of the four Arab countries, I relied mainly on Anthony Cordesman, *The Proliferation of Weapons of Mass Destruction in the Middle East* (Washington, DC: Center for Strategic and International Studies, March 2004); Ian Lesser, "Weapons of Mass Destruction in the Middle East: Proliferation Dynamics and Strategic Consequences," in Nora Bensahel and D. Byman, eds, *The Future Security Environment in the Middle East: Conflict, Stability and Political Change* (Santa Monica, CA: Rand, 2004), pp. 253–298; Mohammad Abdel-Salam, *American Policy towards Nuclear Issues in the Middle East*, Strategic Papers series No. 146 (Cairo: Al-Ahram Center for Political and Strategic Studies, December 2004); Paul Jabber, *A Nuclear Middle East: Infrastructure, Likely Military Postures and Prospects for Strategic Stability* (Los Angeles: Center for Arms Control and International Security, UCLA, September 1977).

254 MOHAMMAD EL-SAYED SELIM

2. Amin Howeidi, *Al-Sira'a Al-Arabi Al-Israeli bayn Al-Radie Al-Nawawi wa Al-Radie Al-Taklidi [The Arab–Israeli Conflict between the Nuclear and the Conventional Deterrents]* (Beirut: Center for Arab Unity Studies, 1983).

3. Eyal Zayser, "Syria and the Question of Weapons of Mass Destruction", *Ara'a Houl Al-Khaleeg [Opinions on the Gulf]* (Dubai), 4 December 2004, pp. 43–48. Nadia El-Shazly and R. Hinnebusch, "The Challenge of Security in the Post-Gulf War Middle East System", in Raymond Hinnebusch and A. Ehteshami, eds, *The Foreign Policies of Middle East States* (Boulder, CO: Lynne Rienner, 2002), pp. 84–85.

    The Iraqis expressed similar motives for developing WMD. Before the 1990–1991 war, they presented three major reasons for developing WMD capability: (i) to deter the Zionist threat, (ii) to deter Iranian ambitions in the Arab world, and (iii) to protect Arab resources. Ahmed Ibrahim Mahmoud, *Al-Irak wa Aslihat Al-Damar Al-Shamel [Iraq and Weapons of Mass Destruction]* (Cairo: Al-Ahram Center for Political and Strategic Studies, 2002), pp. 18–20.

4. Mohammad Selim, "Towards a New WMD Agenda in the Euro-Mediterranean Partnership: An Arab Perspective", *Mediterranean Politics*, Vol. 5, No. 1 (Spring 2000), pp. 133–157.

5. Mohammad Diab, "Regional Arms Control in the Arab–Israeli Conflict: A Syrian Viewpoint", *Review of Palestinian Studies (Majallat al-Dirasat al-Filistinya)*, Vol. 18 (Spring 1994), pp 38–52 (in Arabic). In this respect, the Syrian approach differed from the Egyptian one. The crux of the Egyptian approach to WMD is the simultaneous elimination of all forms of WMD; in other words, the Arabs and the Israelis would join all global regimes for the control of WMD at the same time and Israel would place its nuclear arsenal under international control as a prelude to its destruction. In this context, Egypt links its accession to the CWC to Israel's endorsement of the NPT and its denuclearization within a specified framework. Further, the Egyptians favour the adherence of all actors to the verification measures of the IAEA. The Egyptians call for a ban on the transfer and local production of WMD and their ingredients, arguing that a ban only on the transfer of WMD technology would work in Israel's favour because it manufactures a considerable portion of its needs for WMD locally. They also prefer to begin the process of removing all forms of WMD from the Middle East without necessarily waiting for the completion of the peace process. Removing such weapons, in their judgement, would provide a strong momentum to the peace process. Mohammad Selim, "Conceptualizing Security by Arab Mashreq Countries", in Hans Gunther Brauch et al., eds, *Security and Environment in the Mediterranean* (Berlin: Springer, 2003), pp. 333–344.

6. These issues were dealt with in detail in the draft "Treaty on Declaring the Middle East an Area Free of Nuclear Weapons and Other Weapons of Mass Destruction" prepared by the League of Arab States. The draft treaty called upon the parties to refrain from developing, testing, using, threatening to use, receiving, possessing, providing or deploying all categories of WMD, whether directly or on behalf of a third party. It also obliged the parties to destroy all stored WMD, and established a system of verification. This draft treaty is still under discussion in the League. The draft treaty included in the Middle East all member states of the League, Iran, Israel, Turkey, Cyprus, Malta and Pakistan. The inclusion of countries such as Turkey, Malta, Cyprus and Pakistan is extremely controversial. For example, Pakistan is not likely to accept being included in the Middle East unless India is too.

7. Rashed Uz Zaman, "WMD Terrorism in South Asia: Trends and Implications", *Perceptions* (Ankara), Vol. 7, No. 3 (September–November 2002), pp. 124–139. Niaz Naik, "American and European Perceptions on WMD and Terrorism", in Naveed Ahmad Tahir, ed., *US–European Relations in the Contemporary International Setting: Implica-*

tions for the Developing World (Karachi: Area Study Center for Europe, University of Karachi, 2004), pp. 99–101.

8. *Al-Ahram* (Cairo), 11 October 2004.

9. William Potter, C. Ferguson and L. Spector, "The Four Faces of Nuclear Terrorism and the Need for a Prioritized Response", *Foreign Affairs*, Vol. 83, No. 3 (May–June 2004), pp. 130–132. Alan Lamborn and J. Lepgold, *World Politics into the Twenty-First Century* (New Jersey: Prentice-Hall, 2003), pp. 248–250.

10. Ouyang Liping, "Non-proliferation under Circumstances of Counter-Terrorism", *Contemporary International Relations* (Beijing), Vol. 13, No. 7 (July 2003), pp. 10–19.

11. Quoted in *Al-Ahram*, 17 March 2005.

12. *Arab Strategic Report, 2003–2004* (Cairo: Al-Ahram Center for Political and Strategic Studies, 2004), pp. 127–130.

13. Ibid.

14. Ibid.

13

An Egyptian perspective

Mohamed I. Shaker

On 17 August 1965, the first American draft treaty on the non-proliferation of nuclear weapons was submitted to the Conference on Disarmament in Geneva, known then as the Conference of the Eighteen-Nation Committee on Disarmament (ENCD).[1] The Conference members came from three distinct groups: the North Atlantic Treaty Organization (NATO), the Warsaw Pact and the Non-Aligned Movement (NAM). There were five members each from NATO and the Warsaw Pact and eight members from NAM, among which was Egypt (then known as the United Arab Republic).[2] Egypt found itself entangled in protracted negotiations of the Treaty on the Non-Proliferation of Nuclear Weapons (Nuclear Non-Proliferation Treaty, NPT), which lasted in the ENDC until April 1968 and then resumed at the United Nations General Assembly, which on 12 June 1968 commended the final text of the treaty as it stands today.[3]

Egypt signed the NPT on the first day it was opened for signature, 1 July 1968. It did so on the basis of the active role it played in laying down the principles that guided the NPT negotiations and as a leading party in the negotiations. However, it postponed its ratification for almost 13 years, hoping to ratify the treaty if Israel were to adhere to it. In 1968, Israel already had a nuclear research reactor at Dimona in the Negev Desert that was not under international safeguards administered by the International Atomic Energy Agency (IAEA) and that went critical in December 1963. It was then, and still is, a source of great concern to Egypt and to the Middle East region at large. In the circumstances, it was not possible for Egypt to take a further step down the road and ratify. It did so, however, on 22 February 1981 for two basic considerations.

The first was the realization by Egypt that it would be difficult if not impossible to develop further its electrical power on a large scale through the introduction of nuclear power plants (about 8–10 units) without the ratification of the NPT and the application of full-scope safeguards by the IAEA. To continue with the old policy of linking ratification with the adherence of Israel to the NPT would have meant, in the words of the then deputy prime minister and minister of foreign affairs, Kamal Hassan Aly, in the Shura Assembly (the Upper House), allowing "others to veto the development and promotion of our peaceful programmes needed to achieve prosperity and well being of our people".[4]

A secondary consideration was Israeli support for the establishment of a nuclear-weapon-free zone in the Middle East, an Egyptian–Iranian initiative put forward in 1974. A consensus resolution was adopted at the UN General Assembly in 1980.[5] The initiative, now led by Egypt, receives an annual endorsement by the UN General Assembly.[6]

Alas, Egypt's rationale for its NPT ratification failed to materialize. On the one hand, and as a result of the Chernobyl accident in Ukraine in 1986, Egypt decided to shelve its nuclear power plants project, which was on the verge of opting for its first plant at Dabaa on the north coast of Egypt, west of Alamein. The site of the project is still reserved and fenced round. On the other hand, and apart from continued Israeli support for the yearly UN General Assembly resolution on a nuclear-weapon-free zone in the Middle East, Israel seems as far as ever from joining the NPT as a non-nuclear-weapon state. A few Israeli officials and scholars, supported by others, would like to see Israel, along with India and Pakistan, accommodated within the NPT regime or in the context of a new non-proliferation regime. I shall come back to these attempts later. It is also believed that, if Egypt had not ratified the NPT before the Israeli attack of June 1981 on the Iraqi nuclear research centre, it would have been difficult for Egypt to ratify the treaty in the aftermath of the attack and even beyond.

After ratifying the NPT, Egypt, for years, found in its initiative on a nuclear-weapon-free zone in the Middle East a yearly reminder of the importance of engendering a sense of security in its region along with other initiatives within the United Nations or the IAEA calling upon Israel to adhere to the NPT and to IAEA full-scope safeguards as well as calling for a study on verification of such a zone. The thrust forward of the other initiatives is relentless and is not hindered by occasional setbacks or resentment from certain quarters, including Israel and the United States.

Egypt fully supported the formation of a UN expert group on the establishment of a nuclear-weapon-free zone in the Middle East. The report produced in 1990 by the group remains to this date the only solid attempt to deal with the different aspects of the establishment of such a zone.[7]

On 8 April 1990, Egyptian President Hosni Mubarak put forward another proposal for the establishment of a Middle East zone free of weapons of mass destruction (WMD), thus adding other weapons of mass destruction to nuclear weapons. The new initiative coincided that year with several worrying reports and actions indicating that Iraq was trying to acquire equipment and materials relating to weapons of mass destruction. Egypt seemed keen indirectly to draw the attention of the world community to the importance of averting an escalation in the acquisition of weapons of mass destruction in the region. Israeli nuclear weapons capability was also foremost in the mind of President Mubarak when he put forward this new proposal. President Mubarak emphasized the following:

1. All weapons of mass destruction, without exception, should be prohibited in the Middle East, i.e. nuclear, chemical, biological, etc.
2. All states of the region, without exception, should make equal and reciprocal commitment in this regard.
3. Verification measures and modalities should be established to ascertain full compliance by all states of the region with the full scope of the prohibitions without exception.[8]

The initial reaction to President Mubarak's new initiative was surprisingly lukewarm. For example, the Foreign Office in London issued a statement just taking note of the initiative. There was, however, a delayed reaction to Mubarak's vision. A few months later, in the aftermath of Operation Desert Storm to free Kuwait from Iraqi occupation, revelations about Iraq's weapons of mass destruction attracted the attention of the world in a dramatic way and led to the adoption of Security Council Resolution 687 of 1991 ordering the dismantling of weapons of mass destruction in Iraq, a process that extended well into March 2003 when war on Iraq was launched by the United States, the United Kingdom and the coalition forces.

Following the adoption of Security Council Resolution 687, the then minister of foreign affairs of Egypt, Amre Moussa, forwarded another letter to the UN Security Council in which he pointed out that recent events in the Middle East induced many states to endorse Egypt's latest initiative, which was also endorsed by the Security Council in the context of its Resolution 687 (1991).[9] The resolution indicated that the dismantling of weapons of mass destruction in Iraq could lead to the beginning of the establishment of a WMD-free zone in the Middle East. The minister spoke of according priority to ridding the region of weapons of mass destruction. In order to accelerate the establishment of the Middle East as a zone free of weapons of mass destruction, a number of proposals were put forward by Mr Moussa:

a) Egypt calls on the major arms-producing States – and particularly the permanent members of the Security Council – as well as Israel, Iran and the Arab states to deposit undertakings with the Security Council in which they clearly and unconditionally endorse the declarations of the Middle East as a region free of weapons of mass destruction and commit themselves not to take any steps or measures which would run counter to or impede the attainment of that objective.

b) Egypt calls on the arms-producing States and the parties to the Treaty on the Non-proliferation of Nuclear Weapons to step up their efforts to ensure that all Middle East nations which have not yet done so to adhere to the Treaty, in recognition of the fact that this is a step of the utmost importance and urgency.

c) Egypt calls on the nations of the Middle East region which have not yet done so to declare their commitment:
   i.   Not to use nuclear, chemical or biological weapons,
   ii. Not to produce or acquire any nuclear weapons,
   iii. Not to produce or acquire any nuclear materials susceptible to military use and to dispose of any existing stock of such materials,
   iv. To accept the International Atomic Energy Agency safeguards regime whereby all their nuclear facilities become subject to international inspection.

d) Egypt calls on those nations of the region which have not yet done so to declare their commitment to adhere to the Treaty on the Non-Proliferation of Nuclear Weapons, as well as to the Convention concerning the prohibition of biological weapons of 1972, no later than the conclusion of the negotiations on the prohibition of chemical weapons being conducted by the Conference on Disarmament in Geneva.

e) Egypt calls on Middle East States to declare their commitment actively and fairly to address measures relating to all forms of delivery systems for weapons of mass destruction.

f) Egypt calls on nations of the region to approve the assignment to an organ of the United Nations or another international organization of a role, to be agreed upon at a future date, in the verification of these nations' compliance with such agreements on arms reduction and disarmament as may be concluded between them.[10]

Egypt pursued the 1974 and 1990 initiatives simultaneously. The latter initiative has not affected the yearly submission by Egypt of a resolution on the nuclear-weapon-free zone to the UN General Assembly. It should be deduced from the above-mentioned proposals that Egypt's priority and real worry are nuclear weapons and more particularly Israeli nuclear weapon capabilities. However, Egypt's thrust forward on weapons of mass destruction led to another study, this time in 1996 by the United Nations Institute for Disarmament Research on a zone free of weapons of mass destruction in the Middle East.[11]

Between the 1990 initiative and the 1996 study, the Madrid Conference on the Middle East convened in 1991. Under its umbrella, bilateral Arab–Israeli negotiations took place and multilateral tracks were initiated among which was the establishment of a Working Group on Arms Control and Regional Security (ACRS).[12] The work of ACRS reached a dead end in 1994 as a result of a sharp divergence of views between the Arabs and the Israelis. Whereas the former wanted to pursue the nuclear issue and to force the Israelis to open up on it, the latter wanted to concentrate solely on confidence-building measures, on which some progress was made in the group. Israel's objections to dealing with the nuclear issue have been based on its refusal to forgo the element of ambiguity in its policy, arguing that a discussion of this matter would lead Israel down a slippery slope.[13]

During the same period (1990–1996), the Chemical Weapons Convention was opened for signature on 13 January 1993 and entered into force on 29 April 1997. Egypt and a few Arab countries abstained from adhering to the Convention in the absence of Israel's adherence to the NPT, which raised speculations about Middle Eastern countries' capabilities in waging chemical warfare, or using chemical weapons as a deterrent or an equalizer vis-à-vis Israeli nuclear weapon capability.[14]

In 1995, when the NPT was extended indefinitely, a key resolution on the Middle East closely linked with the three decisions adopted by the NPT Review and Extension Conference called for the creation of a zone free of weapons of mass destruction in the Middle East.[15] There would have been no consensus on any of the three decisions, including the decision on the indefinite extension of the treaty, without the Middle East resolution. However, implementation of the resolution is lagging and facing difficulties. In the words of one US delegate, the resolution was "a mistake". It is worth mentioning that the resolution was sponsored by the depository governments designated by the NPT, i.e. Russia, the United Kingdom and the United States.

The League of Arab States, whose headquarters are in Cairo, is actively contributing to the efforts towards the establishment of a zone free of weapons of mass destruction in the Middle East. A special committee within the League opted for the establishment of such a zone instead of a nuclear-weapons-free zone. It was entrusted with negotiating a draft treaty on the establishment of a WMD-free zone. The committee made great progress but many issues have yet to be agreed upon and settled, such as verification mechanisms within the zone, along with IAEA and possibly OPCW (Organisation for the Prohibition of Chemical Weapons) verifications, as well as the geographical delimitations of the zone, etc.

At the Arab League's annual Summit in Tunisia in May 2004, a statement was issued calling for the convening of an international conference under the auspices of the United Nations for the establishment of a WMD-free zone in the Middle East.[16] It was expected that this move would be followed by specific action within the United Nations to translate this call into an action plan, such as suggesting a new item on the UN General Assembly agenda or submitting a draft resolution under an appropriate agenda item calling for the convening of an international conference. Those are matters that ought to be carefully planned and executed.

In all of this, Egypt has been playing a leading role in moving ahead with its proposal for a zone free of WMD in the Middle East. It is quite interesting that the ruling party in Egypt, the National Democratic Party, at its annual conference in September 2004 asserted in its policy paper *Egypt and the World* the importance of responding positively to President Mubarak's initiative.[17] It confirmed the importance of convening an international conference on non-proliferation and freeing the Middle East from weapons of mass destruction and, more particularly, nuclear weapons. The paper went on to say that the conference would be of great significance, especially in the current international climate in which the tendency was towards tightening restrictions and international norms with regard to non-proliferation of weapons of mass destruction while failing to deal effectively with the nuclear programmes falling outside international control, an implied reference to Israel in particular.

The idea of an international conference on weapons of mass destruction in the Middle East under the auspices of the United Nations is not a completely new idea. Soon after his proposal of 1990, President Mubarak hinted at the possibility of convening an international conference for the elimination of all weapons of mass destruction worldwide. This was long before the conclusion of the Chemical Weapons Convention of 1993 and the recent attempts to improve the verification procedures of the Biological Weapons Convention of 1972.

But why the call now for an international conference on weapons of mass destruction in the Middle East? In my view there are four basic reasons:

• There is a genuine need on the part of the Arab countries for international involvement in establishing a zone free of WMD. It reflects a realization that the countries of the Middle East cannot do it alone, in contrast to what other nations have achieved in their respective zones by their own efforts. One such example is the Treaty of Tlatelolco in Latin America, although the parties to that treaty secured guarantees from the five nuclear-weapon states as defined in the NPT not to use or threaten to use nuclear weapons against the zone.

- Now that the efforts to check the proliferation of weapons of mass destruction have had some success – for example in Iraq (Security Council Resolution 687 of 1991 and successive relevant resolutions), Libya (the dismantling of its WMD in April 2004) and Iran, which signed the Additional Protocol to the Safeguards Agreement with the IAEA and has undertaken to freeze uranium enrichment – Israel's nuclear weapon capabilities still haunt us in the region, especially if we take into consideration the brutal and oppressive practices of the Israeli government in the occupied Palestinian territories.

- The United Nations has so far failed to convene a further special session on disarmament where the issue of a WMD-free zone could have been further elaborated upon and developed. Furthermore, the unlikely possibility of convening a UN conference on disarmament and arms control similar to the UN conferences on population, women, the environment, and so on, led to a tendency to concentrate on a conference on WMD in the Middle East. In any case, if such a conference were to take place, it would have to be linked in some way with the disarmament process in general. This was felt to be important to non-governmental organizations concerned with disarmament. The NPT Review Conference of 2000 prescribed 13 steps on disarmament, and more particularly nuclear disarmament, with the approval of the five nuclear-weapon states, which unfortunately have not done much to comply with the recommendations of the conference. It should also be recalled that, at that conference, Israel was mentioned for the first time by name as the only state in the Middle East not party to the NPT. It was called upon to adhere to the treaty.

- There is a slight opening up on nuclear issues among Israeli scholars. They are not as inhibited as they used to be a few years ago on these issues. Informal gatherings and the so-called second-track meetings have contributed to this new attitude.

The first step in the preparation of the proposed international conference should be taken by the Arab states activating their statement issued in Tunisia by formally requesting the convening of this conference under the auspices of the United Nations. The second step would be to make good preparations for the conference by establishing a preparatory committee that would meet two or three times before the conference takes place. Also, raising the matter at the 2005 NPT Review Conference should have helped attract world attention to this initiative, especially through the UN General Assembly.

In convening such a conference, the factor of non-state actors should not be neglected. In other words, the potential of international terrorism using weapons of mass destruction should not be overlooked. The Middle East has suffered greatly from terrorism, both state and non-state. It is believed that the discussion of weapons of mass destruction in the Middle East with a view to eliminating them from the region would not be complete without dealing with the terrorist factor. It had been widely reported in the media that some equipment and materials disappeared in Iraq in the midst of the chaos of war in the country.

In a draft study in 2004, the Carnegie Endowment suggested a number of commendable measures with regard to the supply of nuclear materials and fuel.[18] However, it must be emphasized that any measures pre-empting nuclear terrorism should not affect the inalienable right of all nations to invest in peaceful uses of nuclear energy without hindrance or obstacles.

There is a tendency in some influential quarters to lament a loophole in Article IV of the NPT, the article that promotes international cooperation in the peaceful uses of nuclear energy. In response to this view, it must be said that, without Article IV of the NPT, there would have been a loophole in the NPT. There would have been no NPT without Article IV. If parties to the NPT such as Iran are to give up their right to invest in certain nuclear technologies, they must in return be assured of the supply of equipment and materials needed for their peaceful nuclear programmes.

Iran is not the only case. Assurances of supply must be given to all parties to the NPT on an equal basis. Unfortunately, the IAEA experience a few years ago is extremely disappointing. The IAEA Committee on Assurances of Supply, which is now defunct, failed to convince the supplier states to give such assurances. Also, the UN Conference on the Promotion of International Co-operation in the Peaceful Uses of Nuclear Energy held in Geneva in 1987 failed to agree on a set of principles in this domain as a result of the major suppliers' reluctance to approve of these principles. Would the suppliers be forthcoming now, or would they rather treat case by case, as in the Iranian case? What is really needed are reliable and legally binding assurances of supply to all. Recipients, especially developing countries, have to have secure supplies. Many of them have experienced a long history of exploitation and deprivation of basic needs for political reasons. The IAEA may be entrusted as the guarantor of supply, as suggested by the report of the UN Secretary-General's High-level Panel on Threats, Challenges and Change referred to below.

This brings us to the export control regimes, which are virtually cartels in which guidelines and policies are planned without consultation with the recipients. Is this in conformity with the spirit and letter of Article IV of the NPT? Certainly not.

Going back to non-state actors, Security Council Resolution 1540 of 28

April 2004 prescribed for the first time under Chapter VII the way to contain, respond and act to face up to potential WMD terrorism. One reservation with regard to this justified resolution is that the Council is trying to legislate for matters that should be legislated by states through treaties and conventions. That is why it is important to call for an international conference on terrorism that would have the opportunity to tackle, among other issues, WMD terrorism and to recommend certain actions or negotiations with a view to concluding international agreements. Here again, Egypt has repeatedly renewed its call for such an international conference, another initiative it is keen to carry through.

Now that the December 2004 report from the UN Secretary-General's High-level Panel on Threats, Challenges and Change entitled *A More Secure World: Our Shared Responsibility*[19] has come up with substantive elements of a definition of terrorism,[20] the way may be open to convene an international conference on terrorism, which has stumbled for many years because of international controversy over a definition.

The same report dealt with weapons of mass destruction: nuclear, radiological, chemical and biological weapons.[21] A key segment of the report says that the "nuclear non-proliferation regime is now at risk because of lack of compliance with existing commitments, withdrawals or threats of withdrawal from the Treaty on the Non-Proliferation of Nuclear Weapons to escape those commitments, a changing international security environment and the diffusion of technology. We are approaching a point at which the erosion of the non-proliferation regime could become irreversible and result in a cascade of proliferation."[22]

This rather pessimistic view needs to be taken seriously. The report was right in pointing to the nuclear-weapon states that should honour their commitments under Article VI of the NPT. It is also recommended that negotiations to resolve regional conflicts should include confidence-building measures and steps towards disarmament. It went on to recommend that "peace efforts in the Middle East and South Asia launch nuclear disarmament talks that could lead to the establishment of nuclear-weapon-free zones in those regions".[23]

All of the above is very much in line with Egypt's known positions and beliefs and, more importantly, with regard to its two initiatives on WMD-free and nuclear-weapon-free zones. If any such zones were to materialize, it would be a boost to the crumbling non-proliferation regime. With the spread of such zones around the world, together with progressive steps towards nuclear disarmament in accordance with Article VI, the NPT might one day become less relevant, not because of violations and non-compliance, but, on the contrary, because of positive steps and parallel effective regional mechanisms.

Lastly, the report recommended that "States not party to the Treaty on the Non-Proliferation of Nuclear Weapons should pledge a commitment to non-proliferation and disarmament, demonstrating their commitment by ratifying the Comprehensive Nuclear-Test-Ban Treaty and supporting negotiations for a fissile material cut-off treaty, both of which are open to nuclear-weapon and non-nuclear-weapon States alike".[24]

The report avoided calling upon states not party to the NPT in the Middle East and South Asia (i.e. Israel, India and Pakistan) to adhere to the NPT. Instead they have been asked to join the CTBT, the cut-off treaty and the nuclear-weapon-free zones, as earlier indicated. Their status as nuclear-weapon states would not be compromised with regard to the first two measures, but would be with regard to nuclear-weapon-free zones or WMD-free zones and certainly the NPT. Nuclear-weapon states are clearly defined in the treaty to mean only the five nuclear-weapon states that happen to be the five permanent members of the UN Security Council.[25] If Israel, India or Pakistan were to adhere to the NPT, it could not but mean that they would be giving up their nuclear weapon capabilities, thus adhering to the treaty as non-nuclear-weapon states, a far-fetched possibility.

In order to get round this dilemma, two trends have emerged, supported by Israeli scholars and others. One suggests inviting Israel, India and Pakistan to accede to an additional protocol to the NPT obliging them to behave "as if" they were members of the treaty.[26] Such a protocol would permit the three states to retain their programmes but would inhibit further development.[27] The second trend advocates a new regime to replace the NPT and include the three non-NPT states. With regard to the latter states, only fissile materials produced for peaceful purposes would be monitored.[28]

Without going into the details of these proposals, it is clear that the three non-NPT nuclear-weapon states would continue with their nuclear weapon capabilities unabated. Either they would undertake to abide by certain provisions of the NPT that would not affect their nuclear weapon status; or they would abide by a new regime that would bring them closer to or on par with the acknowledged five NPT nuclear-weapon states. In other words, nuclear-weapon status would be conferred upon them and endorsed by either the present or the "new" non-proliferation regimes. Israel, a country that has stated that it would not be the first to introduce nuclear weapons into the region, would find itself being forced to accept a status, implicitly or explicitly, that it has so far hesitated to recognize.

Accommodating the three countries, whether within the NPT regime or a "new regime", might encourage further proliferation within the NPT regime. Non-compliance and violations have already plagued the regime, and the suggested accommodation could exacerbate the malaise. In such an atmosphere, the disarmament process in compliance with Article VI of the NPT might also be further downgraded or disregarded.

Moreover, a protocol attached to the NPT would be tantamount to an amendment of the treaty, whose parties have agreed to follow certain procedures and conditions prescribed by the treaty that seem to be rather difficult, if not impossible, to fulfil. In the past, additional protocols to the NPT have been suggested with regard to other issues but they were quickly discarded or withdrawn because of the aforementioned considerations.

In the particular case of Israel, the way is wide open for it to adhere to the NPT and abide by its provisions as a non-nuclear-weapon state. A unilateral declaration of behaviour as if it were a party to the NPT, the alternative proposed by some, is meaningless if Israel's status remains ambivalent and if its nuclear activities are not subjected to the verification system of the IAEA. There is a direct route to inspire non-parties to abide by the NPT regime, simply adhering to the treaty. Why invent other routes that would in fact legitimize the status quo and appear to Israel's neighbours as outright appeasement?

Israel's nuclear programme is a source of great anxiety in the Middle East. Security cannot prevail in the region in the shadow of Israel's growing nuclear weapon capabilities. The establishment of a nuclear-weapon-free or WMD-free zone ought not to wait until a comprehensive peace in the Middle East is established. The two processes should proceed simultaneously. The second phase of the roadmap to peace in the Middle East, which has lately received a boost by its sponsors, the United States, the European Union, the United Nations and Russia (known as the Quartet), prescribes reconvening the multilateral tracks, including the Working Group on Arms Control and Regional Security (ACRS). The latter would be a convenient vehicle for assessing and following up on the progress achieved so far in establishing the free zone.[29]

The way ahead is fraught with serious difficulties and obstacles. The removal of WMD threats should be high on the peace agenda. With vision and determination, we could reach our destination and achieve our targets. And as rightly said by an Egyptian representative at ACRS, "without dwelling on who has what, let us discuss what a nuclear (or WMDs) free Middle East should look like, what conditions are necessary to establish such a region".[30]

Notes

1. Disarmament Commission Official Records, Supplement for January–December 1965, DC/227, Ann.1, Sec.A (ENDC/152, 17 August 1965).
2. After the secession of Syria in 1961, it was decided by the authorities in Cairo to continue with the "United Arab Republic". "Egypt" re-emerged as the Arab Republic of Egypt in 1972.

3. For the history of the NPT negotiations, analysis and early implementation, see Mohamed I. Shaker, *The Nuclear Non-Proliferation Treaty: Origin and Implementation*, 3 vols (Dobbs Ferry, NY: Oceana Publications, 1980).
4. Arab Republic of Egypt, Ministry of Foreign Affairs, *Egypt and the Treaty on the Non-Proliferation of Nuclear Weapons* (Cairo: State Information Services, 1981), p. 76.
5. Ibid., pp. 74–75.
6. See, for example, General Assembly Resolution 59/63, UN Doc. A/Res./59/63, 16 December 2004.
7. UN Department for Disarmament Affairs, Report of the Secretary-General, *Effective and Verifiable Measures Which Would Facilitate the Establishment of a Nuclear-Weapon-Free Zone in the Middle East* (New York: United Nations, 1991).
8. "Letter dated 16 April 1990 from the Permanent Representative of Egypt to the United Nations addressed to the Secretary-General", UN Doc. A/45/219–S/21252, 18 April 1990.
9. "Letter from the Minister of Foreign Affairs of Egypt to the Secretary General of the UN", UN Doc. A/46/329–S/22855, 30 July 1991.
10. Ibid.
11. Jan Prawitz and James F. Leonard, *A Zone Free of Weapons of Mass Destruction in the Middle East* (Geneva: United Nations, 1996).
12. For an analysis of the work of ACRS by an Israeli analyst, see Shai Feldman, *Nuclear Weapons and Arms Control in the Middle East* (Cambridge, MA: MIT Press, 1997).
13. For an Egyptian point of view, see Nabil Fahmy, "Reflections on the Arms Control and Regional Security Process in the Middle East", in James Brown, ed., *New Horizons and New Strategies in Arms Control* (Albuquerque: Sandia National Laboratories, 1999), pp. 173–189. Fahmy was a political adviser to the Egyptian foreign ministry until September 1997, and represented Egypt at ACRS. At present he is the Egyptian ambassador in Washington.
14. See, for example, the detailed study by Anthony H. Cordesman, *The Proliferation of Weapons of Mass Destruction in the Middle East* (Washington, DC: Center for Strategic and International Studies, 2004).
15. For the text of the Middle East resolution and the three decisions of the Conference, see 1995 Review and Extension Conference of the Parties to the Treaty on the Non-Proliferation of Nuclear Weapons, *Final Document*, NPT/Conf.1995/32, Part I (New York, 1995).
16. "Tunis Declaration Issued at the 16th Session of the Arab Summit, Held in Tunis on May 22–23, 2004", ⟨http://www.arabsummit.tn/en/tunis-declaration.htm⟩.
17. *Misr Walaalam* [Egypt and the World], National Democratic Party Annual Conference, September 2004, p. 5.
18. George Perkovich et al., *Universal Compliance. A Strategy for Nuclear Security* (Washington, DC: Carnegie Endowment for International Peace, June 2004), Part Five, pp. 43–60.
19. *A More Secure World: Our Shared Responsibility. Report of the Secretary-General's High-level Panel on Threats, Challenges and Change*, UN Doc. A/59/565 (New York: United Nations, 2 December 2004).
20. Ibid., paras 163–164, pp. 48–49.
21. Ibid., Part V, pp. 38–45.
22. Ibid., para. 111, p. 39.
23. Ibid., paras 120–124, p. 41.
24. Ibid., para. 124, p. 41. The seven foreign ministers of the New Agenda Coalition (Brazil, Egypt, Ireland, Mexico, New Zealand, South Africa and Sweden) were of the view that a fissile material cut-off treaty would impose restraints on India, Israel and Pakistan,

"together with the test-ban treaty, it would go a long way to uphold the nonproliferation treaty and strengthen the norm on nuclear nonproliferation and nuclear disarmament" ("Nonproliferation and Disarmament Go Hand in Hand", *International Herald Tribune*, 22 September 2004).

25. NPT, Article IX, para. 3 stipulates: "For the purpose of this Treaty, a nuclear-weapon State is one which has manufactured and exploded a nuclear weapon or other nuclear explosive device prior to 1 January 1967."

26. Sverre Lodgaard, "Making the Non-Proliferation Universal", *WMDC Papers*, No. 7 (2004). A shortened version of the paper was presented at the 54th Pugwash Conference, Seoul, South Korea, 4–9 October 2004.

27. Avner Cohen and Thomas Graham Jr, "WMD in the Middle East: A Diminishing Currency", *Disarmament Diplomacy*, No. 76 (March–April 2004), pp. 22–25.

28. Ephraim Asculai, *Rethinking the Nuclear Non-Proliferation Regime*, Memorandum No. 70 (Tel Aviv: Jaffee Center for Strategic Studies, 2004) quoted by Brig. Gen. (ret.) Shlomo Brom in his contribution to this volume (Chapter 20). Ephraim Asculai is a former Israeli Atomic Energy Commission official.

29. An Egyptian analyst has suggested that, as a prelude to the resumption of ACRS, a series of two- or three-day official meetings should be held between regional players to discuss the meaning and requirements of security in a "Middle East at peace". He further suggested that, when ACRS reconvened, it should not immediately re-establish an operational basket before it had reached consensus in the conceptual basket on the meaning of security and on how to provide it (the "operational basket" deals with a range of military issues and confidence-building measures; the "conceptual basket" addresses long-term objectives of the arms control process). Fahmy, "Reflections on the Arms Control and Regional Security Process in the Middle East", p. 185.

30. Ibid., p. 187.

Part V

The permanent five: Part of the problem or devising new solutions?

14

An American perspective: The US response to proliferation in weapons of mass destruction

Damon Coletta

The United States homeland, unscathed by two world wars and a 40-year showdown against Soviet nuclear weapons, suddenly appears more vulnerable than it was back in the early days of the republic. In those first years after ratification of the Constitution, the United States contended with great power land and naval forces on all sides. Now, in the opening years of the twenty-first century, any failing state or rogue state can provide the necessary breeding ground to sustain a terrorist network. Al-Qaeda demonstrated that such a network could operate foreign cells embedded in the infrastructure of European allies and the United States itself. The genius of the terrorists' attack on 11 September 2001 (9/11) lay in the modest amount of physical effort needed to spin vital American systems – transportation, communication, finance and skilled training – violently out of control. If four jet-liners could cause such damage, Americans had to wonder what might happen if al-Qaeda or a follow-on terrorist group acquired even a few nuclear weapons.

Proliferation in weapons of mass destruction (WMD) has concerned the United States since the dawn of the atomic age. In previous decades though, the threat came from a state counterpart, one with a bureaucracy to engage and fixed assets to threaten if necessary. Al-Qaeda apparently operates well enough without either of these. If it possessed nuclear weapons, there is little the United States could do to deter or persuade the terrorists from tearing once again at the social fabric of the nation with horribly destructive strikes that could induce widespread panic.

The most likely proliferation sources for instruments of mass destruction are under-secured materials in Russia or arsenals from states that choose to defy international proliferation regimes. While the first problem has already inspired unprecedented multilateral cooperation involving annual contributions on the order of US$1 billion from the United States, the second supply route places enormous pressure on the national security apparatus to act before dangers gather.[1]

At the strategic level, what 9/11 most clearly accomplished was to wrench the American nation-state from its position of majestic repose to that of an eagle on the edge. The olive branches, on the eagle's right in the presidential seal, have fallen away, reserved only for those countries – and international organizations – that stand clearly with the United States. Meanwhile, the arrows on the eagle's left have multiplied for any party that presses too close to the United States' newly exposed vulnerability.

The strategic shift is both rational and foreseeable. It is also dangerous: if the United States strikes too many regimes with its superior conventional forces, it may stop proliferation threats in the short term but, eventually, even allies may resist the United States' assault on the bedrock principle of inviolable state sovereignty. Its military and economic strength notwithstanding, the United States could exceed the limits of its power, exhausting itself in lengthy occupations. The list of countries suspected of sponsoring terrorism or pursuing nuclear weapons programmes could grow as governments opposed to the United States consider a dash across the threshold of secure second-strike capability before the United States decides to eliminate them with a swift, high-tech campaign such as those unleashed against the departed Taliban and Saddam Hussein. Vigorous action by the United States against near-term threats can make the long-term solution to proliferation of weapons of mass destruction more difficult to reach.

In order to better understand the US response to proliferation threats after 9/11, it is useful to note how competing impulses, not always of equal strength, have vied for the soul of US policy in the past. On occasion, the United States has advocated steps toward a permanent solution involving international control. At other times, it has demonstrated willingness to counter impending dangers with a more aggressive response. Once placed in historical context, twists in US non-proliferation efforts after 9/11 and Operation Iraqi Freedom are more easily understood. The dual nature of the US perspective means that the dovish impulse, although not always plainly apparent, is unlikely to disappear forever. Despite current tensions, there remains substantial overlap of interest between the United States, leading supranational bodies such as the United Nations and the European Union, and many individual states that inevitably face consequences from American action.

The historical pursuit of dual goals

From the first atomic explosion, those responsible for US policy understood the instinctive revulsion experienced by atomic scientists who knew
best what they had created.[2] The scientists' horror was compounded by
the urgency with which they had applied their talents to build the bomb.
They raced to prevent Nazi Germany from achieving an atomic monopoly only to fortify new dangers in the aftermath of World War II, namely
a nuclear exchange between the United States and the rising Soviet
Union. Throughout the history of US efforts to prevent proliferation,
America agonized over similar competing concerns: to deter strategic
threats through superior nuclear arms or to cement world recognition
that general use of these weapons in war would be disastrous for civilization as a whole.

Several of the original atomic scientists indeed backed an effort toward
mutual nuclear disarmament in 1945–1946.[3] The plan, presented by US
Representative to the United Nations Bernard Baruch, called for complete nuclear disarmament in order to prevent a catastrophic third world
war, with fissile materials and processing technologies secured under an
international authority tied to the United Nations Atomic Energy Commission.[4] The fear of a world populated by several nuclear states, each
crowding the threshold for launching an attack to avoid becoming the
victim of destruction themselves, prompted the United Nations General
Assembly formally to support international controls in 1948. By that
time, however, the Soviet Union had insisted that the United States give
up its nuclear monopoly, that is, unilaterally disarm in the face of overwhelming conventional imbalance in Europe, before the rest of the world
submitted incipient production facilities to supranational authority.

The US reaction, reinforced after the Soviets' first nuclear explosion in
1949, the invasion of South Korea in 1950 and the election of Dwight Eisenhower to the presidency in 1952, was to keep, as far as possible, design information away from adversaries while permitting limited cooperation with the United Kingdom. In order to maintain the balance of
power in Europe as well as on the periphery of Asia, the United States
veered away from the Baruch Plan principles, increasing its reliance on
nuclear superiority.

Nevertheless, one of the chief implementers of Eisenhower's strategy,
Secretary of State John Foster Dulles, seemed to be of two minds on the
utility of nuclear weapons.[5] In response to communist pressure in Asia,
he brandished nuclear weapons, establishing "brinkmanship" as a diplomatic complement to the New Look force structure. Should an adversary
call the US bet, however, Dulles was aware of the disaster if nuclear
threats led to a large-scale exchange. The era of the New Look emphasis

on nuclear weapons was also the era of proposals such as "Atoms for Peace" and "Open Skies", which sought mutual safety through greater international control of nuclear materials and facilities. Atoms for Peace restricted the availability of fissionable materials by obligating the United States and the Soviet Union to supply a new international body, the International Atomic Energy Agency (IAEA), with uranium. The IAEA would then assist developing countries in constructing reactors for peaceful purposes in return for their commitment to refrain from building atomic bombs.[6] Open Skies was designed to shore up obstacles to vertical proliferation in the Soviet Union and the United States as each of the powers consented to foreign monitoring of their nuclear facilities.

Despite his hard-line reputation, Dulles did not reject these proposals out of hand. Restricting the supply of fissionable materials and detecting expansion of operations were reasonable approaches to preventing the Soviet Union from acquiring a large arsenal that might be used for a devastating surprise attack. Yet, similar to the case of the Baruch Plan, mistrust between the leading powers, and further divisions pitting states vested in the status quo against non-nuclear states, undermined long-term cooperation.

Both the United States and the Soviet Union again raced forward with more weapons and improved missiles. Furthermore, the Soviets rejected the premise of Open Skies, which froze their numerical inferiority in place at the same time that it provided the Americans with more information for a more effective first-strike option. Damage to the prospects for a global non-proliferation regime stemming from civilian assistance under Atoms for Peace became apparent later, after India – one of the largest countries outside either the communist or Western blocs – detonated its own surprise nuclear explosion in 1974.[7]

By that time, aid for civilian purposes and the IAEA had been incorporated into the Treaty on the Non-Proliferation of Nuclear Weapons (Nuclear Non-Proliferation Treaty, NPT). Although not agreeing to place their arsenals under international control, the superpowers, in the somewhat warmer climate of relations following the Cuban missile crisis, did commit themselves before the international community to good-faith efforts for the reduction of their nuclear complexes. This was in return for promises from all declared nuclear powers under the treaty not to transfer – for profit or for purposes of alliance – nuclear weapons technology to aspiring states. Non-nuclear signatories, for their part, pledged to cooperate with the IAEA and restrict themselves to civilian uses; essentially, this meant technology for slow reaction rates, below the threshold required for a nuclear explosion.

The 1968 NPT became one of the crown jewels in a sprawling arms control regime developed during the years of superpower détente. If international agreements constitute conditional delegation of sovereign authority, then the United States in the ensuing decade established a new precedent for accepting international interference in basic national security decisions. The 1972 Interim Agreement on the Limitation of Strategic Offensive Arms (SALT I) placed explicit, albeit light, constraints on the numbers and types of platforms the superpowers could build for long-range delivery, and the 1972 Anti-Ballistic Missile (ABM) Treaty prohibited either side from pursuing a plausible defence against the "assured destruction" of a large-scale nuclear strike. In addition to the drama of superpower summit meetings, the signing of these agreements created institutions, such as the Standing Consultative Commission, and rules of the road, such as those facilitating national technical means of verification, that further narrowed the acceptable range of nuclear behaviour.[8]

Unfortunately for optimists who welcomed a steady, if incremental, march toward international control of nuclear weapons, several events, particularly in the latter half of the 1970s, made it difficult for the United States to refrain from hedging its bets in ways that undermined more ambitious attempts at multilateral cooperation. The surprise 1974 nuclear explosion orchestrated by India served notice that civilian assistance encouraged by the NPT for developing countries could not be entirely separated from the capacity to manufacture weapons-grade materials. On the broader geopolitical chessboard of the Cold War, America's humiliating retreat from Viet Nam in 1975, along with growing Soviet-backed rebellions in Angola and Nicaragua and direct Soviet intervention in Afghanistan by the end of the decade, called into question the linkage between advances in nuclear arms control and the nurturing of more stable, businesslike relations between the superpowers.[9]

In fact, Cold War hawks questioned whether the elaborate catechism of rules and rituals regarding nuclear weapons, purportedly designed to build confidence, might actually lull the United States into a false sense of complacency. To be sure, the United States continued to compete in nuclear dimensions, improving accuracy and expanding the number of warheads on treaty-controlled platforms with multiple independently targetable re-entry vehicles (MIRVs). At the same time though, the United States government hesitated over whether to produce the neutron bomb or the supersonic B-1 bomber. Moreover, the 1979 SALT II Treaty signed by President Carter seemed to codify US numerical inferiority in the arms race without sufficiently guarding against the potential of Soviet breakout. Soviet duplicity might play out in the form of a new "offensive" missile large enough to deliver extremely high-yield warheads to hardened targets.

Responding to these concerns, the early Reagan years featured withering attacks on the international regime for arms control. Consistent with the president's characterization of the Soviet Union as the evil empire, negotiations stalled on several initiatives for international regulation of the superpower arsenals. Yet, even in this climate of mistrust, the Reagan administration continued to abide by the still unratified limits of SALT II and to express a long-term desire for not just ceilings on future expansion but mutual force reductions.

During the early 1980s, when the rhetoric of the mini Cold War was at its most vituperative, arms control advocates suspected that the professed administration goal of arms cuts – conveniently consistent with commitments made under the NPT – actually provided political cover for rejection of the old regime while expansion proceeded under a sharply rising defence budget. Much of this build-up involved the modernization of conventional systems, but many who feared the demise of arms control achievements such as SALT, the ABM Treaty and the NPT could draw a clear link between new radars and interceptors for Reagan's Strategic Defense Initiative and a future that saw even greater superpower reliance on vertical proliferation. Larger numbers of offensive nuclear weapons would overwhelm potential defences and preserve a secure second-strike capability.

As it happened, the ascendance of a new generation of leadership personified by Mikhail Gorbachev inaugurated a turn toward more cooperative superpower relations. By the end of the decade, intrusive monitoring to verify significant arms reductions did not seem far-fetched. The Intermediate-Range Nuclear Forces (INF) Treaty, signed in December 1987, eliminated a class of nuclear-tipped ballistic missiles from Europe and introduced on-site inspections among the nuclear powers. The first Strategic Arms Reduction Treaty (START), completed in 1991, kicked off a steep decline in the number of nuclear warheads held by both sides, from some 11,000 to 6,000 each, that would carry on through the 1990s.[10] This followed after Reagan, during a summit with Gorbachev in Reykjavik, Iceland, nearly committed the United States to a major step in the ultimate vision of NPT: the dismantling of all offensive ballistic missiles.[11]

The stunning achievements at superpower summits spilled over into multilateral forums for restraining the spread of nuclear weapons.[12] The year of the INF Treaty also saw the inauguration of the Missile Technology Control Regime (MTCR). By making it more difficult to acquire delivery systems, signatories hoped to lower the incentives for states on the cusp of acquiring nuclear warheads. As numbers fell in the leading arsenals, all five declared nuclear powers saw greater advantages in expanding and strengthening the NPT. Between 1978 and 1990, 12 states joined the Nuclear Suppliers Group, and stricter controls were advanced through bilateral meetings. Recipient countries of civilian nuclear aid were encouraged to sign more intrusive inspection protocols with the IAEA.[13]

After the fall of the Soviet Union, cooperative non-proliferation with strong support from the United States advanced on two fronts. Several states with highly developed nuclear reactor programmes, including Brazil, Argentina and South Africa, pledged not to build nuclear weapons and acceded to the Non-Proliferation Treaty. Second, the Russian Federation and the United States agreed that intensified cooperation was vital for reducing and securing the former Soviet arsenal. Overriding misgivings in the US Congress about military aid to a strategic competitor, the United States government provided some US$7 billion over 10 years to fund a suite of cooperative threat reduction (CTR) programmes. Broadly speaking, the activities included an effort to "repatriate" nuclear weapons and de-activate related facilities located in newly independent republics such as Belarus and Ukraine. Best practices for destroying platforms, mothballing warheads and securing reactors were shared and financially supported from the United States. A special programme from the US Department of Energy provided funds to create a soft landing for ex-Soviet scientists and engineers who might otherwise lend their services to aspiring nuclear states. CTR funding dipped with the arrival of George W. Bush at the White House but, two years after 9/11, the CTR budget had recovered, reaching US$1.5 billion for 2003.[14]

In short, from the end of World War II to 9/11, despite the frequent outbreak of acute threats, the United States maintained its interest in a long-term solution to the profound security problem presented by nuclear weapons. Although this solution necessitated cooperative regimes and international authority, the United States, at the same time, could never banish its fear of the nightmare scenario in which it lay at the mercy of a nuclear aggressor that somehow managed to escape disarmament verification measures. The next section maintains that the dramatic ascendance of non-state terrorist networks as a primary security threat did not extinguish the cooperative impulse in what has always been a dichotomous approach to nuclear weapons. Despite an apparent shift toward a more aggressive response, including the development of new deployment techniques and a new strategic triad suitable for nuclear superiority after 9/11, the United States remains receptive to multilateral programmes for controlling the spread of mass destruction weapons.

The current policy for non-proliferation

One perspective on the current non-proliferation policy for the United States pays close heed to the unilateralist rhetoric of the Bush administration. Negative reactions to early opportunities for international cooperation such as the Kyoto Protocol on greenhouse gas emissions and the International Criminal Court confirmed the impression of an arrogant "hyper-power" that saw little need to indulge what it viewed as prideful or jealous claims from weak allies. Although the administration was careful not to target the NPT in principle, in certain areas related to proliferation, such as the proposed Comprehensive Nuclear-Test-Ban Treaty (CTBT) and the ailing ABM Treaty, it showed no nostalgia for the Cold War arms control edifice.[15]

The run-up to the Iraq war, billed as both a counter-terror and a counter-proliferation operation after 9/11, reopened wounds in relations between the United States and key interlocutors on both terror and nuclear weapons. The United States walked with the United Nations halfway down the road to disarming Iraq but, when it came time to tighten the legal noose around any remaining WMD programmes, the United States lost patience. In frustration, the Bush administration admonished the international community, arguing that the United Nations Security Council was useless for reducing proliferation as long as it could not muster the will to enforce its own resolutions. The United States would not stand idly by while Saddam Hussein used UN inspections and deliberations to play for time to build his arsenal.

Since no weapons of mass destruction have been found in Iraq, and the congressionally mandated 9/11 Commission found that no operational links tied al-Qaeda to Iraqi agents before the US-led invasion, US nonproliferation policy is ripe for criticism. The US willingness to ignore the results of Security Council deliberations and to carry out unilateral regime change on mere suspicion of nuclear weapons development makes it hard for many international observers to imagine that there might still be room in the US approach for multilateral cooperation and international controls. Despite the watershed events of 9/11 and Operation Iraqi Freedom, however, several American choices indicate enduring hope in international agreements rather than in the use of force as a long-term solution to the conundrum first posed by Bernard Baruch in 1946: namely that an arena of sovereign states armed with nuclear weapons would produce destabilizing crises as each leader confronted a narrow choice between "the quick and the dead".[16]

To be sure, neoconservative hawks in the Bush administration make any olive branches in US policy harder to detect. They place a premium on being quick, rejecting second thoughts on the invasion of Iraq. According to this muscular perspective, decisive pre-emption forestalled a probable attack on the United States that eventually would have been executed or sponsored by Saddam Hussein. Even so, the case of Iraq should be viewed not solely in terms of today's hawkish rhetoric but also against the backdrop of a broader-based scepticism in the twenty-first century about the denial of WMD to determined proliferators.

In an analysis of the indefinite extension of the NPT, a measure that was supported by the United States and passed the Treaty Review Conference in 1995, George Rathjens, a science adviser to President Eisenhower and a long-time advocate of international arms control, described how the technology of nuclear proliferation had evolved since the treaty's first signing in 1968. The scientific and engineering know-how to turn a bundle of fissile material into a bomb had diffused over three decades, and the options for acquiring weapons-grade material through uranium enrichment or the reprocessing of spent fuel from civilian reactors were expanding. Even a relatively small state, if it were willing to spend years and a significant percentage of its gross domestic product, could eventually assemble a fission bomb with a fair chance of deterring the United States.[17]

Rathjens' concerns on technical grounds were supported by various unpleasant surprises throughout the 1990s. Inspectors after the 1991 Gulf war were shocked at how far Iraqi scientists had progressed in their nuclear weapons programme while under the IAEA inspections mandated by the NPT. North Korea, another one-time signatory, held its NPT status hostage while fending off international interference in its programme to divert enough spent plutonium from its civilian reactor at Yongbyon to fashion one or two nuclear bombs.

Well before President Bush's "axis of evil" remarks in his 2002 State of the Union address, America's experts viewed Iraq, North Korea and Iran as the most dangerous aspiring states. Prior to 9/11, it was difficult to envision the United States mobilizing domestic and international support for exercising the full range of options against these would-be proliferators. The so-called rogue states cut themselves off from the constraining influence of the international community in many respects, but even they had fixed assets to hold at risk. If the non-proliferation policy failed, nuclear war might be more likely, but war in any form was not the obvious next step.[18] Proliferation optimism, the notion that new nuclear states would exercise caution to avoid uncontrolled escalation in a foreign crisis, did not convince the United States to abandon efforts for slowing the spread of nuclear weapons, but it did make the more extreme counter-proliferation options of a disarming blow or regime change seem disproportionately costly.[19] The catastrophic union of international terrorism and what might be called WMD tactics in 2001 precipitated a dramatic reassessment of the costs of using force, and particularly regime change, as an instrument for counter-proliferation.

Despite this shift in threat and a recalibration of the costs of aggressive options, other items remained on the counter-proliferation menu. The

Clinton administration, faced with increasingly demanding requirements in its peaceful denial strategy, had previously expanded to the "8 D's" of counter-proliferation, which included "denial" but ranged from "dissuasion" to "destruction".[20] While the Bush administration captured headlines by reasserting the importance of pre-emptive force to deny terrorists access to WMD, the *National Security Strategy* and the *National Strategy to Combat Weapons of Mass Destruction* of 2002 reiterated the full panoply of policy tools.

Because the Bush administration tool-set matched the 8 D's, technically speaking, there was no brand-new US doctrine of pre-emption. Even though the United States appeared more willing to entertain pre-emptive or preventive attacks, it did not lose its sensitivity to war costs. It remains reluctant to drain the treasury in defence of something called "the pre-emption doctrine" that, in principle, would require regime change in every state of concern with evidence of a nuclear weapons programme. Several commentators have already noted US pragmatism in the very different treatment accorded surviving members of the axis of evil after the war in Iraq.[21] An equally valid way of viewing US policy on North Korea and Iran emphasizes the long-term continuity in US efforts oriented toward dissuasion, diplomacy and denial as complementary to the threat of pre-emptive strike.

On North Korea, for example, the Bush administration slowed the pace of negotiations – to the dismay of some arms controllers, who would like to see Kim Jong-il re-engaged in international agreements that, nominally at least, commit his regime to nuclear disarmament. Yet, neither the Clinton administration nor the Republican-controlled Congress was enamoured with the 1994 Agreed Framework, well before Bush administration experts began their review in March 2001. In the face of a vexing problem, including the high cost to Seoul of any of the destruction alternatives, the Bush administration in June 2001 adopted a policy that actually resembled former Secretary of Defense William Perry's recommendation to President Clinton after a similar review in 1998 calling for broader engagement with North Korea.

The most serious deterioration in talks under Bush came later, in the fall of 2002. This followed new evidence of North Korean uranium enrichment that violated the spirit of the 1994 Agreed Framework between the United States and North Korea and the common understanding of commitments under the NPT. The hard-line reaction of the United States probably accelerated the collapse of the Framework and North Korea's withdrawal from the NPT. Yet, even during the darkest months when the US government declined to talk directly with North Korea, there were episodes of back-channel diplomacy: the North Korean visit with Democratic Governor Bill Richardson of New Mexico in January 2003 and the visit by Stanford University researchers in January 2004 after the first, inconclusive round of talks. Every round of those Six-Party Talks, in turn, relied upon international cooperation among several declared nuclear powers under the NPT – the United States, Russia and China – as well as regional, non-nuclear powers – South Korea and Japan. The multilateral forum permitted the Bush administration to engage North Korea without explicitly rewarding it for illicit uranium enrichment activities.

After the third round of Six-Party Talks in June 2004, the United States, in acknowledgment of positions taken by its partners, demonstrated flexibility. It offered a return to the mix of energy and security incentives for North Korea if that country submitted to a rapid and verifiable nuclear disarmament protocol. North Korea spurned the offer, objecting to the sequencing and probably eyeing the upcoming American elections, but the international community took note.[22] In the year following Bush's re-election, North Korea accepted a new round of talks and agreed, in principle, to abandon nuclear weapons along with existing nuclear weapons programmes in exchange for Western security assurances and energy assistance.[23]

The United States and international partners have also cooperated on other initiatives to re-emphasize dissuasion, denial and defence rather than destruction in counter-proliferation. In 2003, the United States and several maritime allies inaugurated the Proliferation Security Initiative (PSI) for interdicting illegal shipments of WMD-related materials. Spain signed on early because of a previous misstep in attempting to help the United States. After acting on US intelligence and performing a daring seizure of North Korean missiles on the high seas in December 2002, it received word that the shipment involved a legal sale to Yemen. In a concession to international procedure, the United States then requested release, and Spain, despite its chagrin, permitted the ship to continue on its way. Spain at that time was a close ally of the United States in pressuring Iraq. More impressively, by May 2003, PSI had attracted key opponents of the Iraq war – France and Germany. Though many physical and legal obstacles to creating a foolproof net for WMD proliferators remain, PSI won broad support from some 60 states before its one-year anniversary in 2004.[24]

The success of PSI notwithstanding, the Bush administration still laboured under a reputation for dismantling cooperative arms control, stemming from its dumping of the venerable Anti-Ballistic Missile Treaty. Yet, the story of ABM and counter-proliferation through missile defence had its cooperative aspects. As mentioned, the Clinton administration understood the low likelihood of perfectly enforcing denial strategies, and "defence" had played a more prominent role toward the end of President Clinton's second term. The technical challenges of protecting cities from a small-scale attack of the type anticipated from a rogue state or terrorist group were continually shifting as were the political-strategic consequences of abandoning the ABM regime.

Though al-Qaeda did not launch missiles on 9/11, the imagery of projectiles crashing into skyscrapers and detonating huge explosions, along with the United States' inability to track and intercept the third and fourth airplanes after the first two struck New York, fired the imaginations of US leaders as well as potential overseas partners. In December 2001, critics highlighted President Bush's unilateral withdrawal from one of the central arms control agreements of the 1970s. Less prominent was the diplomatic triumph implied by the surprisingly mild concerns expressed by Russian and West European leaders. Their countries and other important players such as Japan, South Korea and India were approached in 2002 about the possibility of competing for subcontracts in missile defence, thereby giving substance to the notion that America could think simultaneously in terms of unilateral options and multilateral opportunities. The United States also demonstrated that, consistent with principles of cooperative security if not the ABM Treaty, it had less interest in protecting itself from missile-based WMD attack if like-minded nations would be left completely vulnerable.[25]

Originally, acceptance of ABM constraints had been considered, in the vertical sense, as an anti-proliferation measure. By leaving the leading powers clearly vulnerable to destruction through missile attack, strategic incentives pointed toward a secure second-strike capability and no further. There was no need to pour resources into offensive forces in order to overwhelm defences that did not exist. In 2002, however, cooperative ABM served horizontal anti-proliferation by decreasing the incentives for small-time proliferators. ABM defences reduced the chances of success for a rogue state or terrorist network that could muster only a few ballistic missiles. Technological and strategic obsolescence – not lawless unilateralism – led both the Clinton and Bush administrations to legally weaken and eventually lift the ABM ban. At least in this important case, an American "assault" on one ailing global regime reinforced another, more critical multilateral norm against proliferation.[26]

Even after the shock of 9/11, defence, denial and dissuasion continue to serve as complementary elements of US counter-proliferation policy. Steps toward initial ABM deployment have been accompanied by fresh calls for an international fissile materials ban, along with continuing reductions in both strategic and sub-strategic nuclear weapons.[27] The measures on defence and denial support dissuasion under the NPT. Aspiring states facing the prospects of cooperative missile defence and a multilateral fissile material cut-off have a much longer, more arduous road to

produce an effective strike capability. Adding positive security and economic incentives to the mix – of the sort now on the table in talks with
North Korea – could help encourage general NPT compliance and dissuade states now weighing the potential benefits of nuclear weapons.

That said, not all the 8 D's work together smoothly in all instances.
Completed at about the same time as the new National Security Strategy,
the Bush administration's 2002 Nuclear Posture Review identified a US
vulnerability that might be neutralized most effectively with a new class
of nuclear weapon. The concern relates to hardened deeply buried facilities, within the financial reach of a rogue state or even a global terrorist
network poaching territory within a weak state, that could be used for
developing WMD. The problem is that, even if such a secret facility
were discovered and even if the political will existed to mount a counter-
proliferation strike, the United States would not be able to destroy the
complex using conventional bombs. The surest military solution would
be to deliver a highly explosive package deep under the Earth's surface
and, to keep that package as small as possible, the Bush administration
in 2003 requested and received authorization from Congress to research
custom nuclear warheads.[28]

It may be the case that no new fissile material and no new nuclear testing will be required to develop nuclear bunker busters, and it may also be
true that the net number of US nuclear warheads can decline even as the
tailored warheads are fielded. The United States, however, will struggle
to maintain its NPT obligation to reduce reliance on nuclear weapons
even as it assigns them to new, high-priority missions. Proliferation
destruction and dissuasion do not always go hand in hand.[29] In tacit acknowledgement of this tension, the Bush administration dropped its 2006
congressional funding request for nuclear bunker busters and turned toward more research on conventional alternatives.[30]

Conclusion: Coping with an eagle on the edge

Friction between different elements of counter-proliferation policy fuels
heated arguments at both the domestic and international levels. Although greater emphasis on counter-proliferation through destruction
can skew incentives for potential target states, actually making it harder
to dissuade them or deny them WMD programmes, it also makes
deterrence – one of the other D's in the counter-proliferation suite –
more credible.[31] A higher risk of punishment could help persuade some
states to abandon the road to nuclear weapons. Indeed, some conservative commentators claim that "destruction" in Iraq helped persuade

Muammar Gaddafi in Libya to change course and accept the carrots of denuclearization rather than run the risks of regime-ending attack for several years before his nuclear programme bore fruit.[32]

With respect to those states that can be deterred, the difference between spurring them on and deterring them lies in how judiciously the United States applies its regime-killing capability. The nightmares unfettered after 9/11 haunt US statespersons. Out of a series of surprises related to nuclear programmes in Iraq, North Korea and Iran, only Iraq 2003 has presented a false positive. Taken together, recent intelligence failures make it more, not less, agonizing to wait for inspections. Regardless of political party, a person bearing the responsibilities of commander-in-chief is more likely to hedge against the worst-case scenario and perceive a proliferation threat that merits quick action rather than deliberate hesitation.[33]

Unfortunately, a preference for quick and decisive action not only pulls the chief executive away from the cast of supporting characters in the US foreign policy process, it also pulls the United States away from its partners in the international community. Two high-level UN reports representing the views of the Secretary-General and the General Assembly on the occasion of the 2005 World Summit in New York reiterated the importance of a universal commitment by member states to multilateralism after Iraq.[34] In subsequent paragraphs, these same reports urged measures to make the Security Council work better. US policy makers, more so than their UN counterparts, are likely to link these passages as part of a *quid pro quo*. Without improvements in the Council's efficiency and effectiveness, the United States will ultimately rely on its own volition and capacity to defend its citizens from specific threats. It will resist delegating its security functions as long as the Council remains weak, regardless of the benefits that collective action offers in terms of legitimacy.

For democratically accountable leaders, even small numbers of nuclear weapons in the hands of terrorists pose Baruch's old dilemma between "the quick and the dead". The work involved in multilateral cooperation may be worth extra legitimacy when the counter-proliferation strategy is dissuasion or denial but, when it comes to destruction of a proliferator, transparency, delay and compromise at the international bargaining table undermine the efficiency and effectiveness of US military operations. The UN reports, progressive in their intent, nevertheless reflect truths enduring from the beginning of the nuclear age. US statespersons wrestle with crosscutting incentives: too many concessions to formally correct UN procedures eviscerate the destruction option in the immediate situation; yet too few concessions to collective action drain US striking power over the long term, starving it of international legitimacy.

Returning to the metaphor at the beginning of this chapter, "an eagle on the edge" evokes a once proud creature that retains its fierceness even if fear has suppressed some of its nobility. If America overemphasizes pre-emptive attack, it is not because Americans have completely forgotten the impulse to craft more durable multilateral solutions to the problem of WMD proliferation. Rather, Americans and the US government in particular discount the damage to long-term strategies such as denial and dissuasion in order to make sure near-term WMD threats are destroyed. True to its traditions, the United Nations would like to see the United States restore the balance in its counter-proliferation policies away from unilateral violence and toward international cooperation. For the American eagle, this diplomatic mix is actually a more natural state of affairs, provided that, in those rare instances when diplomacy fails, as a former US Assistant Secretary of Defense under President Clinton recently wrote, there remains a credible prospect of punishment.[35]

Together, the United States and the international community confront mounting proliferation threats from North Korea and Iran. In both cases, the United States and key allies have struggled to preserve a united front to convince these defiant regimes that there will indeed be consequences to pay if they continue to flout international non-proliferation norms. Counter to present inclinations, United Nations members cooperating with the IAEA to bring recalcitrant states – not to mention the irascible American eagle – back into the fold may find better success emphasizing the viability of the destruction option sooner rather than later.

Although hasty counter-proliferation strikes against North Korea or Iran could bring horrific costs in their own right and severely limit the opportunities for multilateral dissuasion in the future, putting off international planning or authorization for the use of force until the last possible moment will strike almost any US president as a recipe for paralysis. After 9/11, "last resort" sounds to an anxious America suspiciously like "never" or "too late". In the circumstances, fastidious commitment to sovereign equality and procedural correctness in collective action may increase the chances of the violent outcomes such steps were established to avoid. If the American eagle senses its own political isolation before the fact, it will have less reason to wait for its prey to acquire nuclear weapons before pouncing in self defence.[36]

Notes

This chapter is academic work and does not represent the opinions, standards or policy of the United States Air Force Academy or the United States government.

1. A sentence from the *National Security Strategy of the United States* is also the epigraph for the follow-on *National Strategy to Combat Weapons of Mass Destruction* (December

2002), available at ⟨http://www.whitehouse.gov/news/releases/2002/12/WMDStrategy. pdf⟩: "History will judge harshly those who saw this coming danger but failed to act."

2. Not all scientists felt the same way, of course. Edward Teller famously advocated accelerating efforts to build the hydrogen bomb and, later, strategic missile defence. Still, a long list of celebrated scientific minds has urged extraordinary caution and greater international controls on nuclear weapons. The list includes Robert Oppenheimer, Enrico Fermi, Leo Szilard, Hans Bethe, Linus Pauling, Richard Feynman, Sidney Drell and Andrei Sakharov.

3. J. Robert Oppenheimer, "The International Control of Atomic Energy", *Bulletin of the Atomic Scientists*, Vol. 1, No. 12 (1946).

4. Henry Sokolski, *Best of Intentions: America's Campaign against Strategic Weapons Proliferation* (Westport, CT: Praeger, 2001), pp. 13–24.

5. Neal Rosendorf, "John Foster Dulles' Nuclear Schizophrenia", in John Lewis Gaddis, Philip Gordon, Ernest May and Jonathan Rosenberg, eds, *Cold War Statesmen Confront the Bomb: Nuclear Diplomacy Since 1945* (Oxford: Oxford University Press, 1999).

6. Sokolski, *Best of Intentions*, pp. 25–37.

7. Peter Lavoy, "The Enduring Effects of Atoms for Peace", *Arms Control Today*, Vol. 33, No. 10 (2003).

8. SALT and the ABM Treaty are more directly relevant to vertical proliferation, but the strengthening of international institutions was not limited to the bilateral superpower relationship. The Nuclear Suppliers Group, in support of NPT restrictions on the transfer of nuclear technology, expanded from 7 to 15 countries during the 1970s (Federation of American Scientists, Summary Sheet on Nuclear Suppliers Group, ⟨http://www.fas. org/nuke/control/nsg/⟩).

9. For a well-known review of the circumstances contributing to the unravelling of détente and its companion linkage policy, see John Lewis Gaddis, *Strategies of Containment* (Oxford: Oxford University Press, 1982), pp. 309–344.

10. Stephen Cimbala, ed., *Deterrence and Nuclear Proliferation in the Twenty-First Century* (Westport, CT: Praeger Publishers, 2001), pp. 145–152 (Appendix B).

11. Melissa Williams and Richard Haass, *The Reykjavik Summit: Watershed or Washout?*, Pew Charitable Trusts Case Studies in International Affairs C-15-88-813.0 (Washington, DC: Institute for the Study of Diplomacy, School of Foreign Service, Georgetown University; Cambridge, MA: Harvard University Kennedy School of Government, 1988), pp. 23–24.

12. The spirit of cooperation also carried over into other classes of "mass destruction weapons". See the 1980s chronology leading to the Chemical Weapons Convention at ⟨http:// www.fas.org/nuke/control/cwc/chron.htm⟩.

13. Tadeusz Strulak, "The Nuclear Suppliers Group", *The Nonproliferation Review* (Fall 1993), pp. 3–4.

14. Robert Einhorn and Michele Flournoy, project directors, *Protecting against the Spread of Nuclear, Biological, and Chemical Weapons: An Action Agenda for the Global Partnership*, Vol. 3 (Washington, DC: CSIS Press, 2003).

15. Thom Shanker and David Sanger, "White House Wants to Bury Pact Banning Tests of Nuclear Arms", *New York Times*, 7 July 2001, p. A1. Also, see a critical review of the recent US approach to multilateral arms control in Andrew Newman, "Arms Control, Proliferation and Terrorism: The Bush Administration's Post-September 11 Security Strategy", *Journal of Strategic Studies*, Vol. 27, No. 1 (2004). In the introduction to this volume, Ramesh Thakur warns that US behaviour toward arms control's *ancien regime* indicates a "systematic belittling" of international agreements that, in turn, weakens global norms against proliferation (Chapter 1, p. 16).

16. See ⟨http://www.federalobserver.com/speeches.php?speech=7415⟩.

17. George Rathjens, "Nuclear Proliferation Following the NPT Extension", in Raju G. C. Thomas, ed., *The Nuclear Non-proliferation Regime: Prospects for the 21st Century* (New York: St. Martin's Press, 1998). In a recent keynote address, Mohamed ElBaradei, Director General of the IAEA, referred to estimates that some 40 countries were now capable of developing atomic weapons. "Nuclear Nations Could Top 40", *Chicago Tribune*, 21 September 2004, p. 12.

18. The debate over the consequences of proliferation for international stability played out in academic circles. The latest edition of widely circulated, contending arguments by Kenneth Waltz and Scott Sagan reflects greater emphasis on allowing only selective proliferation in order to keep nuclear weapons out of terrorist hands. Scott Sagan and Kenneth Waltz, *The Spread of Nuclear Weapons: A Debate Renewed*, 2nd edn (New York: W. W. Norton, 2002).

19. Rathjens' 1998 analysis ("Nuclear Proliferation Following the NPT Extension") was prescient. Short of an international collective security agreement, which he conceded was likely to be a long way off, he identified regime change as the next most effective policy against determined proliferators. A pinprick strike against nuclear facilities was only a temporary fix and could actually spur regimes to accelerate their programme rather than discontinue it. Regime change, he felt, had more permanent character, but the high levels of domestic and international consensus required to sustain it made it impractical for application against a series of proliferators. More than five years later, despite several shocks to the international system, his reading of the situation holds rather well.

20. The 8 D's are dissuasion, denial, disarmament, diplomatic pressure, defusing, deterrence, destruction and defence. In the face of a costly occupation in Iraq, stalemate on North Korea and increased concerns about Iran, Ashton Carter, Assistant Secretary of Defense under the Clinton administration, reviewed counter-proliferation options and evaluated current policy in "How to Counter WMD", *Foreign Affairs*, Vol. 83, No. 5 (September–October 2004).

21. David Sanger, "Bush's Pre-emptive Strategy Meets Some Untidy Reality", *New York Times*, 12 July 2004, p. A10.

22. Andrew Ward, "N. Korea Promised Aid to Scrap Arms Plans", *Financial Times* (London), 22 July 2004, p. 2; David Sanger, "U.S. to Offer North Korea Incentives in Nuclear Talks", *New York Times*, 23 June 2004, p. A3.

23. "Text of N. Korea Talks Agreement", *CNN*, 19 September 2005, available at ⟨http://www.cnn.com/2005/WORLD/asiapcf/09/19/korea.north.text/index.html⟩.

24. John Bolton, "Press Conference on the Proliferation Security Initiative", 31 May 2004, ⟨http://www.state.gov/t/us/rm/33556.htm⟩.

25. A thorough, albeit critical, review of this cooperation is in Nicole Evans, "Missile Defense: Winning Minds, Not Hearts", *Bulletin of the Atomic Scientists*, Vol. 60, No. 5 (2004).

26. In Chapter 1 in this volume, Ramesh Thakur presents a sweeping critique of US legitimacy for enforcing non-proliferation norms (pp. 11–12, 15–17). Indeed, there is some risk that Russia and China could engage in vertical proliferation in order to overwhelm US attempts at ABM defence. In the near-term though, the expected technological and political benefits of doing so are modest. Also, US withdrawal from the ABM Treaty does not appear to have altered these countries' growing willingness to cooperate with the United States in stemming the spread of nuclear weapons beyond the circle of established powers under the NPT.

27. John Zarocostas, "U.S. Seeks Treaty to Ban Fissile Material", *Washington Times*, 30 July 2004, p. 17. For its part, the United States claims that it has not produced fissile material for more than 15 years.

28. Christine Kucia, "Congress Authorizes New Weapons Research", *Arms Control Today*, Vol. 33, No. 10 (2003).

29. In *A More Secure World*, the UN Secretary-General's High-level Panel on Threats, Challenges and Change bemoaned the US precedent for threatening nuclear retaliation against biological or chemical attack by a non-nuclear-weapon state. The threat of nuclear destruction, rather than deterring WMD use, could stampede states into adding the nuclear option to their arsenals. *A More Secure World: Our Shared Responsibility. Report of the Secretary-General's High-level Panel on Threats, Challenges and Change* (New York: United Nations Report, December 2004), p. 42.

30. "US Cancels Bunker Bomb Programme", *BBC News*, 26 October 2005, ⟨http://news.bbc.co.uk/2/hi/americas/4377446.stm⟩.

31. I am using deterrence here in a slightly different sense from Carter's article in which he emphasizes the capacity to deter nuclear attack through a secure second-strike capability. It is also true that a rational state might forgo a nuclear weapons programme altogether if it felt such a move had a credible chance of inducing a counter-proliferation strike against either its assets or its regime. Carter, "How to Counter WMD", pp. 74–76.

32. Bill Nichols, "Pre-Emptive Policy Still Being Debated", *USA Today*, 31 August 2004, p. 6.

33. Indirect evidence for this idea comes out of the range of views in John Kerry's Democratic Party as he sought the presidency in 2004. Primary rival Howard Dean saw the threat as far less compelling than fellow Democrat Joe Lieberman. Kerry, himself, took criticism for his inability to articulate an alternative presidential response to the problems posed by Iraq, in either the spring of 2003 or the fall of 2004. "Kerry, Bush and Iraq", editorial, *Chicago Tribune*, 9 September 2004, p. C20.

34. *In Larger Freedom: Towards Development, Security and Human Rights for All. Report of the Secretary-General* (New York: United Nations Report, September 2005). General Assembly of the United Nations, *World Summit Outcome* (New York: World Summit High-Level Plenary Meeting of the 60th Session of the General Assembly, 14–16 September 2005).

35. Carter, "How to Counter WMD".

36. This danger should be kept in mind as the United Nations ponders its role in reinforcing global non-proliferation norms. "If the United Nations is not able or willing to distinguish between regimes with respect to the risks they pose ... concerned countries will make these tough decisions and act on them outside the UN framework. Such countries are not going to imperil their national security through an idealistic faith ... resting on demonstrably false assumptions" (Thakur, Chapter 1 in this volume, pp. 7–8).

15

UK perspectives on WMD proliferation, arms control, disarmament and WMD use by non-state actors

John Simpson

Introduction: Some core perspectives

The United Kingdom is no stranger to weapons of mass destruction (WMD). The history of its possession of WMD and its support for attempts to develop international controls stretches back for at least a century. The key to understanding its contemporary official position is that it regards possession of one type of WMD – nuclear weapons – as the ultimate guarantor of its security, and this makes it unnecessary to have other types of offensive WMD capabilities. As a consequence, it has supported strongly the global bans on chemical and biological weapons that were a key element of the United Kingdom's past disarmament efforts, backed by the belief that Britain's possession of nuclear weapons would in any event deter use of other forms of WMD against its territory and forces.[1] Nuclear weapons were and are seen as qualitatively in a league of their own in their destructiveness, and thus their deterrent effect, compared with other WMD.

UK policies towards WMD have been, and continue to be, pragmatic rather than logically consistent. Indeed, Britain's current possession of a nuclear deterrent is probably explained more by its past existence, the bureaucratic inertia this has generated, and its relationship to US security decision-making, rather than a response to existing threats. Indeed, if the United Kingdom did not currently possess nuclear weapons, it would almost certainly not seek them.

The world of 2006 is not the world of 1991: security threats have changed, as have assessments of the capabilities necessary to combat them. This is an age of nuclear transition, if not a post-nuclear age, so far as much of Europe is concerned.[2] One consequence is that the invulnerability to surprise attack possessed by the United Kingdom's Trident submarine missile force appears disconnected from current and probable future security challenges. In addition, the UK defence budget is stretched. As a consequence, the time is approaching for a principled policy debate of a type last seen in the 1957–1963 period, asking what are the United Kingdom's nuclear weapons for; why does it need them; do they have priority for scarce resources over conventional security capabilities; and, if they do not, how should the United Kingdom divest itself of them?

UK WMD policies post-1991

The collapse of the Warsaw Treaty Organization (WTO) and the USSR led to major changes in UK defence policy. The United Kingdom abandoned significant elements of its WTO-oriented nuclear war-fighting capability and reoriented its armed forces to peacekeeping roles in support of multilateral UN humanitarian interventions. Decisions were also made to withdraw the existing force of Polaris submarines as soon as the first two of the successor Trident submarines had been commissioned. In 1993, it was made clear that any military response to WMD proliferation would not be a nuclear one,[3] and therefore conventionally armed US Tomahawk cruise missiles were purchased for this and other roles.

Successive annual Defence White Papers during this period emphasized the significant role played by multilateral and bilateral arms control agreements in making these nuclear reductions possible.[4] These were followed in 1998 by a Strategic Defence Review (SDR), which resulted in the dismantling of the remaining UK nuclear gravity bombs. Although retaining the continuous patrolling intended to deter a surprise nuclear attack on the United Kingdom, the Trident force was de-targeted; its alert status was changed from hours to days; and it assumed both a strategic and a sub-strategic role. This force is more closely integrated into the equivalent US capabilities than was its predecessor Polaris force. Its "spare" missiles are held in common with those of the United States, thus locking any future UK missile modernization into US decisions on its force.

From the mid-1990s onwards, work started in both academic and technical circles in the United Kingdom on the practicalities of nuclear disarmament.[5] The SDR announced plans to use the dismantling of its weapons as a test-bed for nuclear disarmament verification techniques,[6] but at the same time concerted pressure for UK unilateral nuclear disarmament declined sharply. At the Review Conference of the Nuclear Non-Proliferation Treaty (NPT) in 2000, the United Kingdom tabled a discussion paper on the practicalities of nuclear disarmament,[7] and this exercise was responsible for the inclusion of this item in the "13 practical steps to disarmament" contained in its Final Document.[8]

One area of latent friction between the US and UK nuclear policies during this period concerned the Anti-Ballistic Missile (ABM) Treaty. There were those who preferred this treaty to remain in place, among other things to constrain any Russian ABM upgrading decisions and their knock-on effects on the technical credibility of the United Kingdom's offensive missile capabilities and on "strategic stability". Unlike Reagan's "Star Wars" proposals of the 1980s, the proposed US national missile defence (NMD) system could not defend both the United States and Europe. Whereas the United States needed infrastructure capabilities in the United Kingdom and elsewhere for its system, Europe, including the United Kingdom, saw no pressing need for an equivalent, and in the United Kingdom it was viewed as likely to divert resources from more pressing defence requirements.[9]

Following 9/11, the debate on NMD lost salience in the United Kingdom. The international consequences of the US withdrawal from the ABM Treaty appeared to be minimal. In May 2002, Russia and the United States signed the Moscow Treaty on Strategic Offensive Reductions, which in effect normalized their relationship, confirmed that they were in a non-adversarial military situation, and implied that further bilateral legal arms control agreements between them were unnecessary. Although politically the UK government could not deny access to the capabilities in the United Kingdom necessary to defend the US homeland, it delayed decisions on this matter as long as was practically possible.

Overall, the nuclear situation in 2005 was one where UK national policy appeared to revolve around two main perspectives. The first perspective was that the UK Trident force and the infrastructure that sustains it were "the ultimate guarantor of the United Kingdom's national security".[10] Linked to this was the argument that, operationally and technically, the force was a minimum one and could not be reduced further without moving to de facto nuclear disarmament because of the time required to re-establish its operational effectiveness. Only if all other nuclear weapon states' warhead numbers were close to those of the United Kingdom would it be prepared to engage in multilateral nuclear disarmament negotiations. Indeed, in the late 1990s it was hoped that the Strategic Arms Reduction Treaty (START) process would lead to negotiations on a multilateral Nuclear Arms Reduction Treaty (NART) covering both strategic and sub-strategic nuclear weapons. The inclusion of non-strategic weapons in such negotiations was an implicit UK prerequisite for engaging in them. This perspective was one of the inspirations for its technical work on nuclear disarmament.

The second perspective was that the technically dependent UK force constituted a key part of the wider politico-military relationship with the United States, because the United Kingdom's independent capability for use gave it direct access to US nuclear decision-making. Although this was a cornerstone of UK security policy, at the same time it generated frictions with another component of that policy – support for arms control agreements. Indeed, the UK government would probably have been prepared to be a more visible advocate of nuclear arms control agreements than it has been in the past, but for pressures not to undermine the national nuclear positions of the United States and France.

Decisions on a replacement of the current Trident nuclear force now seem likely to occur in the 2006–2010 period.[11] Defence Secretary John Reid indicated in June 2005 that "decisions on whether to replace Trident ... are likely to be needed during this Parliament".[12] In March 2006 the Defence Committee of the House of Commons started the first of a number of inquiries into aspects of a Trident replacement decision,[13] while reports indicated that there have been "talks with the US government on a successor to Trident".[14] The technical factors driving the decision remain obscure, although they may focus on the platforms rather than the missiles or the warheads. Above all, the specific threat, if any, that the force is designed to deter is unclear.[15] This suggests a very different replacement debate than in the past: current terrorist WMD threats to the United Kingdom are unlikely to be deterred by a national nuclear weapon capability.[16] This has led to suggestions that the choice may lie between long- and short-term perspectives – between insuring against an uncertain future, and accepting that such an insurance policy is an expensive luxury for the United Kingdom. Cashing it in without direct replacement could free up scarce defence resources for the acquisition of modern network-centric warfare and conventional intervention capabilities.[17] The compromise would be to replace the submarines but not change the missiles and warheads, giving the force at least 15 further years of life.

In these circumstances, the United Kingdom would become a virtual nuclear-weapon state, but with an ability to regenerate it at short notice.[18] What would be the implications of implementing this option for the United Kingdom's strategic alliance with the United States, its relations with NATO and its partners in the European Union, and with France? Answers to these questions are uncertain, and these and other political implications of possible replacement options will need detailed analysis before any decision is taken. For, if sustaining a strong NPT-based multilateral nuclear security regime remains a prime objective of UK policy, as it has been in the past, any positive replacement decision is likely to have a negative impact on the 2007–2010 cycle of the NPT review process. One option to ameliorate this might be to accompany the decision with some very positive UK initiatives in the multilateral nuclear arms control area. However, as William Walker has pointed out, the United Kingdom may find itself constrained from doing this by pressures from the United States and France.[19]

The United Kingdom, the war on terrorism and WMD non-proliferation

In the period since 1991, perceptions of the main WMD security threat to the United Kingdom have switched from the former USSR to global terrorism and, to a much lesser extent, attacks from "states of concern".[20] Public debate on these new threats evolved much more slowly in the United Kingdom than in the United States. It was not until after 9/11 that the issues became fully transparent to UK audiences. Previously, public UK perceptions had often been of a US security establishment seeking new threats to justify its existence. This was particularly so for the counter-proliferation strategy first set out by the Pentagon in the mid-1990s. One consequence was that, although dealing with Iraq's WMD capabilities was a significant issue in UK public decision-making over nuclear proliferation from 1991 onwards, it took 9/11, the intervention in Afghanistan, the 2002/2003 confrontation with Iraq over its WMD, and the revelations about the "commercial activities" of Abdul Qadeer Khan (the "father" of Pakistan's bomb) in Iran, Libya and other states to align UK public perceptions of the WMD threat with those held in the United States.[21]

At the official level, however, perceptions of the threat moved closer to those in the United States at a much earlier date. Walker points to a desire to "keep in step with Washington" as one explanation for the shift at the politico-military level,[22] though the main driver appears to have been secret intelligence information. UK and US intelligence services had been monitoring the activities of both al-Qaeda and the A. Q. Khan procurement network for some considerable time, although a comprehensive understanding of the latter's role in supplying states other than Pakistan took years to evolve.

The role of intelligence is thus central to both UK anti-terrorism and UK anti-proliferation policies. Intelligence-sharing and cooperation comprised the second pillar of the "special relationship" with the United States that developed from 1946 onwards, and its preservation and exploitation remain a core objective of UK policy, as well as an important element in the United Kingdom's international capabilities.[23] At the same time, the evolving intelligence relationships with other European governments indicated they held similar threat perceptions over Iraq, although they differed in how to respond and what mixture of military and diplomatic pressures should be deployed.

This situation placed UK officials and ministers in a difficult situation, because UK intelligence capabilities meant there was a disjunction between governmental and popular perceptions of the proliferation threat. Pakistan's role as both a nuclear proliferator and a base for anti-al-Qaeda operations was known, but the activities of A. Q. Khan remained hidden until Libya decided to disarm. One structural consequence was that the balance between action to support the multilateral non-proliferation regimes and more direct action with allies to counter proliferation threats appeared to outsiders to change visibly in the latter direction after 9/11, although, as Walker comments, the UK government "remained deeply uneasy ... with the aggressive and unilateral approach taken by the Bush administration".[24]

This shift in focus should not be exaggerated, however. UK non-proliferation policy had always depended heavily on UK intelligence capabilities and bilateral diplomacy. This had been the case, for example, over policy towards India and Pakistan after the tests in 1998. The United Kingdom was a major actor in the international Task Force created to manage the resultant regional nuclear tensions and had taken a pragmatic view of the situation, arguing that the first priority was to prevent nuclear war, even if this necessitated engagement with these states rather than isolating and punishing them. The United Kingdom was subsequently able to use its position as a member of the UN Security Council to stimulate action to address this specific situation and more general issues of WMD proliferation and terrorism, such as acting as a prime mover behind Security Council Resolution 1540 on the non-proliferation of weapons of mass destruction. Pursuing both regime policies and direct policies in these areas when confronted by the new proliferation threats was a natural continuation of existing UK policies; by contrast, those outside government tended to focus their attention on the more visible and accessible treaty regimes. From 2002 onwards, however, this gap started to close as more information emerged about clandestine proliferators and international terrorist networks.

After the advent of the Bush administration and 9/11, the emphasis in UK policy changed from non-proliferation to counter-proliferation. One driver of this was the uncovering of information in Afghanistan suggesting that some elements of al-Qaeda had been planning to use WMD for terrorist purposes. There were also concerns that the al-Qaeda network had been attempting to acquire WMD precursors and technology through clandestine A. Q. Khan-type procurement channels. One consequence was a tendency for UK ministers and annual Defence White Papers to make open-ended deterrent statements about possible responses to offensive actions against the United Kingdom, its forces and its interests, rather than emphasize the international legal constraints accepted by the United Kingdom.[25]

The terrorist threat also generated policies of countering threats at source via interventionist counter-proliferation policies, rather than through regime action.[26] This was in part responsible for a change in the name of the relevant sections of both the UK Foreign and Commonwealth Office and the Ministry of Defence to the Counter-Proliferation Department (CPD) and Counter-Proliferation and Arms Control Secretariat (C-PACS).[27] The advent of the Bush administration also had the effect of forcing the United Kingdom to abandon its longstanding leadership of the attempt to create a verification protocol for the Biological Weapons Convention. However, one institutional initiative the United Kingdom was able to advance was the development of the International (later Hague) Code of Conduct on Missile Technology.

UK participation in the military interventions in both Afghanistan and Iraq was the most visible indicator of a move towards the policy stance being adopted by the United States. In the former case, there seemed little alternative if the al-Qaeda network was to be disrupted. In the case of Iraq, it was the consequence of decisions taken by the United Nations years earlier fully to disarm its WMD capabilities and to apply military sanctions if this was opposed. The lack of consensus within the UN Security Council on this matter from the mid-1990s onwards led directly to the US and UK actions. Regime overthrow by force appeared to be the only effective method of resolving the problem in a definitive manner.[28] The United Kingdom sought to do this in the context of an explicit UN Security Council resolution reaffirming previous authorities to act, whereas the United States was content to move ahead without it.[29] Walker argues that, because the United States could not be dissuaded from embarking on military operations in Iraq, the United Kingdom reluctantly supported it as "opposition would ... damage the transatlantic relationship without bringing tangible benefits" and it was driven "towards supporting US policies even when [it considered] them antithetical to its political and security interests".[30] Deploying the military option generated major domestic opposition within both Parliament and the country at large.[31]

One consequence of the move into Iraq was to expose the limitations of basing WMD counter-proliferation policy on intelligence capabilities. Admittedly, the United Kingdom and other states had relied on the UN inspection system for information on Iraq's WMD prior to 1998. It was only afterwards that attempts were made to create national networks within Iraq. Thus reliable human intelligence about intentions was impossible to obtain. By contrast, the case of Libya in late 2003 illustrated the ability of the UK intelligence system to play a pivotal role in international non-proliferation policies. It succeeded in infiltrating A. Q. Khan's network, and its ability to enable centrifuge components to be seized on the *BBC China* precipitated the meeting between the head of Libyan intelligence and his US and UK counterparts in the Travellers Club in London, which resulted in the UK/US-led process for neutralizing Libya's WMD capabilities.[32]

The lessons from Iraq and Libya have thus been radically different from a UK perspective, and to some extent contradictory. On the one hand, Iraq was an intelligence failure that demonstrated the perils of using intelligence information (or the lack of it) as a basis for interventionist counter-proliferation policies.[33] On the other hand, the intelligence services appear to have played the major role in securing Libyan WMD disarmament and in so doing exposing both Iranian and North Korean proliferation activities. The need for effective intelligence capabilities targeted on clandestine proliferation has moved to the heart of UK security policy, but at the same time has sustained the "special relationship" in intelligence with the United States. In so doing, the intelligence services may also have made the "special relationship" with the United States over nuclear weapons relatively less salient in current circumstances.

The United Kingdom and multilateral strategies to combat the WMD threat

The United Kingdom has continued to use its UN position as a significant part of its policy to combat WMD proliferation.[34] It remains publicly unclear where the United Kingdom stood over the WMD language in the September 2005 Millennium Summit Outcome document (particularly on disarmament and the three pillars of the NPT), given that the relevant sections of the draft text were removed as a result of US actions. It was notable, however, that the agreed statement on these subjects generated by the UK-chaired G-8 Gleneagles Statement on Non-Proliferation did cover these issues, and may indicate what the United Kingdom might have been prepared to commit itself to at the Summit had circumstances been different.[35] Moreover, previously the United Kingdom had encouraged the creation of a Security Council Committee to address terrorism, and had sponsored Resolution 1540, which created a similar committee to address national measures to make it more difficult for non-state actors to acquire nuclear weapons and radiological devices. This may eventually link into existing and new international coalitions of the willing designed to address specific aspects of the WMD proliferation problem.

The first of these bodies, the Nuclear Suppliers Group (NSG), was originally called the London Group. It was convened by the United Kingdom in 1974 to harmonize the national nuclear export control list. The United Kingdom has consistently supported this body and a similar informal entity for chemical and biological precursors, the Australia Group, based in Vienna. The United Kingdom was also one of the initial sponsors in the 1980s of the Missile Technology Control Regime (MTCR), which was designed to perform the same function for the trade in missile technologies. The United Kingdom was also one of the initiators in 2003 of the Proliferation Security Initiative (PSI). This was designed to facilitate cooperation among like-minded states in physically interdicting transfers of WMD materials and associated technologies taking place beyond the scope of these export control activities.

More recently the United Kingdom has been a member of the G-8 Global Partnership, created in 2002 to assist the Russian Federation and others to secure stocks of nuclear weapon materials. In 2004, the G-8 established a more comprehensive Action Plan on Non-Proliferation. The UK presidency of the G-8 could have been used as an opportunity to further develop and implement this plan. However, although the Gleneagles Statement on Non-Proliferation indicated that intensive work was taking place on implementation of the Action Plan, little in the way of new commitments emerged from it.

The European connection

The United Kingdom is one of two nuclear weapon states in the European Union, some of whose members are strong advocates of nuclear disarmament. At the same time, the European Union has become an increasingly central body in the international politics of WMD control because, if it can agree on policy initiatives, it is the most coherent voting bloc in the international community. Thus, at the same time as the balance in UK counter-proliferation policy appeared to be tilting away from strengthening the WMD institutions towards more direct action through US-led coalitions of the willing, the United Kingdom was also integrating itself more closely into EU defence and foreign policy, from which the United States was excluded.

This integration has occurred through the EU policy coordination framework, which facilitates common positions to be enunciated at

WMD treaty meetings by the state holding the EU presidency. Member states are legally bound to adhere to these common positions – thus France and the United Kingdom could not start nuclear testing again without being in breach of EU law. Although mechanisms are lacking to change these positions during extended conferences, the EU states do meet more regularly as a caucus group during such meetings than others. Given the range of states involved, the European Union also plays a central role in identifying the areas where compromises are possible.

At the end of 2003 under the Greek presidency, the European Union, as with NATO, sought to play a more independent role in the WMD politics by creating its own strategy against the proliferation of WMD.[36] This sets out a broad range of initiatives and measures to harmonize activities of EU states in this area. In addition, three of the EU states – France, Germany and the United Kingdom – plus representatives of the EU Council have played a leading role in trying to engage with Iran over the future of its nuclear energy programme and its alleged nuclear weapon activities. In doing this they have used the EU states' trade and aid capabilities to engage in "carrot and stick" diplomacy.

In the course of this diplomacy, the United Kingdom has at times distanced itself from the United States on the issue, unless one regards it as engaged in a "good cop, bad cop" routine. Indeed, the United Kingdom's approaches towards Iraq and Iran have been markedly different. There appear to be two main reasons for this. One is that the United Kingdom was committed to a confrontational position over Iraq from the early 1990s onwards. Thus regime change was a natural extension of existing policies and commitments. The second is that the US–Iran relationship remains heavily conditioned by the hostage crisis of a quarter of a century ago, whereas UK perspectives are free of this, enabling the United Kingdom to take a more pragmatic approach.

UK attitudes towards WMD policies are therefore conditioned by the need to walk the tightrope between its European and US interests. On Iraq, Walker observes that "while adopting a special stance on arms control and on multilateralism at variance with Washington's, the alliance with the United States was preserved even when the United Kingdom's and its European partners' multilateral objectives were being thwarted".[37] On Iran, any UK support for a hawkish US policy would have a negative impact on its relations within the European Union, given the lead it has taken on the issue with France and Germany. As Simpson notes, the United Kingdom could find itself in a "much more delicate and difficult position" in Europe than it was over Iraq if it were actively to support the United States in actions against more ambiguous cases of proliferation.[38]

Conclusions

There is no doubt that UK perspectives on WMD have changed significantly since 1991. The core change has been in threat perceptions: Soviet nuclear weapons are no longer the main concern; all types of WMD in the hands of states on the periphery of Europe and of its main trading partners or non-state terrorist entities are now seen as threats. The UK response to the pre-1991 situation was a mixed and pragmatic one. It rested on four pillars: a capability for independent action with its own nuclear weapons; a capability to influence US nuclear decision-making through coordination between US and UK nuclear forces; a significant national intelligence capability partnered with that of the United States; and membership of NATO and the possession of conventional forces capable of fighting a major land battle in Europe. Arms control and non-proliferation policies were shaped by, and supportive of, these central pillars of UK security policy. This resulted in active support and engagement in WMD arms control and non-proliferation activities, and more particularly in the search for bans on biological and chemical weapons.

Significant contradictions were visible in these UK policies, but these were seen to be outweighed by national security necessities arising from the East–West confrontation. The key guides for policy remained to sustain a close UK–US security relationship; to accept nuclear disarmament only if all others did so; and to support bans on chemical and biological weapons as a backstop to UK assumptions that nuclear capabilities would deter their use against UK interests. The limitations on Soviet ABM capabilities were also supportive of the small UK nuclear deterrent force. At times, nuclear weapons and arms control policies were mutually reinforcing; at others radically opposed, but pragmatism rather than strict logic prevailed throughout.

Since 1991, the threat picture has changed radically, yet UK responses still contain many elements of continuity with the past. WMD threats are reduced in scale and more varied in their nature. The UK nuclear capability is the minimum that is technically credible. Defences are no longer seen to undermine the long-term credibility of the existing UK force as they have in the past, but neither are they currently regarded as necessary for the United Kingdom. The elements of continuity are that the nuclear relationship with the United States remains, as does UK operational control over its force. Yet the United Kingdom has no acute adversarial relationship with any other state, and thus no permanent or obvious targets for its assured retaliation capability against surprise attack.

The main UK response to WMD proliferation threats is now a layered series of defence and security capabilities, starting with an ability to destroy the threats at source and then interdict their movement towards the United Kingdom. The former is seen to require specialized intervention forces, as well as conventionally armed cruise missiles and a greater commitment by states to monitor and eliminate non-governmental WMD activities. Interdiction of the means of delivery implies preliminary work on missile defences and closer monitoring of cargoes in transit and entering the United Kingdom. All of these activities place great reliance on accurate and effective intelligence-gathering and analysis, and this has been highlighted by the decision to expand the size of the UK intelligence establishment.[39] US–UK intelligence exchange arrangements thus remain central to UK security policies, but so too does the ability of the European Union to police WMD activities within its member states.

One consequence of this evolution is that, in relative terms, the United Kingdom appears to have moved away from a multinational institutionally based approach to WMD non-proliferation and towards direct action against those perceived to be breaking regime rules. This is seen in the UK role in the development and use of multinational instruments other than the WMD treaties, and its use of military and intelligence capabilities to prevent proliferation in Iraq, Iran and Libya.

Actions, however, often speak louder than words, and in this respect the record of the United Kingdom over the past few years is puzzling and contradictory. Iraq was an example of a failed attempt to use the United Nations; a military intervention to generate regime change that succeeded in that objective but generated no stable successor regime; and a failure in intelligence by all countries concerned. This failure may place domestic limits on the ability to implement similar actions in future. By contrast, Libya was an example of a very successful intelligence-led operation conducted on a US–UK basis that succeeded in preventing WMD proliferation, led to disarmament, and generated the possibility of further such operations. The United Kingdom has also joined with other EU states to engage potential proliferators (notably Iran) diplomatically, and to attempt to persuade them to desist from nuclear activities of international concern.

Overall, what does this mean in terms of UK perspectives on WMD proliferation, arms control, disarmament and WMD use by non-state actors? First and foremost, the United Kingdom will continue to seek to prevent WMD proliferation by using a much wider range of instruments and coalitions of states than before. Although its active security policies appear to have moved it closer to US policies in this respect, the United Kingdom has also developed more effective ties with the EU states, and thus, as in the past, its policy choices are likely to be pragmatic – a matter of matching the means to the objective.

As far as arms control is concerned, the United Kingdom does not appear to be particularly concerned over the lack of movement in verified bilateral arms control between Russia and the United States, or over the consequences of the end of the ABM Treaty. However, it does see a need to engage with declared nuclear-weapon states such as India and Pakistan.

The United Kingdom's disarmament position is that it is expending resources on exploring the technical possibilities of verifying a nuclear disarmament agreement, but the current context is one where "the continuing risk from the proliferation of nuclear weapons" means that "Trident ... is likely to remain a necessary element of our security",[40] despite the friction within NPT forums that this may generate.

Finally, preventing WMD use by non-state actors entails a greater emphasis on states policing all WMD-related activities within their borders. Distinguishing non-state procurement networks from those of state proliferators may be difficult, but the same intelligence and interdiction methods can be used for dealing with both state actors and non-state ones. In short, pragmatism continues to rule!

Notes

1. This pragmatic UK position contrasts sharply with the principled argument advanced by Ramesh Thakur in his introduction to this volume (Chapter 1, pp. 10–11).
2. See John Simpson, "The Nuclear Non-Proliferation Regime: Back to the Future?", *Disarmament Forum*, No. 1 (2004); and John Baylis and Robert O'Neil, eds, *Alternative Nuclear Futures: The Role of Nuclear Weapons in the Post-Cold War World* (Oxford: Oxford University Press, 2000).
3. Minister of Defence Malcolm Rifkind in a speech on "UK Defence Strategy: A Continuing Role for Nuclear Weapons?" at the Centre for Defence Studies, King's College, London, 16 November 1993.
4. See, for example, Ministry of Defence, *Statement on the Defence Estimates 1995: Stable Forces in a Strong Britain*, Cm 2800 (London: HMSO, May 1995), p. 25, para. 250.
5. See Darryl Howlett, Ben Cole, Emily Bailey and John Simpson, "Surveying the Nuclear Future: Which Way from Here?", *Contemporary Security Policy*, Vol. 20, No. 1 (1999).
6. See Ministry of Defence, *Strategic Defence Review. White Paper: Modern Forces for the Modern World*, Presented to Parliament by the Secretary of State for Defence by Command of Her Majesty, Cm 3999, July 1998; and "Verification of Nuclear Disarmament: Second Interim Report on Studies into the Verification of Nuclear Warheads and Their Components", Working paper submitted by the United Kingdom of Great Britain and Northern Ireland, NPT/CONF.2005/PC.III/WP.3, 8 April 2004.
7. See "Systematic and Progressive Efforts to Reduce Nuclear Weapons Globally: A Food for Thought Paper", Submitted by the United Kingdom to the 2000 Review Conference of the Parties to the Treaty on the Non-Proliferation of Nuclear Weapons, NPT/CONF.2000/23, 4 May 2000.
8. See *Final Document of the Conference*, 2000 Review Conference of the Parties to the Treaty on the Non-Proliferation of Nuclear Weapons, 24 April–19 May 2000, New York, Vol. I, Part I, NPT/CONF.2000/28 (Part I).

9. See Mark Smith, "European Perspectives on Ballistic Missile Proliferation and Missile Defences", in *Missile Proliferation and Defences: Problems and Prospects*, Occasional Paper No. 7, Special Joint Series on Missile Issues, Center for Nonproliferation Studies and Mountbatten Centre for International Studies, 2001.

10. See *Delivering Security in a Changing World*, Defence White Paper, Presented to Parliament by the Secretary of State for Defence by Command of Her Majesty, December 2003, Cm 6041-I (London: The Stationery Office, 2003), p. 9, para. 3.11, ⟨http://www.mod.uk/NR/rdonlyres/051AF365-0A97-4550-99C0-4D87D7C95DED/0/cm6041I_whitepaper2003.pdf⟩.

11. Although the SDR indicated that "Trident could remain an effective deterrent for up to 30 years", the December 2003 Defence White Paper noted that "decisions on whether to replace Trident are not needed this Parliament but are likely to be required in the next one". *Delivering Security in a Changing World*, p. 9, para. 3.11.

12. House of Commons, Written Questions, 20 June 2005: Column 666W, "Nuclear Deterrent", ⟨http://www.parliament.the-stationery-office.co.uk/pa/cm200506/cmhansrd/cm050620/text/50620w02.htm⟩.

13. See "The Future of the Strategic Nuclear Deterrent: The Strategic Context", House of Commons Defence Committee, Evidence Sessions, Session 2005–06, 8 March 2006, ⟨http://www.parliament.uk/parliamentary_committees/defence_committee/def060308___no__25.cfm⟩.

14. David Cracknell, "Talks Start with US on Trident's £15bn successor", *Times Online*, 17 July 2005, ⟨http://www.timesonline.co.uk/article/0,,2087-1697246,00.html⟩.

15. For a detailed analysis of the factors involved in the United Kingdom's post–Cold War deterrence policy, see John Simpson, "France, the United Kingdom and Deterrence in the Twenty-first Century", *Contemporary Security Policy*, Vol. 25, No. 1 (2004), pp. 136–151.

16. The diminished deterrence value is alluded to in Ministry of Defence (MoD) and Foreign and Commonwealth Office (FCO) documents, particularly those published following 9/11.

17. William Walker, "Caught in the Middle: The United Kingdom and the 2005 NPT Review Conference", *Arms Control Today*, Vol. 35, No. 1 (2005), p. 18.

18. The United Kingdom would, of course, remain a nuclear-weapon state legally in the context of the NPT.

19. Walker, "Caught in the Middle", p. 18.

20. The SDR emphasized the need to provide deployed British Armed Forces with effective nuclear, biological and chemical protection. This signalled a shift in perception of the perceived nature of UK military vulnerabilities – abroad in scenarios with deployed forces, not within the United Kingdom's borders. It also reflects the strategy of actively countering threats at their source.

21. The Butler Report specifically mentions the effect of 9/11 on British policy towards Iraq. "In his evidence to us, the Prime Minister endorsed the view expressed at the time that what had changed was not the pace of Iraq's prohibited weapons programmes, which had not been dramatically stepped up, but tolerance of them following the attacks of 11 September 2001". *Review of Intelligence on Weapons of Mass Destruction. Report of a Committee of Privy Counsellors*, Chairman: The Rt Hon The Lord Butler of Brockwell KG GCB CVO, 14 July 2004, HC 898 (London: The Stationery Office, 2004), ⟨http://www.official-documents.co.uk/document/deps/hc/hc898/898.pdf⟩, p. 105, para. 427.

22. Walker, "Caught in the Middle", p. 17.

23. The FCO emphasized the importance of international cooperation and intelligence-sharing in a December 2003 document outlining its international priorities. Interna-

tional terrorism and the proliferation of WMD were stated as having "emerged as potentially the most catastrophic dangers to our [the United Kingdom's] national security in the early twenty-first century". *UK International Priorities: A Strategy for the FCO*, Presented to Parliament by the Secretary of State for Foreign & Commonwealth Affairs by Command of Her Majesty, 9 December 2003, Cm 6052 (London: The Stationery Office, 2003), 〈http://www.fco.gov.uk/Files/kfile/FCOStrategyFullFinal,0.pdf〉, p. 1.

24. Walker, "Caught in the Middle", p. 17.

25. In March and April 2002, UK Defence Secretary Geoffrey Hoon made statements alluding to the possibility of nuclear weapon use in retaliation for a chemical and biological weapon attack on British deployed forces. These included the United Kingdom's "willingness and ability to use them in appropriate circumstances" and being "absolutely confident that in the right conditions we would be willing to use our nuclear weapons". Select Committee on Defence, Minutes of Evidence, Questions 236 and 237, Wednesday 20 March 2002, 〈http://www.parliament.the-stationery-office.co.uk/pa/cm200102/cmselect/cmdfence/644/2032008.htm〉. He also stated that the United Kingdom "'reserved the right' to use nuclear weapons if Britain or British troops were threatened by chemical or biological weapons". Richard Norton Taylor, "Bush's Nuke Bandwagon", *Guardian* (London), 27 March 2002, 〈http://www.guardian.co.uk/comment/story/0,,674632,00.html〉. On 29 April 2002, he confirmed that although "the use of nuclear weapons is still a deterrent of last resort ... ultimately and in conditions of extreme self-defence, nuclear weapons would have to be used". See HC Debates, Oral Answers to Questions, 29 April 2002, 〈http://www.publications.parliament.uk/pa/cm200102/cmhansrd/vo020429/debtext/20429-05.htm#20429-05_spnew9〉.

26. The FCO clearly states that, because "there is no panacea" or "one-size-fits-all" policy to counter WMD threats, "the Government uses the tools that it judges will be most effective in each case". *Counter-Proliferation Strategy, Terrorism & Security, UK Priorities*, 〈http://www.fco.gov.uk/servlet/Front?pagename=OpenMarket/Xcelerate/ShowPage&c=Page&cid=1065432164878〉.

27. Walker, "Caught in the Middle", p. 17.

28. According to the Butler Report, "[t]he Government ... saw a need for immediate action on Iraq because of the wider historical and international context, especially Iraq's perceived continuing challenge to the authority of the United Nations". *Review of Intelligence on Weapons of Mass Destruction*, p. 105, para. 428.

29. The Butler Report indicates that "[t]he Government also saw in the United Nations and a decade of Security Council Resolutions a basis for action through the United Nations to enforce Iraqi compliance with its disarmament obligations". *Review of Intelligence on Weapons of Mass Destruction*, p. 105, para. 428.

30. Walker, "Caught in the Middle", p. 18.

31. There were heated exchanges on the war in the House of Commons, and several ministers resigned over the issue. The formal parliamentary debate and decision took place on 18 March 2003. See 〈http://www.publications.parliament.uk/pa/cm200203/cmhansrd/vo030318/debtext/30318-06.htm〉. Public opposition to military action against Iraq was also evident, with massive demonstrations leading up to and during the war. For example, see "'Million' March against Iraq War", 16 February 2003, 〈http://news.bbc.co.uk/1/hi/uk/2765041.stm〉.

32. See Peter Beaumont, Kamal Ahmed and Martin Bright, "The Meeting That Brought Libya in from the Cold", *Observer*, 21 December 2003.

33. Although the Iraq case is often seen as an intelligence failure, the Butler Report indicated that the British "Government's conclusion in the spring of 2002 that stronger action (although not necessarily military action) needed to be taken to enforce Iraqi dis-

armament was not based on any new development in the current intelligence picture on Iraq". *Review of Intelligence on Weapons of Mass Destruction*, p. 105, para. 427.

34. MoD and FCO documents emphasize the United Kingdom's commitment to multilateral organizations, particularly the United Nations. *Delivering Security in a Changing World*, p. 5, para. 2.16.

35. The July 2005 Gleneagles Statement on Non-Proliferation affirmed the G-8's full commitment to all three pillars of the NPT, and that it should form the basis for addressing threats and challenges to the nuclear non-proliferation regime. See *Gleneagles Statement on Non-Proliferation*, July 2005, ⟨http://www.fco.gov.uk/Files/kfile/PostG8_Gleneagles _CounterProliferation.pdf⟩. At the Millennium Summit, however, US insistence on the deletion of the word "disarmament" resulted in the complete omission of the draft section on disarmament and non-proliferation, and thus any reference to the substance of the statements agreed at Gleneagles. More specifically, the US delegation insisted on deleting reference to the NPT having three pillars. See Julian Borger, "Road Map for US Relations with Rest of World", *Guardian* (London), 27 August 2005, ⟨http:// www.guardian.co.uk/usa/story/0,12271,1557488,00.html⟩, and Jim Wurst, "Nonproliferation, Disarmament Matters Dropped from U.N. Summit Document", *Global Security Newswire*, 16 September 2005, ⟨http://www.nti.org/d_newswire/issues/539B1CCD⟩.

36. See Clara Portela, "The Role of the EU in the Non-Proliferation of Nuclear Weapons: The Way to Thessaloniki and Beyond", PRIF Reports No. 65, Peace Research Institute Frankfurt, 2003, ⟨http://www.hsfk.de/downloads/prifrep65.pdf⟩.

37. Walker, "Caught in the Middle", p. 17.

38. Simpson, "France, the United Kingdom and Deterrence in the Twenty-first Century", p. 147.

39. See Mark Huband, "MI6 Steps up Spy Recruits to Cold War Levels", *Financial Times* (London), 5 May 2003.

40. *Delivering Security in a Changing World*, p. 9, para. 3.11.

16

Nuclear non-proliferation after Iraq: A French perspective

Philippe Errera

When voting unanimously on Security Council Resolution 1441, all 15 members of the UN Security Council recognized "the threat Iraq's non-compliance with Council resolutions and proliferation of weapons of mass destruction and long-range missiles poses to international peace and security", and recalled that they had "repeatedly warned Iraq that it will face serious consequences as a result of its continued violations of its obligations". In effect, they were envisaging, for the first time in the organization's history, the possibility of using force in order to achieve disarmament[1] if the Iraqi government refused to seize its last chance to comply with its obligations. The fact that there were other motives behind the US action,[2] expressed both explicitly and less explicitly, both before and after the war, as well as the facts that war was finally declared without UN Security Council authorization and that no weapons of mass destruction (WMD) were found in Iraq, does not alter the fundamental fact that Operation Iraqi Freedom was ostensibly the first war ever fought with a counter-proliferation rationale.

Almost three years after the end of major combat operations in Iraq was declared on the flight deck of the USS *Abraham Lincoln* by President George W. Bush, the net effect of this war on efforts to counter WMD is, at best, mixed. Zhou Enlai's famous assertion regarding the effects of the French Revolution ("It's too early to tell") comes to mind in this regard. It is worth examining the positive and negative impacts of this endeavour on individual proliferation cases and, more broadly, on the elements of the international order whose purpose it is to prevent proliferation in the first place, constrain proliferators when this first level fails and, ultimately, offer possibilities for rolling back proliferation through coercive measures.

The impact of the Iraq war on individual proliferation cases

One aspect of the Iraqi campaign that, surprisingly, was not particularly damaging was its immediate impact on joint transatlantic non-proliferation efforts. Given the degree of resentment between members of the Security Council, and in particular between Washington on the one hand and Paris and Berlin on the other, one would have thought that this situation would have been incompatible with the sense of shared purpose necessary to cooperate closely on the two other pressing proliferation cases, i.e. Iran and North Korea. This cooperation, however, continued.

For example, in the case of North Korea, close coordination was required to get board members of the Korean Peninsula Energy Development Organization (KEDO) to stop heavy fuel oil shipments and then suspend construction of the light water reactors. The Franco-German interception of a ship bound for North Korea (via China) with specialized aluminium tubes for centrifuge production occurred in April 2003 at the height of the Iraqi crisis. Judging from French Defence Minister Michèle Alliot-Marie's assertion on 16 October 2002 that Washington had already informed France of the results of Assistant Secretary of State James Kelly's fateful visit to North Korea barely two weeks earlier,[3] it is hard to see the falling out that one would have expected. To a certain extent, this state of affairs served as a useful reminder that, contrary to the assertions of the US administration (not to mention the US media), the differences over Iraq had not so much to do with alleged differences regarding the importance of dealing resolutely with illicit WMD programmes as with the balance of risks and benefits in dealing with the suspected Iraqi WMD programme through force before having exhausted all non-military options.

As time passed, and it became increasingly clear that the Iraqi endeavour was not turning out to be the initially planned success, the US administration made a resolute effort to mend fences. Bush's second term began with a conscious effort to reach out to European partners, including France and Germany, in order to turn the page. Part of this endeavour – arguably its most visible manifestation – was the decision to support efforts by the EU-3 (France, Germany and the United Kingdom) to solve the Iranian nuclear crisis through diplomatic means. On the European side, it has been argued that Paris, Berlin and London embarked upon the attempt to deal with the Iranian nuclear threat with the intention, among many other motivations, of re-creating a transatlantic sense of purpose and determination in dealing with strategic threats, an objective also present in the European Security Strategy of December 2003.

In sum, as far as the narrow field of transatlantic relations is concerned, it can therefore be argued that the Iraq war had neutral or even, paradoxically, positive effects on the non-proliferation agenda.

The global negative effects of the Iraqi diplomatic campaign and then military operations were, however, more direct and, at least with the limited hindsight that we have today, more forceful than the impact on transatlantic cooperation. The first negative effect can be characterized as the distraction that Iraq represented for Washington from more pressing proliferators: US intelligence assets and, in an even more acute manner, diplomatic capital were fully mobilized to prepare for the Iraqi diplomatic and military campaigns. There were even more direct, inverse correlations between efforts to deal with Iraq on the one hand and North Korea and Iran on the other.

North Korea

North Korea seemed to time each of its provocations in relation to a development in the Iraqi issue. It was helped by the American fixation on Iraq, and by Russian and, especially, Chinese approaches. Insofar as Beijing and Moscow perceived North Korean restraint as something that was more in the US interest than in theirs, and insofar as Washington accepted this view de facto, Washington felt that it had to make a choice between Chinese and Russian pressure on North Korea on the one hand and a "helpful" attitude on Iraq on the other ... and that choice was quickly made. This may have been one of the reasons that Washington was not particularly pressed to refer the North Korean dossier to the Security Council and, once it was placed there, to push harder to try to obtain consensus for coercive measures. In Washington's defence, neither its Asian allies most directly concerned (South Korea and Japan) nor China wished to see the possibility of sanctions raised.

Furthermore, it was important for the Bush administration to dissociate the Iraqi and North Korean issues *domestically*. When US Assistant Secretary of State James Kelly returned to Washington from Pyongyang, after the defiant North Korean admission of a clandestine uranium enrichment programme in October 2002, the foremost preoccupation of the US administration seemed to be to keep the issue out of American newspapers, in order to prevent it from interfering with the congressional vote authorizing the administration to intervene in Iraq. Some isolated democratic Congress members criticized the administration for this behaviour, but they were not heeded by their own party members, let alone the Republican majority.

Thus, in this Iraq-focused environment, Pyongyang was able to cross one American "red line" after another without any consequences: withdrawal from the Treaty on the Non-Proliferation of Nuclear Weapons (NPT), eviction of International Atomic Energy Agency (IAEA) inspectors, reprocessing of spent fuel at the Yongbyon nuclear reactor. Pyongyang may have drawn the conclusion from the American rhetoric and preparations for war that regime survival required a determined, and ostensible, acceleration of its nuclear programme, in order to have available a comfortable deterrence margin once Washington emerged from its Iraqi endeavour. President Bush's 2003 State of the Union address contained an almost explicit recognition of the judicious nature of North Korea's choice to have pressed full steam ahead, and an unhelpful message indeed for the Iranian leadership,[4] which was doubtless monitoring the way the world dealt with the North Korean crisis as closely, if not more so, as it was observing Saddam Hussein's fate.

In the case of North Korea, one could argue that active counter-proliferation (in Iraq) led to accelerated proliferation. However, this had more to do with tactics, i.e. with good North Korean gamesmanship, than with direct causality: North Korean violations of the 1994 Agreed Framework between the United States of America and the Democratic People's Republic of Korea had started well before the Bush administration was in place.

Iran

The case of Iran is more ambiguous. It is possible that Iranian leaders initially thought that they would be able to get away with a dose of "transparency" (i.e. admitting part of what had already been claimed publicly by opposition movements, but casting it in the framework of a civilian nuclear programme[5]), before getting tangled up in their web of omissions, contradictions and, ultimately, lies. The apparent ease with which US forces crushed the Iraqi army in the spring of 2003 may have focused some minds in Tehran and helped, indirectly, the EU-3 to reach an agreement with Iran in the 21 October 2003 Paris accord, by which Iran accepted the suspension of its fuel-cycle activities so long as the dossier was treated in the IAEA and not referred to the Security Council. However slim, there was still a possibility that US troops in Iraq could, at some point down the road, pose a credible military threat to Iran – if not for a full-fledged invasion, at least for a series of destabilizing actions. Relatively quickly, however, the Iranian leadership realized that UK and US forces were largely bogged down in Iraq and that their presence there could provide Tehran with strategic leverage against Washington and London, and not the other way around.

Ali Akbar Hashemi Rafsanjani, chairman of the Expediency Council, thus stated in early 2005 that "[Iran's] defensive power has increased ... and meanwhile the US has become vulnerable after attacking Iraq and Afghanistan. They cannot do anything to us."[6] A week earlier, Iranian Defence Minister Shamkhani had asserted somewhat quizzically that "one can only have deterrent power vis-à-vis an opponent by identifying the opponent's weaknesses and strengths".[7] Iranian Revolutionary Guards actually took eight UK sailors hostage in the summer of 2004, very probably as a signal of what was to come if the United Kingdom, or the United States for that matter, pressed too hard. According to British officials speaking at the end of 2005, Iranian know-how was increasingly shared with Iraqi insurgents against US and UK forces.

Here we have an interesting paradox. For some in the US administration, the main purpose of the Iraq war was to demonstrate the extent of US military strength and new-found determination to the rest of the world, and in particular to regimes in the Middle East. This signal, coming on the heels of the lightning-quick Afghan success, was intended to deter regimes from again attacking America or Americans as they had in the 1990s (for example, the Khobar Towers bombing, attributed by American investigators to Iran using Hezbollah). The problem is that the Iraqi campaign showed the neighbours of Iraq that, no matter how formidable it might be in terms of conventional war-fighting, the US military tool had very serious limitations in achieving non-military objectives, such as state-building, or in fighting non-conventional adversaries.[8]

Furthermore, even though the evidence on the Iranian nuclear programme comes from a United Nations Agency (the IAEA), and even though the IAEA Board of Governors repeatedly considered that "Iran's policy of concealment ... until October 2003 has resulted in many breaches of its obligations to comply",[9] before openly declaring Iran in non-compliance with its Safeguards Agreement in September 2005, the fact remains that in a significant part of the world, and in particular in the Muslim world, US pressure on Iran is seen solely as a continuation of the Bush policy that led to the Iraq war. Iran is seen not as a violator but as a victim, despite the fact that its most direct threat has been eliminated thanks to US action.[10]

Beyond the disappearance of the threat that Saddam Hussein constituted, and the stronger foothold that Shiite Iran has gained in the region, the Iranian regime was, at the end of 2005, thriving in the long and dark shadow of the Iraq war – probably beyond its wildest expectations:

• the shadow of Iraq has seriously undermined the international credibility of US, and more broadly Western, intelligence assessments of clandestine WMD programmes – even when they are, as in the Iranian case, solid and corroborated by data gathered by IAEA inspectors;

- the shadow of Iraq has seriously undermined the credibility of the threat of use of force against Iran, not so much in operational terms (the US Air Force is not subject to the same burdens as the US Army) but in domestic political terms and in diplomatic terms;
- the shadow of Iraq has seriously limited the appetite of a great number of countries to refer the Iranian dossier to the UN Security Council, which is where the IAEA Board of Governors squarely stated that it should be in its September 2005 Resolution. Once the matter is reported to the Security Council, it will have been after much costly hesitation and delay.

The end of this story is, fortunately, not written. For the moment, however, the Iraq war has clearly hampered international efforts to deal with the challenge posed by the Iranian nuclear programme, which is one of the key threats to international peace at the opening of the twenty-first century, while it has boosted Tehran's strength in the region.

Libya

The Libyan case is more interesting. The US administration has cast this clear non-proliferation success as resulting directly from the Iraq campaign: impressed by US military might, Muammar Gaddafi decided that he was better off coming back into the fold. UK officials, who actually took the leading role in setting up and concluding the deal that led to the Libyan renunciation of WMD, have sometimes echoed this assertion but have generally put forward a more subtle analysis to do with the effect of bilateral and UN sanctions and the prospect of having them lifted. Whatever the case may be (and this second view does seem more convincing), the interesting fact is that Washington could take "yes" for an answer in the Libyan case, something that is far from evident in the Iranian case and was clearly not so in the Iraqi case. Given Iraqi failure to comply with all of the requests contained in UN Security Council Resolution 1441 (for example, Iraq's 12,000-page weapons declaration in December 2002), this question was never put to the test. In an instance where prohibited items were discovered (e.g. Al-Samud missiles, whose range was greater than the 150 km authorized by Security Council Resolution 687), their destruction by Baghdad was seen as simply a further sign that the Iraqi leadership was playing games; but then again, by February 2003, it was in any case too late for Washington to take "yes" for an answer.

This question is not purely hypothetical, because it is posed in almost identical terms in the Iranian case; or rather *was* until June 2005 – it can be argued that the election of Mahmoud Ahmadinejad has fundamentally changed the equation. For the Iranian leadership until the summer of 2005, the situation was very different depending on whether it considered that a strategic choice of renunciation of its clandestine nuclear programme would get it closer to normalization with Washington or simply strip it of a possible deterrent and expose it to US military power. To the fundamental question of whether the problem is the Iranian regime or the Iranian regime's behaviour, there was for long no single American answer; rather, there were many, simultaneously held by different actors in the administration. Statements in the spring of 2005 gave greater coherence to US policy vis-à-vis the EU-3's efforts, but in parallel there had been more strident rhetoric on regime change, which undercut the European effort tactically. Today, the question is largely moot anyway, considering the Iranian president's incendiary statements on Israel, the United States and the West more generally.

Reinforcing the nuclear non-proliferation regime

Among the few encouraging signs of the past few years, we may at least take comfort in a common sense of purpose among key international actors in their wish to reinforce the nuclear non-proliferation regime. This sense of purpose does not appear to have been set back by divisions over Iraq – quite the contrary.

The Non-Proliferation Treaty

Despite its shortcomings, the Non-Proliferation Treaty has played an essential role in shoring up the nuclear order. If President Kennedy's prediction that, by the end of the twentieth century, there would be 20 or 30 nuclear nations has turned out to be false, it is essentially thanks to the NPT. However, this does not mean that the NPT cannot be perfected or, rather, that the regime of which it is the core cannot be strengthened.

In the run-up to the 2005 NPT Review Conference, France put forward a series of proposals in this regard, both within the NPT framework[11] and more broadly. Two of the key French proposals to strengthen the NPT can be summarized as preventing the risks stemming from the dissemination of sensitive nuclear technologies and raising the stakes for withdrawal from the Non-Proliferation Treaty.

Preventing the risks stemming from the dissemination of sensitive nuclear technologies

In most cases, developing nuclear energy for peaceful purposes does not require transfers of sensitive and potentially proliferating technologies or materials, such as enrichment, reprocessing, heavy water production facilities, equipment or related technologies. Furthermore, recent proliferation crises (North Korea, Libya, Iran) have demonstrated the need for strengthened export controls on those technologies or materials. Different approaches can be taken.

In terms of sheer effectiveness, the US proposal that enrichment and reprocessing equipment and technologies should no longer be exported "to any state that does not already possess full-scale, functioning enrichment and reprocessing plants"[12] certainly makes sense. The difficulty is two-fold: first, it is politically impractical to obtain consensus among the 40 members of the Nuclear Suppliers Group (NSG) on such a measure; second, it hardens the opposition from third countries, by creating an artificial fault-line between "haves" and "have-nots". The second camp includes countries that would probably never have been interested, in practice, in trying to obtain such technologies had their perceived right to them not been put into question. In other words, we would be doing the bidding of the proliferators for them by rallying countries to their rhetoric.

The approach taken by France aims to avoid these two pitfalls, by focusing on the specific context in which the transfer would take place on a case-by-case basis. The export of such materials, facilities, equipment or related technologies should be envisaged, in the French view, only in the light of the existence of a set of economic and political conditions relevant to the global non-proliferation regime and NPT objectives. In addition, in order to strengthen the legal base and framework for such cooperation, suppliers should commit themselves to linking any transfer of sensitive items and major transfers of non-sensitive items to non-nuclear-weapon states to the signature of intergovernmental agreements. Any transfer *not* covered by such an agreement should be considered illegal, with the necessary legal action being at the national level. This would make proliferation networks, such as the one set up by A. Q. Khan and his associates both inside and outside the Pakistani establishment, more difficult to hide, especially when they involve transhipment through non-NSG countries to and from non-NPT members (witness the role of Dubai and Malaysia).

It is important, at this stage, to set the record straight regarding a so-called "inalienable right" to enrichment or reprocessing technologies. This "inalienable right" has been claimed by Iran, and others, in order to create the impression that they would be giving up something to which they are entitled in accepting a cessation of all enrichment and reprocessing-related activities, and therefore should get something in return. The NPT refers, in Article IV, to "the inalienable right of all the Parties to the Treaty to develop research, production and use of nuclear *energy* for *peaceful purposes*". The text of the treaty therefore does not mention the fuel cycle, even though a reasonable interpretation of Article IV might lead one to a broader perspective. More importantly, according to the treaty, at least two conditions must be met in order to be able to exercise this right:

- The programme must have peaceful purposes. Given the Preamble, and given Article IV, a non-nuclear-weapon state may embark on a nuclear research or energy production programme only if it intends, in good faith, to pursue a nuclear programme for peaceful purposes and these activities are necessary in order to enjoy the benefits of peaceful applications of nuclear energy. This is where the rub is, in the case of Iran, because the peaceful purpose behind the Iranian efforts to master the fuel cycle cannot be established. Iran has no nuclear power plants or an export market justifying the mastering of uranium enrichment. Furthermore, it can obtain from other States Parties the enriched uranium it needs in order to benefit from all of the advantages of peaceful applications of nuclear energy, given the current state of its programme.
- Non-proliferation commitments must be respected. Article IV emphasizes that the rights it recognizes must be exercised in conformity with Articles I and II of the treaty, and more broadly with the non-proliferation obligations identified by the treaty, including the Safeguards Agreements with the IAEA. Here, again, Iran is in a situation where it has very probably forfeited this right by breaching the obligation to comply with its Safeguards Agreement and by possible violation of Article II of the NPT itself, because it received technology exclusively related to nuclear warhead manufacturing as early as 1987 from Pakistan.[13]

Raising the stakes for withdrawal from the Non-Proliferation Treaty

This issue may seem like an arcane legal issue, but even a summary examination of the North Korean crisis underlines the importance of coming to terms with it. Like any treaty, the NPT has a withdrawal clause. But the particular danger with withdrawal from this treaty is that what a non-nuclear-weapon state is entitled to while it is a party – nuclear cooperation, transfers of know-how and materials, etc. – is precisely what is forbidden to non parties, and for good reason: because it is at the core of a military nuclear programme.

The idea is not to limit the sovereign ability of a state to withdraw from a treaty that it is complying with: however politically desirable such a limitation might be in terms of the predictability and stability of the international order, that is legally a non-starter (and politically a non-starter for states that are highly attached to their freedom of manoeuvre, such as the United States, Russia or China). The idea is to limit the ability of a state to withdraw from a treaty that it is *violating*, both by raising the cost of such an action and by limiting the benefits derived from it.

The French proposal initially put forward in the context of the Preparatory Committee (PrepCom) for the 2004 NPT Review Conference was straightforward. First of all, a state that withdraws from the NPT should no longer make use of all the nuclear materials, facilities, equipment or technologies that it acquired before withdrawal. These should be returned to the supplying state, frozen or dismantled under international verification. Second, the International Atomic Energy Agency should be able to implement Safeguards Agreements for a specified time after the withdrawal, which is not the case today. These obligations could be put forward in the bilateral governmental agreement between the supplier state and the recipient state, which would thus be bound. Some may argue that a country that is willing to risk an international crisis is unlikely to be constrained by the letter of these bilateral agreements any more than it was by the spirit of the multilateral treaties that it chose to violate. One advantage would be, however, to change the status of the nuclear installations, whose continued possession and operation would become illegal.

The 2005 NPT Review Conference unfortunately did not achieve consensus on a final document, largely because of the delaying tactics of countries such as Egypt, which precluded any substantive plenary debate until the very last days of the conference. The conference did, however, allow for useful and productive debates on European Union proposals for strengthening the treaty, many of which were inspired by the original French ideas.[14] One can only hope that this debate will continue to be pursued.

Leveraging key international actors

Important as it is to strengthen the NPT, whose initial purpose it was to counter the spread of nuclear weapons, we also need to look at ways of leveraging existing international institutions whose original purpose was either broader than or different from non-proliferation per se.

The United Nations and the Security Council

Obviously, at the core of this approach are the United Nations and the UN Security Council. There may be substantial differences, across the Atlantic and more broadly, regarding the issue of whether the United Nations is the sole, or even the primary, source of legitimacy for the use of force. One element over which there is no difference, simply because it is a fact, is that the UN Security Council is the only body today that can, outside of a contractual framework, adopt internationally binding legal rules that are applicable virtually everywhere around the globe.

The adoption in April 2004 of UN Security Council Resolution 1540, which France co-sponsored, represents a significant achievement, in at least three regards:

- It gives teeth to the Security Council's pioneering Presidential Statement of 31 January 1992, which constituted the Council's first affirmation that the proliferation of weapons of mass destruction represented a threat to international peace and security. Resolution 1540 was adopted under Chapter VII of the Charter.
- It requires states to ensure that they have the necessary infrastructure in place to address the threat posed by non-state actor involvement in any aspect of WMD proliferation. It decides that states shall not support non-state actors involved in such activities and that states shall enact and enforce the necessary laws to prevent these activities on their territories. In a sense, it helps fill a double gap regarding non-state actors and the capabilities of states, building on Security Council Resolution 1373, which was adopted in the immediate aftermath of 9/11.
- Finally, it targets ballistic missile proliferation, essentially becoming the first legally binding international instrument that addresses the proliferation of WMD delivery means.

Resolution 1540 is but one illustration of the extraordinary power provided by the United Nations that can be harnessed in favour of non-proliferation. The report of the High-level Panel on Threats, Challenges and Change, presented to Secretary-General Kofi Annan at the end of 2004,[15] contained several excellent proposals in this field, not all of which were, unfortunately, echoed in the Secretary-General's report *In Larger Freedom* in March 2005.[16] The failure in the fall of 2005 of the 60th Anniversary Summit to reach agreement even on these modest measures was a particularly preoccupying setback.

The European Union

The European Union is another institution that is playing an increasingly important role in the fight against WMD proliferation. The EU Security Strategy, which was adopted at the EU Summit in Thessaloniki in December 2003,[17] correctly identifies proliferation (along with terrorism) as one of the key strategic threats to the European Union, to the European Union's security and to the European Union's interests more broadly. At the December 2003 Summit, the European Union also adopted a "Strategy against proliferation of WMD".[18] Although this document went largely unnoticed, it contains several important innovations. Chief among them is the generalization of a so-called "conditionality clause" in agreements with third countries.

Through this clause, respect for non-proliferation commitments is considered a key element of the agreement, with a breach of these commitments opening a process leading ultimately to the suspension of the agreement if nothing is done to remedy this. This is important because, on top of the European Union's growing diplomatic weight, it is now possible to leverage the economic and commercial power of the European Union toward a non-proliferation objective – "mainstreaming" in Euro-jargon.

In 2005, the picture was encouraging. A non-proliferation clause had been inserted in the Partnership and Cooperation agreement with Tajikistan and the draft Stabilization and Association Agreement with Albania. More importantly, given serious suspicions regarding Syria, negotiations had been completed with this country and the text of the Association Agreement containing a WMD clause had been initialled. Discussions were under way in the context of negotiations of an interregional association agreement with Mercosur, a Free Trade Agreement with the Gulf Cooperation Council countries and the review of the Cotonou Agreement between the European Union and the African, Caribbean and Pacific Group of States (the ACP states). In parallel, the draft Action Plans negotiated with countries of Eastern Europe and the Mediterranean in the context of the "European Neighbourhood Policy" contain WMD chapters based on key elements of the WMD conditionality clause.[19]

The Group of Eight

For the past several years, the G-8 has taken an increasing role in dealing with nuclear non-proliferation. A rapid examination of the statements issued at its Summit meetings shows not only the broad range of tools that its members are mobilizing, beyond financial and technical assistance (the Global Threat Reduction Initiative), but also the growing consensus between its members regarding the key non-proliferation issues of the day. The strong language on Iran contained in the Evian (June 2003), Sea Island (June 2004) and Gleneagles (2005) statements is all the more important considering that the G-8 includes all five permanent members of the Security Council except for China.

What role for the pre-emptive or preventive use of force in counter-proliferation?

Some may see the Iraq war as simply an application of the September 2002 US National Security Strategy[20] and its much-debated policy of pre-emption. In this regard, debating nuclear non-proliferation after

Iraq is synonymous with nuclear non-proliferation after the 2002 National Security Strategy.

For the sake of clarity: the term "pre-emption" is used in this chapter to mean the use of force against an imminent threat, whereas the term "prevention" is synonymous with the use of force against a threat that is not imminent but only potential at best (for example, the Israeli raid on Iraq's Osirak nuclear reactor or the Japanese raid on Pearl Harbor). The authors of the 2002 National Security Strategy tried to blur this key strategic and legal distinction by using the term "pre-emption" when in fact they were referring to "prevention".

The unilateral pre-emptive use of force is legal in certain circumstances,[21] whereas the unilateral preventive use of force is not, in any circumstances. However, the preventive use of force can be authorized by the UN Security Council in cases where it judges that a threat to international peace and security must be dealt with by military means.

US treatment of the three members of the "axis of evil" referred to in President Bush's 2002 State of the Union address is probably the best indication of the (ir)relevance of a declared policy of pre-emption. As a tool for dealing with WMD programmes, such a policy has proven to be either too risky militarily (North Korea, where conventional and non-conventional capabilities have effectively deterred America from acting), too uncertain (Iraq, where the intelligence justifying the attack proved faulty) or, for the moment at least, too risky strategically (Iran, where the certain regional consequences of US military strikes seem to outweigh the uncertain operational effects in terms of setting the nuclear programme back).

Is this to say that there is no room for the use of coercive measures, up to and including the use of force, in dealing effectively, legally and legitimately with a proliferator? Such an assertion would be in direct contradiction to the UN Charter, which calls for the UN Security Council to adopt and enforce whatever measures may be necessary to defend against threats to international peace and security. Then French Foreign Minister Dominique de Villepin, in several speeches in the winter of 2002–2003, defended the role of the UN Security Council to take such measures. More recently, French President Jacques Chirac considered that, if Iran were not to respect its commitments, the international community would take whatever measures it deemed appropriate, the Security Council being the body that could define such measures.[22]

To be sure, military action against Iran, for example, would entail substantial technical and political risks.[23] The fact that such an action would seem legitimate, in terms of upholding the international order, if Iran continued to defy the international community, and would be legal if the

Security Council authorized it after qualifying this Iranian defiance as a threat to international peace and security,[24] would indeed have only a marginal tempering effect on the regional implications of such an action.

However, ruling out such an option in any circumstances seems even less judicious than bringing it to the fore. The day may come when the international community will have nothing but very poor options, the least poor of them being the military option, which would still seem preferable to living with a nuclear-armed Iran. The idea that the problem could be solved by having the United States or Israel intervene unilaterally is illusory: militarily, the effect might be the same as that of a broader coalition, but the consequences of having an NPT member violate its commitments, and then withdraw from the treaty, with the Security Council remaining inactive, would haunt us for a long time to come.

If we wish to avoid being confronted with such a dilemma, we must find the necessary determination today, even if that means having to make unpleasant choices. Had the Security Council acted more resolutely in the early 1990s vis-à-vis North Korea, we would perhaps not be in the situation we are in today.

Dealing with procurement networks

There is, finally, a type of proliferation activities that defies many of these judgements, as well as the possible remedies proposed: procurement networks. Depending on whether one's outlook is optimistic or pessimistic, the Libyan case can be seen as a positive development (thanks to diplomacy, a country makes a strategic choice to give up its WMD) or as a far more worrying one. Indeed, by putting A. Q. Khan in the spotlight, the Libyan case has brought home the effect of globalization on proliferation.

A Pakistani scientist working through a Sri Lankan associate, procuring components from Europe, assembled in Malaysia after transhipment through Dubai, and exporting centrifuges to a North African country (and this may just be the tip of the iceberg) – the limits of supplier regimes in cases such as these are obvious. Despite the progress represented by Resolution 1540, which calls for states to exercise effective controls over their borders and what takes place inside them in the realm of proliferation, we are still a long way from having the necessary instruments always to be in a position to detect and disrupt new Libyan-style networks.

Beyond the question of instruments, there is the question of political will. It is revealing of the current state of affairs that the international community accepted the charade whereby A. Q. Khan was publicly reprimanded by the Pakistani authorities but otherwise not punished, and was not even forced to share his knowledge, which would be precious for the IAEA in the Iranian case (not to mention others – for example, Syria, Saudi Arabia, Egypt).

Conclusions

In conclusion, three thoughts come to mind. First of all, rarely have our responsibilities been so starkly put before us. Usually we can dissect proliferation cases after the fact. What signals did we miss? What actions did we not take that we should have? Our choices will never be easy: intelligence is uncertain; political and military options always carry a price; proliferation does not mobilize public opinion in the same way that, say, a humanitarian crisis does. Yet here we are, in the midst of crises, and we know that our actions, or lack thereof, will shape the world in which we live for years and even decades to come. By their respective regional repercussions, and by their impact on the nuclear non-proliferation regime and the NPT, which is at its core, the Iranian and North Korean crises are far more momentous than were the Indian or Pakistani ones in the late 1990s.

Second, in a relatively bleak environment, there are at least two causes for hope: the unity of purpose of the international community, which has broadly resisted the divisions over Iraq regarding non-proliferation; and a more pragmatic approach – what is important is what works. In the United States, even those officials who were proud to portray themselves as staunch unilateralists are now rediscovering the virtues of the IAEA. In Europe, the stark distinctions such as unilateralism vs. multilateralism or ad hoc initiatives vs. institutions now seem somewhat artificial.

Finally, the fundamental challenge that remains before us is not specific to non-proliferation. Instead, it pervades the whole international order, non-proliferation being but a subset of this broader arena. Put succinctly, this challenge is the pursuit of legitimacy and efficacy. International legitimacy is perhaps a necessary condition for efficacy (in the sense that countervailing attitudes will undermine unilateral action sooner or later), but it is by no means a sufficient one. The reverse is also true: post facto results reflecting the efficacy of the action undertaken alone do not provide legitimacy. Both legitimacy and efficacy must be pursued simultaneously if we wish to reinstate an effective international WMD order. The first years of the new millennium have offered us important lessons on what to do, and what *not* to do, in pursuing this goal.

Notes

The views expressed in this chapter are the author's own. They do not necessarily reflect those of the French government, and should in no case be attributed to it.

1. The first Gulf war occurred after the invasion of Kuwait, a sovereign state, by Iraq. It was only after the conflict that the extent of Iraq's WMD programmes was discovered.
2. "For bureaucratic reasons we settled on one issue – weapons of mass destruction – because it was the one reason everyone could agree on", US Deputy Secretary of Defense Paul Wolfowitz, interview with *Vanity Fair*, June 2003.
3. See the Question and Answer session after Minister Alliot-Marie's speech at the National Defense University, Washington, DC, "Why America and Europe Need Each Other", 16 October 2002.
4. "Our nation and the world must learn the lessons of the Korean Peninsula and not allow an even greater threat to rise up in Iraq", US President's "State of the Union" address, 28 January 2003, ⟨http://www.whitehouse.gov/news/releases/2003/01/20030128-19.html⟩ (accessed 6 March 2006).
5. See President Khatami's speech of 9 February 2003 (Foreign Broadcast Information Service translated text, I.D. IAP20030210000081), commented on at ⟨http://news.bbc.co.uk/1/hi/world/middle_east/2743279.stm⟩ (accessed 6 March 2006).
6. *Jomhuri-ye Eslami*, 25 January 2005.
7. Mehr News Agency, 17 January 2005.
8. From a proliferation perspective, one positive effect of the war has been often overlooked: the downgrading of chemical and biological weapons as an effective deterrent. Coalition troops entered Iraq firmly believing that the probability of biological or chemical weapon use against them was high, but were not deterred, thanks to advances in bio-defensive measures. One can only hope that this lesson was not lost on neighbouring countries, such as Syria or Iran.
9. See, for example, the 26 November 2004 "Resolution on Implementation of the NPT Safeguards in the Islamic Republic of Iran", GOV/2003/81, ⟨http://www.iaea.org/Publications/Documents/Board/2003/gov2003-81.pdf⟩ (accessed 6 March 2006).
10. Revelations of Ahmed Chalabi's dealings with the Iranian security services, as well as the amount of forged intelligence on Iraqi WMD passed on to the US authorities by Chalabi's Iraqi National Congress, have led some commentators to wonder whether Tehran did not, with a deep sense of strategic irony, have a role in pushing Washington to act.
11. "Strengthening the Nuclear Non-Proliferation Regime: Working Paper Submitted by France", NPT/CONF.2005/PC.III/WP.22, available at ⟨http://disarmament2.un.org/wmd/npt/2005/PC3-listofdocs.html⟩ (accessed 6 March 2006).
12. "President Announces New Measures to Counter the Threat of WMD", Remarks by the President on Weapons of Mass Destruction Proliferation, National Defense University, Washington, DC, 11 February 2004, ⟨http://www.whitehouse.gov/news/releases/2004/02/20040211-4.html⟩ (accessed 6 March 2006).
13. See the IAEA Director General's report to the November 2005 Board of Governors, "Implementation of the NPT Safeguards Agreement in the Islamic Republic of Iran", GOV/2005/87, 18 November 2005, ⟨http://www.iaea.org/Publications/Documents/Board/2005/gov2005-87.pdf⟩ (accessed 6 March 2006).
14. See, in particular, the European Union's working paper NPT/CONF.2005/WP.32 on withdrawal from the NPT, available at ⟨http://disarmament2.un.org/wmd/npt/2005/PC3-listofdocs.html⟩ (accessed 6 March 2006). According to the paper, parties would be entitled to withdraw from the treaty only if extraordinary events had precipitated

such a withdrawal. A written notification should be presented to the United Nations three months prior to such a withdrawal, including to the President of the Security Council. It should contain a detailed account of the rationale for withdrawal. If a State Party was preparing to withdraw, the depository states should immediately undertake consultations to resolve problems described in the note of intent to withdraw. The consequences of such a withdrawal should be spelled out clearly. The Security Council would affirm that, in view of the importance of the NPT for peace and security, it should take up any withdrawal as a matter of urgency. The state would remain responsible for any violation of the NPT before the date of its withdrawal. The paper also proposed measures to ensure that all nuclear equipment and materials meant for peaceful purposes under the treaty continued to be used only for those purposes after a country's withdrawal.

15. *A More Secure World: Our Shared Responsibility. Report of the Secretary-General's High-level Panel on Threats, Challenges and Change* (United Nations, 2004), ⟨http://www.un.org/secureworld/⟩ (accessed 6 March 2006).

16. *In Larger Freedom: Towards Development, Security and Human Rights for All. Report of the Secretary-General* (United Nations, 2005), ⟨http://www.un.org/largerfreedom/⟩ (accessed 6 March 2006).

17. *A Secure Europe in a Better World. European Security Strategy* (Brussels: European Council, 2003), available at ⟨http://ue.eu.int/uedocs/cmsUpload/78367.pdf⟩ (accessed 6 March 2006).

18. "Strategy against Proliferation of WMD", ⟨http://ue.eu.int/uedocs/cmsUpload/st15708.en03.pdf⟩ (accessed 6 March 2006).

19. Such draft Action Plans are currently being negotiated with Ukraine, Moldova, Israel, Jordan, Morocco, Tunisia and the Palestinian Authority.

20. *The National Security Strategy of the United States of America* (Washington, DC: Office of the President, September 2002), available at ⟨http://www.whitehouse.gov/nsc/nss.pdf⟩ (accessed 6 March 2006).

21. The classic formulation of the right of pre-emptive attack was given by US Secretary of State Daniel Webster in connection with the famous Caroline incident during a rebellion of Canadians against the British Crown government in 1837. In an exchange of diplomatic notes with British Ambassador to Washington Henry Fox, Webster articulated the two conditions essential to the legitimacy of the pre-emptive use of force under customary international law. In one note he asserted that an intrusion into the territory of another state can be justified as an act of self-defence only in those "cases in which the necessity of that self-defense is instant, overwhelming, and leaving no choice of means and no moment for deliberation". In another note he asserted that the force used in such circumstances has to be proportional to the threat. See Kenneth E. Shewmaker, ed., *The Papers of Daniel Webster: Diplomatic Papers Volume 1, 1841–1843* (Hanover: University Press of New England, 1983).

22. President Chirac, joint press conference with M. Abdoulaye Wade, President of the Republic of Senegal, Dakar, 2 February 2005: "Il est tout à fait essentiel que l'Iran tienne ses engagements et s'il ne devait pas les tenir la communauté internationale devrait imaginer quelles sont les réactions qui pourraient être les siennes et qui ne pourraient être que celles que retiendrait le Conseil de Sécurité des Nations Unies", ⟨http://www.elysee.fr/elysee/elysee.fr/francais/interventions/conferences_et_points_de_presse/2005/fevrier/conference_de_presse_conjointe_du_president_de_la_republique_et_du_president_du_senegal-dakar.27673.html⟩ (accessed 2 May 2006).

23. For some solid discussions of the military option, see, for example, Sammy Salama and Karen Ruster, "A Preemptive Attack on Iran's Nuclear Facilities: Possible Consequences", Center for Nonproliferation Studies, Monterey Institute of International

Studies, 12 August 2004, ⟨http://cns.miis.edu/pubs/week/040812.htm⟩ (accessed 6 March 2006); Michael Eisenstadt, "The Challenges of U.S. Preventive Military Action", in Henry Sokolski and Patrick Clawson, eds, *Checking Iran's Nuclear Ambitions* (Washington, DC: Strategic Studies Institute, 2004); James Fallows, "Will Iran Be Next?", *Atlantic Monthly*, December 2004; Ephraim Kam, "Curbing the Iranian Nuclear Threat: The Military Option", *Strategic Notes* (Jaffee Center for Strategic Studies, Tel Aviv University), Vol. 7, No. 3 (December 2004).

24. Something that would not seem far-fetched given Iranian support for international terrorism, its active ballistic missile programme and its suspected chemical and biological weapons activities, in contravention of its commitments under the Chemical Weapons Convention and the Biological and Toxin Weapons Convention.

17

Russia's perspectives on the world order and WMD proliferation

Andrei Zagorski

"Russia categorically rejects the expansion of the club of nuclear states."
(Vladimir Putin, President of the Russian Federation, 21 September 2004)

The world order, weapons of mass destruction and the Iraq crisis of 2003

The concepts of world order, the challenges of the proliferation of weapons of mass destruction (WMD) and the Iraq crisis of 2003 are certainly all closely interlinked within Russian perceptions of evolving international politics, but indirectly rather than directly. Similar to the Soviet Union just before it broke up, the Russian Federation pursues the policy of a status quo power that is no longer able to resist ongoing change. Having inherited from the Soviet Union the status of a permanent member of the UN Security Council and of one of the five "official" nuclear states under the 1968 Treaty on the Non-Proliferation of Nuclear Weapons (NPT), Moscow finds those two elements to be the only two remaining symbols of its formerly central role within the eroding "Yalta" order. It seeks to capitalize on both symbols while preserving its exclusive place, even if a formal one, in the emerging world order.

The preservation and the strengthening of the central role of the United Nations and especially of the UN Security Council enjoy the highest priority in Russian policy, even if this policy is supposed to accept or even to embrace the idea of the expansion of the exclusive group of permanent members of the Council. Indeed, Moscow has fully embraced that idea by supporting the admission of Germany and Japan to the club, perceiving this as a way of preserving its own status in it.

From the Russian perspective, the major challenge to the preservation of this relevant element of the world order emanates from the increasing unilateralism of US policy and the gradual erosion of the principles of respect for states' sovereignty and of non-interference in domestic affairs. The mounting Iraq crisis in the autumn of 2002 was mainly perceived by Moscow from that perspective rather than from the perspective of non-proliferation policy. The decision of the United States to go to war without an explicit authorization from the UN Security Council has become the second precedent over recent years eroding the role and the credibility of the United Nations in international security. It was certainly a precedent that has had a much deeper impact than the 1999 Kosovo war on the United Nations.

The Russian Federation has also inherited from the Soviet Union another symbol of being an exclusive part of the international security system, namely being recognized as the single Soviet successor state enjoying the status of an "official" nuclear power under the NPT regime. Indeed, in the early 1990s Moscow largely performed as a champion of non-proliferation policies, although its championship was largely reduced to ensuring that the Soviet nuclear weapons deployed in Belarus, Kazakhstan and Ukraine are returned to Russian soil and dismantled. The preservation of a non-proliferation regime that gives Russia an exclusive status certainly has been and remains the focus of Russian policy, which explains Moscow's active promotion of an indefinite extension of the NPT in 1995.

However, although Moscow has reconfirmed its interest in preventing further proliferation of WMD and, most notably, of nuclear capabilities (as the quotation from President Vladimir Putin above suggests), it sees its status as the second-largest nuclear power challenged first of all by the domestic difficulties of maintaining a relevant and credible nuclear capability rather than by the intentions of other state actors to obtain a nuclear capability. Russia finds itself largely in tune with the United States as regards recognizing the need to prevent further proliferation, but it seems to be more important to Moscow to ensure continued international assistance to deal with its own nuclear assets, nuclear and chemical disarmament, and the security of its nuclear facilities. It is this assistance, currently provided through the G-8 Global Partnership against the Spread of Weapons and Materials of Mass Destruction, that largely enables Russia to preserve its residual nuclear capability and gradually to modernize it.

At the same time, although seeing no benefit in further proliferation, Russia does not perceive any direct challenge from the threshold countries challenging or capable of challenging the regime. It therefore believes it has more important interests to pursue in most of the particular cases concerned. Apart from commercial interests and the issue of maintaining regional stability, Moscow reveals uneasiness with the compliance and enforcement discourse pursued by the United States. This discourse might endanger the higher interest of Russia within the emerging world order – preserving the principles of state sovereignty and non-interference in domestic affairs – and thus increasingly encroach on the status quo Moscow seeks to maintain. However, whenever Moscow is unable to resist existing "revisionist" trends while continuing to depend on cooperation with the United States, the resulting vector of Russian policy appears to be a selective hesitant and conditional following of the American lead, including on the issue of non-proliferation.

In that context, the Iraq crisis represents a rather special case. From Moscow's perspective, it is certainly relevant to the world order debate, especially once it is closely linked to the future relevance (or irrelevance) of the UN Security Council and, thus, to the relevance (or irrelevance) of Russia's permanent seat on the Council. At the same time, it was never viewed by Russia from the (non-)proliferation perspective, not even in the early 1990s. Rather, Moscow was concerned with the eventual collateral damage from the United States' interventionist policy, especially if not endorsed by the United Nations.

This chapter addresses the ambivalent Russian policy on (non-)proliferation against the background of world order considerations. I start by looking at the evolution of Moscow's nuclear policy and at the relative relevance of (non-)proliferation for Moscow. I then exemplify the low-profile and rather indifferent, or at least ambiguous, policy of Russia with regard to relevant regional proliferation issues. I follow this with an examination of Russian policies towards recent non-proliferation initiatives. I argue that Russia is pursuing a rather conservative policy, avoiding any major revision of the existing regimes, especially of the NPT, and at the same time hesitantly following the American lead on counter-proliferation while becoming a net recipient of the global non-proliferation policy.

A declining nuclear power and non-proliferation

Russia is currently, and is likely to remain, the world's second-largest nuclear power. It pays special attention to the maintenance of a significant military nuclear capability and reveals no interest in the wider proliferation of nuclear weapons, not only because this would make the world a less safe place but, more importantly from Moscow's perspective, because it would accelerate the erosion of Russia's exclusive nuclear status. This is enough to suggest that Russia is highly unlikely deliberately to play a proliferation game, even though it is often considered part of the problem when expecting commercial benefit from proliferation-related business.

At the same time, Moscow primarily concentrates on maintaining its own nuclear capability at a minimum feasible level rather than on preventing other states from obtaining it. The non-proliferation issue is no longer high on Moscow's policy agenda for all sorts of reasons. The number of countries capable of developing a nuclear capability is limited, and Moscow does not consider itself directly challenged by the countries concerned. In any case, it relies on keeping a deterrent capability of its own sufficient not to feel threatened by any of the eventual "small" nuclear powers. Therefore, it is more concerned about the prospect of WMD (especially radiological weapons) getting into the hands of terrorist groups, or about regional destabilization, particularly in North-east Asia, as a result of a nuclear proliferation chain. This largely explains why, since the indefinite extension of the 1995 NPT, Russia has been pursuing a rather low-profile non-proliferation policy and is unlikely to return to being a proactive international non-proliferation agent.

Since the collapse of the Soviet Union, the Russian Federation, which inherited its nuclear weapons and status, should be largely considered a nuclear superpower in decline. It did not have the resources or, with the end of the Cold War, any longer the need to sacrifice those limited resources for the sake of keeping its nuclear capability at least numerically equal to that of the United States. The Strategic Arms Reduction Treaties (START I and II) have helped Russia to justify deep cuts by maintaining the illusion of keeping parity with the United States. Largely, so does the Strategic Offensive Reductions Treaty (SORT) of May 2002, which provides that Moscow will further reduce the number of its nuclear assets. What Moscow can sell as disarmament based on a mutual commitment with the United States in fact reflects the natural downsizing of Russian nuclear capabilities that Moscow cannot afford, and does not really need to maintain vis-à-vis the United States. Seeking to increase the efficiency of its nuclear policy, Moscow has introduced serious structural changes into its nuclear triad by concentrating on cheaper land-based intercontinental ballistic missiles (ICBMs) at the expense of its sea-based and airborne long-distance nuclear capability.[1]

Still, even the land-based component of the Russian strategic missile forces has significantly declined over the past 15 years. According to information released by the Strategic Missile Command late in 2004, the number of land-based missile brigades and divisions (including medium-range missiles) fell from 36 in 1990 to 15 at the end of 2004. Although all medium-range missiles have been dismantled under the 1987 Soviet–American Intermediate-Range Nuclear Forces Treaty, the number of missiles under the Strategic Command declined from 1,443 to 596 over the same period.[2] Taking the contemporary scale of production and procurement of the new generation of ICBMs to replace those cut, it is realistic to expect that, over the next few decades, the Russian nuclear capability is going to be below the 15,000–17,000 warheads allowed by SORT. According to some experts, it could well decline to about 400 new "Topol-M" ICBMs, half of which would be equipped with multiple independently targetable re-entry vehicles (MIRVs), four submarine carriers (instead of 14 now and 63 in Soviet times) and virtually no air-borne component at all.[3] This still means that Russia would keep its position as the second-largest nuclear power worldwide, followed by China,[4] and this capability is considered to be sizeable enough to provide for meaningful minimal deterrence to whoever might challenge Russia.

The significant reduction in numbers of nuclear weapons has, however, been complemented by dramatic changes in the defence posture of the Russian Federation, which has reinvented the role of nuclear weapons. Seeking to compensate for its increasing conventional weakness, Moscow has abandoned the Soviet policy of no first use and suggested that it would not hesitate to have recourse to its nuclear weapons in order to avert a serious external threat. The wisdom of this policy is disputed by many Russian specialists, but this change in doctrine has stimulated the development and limited procurement of a new generation of ICBMs beginning in 2004.

This development reveals that, while being able to report significant progress in nuclear disarmament under NPT Article VI,[5] the Russian Federation is certainly far from being ready to abandon its nuclear capability. On the contrary, in order to maintain its exclusive status, and within the logic of the evolution of its defence posture, Moscow is seeking to consolidate and modernize its nuclear force, even if it is a smaller one. This capability is no longer considered to address a "residual threat" but, increasingly, to deter any other regional military power, whether nuclear or conventional.

The preoccupation with maintaining a sufficient nuclear capability of its own, as well as with other issues, has resulted in little appreciation for the non-proliferation agenda among the Russian security community. As revealed in a poll conducted within the Russian foreign policy and security establishment in April 2001, the political class of the country is rather

Table 17.1 National security threats, as perceived by the Russian expert community in 2001

		Per cent
1	International terrorism, expansion of Islamic fundamentalism into Russia	61.0
2	Low economic competitiveness of Russia	58.6
3	Technological backwardness compared with the United States and other Western countries	54.8
4	Further eastwards enlargement of NATO at the expense of the former Soviet states (i.e. the Baltic states, Ukraine, Georgia)	52.9
5	Worldwide dominance of the United States and its closest allies	51.4
6	Pressure from international economic and financial institutions seeking to eliminate Russia as an economic competition factor	51.0
7	Danger of the dissolution of Russia	26.2
8	Information warfare against Russia	18.6
9	Demographic expansion of China	17.1
10	Weakening of the United Nations and erosion of the international collective security system	16.7
11	Large-scale technogenic disasters	15.7
12	**Illicit nuclear weapons proliferation**	**11.9**
13	Global threats (climate change, AIDS/HIV, exhaustion of natural resources, etc.)	10.0
14	Territorial claims from neighbouring states	7.1
15	There are no serious national security threats to Russia	3.3

Source: *Vneshnaya politika Rossii: mneniya expertov* [Foreign Policy of Russia: Experts Opinions], an analytical report commissioned by the Moscow Office of the Friedrich-Ebert-Foundation (Moscow: Russian Independent Institute for Social and National Problems, 2001), pp. 20–21.

Notes: The poll was conducted in April 2001 by the Russian Independent Institute for Social and National Problems among 210 experts, including members of both chambers of the Russian parliament (the State Duma and the Council of Federation), the staff and experts of relevant committees, senior officers in ministries and state agencies relevant to foreign and security policy, experts from the relevant governmental and non-governmental think tanks, as well as senior journalists working on foreign policy issues.

indifferent to (non-)proliferation. It is more concerned about the expansion of Islamic extremism, the economic and technological deterioration of the country, the dominance of the United States, and alleged international conspiracies against Russia. All these items are perceived as national security challenges by the majority of the Russian foreign policy and security establishment, whereas proliferation is seen as a relevant national security concern by only 12 per cent of those polled (see Table 17.1). One may dispute the objectivity of the predominant security concerns of the Russian political class. However, the outcome of the poll indicated that (non-)proliferation attracts very little attention among the security community in Moscow.

Russia's ambiguous regional non-proliferation policy

The ambiguity of the Russian policy of "no further proliferation" manifests itself in the treatment of the two current cases of non-compliance with the NPT regime. On the one hand, President Putin readily reached consensus with President George W. Bush by jointly stating that neither Iran nor North Korea should attain a military nuclear capability. On the other hand, in neither case did Moscow act on the presumption of the supremacy of the objective of preventing further proliferation of nuclear weapons. It obviously considered the non-proliferation aspect of each case to be secondary to the wider interest of Russia. In both cases Moscow was neither among the proponents of a proactive compliance enforcement policy nor among the supporters of the alleged proliferators. The stronger the self-interest of Russian lobbyists has been in any particular case, the more ambivalent was Moscow's policy. For all sorts of reasons, in both cases Russia has failed, when pressed to address acute issues on the international agenda, to take steps to strengthen the role of the UN Security Council in handling the problem. Rather it is seeking to maintain some leeway to be able to deal with the problems as they arise on a case-by-case basis.

In both cases Moscow rather is seeking to keep a low profile in order to avoid or limit any serious dispute with the United States and, at the same time, to avert any controversy with the countries concerned. However, the beginning of the war in Iraq in 2003 brought about a significant change in Moscow's policy. Having joined the coalition against the war in Iraq in February 2003, Moscow was obviously seeking to reduce the damage caused to US–Russian relations and to restore a closer relationship with Washington. While doing so, Moscow further lowered the profile of its policy, particularly with regard to Iran and North Korea, by increasing the level of convergence with US policy and, at the same time, avoiding fully joining in the anti-proliferation coalitions emerging around each case.

The case of the Democratic People's Republic of Korea

Moscow has long been alarmed by the nuclear ambitions of Pyongyang.[6] At all stages of the evolution of the more recent North Korean nuclear crises, Moscow sought to avoid the development leading to the DPRK obtaining nuclear weapons. However, it did less to prevent the DPRK from following the nuclear option. It is also important to note that at no time did Moscow really feel directly threatened by the nuclear ambitions of the country.

In the most recent dispute over the DPRK nuclear programme, which started in 2002 when Pyongyang again declared its withdrawal from the NPT and admitted its nuclear ambitions, Moscow reacted cautiously. On the one hand, it has repeatedly reconfirmed that it had no interest in the DPRK becoming a nuclear state. Russian Defence Minister Sergei Ivanov has repeatedly rejected the declared intention by North Korea to withdraw from the NPT, and has called for everything possible to be done "in order to bring this state back into the treaty framework".[7] From the very beginning, Moscow insisted that this should be achieved cooperatively through political and diplomatic means. As stated by former Deputy Foreign Minister Alexander Losyukov, Russia certainly was interested in ensuring a nuclear-free environment in the Korean Peninsula. However, the prior goal was to achieve regional stability, not by coercion but through a political solution by providing North Korea with security guarantees and economic assistance.[8]

It is notable that, from the outbreak of the crisis in 2002, Moscow was reluctant to bring the dispute before the UN Security Council, although not only would this ensure Russia's participation in the discussion but, eventually, it could also serve the purpose of strengthening the role of the Security Council. Instead, Moscow started by supporting the DPRK's rejection of multilateral talks and pushing for a bilateral solution with the United States. It was only with the beginning of the Iraq war that Moscow's policy started to change following the revision of North Korea's policy, which now became open to multilateral talks.[9] Apparently, as in other cases (and initially in the case of Iraq as well), Moscow hesitates to call on the Security Council to address the urgent but controversial issues of world politics because it does not believe it could mitigate the US approach either on its own or together with other permanent Security Council members, and might be confronted with a very unpleasant choice of either siding with the United States, tacitly or explicitly, or resorting to its power of veto.

During the frequently interrupted negotiations, Russia certainly kept a relatively low profile. Having little leverage over Pyongyang, it left the lead to the United States and played a modest role in the various consultations and negotiations by merely pledging to maintain regional stability and granting North Korea security guarantees and economic assistance in exchange for the dismantling of its military nuclear programme. Moscow left the active mediating work to China and avoided being associated with any of the various coalitions within the Six-Party Talks. At different times, the United States, the Republic of Korea and Japan formed a smaller group that maintained deeper and closer consultation over the North Korean nuclear problem.

The case of Iran

There is a strong pro-Tehran lobby in Moscow, coming in the first instance from the Russian atomic energy sector. Russo-Iranian nuclear cooperation has been an issue of controversy between the United States and Russia since the contract to finish the construction of the Bushehr nuclear plant was signed between Moscow and Tehran in 1992. In 1995, under strong pressure from Washington, Moscow withdrew from the militarily relevant parts of the deal, most notably from shipping uranium enrichment equipment, but went ahead with the construction of a light water reactor.

The Iraq crisis, as well as evidence of clandestine uranium enrichment and heavy water production programmes in Iran, pushed Moscow partially to reconsider its policy. Most notably, after a period of deterioration in its relations with Washington because of their diverging policies on Iraq, Moscow obviously decided to avoid any escalation over its nuclear cooperation with Iran. However, despite voicing concerns with regard to the development of the Iranian nuclear programme, Moscow did not reverse the Bushehr project but, instead, made its implementation conditional on tougher safeguards and, more particularly, on an agreement to return spent fuel to Russia. This has helped Moscow to postpone the implementation of the project for more than a year, thus freezing the dispute with the United States as well.

Beginning in the spring of 2003, Moscow has constantly emphasized the progressive convergence of its policy position with that of the United States, as well as of the United Kingdom, France and Germany, which took the initiative in persuading Iran to accept intrusive verification of its nuclear activities by the International Atomic Energy Agency (IAEA) on the basis of the Additional Protocol to the Safeguards Agreement with the IAEA, which allows for challenge inspections of any facility to be conducted. At every difficult moment in negotiations with Tehran on its nuclear programme, Moscow did not hesitate to issue strong warnings, as President Putin did, for instance, on 21 September 2004: "Russia categorically rejects the expansion of the club of nuclear states. Iran must accommodate itself to the demands and rules of the IAEA. I am firmly convinced that Iran does not need nuclear weapons. This would not solve any problems, including those of regional security."[10]

Moscow's position went beyond demanding transparency of the Iranian nuclear programme, to be ensured through full cooperation with the IAEA, and joined the United Kingdom, France and Germany in their demand that Tehran abandon its enrichment programme as well as the idea of developing an independent full nuclear cycle of its own.[11] However, in this case, Moscow was following the same pattern as in the dispute over North Korea. At every stage, it resisted any proposal to pass the issue over from the IAEA Board of Governors to the Security Council. And it never fully participated in the efforts of France, Germany and the United Kingdom to persuade Iran to give up the most controversial components of its nuclear programme and make it subject to tight control from the IAEA in exchange for increasing economic cooperation, including in the peaceful nuclear energy sector.

Furthermore, the increasing cooperation of Tehran with the IAEA provided Moscow with an excuse to go ahead with the construction of the Bushehr plant despite the dispute's being unresolved. After the signing of a bilateral protocol on the return of spent fuel had been postponed several times in the course of more than a year and a half, Russia was no longer able to continue that tactic because the construction work at Bushehr was 80 per cent accomplished by the autumn of 2004 and the designated Russian supplier went on to produce the first portion of the nuclear fuel for the plant. Later, in February 2005, after talks between Presidents Putin and Bush in Bratislava (Slovakia), Moscow went on to sign the spent fuel protocol with Tehran, thus opening the door for the finalization of the plant's construction, although its launch had to be postponed again to 2006.

Responses to the evolving international non-proliferation agenda

Over the past decade, especially since the 1995 extension of the NPT, Russia has been pursuing a rather conservative policy, concentrating on the preservation of the existing non-proliferation regime and instruments rather than on their further development and/or revision. Although recognizing the need to adapt international institutions and mechanisms for non-proliferation, Moscow has proceeded on the basis of the expectation that any major revision in the formal institutional structure of the international order might undermine its rather symbolic position. In a sense, Russia has adopted a status quo policy without, however, possessing the resources to resist emerging changes. Therefore, Russia tends to follow a policy of damage limitation as regards any changes that do occur.

For a long time now, Moscow has not sponsored or co-sponsored any major initiative addressing problems of WMD proliferation. The only exception was the proposal to develop a "global control system" – a vague idea about multilateral surveillance of the global spread of missile technologies. The idea died after a series of conferences held in 1999–2001 because Moscow did not have a vested interest in it. For that reason, Moscow constantly found itself merely reacting to others' initiatives and policies, most particularly to those put forward by the United States.

Thus Russia's policy largely limited itself to deciding whether or not to join this or that initiative, and it often became a subcontracting party of others' non-proliferation policy. This pattern is exemplified in Russia's attitudes towards the Proliferation Security Initiative (PSI) proposed by President George W. Bush in the autumn of 2003, and in Russia's close cooperation within the G-8 Global Partnership framework for the purposes of safeguarding fissile materials in a number of countries that, eventually, could become the subject of terrorist encroachment in an attempt to get hold of those materials.

Once the PSI was launched, Moscow hesitated either to join or to reject it. It admitted that the initiative could be a step forward in cutting illicit trafficking in WMD-relevant components and materials, but raised major concerns as regards the legality of the proposed means, particularly concerning eventual violations of the Law of the Sea. Indeed, Moscow also might have had concerns that any eventual illegal shipments from Russia might become subject to the PSI measures. At the same time, Moscow hesitated to reject the initiative outright and rather opted for "constructive dialogue" with the United States.

However, as more countries joined and signed up to cooperate within the PSI framework, Moscow started to reconsider its policy. In February 2004, Defence Minister Sergei Ivanov implied in an address to the annual international conference on security policy in Munich that Russia might join the initiative. Though his statement was immediately denounced by the Foreign Ministry, Moscow did start gradually to move towards a cooperative approach to the PSI. The first step towards joining it was in October 2004 when, at a meeting of the Russia-NATO Council, Moscow agreed, after lengthy consultations, to join NATO's Operation Active Endeavor, aimed at patrolling in the Mediterranean, by sending two warships to join in the operation.[12]

Russia also turned out to be cooperative with the US desire to remove fissile material from countries that lacked the facilities or the expertise in secure storage of the spent fuel, thus making existing fissile material vulnerable to a terrorist attack. Based on the United States' negotiations with the various countries, Russia subcontracted to take back and dispose of spent fuel of Soviet origin from Romania and Serbia in 2003, and from Libya in 2004. Further action of this sort is being planned.

Moscow's low-profile policy on the various non-proliferation issues and initiatives largely reflects an important trend whereby Russia is no longer a champion and initiator of non-proliferation policy but increasingly is becoming a beneficiary of others' non-proliferation policy. The most obvious example is that Russia is a major recipient of international (predominantly US) assistance aimed at increasing the security of its nuclear materials and WMD components and at providing appropriate treatment of its nuclear assets.

The cuts in the nuclear arsenal, the disassembly and destruction of the nuclear weapons thus cut, the down-blending of weapons-grade nuclear material, the expansion of spent fuel disposal and storage facilities, improving the safety of stored fissile material, preventing a brain drain by providing alternative employment to Russian weapons specialists, the disposal of decommissioned nuclear-powered submarines, the elimination of chemical weapons stockpiles – all these projects have been a growth industry over the past decade and a half and have been made possible largely through funding and cooperation provided within the US Department of Defense's Cooperative Threat Reduction (CTR) programme as well as other bilateral programmes. Implementation of these programmes, although not yet considered sufficient, has made it easier for Russia to keep its residual nuclear arsenal and even slowly to modernize it.

From 2002, projects generated and funded by various individual countries are being integrated within the Global Partnership programme against the spread of weapons of mass destruction, related technologies and components decided upon at the G-8 meeting in Kananaskis, Canada. It is envisaged that the programme will spend US$20 billion over 10 years. Apart from the fact that Moscow is doing its best to convert this promise into cash and to ensure that Russia receives the maximum possible assistance in its priority fields, it is important that the programme receives the attention of the leadership of the country, thus helping to keep the wider problem on the radar of the president.

This is important given that most of the contemporary (non-) proliferation issues are regularly brought to the attention of the Russian leadership by the leaders of other nations, most notably of the United States, although neither Iran, nor North Korea, nor Saddam Hussein's regime in Iraq have been considered a threat in Moscow. Otherwise, the small section of the Russian security community ranging across the governmental and non-governmental sector that is committed to the goal of non-proliferation would hardly be able to push effectively on pending issues within the broader government, which is largely ignorant or uninterested in non-proliferation or seeks to pursue commercial interests related to the proliferation of sensitive technologies.

Conclusions

Russia has no interest in abandoning its goal of ensuring WMD non-proliferation. Having become a status quo power that is no longer able to prevent or resist major change in world politics, it hates anything that supports the trend toward further revision of the world order at the expense of Russia. Being the second-largest of the eight nuclear powers (within and outside the NPT regime), Russia certainly pays attention to maintaining its exclusive status and reveals no interest in the expansion of the nuclear club.

At the same time, for all sorts of reasons, non-proliferation is not high on the agenda of Moscow's world order policy. Keeping its status as a permanent member in the Security Council and thus relevant in international politics, retaining and modernizing a significant, albeit smaller, nuclear capability, avoiding and preventing serious regional instability that would test the validity of either symbol of Russia's being a great power certainly enjoy higher priority in Russian policy, especially since Moscow does not feel directly affected by WMD and especially by nuclear proliferation by other state actors. Apparently, the issue of (non-)proliferation is not considered in Moscow as being *the* or even *a* world order issue. This explains why, once the problem of the nuclear heritage of the former Soviet Union had been settled in the mid-1990s and the NPT had been indefinitely extended in 1995, Russia has been pursuing a rather low-profile non-proliferation policy. Although (non-)proliferation issues are merely put on its agenda by other governments, most notably by the United States, Russia prefers to avoid any serious controversy over them. For this purpose, Moscow regularly reconfirms its commitment to the principle of "no further" proliferation, but seeks to avoid any strong counter-proliferation options suggested by the United States.

Over the past decade, Moscow has largely ceased to be a major initiator of non-proliferation policies, and has instead become a net recipient of non-proliferation assistance, which enables it to keep and to modernize its nuclear capabilities. This has implied an important change in Russian policy. Moscow has not submitted any major initiative on non-proliferation in recent years and has rather hesitantly and selectively followed US initiatives, seeking a compromise between its desire to stick to a conservative NPT policy and the United States' more proactive and interventionist counter-proliferation drive.

This, in turn, implies that Moscow not only does not see the non-proliferation issue from the perspective of the world order debate but has no interest in including this issue on the agenda of this debate. It seems to be content to preserve its current exclusive status and does not feel challenged by the current proliferation trends because these involve very few state actors, none of which is expected to compete with Russia as the second-biggest nuclear power in the world.

Notes

1. For discussion of the structure of the Russian nuclear force, see, *inter alia*, General Vladimir Dvorkin's reprint in *Yaderny Kontrol [Nuclear Control]: Information* (Moscow), No. 8, 8–14 April 2005, pp. 13–17.
2. See ⟨http://www.gazeta.ru⟩, 20 December 2004.
3. *Yaderny Kontrol*, No. 8, 8–14 April 2005, pp. 16–17.
4. The Chinese ICBM capability by 2015 is still estimated not to exceed 75–100 single-warhead ICBMs, with the nuclear submarine carrier fleet remaining at a rudimentary stage. See Igor Bocharov, "Paradoxy yadernogo sderzhivaniya" [Paradoxes of Nuclear Deterrence], *Nezavivimoe yadernoe obozrenie [Independent Nuclear Review]* (Moscow), 22 April 2005.
5. Russia does indeed report significant progress, referring to the deep cuts under START II and the further cuts envisioned under SORT, as well as to its ratification of the Comprehensive Nuclear-Test-Ban Treaty. See the interview with Deputy Foreign Minister Sergei Kislyak in *Voprosy bezopasnosti [Issues in Security]* (Moscow), No. 1 (March 2005), p. 2.
6. The 1985 agreement between the Soviet Union and the Democratic People's Republic of Korea (DPRK) for the supply of two nuclear reactors was signed on condition that the DPRK acceded to the NPT, which it did in 1985, although it hesitated to sign the relevant agreement with the IAEA until 1992. Early in 1990, the KGB head Vladimir Kryuchkov reportedly informed the Soviet leadership that the DPRK had by that time already assembled its first nuclear device, although it had not tested it. See Yurii Fedorov, "Koreiskaya yadernaya programma" [The Korean Nuclear Programme], *IAIR Policy Papers*, Vol. 2, No. 1 (2003), pp. 5–7.
7. See ⟨www.gazeta.ru⟩, 14 January 2005.
8. *Yaderny Kontrol: Information* (Moscow), No. 8, 25 February–3 March 2004, p. 4. The policy did not change over time. See the cautionary statement by Sergei Ivanov in January 2005 at ⟨www.gazeta.ru⟩, 14 January 2005.
9. On the initial suggestion of the DPRK, Russia was not included as a participant in the talks on the North Korean nuclear programme and joined the forum only upon a forceful suggestion by the United States.
10. *Yaderny Kontrol: Information* (Moscow), No. 34, 22–29 September 2004, p. 1.
11. For example, Putin in April 2005: *Yaderny Kontrol: Information* (Moscow), No. 9, 15–28 April 2005, p. 5.
12. *Frankfurter Allgemeine Zeitung*, 15 October 2004, p. 2.

18

China's perspectives on WMD proliferation, arms control, disarmament and related threats from non-state actors

Dingli Shen and Jiadong Zhang

The spread of weapons of mass destruction (WMD) is no longer a new phenomenon, and it is a realistic threat to the contemporary world.[1] Ever since the United States exploded its first nuclear bomb in its own desert some six decades ago, the world has witnessed a remarkable continuation of this development, way beyond US territory. The reason the US government revealed this unprecedented weapon, by bombing two Japanese cities, might have had something to do with deterring all other nations, particularly the Soviet Union, in the post–World War II era. But it will have found that this policy has not been that successful and, in fact, the United States today finds itself deterred to some extent by some other nuclear-weapon countries as well.

The Soviet Union was one such equal to the US nuclear might. Each country has manufactured, in total, over 30,000 nuclear weapons. Clearly, both have seriously violated Article VI of the Treaty on the Non-Proliferation of Nuclear Weapons (NPT). Even if the United States and Russia, the sole legal successor to the Soviet military nuclear assets, fully implemented the 2002 Moscow Treaty on Strategic Offensive Reductions by the end of 2012, Washington and Moscow would still deploy some 2,000 "accountable" atomic weapons at that time.

Owing to US and Soviet threats at various times, primarily in the 1950s and 1960s, the People's Republic of China (PRC) started its own nuclear weapons programme. On 16 October 1964, the PRC exploded its first nuclear weapons on the grounds of calling the US nuclear bluff. Today, the United States, Russia and China constitute the three major independent nuclear forces of the world, although the PRC's current nuclear arsenal is probably just a fraction of that of the United States and Russia.[2]

The proliferation of WMD is continuing. India and Pakistan tested their weapons in 1998 and declared themselves to be nuclear-weapon states. Israel is understood to possess a medium-sized nuclear arsenal. Since October 2002, the Democratic People's Republic of Korea (DPRK) has stressed that it has the right to go nuclear given US hostility, and has even suggested that it may have acquired a certain level of nuclear deterrent. In the meantime, Iraq and Libya have demonstrated their ability to launch and operate clandestine military nuclear programmes, and Iran has been suspected of similar intentions. Iran is being pressed to abandon its programme of uranium enrichment and to make its past covert nuclear programme accountable.[3]

WMD proliferation

The recent revelations of nuclear development by Iraq, Iran, Libya and the DPRK have justified the concern of the international community about WMD proliferation, and especially about the acquisition of such weapons by non-state actors. China's views on these issues are clear: although such proliferation threatens international peace and security, it is important to understand the root cause of the problem. The world needs to help create an international environment in which there is no pressure to go nuclear. Over the past decade, China has taken various measures to strengthen international efforts on WMD non-proliferation.

Iraq

The "regime change" in Iraq in the spring of 2003 has not led to the discovery of significant amounts of WMD in Iraq, but it is obvious that prior to this war the Iraqi government had engaged in the illegal development of such weapons while being committed not to develop them. Even the Israeli air raid on the Osirak nuclear reactor, an extreme and controversial act, did not stop Saddam Hussein's nuclear ambitions.[4] It was understood that Iraq was only a year away from creating a nuclear bomb in 1991 when its invasion of Kuwait was thwarted.

Iraq thus became the first state to be prohibited from possessing any WMD by the United Nations, through Security Council Resolution 687 of 3 April 1991. However, Iraq time and again violated numerous UN resolutions on its WMD and verification, thus inviting suspicion. Despite this, there was very little solid evidence of the Iraqi development of nuclear weaponry in the 1990s. A recent CIA report, authored by chief

US weapons investigator Charles Duelfer, concluded that Saddam had given up all his nuclear programmes after the first Gulf war in 1991. Well before the March 2003 invasion, the International Atomic Energy Agency (IAEA) had drawn similar conclusions.[5] For other types of WMD, however, Iraq secretly acquired considerable amounts of chemical and biological weapon agents (including anthrax) by the mid-1990s.

On the one hand, we believe that the United States' "pre-emptive" war against Iraq in 2003 was neither warranted nor lawful under existing international laws. Moreover, that military operation may have worsened the situation in Iraq, at least in the short run. On the other hand, by the time the war was launched, the Iraqi government had not described in detail where and how those chemical weapon agents had been disposed of, failing the terms of Security Council Resolution 1441.[6] Saddam's defiant act may have constituted a violation of that particular resolution and therefore wasted "a last chance of peace".

Iran

Thus far, the IAEA has not concluded that Iran must have been developing nuclear weapons. However, over the years Iran has built a sizeable uranium enrichment capacity without informing the IAEA properly. Iran has not convincingly explained how its enrichment facility became contaminated by highly enriched uranium. Nor has it detailed where its centrifuge enrichment instruments have come from.

Given these reasonable doubts, the international community has demanded that Iran make transparent its history of nuclear activities previously unaccounted for. Tehran has also been asked to stop uranium enrichment entirely, for fear of a possible rapid breakout from its commitment to the peaceful use of nuclear energy. Nevertheless, Iran has been on an off–on trajectory of action under international pressure. Although all countries, Iran included, have a legitimate right to develop nuclear energy for peaceful purposes, to many Iran's nuclear intentions are suspicious to say at least.

China is aware that Iran's nuclear development is not fully in compliance with its obligations under the IAEA Safeguards Agreement. However, China is not interested in coercing Iran, and has indicated that it will oppose the effort to take this issue from the IAEA to the UN Security Council in New York, because this might increase rather than defuse the tension.[7] We consider that, in order to ensure that Iran does not pursue a military nuclear programme, the international community should take measures to improve Iran's security environment, rather than seeking a confrontational approach. Settling the dispute through negotiations will be better than compulsion.

Libya

Libya has long been suspected of an intention to acquire nuclear arms. Because of the UN sanctions against Libya for its role in blowing up a Pan-Am airplane over Lockerbie in Scotland on 21 December 1988,[8] Colonel Muammar Gaddafi, who replaced Libya's former pro-American king, might have become more interested in nuclear weapons. These suspicions were eventually confirmed at the end of 2003, against the backdrop of the war against Iraq. Libya's abandoning of its nuclear weapons programme might be the most important windfall of the Iraqi war.

Given that Libya joined the NPT as early as 1975, its covert pursuit of nuclear weapons indicates that the IAEA has been insufficient in detecting and deterring a non-nuclear-weapon NPT member state from developing a secret bomb programme. Had the Islamabad–Tripoli centrifuge route not been discovered in 2003, Libya might well be on the verge of starting its enrichment operation now.

Historically, China has been cautious in its dealings with the Arab world. China understands Libya's motivation but cannot accept its demand for WMD. In December 2003, Libya agreed to give up its nuclear, chemical and biological weapons programmes completely. Beijing welcomes Libya's bold shift of position toward nuclear non-proliferation, because this action will help stabilize regional security in the Middle East where China is staking more on oil.

The DPRK

The North Korean nuclear crisis is an extremely complex affair, because Pyongyang not only claims to be threatened and but also may have already acquired a few rudimentary fission bombs.[9] If this is true, North Korea would have become the world's ninth nuclear-weapon power,[10] with implications that could drastically affect Asian security. The confrontation has weakened the NPT and may send a signal to others that obtaining nuclear weapons has geopolitical benefits, especially when facing the United States.[11]

North Korea's claim of external threat should not be underestimated, if the foundation of current international law and the United Nations is still the principle of state sovereignty. For a long time until the end of the Cold War, the United States deployed tactical nuclear weapons, along with conventional forces, on the Korean Peninsula.[12] Although Washington has extended its nuclear protection umbrella to Seoul, Moscow and Beijing have not provided similar protection to Pyongyang. It is a natural response that the North Koreans should search for an A-bomb themselves to counterbalance the US nuclear presence in South Korea.

Both North and South Korea have sought reunification of the whole Korean Peninsula. Because the two sides have made no progress beyond the 1953 armistice agreement, both South and North Korea have resorted to nuclear weapons development at one time or another. In the early 1970s, South Korea was working on a nuclear weapons programme but this was later halted under US pressure. Recent reports of South Korea's unauthorized and unreported laser enrichment of uranium have revived suspicions of Seoul's nuclear intentions.[13]

Given South Korea's logical feelings of insecurity, North Korea may have more reasons to do likewise. President George W. Bush's State of the Union speech in 2002, arguing that the DPRK is part of an "axis of evil", provides further justification that the current US administration is so hostile to the DPRK that the North has to develop nuclear deterrence for its ultimate security. In addition to rhetoric, the United States is actually researching and developing a deep-striking "bunker buster bomb" and "usable" tactical nuclear weapons, with primary targets in North Korea. This will do nothing to alleviate North Korea's security concerns.[14]

China has played a proactive role since 2003 in bringing the United States and North Korea together in Beijing, initially through trilateral talks and then through three rounds of "Six-Party" talks.[15] Reportedly, China demanded that the DPRK participate in the talks, while defending North Korea's legitimate security interests. It is understood that China has used its leverage to seek peaceful nuclear dismantling in the North.

However, the Six-Party Talks have been inactive since mid-2004, owing to the politics of the US presidential campaign and emerging issues of South Korea's unreported nuclear experiments. Now that there has been no "regime change" in the White House, Pyongyang has to be more realistic about returning to the negotiating table, especially as Bush's new administration seems to be presenting a milder posture.[16] China also cannot afford the loss of momentum of the talks, and has been carrying out shuttle diplomacy between the various capitals.

China's measures

China is surrounded by countries/regions of acknowledged nuclear-weapon status, such as Russia and United States (through its nuclear weapons presence in East Asia), by de facto nuclear-weapon states, such as India and Pakistan, by states that still aspire to nuclear weapons, such as North Korea, by states/regions that developed or acquired nuclear weapons in the past, such as Japan (at least during World War II), Kazakhstan, South Korea and Taiwan, or by states that have been suspected of having had nuclear weapons ambitions, such as Indonesia. No other nuclear-weapon state has such a complex nuclear environment on its periphery.

North-east Asia and South Asia are two critical areas immediately adjacent to China where nuclear proliferation either has occurred or is continuing. Such developments are detrimental to China's security environment, but responding to them entails a delicate strategy. Fundamentally, developing nuclear weapons is within the realm of national sovereignty: the United States had the right to develop them when it faced the Nazi threat; China had the right when threatened by the United States; and North Korea also has the right because the United States has been hostile to it for a long time.[17]

However, being entitled to nuclear weapons does not mean that China should be engaged in the process. In fact, China has been exercising a great deal of self-restraint in distancing itself from nuclear weapons aspirants. Since the 1990s, primarily out of recognition of the threat of WMD proliferation, and partly out of the need for international cooperation in this regard, Beijing has taken comprehensive measures on non-proliferation. These involve: self-discipline through the imposition of export controls; international cooperation; and persuasion. The tool of persuasion seeks the peaceful ending of actual or suspected nuclear weapons programmes, if and when suitable external conditions are met. This applies, in particular, to the cases of North Korea and Iran.

China's major self-discipline efforts include the promulgation of domestic regulations on non-proliferation export controls concerning dual-use nuclear technology and chemical, biological and missile components and technology. Various trigger lists have been published that match the major international standards. Taking such measures does not necessarily mean that China will not export, but exports will be on a licence basis whereby recipients must present end-use and end-user assurances about civilian purposes. China has stated that it will not export if a particular transfer would entail a proliferation risk.

For a long time China argued that it had the right to export dual-use technologies and items, because non-proliferation should not deprive it of such rights for non-military development. Since May 2004, China has reversed its position by joining the Nuclear Suppliers Group (NSG) and committing to a "full scope" safeguards obligation; i.e. China will no longer export anything of a nuclear nature to any non-NPT nuclear-weapon state that refuses to accept complete and comprehensive nuclear safeguards at all its nuclear facilities. This will prohibit China's nuclear cooperation with Pakistan, India, North Korea and Israel, even at the civilian level.[18] Furthermore, China has approached the Missile Technology Control Regime (MTCR) for membership.

In May 2003, the United States launched the Proliferation Security Initiative (PSI), and claims to have secured support from 60 countries.[19] China was initially rather concerned about the legality of the PSI in interdicting suspected shipments in international space and waters. It remains concerned but has presented a more understanding stance on this issue recently. In fact, at the prompting of US intelligence, China has reportedly intercepted, on its own territory, a shipment of dubious chemicals to a neighbouring country.

Arms control and disarmament

Although all the above-mentioned cases confirm the seriousness of WMD proliferation, one should also note that the post–Cold War international security environment is very different from the past – emphasizing WMD proliferation while frustrating institutionalized international arms control and disarmament.

The demise of anti-ballistic missiles

Given the current level of missile proliferation, the United States put forward a new Nuclear Posture Review (NPR) after the attacks of 11 September 2001.[20] This NPR formulated a new triad of defence capabilities: offensive strike systems (both nuclear and non-nuclear); defences (both active and passive); and a revitalized defence infrastructure. Obviously, this is a major departure from the strategic offence–defence balance forged during the Cold War.

Subsequently, the United States withdrew from the Anti-Ballistic Missile (ABM) Treaty, effective 13 June 2002, and has since embarked on a course of missile defence R&D, as well as deployment. President Bush was committed to deploying 10 anti-strategic missile interceptors by the end of 2004, and the United States has been in the process of implementing this.

This strategic move, despite its rationale, is frustrating to China. China reportedly has just two dozen intercontinental striking systems, so its strategic deterrence could be substantially neutralized if the United States fully deployed an effective North America-based missile defence system (formerly known as National Missile Defense). The prospects would be grimmer if the United States were to deploy a space-based missile defence system, which it is researching. China will be forced to take hard decisions to modernize its strategic forces to a level that can adequately handle US missile defences. Coupled with the Taiwan issue, in which the United States has been meddling by supplying theatre missile defence equipment to the island, it is hard to cultivate strategic trust between Washington and Beijing.

Going into space

Though there exist international treaties prohibiting nuclear weaponization in space, so far there is no international law that bans the use of space for non-nuclear weapons. In fact, the US Air Force Space Command has been moving rapidly to develop the concept of space control assets and to implement its programme.[21] This trend towards space weaponization has revealed the United States' interest in maximizing its monopoly of outer space, a notion that is unacceptable to the rest of the world. The US space-based military programme has a special bearing on the major powers of the world, in particular the major independent centres. China is concerned about these developments, because its security cannot be dependent on others.

In this context, China has in the past proposed the Prevention of an Arms Race in Outer Space (PAROS) at the Conference on Disarmament, trying to mandate the Conference to negotiate an international convention banning any military use of outer space. However, the Chinese proposal met US opposition. Washington was especially opposed to China's linking of PAROS to the fissile cut-off negotiations. Therefore, the Conference on Disarmament has not been effective for years in the areas of either PAROS or the Fissile Material Cutoff Treaty (FMCT). Recent reports, however, seem to indicate that China is showing a certain flexibility in de-linking the two, while still pushing for the non-weaponization of space.

Nuclear weapons reduction

There has been no significant advancement of bilateral or multilateral nuclear arms control and disarmament in the past decade, except for the opening for signature of the Comprehensive Nuclear-Test-Ban Treaty (CTBT) in 1996 and the signing of the Moscow Treaty on Strategic Offensive Reductions (SORT) in 2002. In terms of entering into force, the CTBT has met a major impasse, especially as the US House of Representatives had refused to ratify it and nuclear weapons tests in India and Pakistan have presented it with further challenges.

The Moscow Treaty is therefore the only outstanding effort at further removing nuclear weapons from the earth. Because this treaty demands that the United States and Russia reduce their strategic nuclear warheads to 1,700–2,200 by 31 December 2012, the US government has considered it "a level nearly two-thirds below current levels".[22] This cut, if implemented, should be commended, but one must remember that the treaty asks only for a reduction in the number of strategic delivery systems; most of the "cut" warheads will be put into storage. In this sense, the traditional nuclear arms reduction treaties per se do not ensure a physically irreversible dismantling of nuclear warheads. This contrasts with the US demand of the DPRK for a "comprehensive, verifiable and irreversible dismantlement" (CVID) of all nuclear weapons capability at Pyongyang's disposal.

With the reduction in deployed strategic weapons systems, inevitably the size of the inactive US stockpile will increase, unless the stockpile itself is reduced. In fact, both the United States and Russia are retiring or disassembling some of their stockpiled warheads, but at a far from satisfactory reduction rate. A recent study pointed out that, by 2012, the inactive US stockpile would still be at a level of 700 (compared with its 2,200 treaty-permitted "accountable" warheads). The de facto active warheads that still exist at that time are projected to be 5,260, whereas the actual total will be 5,960.[23]

R&D of new nuclear weapons

The 2001 Nuclear Posture Review asked for an "earth penetrator", the so-called "bunker buster bomb", in order to defeat hard and deeply buried targets. By 2003, the US Congress had appropriated funds for this research.[24] Although the United States has not produced this low-yield weapon, the very rationale for even carrying out research into this type of nuclear weapon is counter to the ultimate purpose of nuclear weapons disarmament. In fact, it is hard to argue that the current programme is for research only because, in our opinion, research is intertwined with development and the eventual purpose of R&D is to prepare for production – introducing a new type of nuclear weapon to the US arsenal in the name of defeating "evil", whether a state leader or a group of terrorists.

It seems ironical to ask North Korea to accept CVID and relinquish all its nuclear assets while the United States can send "earth penetration" bombs deep underground. Such a US-centric security vision is not far-sighted, and does not help to dispel the concerns of other states. It will be almost impossible to lead other nuclear-weapon states to restrict their nuclear options.

China's modernization

China has reportedly been continuing the modernization of its nuclear weapons.[25] Although the Chinese government has not released any information on this, China is understood to have been undertaking efforts to enhance its nuclear weapons survivability by putting the missiles on mobile launchers. China is believed to be adding multiple independently targetable re-entry vehicles (MIRVs) or multiple re-entry vehicles (MRVs) to its warheads, which would serve the purpose of balancing the strategic missile defence build-up. To foil missile defence, China needs to develop better penetration technology for effective strategic retaliation. In addition, China has been long concerned about space weaponization and has reservations about pushing for a production ban on fissile materials.

These developments have formed the technically hard base of China's position on nuclear arms control and disarmament over the past decade. To allow for flexibility in its modernization, Chinese policies under the CTBT and FMCT have been a mix of enthusiasm and reservations. Over time, China has relinquished some of its demands, such as asking for no-first-use in CTBT negotiations, and has compromised over insisting on the right of peaceful nuclear explosion in the same treaty negotiations. It has lowered its opposition to a US withdrawal from the ABM Treaty and its parallel missile defence build-up. It may even de-link PAROS and FMCT, for various reasons including its image. Nevertheless, it is inconceivable that China will not make an effort to offset the US missile defence. This question has been a determining one in gauging the future strategic balance between China and the United States.

Related threats from non-state actors

At the non-state level, the primary concern is the possibility of the illegal acquisition and use of WMD.

As regards the acquisition of nuclear weapons, so far there has been no evidence that a nuclear weapon has fallen into the hands of non-state actors. All acknowledged nuclear-weapon states should have implemented robust physical protection of their nuclear arsenals, so the breach of a state-owned stockpile is very difficult if not impossible. One realistic concern should be the domestic transportation of nuclear weapons from one site to another. In particular, this has been a concern of some Western countries in relation to the security of nuclear weapons in some non-NPT nuclear states (for example, Pakistan).

The acquisition of fissile material by non-state actors is more likely. According to a report by the Institute for Science and International Security, there are more than 3,000 metric tons of fissile materials in the world, enough for more than 230,000 nuclear weapons.[26] The key problem in this arena is the large stocks of weapons-grade plutonium and uranium that are produced by power reactors. Russia now holds about 150 tons of plutonium and 1,000 tons of highly enriched uranium.[27] Such a great quantity of nuclear materials is not only an important energy resource but also a dangerous resource for making weapons. In fact, there are currently more nuclear materials that pose a greater danger because of a lack of effective global management. About 40 kg of weapons-usable uranium and plutonium have been stolen from poorly protected nuclear facilities in the former Soviet Union during the past decade. Although most of that material has been retrieved, 2 kg of highly enriched uranium filched from a research reactor in the former Soviet Republic of Georgia are still missing.[28] In addition, there are many dangerous scenarios in relation to the transportation and stocking of these nuclear materials.

Many terrorist organizations, such as Osama bin Laden and his al-Qaeda network, might be interested in nuclear weapons, but nuclear weapons are not accessible to them, for now and for a long time to come. Al-Qaeda's interest in and willingness to use unconventional weapons may not be an issue at all, but evidence of its capabilities is fragmentary and reveals the difficulty of finding conclusive proof of a threat capability.[29] However, radioactive bombs ("dirty bombs") may be well within the reach of some determined terrorist groups, because such materials are more available. Fortunately, the lethality of a dirty bomb is much less than that of even a low-yield nuclear bomb.

Chemical weapons are thought of as the nuke of the poor, for their relative convenience of production and the readier availability of precursors, which are often of dual use. During the two world wars, chemical weapons were widely used against civilians and those in uniform. Saddam Hussein used them as late as the 1980s against Iranian soldiers and his own Kurdish people. From a non-state-actor perspective, the 1995 Aum Shinrikyo attack with sarin in a Tokyo subway fully demonstrated the relative ease with which this chemical warfare agent can be made with simple precursor materials available on the market and through unsophisticated processing that can be done at home. Thus, the more plausible and imminent threats from non-state actors are still posed by terrorists' access to dual-use chemical weapons precursors and technology. This certainly presents daunting challenges to humankind.

China is facing a rather serious terrorism threat in its region. In the past few years, quite a few anti-China terrorist groups – for example, the Eastern Turkistan Liberation Organization, the World Uygur Youth Congress, the East Turkistan Information Center, and the Eastern Turkistan Islam Movement (Party of God) – have organized a number of armed attacks against both ordinary Chinese people and unarmed local officials, causing loss of life and property. Considering their close ties with al-Qaeda, it is not inconceivable that these organizations might one day launch an attack with weapons of mass terror.

The Iraq crisis and international security

In the aftermath of 9/11, it is very evident that WMD have already spread to countries such as India, Pakistan and the DPRK. The issue of Iran's nuclear capability is highly controversial and no solution has yet been found for permanently closing its uranium enrichment facility. Terrorists' access to WMD will undoubtedly pose the most serious threat ever in the history of humankind. However, so far they have not succeeded in gaining access to nuclear weapons, but they have already acquired chemical and biological materials.

Arms control and disarmament concern human security and China supports these tasks. However, China opposes any attempt by countries to use arms control and disarmament to serve their own interests. China holds that the international community should act cooperatively to advance arms control and disarmament within the framework of the United Nations. The United States launched the Iraq war to test its theory that a pre-emptive war can be an effective instrument against the spread of WMD. But this theory has not proved to be straightforward. A pre-emptive war could also initiate efforts to attain WMD. North Korea, alarmed by US pre-emption, might feel a greater urgency about obtaining nuclear weapons.

Reviewing the Iraq war, China can understand why the United States would retaliate when faced with serious threats from terrorism and WMD proliferation. However, these two problems are of a global nature and should be dealt with globally. This is the reason for asking whether the US action is one of self-defence or unacceptable retaliation or even outright aggression.

Another question is whether or not a democratic Iraq will seek nuclear weapons. Even if Iraq becomes "democratic", it might still be interested in nuclear weapons or other forms of WMD, as long as Israel possesses them. Iraq used to pose a serious threat to its neighbours – Iran, Israel, Kuwait and Saudi Arabia – and to the international security system. The removal of that threat may offer important non-proliferation gains in the short term, but it will not necessarily lead to a safer regional security environment. For instance, the Iranian nuclear programme began under the Shah, when the United States sold Tehran its first reactor. That programme will likely continue under future Iranian governments, unless regional dynamics change fundamentally.

Finally, in the contemporary world, traditional security matters are more interlinked with non-traditional security issues. In this regard, the major powers' record on non-proliferation, arms control and disarmament policies has not been very encouraging in the past few years, primarily owing to the Bush administration's US-security-centric approach.

Notes

The views expressed in this chapter are solely our own.

1. UN Security Council Resolution 1540 (UN Doc. S/Res/1540), passed on 28 April 2004, reaffirmed that "proliferation of nuclear, chemical and biological weapons, as well as their means of delivery, constitutes a threat to international peace and security".

2. Although the PRC has not revealed these data, the unofficial understanding in the West of the Chinese nuclear arsenal is that China possesses some 20 ICBMS (intercontinental ballistic missiles) and some 200 IRBMs (intermediate-range ballistic missiles) that are nuclear tipped, and that China is slowly modernizing its nuclear forces.

3. The International Atomic Energy Agency (IAEA) has not concluded that Iran was developing nuclear weapons, and Iran has signed the Additional Protocol with the IAEA. At the time of writing, Iran has suspended its enrichment programme but has not agreed to do so permanently.

4. Israel is believed to have acquired nuclear weapons.

5. News Wire, "Saddam's Nuclear Program: CIA vs. the U.N.", 11 October 2004.

6. The resolution asked for Iraq's "complete, immediate, unconditional and unimpeded" cooperation in terms of reporting its history of WMD development and the dismantling of these weapons. The Iraqi government admitted in the mid-1990s that it had possessed large quantities of chemical/biological weapons agents, including anthrax. The existence of these agents and Iraq's possible later unilateral dismantling of them have never been reported and verified. In our view, this represents a "substantial breach" of the terms of the resolution.

7. Whereas China has voiced opposition to taking Iran's nuclear issue to the UN Security Council, it has not opposed similar action on the DPRK's nuclear issue, although it does not agree to the imposition of UN sanctions on North Korea.

8. This incident resulted in the death of 270 people.

9. The CIA estimated in November 2002 that Pyongyang had acquired one, and perhaps two, nuclear weapons.

10. The other eight nuclear-weapon states are the United States, Russia, France, the United Kingdom, China, India, Pakistan and Israel (which has not actually declared its nuclear-weapon status).

11. Robert S. Norris, Hans M. Kristensen and Joshua Handler, "North Korea's Nuclear Program, 2003", *Bulletin of the Atomic Scientists*, Vol. 59, No. 2 (March–April 2003), pp. 74–77.

12. US tactical nuclear weapons were withdrawn from the Peninsula after President Bush announced in 1991 that the United States would bring back overseas tactical nuclear weapons.

13. The IAEA has not concluded that South Korea's covert nuclear experiments were for nuclear weapons purposes.

14. Some would argue that the US threat to North Korea has been decreasing, and that it has no excuse for developing its nuclear programme. However, one should focus more on the arguments of North Korea, which is a weaker state than the United States. It could also be argued that, with the end of the Cold War, the threats posed by other states to the United States are decreasing, although threats from some non-state actors may be on the rise for a while. Why then should the US government decide to develop mini-nuclear weapons at this time, especially as such weapons are not the best response to terrorism?

15. The six parties are the United States, China, Japan, Russia and the two Koreas.

16. In his 2005 State of the Union address, President George W. Bush mentioned North

Korea just once: "We're working closely with the governments in Asia to convince North Korea to abandon its nuclear ambitions", ⟨http://www.whitehouse.gov/news/releases/2005/02/20050202-11.html⟩.

17. On a number of occasions we have argued that North Korea, like all other countries (except for Iraq, because so far it is still prohibited by the United Nations), is entitled to develop nuclear weapons. This may not necessarily reflect the view of the Chinese government.

18. Of those nuclear-weapon states that have remained outside the NPT, China has undertaken civilian nuclear cooperation with both India and Pakistan. There have been no reports of such cooperation with the DPRK or Israel.

19. President George W. Bush, State of the Union Speech, 2 February 2005.

20. The Nuclear Posture Review was submitted to the US Congress on 31 December 2001.

21. See the Air Force Space Command "Vision" at ⟨http://www.peterson.af.mil/hqafspc/library/AFSPCPAOFFICE/chaptertwo.htm⟩.

22. "Fact Sheet on the Moscow Treaty on Strategic Offensive Reduction", US Department of State, Bureau of Arms Control, 5 June 2002, see ⟨http://www.state.gov/t/ac/trt/18016.htm#14⟩.

23. Robert S. Norris and Hans M. Kristensen, "What's Behind Bush's Nuclear Cut?", *Arms Control Today*, Vol. 24, No. 8 (October 2004), pp. 6–12.

24. On 20 November 2004, however, the US Congress refused the White House funding request for the next fiscal year for researching earth-penetrating and low-yield nuclear bombs.

25. The statements in this paragraph are based on many non-Chinese sources.

26. David Albright and Kevin O'Neill, eds, *The Challenges of Fissile Material Control* (Washington, DC: Institute for Science and International Security, 1999), ⟨http://www.isis-online.org/publications/fmct/book/Front%204%20w_intro.pdf⟩.

27. David Isenberg, "Nuclear Materials: More Control Is Vital", Washington, DC: Center for Defense Information, 11 September 2002.

28. Ibid.

29. Since 1980, only four significant attacks by terrorists using poison, disease or radioactive materials as weapons have occurred and there have been a few instances of groups or individuals showing interest in using such weapons. The first incident was in 1984 in Oregon when a religious cult sought to depress voter turnout in a local election by clandestinely contaminating restaurant salad with salmonella, poisoning at least 751 people. In 1990, in northern Sri Lanka, the Liberation Tigers of Tamil Eelam (LTTE) attacked a Sri Lankan Armed Forces base with chlorine gas, injuring more than 60 military personnel and enabling the LTTE to overwhelm the fort. The other two incidents were an attack on the Tokyo subway with liquid sarin in 1995 and the 2001 anthrax attacks in the United States. See John Parachini, "Putting WMD Terrorism into Perspective", *Washington Quarterly*, Vol. 26, No. 4 (Autumn 2003), pp. 39–40.

Part VI

The other nuclear powers and the non-proliferation regime

19

Nuclear disarmament, nuclear proliferation and WMD proliferation: An Indian perspective

Gopalaswami Parthasarathy

Nearly six decades have elapsed since hundreds of thousands of innocent men, women and children perished in the nuclear holocaust that engulfed the cities of Hiroshima and Nagasaki. Marking the fiftieth anniversary of this horrific devastation, India's parliament unanimously condemned the use of nuclear weapons in Hiroshima and Nagasaki. Although the world has fortunately not witnessed such devastation by weapons of mass destruction again, the spectre of nuclear annihilation still haunts humankind. The five nuclear-weapon powers "recognized" by the Treaty on the Non-Proliferation of Nuclear Weapons (NPT) are estimated to have possessed 20,150 warheads in 2002, with the United States and Russia alone possessing 19,200 of them. Three states that have not signed the NPT and have either declared or are known to possess nuclear weapons – Israel, India and Pakistan – are estimated to possess around 300 warheads between them. Israel is reported to have commenced assembly of nuclear weapons in 1967. South Africa had a clandestine nuclear weapons programme and had assembled half a dozen nuclear warheads. In 1993 it acceded to the NPT and destroyed these warheads. Both India and Pakistan tested and declared their possession of nuclear weapons in May 1998, but it is now widely acknowledged that both countries actually developed and assembled their respective nuclear arsenals in the 1980s, with India commencing its weaponization programme around January 1989, after Rajiv Gandhi's 1988 Action Plan for universal and time-bound nuclear disarmament was ignored and implicitly rejected by most of the "recognized" nuclear-weapon powers.

Nuclear disarmament

Global nuclear disarmament has been a cherished goal of Indian foreign policy. Recognizing the dangers posed to humanity by the spiralling nuclear arms race between the United States and the Soviet Union, the UN General Assembly accepted an amendment moved by India in 1953 which reflected the "earnest desire" of the world community for the "elimination and prohibition of atomic, hydrogen, bacterial, chemical and other weapons of mass destruction".[1] The first chairman of India's Atomic Energy Commission, Dr Homi Bhaba, indicated in 1964 (just after China had exploded its first nuclear device and well before the NPT in its present form was conceived) that, even though India had the capability to produce nuclear weapons, it had deliberately then chosen not to make nuclear weapons or to adopt a strategy based on nuclear deterrence. It was this approach that underlay India's championing of the Treaty Banning Nuclear Weapon Tests in the Atmosphere, Outer Space and Under Water (Partial Test Ban Treaty, 1953). As part of its abiding commitment to nuclear disarmament, India proposed a Convention on the Prohibition of the Use of Nuclear Weapons in 1982. The proposal called on the Conference on Disarmament to commence negotiations on an international convention prohibiting the use or threat of use of nuclear weapons in any circumstances, as a first step towards reducing the salience of nuclear weapons. Prime Minister Rajiv Gandhi presented an Action Plan for the total elimination of nuclear weapons within a practical and realistic timeframe to the UN Special Session on Disarmament on 9 June 1988.

India's approach to nuclear non-proliferation was aimed not exclusively at curbing the horizontal proliferation of nuclear weapons, but at laying the basis for outlawing the possession, use or threat of use of nuclear weapons. However, what commenced in the late 1960s was not the adoption of any move towards disarmament but a series of measures designed to perpetuate the nuclear hegemony of the five powers. These five powers are also the only countries that can veto any decision of the United Nations that they deem to be inimical to their national interests. The very first measure for perpetuating this nuclear hegemony was the signing of the Nuclear Non-Proliferation Treaty. India chose not to sign this discriminatory and inequitable treaty because it believed that its own security and the cause of world peace could be guaranteed only in a nuclear-weapon-free world. India was convinced that, if a select group of countries was given the right to preserve their nuclear weapons in perpetuity, possession of these weapons would lead to threats of nuclear blackmail by a privileged few.

Did the signing of the NPT guarantee security for all sovereign states by ruling out the threat of use of nuclear weapons, especially against those that do not possess such weapons? The answer to this question must be a categorical "no". In 1975, during his secret grand jury testimony to the Watergate Special Prosecution Force, President Nixon asserted that, during the Indo-Pakistan war in 1971, the United States had "come close to nuclear war" and that "we had threatened to go to nuclear war with the Russians".[2] Between the time the NPT was signed in 1968 and the end of the Cold War there were at least six instances when the United States contemplated the use of nuclear weapons. We will learn, in the course of time, how often other powers have contemplated the use of nuclear weapons and the occasions on which the United States has contemplated the use of nuclear weapons. But the readiness of the Nixon administration to make common cause with China, contemplate the use of nuclear weapons and dispatch a nuclear-powered and nuclear-armed aircraft carrier near India's shores during the course of a conflict in which India was involved only strengthened the resolve of those in India who had argued for an independent Indian nuclear deterrent.

The indefinite extension of the NPT without any binding commitment from the nuclear-weapon states only encouraged these states to resist moves for nuclear disarmament. It virtually eliminated any possibility of getting a firm commitment from the "recognized" nuclear-weapon states to renounce the threat of use of nuclear weapons against those that do not possess such weapons. The advent of the Clinton administration also saw the emergence of an aggressive policy by the United States to "cap, roll back and eliminate" India's nuclear autonomy. In Indian perceptions, moves by the Clinton administration to push ahead with measures such as the Comprehensive Nuclear-Test-Ban Treaty (CTBT) and the Fissile Material Cutoff Treaty (FMCT) were all a part of this effort. Adding to Indian suspicions of American intentions during this period was the reluctance of the Clinton administration to take any meaningful action against China after substantial evidence had emerged about Chinese missile and nuclear transfers to Pakistan. The Clinton administration's non-proliferation initiatives were seen as a manifestation of a new US–Chinese axis directed against India. It would be no exaggeration to say that it was the overzealousness on the part of the Clinton administration to corner India that significantly contributed to India carrying out its nuclear tests in May 1998.

India saw moves to enact the CTBT and FMCT as designed to perpetuate the possession of nuclear weapons by the five powers under the discriminatory NPT. It was against this background that Indian initiatives led to the Non-Aligned Movement's call for "the renunciation of strategic doctrines based upon the use of nuclear weapons and ... for the adoption of an action plan for elimination of all nuclear weapons, within a time-bound framework" during the Cartagena Summit in October 1995.[3] The Non-Aligned summit was held at around the same time as the World Court was considering a reference from the UN General Assembly on a question of immense international importance. The question was: "Is the threat or use of nuclear weapons in any circumstance permitted under international law?" In its historic ruling on 8 July 1996, the World Court held that countries possessing nuclear weapons have not just a *need* but an *obligation* to commence negotiations leading to nuclear disarmament. The World Court also held that the use or threat of use of nuclear weapons would be generally contrary to the principles of international law, although there was some doubt about the extreme contingency when the "very survival of a State" was threatened.[4] The World Court ruling strengthened India's position in demanding a clear linkage between agreements designed exclusively to curb horizontal proliferation (such as the CTBT and FMCT), on the one hand, and a commitment to nuclear disarmament within a reasonable timeframe, on the other.

The Canberra Commission established by the Paul Keating government in Australia affirmed the need for nuclear disarmament and made two crucial recommendations for reducing the risk of nuclear war. The Commission called for the de-alerting of nuclear weapons systems worldwide and for the removal of nuclear warheads from missiles. India took the lead in co-sponsoring a resolution in the UN General Assembly in 1998 on "Reducing the Nuclear Danger", calling for the removal of warheads from missiles and the de-alerting of nuclear weapons systems. Pakistan and over 100 non-nuclear-weapon states supported this resolution, which would have reduced the risk of accidental nuclear conflict worldwide. The United States and its allies did not support even this minimal effort to reduce nuclear risk. India believes that a global no-first-use agreement would be the first step towards universal de-legitimization of nuclear weapons. Given the nuclear-weapon states' existing strategic doctrines, which do not contain any provision for unconditional and universal adherence to the principle of no first use, it is obvious that, with the exception of India, all other nuclear-weapon states wish to retain the option to use nuclear weapons, whenever their national interests require such use.

Nuclear strategies and doctrines

The United States and its partners in the North Atlantic Treaty Organization (NATO) have indicated that they would be prepared to use nuclear weapons to deal with a variety of threats. Even after the Cold War ended, the US military *Doctrine for Joint Nuclear Operations* released in April 1993 stated: "The fundamental purpose of US nuclear forces is to deter the use of weapons of mass destruction (WMD), particularly nuclear weapons, and to serve as a hedge against the emergence of an overwhelming threat".[5] The document also stated that the use of such weapons would be especially useful in "regional conflicts". This implied that, where the United States cannot achieve its military objectives, even in regional conflicts, by conventional means, it reserves the right to use its nuclear arsenal. Releasing the Bush administration's Nuclear Posture Review in 2002, Defense Secretary Donald Rumsfeld defined the aim of American nuclear strategy as providing "the range of options needed to pose a credible deterrent to adversaries whose values and calculations of risk and of gain and loss may be very different from and more difficult to discern than those of past adversaries".[6] Rumsfeld advocated that, in order to deal with "rogue states and adversaries", the United States would supplement its offensive nuclear weapons with credible missile defences. The Defense Department requires the Energy Department to retain a capability to "design, fabricate and certify new warheads". It envisages the development of nuclear weapons to attack deep bunkers.

US strategic thinking has largely influenced NATO nuclear doctrines. Although all but three of the members of NATO are non-nuclear-weapon states under the NPT, all the alliance members base their security on and promote their security interests by giving primary importance to the concept of nuclear deterrence. The NATO Strategic Concept adopted at the Washington Summit in 1999 asserts that the "supreme guarantee of the security of the Allies is provided by the strategic nuclear forces of the Alliance".[7] It adds that the "fundamental purpose" of the strategic nuclear forces is to ensure "uncertainty" in the minds of any potential aggressor, irrespective of whether or not the adversary possesses nuclear weapons. It has since been reported that a document adopted by NATO on 16 May 2000 allows the North Atlantic Council to advise its members to use nuclear weapons against states using, threatening to use or even simply possessing weapons of mass destruction. Thus, nuclear weapons can be used by NATO members against states armed with biological and chemical weapons even if they have signed the NPT. Further NATO procedures and the US–UK Mutual Defence Agreement of 1958 under which the United States and the United Kingdom improve each other's "atomic weapons design, development and fabrication capability"[8] appear to be in violation of Articles I and II of the NPT, which stipulate that nuclear weapons may not be transferred or received by signatories.

The Russian Federation does not subscribe to a doctrine of no first use of nuclear weapons. Russia did, however, sign a no-first-use agreement with China on 4 September 1994 in response to an initiative by China in

January 1994 for a multilateral treaty between the five "recognized" nuclear-weapon powers. Presidents Yeltsin and Jiang Ze Min signed an agreement not to be the first to use nuclear weapons against each other or to target their nuclear weapons against each other. China proposed a "no-first-use agreement" with the United States in 1996. This proposal was rejected. China and the United States did, however, sign a "Non-targeting" agreement on 1 June 1998 when President Clinton visited China, just after the conduct of nuclear tests by India and Pakistan. Clinton claimed that this agreement would "completely eliminate" the risk of accidental nuclear launch and demonstrate "mutual confidence and trust".[9] He also referred to the agreement as "a helpful counterweight" to recent nuclear tests in South Asia. Clinton's comments, reminiscent of the Sino-US "tilt" against India by the Nixon administration during the Bangladesh conflict of December 1971, were viewed with serious concern in Delhi.

China was a vociferous critic of the NPT for over two decades, but its approach changed after India commenced developing its nuclear arsenal in 1989. China acceded to the NPT in 1992. Although China unconditionally offered pledges of "no first use" of nuclear weapons to all states until it acceded to the NPT, the official policy on security assurances posted on China's Foreign Ministry website now states: "China fully understands the request of the non-nuclear-weapon states to be given security assurances. China has undertaken unconditionally not to use or threaten to use nuclear weapons against non-nuclear-weapon states or nuclear-weapon-free zones. China urges all nuclear-weapon states to make the same commitment and conclude a binding international legal instrument so as to enhance the security of all non-nuclear-weapon states."[10] China obviously knows that, given the nuclear doctrines of the other "recognized" nuclear-weapon states, no such legal instrument is feasible. China's readiness to sign "no-first-use" agreements with the other "recognized" nuclear powers and its commitment not to threaten or use nuclear weapons against non-nuclear-weapon states allow a measure of ambiguity on whether its "no-first-use" pledge will be applicable to India. This became evident when China's Foreign Ministry spokesman on 29 July 2004 rejected a suggestion from Indian External Affairs Minister Natwar Singh that both countries should adopt a "common nuclear doctrine". The Chinese Foreign Ministry demanded that India should observe the provisions of UN Security Council Resolution 1172 that called on India to sign the NPT, disband its nuclear arsenal and refrain from any further tests of nuclear weapons and ballistic missiles. Chinese ambiguity on its "no-first-use" policies is regarded in India as part of its continuing desire to "contain" India.

Although Pakistan has not formally enunciated a nuclear doctrine, Lt.

General Khalid Kidwai, the Head of the Strategic Planning Division of its National Command Authority, told a team of physicists from Italy's Landau Network (an arms control institution) that Pakistan's nuclear weapons were "aimed solely at India".[11] According to the Landau team's report, Kidwai added that Pakistan would use nuclear weapons if India conquered a large part of Pakistan's territory or destroyed a large part of Pakistan's land and air forces. Kidwai also held out the possibility of the use of nuclear weapons if India tried to economically strangle Pakistan or pushed it to political destabilization.[12]

India's nuclear doctrine, first officially enunciated on 4 January 2003, asserts that it intends to build and maintain a credible minimum deterrent.[13] Although adopting a policy of "no first use", it clarifies that its nuclear weapons would be used only in retaliation against a major attack on Indian territory, or on Indian forces anywhere, in which nuclear weapons are used. India also retains the right to use nuclear weapons in the event of major attacks on Indian territory, or on Indian forces anywhere, in which chemical or biological weapons are used.

Although concern has been voiced about strained relations between India and Pakistan leading to a nuclear conflict, the two countries are now working on a series of nuclear confidence-building measures. They acknowledged on 20 June 2004 that "the nuclear capabilities of each other, which are based on their national security imperatives, constitute a factor for stability".[14] India sees its nuclear deterrent as essential to meet the strategic challenges posed by the nuclear capabilities of both China and Pakistan. Pakistan asserts it needs nuclear weapons as an "equalizer" against Indian conventional superiority. Because India's security concerns extend beyond South Asia, it will not agree to any proposal for a South Asian nuclear-weapon-free zone, especially given its experiences of the United States and China working together against its security interests during the Nixon and Clinton administrations.

The Israeli nuclear stockpile is said to consist of several hundred weapons of various types including boosted fission and enhanced radiation weapons. Israel uses its long-range missiles and nuclear-capable aircraft to deter both conventional and unconventional attacks or to launch the "Samson Option" should an all-out attack threaten its population centres. Israel does not have an overt nuclear doctrine apart from its assertion that it will not be the first to introduce nuclear weapons into the Middle East – an assertion that is somewhat redundant, given its existing nuclear stockpiles. The systems it possesses, however, constitute an effective pre-emptive strike force. By possessing nuclear weapons while denying their existence, Israel enjoys the benefits of being a nuclear-weapon state without having to face the repercussions of acknowledging its arsenal. Israel also has a policy of preventing its potential adversaries from acquiring nuclear weapons, as evidenced by its attack on Iraq's Osirak reactor in 1981.

Chemical and biological weapons

India is committed to the goal of ending the production, stockpiling, use or threat of use of all weapons of mass destruction. But it will remain opposed to any treaties such as the NPT that are discriminatory. It is primarily because of the universal applicability of the Chemicals Weapons Convention (CWC) that India became an original signatory on 14 January 1993. In keeping with its commitments under this treaty, India has furnished information on its chemical weapons stocks as well as manufacturing installations and storage facilities. The destruction of India's stocks is taking place in accordance with the provisions of the CWC. But there are some concerns about the lack of progress in implementing some provisions of the CWC that are of interest to developing countries, such as those relating to international cooperation and assistance. The CWC has, however, been signed by only 131 out of 191 member states of the United Nations. Some Arab countries that have signed the NPT have not subscribed to the CWC. It has been argued that chemical and biological weapons are considered "the poor man's nuclear weapons". These countries claim that they stay out of treaties such as the CWC because of Israel's rejection of the NPT. This only strengthens the Indian argument that treaties banning weapons of mass destruction have necessarily to be universal and non-discriminatory.

India ratified the Biological and Toxin Weapons Convention (BTWC) in 1974. It has participated in negotiations of the ad hoc group of States Party to the BTWC with the aim of strengthening the convention with a verification protocol. Discussions are still in progress on issues such as national mechanisms to maintain security and oversight of pathogenic organisms, enhancing capabilities for responding to cases of alleged uses of biological weapons, strengthening national and international mechanisms for surveillance and detection of infectious diseases, and the adoption of codes of conduct for scientists and professionals. India maintains that existing norms against biological weapons, especially in the context of possible WMD terrorism, should be strengthened and pursued through multilateral frameworks.

Nuclear non-proliferation

India regards assurances of stringent action by the United States and others against states that participate in the horizontal proliferation of nuclear weapons with scepticism. This is because of the reluctance of the international community to deal in a firm and non-discriminatory manner with nuclear and missile proliferation across India's borders from China to Pakistan and by Pakistan to states such as North Korea, Libya and Iran, and potentially to Saudi Arabia also. India has never questioned Pakistan's desire or right to acquire nuclear weapons in the pursuit of its own security against a larger and more powerful neighbour. Its strategic perceptions have, however, been shaped by the continuing readiness of China to provide Pakistan with assistance to develop its nuclear and missile programmes – programmes that Pakistan acknowledges are exclusively directed against India.

China's assistance to Pakistan's nuclear programme is extensively documented. The director of the Wisconsin Project on Arms Control, Gary Milhollin, has commented: "If one subtracts China's aid to Pakistan's nuclear program, there probably wouldn't be a program".[15] There is evidence, including hints from Bhutto's prison memoirs, that China formally agreed to help Pakistan to develop nuclear weapons when the then prime minister, Zulfiqar Ali Bhutto, visited China in 1976. It is now acknowledged that by 1983 China had supplied Pakistan with enough enriched uranium for about two weapons and the designs for a 25 kt bomb. Chinese support for the Pakistan programme is believed to have included a *quid pro quo* in the form of Pakistan providing China with designs for centrifuge enrichment plants. China's assistance to Pakistan continued even after it acceded to the NPT. When Pakistan's enrichment programme faced problems in 1995, China supplied Pakistan with 5,000 ring magnets. China has subsequently supplied Pakistan with unsafeguarded plutonium processing facilities at Khushab. There is also evidence that China has supplied Pakistan with a range of nuclear weapons designs. It has been noted that, whereas the nuclear weapons designs supplied by Dr Abdul Qadeer Khan to Libya were of a Chinese warhead tested in the 1960s, the nuclear warheads tested by Pakistan in 1998 were of a more modern design.

China's strategic relationship with Pakistan has included not only supplies and know-how to enable Pakistan to build weapons of mass destruction, but also the means of delivery for WMD. Shortly after the visit of Prime Minister Rajiv Gandhi to China in December 1988, China supplied Pakistan with M-11 missiles, which, it was claimed, had a range of less than 300 km. This was followed by assistance to Pakistan to build M-9 missiles (called Shaheen 1 by Pakistan), which were capable of carrying nuclear warheads up to an estimated distance of 800 km. Indian observers have subsequently noted that the Shaheen 2 missile, with a range of around 1,800 km, recently tested by Pakistan is a replica of the two-stage solid-fuelled Chinese M-18 missile. Although the strategic objectives of the Sino-Pakistan nuclear and missile nexus are clearly understood in India, the approach of the United States and other countries to this relationship has only reinforced India's determination to strengthen its nuclear and missile capabilities. Western commentators have acknowledged that, even though the United States was aware of Chinese assistance to Pakistan's nuclear programme in the 1980s, its strategic relationships with China and Pakistan – designed to counter the Soviet Union – led to nuclear proliferation between these "strategic partners" being deliberately ignored. For similar reasons, the Clinton administration refused to take any meaningful action, despite possessing information about China's assistance to Pakistan's nuclear weapons and missile programmes in the 1990s. There is, however, an acknowledgement that the Bush administration is aware of these factors and has endeavoured to take a realistic view of the security imperatives of India's nuclear and missile programmes.

While explaining the rationale for Pakistan's nuclear programme, Prime Minister Bhutto noted that, whereas the "Christian, Jewish and Hindu" civilizations had nuclear weapons capability, it was the "Islamic Civilization" alone that did not possess nuclear weapons. He asserted that he would be remembered as the man who had provided the "Islamic Civilization" with "full nuclear capability".[16] Bhutto's views on Pakistan's nuclear weapons contributing to the capabilities of the "Islamic civilization" were shared by Pakistan's nuclear scientist Sultan Bashiruddin Mahmood, who, along with his colleague Chaudhri Abdul Majeed, was detained shortly after the terrorist attacks of 9/11. They were both charged with helping al-Qaeda to acquire nuclear and biological weapons capabilities. Mahmood openly voiced support for the Taliban and publicly advocated the transfer of nuclear weapons to other Islamic nations. He described Pakistan's nuclear capability as the property of the whole "Ummah" (Muslim community).[17] Two other Pakistani scientists, Suleiman Asad and Al Mukhtar, wanted for questioning about suspected links with Osama bin Laden, disappeared after it was claimed that they had gone to Myanmar, bordering China. Mahmood and Majeed are reported to have acknowledged that they had long discussions with al-Qaeda and Taliban officials. A "Fact Sheet" put out by the White House stated that both scientists had meetings with Osama bin Laden and Mullah Omar during repeated visits to Kandahar, with al-Qaeda seeking their assistance to make radiological dispersal devices.[18] Documents recovered by coalition forces in Afghanistan also reportedly establish that the two scientists were active members of an Islamic organization (UTN) that was engaged in securing information on biological weapons.

A BBC documentary provided a detailed account of how Libya and Saudi Arabia funded the Pakistan nuclear weapons programme from 1973. There is now conclusive evidence about Pakistan's supply of nuclear weapons designs and know-how to Libya and of uranium enrichment technology to Iran and North Korea. According to US officials, Khan "provided the design, the technology, the expertise [and] equipment, primarily for the centrifuge. He also provided the warhead design."[19] The transfers of nuclear enrichment technology and equipment to Iran are reported to have commenced in 1987. The International Atomic Energy Agency (IAEA) reportedly determined that the centrifuges assembled at the Tapeh military base near Tehran strongly resembled the "Pakistan 2" centrifuge design, while centrifuge drawings acquired by Iran resemble the "Pakistan 1" centrifuges. There is evidence that missile collaboration between Pakistan and North Korea commenced around 1992. The transfer of enrichment capabilities is attributed to Pakistan's lack of foreign exchange to pay for No-dong missiles and is believed to have taken place after a visit by Pakistan's then Army Chief General Jehangir Karamat to Pyongyang in December 1997. Pakistan is reported to have admitted that technical assistance for uranium enrichment continued even after General Musharraf became president in 1999.

In a recent interview, the former US ambassador to Riyadh, Charles Freeman, stated that King Fahd had told high-level US officials that Saudi Arabia would need a nuclear deterrent if Iran developed nuclear weapons. There have been credible reports about Saudi Arabia funding Pakistan's nuclear programmes in the 1970s. Saudi Arabia has continuously provided Pakistan with considerable economic assistance, including in the wake of sanctions that Pakistan faced after its nuclear tests of May 1998. Saudi Arabia's defence minister, Prince Sultan, was given unprecedented access to Pakistan's nuclear weapons facilities in Kahuta in March 1999. Shortly thereafter Dr A. Q. Khan paid a visit to Saudi Arabia at the invitation of Prince Sultan in November 1999. Khan's visit was followed by a visit to Pakistan's nuclear facilities by Saudi scientists who had been invited by him to visit Pakistan. Given these developments and the fact that China has supplied long-range CSS-2 missiles to Saudi Arabia in the past, there is interest about the precise directions that nuclear and missile collaboration between Pakistan and Saudi Arabia could take. Pakistan could, for example, justify deployment of nuclear weapons and missiles on Saudi soil by asserting that such deployment was akin to the deployment of American nuclear weapons and missiles on the soil of its NATO allies and did not, therefore, constitute a violation of the NPT.

The United States recently imposed sanctions on 14 "entities" from China, Russia, Belarus, Ukraine, Spain, North Korea and India, claiming that it had "credible information" that these entities had transferred unconventional weapons and missile technologies. The Indian "entities" named were two scientists, C. Surendar and Y. S. R. Prasad, who had worked in India's Nuclear Power Corporation. Both scientists were said to have visited and transferred nuclear technology to Iran. The Indian government rejected the US charges, pointing out that the scientists had visited Iran under IAEA-supported nuclear safety projects. It asserted that no sale of material, equipment or technology was involved and that no transfer of sensitive technology had taken place. It therefore requested the US government to review the issue and to withdraw the sanctions. India has invariably rejected requests to transfer nuclear technology. Colonel Gaddafi's erstwhile deputy, Major Jalloud, asked for Indian nuclear technology during a visit to India in 1978. The request was rejected even though there were hints of Libyan oil supplies on concessionary terms. A few years later, the former chairman of India's Atomic Energy Commission and the architect of its 1974 nuclear blast, Dr Raja Ramanna, turned down a personal request from President Saddam Hussein of Iraq for assistance in nuclear development. Iran was interested in acquiring a nuclear research reactor from India in the 1990s. Responding to international concerns, New Delhi did not go ahead with the proposal. More recently, a North Korean ship carrying missiles was detained and its cargo unloaded at an Indian port.

UN Security Council Resolution 1540 (28 April 2004) focuses on measures to be taken nationally and internationally to prevent the acquisition of WMD by non-state actors. Although India has expressed support for this resolution, it has made clear that it will not accept externally prescribed norms, whatever their source, pertaining to the jurisdiction of its parliament. Spelling out India's concerns during the debate that preceded the adoption of Resolution 1540, India's Permanent Representative, Vijay Nambiar, observed on 22 April 2004:

Our recognition of the time imperative in seeking recourse through the Security Council does not, however, obscure our more basic concerns over the increasing tendency of the Council, in recent years, to assume new and wider powers of legislation on behalf of the international community, and binding on all states. In the present instance, the Council seeks to both define the non-proliferation regime and monitor its implementation. *But who will monitor the monitors?*[20]

India is thus ready to join in measures to prevent the proliferation of WMD, provided these measures are universal and non-discriminatory. India will in no circumstances export materials, equipment or know-how that could give recipients the capability to develop WMD. Its own experience has, however, been that, despite its virtually spotless record on this score, countries that are members of arrangements such as the Nuclear Suppliers Group and the Missile Technology Control Regime use alleged concerns about the need for greater export controls to deny legitimate high-technology transfers.

India is now engaged in a dialogue with the Bush administration on issues pertaining to high-technology transfers and transfers in the space and nuclear power related sectors. Cooperation in the area of missile defence is also envisaged. There has been some progress in this dialogue thus far. There is continuing concern in India that the implementation of non-proliferation measures is selective, arbitrary and entirely subordinate to the strategic interests of the nuclear-weapon powers. Whereas recipients of nuclear weapons designs, equipment and technology such as Libya, Iran and North Korea face threats and sanctions, the culpability of those who actually supply and transfer such technology and know-how is ignored, especially if they are regarded as "strategic allies" or are permanent members of the Security Council.

The world cannot be permanently divided between those who possess and retain the right to use nuclear weapons on the one hand and others who have to live in constant fear of when these weapons will be used. There has to be a vision and commitment to building a nuclear-weapon-free world within a reasonable timeframe. In the meantime, there should be moves to seek a broad consensus to declare the use or threat of use of nuclear weapons to be a crime against humanity. Speaking to the UN General Assembly on 23 September 2004, Prime Minister Manmohan Singh asserted: "The Chemical Weapons Convention is a good model to follow in respect of other weapons of mass destruction, including nuclear weapons. It is through representative institutions rather than exclusive clubs of privileged countries that we can address threats posed by proliferation of weapons of mass destruction and their means of delivery." He added that "progressive steps towards the elimination of weapons of mass destruction must be based on a balance of obligations between those who possess such weapons and those who do not".[21] There naturally has to be a global consensus while moving in this direction – a consensus that differentiates between states that knowingly transfer nuclear weapons designs and technology, on the one hand, and those that do not create nuclear and missile marketing chains, on the other.

Notes

1. United Nations General Assembly Resolution 715 (VIII), "Regulation, Limitation and Balanced Reduction of all Armed Forces and all Armaments: Report of the Disarmament Commission".
2. S. M. Hersh, *The Price of Power* (New York: Simon & Schuster, 1983), p. 457.
3. The Non-aligned Movement, XI Summit, Cartagena (Colombia), 18–20 October 1995, *Basic Documents: Final Document*, ⟨http://www.nam.gov.za/xisummit/chap1.htm⟩ (accessed 7 March 2006).
4. International Court of Justice Advisory Opinion, "Legality of the Threat or Use of Nu-

clear Weapons", 8 July 1996, ⟨http://www.lcnp.org/wcourt/opinion.htm⟩ (accessed 7 March 2006).

5. *Doctrine for Joint Nuclear Operations*, Joint Pub 3-12 (Washington, DC: Joint Chiefs of Staff, 15 December 1995), p. v.

6. US Defense Department, *Nuclear Posture Review Report*, 8 January 2002, excerpts at ⟨www.globalsecurity.org/wmd/library/policy/dod/npr.htm⟩ (accessed 7 March 2006).

7. North Atlantic Treaty Organization, "The Alliance's Strategic Concept", Press Release NAC-S(99)65, 24 April 1999, ⟨http://www.nato.int/docu/pr/1999/p99-065e.htm⟩ (accessed 7 March 2006).

8. See ⟨http://www.basicint.org/nuclear/MDA.htm⟩ (accessed 7 March 2006).

9. "China Profiles: US-China Non-targeting Agreement", June 1998 (Monterey Institute of International Studies for the Nuclear Threat Initiative, 2003), ⟨http://www.nti.org/db/china/chusdet.htm⟩ (accessed 7 March 2006).

10. "China Profiles: Nuclear Weapons Declaratory Policy" (Monterey Institute of International Studies for the Nuclear Threat Initiative, 2003), ⟨http://www.nti.org/db/china/ndeclar.htm⟩ (accessed 7 March 2006).

11. P. Cotta-Ramusino and M. Martellini, *Nuclear Safety, Nuclear Stability and Nuclear Strategy in Pakistan: A Concise Report of a Visit by Landau Network – Centro Volta*, 21 January 2002, ⟨http://www.mi.infn.it/~landnet/Doc/pakistan.pdf⟩ (accessed 7 March 2006).

12. Ibid.

13. See Ministry of External Affairs, India, press release, "The Cabinet Committee on Security Reviews Operationalization of India's Nuclear Doctrine", 4 January 2003, ⟨http://meaindia.nic.in/prhome.htm⟩ (accessed 10 May 2006); also see Ministry of External Affairs, India, *Draft Report of National Security Advisory Board on Indian Nuclear Doctrine*, 17 August 1999, ⟨http://meaindia.nic.in/disarmament/dm17aug99.htm⟩ (accessed 7 March 2006).

14. "Joint Statement, India-Pakistan Expert-Level Talks on Nuclear CBMs" (New Delhi: Ministry of External Affairs, India, 20 June 2004), ⟨http://www.iiss.org/showpage.php?mixedPagesID=99#20_June_2004⟩ (accessed 7 March 2006).

15. "Testimony of Gary Milhollin Before the Committee on Governmental Affairs, Subcommittee on International Security, Proliferation, and Federal Services United States Senate, June 6, 2002", ⟨http://www.senate.gov/~gov_affairs/060602milhollin.pdf⟩ (accessed 7 March 2006).

16. P. Hoodbhoy, "Nuclear Temptations: Myth-Building: The Islamic Bomb", *Bulletin of the Atomic Scientists*, Vol. 49, No. 5 (June 1993), p. 43.

17. Ibid.

18. "Day 100 of the War on Terrorism: More Steps to Shut Down Terrorist Support Networks", 20 December 2001, ⟨http://www.whitehouse.gov/news/releases/2001/12/20011220-8.html⟩ (accessed 10 May 2006).

19. Cited in C. Clary, "Dr. Khan's Nuclear Walmart", *Disarmament Diplomacy*, No. 76 (March–April 2004), ⟨www.acronym.org.uk/dd/dd76/76cc.htm⟩ (accessed 7 March 2006).

20. "Statement by Mr. V. K. Nambiar, Permanent Representative, on Non-Proliferation of Weapons of Mass Destruction at the Security Council on April 22, 2004", ⟨http://www.un.int/india/ind954.pdf⟩ (accessed 7 March 2006), emphasis added.

21. "Address by Dr. Manmohan Singh", at the 59th Session of the United Nations General Assembly, 23 September 2004, ⟨http://www.un.org/webcast/ga/59/statements/indeng040923.pdf⟩ (accessed 7 March 2006).

20

Israel's updated perspective on WMD proliferation, arms control, disarmament and related threats from non-state actors

Shlomo Brom

Israel's present perspective on WMD proliferation, arms control, disarmament and related threats from non-state actors is shaped by its basic positions and a number of developments that have occurred in recent years: the war in Iraq, the uncovering of the Iranian nuclear projects, the roll-back of the Libyan WMD projects, the attacks of 11 September 2001 and their aftermath, and the prolonged conflict with the Palestinians.

The effect of recent developments on Israel's threat perceptions

The war in Iraq

Although now it is becoming quite clear that Iraq did not possess the WMD capabilities of which it was suspected on the eve of the war, the preparations in Israel for the war increased Israel's awareness of the dangers of WMD proliferation in the Middle East. Given the experience of the first Iraq war in 1991, in which Iraq launched ballistic missiles at Israeli cities, Israel had to be prepared for similar Iraqi action even if Israel was not participating in the coalition fighting in Iraq. Based on the intelligence picture at that time, it was assumed that Iraq might also launch chemical and biological warheads at centres of population in Israel. Once again, protective equipment against chemical and biological agents was distributed to the Israeli population, who were alerted to the possibility of such attacks. That has once again put WMD proliferation at the centre of public debate.

The swift occupation of Iraq had several significant ramifications for Israel. On the one hand, it presented an opportunity to halt the proliferation of WMD in the Middle East. Israel could assume that Iraq would be disarmed of its WMD capabilities if it had any prior to the war, and would not be capable of resuming its efforts in these areas for many years, because of the US insistence on reforming Iraq and making it a part of the democratic world. It was also believed that the war and its outcome provided an opportunity for the United States and its allies to deter other proliferators and potential proliferators in the Middle East from taking the path of proliferation and even to roll back existing WMD programmes. The United States could use its military presence in the Middle East and the manifestation of its willingness to engage militarily with proliferators based on its new pre-emption doctrine to put pressure on states involved in programmes that threaten the security of the United States and its allies.

On the other hand, there is concern in Israel that the war in Iraq might also have increased the motivation of some Middle Eastern states to acquire WMD capabilities and especially nuclear capabilities. The war demonstrated the huge gap in conventional military capabilities between the Muslim and Arab states and the United States and its allies and the futility of attempts by the Muslim and Arab states to acquire conventional military capabilities that could balance US capabilities for the foreseeable future. What is left to the states and sub-state actors that oppose US policies is to try and use asymmetric responses to balance the US supremacy. One type of asymmetric response is to engage in terror and guerrilla warfare and the other is to develop WMD capabilities that will deter the United States. In this context the comparison between Iraq and North Korea offers some very tempting conclusions. It can be argued that the United States did not engage North Korea militarily, although its record as an oppressive authoritarian regime and irresponsible proliferator was worse than Iraq's, because it is assumed that North Korea already possesses a few nuclear warheads and that is sufficient to deter the United States.

It is believed in Israel that future developments in Iraq and the way the United States handles other proliferators in the Middle East will decide which trend will be more powerful – yielding to US deterrence or surrendering to the temptation of achieving relative immunity through the acquisition of a nuclear capability. There is concern in Israel that the US failure to stabilize the security situation in Iraq will have a detrimental effect on its deterrence vis-à-vis other states in the Middle East and on its willingness to act against other proliferators. On the one hand, the US difficulties in Iraq are eroding its image as a superpower and are encouraging challenges to its policies from states and sub-state actors in the Middle East. On the other hand, the same difficulties are likely to have a discouraging effect on the US willingness to be engaged in other tests of will that might involve the use of force, and that will contribute to further erosion of its deterrence. It is becoming clear that the new US doctrine of pre-emption will become a dead letter unless events in Iraq change course and the occupation of Iraq and the reforming of its regime turn out to be a US success (to the surprise of most observers).

The uncovering of the Iranian nuclear projects

Iran is a key test case for the contradictory effects of the war in Iraq. It is assumed that the way this case is handled will have a decisive influence on WMD proliferation in the Middle East. From the Iranian perspective, the war in Iraq has put Iran under a complete US siege. Iran is surrounded by US military forces in Iraq, Afghanistan, Turkey and the Gulf states, and even the Central Asian republics are under US influence. Iran does not have a single friendly neighbour anywhere along its long borders. The United States has adopted a new doctrine of pre-emption against hostile states that develop WMD capabilities and has demonstrated its willingness to use force to implement this doctrine. All these considerations imply that Iran needs to exercise caution in dealing with WMD if it wants to avoid becoming the United States' next target. Indeed, there were indications that the Iranian government fully understood the implications of the war and was willing to cooperate with the United States and not provoke it during the war and immediately after the war.[1]

At the same time, the strengthening of the feeling of siege is contributing to Iranian paranoia and the wish to find ways to neutralize the US threat and achieve a mutual deterrence balance with the United States. In this context it is no coincidence that, in a recent military parade in Tehran, Sheab ballistic missiles developed by Iran were covered with slogans threatening the United States and Israel. On the Sheab-2 missile was written "We shall erase Israel from the map" and on the longer-range Sheab-3 missile was written "We shall crush the Americans under our feet".[2]

The uncovering of Iran's secret nuclear projects has put the power of these two opposing forces to the test. From Israel's perspective, the two nuclear installations that were uncovered – the uranium enrichment facility at Natanz and the heavy water production facility at Arak – indicate the existence of a redundant military nuclear project to pursue two alter-

native tracks for the acquisition of fissile material: the uranium enrichment track and the plutonium separation track. The facility at Natanz
will be capable of enrichment up to the level of weapons-grade uranium
and the heavy water production facility is a necessary stage in the construction of a plutonium production reactor. It was believed in Israel
that 2005 would be critical in determining whether the Iranian nuclear
programme would be halted or proceed to a full-scale military programme that could not be stopped. In this context, Major General Giora
Eiland, the National Security Advisor to Prime Minister Sharon, told his
US counterparts on a visit to the United States that November 2004
would be a critical date for the Iranian nuclear programme. After this
date Iran might pass the no-return point in its race to acquire a nuclear
capability.[3] He probably meant that, if the Board of Governors of the International Atomic Energy Agency (IAEA) meeting on that date did not
impose tough measures that would make Iran change its stance, such as
moving the issue to the UN Security Council, most probably it would
not be possible to stop the production of fissile material in Iran, and that
would remove the most important obstacle to Iran's achievement of a full
military nuclear capability. The uncovering of the secret facilities and the
consequent monitoring and criticism of Iran by the IAEA surprised the
Iranians and probably caused delays to the Iranian programmes but it
did not stop them. The next test will come if the Iranian dossier is referred by the IAEA to the UN Security Council.

Israelis believe that Iran's insistence on continuing these programmes
demonstrates one of the main weaknesses of the Treaty on the Non-
Proliferation of Nuclear Weapons (NPT). The treaty enables any would-
be proliferators to make the technological and industrial progress needed
for military nuclear programmes under the cover of civilian nuclear activities. The NPT allows any signatory to be involved in nuclear fuel-cycle
activities as long as they are reported and monitored. Proliferators can
then choose one of two tracks. Either they can fully develop all the necessary capabilities without violating any of the provisions of the NPT and
then withdraw from the treaty at a convenient moment and acquire a military nuclear capability in a very short space of time. Or they can use the
technologies developed in overt civilian nuclear programmes to establish
a parallel unreported and unmonitored programme to produce weapons-
grade fissile material. Once weapons-grade fissile material is available, the
rest is only a matter of decision, time and the investment of some financial resources in developing and producing the components of a nuclear
device. These types of activities are much less transparent than the production of fissile material and it is extremely difficult to monitor them and
stop them.

It would appear that Iran made a mistake when it chose to keep its nuclear fuel production facilities unreported, thus violating its NPT commitments, but it is not at all certain that these violations are sufficient to make the IAEA and the Security Council take the necessary steps against Iran. That depends to a great extent on the cooperation of some major actors in addition to the United States, namely the European Union, Russia and China. So far, the limited achievements in delaying the operation of the Iranian uranium enrichment facility can be attributed to the willingness of the three major European states – the United Kingdom, France and Germany (the EU-3) – to put pressure on Iran, but it is doubtful whether these states are determined enough and willing to push Iran further by supporting an IAEA decision to refer the Iranian violations to the Security Council and then support effective measures against Iran in the Security Council. It is even more doubtful that Russia and China would support such steps. Without the support of these states, the IAEA cannot take effective action to stop Iran's programmes because Iran enjoys the support of the third world bloc of states, which can be easily persuaded that this is another case of first world states denying technology to a third world state because they wish to preserve their technological monopoly. So far, the EU-3 have shown a surprising willingness to close ranks with the United States because of their awareness of the dangers of the nuclearization of Iran, but the meeting of the IAEA Board of Governors in September 2004 indicated that the rift between the United States and Europe on this issue was reopening.

The difficulties of the United States in Iraq, the growing hostility in the Arab and Muslim world towards the United States and the rift between the United States and its European allies are weakening the credibility of the US military threat vis-à-vis Iran. There are enough reasons to assume that the United States will hesitate to get involved in another quagmire in Iran. That is directly weakening the United States' coercive power against Iran and indirectly it makes it easier for the other powers to oppose US policies in the IAEA and elsewhere because they do not have to consider that, if they do not cooperate with the United States, it will take unilateral military steps against Iran that will be detrimental to their interests.

Israel is carefully observing this ongoing saga. It cannot be indifferent to Iran's progress towards a military nuclear capability when Iran's leadership openly declares that it aims to destroy Israel and when Iran is translating its ideology into action by actively supporting and guiding terror groups that operate against Israel. Israel is also concerned that, if Iran is not stopped, this will cause a domino reaction in the Middle East and other states such as Egypt, Saudi Arabia and Syria will not be able to oppose domestic pressures to enter the fray and initiate their own nuclear programmes. Israel would prefer the international community to deal with the problem of Iran, but it has to take into account a scenario in which the international community fails, and consider its options for unilateral action.[4]

The roll-back of the Libyan WMD projects

The case of Libya is different. It is an example of the potentially positive effect of the war in Iraq on the international community's ability to roll back proliferators in the Middle East. Following the war, Libya's leader, Muammar Gaddafi, concluded that proceeding with WMD programmes involves too much risk and he decided to give them up. He even gave up his ballistic missiles inventory. One can argue that the war was not the only determining factor and that Gaddafi had decided quite a long time ago to mend fences with the United States following the Lockerbie bombing and the UN sanctions against Libya. Nevertheless, it is difficult to argue that the war did not have a central role in the timing and abruptness of this dramatic decision.

From Israel's point of view, another significant lesson of the Libyan case is the importance of proactive counter-proliferation policies. This is concluded from the significant role played by the Proliferation Security Initiative (PSI)[5] operation against Libya in the Libyan decision. Under this initiative, a ship carrying centrifuge parts supplied by Abdul Qadeer Khan's network was intercepted in Italy on its way to Libya. Libya was caught red-handed and, against the background of the war in Iraq, this increased Libyan concerns that it might risk a harsh reaction from the United States.[6]

Israel believes that the Libyan example has both positive and negative implications. On the one hand, it shows that the war in Iraq could be used to put effective pressure on other proliferators such as Iran to divest themselves of their WMD programmes and infrastructure. On the other hand, it is another manifestation of the IAEA's failure in its monitoring of NPT signatories to discover such huge violations of the treaty. This failure joins earlier failures in Iraq and Iran, and it makes it very difficult to trust the Safeguards Agreements and the monitoring mechanisms of the IAEA as a credible base for a non-proliferation regime. There was also some concern initially in Israel that the Libyan move would increase the pressure on Israel to join the NPT and sign a Safeguards Agreement,[7] but it dissipated after a short time.

The attacks of 11 September 2001 and their aftermath

The 9/11 attacks and their aftermath raised concerns in Israel about the deadly combination of terror and WMD. The incident of the anthrax letters in the United States sharpened this concern. From Israel's perspective, that should add impetus to the efforts to curb proliferation in the Middle East. Israel is especially concerned about the close relationship between Iran, Hezbollah in Lebanon and the Palestinian terror groups. Iran has already supplied Hezbollah with long-range artillery rockets that are able to threaten Israeli population centres, and there are concerns that WMD agents will be the next stage. The uncovering of the A. Q. Khan network raised the possibility that terror organizations might have access to nuclear technologies as well. This network was not selective in the choice of its clients. A. Q. Khan and his team had some relationship with the Taliban regime in Afghanistan and through it possibly also with al-Qaeda.[8] This demonstrates how easy it is to trade in nuclear technologies in spite of all the counter-proliferation regimes. It can be assumed that it is still difficult for a terror organization to build the industrial infrastructure necessary for constructing nuclear warheads, but such organizations could have the capability to build "dirty bombs" that disperse radioactive material.

The conflict with the Palestinians

The prolonged violent round of conflict between Israel and the Palestinians that started in September 2000 has an effect on Israel's attitude towards non-proliferation and arms control. First, it is widening the rift between Israel and the Arab states of the Middle East. That leaves no place for a confidence-building process, which is a precondition for the reduction of tensions that could lead to real arms control dialogue in the Middle East. The numerous manifestations of Arab hostility towards Israel are increasing Israelis' awareness of their vulnerabilities. In such an atmosphere, talk about a Middle East free of WMD based on agreements with credible Arab partners is met with suspicion and disbelief. Second, Israel has formally declared that it would be willing to consider arms control talks aimed at the establishment of a WMD-free zone in the Middle East, but only after a stable comprehensive peace has been established in the Middle East. In the present circumstances, it seems unlikely that a comprehensive peace will be achieved in the foreseeable future and that is making real discussion of arms control agreements in the Middle East a distant prospect. Third, the Israeli leadership is so preoccupied by the struggle with the Palestinians that no attention is given to subjects that are not seen as having real urgency. That means that only a very small community in Israel within the establishment and outside the establishment is interested in these questions. The leadership and the public at large are more interested in the immediate threats and the operational responses to these threats.

Developments in Israel's response strategy

Summing up the effect of the developments of recent years, it is possible to say that they are generally pushing Israel to put much more emphasis on counter-proliferation efforts than on arms control agreements. According to this perspective, counter-proliferation should be based first on political action by the international community against the proliferators. The Libyan roll-back and the limited successes with Iran are proof of the effectiveness of such political action, but this depends on the willingness of the major powers to cooperate in fighting proliferation. In parallel, military counter-proliferation options and the ability to engage in pro-active counter-proliferation operations have to be maintained. Military options are necessary to make the political action by the international community credible and to be used as a last resort. The PSI is a good example of proactive counter-proliferation. It aims to impede and stop trafficking in WMD, their delivery systems and related materials by any state or non-state actor engaged in or supporting WMD proliferation programmes, at any time and in any place by interdicting transfers by land, sea and air.[9] In this context, Israel is retaining the right to act unilaterally along the same lines when its vital interests are at stake. Israel is also investing a lot of resources in the deployment of a national missile defence system based on the Arrow anti-ballistic missile. Although no system can provide a fully protective umbrella against ballistic missiles, it is believed that such a system can minimize the damage and have a strong deterrent effect.

It is evident that developments in recent years have decreased the emphasis on arms control in Israel's foreign policies, but have they also changed some of these policies?

Since the nuclear tests by India and Pakistan, Israel retains a unique status as a suspected non-declared nuclear-weapon state. There are no indications that Israel intends to change its policy of nuclear ambiguity. The widespread view is that it has nothing to gain from a change and a change might only cause harm by provoking Arab and international reactions. Nor is Israel considering joining the NPT. The reasons for Israel's entry into the nuclear field are still valid: it is in the unique situation of existing in a hostile environment in which there are still powerful elements that are calling for its destruction, and its nuclear policy provides a kind of insurance policy.

The most authoritative presentation of Israel's arms control policies was made by the former director general of the Israeli Ministry of Foreign Affairs, Ambassador Eytan Bentsur, in a statement before the UN Conference on Disarmament on 4 September 1997.[10] In this statement he listed the guiding principles of Israel's approach to regional security, arms control and disarmament. He started with general principles:

1. Peace must come with security – that means that, even in times of comprehensive peace, Israel cannot give up the security capabilities that offset its strategic vulnerabilities and disadvantageous disparities vis-à-vis its neighbours.

2. The peace process should be free of terrorism and violence – states using these instruments cannot be partners in any regional security process and arms control negotiations.

3. Regional cooperation is an essential part of security and stability.

4. Peace and normalization are one and indivisible.

The first conclusion of these principles is that Israel supports the adoption of a regional approach to the Middle East's security problems. Global conventions and regimes are important, but they do not respond effectively to the specific problems of this region. This basic position is also reflected in Israel's acceptance of the idea of establishing in the Middle East a mutually verifiable zone, free of surface-to-surface missiles and of chemical, biological and nuclear weapons.[11]

Based on that, Ambassador Bentsur developed several basic premises:

• Arms control and the regional security process should enhance the security of every state participating in it. This premise reflects the perception in Israel that, from the point of view of the Arab states, the purpose of arms control and the regional security process is to weaken Israel by denying it the capabilities that offset its vulnerabilities.

• All steps taken in such a process should increase the overall stability of the region.

• Each state is entitled to equally high levels of overall security, defined as freedom from threats to its existence and well-being.

• Every state has the right to define the threats it considers relevant to its own security – arms control and the regional security process should provide adequate responses to these defined threats.

• The process should take into account not only individual states but also possible coalitions – any agreement that is based on a conception of a balance of forces should take into account that Israel may face different potential Arab/Muslim anti-Israel coalitions in the Middle East.

Against this background, the government of Israel has some process guidelines:

1. The peace process is paramount and the eventual peace must be durable and comprehensive.

2. The peace process must be regional and embrace every state in the region. Confidence-building and security measures have to be developed within this framework.

3. A step-by-step approach is required – any attempt to rush the process will make it collapse.
4. The progress achieved in the transformation of the region into a more peaceful, stable and secure environment will govern the pace and scope of the negotiation and implementation of arms control measures.

At the end of his statement, Ambassador Bentsur elaborated the specific Israeli policies on the different arms control regimes. The significant WMD regimes are as follows:

- The Non-Proliferation Treaty – Israel supports the NPT but does not find it an adequate response to its own security problems and regional concerns, so Israel does not intend to become a signatory.
- The Chemical Weapons Convention (CWC) – Israel is a signatory of the CWC but it did not ratify it. Israel does not intend to do so as long as the chemical weapon capable states in the Middle East do not join the CWC.
- The Comprehensive Nuclear-Test-Ban Treaty (CTBT) – Israel joined the CTBT and is cooperating in making its monitoring mechanism reliable.
- The statement did not mention the Biological and Toxin Weapons Convention (BTWC) to which Israel is not a signatory on the grounds of its unverifiability.

The main question is whether the dramatic events of recent years have made a dent in this strong policy approach. So far there are no indications to that effect. In fact, the opposite is true. Israel's positions have become more entrenched, and the little optimism that existed in Bentsur's statement has faded. What seemed to be possible in the atmosphere of a peace process appears now to be fantasy. There is no active peace process in the Middle East and the violent conflict between the Palestinians and Israel has poisoned the Middle East atmosphere. No confidence- or security-building measures are being undertaken and the level of trust in the ability to find a credible Arab partner to any agreement is at its lowest. Mistrust and suspicion reign. In this atmosphere there is a growing tendency to take unilateral steps. Prime Minister Sharon's plan of unilateral disengagement from some of the Palestinian territories is only one indication of this trend. Proactive counter-proliferation is given a clear preference vis-à-vis arms control. The changes in US policies towards rejection of multilateralism and adoption of unilateralism and preemption make it easier for Israel to adopt a similar course.

There is less discourse on regional cooperation. Because of the deep sense of disappointment dominating the Israeli scene the public do not want any more illusions. Past statements by former Prime Minister Shimon Peres about a New Middle East that cooperates economically and in other areas are being ridiculed. Cooperative security concepts cannot be absorbed in such an atmosphere.

All this implies that, although there has been no declaratory change in the basic set of principles and premises listed above, they are related to as a set of conditions that cannot be fulfilled at any foreseeable future date, and therefore it is not realistic to expect any real progress in arms control in the Middle East at the moment. The shelving of the idea of being more engaged in arms control became easier because of a corresponding change in US arms control policies. It is usually more convenient for Israel to follow US policies because of the very close relationship between the two states. Moreover, Israel can expect no real pressure to change its arms control policies as long as the United States holds its present policies.

Another important facet of this approach is a change in Israel's approach to confidence- and security-building measures (CSBMs). There is no trust in the intentions of the Arab states and CSBMs are looked upon as insignificant measures sometimes suggested by Arab states to lure Israel into making much more significant concessions. The indifference of the Israeli leadership and media towards the Arab Peace Initiative adopted at the Arab League's Beirut summit in 2002, which was generally based on a Saudi peace plan, is an example of this disillusioned approach.

There have also been some developments in concrete arms control issues. The perception that the NPT does not respond adequately to security problems in the Middle East was strengthened because of more cases of states signatories to the NPT being actively involved in military nuclear programmes that were not uncovered by IAEA monitoring. Israel is especially concerned about the ability of more states using their right under the NPT to engage in nuclear fuel production to divert the technology and the industrial capacity needed to the production of nuclear warheads.

In this context, efforts are being made in Israel to develop new conceptions of arms control regimes that will close this wide gap.

The NPT

According to Ephraim Asculai, a former Israel Atomic Energy Commission official, the main problems of the present NPT regime are: the illicit quest of member states for nuclear weapons; the provision of illicit assistance to such states; the failure to implement Article IV of the NPT relating to access of signatories to civilian nuclear technology; the possibility of withdrawal from the NPT, which can be used by states such as North Korea and Iran; and the problem of the three non-NPT states (India, Pakistan and Israel).[12] To solve these problems, he suggests a new regime to replace the NPT that would include the three non-NPT states.

The main elements of the suggested regime are:

1. All states will sign Safeguards Agreements; that includes the NPT nuclear-weapon states and the non-NPT nuclear states.
2. Only fissile materials will be monitored. In weapon states, only fissile materials produced for peaceful purposes will be monitored. The purpose of this suggestion is to remove from the IAEA the huge number of tasks that prevent it from implementing an effective monitoring function where it is needed.
3. The nuclear fuel cycle will be internationalized. No individual state will be allowed to produce nuclear fuel. That will prevent diversion of machinery and fissile material to military projects.
4. The nuclear suppliers' regime will encompass all potential suppliers, including the non-NPT weapon states. This would close a major potential source of leakage of nuclear technology, as was manifested by the A. Q. Khan network. It would also limit the possibilities for non-state actors to acquire nuclear technologies.

It is difficult to assume that the international community will be capable of accepting a new non-proliferation regime based on this full set of principles because of the tension between the non-weapon states and the weapon states and because of the expected opposition of the Arab states to any implied legitimization of the nuclear status of Israel. However, practical elements of this proposal, such as the internationalization of nuclear fuel production and introducing some elements of monitoring of all weapon states and potential suppliers, are worthy of attention.

The CTBT

Israel has not given up its support for the CTBT and it still cooperates in the monitoring system developed for this treaty, although it did not ratify it because it decided to follow the lead of the United States.

The CWC

There is no change in Israel's approach to the CWC. It is still postponing its ratification until the other states in the region sign the treaty. In recent years, only Libya has decided to give up its chemical weapons and join the CWC; other Arab states have only accelerated the development and production of chemical weapons. Therefore Israel does not see any reason to reconsider its position. From Israel's perspective, the CWC organization has not yet proved its effectiveness, mainly because of four groups of problems:

- no challenge inspections were put in place;
- huge delays have occurred in the necessary legislation among many member states;
- no regular reports are made by most states and there are discrepancies in the existing reports that are not dealt with;
- the monitoring system does not currently cover chemical factories, which can easily be converted into weapons-producing sites.[13]

The BTWC

There is no change either in Israel's attitude towards the Biological and Toxin Weapons Convention, which is viewed as an unverifiable regime that is stagnating.[14] Israel is not considering joining this regime. One can assume that, if the attempts to develop a verifiable biological weapons treaty bear fruit, Israel will have to rethink its position. This time, the decision to sign such a treaty would be much more difficult because of Israel's generally negative approach to arms control and because of its negative experience of the CWC. Israel hoped that its signing of the CWC would be followed by the Arab states, but it was disappointed and therefore remains in the awkward position of a signatory that has not ratified the treaty. Israel can assume that the Arab reaction to its future signing of a biological convention would be no different and it would avoid the inconvenience by not signing it.

Conclusion

There is much concern in Israel about WMD proliferation in the Middle East. It is mostly focused on the Iranian nuclear project. The engagement of the international community with this issue is helping Israel to delay a decision on taking unilateral action until it has seen the results of this engagement.

Notions of cooperation on arms control and regional security are going through a difficult period in Israel. Their revival is dependent on a change of atmosphere in the Middle East. This implies that the international community will have to give first priority to ameliorating the Arab–Israeli conflict and specifically the Israeli–Palestinian conflict if there is a wish to start a real dialogue on regional security arrangements, including regional arms control. Recent developments in the Israeli–Palestinian arena and their positive impact on the Israeli–Arab relationship in general may raise hopes that in the not too distant future some sort of a resumption of a dialogue on arms control will be possible.

Because of its growing proliferation concerns, Israel is probably still examining different proactive counter-proliferation options. Some of them may lead to a clash between Israel and Iran. All of this is adding an additional element of instability to the Middle East, which has to be addressed by the international community.

Notes

1. Elizabeth Farnsworth, "The View from Iran", Public Broadcasting Service, 6 March 2003; Donna Bryson, "Iraq War Leaves Iran with Few Options", *Associated Press*, 23 April 2003; Ayelet Savyon, "Iran and the War on Iraq", *MEMRI*, 28 March 2003.
2. Yossi Melman, "Iran: We Started the Preparation for the Re-operation of the Uranium Enrichment Program", *Haaretz*, 22 September 2004, web archive (in Hebrew).
3. Ben Kaspit, "Approaching the No-return Point in Iran's Nuclear Race", *Maariv*, 27 September 2004, p. 3 (in Hebrew).
4. Yossi Melman, "The Problem Is That Even an Unpleasant Regime Is Allowed to Erect a Civilian Nuclear Reactor", *Haaretz*, 22 September 2004, web archive (in Hebrew).
5. Mike Nartker, "U.S. Response I: Bush Proposes New Initiative to Block Suspect Cargo Shipments", *Global Security Newswire*, 2 June 2003.
6. Michael Roston, "Polishing up the Story on PSI", *The National Interest*, Vol. 3, No. 23 (2004).
7. Nancy Palus, "Muammar's Big Move – Can Israel's Nuclear Program Survive the Current Trend?", *Slate*, 22 December 2003.
8. William J. Broad and David E. Sanger, "The Bomb Merchant: Chasing Dr. Khan's Network; As Nuclear Secrets Emerge, More Are Suspected", *New York Times*, 26 December 2004; William J. Broad, David Rohde and David E. Sanger, "A.Q. Khan's Secrets", *International Herald Tribune*, 31 December 2004; B. Raman, "A.Q. Khan and Osama Bin Laden", Paper No. 960, South Asia Analysis Group, 24 March 2004, ⟨http://www.saag.org/papers10/paper960.html⟩.
9. "Statement of Interdiction Principles", declaration issued by the Proliferation Security Initiative (PSI), Paris, 4 September 2003, ⟨http://www.acronym.org.uk/docs/0309/doc06.htm⟩.
10. "Israel's Approach to Regional Security, Arms Control and Disarmament", statement by H.E. Mr. Eytan Bentsur, Director General of the Ministry of Foreign Affairs, before the Conference on Disarmament, Geneva, 4 September 1997, ⟨http://www.newyork.israel.org/mfa/go.asp?MFAH00js0⟩.
11. "A Farewell to Chemical Arms", address by the Foreign Minister of Israel, Mr. Shimon Peres, at the Signing Ceremony of the Chemical Weapons Convention Treaty, Paris, 13 January 1993, ⟨http://www.fas.org/news/israel/930113-peres.htm⟩.
12. Ephraim Asculai, *Rethinking the Nuclear Non-Proliferation Regime*, Memorandum No. 70 (Tel Aviv: Jaffee Center for Strategic Studies, June 2004).
13. Shmuel Limone, "The Chemical and Biological Weapons Conventions", *Strategic Assessment*, Vol. 7, No. 1 (2004).
14. Ibid.

Part VII

Broadening the scope of the non-proliferation regime

21

Nuclear threats from non-state actors

William C. Potter

Introduction

The subject of non-state actors and weapons of mass destruction (WMD) has been the focus of sporadic scholarly research and policy analysis for decades.[1] A major surge of research and US government spending on chemical and biological weapons terrorism followed the 20 March 1995 sarin attack on the Tokyo subway by the Japanese doomsday cult Aum Shinrikyo, and an even greater and sustained level of international attention to all dimensions of WMD terrorism has occurred since 11 September 2001. In the aftermath of the sophisticated attacks by al-Qaeda on multiple US targets, the issue of nuclear terrorism has generated particular attention as many analysts have revised their assessments about the readiness and ability of non-state actors to resort to different forms of nuclear violence. This chapter provides a brief introduction to the four principal kinds of nuclear terrorism, the motivations of potential nuclear terrorists, the barriers to nuclear terrorism, and the means available to the international community to reduce the probability of nuclear terror acts with the highest consequences.

The four faces of nuclear terrorism

Non-state actors have essentially four mechanisms by which they can exploit civilian and nuclear assets internationally to serve their terrorist goals:

- the dispersal of radioactive material by conventional explosives or other means – a radiological dispersal device (RDD);
- attacks against or sabotage of nuclear facilities, in particular nuclear power plants, causing the release of radioactivity;
- the theft or purchase of fissile material leading to the fabrication and detonation of a crude nuclear weapon – an improvised nuclear device (IND); and
- the theft and detonation of an intact nuclear weapon.

All of these nuclear threats are real, all merit the attention of the international community, and all require the expenditure of significant resources to reduce the likelihood and impact of their occurrence. The threats, however, are different and vary widely in their probability of occurrence, their consequences for human and financial loss, and the ease with which one can intervene to reduce their destructive outcome.[2]

The risk of nuclear terrorism can be defined as the probability of an event multiplied by its consequences. Thus, the greater the probability *or* the greater the consequences, the higher the overall risks.

Nuclear terrorism experts generally agree that the nuclear terror acts with the highest consequences – those involving nuclear explosives – are the least likely to occur because they are the most difficult to accomplish.[3] Conversely, the acts with the least damaging consequences – those involving release of radioactivity but no nuclear explosion – are the most likely to occur because they are the easiest to carry out. Constructing and detonating an improvised nuclear device, for example, is far more challenging than building and setting off a radiological dispersal device, because an IND is much more complex technologically and the necessary materials are far more difficult to obtain. Thus, an IND presents a less likely threat than does an RDD. In contrast, the consequences of an IND explosion are orders of magnitude more devastating than the damage from use of an RDD.

The probability component of the terrorism risk equation includes both ease of access to nuclear assets and the readiness of non-state actors to employ those assets. Most analyses to date have focused on the important issues of terrorist capabilities and their access to nuclear weapons and material, but largely have ignored the question of terrorist motivations to undertake different acts of nuclear destruction.

Motivations

The conventional wisdom about terrorists – until recently – was that very few would be inclined to carry out an attack using WMD even if they had the capability to do so.[4] This perspective was perhaps best stated by

Brian Jenkins of the RAND Corporation who observed that "[t]errorists want a lot of people *watching*, not a lot of people *dead*".[5] Historically, this assessment probably is correct, at least for terrorist organizations with clear political agendas. Such groups generally have viewed mass-casualty attacks as counter-productive, having the potential not only to alienate current and prospective supporters of the organization but also to jeopardize group cohesion by violating widely shared taboos, as well as to provoke severe government repression.[6] There is little evidence to suggest that most terrorist groups have abandoned this aversion to WMD terrorism. The growing lethality of conventional terrorist attacks during the past two decades, however, indicates the emergence of a new breed of terrorist ready to inflict mass violence in pursuit of a variety of goals often unrelated to concrete political objectives.[7]

Amy Sands identifies at least four general categories of non-state actors that might pursue nuclear terrorism. They are apocalyptic groups, politico-religious organizations, nationalist/separatist groups, and single-issue terrorists.[8] Apocalyptic groups that perceive the end of the existing world order as near often are driven by an extreme passion to hasten events, and may resort to violence. These groups, which have long existed, today include the Christian Identity Movement, who possess a deep conviction of the need to purify the world by eliminating non-believers. This self-righteous conviction is shared by politico-religious terrorists, who combine both political and religious motivations. At least one of these hybrid groups, al-Qaeda, is known to advocate catastrophic terrorism against Western targets. Nationalist/separatist terrorist groups such as the Irish Republican Army, the Tamil Tigers in Sri Lanka and various rebel factions from Chechnya generally have more narrowly focused political objectives for a specific ethnic group than do apocalyptic or politico-religious terrorists. Typically, these include the pursuit of political independence. Violence often is employed as a means to this end, but also may arise to exact revenge. Single-issue terrorists also usually have a very focused political or social agenda, such as anti-abortion and animal liberation. Such groups in the past have rarely expressed interest in mass-casualty attacks, although some include violence-prone extremist factions.[9]

It is beyond the scope of this chapter to probe very deeply into the nuclear terrorism motivations of these categories of terrorist groups. It would appear, however, that the defining characteristics of these groups are likely to influence significantly their attraction or aversion to specific forms of nuclear terrorism.

Apocalyptic and politico-terrorist groups are most likely to be attracted to the acquisition/manufacture and use of nuclear explosives (i.e. intact nuclear weapons or INDs). Demonstration of such a capability might be perceived by these groups as conferring upon them a near state-like status and prestige, as well as considerable political and military leverage. As Sands notes, apocalyptic groups may also believe that a nuclear detonation will hasten the end of the world by causing mass terror and destruction, and, for a politico-religious group such as al-Qaeda, even the credible threat of a nuclear detonation would have an extraordinary psychological impact on the enemy.[10] Were al-Qaeda either to acquire an intact nuclear weapon or to manufacture an IND, one would have to anticipate its use since a nuclear detonation would represent the ultimate blow against the perceived enemy.

It is much more difficult to envisage the use of high-end nuclear terrorism by either nationalist/separatist or single-issue groups. Both would be hard-pressed to reconcile any potential benefits in perceived military prowess with the enormous political costs of a nuclear explosion. However, some nationalist/separatist groups might believe they could benefit from the perception by their adversaries that they possessed an enormous capacity to inflict punishment. Given the political aims of traditional nationalist/separatist groups, one might assume that, to the extent they are drawn to nuclear terrorism, they are likely to prefer lower-consequence varieties. Employment of a radiological dispersal device, for example, could be perceived as having a greater symbolic impact than a plain conventional explosive but without inflicting such high casualties as to rule out a negotiated political settlement. An attack on a nuclear facility, especially if it were located at a considerable distance from the organization's ethnic support base, might be regarded in similar terms. That being said, the extraordinarily irrational and brutal attack by fanatical Chechen terrorists against hundreds of schoolchildren in Beslan, Russia, in September 2004 requires one to reassess the force of the disincentives against high-end nuclear violence usually attributed to nationalist/separatist groups.

To the extent that single-issue terrorist groups contemplate nuclear threats, their objectives are more likely to be mass disruption than destruction, with the aim of influencing policy. An anti-nuclear-power terrorist group, for example, might condone attacks on nuclear facilities as a means of discrediting the nuclear power industry. Historically, most attacks of this nature have been directed at nuclear facilities that were not yet operational.[11]

The aims and obsessions of the terrorist organization's leadership are apt to have a significant impact on the attractiveness of nuclear weapons to the group. Shoko Asahara, the leader of Aum Shinrikyo, for example, was obsessed with nuclear weapons and sought unsuccessfully to obtain them.[12] Osama bin Laden also has emphasized the need for al-Qaeda to possess the same weapons as its adversaries – a need he has characterized as a "religious duty".[13]

Although charismatic and authoritarian leaders such as Asahara and bin Laden may be able to impose their nuclear aspirations on the group, it also is possible that a leadership struggle within a terrorist organization could produce a more radical splinter group. When such fissures occur, they often produce more extreme behaviour as the factions jockey for power. Sands suggests that, in such circumstances, "the resort to nuclear terrorism might provide the new, more violent faction with just the right display of innovative destructiveness to claim center stage and power within the larger organization".[14]

Fortunately, even for those terrorist organizations that are not dissuaded from nuclear terrorism by moral considerations or fears of reprisal, there are major implementation challenges. These include technical hurdles and access to nuclear assets, barriers that vary significantly across the four categories of nuclear terrorism.

Barriers to nuclear terrorism

Radiological dispersal devices

A terrorist organization intent upon nuclear terrorism involving a radiological dispersal device would have to accomplish four basic tasks:

- acquire radioactive materials through theft, purchase, gift, diversion or discovery of a lost radioactive source;
- utilize the materials to construct a device to release radiation;
- deliver the radiological weapon to a high-value target; and
- detonate the RDD or disperse the radioactive material through some other mechanism.

In this "chain of causation", acquiring the radioactive material would be the most difficult step for a terrorist group to accomplish. Yet many scenarios offer pathways for terrorists to obtain potent radioactive materials. They include deliberate transfer by a national government, unauthorized "insider" assistance, looting during times of political or social unrest, licensing fraud, organized crime, theft from facilities, and the recovery of "orphan sources" that are outside regulatory controls owing to abandonment or lax accounting.[15]

Millions of tons of radioactive material exist globally, much of it in the form of spent nuclear fuel. Highly radioactive sources such as cobalt-60, caesium-137, irridium-192 and strontium-90 are also used widely in agriculture, industry, medicine and research. No reliable inventory of these materials exists, and a large percentage of these sources are no longer in use, having been discarded or lost. Although many radiological sources are neither readily accessible nor easy to incorporate into an RDD, "orphan" sources have turned up repeatedly on the black market and are known to have been acquired by Chechen rebels in Russia.

The "dirty bomb" variant of RDDs can be produced by matching radioactive sources with conventional explosives. In principle, sources could range from low-level industrial, research or medical waste to spent nuclear fuel and high-level defence waste. In addition, RDDs could involve non-explosive dispersal means such as the concealment of radiation sources in the ventilation systems of public buildings or in other confined and crowded venues.

Should a terrorist group succeed in acquiring radioactive materials and make a radiological weapon, it still would confront the task of delivering the device to the group's intended target. However, because high-risk radioactive materials are prevalent in the United States and practically all other nations, a terrorist organization would not necessarily need to import the device or transport it over a long distance.

RDDs probably constitute the most immediate nuclear terrorist threat because of generally lax security for radiological sources, their widespread availability and the relative ease with which RDDs can be assembled. These weapons, however, are unlikely to pose a major threat in terms of human casualties. The greater risk concerns their potential for disrupting society by instilling widespread panic and necessitating costly clean-up operations.[16]

Sabotage of nuclear facilities

A terrorist group that wants to damage a nuclear facility for the purpose of releasing radioactivity to the surrounding environment would need to:
- identify a nuclear power plant or other nuclear facility that is vulnerable to attack;
- decide how to strike the facility; and
- overcome the facility's protective measures to cause an off-site release of radioactivity.

According to a report by the International Atomic Energy Agency (IAEA), worldwide there are 438 nuclear power reactors, 277 operational research reactors and hundreds of fuel-cycle facilities, including uranium mills and conversion plants, enrichment plants, fuel fabrication plants, interim storage sites and reprocessing facilities.[17] Many of these facilities, which are distributed throughout much of the world, are deficient in such basic defensive elements as intact perimeter defences, vehicle barriers and surveillance cameras. Others lack armed guards for both cultural and economic reasons. Many have never been subject to design basis threat analyses to determine their vulnerability to terrorist attack or sabotage, and few have been subject to performance-testing based upon realistic threats. Moreover, there are no binding international regulations requiring states to meet minimum security standards at either research or power plants.

Nuclear facilities vary widely across type and country, and terrorists would certainly tailor their attack to the peculiarities of the target. In most instances, they probably would seek to recruit an insider at the facility who was familiar with its specific vulnerabilities and protective measures. Among the means terrorists might employ to attack nuclear facilities are hijacked commercial airplanes, truck bombs, waterborne attacks and commando-type attacks by land.[18] Terrorists also might seek to employ cyber-terrorism in order disable a facility's safety systems.[19]

An attack with conventional weapons on or sabotage of a nuclear power facility have the potential to cause far more casualties and economic chaos than an RDD, although both involve the release of radioactive material. The risk of a catastrophic accident is especially acute for those nuclear power plants that lack containment structures and redundant safety features. In this regard, the consequences of the 1986 Chernobyl nuclear accident are illustrative. In addition to the 31 workers who were killed directly as a consequence of their emergency on-site response efforts, approximately 1,800 excess thyroid cancers developed among the surrounding populace exposed to radioactivity from the accident. It has been estimated that an additional 24,000 leukaemia cases may result from the Chernobyl accident, although it is difficult for public health researchers to determine definitively how many deaths ultimately are linked to the nuclear disaster.[20] The impact of Chernobyl also included the permanent evacuation of more than 100,000 people from the area surrounding the nuclear plant and staggering economic costs of upwards of several hundred billion dollars related to the site clean-up, contamination of arable land, medical care, the building of a giant sarcophagus to enclose the destroyed reactor, and the construction of replacement energy generation capacity.[21]

Research reactors, spent fuel storage sites and reprocessing facilities also constitute potential terrorist targets. In the United States, for example, there are three dozen research reactors in 23 states, many of which are located at universities. Research reactors, however, generally are much less vulnerable to core accidents than are power reactors, contain less radioactive fuel than do power reactors, and therefore represent a lower risk in terms of the potential consequences of a terrorist attack designed to disperse radioactive debris.

Because of the sheer amount of radioactive material present, terrorists might be attracted to spent nuclear fuel storage sites. In most countries, spent fuel is stored near the reactors where it was produced. In the United States, for example, over 40,000 metric tons of spent fuel are stored under water in cooling ponds adjacent to the power reactors. A much smaller quantity of spent fuel is stored in dry casks. Although the consequences of a terrorist attack on spent fuel storage sites are very dependent on the characteristics of those facilities, an assessment by the National Research Council of the US National Academies concludes that, in most instances, little or no release of radioactivity is likely, owing to the robust nature of the storage casks and the ability to provide emergency cooling of the fuel using "low-tech" measures. The National Research Council report also minimizes the threat posed by spent fuel in transport in the United States because of the protection provided by the fuel containers.[22] These optimistic conclusions, however, are not shared by other analysts, who are especially worried about the potential for spent fuel in cooling ponds to catch fire, with possibly catastrophic loss of life and environmental damage.[23]

Although not widely known, there have been a number of incidents in which nuclear power facilities were the target of criminal or terrorist actions. One of the most serious acts of sabotage occurred in 1982 in South Africa when four bombs were detonated at the nearly commissioned Koeberg nuclear power station. At least four incidents also involved nuclear power plants in Lithuania and Russia in the mid-1990s.

Improvised nuclear devices

A terrorist group motivated to manufacture and detonate an IND would need to:[24]

- acquire sufficient fissile material to fabricate an IND;
- fabricate the weapon;
- transport the intact IND (or its components) to a high-value target; and
- detonate the IND.

In the chain of causation, the most difficult challenge for a terrorist organization would most likely be obtaining the fissile material necessary to construct an IND. Terrorists could attempt to exploit many acquisition routes. In particular, a state might voluntarily share fissile material with a terrorist group or sell the material to it; a senior official or governmental element with authorized access to such materials might, for ideological or mercenary motives, provide them to terrorists, without the express approval of government leaders; the immediate custodians of the material, for money or ideology or under duress, might provide highly enriched uranium (HEU) or plutonium (Pu) to the organization or assist it in seizing the material by force or stealth; or terrorists might obtain the material by force or stealth without insider help. Finally, nuclear weapon materials could come into the hands of terrorists during a period of political turmoil, including one brought on by a coup or revolution. Such scenarios are not far-fetched. The IAEA's Illicit Trafficking Database, as well as other databases, has recorded a number of incidents in which proliferation-significant quantities of fissile material have been stolen – most involving material from the former Soviet states.[25]

The problem of protecting fissile material globally has many dimensions, the most significant of which is the vast quantity of HEU and plutonium situated at approximately 350 different sites in nearly five dozen countries. It is estimated that there are more than 2,000 metric tons of fissile material – enough for over 200,000 nuclear weapons. Many of the sites holding this material lack adequate material protection, control and accounting measures; some are outside of the IAEA's safeguards system; and many exist in countries without independent nuclear regulatory bodies or rules, regulations and practices consistent with a meaningful safeguards culture.

The special dangers of HEU

In a pre-9/11 world, where states constituted the main proliferation challenge, it made sense to treat Pu and HEU as roughly equivalent dangers. Today, however, in a world where non-state actors pose greater threats in terms of the likely use of nuclear weapons, efforts must be focused much more on rapidly securing, consolidating and eliminating the vast stocks of HEU globally. The principal reason for this needed shift in emphasis, which is not yet evident in the policies of either national governments or international organizations, is the much easier task for terrorists of building an HEU-based nuclear weapon. Many experts, for example, have concluded that a gun-type improvised nuclear device is well within the technical reach of some non-state actors with access to HEU.

The most basic type of nuclear weapon is a gun-type device.[26] As its name suggests, it fires a projectile. The projectile in this type of weapon is a piece of highly enriched uranium. Moreover, like a gun, a gun-type device would use a gun barrel to direct the projectile. To ignite a nuclear explosion, the HEU projectile would travel down the barrel to another piece of HEU. The HEU pieces would both be sub-critical – that is, each one by itself could not sustain an explosive chain reaction – but once they combined they would form a super-critical mass.

Weapons-grade HEU – uranium enriched to over 90 per cent U-235 – would be the most effective material for a gun-type device. However, even HEU enriched to less than weapons-grade can lead to an explosive chain reaction. The Hiroshima bomb, for example, used about 60 kg of 80 per cent enriched uranium. Terrorists would probably need about

40–50 kg of weapons-grade or near weapons-grade HEU to have reasonable confidence that the IND would work.[27]

Most physicists and nuclear weapons analysts have concluded that construction of a gun-type device would pose few technological barriers to technically competent terrorists.[28] In 2002, the National Research Council warned that "[c]rude HEU weapons could be fabricated without state assistance".[29] The Council further specified: "The primary impediment that prevents countries or technically competent terrorist groups from developing nuclear weapons is the availability of [nuclear material], especially HEU."[30]

Although there appears to be little doubt among the experts that technically competent terrorists could make a gun-type device given sufficient quantities of HEU, the question remains of how technically competent they have to be and how large a team they would need. At one end of the spectrum of analysis, there is the view that a suicidal terrorist could literally drop one piece of HEU metal on top of another piece to form a super-critical mass and initiate an explosive chain reaction. Nobel laureate Luis Alvarez's oft-cited quote exemplifies this view:

With modern weapons-grade uranium, the background neutron rate is so low that terrorists, if they have such material, would have a good chance of setting off a high-yield explosion simply by dropping one half of the material onto the other half. Most people seem unaware that if separated HEU is at hand it's a trivial job to set off a nuclear explosion ... even a high school kid could make a bomb in short order.[31]

However, to make sure that the group could surmount any technical barriers, it would likely want to recruit team members who have knowledge of conventional explosives (needed to fire one piece of HEU into another), metalworking, draftsmanship and chemical processing (for example, in order to extract HEU metal from other chemical forms, such as oxide- or aluminium-based reactor fuel). A well-financed terrorist organization such as al-Qaeda would probably have little difficulty recruiting personnel with these skills. Concerning the size of the team and the preparation time required, Albert Narath has estimated that "[o]nce the HEU in metallic form is in hand it might require only a dozen individuals with the right set of skills to accomplish the design and construction over a period of perhaps a year".[32] The period of preparation would allow for "rapid turn around", that is, "the device would be ready within a day or so after obtaining the material". Carson Mark et al. also concluded that "[s]uch a device could be constructed by a group not previously engaged in designing or building nuclear weapons".[33] In a later analysis in November 2001, the Pugwash Council echoed this view by underscoring that "sub-national terrorist groups could accomplish the challenge".[34]

There are many potential sources of HEU for would-be terrorists or state proliferators. Particularly high-risk sites are present in Russia, Kazakhstan, Ukraine and Belarus, as well as other countries that received Soviet-origin HEU. Many of these sites contain HEU fuel for research reactors. Also vulnerable is HEU in the form of fuel for naval reactors. Indeed, a number of the confirmed cases involving illicit nuclear trafficking involve naval fuel.

Assuming that nuclear terrorists were able to acquire the necessary fissile material and manufacture an IND, they would need to transport the device (or its components) to the target site. Although an assembled IND would likely be heavy – perhaps weighing up to 1 ton – trucks and commercial vans could easily haul a device that size. In addition, container ships and commercial airplanes could provide delivery means. Terrorists also might try to assemble and detonate a gun-type device at a fissile material storage site, assuming that this site contained sufficient quantities of readily usable HEU metal, the terrorists were suicidal, and the assault team included members versed in the relevant technical skills of gun devices.[35] Inasmuch as, by definition, terrorists constructing an IND would be familiar with its design, the act of detonating the device would be relatively straightforward and present few technical difficulties.

The risk of state-sanctioned nuclear assistance

Acquiring weapons-usable fissile material directly from a sympathetic national government would simplify significantly the requirements for a terrorist organization intent upon acquiring an IND. Presumably such a state sponsor would also provide assistance in fabricating an IND, perhaps by providing a design or the non-nuclear components or by machining the HEU or plutonium into appropriate shapes before handing it over. Such material might be provided to terrorist groups by a state that hoped to see an IND used against an opponent but wanted to be in a position to deny its involvement and reduce the threat of retaliation.

Prior to Operation Iraqi Freedom in Iraq, the Bush administration expressed fear that Saddam Hussein might provide nuclear weapons support to terrorist groups. It is now clear, however, that there was neither credible evidence at the time of an active Iraqi nuclear weapons programme nor any plans on the part of Saddam Hussein to provide nuclear assistance to non-state actors. Today, the greatest sources of concern regarding the deliberate transfer of nuclear weapon material and/or know-how by a national government to a terrorist organization are Pakistan, North Korea and Iran.

Regarding Pakistan, questions remain about the nature and extent of government complicity in Dr Abdul Qadeer Khan's transfers between 1989 and 2003 of highly sensitive material for nuclear weapon programmes in Iran, Libya and North Korea – all of which were considered by the United States to be state sponsors of terrorism. If the government of Pakistan was involved, it was apparently unconcerned about whether terrorists might obtain fissile materials, and potentially an IND, from these sympathetic governments. Moreover, although Pakistani President Pervez Musharraf has given his support to the US-led "war on terror", including the ousting of the Taliban regime in Afghanistan and the elimination of al-Qaeda, some senior elements of the Pakistani political establishment oppose this support, and Musharraf was the target of two assassination attempts in December 2003. This history raises concerns that individuals supportive of radical Islamist groups may come to power in Pakistan and might give Pakistani nuclear weapon material to a terrorist organization, although it is assumed that the Musharraf government would not do so.

Although some North Korean officials have provoked concern that North Korea might transfer nuclear materials outside of that country, their statements have not specifically mentioned transactions with terrorists. In addition, there are no known ties between the North Korean government and extremist terrorist groups. However, North Korea has had ties to international terrorism in the past. Moreover, it has sold ballistic missiles to other states of concern, and it has engaged in counterfeiting currency and selling illicit drugs. Such transactions indicate the desperate condition of North Korea and raise the risk that Pyongyang may decide to sell nuclear materials, either directly or indirectly, to terrorist groups. In April 2004, US intelligence analysts revised their estimate of the size of the North Korean nuclear arsenal, assessing that it had grown from two to eight weapons. The increase would make it possible for North Korea to sell one or perhaps two weapons, or the fissile material needed to make them, while retaining a significant nuclear deterrent.[36]

In May 2004, news reports raised suspicions that North Korea might have sold uranium to Libya, a country that had been of proliferation concern until December 2003. According to the reports, it is possible that in early 2001 North Korea provided Libya with almost 2 metric tons of uranium that was not enriched for weapons use but that could have been fed into a uranium enrichment cascade that Libya had been manufacturing.[37]

Although evidence has yet to emerge that North Korea has used a nuclear trading network to sell nuclear material intentionally or inadvertently to terrorist organizations, the apparent North Korean–Libyan connection should serve as a warning about North Korean readiness to export nuclear commodities with little regard to the end user. That being said, there are also reports that North Korea is prepared to reassure the United States that it has no intention of providing nuclear materials to terrorists. Selig Harrison, an American analyst specializing in North-east

Asian security issues, reported in May 2004 that North Korean officials said that they would pledge never to transfer such materials to terrorists, suggesting that this commitment could be part of a larger security package between the United States and North Korea.[38]

Unlike North Korea, Iran presently does have ties to Islamist terrorist groups. Although Iran is widely believed to be seeking nuclear arms, there is no evidence to date to indicate that it has acquired these weapons. Moreover, there is no indication that Tehran has given WMD of any kind to terrorist organizations. Nonetheless, future transactions cannot be ruled out.

As of mid-2005, no other states possessing sizeable quantities of nuclear-weapons-usable materials are thought to have close ties to terrorist organizations. Moreover, even states that actively support terrorist groups would be highly unlikely to transfer such materials to terrorists. The transferring state would risk massive retaliation from the United States and its allies if the material were traced back to the state. The fear of discovery would likely serve as an effective means of deterrence in most situations.

However, the greatest risk of such transactions is likely to involve states that are facing imminent regime change. These states might have little to lose by handing the ingredients for an IND to a terrorist group as a last means of striking against an opponent.[39] For example, some observers expressed concern prior to the 2003 US-led war against Iraq that regime change might provoke Saddam Hussein to transfer WMD material to non-state actors.[40] Thus, an unintended consequence of overthrowing the governments of states possessing HEU or plutonium could be to provoke them to aid or abet nuclear terrorists.

Intact nuclear weapons

In order for terrorists to detonate an intact nuclear weapon at a designated target they would have to:
- acquire an intact nuclear charge;
- bypass or defeat any safeguards against unauthorized use incorporated into the intact weapons; and
- detonate the weapon.

By far the most difficult challenge in this chain of causation would be acquisition of the intact weapon itself. Possible pathways for acquisition include deliberate transfer by a national government, unauthorized assistance from senior government officials, assistance from the custodian of the state's nuclear weapons, seizure by force without an insider's help, and acquisition during loss of state control over its nuclear assets owing to political unrest, revolution or anarchy.[41]

According to conventional wisdom, intact nuclear weapons are more secure than are their fissile material components. Although this perspective is probably correct, as is the view that the theft of a nuclear weapon is less likely than other nuclear terrorist scenarios, one should not be complacent about nuclear weapons security. Of particular concern are non-strategic or tactical nuclear weapons (TNWs), of which thousands exist, none covered by formal arms control accords. Because of their relatively small size, large number and, in some instances, lack of electronic locks and deployment outside of central storage sites, TNWs would appear to be the nuclear weapon of choice for terrorists.

The overwhelming majority of TNWs reside in Russia, although estimates about the size of the arsenal vary widely.[42] The United States also deploys a small arsenal of under 500 TNWs – in the form of gravity bombs – in Europe.

A major positive step towards enhancing the security of TNWs was taken following the parallel, unilateral Presidential Nuclear Initiatives of 1991/1992. In their respective declarations, the American and Russian presidents declared that they would eliminate many types of TNW, including artillery-fired atomic projectiles, tactical nuclear warheads and atomic demolition munitions, and would place most other classes of TNW in "central storage". Although Russia proceeded to dismantle several thousand TNWs, it has been unwilling to withdraw unilaterally all of its remaining TNWs from forward bases or even to relocate to central storage in a timely fashion those categories of TNW covered by the 1991/1992 declarations. Moreover, in recent years, neither the United States nor Russia has displayed any inclination to pursue negotiations to reduce TNWs further or to reinforce the informal and fragile TNW regime based on parallel, unilateral declarations.

Although Russia has been the focus of most international efforts to enhance the security of nuclear weapons, many experts are also concerned about nuclear weapons security in South Asia, and particularly in Pakistan. Extremist Islamist groups within Pakistan and the surrounding region, a history of political instability, uncertain loyalties of senior officials in the civilian and military nuclear chain of command, and a nascent nuclear command and control system increase the risk that Pakistan's nuclear arms could fall into the hands of terrorists. Little definitive information is available, however, on the security of Pakistan's nuclear weapons or of those in its nuclear neighbour, India.

Should a terrorist organization obtain an intact nuclear weapon, in most instances it would still need to overcome mechanisms in the weapon intended to prevent its use by unauthorized persons. In addition to electronic locks, known as permissive action links (PALs), nuclear weapons may be safeguarded through so-called "safing, arming, fusing, and firing"

(SAFF) procedures. For example, the arming sequence for a warhead may require changes in altitude, acceleration or other parameters verified by sensors built into the weapon to ensure that the warhead can be used only according to a specific mission profile. Finally, weapons may be protected from unauthorized use by a combination of complex procedural arrangements (requiring the participation of many individuals) and authenticating codes authorizing each individual to activate the weapon.[43]

All operational US nuclear weapons have PALs. Most authorities believe that Russian strategic nuclear weapons and modern shorter-range systems also incorporate these safeguards, but they are less confident that older Russian TNWs are equipped with PALs.[44] Operational British and French nuclear weapons (with the possible exception of French submarine-launched ballistic missile warheads) are probably protected by PALs. The safeguards on warheads of the other nuclear-armed states cannot be determined reliably from open sources, but are more likely to rely on procedures other than PALs to prevent unauthorized use (e.g. a three-man rule).[45]

Unless assisted by sympathetic experts, terrorists would find it difficult, though not necessarily impossible, to disable or bypass PALs or other safeguard measures. If stymied, terrorists might attempt to open the weapon casing to obtain fissile material in order to fabricate an IND. However, the act of prying open the bomb casing might result in terrorists blowing themselves up with the conventional high explosives associated with nuclear warheads. Thus, terrorists would likely require the services of insiders to perform this operation safely.

Assuming a terrorist organization could obtain a nuclear weapon and had the ability to overcome any mechanisms built into the device to prevent its unauthorized detonation, it would still face the formidable task of delivering the weapon to the group's intended target. If the loss of a nuclear weapon were detected, as would be expected unless a state provided one to a terrorist organization, a massive hunt for the weapon would be launched, involving law enforcement and military personnel from many nations, assisted by nuclear specialists. This effort would be accompanied by greatly intensified security over transportation links and points of entry.

It is also possible terrorists might adopt strategies that minimized transportation, such as detonating the weapon at a nearby, less than optimal target, or even at the place of acquisition. Nuclear detonation by a non-state group virtually anywhere would terrorize citizens in potential target countries around the globe, who would fear the perpetrators had additional weapons at their disposal. The organization could exploit such fears in order to blackmail governments into political concessions – for example, demanding the withdrawal of military forces or political support from states the terrorists opposed. Indeed, the group might achieve these results without a nuclear detonation, by providing proof that it had a nuclear weapon in its possession at a location unknown to its adversaries.

If a nuclear weapon were successfully transported to its target site and any PALs disabled, a degree of technical competence would nonetheless be required to determine how to trigger the device and provide the necessary electrical or mechanical input for detonation. Moreover, detonation could be daunting unless the detonators and the arming and firing sequence mechanisms had been preserved. Here, again, insider assistance would be of considerable help. Thus, even this seemingly straightforward aspect of the chain of causation would pose an obstacle to the terrorists' goals.

Priority corrective measures

Major new initiatives to combat nuclear terrorism have been launched by the US government, as well as by other states and international organizations, and considerable sums of financial and political capital have been committed to new and continuing programmes to enhance nuclear security. These initiatives include the adoption in April 2004 of UN Security Council Resolution 1540, the US Department of Energy's May 2004 Global Threat Reduction Initiative, the expanded G-8 Global Partnership, and the Proliferation Security Initiative. Although these and other efforts are worthy of support, it is not obvious that most are the product of a careful and systematic assessment of the full range of nuclear terrorist threats or are well informed about or coordinated with other relevant initiatives. They also lack a sense of urgency and a clear ordering of priorities. As a consequence, not enough attention is being given to reducing the probability of nuclear terror acts with the highest consequences – that is, preventing the terrorist detonation of a nuclear explosive device – or to mitigating the consequences of the most likely nuclear terror acts.

Reducing the probability of nuclear terrorism with improvised nuclear devices and nuclear weapons

At least five steps should be undertaken as priority measures: (1) pursue an HEU-first strategy; (2) secure, consolidate and/or eliminate HEU in Russia and globally; (3) focus on the South and Central Asian peril; (4) promote the adoption of stringent global security standards; and (5) secure vulnerable tactical nuclear weapons.[46]

Pursue an HEU-first strategy

Because of the relative ease of construction of an IND with highly enriched uranium, US and international non-proliferation assistance programmes in Russia should implement an HEU-first strategy that would secure, consolidate and down-blend all excess stocks of HEU before disposing of weapons-grade plutonium as reactor fuel. Specifically, priority should be given to the acceleration of down-blending of Russian HEU to a non-weapons-usable enrichment level; and the use of the recently opened high-security Mayak Fissile Material Storage Facility for the storage of up to 200 tons of HEU.

Secure, consolidate and/or eliminate HEU in Russia and globally

Significant quantities of fissile materials exist in Russia and globally that are not needed, are not in use and, in many instances, are not subject to adequate safeguards. From the standpoint of nuclear terrorism, the risk is most pronounced with respect to stockpiles of HEU in dozens of countries. It is imperative to secure, consolidate and, when possible, eliminate these HEU stocks. The principle should be one in which fewer countries retain HEU, fewer facilities within countries possess HEU, and fewer locations within those facilities have HEU present. Important components of a policy guided by this principle include conversion of research reactors to run on low-enriched uranium (LEU), rapid repatriation of all US- and Soviet/Russian-origin HEU (both fresh and irradiated), international legal prohibitions on exports of HEU-fuelled research and power reactors, and down-blending of existing stocks of HEU to LEU. A policy to accomplish these objectives must be informed by an understanding of the significant bureaucratic, technical, economic, political and national security impediments to HEU consolidation and elimination, in addition to the development of compelling incentives to overcome these obstacles.

Focus on the South and Central Asian peril

The international community should be more attentive to the nuclear terrorism danger with respect to INDs in South and Central Asia, a zone where Islamist militant groups are active and where the risk of their gaining access to nuclear materials – especially from unreliable elements within the Pakistani establishment or from certain vulnerable sites in Kazakhstan – is highest. It is of urgent importance, therefore, to remove the relatively small – but significant in terms of nuclear terrorism (and proliferation) – quantity of fissile material from Central Asia and to enhance Pakistani fissile material protection, control and accounting.

Means to accomplish the former objective are identified in the preceding paragraph; the latter objective should be pursued by maximizing the sharing of unclassified technology to help Pakistan securely manage its nuclear assets in a manner consistent with the requirements of the Treaty on the Non-Proliferation of Nuclear Weapons (NPT). The NPT-recognized nuclear-weapon states also should develop contingency plans, including the use of nuclear recovery teams, to help secure Pakistani nuclear assets in the event of instability. In most circumstances, such recovery efforts would require the cooperation of knowledgeable Pakistani authorities.

Promote the adoption of stringent, global security standards

A modest step forward in enhancing the physical protection of nuclear material was taken in July 2005 when delegates from 89 countries approved an amendment to the Convention on the Physical Protection of Nuclear Material. The amended convention, which still must be ratified by member states, extends a legally binding obligation to protect nuclear material to domestic use and storage in addition to material in international transport. Unfortunately, however, no specific security standards were adopted as amendments, and only general principles for nuclear security were adopted. As a consequence, it is desirable for as many like-minded states as possible to agree immediately to meet a stringent material protection standard, which should apply to all civilian and military HEU.

Secure vulnerable tactical nuclear weapons

The last issue that must be addressed to reduce the likelihood of highest-consequence nuclear terrorism is securing Russia's most vulnerable nuclear weapons, in particular those TNWs that are forward deployed and portable and that may lack permissive action links. Specifically, the United States must encourage Russia to implement fully its pledges under the 1991/1992 Presidential Nuclear Initiatives, including the removal to central storage of all but one category of TNW. Ideally, all TNWs should be stored at exceptionally secure facilities far from populated regions. In parallel, the United States should declare its intention to return to US territory the small number of air-launched TNWs currently deployed in Europe. Although probably less vulnerable to terrorist seizure than tactical nuclear weapons forward deployed in Russia, there is no longer a military justification for their presence in Europe. The US action, although valuable in its own right, might be linked to Russian agreement to move its tactical nuclear arms to more secure locations.

Mitigating the consequences of the most likely nuclear terror acts

The use of radioactive materials to cause massive disruption and economic loss is by far the most likely nuclear terror act.[47] Although the loss of life and destruction of property would not begin to rival that from a nuclear detonation, the harm caused would be grievous, particularly if radiological attacks were launched in multiple locations. Given the significant quantities of radioactive material currently outside regulatory control around the world, the unambiguous evidence of terrorist interest in using these materials to cause harm, and the ease of carrying out a radiological attack, such an attack is all but inevitable. Thus, even as the United States and other governments pursue measures to reduce the availability of radioactive materials, they should greatly increase preparations for a radiological terror event by training federal, state and local governments to cope with a radiological attack and developing decontamination technologies and post-attack therapies.

One of the most dangerous elements of a radiological attack is the panic that it can spur, which would likely lead to more immediate casualties than the ionizing radiation itself triggered by the attack. It is therefore imperative that the public be psychologically immunized against the threat of a radiological attack through an extensive public education campaign. Such public education should help citizens to understand that radiological attacks are unlikely to pose immediate threats to life and that proper treatment can greatly reduce long-term health effects in many instances.

Even as one prepares for the eventuality of a radiological attack, it is essential to improve controls over radioactive materials so that over time the likelihood of this form of nuclear terrorism can be reduced. For the near term, the following initiatives can have the greatest impact:

- locate and secure the remaining radio-thermal generators in the former Soviet Union, arranging for substitute technologies in remote locations requiring electricity;
- impose mandatory physical security and accounting controls over the most dangerous classes of radioactive sources, beginning with the most potent;
- impose rigorous domestic licensing and import and export controls over high-risk radioactive sources that include pre-licensing determinations of credentials and end users;
- actively promote the use of alternative technologies to radioactive sources, where appropriate.

An attack on nuclear facilities constitutes a second variety of lower-end nuclear violence that is more likely to occur than terrorist detonation of a nuclear explosive. Although nuclear power plants with containment structures and redundant safety features pose considerable obstacles to would-be terrorists, important security gaps remain at nuclear facilities in the United States and abroad. These gaps include a "design basis threat" (which probably does not adequately reflect the magnitude of the 9/11 attack – 19 motivated and well-trained terrorists operating in four separate teams), the vulnerability of reactor control rooms and some types of spent fuel ponds to attack from the air or from stand-off weapons, too great a reliance on compliance-based (as opposed to performance-based) approaches for evaluating plant security, and limited physical protection at many research reactor sites. These security gaps can and should be fixed. However, they probably pose a lower risk than either form of high-consequence nuclear terrorism or a radiological dispersal device and, therefore, require less urgent action.

Conclusion

Implementation of the priority measures listed above will not entirely eliminate the risks posed by nuclear terrorism. Those risks will persist at some level as long as nuclear weapons, weapons-usable nuclear material, potent radioactive sources and nuclear power and research facilities continue to exist. As a consequence, national governments and international organizations must carefully weigh the risks of nuclear terrorism when making decisions about both civilian and military nuclear programmes. Their choices will determine to a large degree the opportunities that non-state actors will have in the realm of nuclear terrorism.

Notes

1. Among the more influential early studies are Brian Jenkins, "International Terrorism: A New Mode of Conflict", in David Carlton and Carlo Schaerf, eds, *International Terrorism and World Security* (London: Croom Helm, 1975); and Paul Leventhal, *Nuclear Terrorism: Defining the Threat* (Washington, DC: Brassey's, 1986).
2. For a detailed analysis of these different threats, see Charles D. Ferguson and William C. Potter with Amy Sands, Leonard S. Spector and Fred L. Wehling, *The Four Faces of Nuclear Terrorism* (New York: Routledge, 2005).
3. See, for example, Matthew Bunn and George Bunn, "Strengthening Nuclear Security against post-September 11 Threats of Theft and Sabotage", *Journal of Nuclear Materials Management* (Spring 2002), pp. 48–60; Siegfried S. Hecker, "Nuclear Terrorism", in Committee on Confronting Terrorism in Russia, *High-Impact Terrorism: Proceedings of a Russian-American Workshop* (Washington, DC: National Academy Press, 2002), pp. 149–155, and "Nuclear and Radiological Threats", Chapter 2 of Committee on Science and Technology for Countering Terrorism, National Research Council, *Making the Na-*

tion Safer: The Role of Science and Technology in Countering Terrorism (Washington, DC: National Academy Press, 2002).

4. This section draws extensively from Chapter 2 in Ferguson and Potter, *The Four Faces of Nuclear Terrorism*. Amy Sands was the principal author of that chapter.

5. See Brian Michael Jenkins, "The Future Course of International Terrorism", *The Futurist* (July–August 1987); reprint available at ⟨http://www.wfs.org/jenkins.htm⟩ (accessed 8 March 2006).

6. For a discussion of this thesis, see Jonathan Tucker, ed., *Toxic Terror: Assessing Terrorist Use of Chemical and Biological Weapons* (Cambridge, MA: MIT Press, 2000), pp. 9–12.

7. Ibid., p. 10. Significant high-casualty terrorist events include the PanAm 103 bombing over Lockerbie (1988); the Buenos Aires car bomb (1992); the World Trade Center truck bomb (1993); the Oklahoma City bombing (1995); the Sri Lanka truck bomb (1996); the Saudi Arabia truck bomb (1996); US embassy in Kenya truck bomb (1998); bombs in a Moscow apartment block (1999); the World Trade Center, Pentagon and Pennsylvania hijackings (2001); the Bali bomb (2002); the Madrid bombings (2004); and, most recently, the Beslan hostage crisis in Russia (2004). For more details, see Ferguson and Potter, *The Four Faces of Nuclear Terrorism*, p. 15. The WMD Terrorism Database of the Center for Nonproliferation Studies also indicates an increase in the number of terrorist incidents involving WMD.

8. See Ferguson and Potter, *The Four Faces of Nuclear Terrorism*, p. 18.

9. See Gary Ackerman, "Beyond Arson? A Threat Assessment of the Earth Liberation Front", *Terrorism and Political Violence*, Vol. 15, No. 4 (Winter 2004).

10. See Ferguson and Potter, *The Four Faces of Nuclear Terrorism*, p. 22.

11. Ibid., p. 25.

12. See Ferguson and Potter, *The Four Faces of Nuclear Terrorism*, pp. 28–31. See also David E. Kaplan, "Aum Shinrikyo", in Tucker, ed., *Toxic Terror*, pp. 207–226.

13. See ABC News Interview, "Terror Suspect: An Interview with Osama Bin Laden", 22 December 1998 (conducted in Afghanistan by ABC News producer Rahimullah Yousafsai), published 26 September 2001; available at ⟨http://jya.com/bin-laden-abc.htm⟩ (accessed 8 March 2006).

14. See Ferguson and Potter, *The Four Faces of Nuclear Terrorism*, p. 30.

15. For a discussion of these scenarios, see Ferguson and Potter, *The Four Faces of Nuclear Terrorism*, pp. 271–277.

16. One point of reference is the September 1987 accident in Goiania, Brazil, involving a discarded radiotherapy machine. During the course of one week, more than 240 persons were contaminated by caesium powder from a canister dismantled by scavengers; 4 of them died and 54 were hospitalized, and more than 34,000 people were inspected by the health authorities. See Alex Neifer, "Case Study: Accidental Leakage of Cesium-137 in Goiania, Brazil, in 1987", Camber Corporation, ⟨http://www.nbc-med.org/SiteContent/MedRef/OnlineRef/CaseStudies/csgoiania.html⟩ (accessed 8 March 2006).

17. See Anita Nilsson, "The Threat of Nuclear Terrorism: Assessment and Preventive Action", Symposium on Terrorism and Disarmament, United Nations, New York, 25 October 2001.

18. For a discussion of these scenarios, see Ferguson and Potter, *The Four Faces of Nuclear Terrorism*, pp. 210–225.

19. A cyber-attack is reported to have penetrated the defences of a US nuclear facility but not a commercial power plant. See Ferguson and Potter, *The Four Faces of Nuclear Terrorism*, p. 224.

20. See Richard L. Garwin and Georges Charpak, *Megatons and Megawatts: A Turning Point in the Nuclear Age?* (New York: Knopf, 2001), pp. 189–195.

21. Although it is difficult, if not impossible, to add up the total costs, Belarus has estimated that "losses over the 30 years following the accident will amount to $235 billion". Ukraine has estimated "the loss at $148 billion over the period from 1986 to 2000". *The Human Consequences of the Chernobyl Nuclear Accident: A Strategy for Recovery. A Report Commissioned by UNDP and UNICEF with the support of UN-OCHA and WHO*, Chernobyl Report-Final-240102, United Nations Development Programme, 25 January 2002, p. 63.
22. National Research Council, *Making the Nation Safer*, pp. 46–88.
23. See, for example, Robert Alvarez, "What about the Spent Fuel?", *Bulletin of the Atomic Scientists* (January–February 2002), pp. 45–47.
24. This section draws extensively from Charles D. Ferguson and William C. Potter, "Improvised Nuclear Devices and Nuclear Terrorism", Paper No. 2, Weapons of Mass Destruction Commission, 9 June 2004, ⟨http://www.wmdcommission.org/files/No2.pdf⟩ (accessed 8 March 2006).
25. See William C. Potter and Elena Sokova, "Illicit Nuclear Trafficking in the NIS: What's New? What's True?" *Nonproliferation Review* (Summer 2002), pp. 112–122.
26. The other basic weapons design is an implosion device, which squeezes a sphere of fissile material from a relatively low-density sub-critical state to a high-density super-critical state. If the implosion does not occur smoothly, the bomb will be a complete dud or result in a fizzle yield much lower than expected from a properly designed implosion weapon. In contrast to a gun-type device, an implosion-type device requires more technical sophistication and competence. A terrorist group, for example, would need access to and knowledge of high-speed electronics and high-explosive lenses, a particularly complex technology. This equipment is necessary to result in a fast and smooth squeezing of the fissile material into a super-critical state. Unlike a gun-type device, an implosion-type device can employ highly enriched uranium or plutonium.
27. John McPhee, *The Curve of Binding Energy* (New York: Farrar, Straus & Giroux, 1974), pp. 189–194.
28. See, for example, Carson Mark, Theodore Taylor, Eugene Eyster, William Maraman and Jacob Wechsler, "Can Terrorists Build Nuclear Weapons?", in Paul Leventhal and Yonah Alexander, eds, *Preventing Nuclear Terrorism: The Report and Papers of the International Task Force on Prevention of Nuclear Terrorism* (Lexington, MA: Lexington Books, 1987), pp. 55–65; Luis W. Alvarez, *Adventures of a Physicist* (New York: Basic Books, 1988), p. 125; Frank Barnaby, "Issues Surrounding Crude Nuclear Explosives", in *Crude Nuclear Weapons: Proliferation and the Terrorist Threat*, IPPNW Global Health Watch Report No. 1 (Cambridge, MA: International Physicians for the Prevention of Nuclear War, 1997); Morten Bremer Maerli, "Relearning the ABCs: Terrorists and 'Weapons of Mass Destruction'", *Nonproliferation Review* (Summer 2000); Frank von Hippel, "Recommendations for Preventing Nuclear Terrorism", *Federation of American Scientists Public Interest Report*, November–December 2001, p. 1; Matthew L. Wald, "Suicidal Nuclear Threat Is Seen at Weapons Plants", *New York Times*, 23 January 2002, p. A9; Robert L. Civiak, *Closing the Gaps: Securing High Enriched Uranium in the Former Soviet Union and Eastern Europe*, Report for the Federation of American Scientists, May 2002; Committee on Science and Technology for Countering Terrorism, National Research Council, *Making the Nation Safer*; Richard L. Garwin and Georges Charpak, *Megawatts and Megatons: A Turning Point in the Nuclear Age?* (New York: Alfred A. Knopf, 2001); Jeffrey Boutwell, Francesco Calogero and Jack Harris, "Nuclear Terrorism: The Danger of Highly Enriched Uranium (HEU)", Pugwash Issue Brief, September 2002; Union of Concerned Scientists, "Scientists' Letter on Exporting Nuclear Material", to W. J. "Billy" Tauzin, Chairman of the House Committee on Energy and Commerce, 25 September 2003, ⟨http://www.ucsusa.org/global_security/

nuclear_terrorism/page.cfm?pageID=1256⟩ (accessed 8 March 2006); and Gunnar Arbman, Francesco Calogero, Paolo Cotta-Ramusino, Lars van Dessen, Maurizio Martellini, Morten Bremer Maerli, Alexander Nikitin, Jan Prawitz and Lars Wredberg, *Eliminating Stockpiles of Highly Enriched Uranium: Options for an Action Agenda in Co-operation with the Russian Federation*, report submitted to the Swedish Ministry for Foreign Affairs, SKI Report 2004: 15 (Stockholm: Swedish Nuclear Power Inspectorate, April 2004).

29. National Research Council, *Making the Nation Safer*, p. 45.
30. Ibid., p. 40.
31. Alvarez, *Adventures of a Physicist*, p. 125.
32. Albert Narath, "The Technical Opportunities for a Sub-National Group to Acquire Nuclear Weapons", XIV Amaldi Conference on Problems of Global Security, Helsinki, 27 April 2002.
33. Mark et al., "Can Terrorists Build Nuclear Weapons?".
34. Pugwash Conferences on Science and World Affairs, "The Dangers of Nuclear Terrorism", Statement of the Pugwash Council, London, 12 November 2001, ⟨http:// www.pugwash.org/september11/pcstatement.htm⟩ (accessed 8 March 2006). See also Morten Bremer Maerli, "Crude Nukes on the Loose?", PhD dissertation, University of Oslo, March 2004.
35. Wald, "Suicidal Nuclear Threat Is Seen at Weapons Plants", p. A9.
36. Glenn Kessler, "N. Korea Nuclear Estimates to Rise", *Washington Post*, 28 April 2004, p. A1.
37. David E. Sanger and William J. Bread, "The North Korean Nuclear Challenge", *New York Times*, 24 May 2004, p. A9.
38. Victor Mallet, "N. Korea Offers US Pledge on Weapons", *Financial Times*, 3 May 2004.
39. See Jasen J. Castillo, "Nuclear Terrorism: Why Deterrence Still Matters", *Current History* (December 2003), pp. 426–431.
40. See William C. Potter, "Invade and Unleash?" *Washington Post*, 22 September 2002, p. B7.
41. For a discussion of these scenarios, see Ferguson and Potter, *The Four Faces of Nuclear Terrorism*, pp. 54–61.
42. See, for example, estimates by Nikolai Sokov, W. M. Arkin et al. and Alexei Arbatov in William C. Potter, Nikolai Sokov, Harald Müller and Annette Schaper, *Tactical Nuclear Weapons: Options for Control* (Geneva: United Nations Institute for Disarmament Research, 2000), pp. 58–60.
43. See, for example, Bruce Blain, *Strategic Command and Control* (Washington, DC: Brookings Institution, 1985).
44. See Nikolai Sokov, *Tactical Nuclear Weapons* (Monterey, CA: Center for Nonproliferation Studies, May 2002), ⟨http://www.nti.org/e_research/e3_10a.html⟩ (accessed 8 March 2006).
45. See Ferguson and Potter, *The Four Faces of Nuclear Terrorism*, p. 62.
46. These measures are elaborated on in Ferguson and Potter, *The Four Faces of Nuclear Terrorism*, pp. 325–329. They correspond in many respects to the recommendations on preventing catastrophic terrorism outlined by United Nations Secretary-General Kofi Annan in his report *In Larger Freedom: Toward Development, Security and Human Rights for All* (New York: United Nations, 2005); see especially para. 92, p. 35.
47. This section draws heavily on the work of Charles Ferguson. See Ferguson and Potter, *The Four Faces of Nuclear Terrorism*, pp. 330–335.

22

Managing missiles after Iraq: Going off course

Christophe Carle and Waheguru Pal Singh Sidhu

Introduction

Missiles have been a central aspect of the drawn-out crisis involving Iraq since the 1980s for at least three reasons. First, Iraq has witnessed the largest use of missiles – both ballistic and cruise – since the end of World War II. Although it is impossible to ascertain with any certainty the exact figures, conservative estimates suggest anything from 1,000 to 3,000 conventionally armed ballistic and cruise missiles have been used in the three conflicts involving Iraq since 1980.[1] Second, although missiles, especially those armed with nuclear weapons, have been a particular cause of concern for international peace and security, the massive use of conventionally tipped cruise and ballistic missiles in the region has highlighted the serious threat posed even by non-nuclear-armed missiles. In fact, despite persistent fears that missiles tipped with nuclear, biological or chemical weapons might be used, there has been not a single instance of the use of a non-conventionally armed missile in this region.[2] Third, the challenges posed by missile use in Iraq spurred on a series of political, military and technological efforts at the unilateral, plurilateral and multilateral levels to manage missiles and missile-related behaviour not only in this region but also in other regions of concern. Among the political initiatives are the Missile Technology Control Regime (MTCR) and its off-spring, the Hague Code of Conduct (HCoC) against Ballistic Missile Proliferation, as well as the two United Nations (UN) panels of governmental experts on missiles. The military efforts include a shift from deterrence to pre-emption and defence. The technological efforts include the development of a new generation of ballistic and cruise missile defence systems with far-reaching implications, notably for the weaponization of outer space.

These developments are occurring amidst a remarkable lack of negotiated international instruments focusing on missiles in themselves, rather than on missiles as a way of controlling nuclear weapons. Indeed, today there is "[no] universal norm, treaty or agreement governing the development, testing, production, acquisition, transfer, deployment or use specifically of missiles".[3] The disproportion between this paucity of regulations and the centrality of missiles – both conventional and non-conventional – in contemporary international security, as evident in the Iraq crisis, is becoming a yawning gap in the panoply of arms control. To further complicate matters, the potential acquisition, possession, use and transfer of certain types of missiles by non-state actors, especially in the wake of the events of 11 September 2001, have also emerged as significant international concerns.[4]

In light of these developments, this chapter will focus on the Iraqi experience in particular and will seek to draw some lessons for managing missiles in general. We will begin with a brief historical overview of the three Iraqi conflicts and the role of missiles in them and will lead up to the effective disarmament of Iraqi missiles by the UN Special Commission (UNSCOM) and the UN Monitoring, Verification and Inspection Commission (UNMOVIC) before the start of the latest conflict.[5] The next section will examine the lessons drawn by the key actors from the Iraqi experience. We will note that two trends have become discernible: first, an attempt by most states to address the issue of missiles through political and diplomatic means; second, an effort by some states to deal with the challenge through a combination of military and technological means. A third trend was also evident in the form of the UNSCOM/UNMOVIC inspections in Iraq: a combination of the political, diplomatic and military means to disarm Iraq's missiles and related nuclear, biological and chemical weapons. In the final section we will note the relative successes or shortcomings of these trends and suggest possible ways forward in trying to manage missiles in an effective and universally acceptable way.

Historical overview

At a time when intra-state wars appear to be the norm, Iraq has had the dubious distinction of being involved in three inter-state wars. At least two of these – the war with Iran and the invasion of Kuwait – were of its own making. It is less clear to what extent Baghdad can be held solely responsible for the latest US-led attack and occupation. Although initial evidence, particularly from the United States and the United Kingdom as well as from the United Nations, seemed to indicate that Iraq remained in violation of UN Security Council resolutions, recent evidence suggests otherwise – Baghdad was probably in reluctant or even unbeknownst compliance with them.[6]

The Iran–Iraq war, 1980–1988

Although the origins of the eight-year Iran–Iraq war remain complex and need not be discussed here in detail, it is important to note that this was the first war that witnessed extensive use of all types of missiles, including ballistic and cruise missiles.[7] According to most accounts, Iraq launched the so-called "war of the cities" by using FROG (free-rocket-over-ground) 7 missiles against Iranian border towns. By the mid-1980s Iraq had escalated to using Scud-B missiles, and between February and April 1988 Baghdad is reported to have launched about 160 al-Husayn extended-range Scud missiles at Tehran, Isfahan and Qom. UNSCOM's findings indicated some 516 Scud-class missiles fired by Iraq during the course of the war. During the mid to late 1980s, Iraq developed one of the most active, if sometimes haphazard, delivery vehicle programmes in the world, with a strong emphasis on ballistic missiles. Through a mix of imported technology and equipment, foreign technical assistance and local expenditure and infrastructure, Iraq made undeniable progress in extending missile ranges and in clustering liquid-fuelled engines. More exotic forms of long-range deliverers such as the infamous and ill-fated "supergun" were also experimented with. Iran, which appears to have had a limited inventory in the early part of the war, is reported to have retaliated with between 88 to 100 Scud missiles aimed at Baghdad during the same time period.[8] Although none of these missiles were tipped with nuclear, chemical or biological weapons and inflicted only limited military damage, they appear to have dealt a psychological blow to the Iranian leadership, who capitulated to bring this war to an end.

According to Richard Russell, two lessons were learnt from this war: "first that conventionally armed ballistic missiles can be used for political advantage, and second, ... either they have to be used in massive barrages or greater emphasis needs to be placed on ... nuclear warheads".[9] Remarkably, Iraq emerged from this war with a vastly improved missile and nuclear programme. The advanced stage of the nuclear programme was particularly impressive given the destruction of the Osirak reactor in a spectacular Israeli raid in 1981. It also indicates the limits of preventive strikes.

Operation Desert Storm, 1991

The 1990 invasion and occupation of Kuwait by Iraq formed the basis for the 1991 Operation Desert Storm, which was mandated by the United Nations to liberate Kuwait. Again, although the precise details of the war are not essential here, it is important to note that this war too saw Baghdad and the Washington-led coalition extensively use ballistic and cruise missiles, respectively. Exact numbers are difficult to come by, but estimates suggest that Baghdad fired as many as 93 extended-range Scud missiles at Israel, Saudi Arabia and Bahrain. Thus, in the three-year interval between the Iran–Iraq war and the 1991 war, Baghdad had not only maintained production of the 600 km al-Husayn but also developed the 900 km al-Abbas missile; it also started developing the al-Abid, which was purportedly a space launch vehicle but designed to be capable of ranges up to some 3,000 km in ballistic mode. The range of the Soviet-supplied missiles was extended by reducing warhead weights – as little as possible – and increasing the fuel capacity – as much as possible.[10] In addition, they manufactured mobile launchers, and after the war there was no conclusive evidence that a single mobile launcher had been destroyed by the US-led forces. The US-led coalition forces fired some 333 cruise missiles (298 BGM-109 Tomahawk Land Attack Missiles and 35 AGM-86C Conventional Air Launched Cruise Missiles) at various targets in Iraq during the 1991 war.

As in the case of the previous war, although the conventionally armed Iraqi ballistic missiles had negligible military effect, they appear to have had a significant political and psychological impact in both Saudi Arabia and Israel. In contrast the conventionally armed cruise missiles and other "smart" bombs used by the US-led coalition had a dramatic military impact; they literally defeated the Iraqi military capability to wage war and led to the withdrawal of Iraqi troops from Kuwait.

Following the war and the constitution of UNSCOM, Iraq's missile programme was comprehensively dismantled. According to the Amorim Report (named after Brazilian diplomat Celso Amorim who, as president of the UN Security Council, led a panel to determine the progress made by UNSCOM in 1999):

UNSCOM was able to destroy or otherwise account for: (a) 817 out of the 819 imported operational missiles of proscribed range; (b) all declared mobile launchers for proscribed Al Hussein class missiles, including 14 operational launchers; the disposition of 9 of the 10 imported trailers used for the indigenous production of mobile launchers; and the destruction of 56 fixed missile launch sites; (c) 73 to 75 chemical and biological warheads of the declared 75 operational special warheads for Al Hussein class missiles; 83 of the 107 imported and some 80 of the 103 in-

digenously produced conventional warheads declared by Iraq to be in its possession at the time of the adoption of resolution 687.[11]

The report also noted that "UNSCOM had also concluded that Iraq does
not possess a capability to indigenously produce either BADR-2000 missiles or assets known as the Supergun".[12]

UNMOVIC, which succeeded UNSCOM in late 1999 following the
adoption of UN Security Council Resolution 1284 on 17 December 1999,
conducted as many as 731 inspections in 111 days. Around 30 per cent
(or 219 inspections) of UNMOVIC's inspections were conducted by the
missile teams.[13] UNMOVIC also confirmed UNSCOM's accounting of
817 out of 819 imported Scud-B missiles.[14] In addition, "Iraq declared
the production of 76 Al Samoud-2 missiles" and also admitted to UN-
MOVIC that the range of these missiles was around 183 km.[15] Among
the very last tasks carried out by UNMOVIC before it withdrew from
Iraq in March 2003 was the verified destruction of as many as 70 of the
100 al Samoud-2 ballistic missiles. As UNMOVIC chief Hans Blix noted
in an uncharacteristic outburst before the UN Security Council: "We are
not watching the breaking of toothpicks."[16] These missiles were assessed
by a specially convened group of technical experts as capable of ranges
of 10–20 km in excess of the threshold of 150 km imposed on Iraq by
UN Security Council Resolution 687. The very fact that Iraq's tampering
with missile ranges was of that order of magnitude (rather than hundreds
of kilometres), given how easy it is to alter a ballistic missile's maximum
reach simply by reducing its payload and/or increasing its fuel load, and
given Iraq's production of ballistic missiles with ranges of some 600–900
km before 1991, attests to the effectiveness of the constraints successively
monitored and imposed by UNSCOM and UNMOVIC. This was the last
instance of the UN-led international community playing a disarming role.

Operation Iraqi Freedom, 2003

Among the various reasons offered by the George W. Bush administration to justify the US-led invasion of Iraq in March 2003, the alleged
presence of nuclear, biological and chemical weapons along with their
missile-based delivery systems was one of the most forceful assertions
made by Washington. One indication of this was the establishment of the
Iraq Survey Group (ISG), initially led by David Kay and later by Charles
Duelfer, to locate Iraq's hidden arsenal, which Washington claimed that
UNMOVIC had been unable to find.

In the course of the brief pre-emptive war, the United States by conservative estimates used 900–1,000 conventionally armed cruise missiles
against various Iraqi targets. In contrast, Iraq is reported to have used

fewer than a dozen randomly fired conventionally armed ballistic missiles. Again, whereas Iraq's missiles had practically no military or psychological impact, the US cruise missiles and "smart" bombs rendered Iraq defenceless in the face of the subsequent invasion by US ground troops.

Operation Iraqi Freedom was also the second instance of combat use of anti-ballistic missile defences. Their performance in 1991 had been a subject of intense debate. With a few exceptions,[17] missile defences were a less broadly commented feature of the second Iraq war, not only because Iraq had few missiles to fire at all, but also as a result of the strengthening consensus on missile defences. Missile defences deployed during the conflict apparently managed to intercept three al-Samoud and six Ababil-100 missiles, but they were blind to low-flying rudimentary cruise missiles fired by Iraq. On the other hand, these defensive missiles did manage to shoot down a British Tornado and a US Navy F-18 aircraft.

Although the ISG had unfettered access and generous resources (its budget in the first three months was significantly more than the annual budget of UNMOVIC) to seek the missing missiles and related weapons, it could not find any. As David Kay candidly noted in his statement before the Committee on Intelligence, "[w]e have not yet found stocks of weapons, but we are not at the point where we can say definitively either that such weapon stocks do not exist or that they existed before the war and our only task is to find where they have gone".[18] Although Kay spoke about "plans and advanced design work for new long-range missiles" and "clandestine attempts" to obtain missile technology as well as efforts to re-initiate work on missiles, fuels and launchers, he was unable to produce a single missile, launcher or fuel complex, let alone dismantle them. Kay's inability to find missiles was reiterated by his successor in October 2004.

Implications and two trends

One reason for the central role of missiles in contemporary international security is their close connection with non-conventional weapons, especially nuclear weapons. It is axiomatic that countries that have pursued nuclear weapon programmes have also carried out ballistic missile activities, whether through indigenous development, imports or, as is more common, a combination of both. Ballistic missiles, notably their flight tests, have become one of the most visible signs that some nuclear weapons ambition may be afoot. To date, the only country that has acquired ballistic missiles without any identifiable nuclear-weapons-related activities is Saudi Arabia. But this is also the exception that proves the rule, since it is commonly acknowledged that the acquisition of the Chinese CSS-2 (DF-3) armed solely with conventional explosives makes little if any sense other than as a somewhat profligate reaction to the exchanges of missile fire during the Iraq–Iran "war of the cities". None of this is to suggest that missiles, particularly ballistic ones, are of legitimate security concern only if they are mated with nuclear warheads. Civilian populations on the receiving end of conventionally armed V1s and V2s during World War II, as well as those subjected to Scud and Scud-variant fire during the Iran–Iraq war, could probably attest to that. The observation is merely intended to stress that such concerns take on an altogether greater order of magnitude if and where the nuclear element is factored in.

A second set of reasons for reflecting on arms control and disarmament measures applicable to missiles indeed focuses on missiles other than nuclear. The underlying security concerns on this point rest less on the potentially catastrophic impact of the use of one or a few nuclear armed missiles, but rather on the actual use in warfare and other military operations of conventionally armed missiles, including cruise and other air-to-surface precision missiles. Recent military operations, whether in Kosovo, Afghanistan or Iraq, have made unprecedented and plentiful use of precision-guided conventional munitions and missiles, including cruise missiles of several types.

A third reason is the continuing spread and improvement of missile technology. The spread of technology is usually emphasized over its improvement. But this is only part of the reality. While admittedly not undergoing the outburst of innovative breakthroughs that characterizes the life sciences and biotechnology in particular (with obvious implications for the control of biological weapons), missile technology can hardly be described as at a standstill.

Given the perceived salience of missiles – both conventional and non-conventional – as well as concerns related to them, two trends have become evident over the past two decades. The first is political and diplomatic and the second is military.

Political and diplomatic initiatives

Political and diplomatic efforts to control missiles have a history of being subordinate to the ulterior and superior objective of dealing with nuclear weapons – and understandably so. Although a number of arms control, non-proliferation and disarmament arrangements do have some bearing on missiles, most of these arrangements address missiles incidentally, rather than in themselves. Such provisions as those that appear in the preamble to the Treaty on the Non-Proliferation of Nuclear Weapons (NPT) on delivery vehicles, or in such bilateral Cold War treaties as the Strategic Arms Reduction Treaties I and II or the Intermediate-Range Nuclear Forces Treaty about certain selected missiles and/or their launchers, are very clearly conceived with a view to constraining nuclear weapons.

Such was also the rationale behind the elder of the missile-specific international arrangements: the MTCR, initiated in 1987 at American instigation among the G-7 states. Essentially a "suppliers' club" for coordinating export controls of missiles and missile technology among participating countries, the MTCR was originally designed to cover ballistic missiles (and their relevant technologies and equipment) deemed to be capable of delivering a first-generation nuclear weapon, hence the range/payload trade-off of 300 km/500 kg established by the regime. There is a strong correlation between the emergence of the MTCR and the presence and extensive use of ballistic missiles in the Iran–Iraq war. Only later did the coverage of the MTCR expand to other types of missiles, including cruise missiles, and to missiles capable of delivering other non-conventional warheads besides nuclear ones.

In parallel, the membership of the MTCR also expanded (it stands at 34 states today), but conditions on most new entrants have become rather more drastic than on the founding participants, resulting in a distinctly two-tiered structure. Thus, the Russian Federation's adherence in 1995 changed nothing in Russia's own missile or space launch capabilities. On the other hand, South Africa's admission as an MTCR participant that same year was made conditional, at US insistence, on its relinquishment not only of ballistic missiles but of its space launch vehicle activities as well. China is now apparently on the verge of being admitted as a full participant in the MTCR, obviously not on the terms applied to South Africa. Conversely, in at least another case, joining the MTCR actually stretched rather than further constrained the permissible missile activities of a participating state. Prior to joining in 2001, South Korea secured the abrogation of a bilateral agreement of 1979 with the United States limiting its development of ballistic missiles to a range of 180 km.

However, it was the growing recognition of the limitations of the MTCR in curtailing the increasingly indigenous missile programmes that prompted the regime's members to conceive of the Hague Code of Conduct (HCoC), hitherto know as the International Code of Conduct (ICoC). The HCoC recognized the need for "confidence and security building measures in the field of responsible missile behaviour" in addition to the MTCR's export controls.[19] However, the lineage of the Code to the MTCR made it particularly unattractive not only for non-MTCR members, such as India, Iran, Israel and Pakistan, but also for MTCR members such as Brazil, leading Mark Smith to note that the Code (with 116 signatories) is "high on quantity ... but low on quality".[20]

Yet another initiative was the Moscow-sponsored Global Control System for the Non-Proliferation of Missiles and Missile Technology (GCS). The initiative was discussed at two international meetings in Moscow in March 2000 and February 2001. Although 71 states, notably including North Korea, took part in the 2001 meeting, the GCS appears to have faded into oblivion, leading some to suspect that it was a valiant effort to keep Washington faithful to the 1972 Anti-Ballistic Missile (ABM) Treaty.[21]

In contrast, the first United Nations Panel of Governmental Experts (UNPGE) on missiles, proposed by an Iranian resolution and set up in 2001, marked the first effort within the United Nations to address the specific issue of missiles, albeit "in all its aspects". Though numerically the smallest of the other initiatives, the UNPGE was also the most deliberately balanced in its membership. Its 23 participants included governmental experts from 12 MTCR members and from 11 non-MTCR states, drawn from diverse regions and providing a representative cross-section of the current missile club of countries possessing or capable of producing missiles of global or regional strategic significance. In its report, however – proving the price for the required consensual adoption of the text – the UNPGE could not even agree on the exact nature of the problem, let alone recommend any particular course of action. Soon after the adoption of the report by the General Assembly in September 2002, a further Iranian resolution calling for the convening of a second Panel to examine the issue of missiles in (once again) all its aspects was passed in November 2002. However, the failure of the second UNPGE to reach consensus after three extremely thorough sessions in 2004 against the backdrop of the ongoing Iraq crisis can be taken as testimony to just how sensitive the security and arms control and disarmament implications of the possession and use of missiles remain. Points of view are simply too far apart on the desirability of any given form of control on some of the most strategically significant missile systems (ballistic and cruise, be they conventionally or non-conventionally armed) for any concrete steps to be envisioned for the time being.

The provisions of the HCoC, watered down though they are, constitute a certain degree of like-mindedness among a growing group of countries. But, for the foreseeable future, these provisions will not be broadened to a number of states with significant missile activities. The price to pay for such stipulations as the HCoC does – laudably – make is non-universality; and the price to pay for the high degree of representation in the second UNPGE of views held across the international community is absence of consensus. Combined, both are a sobering barometer of arms control and disarmament prospects in the area of missiles.

Since 2002, a novel set of measures relevant to missiles has emerged, which operates at the juncture of the diplomatic and the military realms. These are the principles and (evolving) procedures known as the Proliferation Security Initiative (PSI) announced by the President of the United States in Krakow, Poland, on 31 May 2003. The overall idea is to complement existing non-proliferation arrangements by promoting international coordination in impeding and intercepting shipments of non-conventional weapons and of the missiles to deliver them. The case of missiles is rather particular under the PSI, given that, unlike nuclear, biological and chemical weapons, there is no multilateral convention of any sort forbidding or otherwise regulating missile transfers. This was exemplified in the case of a shipment of missiles and missile parts intercepted by the Spanish Navy in December 2002, which was allowed to continue to its destination in Yemen. The extent to which the PSI may involve the use of military force, its compatibility with international law, in particular the right of innocent passage of ships on the high seas, and the willingness of more states to associate themselves with the initiative all remain open to question.

In the absence of universally accepted norms relating to missiles and given the inherent difficulties in attempting to reach consensus on such norms in the present highly divisive international environment, several states have sought to follow a series of military and technological initiatives either individually or collectively to deal with missiles.

Military and technological initiatives

The invasion of Iraq was intended as the exercise of pre-emptive counter-proliferation. The use of force, ostensibly against a possessor and prospective user of non-conventional (including ballistic) missiles, was meant to have an immediate disarming impact on Iraq to be sure, but also an indirect dissuading effect on other potential possessors and wielders of similar capabilities.

Libya's epiphany was (and still is) heralded as shining proof of the success of the use of force as a method of disarmament. Having observed Iraq's fate, the Libyan authorities drew the conclusion foreseen by UK and US office holders and announced in December 2003 their decision to abandon all "weapons of mass destruction". On the specific issue of missiles, the official statement from Tripoli specified that "Libya has ... decided to restrict itself to missiles with a range that comply [*sic*] with the standards of the MTCR surveillance system",[22] which one infers means ranges not in excess of 300 km.[23] Whatever the fate of its Scud-class missiles, Libya never stood out as having any particularly advanced indigenous missile development programme. Its relinquishment of missiles with ranges over 300 km is more significant in terms of possibly forgone missile imports than of actual disarmament. The Libyan initiative is of more symbolic than strategic value. But the symbol, it appears, also has limits and the bigger fish would appear rather more difficult to catch.

Indeed, if one considers countries with missile and nuclear programmes far in excess of what Libya ever had, such as Iran and North Korea, it would appear that the lessons drawn from the invasion of Iraq are exactly the reverse of what advocates of pre-emptive counter-proliferation had (prematurely) boasted of. Rather than hoist a white flag and give up contentious missile, nuclear and other programmes, Iran has held its ground on uranium enrichment and announced the testing of Shahab-3 missiles capable of delivering a 1 ton warhead to over 2,000 km, and North Korea has become continually more explicit in its statements that the 8,000 fuel rods from its Yongbyon reactor had been reprocessed for plutonium and weaponized, amidst persistent rumours of resumed missile testing.

Rather than yield and throw themselves on the mercy of the United States for fear of incurring the fate of Saddam Hussein's regime, governments with significant nuclear and associated missile programmes appear to have concluded that a credible nuclear option and effective missiles to back it up constitute a preferable guarantee of national and regime security. The use of the most overwhelmingly powerful conventional forces the world has ever known may be less a providential counter-proliferation and disarmament tool than a boost to the determination of some countries to endow themselves with a nuclear equalizer, complete with ballistic missiles as delivery vehicles.

A crucial complementary device in the panoply of missile counter-proliferation instruments is active missile defences. Missile defences of course existed in previous incarnations with the limited systems allowed in the United States and the USSR/Russia by the ABM Treaty, and tactical missile defences were used for the first time in the first Iraq war. With the now ongoing deployments of interceptor missiles in the United States, continued reliance on the Arrow system in Israel, prospective deployments by US friends and allies in North-east Asia, an ongoing missile defence study in NATO, speculation about the deployment of some US defence systems in Eastern Europe, the – geographically surrealistic – espousal of missile defences by Australia, heightened interest in such systems in India, and the use of specialized radars in the United Kingdom and Greenland (to name but a few significant recent developments), the dynamics of missile defence have undergone a distinct boost to say the very least.

For some time prior to the 2000 US presidential elections and the subsequent abrogation of the ABM Treaty, there was a semblance of debate on the issue. This has now fizzled out comprehensively. Whether enthusiastically or grudgingly, missile defences have now become accepted as a fact of life. The ineffectuality of opponents of missile defences remains an interesting phenomenon. Part of it was due to a technical fixation. The often-heard prediction that "missile defences will not work and will therefore never be deployed" neglected the human factor, and failed to comprehend that single-minded determination would play havoc with reason. Any political argument to the effect that the – then incoming – Bush administration was doctrinally set on deployment in any case was derided by a whole breed of arms controllers as techno-scientifically naive and countered with equations, graphs and trajectories. The arguments mustered against ABM deployments in the 1970s and against the Strategic Defense Initiative in the 1980s were widely beside the point in the early 2000s. Recurring arguments from self-professed Washington insiders to the effect that the cost of missile defence would be its death-knell "on the Hill" proved equally wrong.

In polarizing the debate on the ABM Treaty and the perils of its abrogation, opponents of strategic missile defences overstated their case. They scaremongered so enthusiastically about ABM abrogation unleashing a new arms race that ensuing events appeared benign in comparison. The net result is that not only are missile defences going full steam ahead regardless of their ineffectiveness, but their proponents can gloat that deployment has caused none of the detrimental side-effects prognosticated by the nay-sayers: "The sky-is-falling group was wrong"[24] is now conventional wisdom. Although no such thing as a full-blown arms race has predictably been unleashed overnight by the US withdrawal from the ABM Treaty and by currently ongoing and prospective deployments in the United States and abroad, Russia's testing of a manoeuvrable warhead for its Topol-M ballistic missile, as well as Moscow's declaratory reactions to discussions about the deployment of some US anti-missile components in Eastern Europe and to the modernization of the Thule radar station in Greenland, very clearly indicates rather less than the fullest confidence in long-term US intentions.[25]

In addition, the urge not to be left behind in another round of military technological innovation (for potential foes) and the urge to participate in substantial R&D and procurement for friends and allies are resulting in increased missile defence research as well as international technology transfers and cooperation. It is often argued that such cooperation is necessarily innocuous, since missile defences are, by definition, defensive. One may then wonder why the United States has been so wary of the prospects of Israeli–Indian cooperation on an anti-missile system derived from the Israeli–US Arrow. The ability to intercept a ballistic missile with another projectile is obviously not irrelevant to the ability to design accurate ballistic missiles for offensive purposes. The overlap between purportedly distinct defensive and offensive technologies is nowhere better illustrated than by the use in tests of the latest generation of Patriot interceptor missiles and of modified earlier Patriots as targets simulating an incoming ballistic missile.

Whatever their performances in warfare in Iraq and in tests, missile defences are being deployed, alongside rather than as a substitute for doctrines of pre-emption. The net result is the worst of both worlds: a defensive system that fails to offer reliability but that does succeed in spurring the further refinement of offensive missile forces.

Beyond Iraq

Given the inherent hurdles in both the political–diplomatic and military–technological approaches and the benefit of hindsight, it could be argued that the UNSCOM/UNMOVIC approach was probably the best way to carry out verifiable disarmament. In fact, based on this experience, some scholars have argued in favour of retaining the UNMOVIC approach post-Iraq for future contingencies.[26] However, it is important to note that the UNMOVIC approach probably worked because of the unique circumstances: the unanimous UN Security Council resolutions and the fact that the Commission was backed by military might, which not only threatened but also used force to ensure implementation. This particular set of conditions is unlikely to be replicated in any possible future scenario, especially related to Iran or North Korea.

At the same time, it is also crucial to acknowledge that missiles of some type or another are present in the military equipment of virtually all states around the world. They are such an integrally central part of operational and strategic doctrines that controls across the board simply cannot be envisaged.

In this context, confidence-building measures (CBMs) are a well-trodden path in many areas of international security. Through the experience of the Organization for Security and Co-operation in Europe and other processes, as well as in a large corpus of expert studies, CBMs tailored to numerous kinds of weapons systems and strategic settings have been evolved, discussed, negotiated and implemented. In comparison, CBMs specifically adapted to the security concerns created or worsened by missiles of various types remain a significantly underdeveloped field. In principle, however, the options are numerous, depending on the kind of action envisaged (from information exchange to restrictions and bans, whether bilateral, plurilateral, regional or even multilateral) and on the stage(s) in the life cycle of missile systems (whether ballistic or cruise, selected according to criteria such as range, mobility or payload) to which they would apply (such as R&D, flight testing, procurement, deployment, storage and use). If and when international and particular regional strategic conditions become more auspicious for consequential arms control discussions and negotiations, such options will need to be explored to a much greater extent than has hitherto been the case. Missile defences, in time, will also need to be addressed (or re-addressed, since the demise of the ABM Treaty) by arms control. This, of course, applies only to states and state-held missiles and does not even begin to address the challenges posed by non-state actors, who are likely to remain outside the purview in the world beyond Iraq.

Notes

1. The three conflicts were the 1980–1988 Iran–Iraq war; the 1991 US-led war on Iraq following the latter's invasion and occupation of Kuwait; and the 2003 US-led war and occupation of Iraq. Missiles were also used against Iraq in 1998 as part of the US–UK Operation Desert Fox. Although these are not the only instances of the use of such missiles, they are probably the most significant military use. Other instances include a barrage of Scud ballistic missiles used by the government forces to break the siege of Jalalabad during the Afghan civil war in the 1990s; the Chinese "testing" of several ballistic missiles north and south of Taiwan during the 1996 crisis; and the use of cruise missiles by the United States in Kosovo (1998), Sudan (1998) and Afghanistan (1998 and 2001–2002).
2. Although mustard and nerve agents were used during the 1980–1988 Iran–Iraq war, they were not delivered via missiles.
3. *Report of the Secretary-General: The Issue of Missiles in All Its Aspects*, UN Doc. A/57/229 (New York, 23 July 2002), p. 13.
4. For the purposes of this chapter, a non-state actor is understood to be an individual or entity not acting under the lawful authority of any state. This definition is derived from United Nations Security Council Resolution 1540 (2004) (UN Doc. S/Res/1540, 28 April 2004).
5. UNSCOM and UNMOVIC were set up in line with UN Security Council Resolution 687 (1991) (UN Doc. S/Res/687, 3 April 1991), and UN Security Council Resolution 1284 (1999) (UN Doc. S/RES/1284, 17 December 1999), respectively. See also Richard Butler, *The Greatest Threat: Iraq, the Weapons of Mass Destruction and the Crisis of Global Security* (Cambridge, MA: Public Affairs, 2001); Hans Blix, *Disarming Iraq: The Search for Weapons of Mass Destruction* (London: Bloomsbury, 2004); and Trevor Findlay's chapter "Lessons of UNSCOM and UNMOVIC for WMD Non-proliferation, Arms Control and Disarmament" in this volume.
6. See *Iraq's Weapons of Mass Destruction – The Assessment of the British Government* (London: The Stationery Office, September 2002), available at ⟨http://www.archive2.official-documents.co.uk/document/reps/iraq/iraqdossier.pdf⟩ (accessed 8 March 2006), which admits that UNSCOM was successful in "destroying very large quantities of ... missiles as well as the infrastructure for Iraq's nuclear weapons programme" (para.

13); Blix, *Disarming Iraq*; and Douglas Jehl, "U.S. Report Finds Iraqis Eliminated Illicit Arms in 90's", *New York Times*, 7 October 2004.

7. For details of the origin of this war, see David M. Malone and James Cockayne, "Lines in the Sand: The United Nations in Iraq, 1980–2001", in Ramesh Thakur and Waheguru Pal Singh Sidhu, eds, *The Iraq Crisis and World Order: Structural, Institutional and Normative Challenges* (Tokyo: United Nations University Press, 2006).

8. See Richard L. Russell, "Swords and Shields: Ballistic Missiles and Defenses in the Middle East and South Asia", *Orbis* (Summer 2002), pp. 486–488; Anthony H. Cordesman, *Iran and Iraq: The Threat from the Northern Gulf* (Boulder, CO: Westview Press, 1994), p. 90; Paul F. Walker, "High-tech Killing Power", *Bulletin of the Atomic Scientists*, Vol. 46, No. 4 (May 1990); and the Terrorism Files website: "Weapons & Terrorism: Missiles, Nuclear, Biological, Chemical Weapons, and Conflict in the Middle East", ⟨http://www.terrorismfiles.org/weapons/use_of_wmd_middle_east.html⟩ (accessed 8 March 2006).

9. Russell, "Swords and Shields", p. 488.

10. Ibid.

11. See *Report of the First Panel Established Pursuant to the Note by the President of the Security Council on 30 January 1999 (S/1999/100), Concerning Disarmament and Current and Future Ongoing Monitoring and Verification Issues*, Annex I, ⟨http://www.un.org/Depts/unmovic/documents/AMORIM.PDF⟩ (accessed 8 March 2006) para. 16.

12. Ibid., para. 17.

13. Findlay, "Lessons of UNSCOM and UNMOVIC".

14. *Unresolved Disarmament Issues: Iraq's Proscribed Weapons Programmes*, UNMOVIC Working Document, 6 March 2003, p. 21, ⟨http://www.un.org/Depts/unmovic/new/documents/cluster_document.pdf⟩ (accessed 8 March 2006).

15. Ibid., p. 28.

16. Blix, *Disarming Iraq*, pp. 188–190.

17. See, for example, Theodore A. Postol, "An Informed Guess about Why Patriot Fired upon Friendly Aircraft and Saw Numerous False Missile Targets during Operation Iraqi Freedom", MIT Security Studies Program, 20 April 2004, ⟨http://www.globalsecurity.org/space/library/report/2004/patriot-shot-friendly_20apr2004_apps1-2.pdf⟩ (accessed 8 March 2006).

18. "Statement by David Kay on the Interim Progress Report on the Activities of the Iraq Survey Group (ISG) before the House Permanent Select Committee on Intelligence, the House Committee on Appropriations, Subcommittee on Defense, and the Senate Select Committee on Intelligence, October 2, 2003", ⟨http://www.cia.gov/cia/public_affairs/speeches/2003/david_kay_10022003.html⟩ (accessed 8 March 2006).

19. W. Pal S. Sidhu and Christophe Carle, "Managing Missiles: Blind Spot or Blind Alley?", *Disarmament Diplomacy*, No. 72 (August–September 2003), ⟨http://www.acronym.org.uk/dd/dd72/72op3.htm⟩ (accessed 8 March 2006).

20. Mark Smith, "Stuck on the Launch Pad? The Ballistic Missile Code of Conduct Opens for Business", *Disarmament Diplomacy*, No. 68 (December 2002–January 2003), pp. 2–6.

21. See Viacheslav Abrosimov, "Preventing Missile Proliferation: Incentives and Security Guarantees", *Disarmament Diplomacy*, No. 57 (May 2001), pp. 4–8. The GCS proposal contains some interesting elements, including: a multilateral transparency regime on missile launches (possibly based on the Russian–American Centre for the Exchange of Data from Early Warning Systems and Notification of Missile Launches in Moscow); security assurances, guarantees or other measures to ameliorate the security of states which renounce ballistic missile programmes; measures to promote access to space launch services to countries not possessing such capacities domestically; and multilateral

consultations with the aim of negotiating a legally binding agreement on missile non-proliferation. The Russian Federation also proposed placing GCS activities under the auspices of the United Nations.

22. "Libyan WMD: Tripoli's Statement in Full", BBC News, 20 December 2003, ⟨http://newsvote.bbc.co.uk/mpapps/pagetools/print/news.bbc.co.uk/2/hi/africa/3336139.stm⟩ (accessed 8 March 2006).

23. See, for example, Carol Giacomo, "Libya May Be Allowed to Keep Some Scud Missiles", *Reuters*, 9 March 2004.

24. US Secretary of Defense Donald Rumsfeld, commenting on his cordial discussions with Russian officials about missile defences and chiding arms control advocates who had forecast that the US initiative would upset relations with Moscow. Bradley Graham, "Interceptor System Set, but Doubts Remain", *Washington Post*, 29 September 2004.

25. See "Letter Dated 16 August 2004 from the Permanent Representative of the Russian Federation to the Conference on Disarmament Addressed to the Secretary-General of the Conference Transmitting the Text of a Press Release Issued by the Ministry of Foreign Affairs of the Russian Federation on 9 August 2004 Concerning the Modernization of the United States Radar Station in Thule, Greenland" (UN Doc. CD/1742, 25 August 2004), which states: "The United States has repeatedly assured us that the future ... anti-missile defence will not be directed against Russia. Yet the very geographical details of the location of [the] radar station in Greenland offer grounds for supposing that the ... anti-missile defence is in fact already being equipped with a definite potential for harming Russia's security. The signal is all the more alarming for us since the United States is also contemplating the deployment of elements of its anti-missile defence in Eastern Europe, in immediate proximity to Russia's borders ... the Russian Federation will carefully analyse the evolving situation in the light of its own security interests, and reserves its right to take all necessary steps to maintain its security at the appropriate level."

26. Trevor Findlay, "Preserving UNMOVIC: The Institutional Possibilities", *Disarmament Diplomacy*, No. 76 (March–April 2004).

23

Conclusion: Managing nuclear threats after Iraq

Cyrus Samii

Introduction

The diplomatic crisis and the subsequent fallout that surrounded the US-led invasion of Iraq – ostensibly to deal with the nuclear, biological and chemical weapons threat – opened fissures among parties to the non-proliferation regime. As the chapters in this volume show, some have argued that the Iraq crisis clearly demonstrated the dysfunction of the regime, whereas others have suggested that the Iraq experience provided a foundation for an effective multilateral non-proliferation toolbox. What *has* the Iraq experience revealed about the adequacy, or inadequacies, of the non-proliferation regime for dealing with today's nuclear threats? What are the implications for enhancing the international community's efforts to manage future nuclear threats?

Unfortunately, the diplomatic fallout in the wake of the Iraq crisis has inhibited proper dialogue within official forums. Washington decided to distance itself from the United Nations Monitoring, Verification and Inspection Commission (UNMOVIC) in forming the Iraq Survey Group. Bitterness lingered among many in the administration of US President George W. Bush and in the UN Secretariat in relation to the Iraq episode. These after-effects inhibited the sharing of lessons and compiling of a complete picture from which to learn. To date, parties have still not been able to clarify the terms of key debates that would have to be resolved for regime-based policy processes to move forward. Lack of direction and of consensus in the non-proliferation regime resulted in complete deadlock at the May 2005 Review Conference for the Treaty on the Non-Proliferation of Nuclear Weapons (NPT) and the failure to identify any points of agreement to include in the *2005 World Summit Outcome* document.[1]

The clarification of lessons from Iraq and the implications for the non-proliferation regime have been the goal of this volume. The contributions touch on nuclear, biological and chemical weapons (NBC), but central attention is given to nuclear proliferation and the multilateral nuclear non-proliferation regime.[2] This conclusion will examine ideas expressed in this volume in relation to the questions posed above and in relation to issues concerning nuclear threats in particular. The focus will be on political and strategic lessons. In many cases, the ideas could be extended to biological and chemical weapons cases. This conclusion will draw not only on the volume chapters but also on discussions among the authors themselves.[3]

There are certainly limits to what can be learned from the Iraq case, given its particularities and that much important information has yet to be revealed. But the Iraq case has already shed considerable light on many of the assumptions undergirding proposals for addressing today's nuclear threats. The first part of this conclusion examines some key issues concerning successes and failures of the international community's efforts to manage the Iraqi proliferation threat. The second part summarizes discussions on broader non-proliferation policy options in the "post-Iraq" era.

Learning from the Iraq experience

The international community's massive effort to manage the threat posed by Iraq's proliferation of weapons of mass destruction was unprecedented in scale. But the international community would be remiss in assuming that such tasks may not arise again. Although it may be too early to assess all of the outcomes of the international community's nearly 15-year effort to manage the Iraqi proliferation threat, a preliminary exploration of the lessons learned from the Iraq experience is warranted.

In particular, it is worthwhile to examine the inadequacies that efforts vis-à-vis Iraq revealed in the regime to deal with today's proliferation threats. This is not only to balance against the optimism that tends to flow within official institutional circuits. It is also to grasp the lessons on evasion that would-be proliferators may have learned. At issue is whether or not one should declare the inspections, destruction and sanctions strategy on Iraq a success or a failure, or whether there were successful bits that could be identified amidst particular failures. Similarly pertinent are the implications from the Iraq experience for future proliferation challenges in the Middle East and North-east Asia.

The international community and Iraq: A post mortem

The contributions to this volume examining the international community's performance vis-à-vis Iraq focus on the efforts initiated by UN Security Council Resolution 687 (1991) and continuing, through a number of turning points, up to the US-led invasion of Iraq in March 2003.[4] It should be noted that this engagement began a decade after the 1981 Israeli strikes on the Osirak reactors,[5] and that international inspectors had been shocked to discover in 1991 that significant progress had been made in regenerating a clandestine Iraqi nuclear programme within 10 years. It should also be noted that the international community's approach was augmented by significant and costly efforts that were not explicitly endorsed by Security Council resolutions, including the no-fly zones and other US-led demonstrations of force in the region.[6] In the post-1991 context, inspections, verification and sanctions were the key components of the international community's approach to Iraq.

One interpretation is that the international community's approach was, essentially, successful. According to this view, Iraqi NBC capabilities were destroyed and Saddam Hussein's regime did not have the space or means to regenerate an arsenal. Such is the conclusion to be drawn from the findings of the United States' Iraq Survey Group reported to the Central Intelligence Agency and from post-invasion revelations by Iraqi scientists.[7] The escalation in 2002–2003 was puzzling, taking place despite the removal of the "object" of the international community's confrontation with the Iraqi regime: the weapons. But this puzzling outcome was simply the product of misperceptions and diplomatic blunders.[8] Technical progress and deepened knowledge had made inspections by the International Atomic Energy Agency (IAEA) and UNMOVIC significantly more effective than had been the case with the IAEA and the United Nations Commission (UNSCOM).[9] Targeted "smart" sanctions were significantly less damaging to innocent Iraqis but no less effective in closing off NBC development opportunities. In the end, the argument goes, the real lesson is that the international community's approach was working. Had cool-headed thinking prevailed, the world could have been assured that the Iraqi threat would be eliminated.

But a less generous interpretation can also be constructed with as much, if not more, plausibility. Even if the international community's approach was generally successful in containing Iraq's proliferation interests, this success was experiencing diminishing returns.[10] Containment could work only if inspections were paired with credible threats and sanctions were consensually upheld.[11] But half-measure applications of force were decreasing in their effectiveness and threats were losing their credibility. Divergences in threat perceptions among the permanent five members of the Security Council were pulling apart the tightness of sanctions. Thus, the containment strategy might have had a time limit to effectiveness.

In addition, despite the technical improvements in the inspections process, informational failures still undermined any other successes. The international community did not confidently come to know whether it was successful. Inspections and verification procedures did not develop the information necessary for the formation of consensus. Sanctions may have been successful in denying the means to regenerate weapons, and inspections may have been successful *as deterrents*. But the IAEA/ UNMOVIC inspections hardly improved upon the IAEA/UNSCOM inspections in quelling doubts among key players in the international community.[12] Their inability to do so was because of a characteristic logical problem: the impossibility of "proving a negative". Because of this impossibility, such inspections rely on the willingness of the authorities from within the state in question to dispel doubts. But Iraqi scientists were muzzled by threats to them and their families, and Saddam Hussein's regime showed no intention of unequivocally demonstrating its benign intentions. Finally, even if Saddam Hussein and his associates wanted to come clean, they may not have been able to do so. As Patricia Lewis explains in Chapter 8 in this volume, orders concerning WMD programmes were often delivered in person. "[O]wing to Saddam's tight control on decision-making, instructions to subordinates were rarely documented and often shrouded in uncertainty."[13] It would seem that the international community could only have *the word* of Saddam Hussein and his associates upon which to base their judgement that the WMD threat had been removed. But, as Lewis also asks, "[h]ow does one believe a liar, even when he is telling the truth?"[14] A number of unfortunate conditions thus conspired to make it unlikely that inspections would ever quell doubts.

Outside intelligence was also compromised in a number of ways. On the one hand, the United States and the United Kingdom had shattered others' trust by broadcasting intelligence assertions that proved to be faulty at best, conniving at worst.[15] Political taint thus spoiled the quality of the inspections process. On the other hand, the implementation of the Amorim Report's recommendations for "one-way" intelligence flows of intelligence also had a compromising effect.[16] As much as this arrangement helps to protect the neutrality of the inspections, it significantly compromises effectiveness. This is especially so for discovery operations, in which national intelligence is often crucial, but with which national intelligence agencies are reluctant to cooperate without two-way information flows.

Finally, one could argue further that IAEA/UNMOVIC inspections did not face a "real test" in 2002–2003 because there were no weapons. The Iraq experience does little to instil confidence in the international community's ability to tackle a genuine proliferation problem, where actual weapons exist. Thus, any conclusions about the success of IAEA/UNMOVIC in the run-up to the 2003 invasion must be qualified, if not rejected.

In addition to these inspections-related failures, one is struck by the marginal impact of the international community's approach on the intentions of the Baghdad leadership. The attitudes and intentions of Saddam Hussein and his close associates, it seems, were hardly changed.[17] Arguments proposing that containment suffered from diminishing returns provoke consideration of how the containment approach could have possibly concluded. Was "regime change" the inevitable conclusion? Were the interests of the Iraqi regime manipulable through inducements, or was war inevitable? If the latter was likely to be true, then should not the timing of that military action have been chosen on the basis of operational propitiousness? This inability to affect the Baghdad leadership's attitudes and intentions was based on how little the international community understood about the domestic and regional dynamics that were playing into Saddam Hussein's calculations. It is puzzling to note that, even though evidence suggests that Saddam Hussein may have been acting on the basis of high domestic and regional insecurity, the international community seemed almost powerless to raise the costs of his defiance sufficiently to change his interests and attitudes.[18]

One final point should be made: a sophisticated assessment of the international community's approach to Iraq should distinguish between different policy areas. This would certainly be true for different classes of weapons; for example, although the Baghdad regime was never forthcoming about biological weapons capabilities, dismantlement of nuclear facilities was less obstructed.[19] In addition, it might be noted that UNSCOM demonstrated great proficiency with ongoing monitoring and verification but was less successful with discovery and initial verification.[20]

Implications for future non-proliferation efforts

Proliferation motivations seem to be closely linked to the imperatives of political survival for leaderships fighting to maintain domestic and regional authority. However, the international community faces a knowledge deficit in ascertaining the threat perceptions and motivations of these leaderships. This became clear in relation to Saddam Hussein's regime. It is just as applicable in the context of proliferation dynamics elsewhere in the Middle East and in North-east Asia, today's two proliferation flash points.

Traditional analyses of proliferation tend to build on the core concept of national survival, but the cases of Iraq, Iran and North Korea suggest that "state leadership survival" may be more useful analytically. An emphasis on state leadership survival forces one to look past the national veneer and into domestic dynamics and the more parochial interests of the leaders vis-à-vis their people and vis-à-vis the world. In the case of Iraq, such an approach may help to explain the puzzling posturing of Saddam Hussein in the run-up to the 2003 invasion.[21] In this vein, economic reforms within North Korea might have important effects on Pyongyang's proliferation motivations. Recognition of the importance of state leadership survival provides the international community with another entry-point for policies aimed at reducing the demand for unconventional weapons.

But even if such an approach is analytically compelling and provides an important entry-point for policy, it faces a number of inherent limitations. First is the problem of opacity. Difficulties in ascertaining a state leadership's motivations should be expected as a likely element of proliferation dynamics and crises. This is because of the strategic value of ambiguity. For Iraq, Saddam Hussein reportedly disclosed in interviews after his capture that ambiguity about his NBC capabilities was part of a strategy to deter neighbouring Iran while simultaneously forestalling the emergence of an international consensus against him.[22] For Iran and North Korea, artful obfuscation and opacity have similarly divided international responses and thus have been sources of bargaining leverage in negotiations over their nuclear capabilities. Strategic opacity compounds the already difficult task for outsiders in penetrating the "black box" of a state and discovering threat perceptions and possible proliferation motivations. Related to such obfuscation by these would-be proliferators is the policy of "strategic ambiguity" to which Israel adheres.[23] On the surface, it would seem that progress in arms control in the Middle East hinges on Israeli transparency. But if one considers the reputational concerns of leaders in the region, it is possible that, for the sake of regional stability, such ambiguity is more desirable than transparency. This is because the ambiguity provides face-saving cover for neighbouring leaders, lessening domestic pressure to develop a balancing arsenal.[24] Judging whether one argument is more or less true relative to the other depends, unfortunately, on knowledge of the leaders' primary concerns in dealing with domestic and regional threats.

The international community's knowledge deficit about proliferation motivations, combined with the logical impossibility of "proving a negative", reinforces the conclusion that the onus during inspections and verification processes is on the authorities of the state in question. On the one hand, this is a rather pessimistic conclusion about the potential of multilateral inspections given current technology and knowledge. On the other hand, it also helps to protect against the lulling effect of an overly generous interpretation of what inspections can accomplish. Such lulling would increase a would-be proliferator's ability to use inspections as a deceptive cover. Perhaps the international community could do more to rally around a particular interpretation of what inspections are all about: as Hans Blix expressed it during the UNMOVIC inspections in 2002–2003, inspections are not punishment but rather an opportunity for a state to show that it has nothing to hide.

Reshaping the repertoire

The inadequacies in the central pillars of the non-proliferation regime are apparent. The bargain enshrined in the NPT leaves a "loophole" whereby states interested in clandestinely developing enrichment capabilities for a weapons programme can do so too easily.[25] Because of technological diffusion, would-be proliferators are not as hampered by the need to import know-how and materials as they would have been when the NPT was negotiated.[26] In addition, the "chronological" basis of the privileges granted to the nuclear-weapon states (NWS) in the NPT accords badly with current realities.[27] This problem also affects the legitimacy of the Security Council as the prime enforcement body of the regime, given that the permanent five members of the Security Council (the P-5) are the same five nuclear-weapon states. The IAEA has never lived up to its purported role as a confidence-building measure and an early warning system triggering responses by the international community. In the cases of Iraq, North Korea, Iran and Libya, the IAEA's role was introduced in *reaction* to startling revelations that came about in ways independent of the agency's work. Finally, the Security Council's centrality was undermined by the diplomatic crisis surrounding the US-led invasion of Iraq. This comes on top of the erosion of the Security Council's credibility owing to the large number of unenforced resolutions, not to mention its antiquated distribution of veto power and representation.

Given these inadequacies, one may debate the degree of change that is needed. For some, change need be only selective and incremental. For example, the "chronological" basis of NWS/P-5 privilege is a serious concern worth addressing only if there exists some other attainable solution to the problem of coordinating international action. Such coordination is the key benefit, and an extremely important one, that the NPT and the

Security Council provide. So long as the current arrangement represents the best of the feasible coordination solutions, it ought to be maintained as the centre of the regime, perhaps only incrementally adjusted. Another perspective is that the institutional structures themselves are sound but they have simply received insufficient resources. The key problem, on the basis of this argument, is identifying more effective financing arrangements. Some may also argue that there has been significant progress in reforming the regime, and that it is too early to pass judgement. The IAEA Additional Protocol may be noted in this regard. And finally, as a continuation of the optimistic assessments of the UN-centred approach to Iraq, some may note that this success is a clear demonstration of the potential of the existing non-proliferation regime. The international community needs only to appreciate the significance of this success.

However, such incremental and selective tinkering is not likely to produce a regime that could truly manage today's non-proliferation threats. The feasibility of closing the NPT "loophole" is blocked by deadlock, because closing the loophole would require renegotiating Article IV rights. Given prevailing perceptions among the non-nuclear-weapon states that the nuclear-weapon states' progress on fulfilling their Article VI commitments has been insufficient, willingness among non-nuclear-weapon states to give up any rights granted in the NPT, including in Article IV, would not be forthcoming. If making "sufficient" progress on Article VI is out of the question for the nuclear-weapon states, then much of the issue of reforming the NPT becomes trivial. The pitiful outcome of the 2005 NPT Review Conference is a good example in this regard.

Aside from deadlock on NPT reform, there is the disconnect between the principles undergirding the multilateral regime and contemporary proliferation threats. Because of the diffusion of know-how and the increase in available sources of equipment and fissile materials, reform efforts must stress enforcement of compliance with non-proliferation obligations. But the NPT is a good faith treaty with no explicit enforcement provisions. The de facto enforcement structure – based on the linkage between the NPT, the IAEA verification mechanisms and the Security Council – suffers from a number of problems. Even with the Additional Protocols, the IAEA operates on the basis of the goodwill of states. As for the Security Council, members of the permanent five have exhibited different perceptions and priorities towards proliferation threats and thus have not often found consensus on WMD-related matters. When they have, as with Security Council Resolution 1540 (2004), the result is weak implementation.[28] Finally, the Security Council's enforcement role suffers from an "enforcement contradiction", in which the enforcers themselves are seen by many in the world as being in non-observance of their Article VI obligations.

Given this mixed assessment, one is compelled at least to consider some alternatives to the current regime-based approach to managing nuclear proliferation threats. One could view these as substitutes for the existing regime, if one deemed that such substitution is necessary given the unreformability of the regime. Alternatively, one could view these as possible auxiliary policies that could bolster the regime.

Evaluating ad hoc approaches

Ad hoc approaches are those that are organized outside the terms of the NPT-centred regime and do not function according to the procedural stipulations of the regime. The Proliferation Security Initiative (PSI) is one example; another is the Nuclear Suppliers Group (NSG). Argument exists about whether "legislative" Security Council resolutions such as Resolution 1540 are ad hoc, given that they do not carry the explicit endorsement of all relevant parties but they are the products of legally sound procedure. In February 2004, US President George W. Bush and IAEA Director General Mohamed ElBaradei exchanged views on how to improve international non-proliferation efforts. Bush's proposals included emphasis on ad hoc initiatives; ElBaradei warned of problems with such approaches, which he described as unpredictable "gentlemen's agreements".[29] The debate is over the merits of ad hoc approaches and whether they are a sustainable substitute in addressing concerns over which the regime is politically crippled.

One proposition favouring ad hoc approaches is that unity of purpose is often difficult to fashion in rigid multilateral institutions, and that an ad hoc grouping may achieve a deeper consensus that is more conducive to tackling difficult security problems. Such is the logic behind the "effective multilateralism" approach promoted by the United States at recent international conferences.[30] The logic would seem to be sound. If actors are assembled on the basis of a particular common interest, then a higher level of consensus should be forthcoming. But if actors are procedurally included in decision-making and they do not have a direct stake in the problem at hand, then they are likely to act on the basis of principles, such as inviolable sovereignty, to ensure that such principles are protected. PSI is a good example of this logic, having been established and put into action quickly. In addition, proponents hold that PSI operates within the framework of international law.

The world is not always so simple, however. The sets of actors needed to tackle particular proliferation problems are not invariably the most willing. The Six-Party Talks on North Korea are a manifestation of this complicating reality: clearly, all of the six parties that are involved in the talks *must* be involved.[31] But the pace of the talks nonetheless suffers because the different parties have different priorities. The Chinese and Russian leaderships, for example, may have an interest in seeing North Korea roll back its weapons programmes, but only to the extent that regional stability is maintained. A similar issue holds for South Korea's leadership, in relation to its own interests in pursuing better relations with Pyongyang. The ordering of priorities is thus inconsistent between the United States and its Six-Party Talks partners. One might add that North Korea has made some of its most pointed exhortations in reference to the possibility of referral to the Security Council. The Six-Party Talks thus seem to sit below the Security Council in the escalatory ladder of diplomatic engagement.

Ad hoc approaches may be the only way to work with the "de facto nuclear-weapon states": Israel, India and Pakistan. To some degree, the de facto nuclear-weapon states prefer to be outside the regime and may derive strategic value from the ambiguity surrounding their capabilities.[32] On the flip side, many of the non-NWS signatories to the NPT are unwilling to allow for the legitimization of the de facto nuclear-weapon states' nuclear arsenals through accommodations within the NPT. Finally, the P-5 have shown little willingness to push the de facto nuclear-weapon states into the regime. Another approach exists to bring the de facto nuclear-weapon states into a regime amended with a Fissile Material Cutoff Treaty (FMCT). But, at the time of writing, the FMCT proposal also faces seemingly irreconcilable disagreements.[33] Given this situation, the integration of the de facto nuclear-weapon states into fissile material control programmes, for example, would necessitate arrangements outside of the regime. Of course, the sustaining of extra-regime status for the de facto nuclear-weapon states raises some uncomfortable issues. What are the implications for the regime if (or, perhaps, when) India takes a permanent or "quasi-permanent" seat on the Security Council?

Another argument for the necessity of ad hoc approaches is based on regional particularities. In the Middle East and South Asia, proliferation dynamics involve de facto nuclear-weapon states. In South Asia and North-east Asia, the fact that a P-5 country, China, is deeply entangled in regional proliferation dynamics suggests that the Security Council is compromised in its enforcement role. As a result, the regime's compliance and enforcement mechanisms are hindered in dealing with regional proliferation dynamics in the most sensitive regions! In addition, regional security dynamics may be better dealt with separately from the global politics that accompanies the regime. Such a regional approach would prevent "principle" from interfering with problem-solving, in the manner discussed above. Moreover, and perhaps more importantly, such an approach would allow non-proliferation efforts to be linked with other regional security interests, which could open up avenues toward achieving agreement on non-proliferation objectives. Of course, the mechanisms of the multilateral regime could be linked to such a regional security arrangement.

Another question is whether such ad hoc approaches necessarily undermine the regime and, if so, whether they leave the international community in a worse position. To the extent that they generate resentment that unravels cooperation more generally, this may certainly be the case. But such ad hoc approaches could conceivably bolster the regime, so long as they do not violate the spirit of the regime. Such may be the case for the PSI and the NSG, which may ultimately lay the groundwork for a treaty-based export and transhipment control system. Until that treaty-based system is put into place, these ad hoc approaches fill a necessary gap. Along those lines, UNSCOM and UNMOVIC were, arguably, ad hoc approaches that may now serve as the basis for a more permanent inspection capability maintained by the United Nations as a regularized part of the non-proliferation regime.

Given the mixed value of ad hoc approaches in relation to different types of proliferation problems, perhaps "mixed multilateral" approaches might offer avenues for progress. Outside the realm of proliferation, mixed models have been used to structure political will in relation to the particularities of the problem. The Quartet (the United States, the United Nations, the European Union and Russia) established to revitalize the Middle East peace process in 2003 is the most prominent example. Perhaps a similar model, involving the United States, the IAEA Director General and other key partners, could provide a diplomatic framework more conducive to progress in arms control, disarmament and non-proliferation in the Middle East, South Asia and North-east Asia.

Debating discriminating approaches

Another key issue, as Ramesh Thakur proposes in his introduction to this volume, is whether the multilateral non-proliferation regime suffers as a result of resting on an untenable "Westphalian fiction" of equal status, and whether some form of "legitimate discrimination" should be introduced. For those advocating legitimate discrimination, the acquisition of nuclear weapons by some states should elicit extra worry, and thus efforts to prevent their acquisition of NBC should be given sharpened attention. Of course, the NPT codified the notion that not all states are equal when it comes to proliferation, giving special rights to the five nuclear-weapon states. In effect, arguments for legitimate discrimination are arguments for the creation of a second tier of differentiation, subdividing the class of non-nuclear-weapon states into "states of concern" and, presumably, states of "non-concern". Members of the "non-concern" class could, for example, maintain uranium enrichment facilities as part of peaceful energy production programmes, whereas such privileges would be denied to "states of concern". Auxiliary conventions could be established, presumably through the Security Council, to enforce this differentiation in rights. This would represent a fundamental shift in the nature of the regime.

As Thakur points out, the argument that such a discriminatory approach is warranted rests on a number of observations. First is the observation that differences abound among states and, thus, so should treatment. States vary in their relative power and wealth, and these differences are appreciated in the multilateral regimes. If some differences translate into different privileges, then why should not different behaviours translate into different treatment? An analogy can be made with the Brahimi Report on peace operations, which stated that the political neutrality of the United Nations should not be misunderstood as moral equivalence, and that there ought to be recognition of the difference between victim and perpetrator. In the context of non-proliferation, this would translate into granting differentiated rights; this differentiation would be based on judgements of whether or not a state demonstrates its responsibility in international affairs. For example, Japan's maintenance of a latent nuclear "breakout" capacity should be recognized within the regime as benign, on the basis of its otherwise responsible international behaviour.

Second is the observation that technological diffusion and the resulting ability for states increasingly to seize advantage of the NPT's proliferation "loophole" have increased the general likelihood of proliferation. Related to this is a third observation that shadowy threats from transnational militant networks require the international community to increase its capacity to mobilize quickly. Based on these observations, one may propose that trigger mechanisms and selectivity criteria should be established in operationalizing such legitimate discrimination. Such trigger mechanisms would force a state of concern to accept more intrusive inspections or face automatic referral to the Security Council in connection with proliferation risk. Selectivity criteria would provide a legal basis on which to determine whether particular states would be subject to export controls on sensitive materials and equipment. If the international community were to settle upon such a set of criteria for declaring that a state is in non-compliance, then it might be easier to mobilize international collective action. Such a discriminatory approach would have the additional benefit of making the regime more efficient, freeing up resources now applied to inspecting states that are not of concern to the international community.

The chief criticism of this view relates to whether such "legitimate discrimination" could possibly serve to undergird a regime.[34] Indeed, there is no way to identify mechanistic criteria for determining whether a state is responsible or not. State regime types such as democracies or dictatorships have not historically been associated with either more or less irresponsibility in nuclear proliferation or NBC use. Any litmus test of political virtue is a political decision in itself; thus a regime founded on such a litmus test would be ,a readily apparent instrument serving the political interests of some group of states. But this criticism does not obviate the need for specialized treatment of "states of concern". Indeed, what it does do is affirm the centrality of case-by-case Security Council deliberation in making legitimate discrimination a reality.

Forceful prevention

In the context of nuclear non-proliferation today, the concept of "prevention" has come to mean more than just structuring regimes to induce states not to proliferate. The amended meaning includes the use of force or the threat of force to neutralize proliferation problems. The argument for preventive approaches proposes that credible threats against would-be proliferators can be used to deter proliferation. If the threats fail, then military action can directly neutralize the proliferation problem and restore credibility for future threats against proliferators. The approach has been most forcefully promulgated in the 2002 US National Security Strategy.[35] The 2003 US-led invasion of Iraq was the most intense exercise of this approach. The 1981 Israeli strike on Iraq's Osirak reactors was a previous manifestation. Veiled pronouncements about US and Israeli military planning vis-à-vis Iran are an application of the approach in principle. The Report of the UN Secretary-General's High-level Panel on Threats, Challenges and Change proposed that such preventive action might be justified under certain conditions.[36]

The invasion of Iraq could be used as a test case for addressing whether the prevention alternative represents an effective approach to non-proliferation and whether it might be considered as an auxiliary approach for the regime. US administration officials have pointed to Libya as an example of how the invasion of Iraq restored the United States' deterrence credibility against would-be proliferators. But a number of issues detract from this argument. Libya had been making normalization overtures to Europe and the United States for years, and it is unclear whether the United States simply took advantage of the situation to claim success vis-à-vis Libya as justification for Iraq.

In addition, it is difficult to argue that North Korea's or Iran's strategies have become more pliant towards the United States. Immediately after the war began, North Korea agreed to the Six-Party Talks. But it seems that, once North Korea had observed the complications that erupted in post-invasion Iraq, the Pyongyang leadership acted as if the invasion was more of an opportunity than a frightening example. With US forces tied down in Iraq, North Korea and Iran may have felt that the pressure had lightened. The visible costs to the United States in dealing with the aftermath of the invasion make it difficult to believe that such an approach could become conventional.

Aside from the dubious contribution to livening deterrence, the manner in which prevention was carried out in relation to Iraq had other costs. These include undermining the trust of long-time partners, not only as a direct effect of the fallout from the 2003 diplomatic crisis but also as a result of the reputation that the United States has acquired for being strategically myopic. Military-operational considerations and geopolitical goals notwithstanding, the findings of the US-commissioned Iraq Survey Group have cut away the core of the justification for acting beyond the regime to address the Iraqi proliferation threat.

Finally, as mentioned above, such forceful prevention is not entirely new, as evidenced by the Israeli strikes on the Osirak reactors in 1981. Nonetheless, the eventual regeneration of Iraq's programme demonstrates how forceful prevention may be only a short-term solution. If so-called "demand-side" issues are not addressed – that is, if no arrangements are made to mitigate the threats that actually propel proliferation interests – then such preventive measures may only set back progress towards weapons control for the short term. The logic of forceful prevention, in the absence of viable threat reduction, descends rapidly into the logic of "regime change". Also, one may take issue with whether the Osirak strikes significantly set back Saddam Hussein's progress towards a nuclear weapon, given the speed with which the facilities were regenerated. In addition, it is apparent the he learned the necessity of making the Iraqi programme more hidden and more resilient. Arguably, the problem for the international community was ultimately made much more difficult after the Osirak strikes.

Thus, the costs of forceful prevention are abundantly clear whereas the benefits are hardly apparent. Forceful prevention in the mode of the Osirak strikes in 1981 amounts to a one-shot, diplomatically costly way to buy time for managing proliferation threats. Such short-term fixes also allow proliferators to learn, adapt and make their programmes even more hidden and resilient. Nonetheless, if other preventive means have failed and if the consequences of a new state crossing the nuclear threshold are serious enough, then such time-buying might be sufficiently valuable to warrant the cost. Forceful prevention in the mode of the 2003 invasion, however, amounts to a staggeringly costly manner of neutralizing a single proliferation threat. In all accounts, such an approach would be un-conventional and extreme. Such historically informed analysis is crucial when weighing forceful prevention against other less-than-perfect strategies, such as inspections and sanctions.

Whither disarmament?

What of the role of disarmament in relation to managing nuclear proliferation threats? As is the subject of Chapter 4 by Rebecca Johnson in this volume, the key issue is whether slow movement or regression in fulfilling NPT Article VI commitments undermines non-proliferation efforts. The issue is linked to the debate over whether discriminatory approaches to non-proliferation are desirable or feasible. The current regime would not exist were it not for Article VI.[37] But the question remains whether the relevant conditions under which this grand bargain was negotiated still hold.

One could argue that perceptions of lack of progress on Article VI and related problems are unfounded. First, under Cooperative Threat Reduction (CTR) programmes initiated in recent years, the world has seen more progress on disarmament than ever during the Cold War. Second, it is not clear that disarmament by the nuclear-weapon states would change the minds of those that are currently seeking nuclear technologies. There is good reason to believe that the United States' conventional superiority, for example, is impetus enough to motivate some states to pursue nuclear capabilities. In other cases, proliferation dynamics are based on regional security concerns and are clearly far removed from the likely effects of Article VI, as in the case of South Asia.

But those who defend the need to put pressure on the nuclear-weapon states to move more quickly on Article VI are quick to reiterate its centrality to the maintenance of the NPT bargain. So long as commitment to the NPT is strong, the international normative and political climate creates costs to proliferation. These costs would evaporate if expressed commitments to the NPT were to wither. In line with this reasoning, those who argue that world perceptions of non-progress on Article VI commitments are insignificant should stop to think about whether an unravelling of the NPT is an acceptable consequence. This is in addition to the self-interest-based arguments that propose progress in disarmament simply lessens both the material available and the positive incentives for proliferation.[38]

A related debate is over the United States' plans, as reportedly announced in the United States' 2002 Nuclear Posture Review, to develop new types of tactical nuclear weapons.[39] The issue is whether such weapons development increases or decreases the difficulty of stemming nuclear proliferation. On the one hand, such "mini-nuke" development could actually deter would-be small-scale proliferators, because they would calculate that the odds of succeeding with a clandestine programme would be sufficiently diminished by a US capability to destroy. But such new weapons development would erode the moral authority of the United States in non-proliferation affairs. This would severely complicate any attempt to halt or roll back proliferators that decide, despite the mini-nuke threat, to take the risk to go forward with programmes.

Conclusion

In some senses, the contributions to this volume and the analysis above lead to a rather banal conclusion: none of the approaches available for managing nuclear threats is without important drawbacks and limitations. Nonetheless, clear identification of such drawbacks and limitations is a crucial first step in effective and rational policy-making. The experience in trying to manage the Iraqi proliferation threat has highlighted the importance of information problems, the relationship between the political climate and intelligence, and the need for deeper assessments of how calculations of political survival factor into proliferation motivations. In the post-Iraq era, some approaches that have been initiated outside the terms of the non-proliferation regime hold significant potential whereas the promise of others may have been overblown.

The international community would do well to keep in mind two key considerations. First, ad hoc approaches, legitimate discrimination and forceful prevention reflect altered beliefs in the wake of the Iraq experience and the 9/11 terrorist attacks. The question arises: *can these changed beliefs be harnessed to further enhance the international community's ability to neutralize today's true nuclear threats?* The question applies most particularly to the deadlock induced by world politics that has set in over the NPT. Second, the very existence of ad hoc and other "alternative" approaches also reflects how the non-proliferation regime has *not* adapted to changing nuclear threats. But, even if these approaches appear to challenge the regime, it is important to raise the question: *to what extent and in what ways do these seemingly alternative approaches actually depend on the existence of the multilateral regime for their success?*[40] A few instances of such dependence were mentioned above, including the relationship between the Six-Party Talks and the latent threat of Security Council referral and the relationship between the PSI and multilateral frameworks such as those governing maritime cooperation. One might also add that the United States' Iraq Survey Group made no apparent gains operating as a unilaterally conducted entity, dissociated from UNMOVIC and the IAEA, and the Survey Group certainly lost out from the disruption of an information-sharing network that such dissociation imposed. This should be a lesson to focus minds on pushing the agenda forward.

Notes

1. Non-proliferation issues are completely absent from the *2005 World Summit Outcome* document (UN Doc. A/60/L.1, 15 September 2005).
2. The regime consists of the interlinked Treaty on the Non-Proliferation of Nuclear Weapons (NPT), the International Atomic Energy Agency (IAEA) and related statutes, bodies of the United Nations and a small set of United Nations Security Council resolutions, as well as a small collection of other more specialized treaties.
3. These discussions took place during a series of seminars upon which the present volume is based. The seminars were hosted by the United Nations University (UNU), the International Peace Academy (IPA), Ritsumeikan University (RU), and Ritsumeikan Asia-Pacific University (APU) in Beppu and Kyoto, Japan, 18–23 October 2004.
4. Refer specifically to Chapters 5–8 in the present volume by Kono, Müller, Findlay and Lewis.
5. From a normative standpoint, it is also worth recalling that the Security Council passed Resolution 487 (19 June 1981) to condemn the 1981 Israeli preventive attack on Osirak.
6. Indeed, David Malone and James Cockayne argue that Western "unilateralism" was thus initiated well before the 2003 invasion. Malone and Cockayne, "Lines in the Sand: The United Nations in Iraq, 1980–2001", in Ramesh Thakur and Waheguru Pal Singh Sidhu, eds, *The Iraq Crisis and World Order: Structural, Institutional and Normative Challenges* (Tokyo: United Nations University Press, 2006).
7. Iraq Survey Group, *Comprehensive Report of the Special Advisor to the DCI on Iraq's WMD* [Duelfer Report], 30 September 2004, available at ⟨http://www.cia.gov/cia/reports/iraq_wmd_2004/⟩ (accessed 10 March 2006). See also Mahdi Obeidi and Kurt Pulitzer, *The Bomb in My Garden: The Secrets of Saddam's Nuclear Mastermind* (Hoboken: John Wiley, 2004).
8. Müller (Chapter 6) and Lewis (Chapter 8) emphasize such misperceptions.
9. See Chapter 7 by Findlay on the details of these technical improvements.
10. Kono makes this case in Chapter 5.
11. Chapter 14 by Coletta emphasizes the importance of such credible threats in any regime-based management of proliferation.
12. In Chapter 8, Lewis acknowledges that, even if politicians and bureaucrats in Washington and London were ultimately responsible for a too-hasty end of inspections, analysts and officials who had no interest in the US invasion, including some at the United Nations, also took for granted that Iraq was lying about whether it had come clean.
13. Chapter 8, p. 163. Of course, this raises a new puzzle: why would any member of Saddam's regime choose not to document these orders if documentation of those orders could potentially be of such enormous value in a future crisis? Could this really have been the result of mindless routine and short-sightedness?
14. Ibid., p. 161.
15. Müller makes an important point in Chapter 6 in highlighting that, after then-US Secretary of State Colin Powell presented supposed evidence of Iraqi disingenuousness to the UN Security Council, "there was no scrutiny in the Council of the validity and reliability

of this evidence. Rather, Powell's one-hour multimedia presentation was followed by the reading of prepared statements by the other foreign ministers. There was never really a careful probing of the reasoning of those opting for war, just retaliatory propaganda" (p. 128 in the present volume).

16. *Report of the First Panel Established Pursuant to the Note by the President of the Security Council on 30 January 1999 (S/1999/100), Concerning Disarmament and Current and Future Ongoing Monitoring and Verification Issues* [Amorim Report], UN Doc. S/1999/356, 27 March 1999, ⟨http://www.un.org/Depts/unmovic/documents/Amorim%20Report.htm⟩ (accessed 10 March 2006), para. 57.

17. Indeed the US Iraq Survey Group, in the *Comprehensive Report of the Special Advisor*, emphasized the constancy of Saddam Hussein's attitude and intentions. The administration of US President George W. Bush and its allies would use this in fashioning *ex post facto* justifications for the 2003 invasion. See, for example, the text of Bush's national radio address on 9 October 2004. "President's Radio Address", White House Press Release, 9 October 2004, ⟨http://www.whitehouse.gov/news/releases/2004/10/20041009.html⟩ (accessed 10 March 2006).

18. On the "domestic and regional insecurity" thesis, see Kenneth W. Pollack, "Spies, Lies, and Weapons: What Went Wrong", *Atlantic Monthly* (January/February 2004).

19. Lewis makes this clear in Chapter 8 in this volume.

20. This observation was made by a UN official participating in the UNU-IPA-RU-APU seminars (see note 3).

21. Pollack, "Spies, Lies, and Weapons".

22. "Regime Strategic Intent", in *Comprehensive Report of the Special Advisor*, Vol. I, Chapter 1.

23. See chapters by Roshandel (Chapter 11), Selim (Chapter 12), Shaker (Chapter 13) and Brom (Chapter 20) in the present volume.

24. Such was an argument put forward in defence of Israel's "strategic ambiguity" policy during the UNU-IPA-RU-APU seminars (see note 3).

25. The NPT "bargain" refers to the implicit trade-off between (i) the NPT's acceptance of nuclear-weapon-state status for the United States, the United Kingdom, the USSR/Russia, China and France, and (ii) the obligations put on the nuclear-weapon states in Articles IV and VI. Refer to the NPT text for details (available at ⟨http://www.un.org/events/npt2005/npttreaty.html⟩, accessed 10 March 2006).

26. This change is the result of an increase both in indigenous know-how as well as in suppliers of know-how and materials.

27. The "chronological" basis refers to the fact that the only factor that determines whether a state is granted NWS status in the NPT is whether it had tested nuclear weapons by the time the NPT came into effect (1970).

28. See Chapter 5 by Kono in the present volume. Security Council Resolution 1540 (UN Doc. S/Res/1540, 28 April 2004), passed under Chapter VII of the UN Charter, calls upon states to act against non-state actors' acquisition or development of NBC and their delivery systems, establish controls over the flow of NBC-related materials, promote strengthening of the regime, and ensure their own compliance with treaties that they have ratified. A Committee of the Security Council was established under the resolution to report on its implementation.

29. "President Announces New Measures to Counter the Threat of WMD: Remarks by the President on Weapons of Mass Destruction Proliferation" (Washington, DC: National Defense University), White House Press Release, 11 February 2004), ⟨http://www.whitehouse.gov/news/releases/2004/02/20040211-4.html⟩ (accessed 10 March 2006); and Mohamed ElBaradei, "Saving Ourselves from Self-Destruction", *New York Times*, op/ed, 12 February 2004.

30. See, for example, International Organizations and Nonproliferation Program, *Overview of the 58th Session of the First Committee: Assessing the United Nations Role in International Nonproliferation and Disarmament* (Monterey, CA: Center for Nonproliferation Studies, 15 January 2004), ⟨http://cns.miis.edu/pubs/week/031103.htm⟩ (accessed 10 March 2003).
31. The six parties are the United States, China, Japan, Russia, South Korea and North Korea.
32. See Chapter 19 by Parthasarathy and Chapter 20 by Brom in the present volume.
33. One point of disagreement is over verification measures, which some states (most notably the United States) deem excessively intrusive without offering sufficient assurances. Another is over whether the treaty should call for a drawdown of existing fissile material stockpiles or allow for the maintenance of existing stockpiles. Finally, as with the NPT, the de facto nuclear-weapon states seem to prefer not to come under treaty restrictions, although Pakistan has shown more of a strategic interest in the FMCT.
34. Such criticisms were raised in the authors' discussions at the UNU-IPA-RU-APU seminars (see note 3 above).
35. Office of the President of the United States, *The National Security Strategy of the United States of America* (New York: The White House, September 2002).
36. The report argues that preventive force *can* be used legally if the Security Council invokes Chapter VII to do so, but that it should be used only when "there is credible evidence of the reality of the threat in question ... [and when a] military response is the only reasonable one in the circumstances". United Nations, *A More Secure World: Our Shared Responsibility. Report of the High-level Panel on Threats, Challenges and Change* (United Nations Department of Public Information, December 2004), pp. 63–64 and 67, paras 190, 193, 195 and 207.
37. During the UNU-IPA-RU-APU seminars (see note 3 above), this was stated bluntly by an individual who was part of the original NPT negotiations.
38. See Chapter 4 by Johnson in the present volume.
39. Excerpts from the classified document are available at ⟨http://www.globalsecurity.org/wmd/library/policy/dod/npr.htm⟩ (accessed 10 March 2006).
40. For an argument that the success of ad hoc approaches depends on the framework provided by the multilateral regime, see Natasha Bajema, with Cyrus Samii, "Weapons of Mass Destruction and the United Nations: Diverse Threats and Collective Responses", *IPA Report* (New York: International Peace Academy, June 2004), ⟨http://www.ipacademy.org/PDF_Reports/WEAPONS_OF_MASS_DEST.pdf⟩ (accessed 10 March 2006).

Index